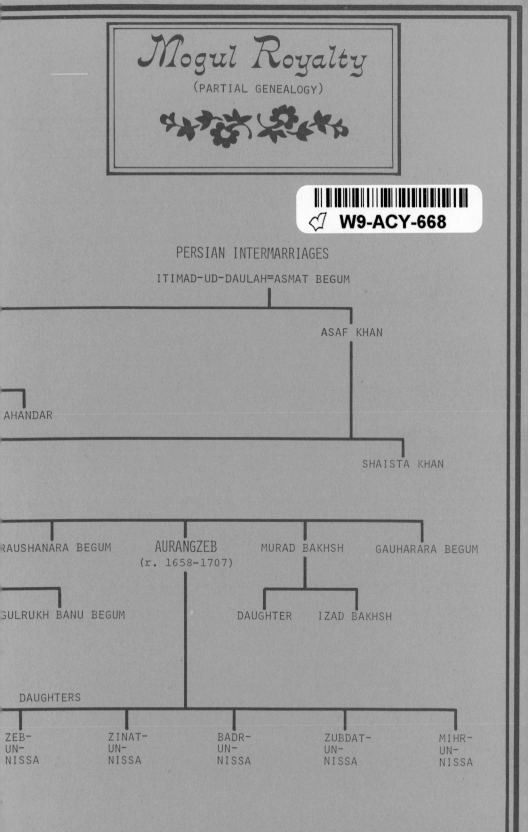

Mogul Royalty

(PARTIAL GENEALOGY)

PERSIAN INTERMARRIAGES

ITIMAD-UD-DAULAH=ASMAT BEGUM

ASAF KHAN

AHANDAR

SHAISTA KHAN

RAUSHANARA BEGUM   AURANGZEB   MURAD BAKHSH   GAUHARARA BEGUM
(r. 1658-1707)

GULRUKH BANU BEGUM   DAUGHTER   IZAD BAKHSH

DAUGHTERS

ZEB-   ZINAT-   BADR-   ZUBDAT-   MIHR-
UN-   UN-   UN-   UN-   UN-
NISSA   NISSA   NISSA   NISSA   NISSA

THE
Peacock
Throne

THE TAJ MAHAL

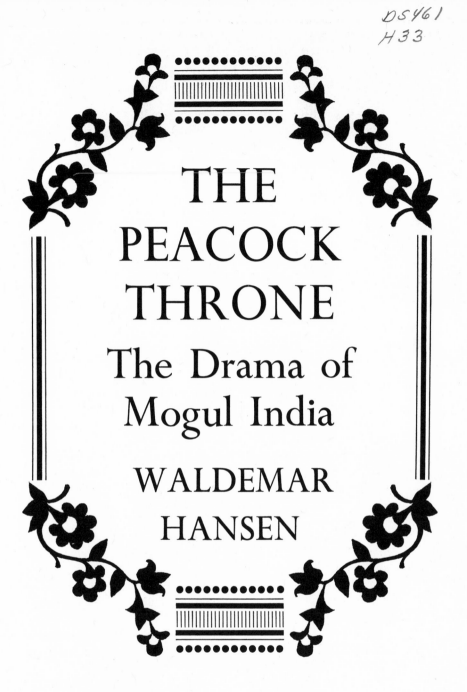

THE PEACOCK THRONE

The Drama of Mogul India

WALDEMAR HANSEN

Holt, Rinehart and Winston

NEW YORK • CHICAGO • SAN FRANCISCO

Published simultaneously in Canada by Holt, Rinehart
and Winston of Canada, Limited.

ISBN: 0-03-000271-0

Library of Congress Catalog Card Number: 72-78094

First Edition

PRINTED IN THE UNITED STATES OF AMERICA

The author is grateful to the following for permission to print quotations:

Central Book Depot, Allahabad, India, for quotations from *History of Shah Jahan of Dihli,* by Banarsi Prasad Saksena.

Kitab Mahal (Wholesale Division) Private Ltd., Allahabad, India, for quotations from *The History of India as Told by its own Historians,* Elliot and Dowson.

Macmillan London and Basingstoke, for quotations from *Travels in India* by Jean Baptiste Tavernier; translated by V. Ball.

Oxford University Press, for quotations from *Travels in the Mogul Empire, 1656–1668* by F. Bernier, translated by A. Constable and revised by V. A. Smith.

Shri Santosh Kr. Sarkar and Mrs. Reba Sarkar for quotations from the works of Sir Jadunath Sarkar (Publisher: Orient Longmans Ltd., Calcutta).

The Hakluyt Society and Cambridge University Press for quotations from *The Travels of Fray Sebastien Manrique,* translated by C. Eckford Luard and H. Hosten.

Visva-Bharati University research publications, Santiniketan, India, and the authors, for quotations from *Dara Shikuh: Life and Works,* by Bikrama Jit Hasrat; and from *Rubaiyat-i-Sarmad,* edited and translated by Fazl Mahmud Asiri.

For My Mother

ANNIE
HANSEN

1882–1953

CONTENTS

Contents

ILLUSTRATIONS
AND MAPS

[ix]

Fig. 11. Shah Jahan, his four sons, a courtier, and two attendants visit an ascetic outside a leaf hut. Murad is the small figure above the horse's tail. (Courtesy of the India Office Library and Records, London)

Fig. 12. Shah Jahan with child and women attendants (By permission of the Victoria and Albert Museum, London)

Fig. 13. Shah Jahan presents a jewel to Dara Shikoh. (Courtesy of the Chester Beatty Library, Dublin)

Fig. 14. Shah Jahan in old age (By permission of the Victoria and Albert Museum, London)

Fig. 15. The Red Fort of Delhi (Courtesy of the Government of India, Ministry of Information)

Fig. 16. The wall of Agra's Red Fort (Courtesy of the Government of India, Ministry of Information)

Fig. 17. Shah Jahan's Hall of Private Audience in the Red Fort, Delhi (Photograph by the Author)

Figures 18 through 39 follow page 370

Fig. 18. The Victory Gate, Fatehpur Sikri (Photograph by the Author)

Fig. 19. Shah Jahan's Friday Mosque, Delhi (Courtesy of the Government of India, Ministry of Information)

Fig. 20. Gwalior fortress (Courtesy of the India Office Library and Records, London)

Fig. 21. Aurangzeb's tomb (Courtesy of the India Office Library and Records, London)

Fig. 22. Jahanara's tomb (Photograph by the Author)

Fig. 23. Akbar's tomb (Courtesy of the Government of India, Ministry of Information)

Fig. 24. Dara Shikoh's tomb (Photograph by the Author)

Fig. 25. Humayun's tomb (Courtesy of the Government of India, Ministry of Information)

Fig. 26. The Taj in its garden setting (Courtesy of the Government of India, Ministry of Information)

Fig. 27. Sir Thomas Roe (By permission of the National Portrait Gallery, London)

MAPS

[xi]

Twelve dervishes may sleep together
under one blanket, but two kings cannot
dwell in one kingdom.
　　　　—EASTERN PROVERB

Prologue: The Taj Mahal

ROYAL HISTORY HAS always demanded nothing less than the theater of the world. Posterity is the audience, fascinated by events whose meaning looms large because the protagonists were large. In the case of the Moguls of India, they positively usurp the stage; they even created their own stage setting in a work of art instantly recognizable to almost everyone on earth—the mausoleum of the Taj Mahal.

Only the Taj could serve as a backdrop to the Moguls' enigmatic origin, and the enormity of their rise and fall. Their dynasty effectively ruled India for less than two hundred years—a drop in the Indian bucket of eternity; but the impact still haunts the subcontinent. Relentless nomads, the Moguls swept to conquest in 1526 as aliens—Moslems in a predominantly Hindu land which had suffered millennia of parochial turmoil. Yet they were the geniuses who unified India; they hypnotized her, they branded her, they left their legacy in a sequence of events which reflect their charisma.

It is all there, embodied in Mogul architecture. In India the Mogul past does more than linger; it overwhelms. Travelers inevitably marvel at the Red forts of imperial Delhi and Agra, whose massive sandstone walls still enclose exquisite palaces and mosques, along with halls of public and private audience inlaid with amethyst and carnelian. Yet nowhere is the mystery of the Moguls more palpable than in the presence of the Taj Mahal. Ostensibly the tomb of an empress, it became the tomb of the entire dynasty—a transcendent embodiment of glory and doom.

What pilgrim arriving in Agra city has not hesitated before approaching the world's most famous monument—from fear of being disappointed? At the vast Saracen entry gate, signs in English and Hindi announce the holy of holies: "Taj Mahal was built between 1631 and 1653 by Emperor Shah Jahan as the tomb for his wife Arjumand, better known as Mumtaz Mahal, ornament of the palace. Born in 1592, the daughter of Asaf Khan, she married Shah Jahan in 1612 and died in 1631 after the birth of her fourteenth child. After his death, the Emperor was buried by her side."

Beyond, through that dark arch of Islam, every visitor for over three hundred years has had the same first glimpse. There is only one approach: no one comes by the adjacent Jumna River, and high surrounding walls preclude indiscriminate views. Almost too perfectly framed, the long mall and reverberating pool lead to a colossal white ghost—the Taj itself. Indeed, this sepulcher is a ghost haunted by unquiet ghosts: Mumtaz Mahal and Shah Jahan, together with their children.

The immediate impact of the Taj is dazzling: a spiritual wonder hovering between the real and unreal, incredibly beyond all the clichés that have ever been written about it. Some esthetes have been known to stay for days, lingering in the garden and observing subtle metamorphoses of the tomb as changing hours lend chiaroscuro—a veil of shadows which the Moslem architects must deliberately have made use of to preserve a delicate mystery from the harsh Indian sun. Experts can even tell daylight hours by shadows that fall on the alcove beneath the great central arch; they become Taj-haunted. By moonlight the monument is utterly beautiful, glowing with a silver effulgence that seems to come curiously from within rather than from without.

Having passed through the entry arch, the spectator is still almost a thousand feet from the mausoleum, and its astonishing amplitude has yet to be appreciated. No long-range inspection can encompass precious-stone inlay or other details; white marble is all, and white is Islam's color of death. The four sentinel minarets are obviously masculine yet something more: they keep the Taj from being earthbound. Remove them and the tomb at once loses its ethereal aspect; it is all very odd. The pear-shaped dome is a feminine miracle, made weightless through perfection of form.

From the top of the mall, the layout seems like that of every other Mogul sepulcher set within a fourfold garden symbolic of the Moslem paradise. Yet unlike other Mogul tombs which always occupy the center of their plot, the Taj stands aloof from its Eden on a great raised platform overlooking the Jumna River.

Looming $243\frac{1}{2}$ feet from garden level to the dome's gold surmounting needle, the mausoleum dwarfs visitors by its grandeur. Inside of that gigantic central arch, vaulted marble has been chiseled into diamond shapes; while black-jet inscriptions from the Koran weave stylized Arabic calligraphy like a giant's puzzle around the entryway. "Conceived by titans and finished by jewellers," the entire edifice reveals a wealth of dadoes, panels in bas-relief, and precious-stone inlay. Flower motifs repeated endlessly in a geometric profusion of bloom are surprisingly naïve. Dominant in the white marble bas-relief is the iris, that graveyard bulb which grows only in shadows away from the Indian heat.

At the entrance, a flight of steps leads down to the real sarcophagi in the crypt: above are only their cenotaph counterparts. Along the corridor surrounding the upper chamber, bas-relief flowers bloom again—only white here, the ghost flowers of death. Daylight filters through the grillwork of four arches surrounding the coffins.

These are the cenotaphs, enclosed by an octagonal screen of white marble amazingly filigreed in floral pattern— a triumph of Oriental decorative art. Dead center within lies the small cenotaph of Mumtaz Mahal; while unsymmetrically adjacent to it, almost rudely crowded against the marble screen, is Shah Jahan's larger cenotaph surmounted by the pen staff symbolic of males. The superfluous addition of his coffin is disturbing—a striking discord in a compulsively

[3]

perfect mausoleum. Even an ignorant stranger would know that something had gone very wrong in history. One of the caretakers utters soft cries to demonstrate the dome's remarkable echo, which lingers weirdly for twenty-two seconds.

Outside, the Indian sun can sometimes be relentless. Visitors shield their eyes from an onslaught of white marble. A slow walk around the edifice reveals that everything is quadrated: the great arch has been repeated four times north, south, east, and west; the four minarets rise like a prayer at each corner of the huge square platform. Yet the shape of the Taj is not square: those outer rows of two-storied arches flanking the great arch are beveled, creating what Moslem architects call a Baghdad octagon. In its insistent symmetry, the whole is soft and lulling.

The river at the rear of the tomb can look very pastoral at dawn. Just across the water, a solitary Mogul cupola shares the scene with what might plausibly be foundation stones for that black marble twin Taj which it is said Shah Jahan intended to build. Agra fort is visible from here, a mile or so along the curve of mud-gray river. In the shimmering air of summer it rears up as a gargantuan red blur, a Mogul mirage.

Inspection ends where it began: facing the great facade. Observant eyes register with something of a shock that a narrow metal lightning conductor runs entirely down one side of the main arch.

No one retreats through the garden without backward looks. A few Indian families have perhaps wandered onto the lawn, the Sikhs in turbans and the women timelessly graceful in saris. Shadows have already begun to appear in the arcades, reviving a mystery which was held at bay during close appraisal. And the mystery will deepen as the afternoon wanes. What is it?

Whatever it is, it seems native to India: an enigma embracing its own history yet curiously impervious to any moment in time. The Taj suggests an endurance beyond now or then, beyond the tideless Jumna River that seeps at its foundations. Now or then are *maya*—illusion, a freakish pattern of impermanence. Three hundred and more years of history can be palimpsested with the transparency of layers of cellophane, and may well be an Indian illusion. Now or then, Mahatma Gandhi stood in this garden and saw the Taj in *his* way—as a symbol of oppression. Sometimes the illusion was even comic. In 1836 the Englishman Colonel Sleeman pitched his tent on the Taj lawn, while his wife exclaimed, "I would die tomorrow to have such a tomb over me!" Sleeman tells how the band of his friend Major Godby's regiment tootled away martial evenings on the terrace of the mausoleum.

At least they were admirers, tiffin parties and all. Not so many years before, picnicking civil servants of the new British raj had armed themselves with hammer and chisel for an enthusiastic afternoon's work on the precious-stone inlay, and helped themselves to petals from that never-fading garden of flowers. Lord William Bentinck, governor-general of India from 1828 to 1835, had already sold by auction the bath in Shah Jahan's palace at Agra, and thought so little of the Taj that he was on the point of destroying it for the value of its marble!

Backward in time, the Taj survived far greater outrage. Its treasures—those Turkish and Persian carpets, those curtains and lamps and gold chains, that priceless pearl canopy for Mumtaz Mahal's tomb—were stolen in the twilight of the Mogul Empire; and the legendary silver doors were looted and melted down by Jats.

Now or then, the chill of the absolute hangs over the tomb. Some ears can even hear a perpetual murmur: the emperor's long-forgotten mullahs weaving litanies of prayer over a never-to-be-forgotten woman. On the anniversary days of her death, Shah Jahan himself knelt to pray at a gem-encrusted balustrade surrounding her coffin. The edifice stood perpetually illumined at night by lamps of gold; and in the vault hung a gold globe garnished with convex mirrors from Aleppo, spangling sensuous patterns of light over the irretrievable dead.

[5]

Death: the essence of the Taj Mahal, yet more than death is here. No photograph or film can convey the spirit emanating from the masterwork; like ectoplasm, it produces gooseflesh only for living witnesses. Spirit rises from that central Islamic arch, a gothic pointer straining toward the white marble dome. It all becomes eerie and glorious, an invocation transforming death into some ultimate luxury.

Against this perfect symbol, the Moguls acted out their violent obsession. Death was the impulse behind their power, their couchant lion against a rising sun.

Part I

PRIDE AND
A CROWN

A Note on Dates and Names

THE MOGULS RECORDED EVENTS according to their Moslem lunar calendar which reckons from A.D. 622, the year of Mohammed's Hegira (abbreviated A.H.). Any Moslem date can be converted to its Christian time equivalent. It must be remembered, however, that Englishmen in Mogul India abided by the old style Julian Calendar (O.S.) which prevailed in Great Britain until 1752, whereas continental Europe had converted to the new style Gregorian calendar (N.S.) in 1582. Thus, there is eleven days' difference between Julian and Gregorian dates of the seventeenth century. All dates in this book (but not dates in the Epilogue) are given in old style; for those who feel compelled to make the adjustment, thirteen days must now be added (since 1900).

NAMES IN MOGUL HISTORY constantly underwent changes; not merely titles but epithets were conferred upon those who performed deeds of distinction or who for various reasons rose in the peculiar Mogul hierarchy. Hence the young Shah Jahan was known as Prince Khurram, and other members of the royal family as well as nobles of the realm all had several different names. In order to avoid confusion, the names often used here are those by which the persons were best known.

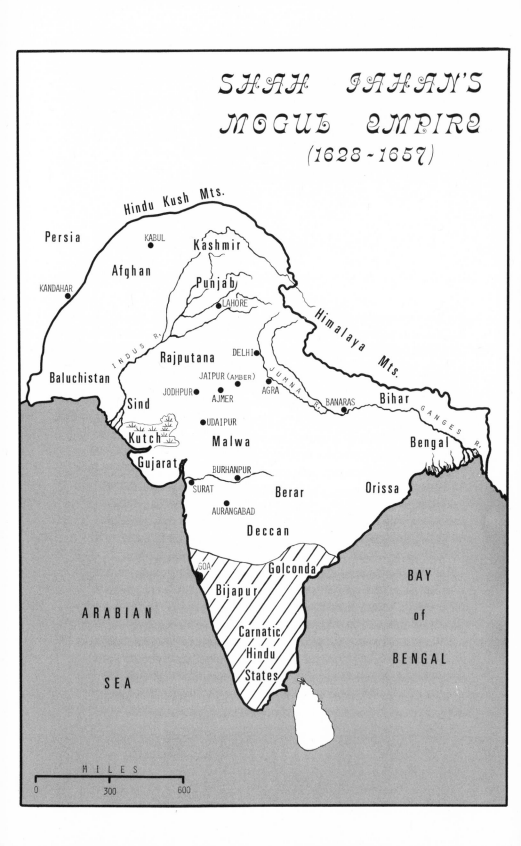

CHAPTER

I

The Standard of Revolt

O N OCTOBER 17, 1605, the third and greatest Mogul ruler
of all—a blunt and unschooled genius who had single-
handedly accomplished the miracle of absolute dominion
over a lion's share of intractable India—lay dying of dysentery in his palace at imperial Agra. By his side sat a devoted
thirteen-year-old grandson. The child's Rajput mother, Princess Manmati, tried in vain to persuade him to abandon the
spectacle of death. "No! So long as there is one breath of life
in Shah Baba, nothing can induce me to leave him." It was
inspired stubbornness: outside the royal apartments, conspirators had appointed henchmen to seize the boy when he
came out. The grand old emperor could only be Akbar the
Great; his grandson could only be Prince Khurram, destined
to become Shah Jahan the Magnificent.

Within the hush of Agra's massive Red Fort, begun and
largely consummated during Akbar's fifty-year reign, agi-
tated grandees of the realm—Moslem khans and Hindu
Rajput chiefs—had been embroiled in a series of plenary ses-
sions, plots, and counterplots ever since the start of the old
man's illness a month before, on September 21. There was
good reason to be disturbed: this emperor of India was no
ordinary regent, but a virtual god-king who alone had held
together a complex and heterogeneous subcontinent which
without him might fly into pieces again. The question of succession loomed large.

As is often the case with genius, Akbar had sired an ungenial brood; in fact they were downright dissolute. Of his three male offspring, Murad and Daniyal had died of drink, with Murad ending in a horrible state of delirium tremens. Only Shah Jahan's father, Prince Salim, remained alive. He was the eldest, born in 1569 of a Rajput consort after previously childless Akbar had made a pilgrimage by foot to saintly Sheikh Salim Chishti of Fatehpur Sikri, some twenty miles from Agra. The holy man had promised a trinity of boys; in gratitude Akbar established a bizarre capital on the spot, embellishing it with strange sandstone palaces—abandoned when the local water source mysteriously dried up.

Salim's loose morals and addiction to both alcohol and opium infuriated Akbar. But a deeper estrangement had come between father and son in the last five years of the emperor's life: for all his debauchery, Salim proved so ambitious that he could hardly wait for Akbar to die. When the prince was barely twenty-two, the great old man had suspected his son of attempting to poison him (the suspicion was groundless). But by the age of thirty or so, Salim, on the advice of counselors, had burst into sulky rebellion; boldly seizing provinces with his army of horsemen, he unsuccessfully attempted to crown himself. In a spider-web intrigue, he had unquestionably instigated the murder of Akbar's beloved scholar-prime minister, Abul Fazl. "He was not my friend," Salim would tersely confess in his memoirs.

Grief-stricken, Akbar yet had to be practical: Murad was dead by then, and Daniyal already dying. Salim's sons, Khusrau and Shah Jahan, were much too young to be considered. A private Dutch chronicle (concerned with Mogul politics as they affected nascent Dutch trade) rendered the dialogue for superiors in Holland: "There is no one left but you. Why do you vex me so? You are bound to inherit the kingdom."

At the intercession of highly placed ladies of the harem, capricious Salim won forgiveness for his rebellious bouts; but he indulged himself in a final revolt before yielding once and for all. At Agra, he performed obligatory ceremonial prostration at Akbar's feet. The emperor, in front of attending no-

1 · *The Standard of Revolt*

bles, accepted this display of submission. But the Dutch record maintains that later, in the privacy of the palace, Akbar struck Salim in the face two or three times with his fist, exclaiming furiously, "You have paid no attention to my commands or letters which I have so often written to you. You raised the standard of revolt against me and made yourself king, which has put me to shame before all kings. Further you minted gold and rupiahs in your name. You became a rebel. What did you mean by doing all this while I am still living? And were you not a fool, to come to me led by fear, like a coward? You hope to become king after my death; but if you rule in the same manner in which you have acted so far, your empire will not last long." The scene is very likely accurate. Akbar further made his son a temporary prisoner, depriving him of opium until powers of the harem again interceded successfully on his behalf.

With princely anarchy at an end, Salim's personal army of horsemen apparently dispersed for lack of employment: he was allowed only four attendants when visiting his father's palace. It was then, during Akbar's remaining year of life, that court intrigue started. One powerful faction headed by the two most influential grandees of the realm—Aziz Koka, Akbar's foster-brother, and Rajah Man Singh of Amber—candidly hoped to preempt Salim and place his eldest son Khusrau (now seventeen) on the throne. Rumor had it that Akbar himself was toying with this idea: Salim had manifested an unpleasant sadistic streak in his treatment of even high-ranking personages, while his narcotic addiction alone provoked alarm.

In the frenzied month between September and October, when it became apparent that Akbar could not live, the two conspirators decided to bring matters to a head: Salim would be seized when he came to visit his dying father. But on arriving at the water gate of Agra fort by boat, the prince received warning as he was about to step ashore; and he retreated.

Desperate, the opposition now convened court nobles and attempted to persuade a majority to repudiate Salim. The suggestion met with stiff resistance from grandees loyal to orthodox rules of succession; but though the meeting broke up without any decision having been reached, matters were later settled by one determined rajah who posted a guard of faithful Hindu Rajputs to watch over the treasury on Salim's behalf. A sheikh also rallied the brave Sayyids of Barha, who declared for the legitimate heir. Realizing that his plot had effectively misfired, Man Singh decided to withdraw to his governing province of Bengal; he would take his pawn Khusrau with him.

In all this intrigue, Prince Salim had understandably remained aloof from his ailing father. He was, in fact, paralyzed by anxiety. Akbar might even rally: five days before the end, several Jesuits had come to pay affectionate respect to the liberal Mogul ruler who welcomed Christianity in his realm; they found the royal patient cheerful. But death was very near, impelling Salim to take action. Sustained by a body of nobles who had prudently extracted a few concessions from him, he appeared before the dying emperor. Unable to speak a word, Akbar was nonetheless fully conscious. The prince dutifully prostrated himself. By gesture, the genius of Mogul India ordered his imperial turban to be placed on the dissolute head of his son; his sword was hung at Salim's side. He then motioned Salim to leave the room, and the incumbent was received outside to the applause of a crowd of grandees. Henceforth, Prince Salim would take the name of Emperor Jahangir—"World Grasper."

Only a few faithful friends were permitted to remain in the death chamber. Worried by their monarch's eclectic religious proclivities in his lifetime, they soberly reminded him of Allah and the Prophet Mohammed. But though he tried several times to oblige them by uttering the name of the one God, no sound came forth. Akbar the Great died as he had lived—an unremitting pantheist. By historical accident, the span of his reign very nearly coincided with that of a sovereign who had died just two years before in her kingdom thousands of miles away—Queen Elizabeth of England.

● ● ●

The Great Mogul might well have been gloomy about

the future of the vast empire which he was leaving in peril to his descendants. He had consolidated India as an absolute autocracy, in which the character of a single sacrosanct ruler determined the fate of everyone. No soothsayer dared to conjure up dark visions. But before long a shrewd Jacobean ambassador to Jahangir's court would uncannily predict: "The time will come when all in these kingdoms will be in combustion, and a few years' war will not decide the inveterate malice laid up on all parts against a day of vengeance."

It would be a terrifying day, in the light of those unbridled emotions which the Moguls so freely displayed. Where had they come from—these strangers with such consuming energy, such a passion for creation and destruction? Inculcated by court scholars, the child Shah Jahan already knew every detail by heart: no Mogul prince could be ignorant of his family's great history. They were (or claimed to be) of noble central Asian blood—nothing less than fifth-generation descendants of mighty Genghis Khan and just as mighty Timur the Lame, or Tamerlane as we know him. In 1398 Tamerlane had even invaded India for a whirlwind moment of mayhem, and Mogul emperors proudly boasted their continuation of "the House of Timur." Perhaps; but in shadowy central Asia, where a thousand Adams had fornicated with a thousand Eves over centuries of nomadic migration, nothing could be certain. Mogul founder Babur had certainly been a prince, but his principality at best constituted a two-by-four realm buried in today's Soviet province of Tajikistan. The Moguls were of inscrutable origin.

Whatever his forebears, there could be nothing uncertain about Babur's achievement in 1526. Between towering Himalayas and Hindu Kush mountains, he stabbed his way into India through that uterine northwest passage used by every aspirant to power except the British. Other Moslems had preceded him in the nine hundred years since Islam's seventh-century birth in Arabia; but none ever controlled more than patches of the Hindu subcontinent, and those who now represented the waning Delhi sultanate proved no match against such an implacable adversary. The sun was in the sign of the Archer and "spear-high" (the phrase is Babur's) for that spectacular battle of April 21, when twelve thousand unassailable Mogul horsemen defeated Delhi's army of a hundred thousand—a triumph of central Asian field strategy in the face of overwhelming odds.

Soldier and poet, Babur had thus inaugurated the dynasty by conquering a three-hundred-mile-wide strip below the Himalayas. But though he swam the Ganges in thirty-three strokes and planted gardens in Agra, he admitted in his memoirs that he loathed India. If Mogul child-princes were allowed to read those candid memoirs uncensored, they also learned that their ancestor had displayed strong homosexual tendencies—which in no way precluded a masculinity capable of leaping between rampart gaps with a man held under each arm. Babur further acknowledged alcoholism, in spite of stern Koranic injunctions against drinking; and he was addicted to opium (Jahangir inherited the double curse). Yet by contrast this founding father had been an esthete, falling into contemplative ecstasies over the autumn leaves of apple trees or composing Persian verse. Babur was the paradoxical model for all his Mogul descendants—a restless warrior energy presumably inherited from Genghis and Tamerlane found itself combined with poetry, with intellectual pursuits and an extreme refinement matched only by the medieval Japanese court of Lady Murasaki.

Babur's son, Humayun, doubtless presented a problem for Mogul historians entrusted with firing the imagination of their royal pupils. Humayun had achieved next to nothing, preferring the company of Moslem mystics to power; he even lost India for eighteen years to an interim Afghan ruler, and fled in misery through sandy deserts of Rajputana and salt wastes to humiliating refuge in Persia. In the midst of flight, he had met and married Hamida Begum, the fourteen-year-old daughter of one of his brother's spiritual advisers. Her hand could hardly reach his collar, but she would become the mother of Akbar the Great. Persia helped Humayun to regain India, supplying him with cavalry for a price: he must wear the twelve-pointed conical cap of their Shia sect of

Islam and promote its schismatic faith. This insult to Mogul orthodoxy had to be borne with patience; Persia would often be high-handed with Humayun's descendants. He, too, took opium, and wound up fatally tumbling down the steps of his library from an overdose. The dynasty's second emperor was then promptly commemorated out of all proportion, with an imposing and very beautiful tomb at Delhi.

It was Akbar who first displayed imaginative Mogul genius. In 1556, at the age of thirteen, he acceded to what was left of Babur's domains; by 1560 he had seized the reins of government from a regent, and within forty-five years achieved the impossible feat of welding together two-thirds of India (including all of today's Pakistan). Short and stocky with a lucky wart on the left side of his nose, indefatigable Akbar literally mesmerized the subcontinent. By war and persuasion he won over those proud rajahs who ruled enormous desert realms in Rajputana. His tolerant harem blended Indian and Mogul, Persian, and even Armenian women. He abolished Islam's hated religious poll tax, established an effective reform of land levy, and inaugurated a daring liberalism which placed Hindu on a par with Moslem. In that momentary exotic capital at Fatehpur Sikri he even concocted his own weirdly eclectic religion—really a spiritual syncretism far in advance of its time. Akbar flouted orthodox Moslem bigotry by making himself virtual pope of India. All these innovations went side by side with hard-pressed military campaigns enlarging the empire: Gujarat and Bengal were conquered, quarrelsome Afghans took heed, Kashmir found itself annexed along with fortresses on the very borders of Persia's domains. Akbar seized hitherto unseizable areas in a stubbornly resistant mid-India.

These achievements were quite untypical of either his progenitors or descendants: no esthetics, no cunning, only a majestic elemental force—"like handling ducks' eggs after hens'." Akbar's physical prowess exceeded Babur's. His passions could terrify: flaring up at the treachery of a foster-brother caught in palace intrigue, he stunned the man with a blow of his fist and then had him thrown from a parapet with the judgment "son of a bitch" punctuating his fall. Yet, though steeped in violence and war, Akbar could also be deeply humane. Virtually untutored, he sparked intellectual curiosity and surrounded himself with eminent scholars. Akbar the Great, third of the Mogul emperors, compared favorably with any European monarch of his period.

Perhaps he was even greater than they: to unify seventeenth-century India required more than ruthless Oriental tyranny, while charitable humanism would have been laughed at. Yet this Hercules had combined authority with stunning broadmindedness, exerting such powers of conciliation that he was able to unite India's disparate religious and ethnic components at a time when abstract national concepts were totally unknown (at least to India). Then, to ensure respect for himself and his descendants, the miracle worker had hypnotized Hindu and Moslem alike into accepting holy monarchic transcendence: both religions must obey the Mogul emperor, and any opposition was sacrilege. Abruptly, haloes began to appear behind the royal head in Mogul court painting. Akbar's strange pantheistic religion may have died with him, but the imperial sanctity he created would linger until 1857—long after the cessation of effective Mogul power.

Akbar's son Jahangir and grandson Shah Jahan could literally coast on all his glory. In the tradition created for them, they were nothing less than semi-divine; tinged with mystique, they ruled a Moslem church and a Hindu-Moslem state.

Hindus hoped that their interference might be limited to the collection of revenues. And revenues were indeed great: the wealth of the Mogul Empire was by now so enormous that all attempts at inventory would be given up after four hundred pairs of treasury scales oscillated day and night for five months.

● ● ●

Behind this House of Timur lay India—ageless, heterogeneous, overwhelming. Moslem strangers had brought a linear Mohammedan calendar in their saddles, hoping to challenge Hindu cyclical time. In that sense they represented something new, though nothing could really be new to India. From the standpoint of Hindu metaphysics she had even known the Moguls before, in staggeringly endless repetitions of the universe known as the day and night of Brahma. These Moguls were a part of Kali Yuga, the blackest age in the throw of cosmic dice. They would act out their tragedy, and India would watch them with compassion but without tears: she had witnessed too many tragedies.

Quite aside from Hindu metaphysics, the Moguls could only take possession for a historical moment. Like Egypt, India looked back on an incredibly long past in which she had always conquered her conquerors. Pastoral Aryans had come through those northwest passes to mingle over millennia with dark-skinned Dravidians, and only the complexities of Hinduism were left to reflect their absorption. Nobody even remembered the overrated intrusion of Alexander the Great. True, brilliant King Ashoka—a would-be Indian Constantine who converted to Buddhism—had briefly held universal sway long before the birth of Christ. But his dynasty disappeared, just as Buddhism itself had almost disappeared from India. In the endless welter of tuppenny kings and limited empires that followed, nothing emerged but the fatal weakness of men whose narrow loyalties precluded grander unity. One final attempt to impose central imperial control had been made by the Guptas, who rose even as Rome was declining in the West. Then came invading Huns, and an interim period not unlike Europe's Dark Ages, with feudal states crystallizing into jigsaw pieces of power.

Now it was the turn of the Moguls. It was their India, impressive in variety and scope. A peregrine falcon soaring upward from some gloved Mogul wrist could have cast its rapacious eye over an empire which extended from Afghanistan to the Bay of Bengal, from the foot of the Himalayas to nervous southern kings of Bijapur and Golconda who lived in fear of annexation.

Skewered together, the fifteen provinces of Mogul Hindustan represented extreme ranges of climate and topography: deserts where water was more precious than gold, snow peaks, and saffron-dotted Kashmir valleys; there was the five-fingered river network of the Punjab, together with rice deltas of Bengal, alluvial tracts of Ganges and Jumna, black cotton soil of Nagpur plain, and wheatfields of a rich Narmada valley. In addition the Moguls had annexed an impressive slice (and intended to appropriate even more) of that mid-India which would later become their coffin—the Deccan. Enclosed by natural barriers of Western Ghats and northern hills, the Deccan was itself a varied enclave of lakes, tablelands which eons of erosion had sculpted into fantastic shapes, water-slashed ravines, and forests where the Asian lion was making its last stand.

Pullulating within these cells of empire, a hundred million subjects fell under Mogul hegemony—the Moslems an ironic minority amid a mass of Hindus whose potential for rebellion against alien rule seemed for the moment neutralized by regional division, jealousy, and mistrust. It was all an ethnic beehive: heroic Rajput clans, fierce tribes swarming over Afghanistan plateaus, sturdy Jats, bearded Sikhs of the Punjab with combs gathering together the woman's-length hair which their religion forbade them to cut, and white-garbed Jains who considered all life so holy that they wore masks to avoid killing even a gnat by breathing. Islam alone bristled with sects and intrareligious frictions, to say nothing of the enormous complexities of a coexisting Hinduism with its rigid caste system and stubborn village autonomy. In addition, a heterogeneous assortment of adventurers—Turks, Persians, Tartars, Uzbeks, Circassians, and Georgians, even Africans and Europeans—made their way to the Mogul court.

Though Humayun had shown a predilection for Delhi, Agra still remained the chosen imperial capital. Both centers of empire were situated in north-central India on the Jumna River, which flowed southward until it finally conjoined with the holy Ganges at the stronghold of Allahabad. Aside from these royal twins, the realm vaunted other large cities—holy Hindu Banaras on the Ganges, Ajmer in the heart of Rajputana, Burhanpur in the Deccan, and Lahore, the great Punjab capital. The port of Surat (somewhat north of the Bombay which did not yet exist) was on the verge of becoming a busy target for foreign commerce and trade: English ambassadors seeking greater foothold for the newly formed East India Company, French gem merchants or doctors, Italian adventurers, and Portuguese intriguers sailing up the coast from their tiny enclave of Goa—droves of them would soon be arriving at Surat, making their way overland by bumpy ox caravan through certain key towns that led to Mogul Hindustan's heart.

But the great masses lived as they had always lived, in thatched and mud-baked huts of myriad villages which defined agrarian India. They grew rice and wheat, barley and millet and vegetables, tending their plots while water buffalo chewed cuds and wallowed in irrigation ditches. Goats, ducks, and skeletal cows wandered these rural precincts; every well had its cluster of bullock carts, swarthy men with burdens, women balancing water pots on their heads, and soulful children with great black eyes and black hair. Inevitable snake charmers and bear tamers heralded the approach to larger towns. Yet parts of the subcontinent also undulated in stretches of desolate wasteland. India then became a curious void, where people could only be invoked as part of a conjuring act.

Helping his descendants to rule such huge domains, Akbar had refined a practical realm based on familiar sources. No one could fail to recognize its affinity to old Baghdad and Ispahan and the whole fairy-tale East: a quasi-Arab, quasi-Persian hierarchy had simply been adapted to an Indian setting. The emperor presided over his typically opulent Oriental court; he enjoyed an exclusive harem, where mysterious ladies were strictly veiled by jealous laws of purdah—the very word referred to screens of state behind which they viewed the spectacle of durbar. Most of these women would be hidden from history in this candidly masculine Mogul world, though a few empresses and princesses asserted their vivid characters. Four in particular would become significant enough in Jahangir's and Shah Jahan's reigns to exert considerable influence on affairs of the realm.

Right hand to the emperor, the vizier or prime minister handled many important matters of state. There was, of course, no cabinet or parliament, though a few trusted officials might sometimes be consulted for advice. But the real pillars of empire in this bellicose Mogul autocracy were the nobility—soldier-grandees who did not inherit their rank but earned it, since every last man had to be ready for combat. Flowery imported titles of khan and khan khanan could be conferred on "holders of command" only by the Mogul emperor, who withdrew distinction whenever he liked. It was a dangerously arbitrary setup for such vital aristocrats; Mogul nobles constituted the very bulwark of bureaucracy, theoretically assigned to high civil and military appointments regardless of caste, creed, or race.

Qualifications naturally counted: a background in martial tradition, and the leadership to attract followers. Happy appointees enjoyed pay clearly defined according to status and length of service. New lords rustled up cavalry contingents, while those who advanced enlarged their already-existing forces. New or old, it stood to reason that a grandee would select followers from his religious caste or clan. Fidelity could be counted upon, especially since master was paymaster directly remunerating troops from his own income. For reasons of cash or kinship, parochial loyalty to Rajput or Afghan chief often exceeded or even defied obeisance to the emperor.

Mogul chronicles become turgid with references to military rank. According to the number of cavalry under his aegis, a nobleman might be commander of five hundred horse or five thousand horse; highest officials—Hindu maharajahs, Moslem generals, and princes of the royal blood—could even command ten thousand horse and more. In war, members of the aristocracy were expected to fight valiantly; in peace, they had to be capable civil administrators. Promotion depended on performance in both categories, or on the emperor's whim.

[22]

1 · *The Standard of Revolt*

Salaries were astronomical, especially for those days: commanders of five thousand horse could pay all their cavalrymen and still have surpluses of eighteen thousand Mogul rupees a month—the equivalent of $60 thousand in actual purchasing power! Petty lords received direct cash, but important persons obtained income in a freakish manner: by imperial grant, they were assigned temporary ownership of territory. Only Rajput rajahs possessed hereditary domains, and even they were subject to fixed tribute. In effect, all of India was crown land—endless acres belonging to an emperor who could relegate them or take them back whenever he pleased. Under his ephemeral proprietary rights a lord merely collected revenue, and (particularly with Shah Jahan) had to sign a bond promising not to exploit peasants or levy excess taxes. When any courtier died, assets were immediately confiscated.

To protest these quixotic aspects of nobility would have been useless if not rank treason. And in point of fact, leftover relatives received preferential treatment: sons of dead grandees could count on liberal education, often receiving titles in short order. It might even be argued that hereditary nobility is itself an arbitrary distinction, based on the accident of birth rather than actual merit. But hereditary nobles are not easily made or broken by an emperor's autocratic command; too often in Mogul India, self-seeking masters of horse watched which way the horse jumped, cynically pledging or withdrawing allegiance at moments when the imperial crown was being contested—a significant factor in tragedy to come.

In any event, such a whirligig of Moslems and Hindus perpetually threatened to shatter into pieces through the accelerations of hatred, jealousy, and religious strife. Their centripetal bond was the powerful personality of the emperor himself—exactly what Akbar had in mind. It was all really a variation on knights in armor, an Oriental round table imported from the steppes of central Asia. Refined by India, the system intermittently worked in its own bizarre way; not a few nobles even proved loyal.

[23]

Provincial Mogul power balanced on a clever teetertotter of military governors and nonmilitary tax collectors. Governors wielded power through armed forces, keeping contact with their village network by means of lesser functionaries; but only tax collectors could garner revenue through a retinue of appointed collections men, sending proceeds to the imperial treasury which then paid governor and collector alike. A spy fabric further assured royal control: news reporters sent weekly official reports to the capital, while there were secret agents whom no one knew.

Rounding out Mogul administration, Islamic justice prevailed. Every town had its Moslem chief of police and mullahs to apply Koranic law, though Hindu pandits were allowed to deal with transgressions in their own communities—a practical concession. Religion served additionally in matters of education: no public schools existed, and teaching reverted to mosque or Hindu temple.

Unable to leave wealth or property to their families, Mogul grandees lived in wild ostentation. Why invest private capital when accumulation might conceivably be appropriated by royal command? Such a system of escheat and obeisance made human volcanoes smolder. No wonder the nobility were forever revolting and the emperor obligingly forgiving them—a cheerful symbiosis. No barons extorted a Magna Charta, no court went into voluntary exile if the emperor found himself dethroned, no mercantile class acted as buffer for the multitudes. Industry remained confined to state enterprises for the emperor, while art or literature found encouragement only by imperial prerogative. Europeans would soon be shocked at the sight of monarchic power carried to such excess. But then, the rules of any society are capricious on final examination.

If the Moguls had created this world of Eastern imperialism, what Atlas sustained it on his back? In agricultural India, Atlas could only be plural: he was the anonymous Hindu peasant. Amorphous and scorned by history, Hindustan's millions tilled the fields that fed an empire; assuredly much of the fruit of their hard work was appropriated (forcibly if need be) by Mogul revenue officers. In some districts, dark clouds obscuring the sky would be followed by hailstones as large as hens' eggs. The specter of famine hovered over masses already haunted by guinea worm, dysentery, cholera, plague, poxes, fevers, and venereal disease. Not that a Moslem court could ever be uncharitable—alms constituted one of Islam's five pillars—but sprays of silver and gold coins from imperial elephant processions could only afford momentary relief for rampant unimperial squalor.

Where exploitation is familiar, it endures for generations. Mogul land assessment was not so very different from Hindu methods rooted in thousands of years of *dharma* or sacred law—Akbar's revenue genius, Todar Mal, merely improved on a long-existing situation. There had always been a ruler who took from the Indian people; farmers had land tenure, it was their duty to pay. The trouble under Mogul rule was the amount of tax. Traditional Hindu assessment had been one-sixth of the land; but with these new conquerors, taxes increased from cupidity until (in spite of Akbar's or other emperors' good intentions) a third or even a half suffered appropriation, every dishonest Mogul official receiving his cut. Obviously, the system must ultimately break down from sheer greed; there was an end even to Hindu patience.

Influential beyond measure, that Hindu majority contributed more to Mogul India than brow sweat. They and their ruling Moslems would and did interchange customs, clothing, ways, language. Members of the royal family already condescended to speak Hindustani in preference to Babur's Turkish tongue, though snobbish Persian had become the official court medium of exchange.

Still, religious differences were harder to reconcile, and Hinduism made orthodox Moslems uneasy. There was something ominous about an ageless theology which crammed everything into its maw—one godhead but endless gods, good and evil, light and dark, gentleness and violence. How could restless Moguls not be disturbed by "infidel" permissiveness? The holiest Hindus even blessed their conquerors with that same acceptance which over thousands of years had embraced everything mankind ever thought or felt or dreamt. Extremes of eroticism and repression, indulgence and abnegation found outlet in Hindu life. Weird sacrifice abounded: ecstatics pitched headlong beneath the wheels of Jagganaut on processional days, and women burned themselves alive in acts of suttee. Yet Hinduism revered creation as much as destruction, fecundity as much as the ascetic. Hindus believed in Laxshmi, goddess of overflowing; reverence for life went to such lengths that bowls of milk were offered to temple cobras.

In its stubborn patterns of eternity, Hinduism passively rebuked those ticktock hours of Moslems and Christians. For Hindus, reincarnation and repetition transcended notions of once-only. Timeless Banaras, the Hindu Rome, afforded the same spectacle for the seventeenth century as it does today or did two thousand years ago. Multitudes of Hindus bathed in the holy Ganges by dawn, assumed the cross-legged lotus posture to greet a rising sun, and worshiped in tilting, half-submerged temples crowding the foreshore. Brahman priests sat under umbrellas by heaps of colored powders to be smeared on cheek or forehead. Cremation fires burned day and night while dogs lurked about the pyres; ashes of the dead were shoveled into a river already crowded with the living, so that posthumous union with the Hindu godhead might prevent endless rebirth in a world of suffering. Moguls saw the same penitents, wanderers, and stark-naked *sadhus* who can still be found along India's roads, together with costumes of dhoti and sari which have changed little over centuries. Indians were so profoundly conservative that they would "prefer an old Hell to a new Heaven!" It was all inordinately strange.

Of course, not everyone conformed or lived as a saint; Mogul India seethed with devils and rebels and crime. A random sampling of standard punishment seems more than revealing: captured thieves had their right hands cut off, apprehended highwaymen lost both hands and feet, and robbers and apostates suffered decapitation so that their heads could be immured in edifying cement turrets. Even adulterers got stoned to death, while fornicators could look forward to a hundred lashes.

Such extreme penalties could only be designed to suppress extreme disorder. Under Jahangir's new reign, lone subjects without caravans were hardly safe on insecure public highways. Before long, the road from Delhi to Agra would become infested with professional assassins called thuggees. Devotees of Kali, the Hindu goddess of death and destruction, thugs offered up prayers for the success of their violent enterprises. Murder represented the apotheosis of devotion and sacrifice, pickaxe and dagger being symbolic of the goddess's teeth and ribs. In remote areas, cutthroat bands dominated whole provinces.

Everything added up to a sum of savage contrasts. Without ever having known this East, John Milton would soon encompass its dazzle and brutality in a single poetic epithet —"barbaric pearl and gold."

• • •

This was the spectrum of Jahangir's and Shah Jahan's inherited world. This was that mightily expanded Hindustan of the Moguls, consolidated by the genius of Akbar the Great and left in jeopardy to his descendants.

In fact, jeopardy seemed to be accelerating. Jahangir's rebellion against Akbar merely preluded his own paternal troubles, which now came only a few months after his accession: his eldest son Khusrau fled and revolted in turn. Again the independent Dutch chronicle offered telling and probable details to Amsterdam; on their way out of Agra, Khusrau and rebel troops "plundered all sweetmeat shops, to have enough to eat for some time."

Khusrau's insurrection failed near Lahore, in May of 1607. Encamped nearby, Jahangir had him brought handcuffed and chained to durbar, where the rebel shook uncontrollably, cried, and tried to prostrate himself. In the Dutch version of events, sadistic Jahangir ordered peasants to cut down trees and make pointed stakes along the road; every treacherous noble who helped Khusrau was then impaled or hanged. "The King personally went to see the sight as a pastime, taking his son Sultan Khusrau, mounted on an elephant, with him. They rode through the dead nobles, who filled both sides of the road. Mahabat Khan [the leading Mogul general] was seated behind the Prince, in order to tell him their names. And as the corpses were dangling or swinging on account of the wind, he said to Khusrau, 'Sultan, see how your soldiers fight against trees.' " The account is more than hearsay: Jahangir himself corroborates details of Khusrau's defecting, and tells how "for the sake of good government I ordered them to hang up and impale [those] who had taken part in the rebellion."

In the aftermath, Khusrau's remaining followers doggedly decided to assassinate the emperor. But young Shah Jahan got wind of the matter and alerted his father in time. The conspirators were seized and their ringleaders put to death. Hapless Khusrau suffered imprisonment and had his eyes either sealed up with stitches, covered with clay, or rubbed with the juice of a baneful leaf—all versions prevail. Only later did Jahangir relent: the eyes were unsealed or unstitched; one regained its vision and the other did not.

Inevitably, Shah Jahan acquired distinction as his father's favorite and the most likely candidate for the throne. All seemed peacefully assured, but Mogul themes had already become too well established. It was only a question of time before the standard of revolt would be raised again.

CHAPTER

2

Henna and Intrigue

IN THE SPRING OF 1612, no Taj Mahal existed. Far from being preoccupied with Mumtaz Mahal's death, Emperor Jahangir and the entire Mogul court were about to celebrate her wedding to Shah Jahan. Nineteen years old and radiantly beautiful, the bride herself would certainly have no fore-knowledge that in another nineteen years she would inspire her husband to commission the greatest monument in the world—a tomb unrivaled by any Medici.

Her real name was Arjumand Banu Begum. But history calls her the Lady of the Taj; and of course only the Moguls could give her that royal title—Mumtaz Mahal, "Exalted One of the Palace"—which with slight corruption designates the mausoleum. Whatever her titles she remains enigmatic, her secrets enclosed by a white marble coffin inlaid with gem flowers of eternal summer. The most important single woman in the Mogul Dynasty emerges as a provocative shadow, out-lined but undelineated.

Research yields nothing but scraps and pieces—frag-ments in Mogul chronicles, or the unsubstantiated romantic embellishments of sentimentalists. The only really significant facts are the Taj itself, together with Mumtaz Mahal's very obvious fecundity: in a Mogul Empire of harems, polygamy, and high infant mortality, Shah Jahan's seven children (and seven others who died in infancy or childhood) were remark-ably the fruit of her particular womb. However unwittingly, she was the real author of first-degree consanguineal tragedy

—the mother without whom there could have been no cataclysm.

A Mogul portrait by a court artist depicts the young bride for us: aristocratic features of striking loveliness, with a somber but amused gaze as the shadow of a Mona Lisa smile plays about her little mouth. Spilling out from under a jeweled headdress, her black plaited hair frames an oval face. She wears rich earrings and a richly embroidered dress, while one hand delicately inclines to her nostrils a single Persian rose held between thumb and forefinger. Indeed, not only the rose but she herself was of Persian descent. Yet for now, she can be seen only in the context of the rarefied court into which she was marrying, just as that court gains definition against a larger background—imperial Agra.

● ● ●

Competent stargazers had selected April 30 of this year 1612 as Prince Shah Jahan's and Mumtaz Mahal's wedding day—a day when nothing need be feared and perfect happiness would prevail. Agra rallied to the occasion, with vivid processions by day and elaborate fireworks lighting up the Red Fort at night.

The Mogul capital was an ideal setting for these important nuptials. Written history might only trace the city back to the last of the Delhi sultanate, but it was much older than that. Epic Hindu legends mentioned Agra, its name deriving from a Sanskrit root meaning "prior" or "first." Here along the river, in mythical time, Vishnu had assumed graceful incarnation: like Pan, the sporting Hindu shepherd-god had blown his pipe and captivated dairymaids and princesses. Agra had witnessed or would witness half the history of Moslem Moguls: it was Babur's founding center, and (aside from Humayun's partiality for Delhi) had remained the seat of power for Akbar, and now for Shah Jahan's father, Emperor Jahangir. Agra assuredly had become the exotic capital of all Asia, far more famous in pomp and magnificence than Haroun-al-Raschid's earlier Baghdad.

Renamed Akbarabad in honor of that great sovereign, the city had swollen since Akbar's day to three quarters of a million people, including many strangers continually filling some ninety caravanserai scattered about town. Mosques abounded, and the high steeple of the Jesuit church sounded its bell to every district. There were eight hundred *hamams* or baths; vaulted avenues lined with merchant shops boasted velvets and silks of Persia, together with gold cloth from China. The swarm of crowds everywhere became so dense that people could hardly pass. Agra, twice as big as Persia's Ispahan, could hardly be circumscribed in a day by a man on horseback.

Only the poor went on foot. Bullock carts rumbled past as best they could, making way (especially on durbar days) for rich men's gilded chariots drawn by white oxen with copper-sheathed horns. Elephants were a sure sign of royalty; golden howdahs hid court ladies; every horse had been imported from central Asia, and only manly soldiers rode them. More effete or elderly nobles preferred palanquins borne on the shoulders of four to six lackeys. They sat cross-legged on cushions, smoking water pipes or chewing betel on their way to court; they spat red juice into silver spittoons while other lackeys shooed away flies or brushed off dust with peacock fans. Often the nobles' women could be glimpsed peeping from luxuriously swaying *chandoles*–the windows adorned with silk, and tiger skins beneath their feet. Boats and rafts made the Jumna a colorful scene.

Heading through Agra's streets on their way outward to the network of empire, royal foot couriers, light-headed from opium or bhang, ran along with whip in hand and small bells on their heads. Operating day and night like an olympic relay, they delivered letters at incredible speed: they often went a thousand miles in a fortnight.

The heart of Agra was the Red Fort on the Jumna River. Its massive sandstone battlements kept watch over outlying mansions of important nobles which stretched along the river bank as far as where the Taj Mahal stands today, and even beyond. These nobles were so rich they kept a thousand torch bearers to cast light by night; behind those facades lay fountains, gardens, harem quarters, and cool subterranean apartments to ward off summer heat. Costly carpets from Persia and Kashmir adorned gilded interiors strewn with brocaded cushions; artistic niches coddled precious porcelains, but aside from beds there was little furniture as we know it. No less wealthy though considerably more discreet, Hindu merchants hid their lofty castles among greenery—a secretive flamboyance conditioned by justifiable fears that orthodox Moslem bigots might yet reverse the notorious liberalism begun with Akbar.

But all this was wealthy suburbia. Within Agra proper an unattractive jumble of streets displayed considerably more modest dwellings, tradesmen and petty lords making do with brick and burned tile; clay houses lodged common soldiers and camp followers. Mud huts of the anonymous poor were omnipresent: miserably thatched one-room affairs entered only by stooping. Entire families lived in these cramped conditions, their earth floors glossed daily with fresh cow dung, their inventory limited to sleeping mats and a pit for beating rice and a pot or two for cooking. Hot winds of summer made fires a nightmare conflagration with thousands of huts and lives lost, especially by women in purdah who preferred death to exposing their faces to strangers. In effect the city could hardly be considered more than a military encampment, affording few amenities to any but the privileged. Yet in an age when even London ladies carried nosegays to fend off the stink of garbage, Agra's fame had already spread as far as a now-curious Europe.

During high moments of durbar, Rajput chiefs poured in from desert strongholds, together with Afghan nobles and motley khans of Turkish, Uzbek, or Persian blood. The environs of the Red Fort would swirl then with elephants, horses, coaches, soldiers, and rabble. In the outer bazaar, even ordinary days afforded a potpourri. Jugglers entertained throngs of spellbound admirers; snake charmers coiled snakes round neck and shoulders. Fortune tellers and bazaar astrologers promised children to sterile women, or listened intently to whispered indiscretions of other ladies wrapped from head to foot. For poor people, foretelling cost exactly one pice—the mere bronze fraction of a rupee. Apothecaries sold opium or bhang pellets compounded with drugs and spices; rogues, pickpockets, and ragged children ogled tinseled dancers; cheek by jowl were walnut vendors, wrestlers, hunters and soldiers—everyone jostling to a pitch of confusion.

Though Hindus ate no meat, Moslems did: marketers offered pigeons and turtledoves, beef, mutton, goats, and even pigs for Christians. Fish seemed limited to carp, but a great store of fruits embraced oranges, muskmelons, and raisins from Persia.

An observant East India Company clerk would soon ferret out other markets—"not so commendable, yet much frequented and allowed of, not only here but all India over, namely the Common Stews. Each of them every evening is like a fair, where they resort, make their bargains, take and choose the whores sitting and lying on their cots." For more discriminating sexual appetites he notes that "daucing wenches" can be hired to sing and shimmy at feasts. The wenches made extra money on little slave girls whom they bought and trained, "selling their maidenheads at first at dear rates, after prostituted for a small matter."

In contrast to vulgar joys, prince and pauper alike could bask in the splendor of the emperor's durbar; always followed by elephant fights, wrestling and fencing matches. Jahangir's Roman proclivities were now encouraging combat between men and beasts. Inclined to spectacle, Shah Jahan would later raise these durbars to an even more lavish pitch of Oriental pageantry.

The main gates of the Red Fort had drawbridges raised at night by thick iron chains, with contingents of noble guardsmen day and night. From the hubbub of the bazaar, where a wretched parrot fixed on a high pole was forever being shot at by nobles and even the emperor himself, only the privileged few entered that inner elephant gateway flanked by two carved stone beasts and riders. And men had to be still more privileged to pass yet another entrance, beyond which lay halls of public and private audience, the treasury, the garden, the emperor's palace, and fine apartments for the royal ladies. The outer fort enclave held royal workshops for silversmiths and goldsmiths, for tailors, carpenters, shoemakers, and many artisans; there were officers' dwellings, and a music gallery where court drummers pounded kettledrums until the palace seemed to shudder, while trumpets added to the din.

● ● ●

If Mumtaz Mahal's imminent royal bridegroom looked out on all this panorama, it could hardly have been from inside the precincts of the Red Fort: prevailing etiquette had already given him a proper residence of his own, away from his father's harem. Shah Jahan (still called Prince Khurram, since his imperial epithet had not yet been conferred upon him) was just past his twentieth birthday: born at Lahore in January of 1592, under the sign of Libra. Overjoyed with a grandson, Akbar had named the young prince "Khurram" or "joyous." One of Akbar's barren wives even adopted the child for her own, so that his real Rajput mother played second maternal fiddle in his upbringing. Tutored by eminent scholars, Shah Jahan displayed prodigious memory—a love of exacting details and an industrious ability to master them. In his personal habits he quickly became compulsively clean, having a special taste for perfume that saturated his wardrobe. He was so polite that he avoided "thou" when addressing even the lowest servant.

As the prince dressed for his wedding, royal mirrors doubtless reflected the handsome face we know from Mogul miniatures: almost Assyrian in its regal hauteur, with slanted almond eyes, firm nose, and a mouth hovering between youthful determination and the lurking sensuality still to spell disaster. Now, in his youth, he was dominated by two emotions—pride, and an overweening ambition to become emperor. But it was still early in the reign of his father Jahangir.

Nuptials were always expensive in India, and this royal affair stinted at nothing. Four precious gifts along with red dye had been duly sent in advance to the bride; Mumtaz Mahal received fruits and sweetmeats on beautiful trays, and no little actual cash—perhaps many thousands of rupees. Accompanied by music, Prince Khurram's friends personally carried the gifts to her father's house.

The wedding ceremony which now took place (probably in the great inner quadrangle of the Red Fort amid tents, pavilions, bunting, and carpets spread for the occasion) would seem odd to us: a *hennabandi* ritual of Moslems. According to prescribed form, the groom submitted his hands to be dyed red with a mixture of henna and turmeric by ladies concealed behind a curtain; noble wedding guests also had their hands stained by the auspicious dye. Curiously, nobody expected the bride's father to be present at the actual marriage. But Mumtaz Mahal's father loved pomp, vying with Emperor Jahangir in providing his part of the magnificent display prompted by the occasion. The emperor himself attached the wedding wreath of pearls to the bridegroom with his own hands. Possibly the *qazi*, as Moslem legal expert of Agra and a very holy mullah to boot, presided over the official conjoining with two male witnesses. The bride then gave her formal consent, the bridegroom recited the usual prayers, and custom dictated announcement of the marriage settlement—a matter of no small importance, since dowry was rigorously observed. Dowry being a dual affair, both the groom's and the bride's family proffered gifts. Mumtaz Mahal's father may well have sent Arabian and Turkish horses, together with a hundred elephants, Abyssinian and Circassian slaves, gold goblets and costly silks. Each of the wedding guests received a present. One hour later, Shah Jahan's hands were washed with rosewater, and he drank a glass of water to confirm the holy tie. The great state banquet which followed in the house of the bride's father was honored by the presence of Emperor Jahangir himself. Musicians, singers, and dancers capped the day.

Further marriage celebrations lasted a whole month, shared with the multitudes through pageanted parades and ingenious pyrotechnical displays. Even as late as the end of May, Jahangir went to Prince Khurram's apartments in company with ladies of the royal harem and high nobles. Shah

Jahan dutifully trotted out presents for his father, jewels for the begums and female servants, and robes of honor for the gentlemen. Jahangir stayed a day and a night, under a pavilion erected by the master of ceremonies.

Considering the potential dispersal of affections in a polygamous Mogul house, the marriage proved a real union of hearts. Two other wives of Shah Jahan count for nothing in history. Prince Khurram had first been engaged to Mumtaz Mahal when he was fifteen and she fourteen—almost a Romeo and Juliet. In the interim his father had contracted another marriage for him, a diplomatic alliance with a Safavid princess descended from the shah of Persia. There would be still a third wedding, for private political reasons: five years after these festivities with the Lady of the Taj, Shah Jahan would look to the future and choose the daughter of Shahnawaz Khan, a canny soldier vital to his growing circle of adherents. Sparse facts are accorded these other wives. Shahnawaz Khan's daughter bore Prince Khurram a son who died in infancy; and the lady of Persian blood produced an obscure daughter.

As for anonymous harem concubines, we know little at this point of his life. Many women in the zenana served other than amorous purposes: ladies-in-waiting, female guards, and attendants swelled the count. Not all of them could be the object of lust—not yet, at any rate. There is no reason to doubt Shah Jahan's relative fidelity to Mumtaz Mahal—a fidelity conditioned by a Moslem framework within which even royal women had no choice but to accept rigidly restricted lives. Yet behind even this true marriage, politics were also at work; if not his, then someone else's.

Mumtaz Mahal's Persian family loomed large at the Mogul court. Persians, the "Frenchmen" of Asia, were esteemed as disseminators of a complex Islamic culture, however much the Moguls might exchange insults with high-handed regents in Ispahan. Official court language was Persian; Mogul historians wrote florid Persian chronicles; Mogul poets composed odes in Persian. Everyone who was anyone could quote chapter and verse from Omar Khayyám or Hafiz. Persian artistry lay like a golden mantle over the sordid materialism of India's empire. In 1577 during the great Akbar's reign, Mumtaz Mahal's noble Persian grandfather, Mirza Ghiyas Beg, had been reduced to poverty in his native Khurasan. Helped by a merchant prince, he survived the rough journey to Agra with a pregnant wife and promptly joined Akbar's court. Cunning, persistent, charming, and as always a refined adventurer, he had raised himself up by his bootstraps. Honored and renamed Itimad-ud-Daulah by Akbar, he now held the most dignified position in the Mogul realm—prime minister to Emperor Jahangir.

Two of Itimad's children shared his political prominence. His crafty son, Asaf Khan, was the father of Mumtaz Mahal, and would himself become prime minister under Shah Jahan. Itimad's daughter, the intriguing Nur Mahal, had recently risen to first lady of the realm by marrying Jahangir. This formidable Persian triumvirate would literally dominate court politics for a decade to come.

In modern blunt idiom, Nur Mahal might be labeled a scheming bitch; but she was a highly clever and fascinating bitch. Basking in her new title of Nur Jahan ("Light of the World"), she had slowly but steadily begun to widen her sphere of influence. Father and brother would soon witness her ascendance; before long she would become nothing less than virtual ruler of Mogul India, with coins minted in her name and imperial orders bearing her signature. She would hypnotize the infatuated Jahangir, and rock him to sleep like a baby after his drunken orgies and opium bouts. At this particular moment, the empress unquestionably had her eye on Shah Jahan as the most ambitious and likely to succeed of Jahangir's sons (there were now five). She could hardly resist showing her initial power before entrusting a niece to this enterprising stepson. One month before the wedding, Nur Jahan wangled Shah Jahan a promotion in rank: he was now commander of thousands of cavalry.

It seems surprising that with this family of Persian plotters Mumtaz Mahal should emerge from history so innocent. Yet with the exception of doubtful allegations that she once succumbed to a momentary anti-Christian pique, we find no record of intrigue on her part—quite the contrary. She grew up under the influence of grandparents and parents; Asaf Khan doted on her, Itimad dandled her. Her mother, Diwanji Begum, was herself the daughter of Persian nobility. Mumtaz would be a beauty in any age, but character added luster. She seems to have been that rare combination of modesty and candor, a woman warmly straightforward yet bemusedly self-possessed. Highly intelligent but happily not shrewd, she became well versed in Persian and Arabic. Early in adolescence, she attracted the attention of important nobles of the realm. Jahangir must have heard about the girl, since he readily consented to Prince Khurram's engagement five years prior to the actual marriage; and he even put the betrothal ring on her finger.

So little is known about Mogul women, so much must be imagined. When, for instance, did Shah Jahan first lift the veil of purdah to gaze on his beloved? Obligingly, later embroiderers conjure up an appropriately cloying encounter. Young Prince Khurram supposedly meets younger Mumtaz Mahal at the Moslem New Year's festival, when Agra's imperial gardens blaze with lights and echo to music. Such festivities did, of course, take place. Akbar had long ago instituted a kind of mock bargain fair for New Year's—a flirtation sale with vending stalls for court ladies to exert their wiles on nobles and sell jewels or worthless trinkets at outrageous prices. A schoolgirl might possibly swallow the story: exquisite Mumtaz Mahal ("black plaited hair, soft black eyes, delicately penciled eyebrows and long silky lashes, velvet skin like a lily") rivals her beautiful aunt, Nur Jahan, and stands shyly behind her stall while Shah Jahan approaches, talks to her, becomes infatuated. "O, that I were a glove upon that hand."

This story of their first meeting is probably apocryphal, the love was not. Mumtaz Mahal symbolized for Shah Jahan an uncorrupt haven, far from imperial games of power. He played them; she did not. She remained generous, unsullied, good spirited and patient. She loved Shah Jahan body and soul, and he reciprocated beyond politics. She even fascinated him, as Nur Jahan was now fascinating Jahangir. One doubting scholar concludes that the two ladies "played their parts in the drama of love admirably well." But Shah Jahan was no Jahangir, no drugged fool giving his utter confidence to a scheming woman. Mumtaz Mahal would never falter in the stark rebellion and flight soon to attend ambitious Prince Khurram's jockeyings for power. On endless journeys and with swollen belly, she would accompany her husband to Udaipur state and even distant Bengal. Princess Royal Jahanara would shortly be born in that Udaipur campaign; Raushanara and Gauharara, their other daughters, were yet to be born at Burhanpur in the fateful Deccan. Four sons—Dara and Shuja and Aurangzeb and Murad—would be slapped into crying life on military campaigns. Mumtaz Mahal was a good woman, she deserved her monument.

● ● ●

Emperor Jahangir ("World Grasper") was forty-three at the time of his son's marriage; he would somehow live fifteen years more. Fleshy, sensual, corrupt, violent in temper, and by now incorrigibly steeped in his vices, he springs to life across the centuries in many portraits. The best capture him exactly: handlebar moustache, bags under his eyes, full lips, and the usual pearls and dagger at his belt.

Vaguely he invites a Roman comparison as the Claudius of the Moguls; but analogy is only partly apt. Jahangir was really an incongruous mixture of decadence, childish naïveté and candor. Pious Moslems must doubtless have been shocked to their five o'clock prayers by the frankness with which he displayed himself, even holding a drinking cup in hand on Mogul coins! In his extraordinary memoirs, he boasts about being more alcoholic than his great-grandfather Babur. He confesses that he began wine drinking at fourteen, to relieve fatigue; when wine stopped having effect Jahangir resorted to *arak*, the heady licorice spirits of the East. "In the course of nine years I got up to twenty cups of double-distilled spirit," he confesses, "fourteen of which I drank in the afternoon, and the remaining six at night. My food in those

days was one fowl and some bread. No one dared to expostu-
late with me, and matters reached such an extreme that when
in liquor I could not hold my cup for shaking and trembling.
I drank, but others held the cup for me." One of Akbar's doctors finally told Jahangir bluntly that six months more of
drinking would put him in his coffin. "His advice was good,
and life is dear." So Jahangir tapered off to six cups of mixed
wine and spirits daily; then, "I took to opium." He was now,
in 1612, taking opium twice a day besides the liquor. He had
the stamina of an elephant.

Prior to all this wild self-indulgence, Jahangir had been
thoroughly schooled to foster the qualifications expected of a
Mogul regent—especially culture, which Akbar had stressed
to compensate for his own lacuna. Brought up at Fatehpur
Sikri in days before the city's total abandonment, Jahangir
had been taught Persian, Turkish, Arabic, and Hindi, together with arithmetic, history, geography and other sciences.
Duly he learned to compose Persian verse, to take an interest
in botany, zoology, music, painting and the fine arts. Along
with culture went sports—archery, riding, swordsmanship,
rifle shooting—and Jahangir developed into a good shot and
a great hunter. It was the same education which would later
be imposed on Shah Jahan.

Oddly, and alone among Moslem rulers, Jahangir had
never been circumcised: an eclectic Akbar may have taken
Saint Paul's "What does it matter?" to heart. Whatever the
reason for this lapse from accepted Islamic practice, it was
far from being the only one. Strictly orthodox Sunni Islam,
though still given lip service by the Mogul emperor and
many Moslems at court, had long since been modified by the
liberalism of Akbar's Hindu-Moslem entente. In marriage
matters alone, Mogul blood was fast mixing with Hindu; Akbar's mingled harem had become an acceptable norm. Continuing the dilution, Jahangir had married a Hindu Rajput
cousin at sixteen; it was she who produced his eldest son,
Khusrau. She vindicated Rajput honor by committing suicide in 1604 out of shame for Khusrau's rebellion. Among
other Hindu wives, Jahangir married the noble mother of

Shah Jahan; by blood alone, Shah Jahan was more Indian than Mogul. Later, Jahangir's harem had swelled to eight hundred women, but final infatuation now focused exclusively on Nur Jahan.

Tamerlane's violence ran through the Mogul line, but with Jahangir it went to extremes. He liked to watch men being flayed alive; he ordered a man killed and two others hamstrung simply because they accidentally intruded on a royal hunt and frightened away game. He reveled in combat between man and beast, and especially enjoyed the sight of lions clawing out human guts. But by divine contradiction Jahangir was also a lover of justice, ordering a gold chain with sixty bells on it attached to a battlement of Agra fort, so that injured parties might circumvent court intrigue and make the bells ring in direct notice of their wrongs—not that anybody ever did. He could murder his father's prime minister and at the same time order lukewarm douches for the royal elephants "because they shivered in winter when they sprinkled themselves with cold water." He tells us charmingly: "This was entirely my own idea. Nobody had ever thought of it before."

Quite aside from the contrasts of cruelty and tenderness, justice and injustice, Jahangir runs a whole gamut of contradictions and curiously emerges likeable. There is something attractive about the unorthodox despot who shocks his mullahs by eating pork and refusing to fast at Ramadan; who shoots blunt wooden arrows at his annoyed physician while Nur Jahan soothes him; who gives gold to fakirs and embraces ash-soiled holy men, taking dirty bread at their hands. We enjoy (even though it may not be true) the Rabelaisian coarseness when he allegedly pits Moslem holy men against Jesuit fathers. On one occasion, a Jesuit presumably offers to trust his faith to flames with Bible in hand if a mullah holding the Koran will do likewise, thus proving Christianity the greater religion; prone to accept the challenge, Jahangir so frightens his mullah that (in an unreliably scatological anecdote) the holy man "dropped his head, the color left his face, and trembling he defiled himself, filling the whole court with

[41]

the odor but answering never a word. When the smell reached Jahangir, he held his nose as also did the courtiers."

And of course there is the romantic Jahangir who woos Nur Jahan. Here, legends crop up again. Nur Jahan is supposedly born while Itimad-ud-Daulah and his wife are making that rough journey from Persia; weakly, they abandon the child under a tree, returning out of guilt to find the indomitable future queen protected from the sun by a hooded cobra. Growing up, Nur Jahan marries a Persian refugee, Sher Afghan, who wins from Jahangir an appointment as a Bengalese subofficial. Sher Afghan finds himself accused of vague indiscretions; hauled before the Bengal governor, he kills him in a rage and is himself hacked to pieces by the governor's men. A bereft Nur Jahan, ordered back to the court at Agra, is told en route by a dervish of her future greatness. No longer a girl but still a beauty, she comes to the emperor's attention. Jahangir is infatuated, if indeed he has not been infatuated years before: there are dark rumors that he had Nur's husband killed in order to fulfill a long-standing love denied by his father Akbar. Whatever the matter, Jahangir will court her assiduously. The Dutch will romantically write to Amsterdam that the emperor "every evening went by water in a boat to the house of Itimad-ud-Daulah on her account. He used to remain there the whole night, and returned again by water to the castle in the morning." These love-sick water journeys lasted forty days, at the end of which Nur Jahan consented to become his queen.

In the welter of conflicting accounts, Dutch and otherwise, truth is hard to ferret out. Why would Akbar object to his son Jahangir marrying young Nur Jahan in the first place? Why would Nur Jahan marry the murderer of her own husband? Schemer she might have been, but she was bound by certain codes of womanly honor. On the other hand, the Jahangir who dotes on trivia in his memoirs says nothing at all about his courtship; he does not even record Nur Jahan's name until three years after their marriage. And why would he order this particular widow to be brought back to Agra and placed in the imperial harem under his mother, the queen dowager? The Dutch imply that Nur Jahan lived during courtship at her father's house. By any addition, the sum remains a puzzle. Why should Jahangir wait four years from the day of her husband's death to marry her? Could this be to lull public suspicion?

Whatever the truth, we know that Jahangir did love her; he wooed her, married her when she was thirty-four, and elevated her to the eminence she now enjoyed. Nur Jahan in any event had become famous in her own right—for her long black hair and horsemanship, her tiger hunts, her high intelligence, and spontaneous composition of Persian verse. Extant profile portraits suggest much: the nose is strong, the mouth too revealing, the eyes a marvel of Persian intensity. Often she is adorned with pearls and earrings, and holds a scent bottle unstoppered in her hands.

Nur Jahan was endlessly inventive: she would soon devise new dresses with long trains (the Peshwaz); she would create new fashions in silk and cotton, new jewelry and ornaments, new banquet-table decorations for the court. Indeed, her fashions would dominate society for many years, until the end of Shah Jahan's reign; some romantics claim that even today India's culture bears the mark of her genius.

So privately scheming that the Dutch merchants in Agra labeled her "that vicious woman who is filled with cunning up to the throat," Nur Jahan was yet outwardly magnanimous. Her daily charity conformed to standards, she provided dowries for orphan girls and succored the poor. But underneath the perfume and the soft gestures was an astute brain, busily assessing political and administrative problems of the realm. Her compulsion to dominate everyone and every situation would soon become apparent, together with no little courage and cool-headedness. She just possibly may have been even a murderess: one source claims that she invited Khusrau's mother to look with her by moonlight down a well in the courtyard of her apartments, and then pushed the lady into the well—giving the alarm only after all splashing had ceased. This is, of course, sheer gossip, but the motive is plausible enough: by getting rid of the mother of the heir apparent, Nur would be preparing the throne for a puppet of her own choosing.

With the marriage in 1612 of Shah Jahan to her niece, Mumtaz Mahal, Queen Nur's junta crystallized. Events kept pace with an itinerant court as Mumtaz Mahal began to produce children—Jahanara (the future princess royal) born in 1614 at the important city of Ajmer, and Dara Shikoh (the future crown prince) also born at Ajmer the following year. Jahangir welcomed a grandson: "Two watches of the night had passed on . . . Monday, the 29th Safar [March 30, 1615], in the ascension of Sagittarius, when a boy was born to Baba Khurram by the daughter of Asaf Khan; I gave him the name of Dara Shikoh. I hope that his coming will be propitious to this state conjoined to eternity and to his fortunate father."

Confident of an endless Mogul future, Jahangir blissfully ignored the present and continued to indulge himself; sinking gradually deeper into vice and sloth, he was glad to give his passionate and capable consort full rein. The mighty empire of Hindustan was in effect being run by the empress, aided and abetted by her father, Itimad, her brother, Asaf Khan, and ambitious young Shah Jahan. Even Nur Jahan's mother was included in family politics: Asmat Begum balanced matters, perhaps acting as counselor to her power-smitten daughter. After all, Nur Jahan's mother was no insignificant character herself—history remembers her as the inventor of attar of roses.

CHAPTER

3

A Foothold in the Realm

IN 1616, JAHANGIR AND the entire Mogul court still so-
journed at Ajmer in the heart of Rajputana. Here they
dallied almost three hundred miles west of imperial Agra,
surrounded by forested hills that enclosed large lakes. But
Ajmer afforded more than a sylvan cadre for impermanent
royal residence; it was also conveniently close to Rajput
strongholds, to Jaipur and notably Udaipur, with whose ruler
Jahangir had recently been at war.

Such prolonged divagations away from the settled luxu-
ries of the royal capital were by no means uncommon for
Mogul rulers. Quite aside from rebellious provinces and subjects—the troublesome Deccan, truant Afghans, and wayward Rajputs to be squelched—there was pleasure to be had
in other parts of the realm: hunting trips for tiger and deer,
summers in Kashmir, and sojourns in the Punjab capital of
Lahore. Mogul emperors proved traditionally migratory,
moving about their enormous domains with a staggeringly gigantic retinue of court attendants, slaves, noble Moslem
khans and Hindu chiefs, artillery, cavalry, foot soldiers, bazaar keepers, elephants, horses, camels, oxen, tents, cooks,
banners, palanquins, hangers-on, and of course the imperial
zenana.

Jahangir continued his starkly degenerate life. Alcoholic
and opium-addled, he remained a helpless but feared mikado
sustained in an aristocratic vacuum. Somehow he managed
his morning prayers and the obligatory public display to

Ajmer's populace: "If he were unseen one day and no sufficient reason rendered, the people would mutiny; two days no reason can excuse." He staggered on to noonday court, elephant fights, and a harem interlude, winding up his day in total stupefaction. How he continued for so long nobody knew. Seven years before, the English opportunist, William Hawkins, had recorded the extent of the emperor's addiction. "He drinketh . . . five cupfuls, which is the portion that the physicians allot him. This done, he eateth opium and . . . layeth him down to sleep. . . . And after he hath slept two hours, they awake him and bring his supper to him; at which time he is not able to feed himself, but it is thrust into his mouth by others; and this is about one of the clock, and then he sleepeth the rest of the night."

Hawkins knew what he was talking about: a heavy drinker himself, his pretensions as England's first unofficial ambassador to the Mogul Empire had won several years of glass-clinking with Jahangir. Yet what was he really?—only a postman bearing a royal letter which the East India Company had solicited from King James. In ignorance the letter addressed Akbar, vaguely requesting "liberty of traffic and privileges" for the benefit of both kingdoms. Hawkins, who had spent time in the Middle East (probably in trade) and spoke fluent Turkish, influenced company officials to make him "Lieutenant General" of their Third Voyage. His lone ship, the *Hector*, significantly had displayed the English flag for the first time along the coast of India when it arrived at Surat port on August 24, 1608. Delayed by Portuguese intriguers determined to prevent English intrusion on their trade monopoly—King James was "King of Fishermen, and of an island of no import, and a fart for his commission"— Hawkins took eight months to reach Agra. He quickly became Jahangir's boon companion: depraved the Mogul emperor might be, but he had inherited Akbar's curiosity for the strange. This Englishman spoke the mother tongue of the Moguls; a raucous elbow bender, Hawkins enjoyed jabbering away day and night about England and the world.

Still, Jahangir was capricious. At first holding out hopes

for English commerce, he had made Hawkins commander of four hundred horse and dubbed him "English Khan." Yet in the end, English Khan's chin-wagging failed to obtain what was promised—a firman or imperial order permitting British trade. Jahangir gave ear to pro-Portuguese nobles, while Portuguese Goa persuaded Surat's Mogul governor of the misfortunes which would attend any British footing in India.

Hard on Hawkins's heels in 1613, a new batch of English "ambassadors" had arrived in Agra, with a fresh letter from King James and two musicians incongruously in tow. One named Lancelot played the virginals for Emperor Jahangir and nobles; presumably Shah Jahan and his Persian relatives were present at these odd musical rites, with Nur Jahan and Mumtaz Mahal hidden behind harem grillwork. The virginals player flopped; but the other musician, Robert Trully, astonished the entire Mogul court by playing the cornet. Jahangir himself tried to manage this weird instrument, then ordered workmen to make six more cornets (all of which were failures). Trully received instructions to give lessons to one of the emperor's chief musicians; and after five weeks the Indian player managed tolerably well, but blew so strenuously that he died two weeks later. Robert Trully remained the only cornet player in the Mogul Empire—not a happy lot, since for all the times he was called on to play he received a total of only fifty rupees.

Such bizarre high comedy belied the stakes, but who could have known? Hawkins and King James's wandering minstrels seemed only a novel interlude to the Moguls; they tootled an insignificant leitmotif from some pipsqueak island kingdom thousands of miles away. True they were bent on securing small trading privileges in a vast India, but profound irony would have to wait. The East India Company and King James himself would certainly have been overwhelmed at the thought of ruling a subcontinent; they had only just got through the door, with Portuguese and even Dutch rivals well ahead of them and Frenchmen soon to come.

The foreign invasion of India had begun. Yet, infinitely

more important to Jahangir, immediate peril lurked like a spider in that web of machinations which he dimly sensed was controlling him. Five imperial sons had their eyes on the throne. Khusrau still remained a prisoner, a threat dormant for the moment; for distance's sake, Prince Parwiz held ineffectual command of Deccan forces to the south; and Hawkins had taken note of seven-year-old Shahriyar's refusal to cry when his father slapped him, beat him, and even stuck a bodkin in his cheek. Now an adolescent, Shahriyar attended the emperor in Ajmer, along with obscure Jahandar (who never counted as a potential successor and would soon inexplicably disappear from Mogul history).

Then there was Shah Jahan: the most capable, the most loved by Jahangir, the most loyal but certainly the most ambitious. In-laws hovered behind this prince—Persian gray eminences, with Empress Nur Jahan's power growing daily. In the end, of course, Jahangir's imperial word remained absolute; he still frightened them all. But years of narcotics had befuddled him, or produced wildly fitful outbursts of arbitrary power. Nur Jahan wheedled and soothed him for her own ends, which for the moment in Ajmer coincided with Shah Jahan's: prince and Persian contingent colloquied together, as thick as thieves. Nur's father Itimad was prime minister but aging, so that her brother Asaf Khan exerted no little pressure on the administration of Mogul affairs. Since Shah Jahan had married into the family through Mumtaz Mahal and in any event seemed fit to wear the crown, all three Persian relatives busily promoted his interests. Yet no one could forget that elder brothers Khusrau and Parwiz were technically first in line, while even Shahriyar or Jahandar could be serious contenders if Jahangir were to exert a freakish whim. So Shah Jahan had four obstacles to overcome.

In fact, he had five: the designs of a power-mad woman had been advancing too rapidly, and before long she would want a more obedient marionette. Far from dancing to strings, determined young Prince Khurram could only clash with Empress Nur Jahan's vanity in his headstrong determination to rule India.

● ● ●

One important strand was missing from this royal cat's cradle of Oriental intrigue: a skilled European observer. How else would posterity ever evaluate character and sift truth from the panegyric of Mogul scribes who flattered their rulers by distorting personages and events? Only an outsider—a shrewd stranger at the Mogul court—could provide "the necessary correction of life-like detail."

Predictably English, the stranger arrived in Ajmer just before Christmas of 1615, so desperately ill that he was carried in a palanquin. One of his retinue had already died enroute from India's west coast. Thus the newcomer did not rally to be presented at the Mogul court until mid-January of 1616. He bore the inevitable letter from King James, but it was clear from the start that this time the East India Company had sent a person of consequence—a highly literate diplomat with full credentials.

From a period portrait, Sir Thomas Roe emerges appropriately grand: a stately and straightforward Jacobean with Vandyke beard, eyes that flinch from nobody, a high, almost noble forehead, and a mouth clearly made to speak the truth. At thirty-five he was in the prime of life; he was a graduate of Oxford and had received his knighthood from King James. Though he had also sat in Parliament, foreign service seemed the best career and the East India Company had made a good offer: £600 a year, a chaplain and surgeon, wages for his retinue, and all living expenses in India (unless the emperor wished to provide bread and board!).

Thomas Roe was to play a double role, inadvertently important as an observer and yet totally preoccupied with his own insular motives, just as the Moguls were with theirs. Roe's were frankly political. In effect, his mission was vital: England's very future in India hung on the skill of a single envoy to the court of The Great Mogul.

Admittedly, Englishmen were still only trying to establish an innocent wedge of commerce, though Roe would soon be writing to King James that "the trade here will doubtless in time be very profitable for Your Majesty's kingdom." In a canny assessment of Mogul strength, he could conclude that "they fear the Portugal, they fear us, and between both patch up a friendship; but in heart (if we were of force) more unsound to them than to us." Clearly, Sir Thomas Roe was a shrewd power politician.

Even more clearly, all of Europe was greedy: Europe wanted opium, indigo, muslin, silks, diamonds, pepper and ginger and other spices, ghee, sugar, lac, wax, and saltpeter for wars. These outsiders meant to shake India's proverbial pagoda tree, though a few would be driven by respectable wanderlust or missionary hopes.

It had, of course, taken time to get there. Before 1600 only a handful of Europeans personally knew Hindustan, which was terra incognita to all except a few Jesuits residing in Agra. Long-established Portuguese pockets such as Goa existed along its coasts, but Renaissance maritime daring accounted for them. Portugal had obtained a good head start over European rivals, shrewdly appropriating Mogul India's trade and providing pilgrim ships to Mecca; indeed, if Portugal had not been so small her hero Albuquerque might well have realized his dream of Indian dominion. As for the prudent Dutch, the Portuguese had driven them to seek the spice islands of Indonesia, later tolerating a Dutch warehouse at Agra.

Latecomer England found all the musical chairs occupied. Hoping to avoid a European war with the double crown of Spain and Portugal, Queen Elizabeth had refused to sanction mercantile rivalry abroad—the East India Company received no charter until the last day of the sixteenth century. No wonder it had taken sixteen years to establish enough of a wedge in Hindustan for diplomatic argument. Portuguese were dogs in the manger, prepared to give up nothing; if they had moved over for the Dutch they were not now going to move out for the English. There had already been skirmishes between English and Portuguese fleets off India's west coast.

As for the Moguls, they watched arrogantly from the sidelines: commerce was the vulgar profession of Hindus and Europeans. Yet there were private reasons for holding aloof —perhaps to see which foreign power would prove stronger and therefore most useful. The powerful Persian party at court influenced Shah Jahan, who now at least nominally exerted personal rule over lucrative Surat port. An open door to the English might well lead to trouble. Unless they proved indomitable, it seemed wise not to kick out the long-established Portuguese.

● ● ●

From the moment of his arrival in India, Sir Thomas Roe had decided that the only way to handle Mogul obliquity was to command respect as an important representative of a king no less mighty than Jahangir himself. Bitterly squabbling with Shah Jahan's governor, he threatened to leave his seized goods to rot in Surat's customs house. The governor, in turn, scorned the English coach intended as a gift for Jahangir: "We bought ill velvet of the Chinese," Roe wrote, "and sent it his Master in coaches." But Jahangir's greed and curiosity saved the day: he issued an official letter of command for safe passage inland of Roe and his effects.

For their journey, the English retinue had followed an established route. Stopping at Burhanpur, the seat of Mogul administration in the north Deccan, Roe soon encountered Prince Parwiz at the local Red Fort. Parwiz sat in haughty state, but an equally haughty envoy refused to perform ceremonial prostration. Would the prince grant permission for an English warehouse to be set up in Burhanpur? Parwiz agreed as soon as presents were offered. Unfortunately, one of the presents—a case of spirits—had been unwise; after waiting for further private audience, Roe heard from an embarrassed attendant that Parwiz was drunk.

Recounting his later reception by Emperor Jahangir at Ajmer's court, the ambassador conjured up an ambiance of velvet and silk canopies, carpets, and an elevated throne set above railed precincts. "When I entered within the first rail I made a reverence; entering in the inward rail another; and when I came under the King a third. The place is a great court, whither resort all sorts of people . . . . This sitting out hath so much affinity with a theatre—the manner of the King in his gallery: the great men lifted on a stage as actors; the vulgar below gazing on."

King James's letter was now presented, together with Roe's credentials and gifts. Not only did Jahangir not spurn the English coach, he clambered into every corner of it that very evening and had English coach attendants take him for a short outing. Two days later, he "sent a gentleman for my commission to show his Queen the seal": shrewd Nur Jahan wanted to ascertain that this was a genuinely accredited diplomat and not merely a stooge of the East India Company.

Roe was actually to stay well over three years in the Mogul Empire, with many months now spent in Ajmer attempting to obtain a formal treaty for English trade. Quickly apprising himself of the real powers behind Jahangir's throne, he began fruitless rounds of conciliatory visits. Mumtaz Mahal's father, Asaf Khan, at first treated the English ambassador with initial contempt by keeping him waiting "in an outward room much against my stomach." The supreme insult followed: Asaf Khan ignored his visitor and began to eat supper with friends. On that occasion Roe left in fury, sending a message that "if his greatness were no more than his manners he durst not use me so: I was an ambassador from a mighty and free Prince and in that quality his better, and scorned to attend his banquetings." But Roe would be back.

Shah Jahan, too, proved galling at first. "His pride is such as may teach Lucifer," Roe scratched in his journal. On one occasion, a tête-à-tête intended to clarify treaty terms ended typically, with the prince requesting something for himself—this time a white feather from the ambassadorial hat. Roe said that the feather was worn. "He asked if I had any more. I answered: three or four of other colours. He replied if I would give them all, for that he was to show his horses and servants to the King within two days and that he wanted some, being very rare in these parts."

The master strategist himself, old Prime Minister Iti-mad, softened insolence by coming to the ambassador's mud house; he even stayed to dinner but declined to eat. "He begged everything, but I pleased him with a feather, 3 or 4 paper pictures, and an old pair of spurs." Itimad, acknowl-edging Roe's potential as a troublemaker, sent him a basket of muskmelons presumably picked by Nur Jahan herself.

It is tempting to wonder whether Roe could not have made headway sooner by sending lavish gifts directly to the all-powerful empress. Yet early on he had a poor stock of gifts, and self-righteously held back from giving bribes; even when he did they often proved inadequate—Asaf Khan re-turned a ring as "too poor of value," while Jahangir repudi-ated a Mercator's map of the world which depicted India as being of lesser scope than he imagined. Then too, Nur Jahan remained invisible. Only once did Roe even catch a partial glimpse of her: "At one side in a window were his [Jahan-gir's] two principal wives, whose curiosity made them break little holes in a grate of reed that hung before it to gaze on me. I saw first their fingers, and after laying their faces close now one eye, now another; sometime I could discern the full proportion. They were indifferently white, black hair smoothed up; but if I had had no other light, their diamonds and pearls had sufficed to show them. When I looked up they retired, and were so merry that I supposed they laughed at me."

Interestingly enough, an obscure foreigner's candid pressure for something as minor as trading privileges pre-sented a considerable threat to Shah Jahan and the Persian triumvirate. Jahangir in a rage could yet undo them all; sub-ject to an absolute despot, they had good reason to worry about falling from favor.

Roe soon had vivid evidence of this. Circumvented and stalled for too long, he appealed one evening to a drugged Jahangir at court. Fearing the worst, Asaf Khan attempted to bar Roe's interpreter, an Italian named John Veronese (who for his services would later receive as gifts a knife and a bot-tle of "strong waters"). But the determined Englishman soon got his aide admitted, and fireworks began. Squarely, Roe countered even Shah Jahan, who tried to pull the interpreter away from the attention of his imperial father. "So I commanded the Italian to speak aloud that I craved audience of the King, whereat the King called me and they made me way." The ambassador complained that he had been in India for two months of illness and compliments and achieved nothing—no agreement from one sovereign to another that would establish "fair and secure trade and residence for my countrymen." Jahangir's firmans were too vague and temporary (Roe dared not say that they had been impeded by Shah Jahan and the Persian triumvirate); a formal and definite agreement was needed.

Jahangir responded childishly: "he desired an English horse." Here the Englishman foresaw difficulties: no horse could be brought via Turkey, and surely none would survive a sea voyage. The emperor remained unconvinced: "If six were put into a ship one might live, and though it came lean he would fat it."

Roe agreed to write to England for the horse, then pressed for immediate action: would Jahangir confirm his previous commands by personally signing conditions to rectify the abuses English traders suffered? Asaf Khan was now desperate to have the interpreter withdrawn; "but I held him, suffering him only to wink and make unprofitable signs. The King hereat grew suddenly into choler, pressing to know who had wronged us, with such show of fury that I was loath to follow it." Roe went on, saying in broken Spanish through the Italian interpreter that what was done was done; he didn't really want to trouble Jahangir about it, and would take the matter to Prince Shah Jahan. "The King, not attending my interpreter but hearing his son's name, conceived I had accused him, saying 'mio filio, mio filio,' and called for him; who came in great fear, humbling himself. Asaf Khan trembled, and all of them were amazed."

In the ensuing debacle, Shah Jahan was raked over the coals while Roe hastened to assure the emperor that he had not accused the prince of anything. Defensively, Shah Jahan said that he had offered the English a firman, which had been refused. Roe brought up a debatable clause about Portuguese trade, which promptly provoked a storm from pro-Portuguese nobles as well as from Jesuits in attendance. After much argument ("for we were very warm") Asaf Khan adroitly settled the issue: the ambassador would make a formal draft of his demands, and if they were reasonable the emperor would sign them with Prince Shah Jahan's confirmation.

Flattered by Jahangir's courtesy, Roe for the moment soft-pedaled in his journal and letters the full implications of this monstrous Eastern absolutism. Besides, he might have been tempted to reflect treasonably on the abuses of European royalty within his own memory: Henry VIII's or Elizabeth's whims, the beheading of a few expendable queens or Lord Essex's fate. Between whimsical European and Oriental monarchies, it was finally only a question of degree.

Roe quickly prepared his treaty; but the Persian in-laws and Shah Jahan would propel him in circles for some time to come. In the midst of frustration, he recorded fine descriptions of the lavish Mogul court. Shortly after the evening quarrel, Jahangir was invited to a propitiatory banquet at Asaf Khan's house, with the queen and Shah Jahan in attendance. Scornfully, Roe noted that velvets and silks rolled on for a whole English mile from court to banquet site, while the feast and gifts together cost £60 thousand!

For the Moslem New Year, durbar proved especially brilliant, though the ambassador wittily compared glitter to "a lady that with her plate set on a cupboard her embroidered slippers." Yet sometimes Roe misunderstood spectacle; once he wrote of a performance of nautch girls that "some whores did sing and dance." It was even ungracious to question the taste of an emperor who, on one occasion, rounded out formal display with "pictures of the King of England, the Queen, my Lady Elizabeth, the Countesses of Somerset and Salisbury, and of a citizen's wife of London."

More hidden in the background than Nur Jahan but about to come to the fore again was Mumtaz Mahal; busy with three children and pregnant again, she suddenly lost her first-born daughter, aged three. Jahangir and all his family plunged into gloom for the better part of a month. Roe could only receive the news indirectly.

Then too, the court was preoccupied with other matters of considerably greater interest to Mogul politics than an obscure English ambassador seeking trading privileges. War in the Deccan against stubborn sultanates had reached a stalemate and Prince Parwiz would soon be summoned home in disgrace, to be replaced by Shah Jahan himself.

Toward the end of June 1616, death yielded to birth: Mumtaz Mahal gave her husband a new son, Prince Shuja. The fecundity of his wife combined with his own imminent departure turned all eyes upon Shah Jahan—"either for flattery, gain or envy, none for love," Roe reported with bitterness. Shah Jahan's cold contempt for almost everyone may well have fitted a future emperor, but it abraded England's fiery ambassador. By contrast, if Shah Jahan had kept a diary his impression of Roe might well have been that of a tiresomely aggressive European impudently circumventing princely authority in efforts to win trade terms and favors. Roe did not yet understand that the binding treaty he hoped for was totally contrary to Oriental notions of rule. Europeans were simply flies in the Indian ointment. Jahangir himself, if pressed, would probably have agreed with Asaf Khan and Shah Jahan; his own memoirs took note of every trivial detail of empire—except Englishmen.

● ● ●

Roe now found himself passively witnessing military history in the making. Ajmer bustled, the court prepared to break up. As rumored, Parwiz had been removed from his Deccan post, and efforts to see his own father were rebuffed by the empress, who effected his transfer to Bengal—the very province of disgrace. Shah Jahan was now to take command of the Deccan army. Nur Jahan's junta decided that the emperor should move southward, conveniently close to the Deccan to sustain the prince's operations. The ambassador had no choice but to follow like a puppy dog.

Without Shah Jahan by his side, Jahangir faced the problem of what to do with the imprisoned rebel, Khusrau. Hatred of Shah Jahan momentarily prevented Roe from accurately assessing the situation. He believed that Jahangir still intended to make Khusrau his heir and was simply playing one son off against the other; civil war would predictably attend the emperor's death. Roe did, however, correctly divine the gruesome purpose of the influences behind the throne. Drunk with power, Nur Jahan and her brother and father, together with Shah Jahan, had to force Jahangir to make Khusrau their hostage; they would then do the rest to get rid of a potential threat to Shah Jahan's accession. Khusrau's days were numbered.

With their favored prince about to leave for the Deccan, the Persian plotters achieved their end: Khusrau was actually delivered up to soldiers of Asaf Khan. Whatever Roe's interpretation of the event, it seems likely that Jahangir feared Khusrau's sympathizers might well attempt a coup with Shah Jahan away. By surrendering Khusrau as hostage, the emperor ensured his own life—or so he may have reasoned.

On November 1, 1616, Shah Jahan reviewed his troops before Jahangir at noon durbar. Roe estimated six hundred richly trapped elephants and ten thousand cavalrymen, many sporting gold cloth and egret feathers in their turbans; the prince himself wore a silver coat embroidered with pearls and diamonds. Jahangir embraced him, kissed him, and presented him with costly gifts.

A plague had now broken out in Agra, and it was expected that the emperor would take his wife's advice and follow Shah Jahan's campaign at a distance. On moving day, the ambassador viewed Jahangir at the *jharoka* window in a startling ritual: eunuchs fanned the monarch while gifts were raised to him on a silk string. Roe and others sat on carpets awaiting the emperor. Jahangir delayed departure for half an hour while the harem ladies mounted fifty elephants, clambering into howdahs of gold surmounted by canopies of silver cloth and provided with gold-mesh grating so that they could see without being seen. At last His Majesty descended the palace stairs, and Ajmer's assembled populace "outcried cannons," shouting *"Padshah salamat"* ("health to the King"). Attendants rushed to buckle on Jahangir's sword and scabbard, encrusted with huge diamonds and rubies; his hunting quiver was attached; each side of his turban blazed with rubies and diamonds the size of walnuts, while in the middle a huge heart-shaped emerald gleamed. The emperor stood bedecked in jewels: a chain of pearls, rubies, and diamonds covered his midriff; a three-strand pearl necklace vied in splendor with jeweled bracelets and armlets set with diamonds, and every finger boasted a ring.

Roe might have felt it a tribute that Jahangir now entered his English coach lined with crimson Chinese velvet and replete with English coachman and four horses garnished by gold velvet trappings; but it was only a copy! Two eunuchs carrying gold maces set with rubies ran along on either side of the emperor's vehicle, shooing away flies with white horsetail switches. Drums and trumpets and loud music vanguarded the procession, together with canopies, umbrellas of state, and Mogul ensigns on gold cloth decorated with rubies, pearls, and emeralds. Three palanquins trailed in Jahangir's wake, gold-plated and also adorned with precious stones; a footman carried a gem-encrusted footstool of gold. Nur Mahal now followed in the original English coach, newly covered and trimmed. But it was overdoing matters when a third English coach rolled by, another copy, bearing Shahriyar and Jahandar, Jahangir's younger sons. Then followed harem elephants, and nobles on foot. Impressed, Roe walked along as far as the palace gate.

Several days later, he rode five miles to Shah Jahan's encampment to wish him victory and a safe return. King James's representative was the prince's humble servant, and hoped to gain protection for Englishmen in the realm. Shah Jahan sat in state on a silver-plated throne inlaid with gold flowers. Roe set aside his active dislike and cannily assessed India's future emperor:

> The watch was set, for it was evening. When he came
> abroad, I observed him now he was absolute, and curi-

ously his fashion and actions. He received two letters, read them standing, before he ascended his throne. I never saw so settled a countenance, nor any man keep so constant a gravity, never smiling, nor in face showing any respect or difference of men; but mingled with extreme pride and contempt of all. Yet I found some inward trouble now and then assail him, and a kind of brokenness and distraction in his thoughts, unprovidedly and amazedly answering suitors, or not hearing. If I can judge anything, he hath left his heart among his father's women, with whom he hath liberty of conversation. Nur Mahal in the English coach the day before visited him and took leave. She gave him a cloak all embroidered with pearl, diamonds and rubies; and carried away, if I err not, his attention to all other business.

Roe did err: Shah Jahan's distraction had nothing to do with his father's women, least of all Nur Jahan. Or if she distracted him, it was purely political; the alliance between empress and prince had probably already begun to weaken. No longer able to control him, she would soon turn to other quarters in her bid to rule the Mogul Empire after Jahangir's death—which, in the condition he was in, might occur at any moment.

Urgently, Shah Jahan now sent for Roe on the eve of his Deccan campaign. Kept waiting, the ambassador fell into preoccupied anxiety; he wanted to return to Ajmer before nightfall. At last attendants brought him to the prince who was playing cards, a favorite Mogul pastime (144 cards in the deck afforded scope for invention!). There had been vague rumors that the Englishman would be asked to accompany Shah Jahan southward, but no such request seemed forthcoming. Instead, Shah Jahan merely presented the visitor with a gold cloak, which having previously been worn constituted a sign of honor. And the curious pourparler ended with a special cavalry escort back to Ajmer. Henceforth, Roe's journal would treat the future ruler of India less astringently.

Now in mid-November, Ajmer was fast becoming deserted. By Jahangir's orders remnants of the imperial camp would be destroyed, compelling any and all recalcitrant followers to move with the court. Roe found himself stuck with no camels or carts for his own departure; he applied to court nobles for transportation, while he tried to ferret out further details of royal intrigue. Though Khusrau had been handed over to Mumtaz Mahal's father, the emperor could still be childishly wrathful. Hearing that Asaf Khan had visited the prisoner and treated him cavalierly, Jahangir laced into his Persian in-law: "The King told him he would make his proud heart know [Khusrau] to be his eldest and beloved heir, his Prince and Lord; and if he once heard of any the least want of reverence or duty toward him, he would command his son to set his feet on his neck and trample on him: that he loved Sultan Khurram well, but he would make the world know he did not entrust his son among them for his ruin." The Persian contingent had to proceed with caution.

Roe had now been a year in India, and wrote to the East India Company to report his progress to date. Lacking suitable presents he had been unable to effect "articles of treaty on equal terms," but bit by bit had managed to retrieve bribes, extortions, and debts taken from company merchants, and had obtained several firmans which afforded some measure of security for company warehouses and agents in Surat, Agra, Lahore, Ajmer, and elsewhere. He would try to settle a trade treaty in due time, and if that were achieved there could be no further need for an English ambassador at court: "a meaner agent . . . would better effect your business." He was sick of moderating.

The court now traveled south, away from the plague in Agra. Urged by Empress Nur's junta to be an awesome rear guard for Shah Jahan, Jahangir headed for Mandu city, only ninety miles from Burhanpur in the strange Deccan. The three-month journey would take Roe through landscape of vital import in later events of the realm. Through woods and over mountains the court and its ambassador went, with camels dying, deserters leaving for Agra, bandits murdering stragglers, and everyone cursing Jahangir and particularly

Empress Nur Jahan who seemed to have instigated this bleak journey.

The ill-starred prisoner Khusrau was actually not with Shah Jahan, but remained under Asaf Khan's surveillance at the royal camp. An unusual meeting now occurred. Stopping to rest one day under a tree, Roe saw Khusrau riding along on an elephant with no great guard or attendance. Escorts called to Roe to clear the way; Khusrau then summoned the English ambassador, and the two conversed. Roe thought him of cheerful countenance and princely bearing, noting that his beard hung to his midriff in token of dishonor. Years of imprisonment had made Khusrau very out of touch with the world; he was almost like a ghost. He wanted to know how far England was from India, what goods the English brought and took away, how Jahangir had treated the ambassador, and whether the emperor had given gifts? Roe replied that he had come to obtain free trade for the English; if he accomplished this, he wanted no royal presents. Khusrau replied that surely a treaty would be forthcoming for strangers who had come so far. He asked how long the ambassador had been in India; told it was two years, he seemed amazed that his father could suffer such a man of quality to stay so long without giving him a single royal gift. He, Khusrau, was a prisoner and could do Roe no good; but he would pray for him. And so he departed.

Gifts would be given under comic duress, not from but to the emperor. In mid-February 1617, Roe found himself once more treated with disdain. His chaplain had died a short while before; and the replacement, Edward Terry, was at last coming from Surat port with presents brought months ago by the 1616 fleet but only recently released after an interminable customs delay. On their way to the royal camp Terry and his party had encountered Shah Jahan advancing to Burhanpur, and were now forcibly detained by the prince who was curious to see English wares. Furious, Roe made immediate appeal to Jahangir but was preempted: "My son hath taken your goods and my presents: be not sad, he shall not touch nor open a seal, nor lock: at night I will send him a command to free them." A dissatisfied ambassador pursued the matter that evening, seeking redress; but Asaf Khan countered sparks with soothing words. Drunk and babbling, Jahangir rambled away. "Am I a king? You shall be welcome: Christians, Moors, Jews, he meddled not with their faith: they came all in love and he would protect them from wrong: they lived under his safety and none should oppress them." The emperor started to weep, and kept everyone till midnight.

Shah Jahan received imperial orders to release the impounded English goods, and dutifully sent them under escort to the royal camp; but before Thomas Roe could claim his cargo, Jahangir greedily dipped into the spoils. An irate diplomat with blood in his eye now confronted India's ruler. His guilty majesty admitted having taken certain items: two embroidered cushions, a folding mirror, and live English dogs. But what were those pictures? Jahangir hauled forth art, becoming so intrigued by a painting of "Venus and Satyr" that he asked all his nobles their opinion. Roe politely suggested a poetic interpretation (but later wrote the East India Company to be careful what they sent: that dark-skinned, naked satyr held captive by a white Venus seizing his nose might well be construed as a devious allegory scorning Asiatics). Allegory or not, Jahangir rolled up the paintings; he would take them. Now if Roe could only rustle up that English horse, he could have any wish his heart desired.

Frustrated, Roe marked time with his quill until summer and autumn of 1617 brought significant political possibilities to the Mogul court. Khusrau received some provisional liberty, and it was even rumored that he would marry Nur Jahan's daughter by her first marriage to Sher Afghan. Roe's journal assumed that Prime Minister Itimad and Asaf Khan were involved in the plot; but it seemed mainly the empress's doing: her rift with Shah Jahan had become overtly manifest. If Khusrau espoused her daughter then the empress could control Khusrau, wretched ghost that he was. At the moment all was speculation; yet for Thomas Roe it could mean a change in Nur's attitude toward the English, and he decided to take advantage of it—he had adapted to devious Mogul politics.

Jahangir's birthday came round, and Roe witnessed ceremonial weighing in a very large and beautiful garden where he joined court nobles sitting on carpets. Greatly bejeweled, the emperor entered royal scales, sitting "like a woman on his legs" while being balanced against silver, gold, and gems. The gems were in bags, and doubting Thomas thought they "might be pebbles." Endless weighings followed—against gold and silk cloth, spices, then meal, butter, and wheat. The weighing over, Jahangir ascended his throne and threw basins of silver nuts and fruits to scrambling nobles. Seeing that British dignity refused to stoop, the Mogul poured a basin of silver knickknacks into Roe's cloak; but greedy nobles "were so bold as to put in their hands."

On October 2 Shah Jahan returned triumphant from the Deccan: intransigent southern rulers had come to terms, sending rich tribute. Roe's assumptions about court politics led him to believe that the victor would not be so royally welcomed home, but gossip had not taken account of Jahangir's mercurial stubbornness. If Nur Jahan was now shifting her position, results were not immediately apparent. Young Prince Khurram found himself embraced by Jahangir; amid pomp and splendor the emperor gave him an unprecedented numerical rank of many thousands of horse, together with the new title of Shah Jahan. Later Roe rode out to pay his respects, but was told that he should come next morning at sunrise when the prince "sat to be worshipped."

Still seeking to profit from the rumored disenchantment of Persian in-laws with their proud prodigy, the ambassador now renewed overtures toward Asaf Khan by secretly selling him a pearl at less than cost. Pleased, Mumtaz Mahal's father promised to mediate with the prince. At the same time it was to the empress's advantage also to welcome English advances, since she no longer supported Shah Jahan and could thereby weaken the prince's position at Surat port. But if Asaf Khan for the moment seemed to be following his sister

Nur's behest, he was actually playing a double game: why lose favor with his own son-in-law when the prince might emerge the winner?

Within a few days, Mumtaz Mahal's father had sanguinely wangled Roe an interview with Shah Jahan, obtained several royal permits favorable to English trade, and was even soliciting princely promise for a Bengal writ. Shortly afterward, Nur Jahan actively entered the picture: she obtained an order from Shah Jahan assigning protection of English goods to her aegis. There would be no more trouble, though of course it would be nice if she and her brother Asaf Khan could have first opportunity to buy certain goods of incoming English cargo! A possibility even arose that Shah Jahan, now about to become governor of entire Gujarat province, would surrender his "ownership" of Surat to Asaf Khan—in which case all Englishmen would be happy. But Asaf Khan's promises were never to bear fruit, as Roe would find out: English ambassadors had to get up very early in the morning to analyze the power play of a man destined to become prime minister of Mogul India.

Toward the end of October Jahangir broke camp at Mandu and moved to Ahmadabad, Gujarat's principal city some fifty miles inland from the Arabian Sea. Here Roe would almost exclusively spend his remaining time in India. Once again, English troubles with Shah Jahan erupted: a cargo of new gifts had arrived at Surat and received the prince's seals; but after waiting for official permission for three weeks, Roe had broken the seals and taken possession of his own goods. Shah Jahan, affronted, complained bitterly to the emperor, and Roe was rudely herded back to court; the shoe was on the other foot now. Jahangir angrily accused the Englishman of deception. Bravely Roe stood his ground, saying that he had done no wrong and "held it fit to give freely." If he had offended Mogul custom it was through ignorance, and he must be pardoned. At last everyone calmed down, even Shah Jahan offered his friendship. The disputed chests were opened, Jahangir and the prince received their gifts, and presents were sent to the empress. Jahangir found one English cloth too coarse, but liked another material and wanted a suit made of it. Roe's last written glimpse of the monarch is recorded: "The King sat in a hat I gave him all night."

In the middle of February 1618, the ambassador made a yearly report to the East India Company: "You can never expect to trade here upon capitulations that shall be permanent. We must serve the time." He had obtained the best he could; he was now on much better terms with Shah Jahan, who within ensuing months would publicly become the Englishman's "protector and procurator."

By August 1618, Jahangir and the court were about to leave Ahmadabad for imperial Agra; "infinitely weary of this unprofitable employment," Roe felt that little more could be accomplished. He took formal leave of India's monarch, carrying away a letter to King James and a general writ for the reception and continuation of Englishmen in Mogul domains. On February 17, 1619, England's ambassador left India on board the good ship *Anne*. He went on to a reception given by King James at Hampton Court, where he reported his mission in detail; the East India Company was happy and awarded him a £1,500 grant.

What had Sir Thomas Roe actually achieved? Too modestly, he himself deprecated the results—nor could he have known they would be twofold. For history he proved to be inestimable: no other European ever provided or would provide such a detailed daily picture of the Mogul court with all its underlying plots. His pen brought to life a vivid portrait gallery of characters: an inimitably capricious Jahangir; a proud Shah Jahan, future emperor and architectural genius of Agra and Delhi; a totally unscrupulous Asaf Khan; and even Nur Jahan, whom Roe never met, emerges as a palpable if invisible force. Details of durbar and military pomp, birthday weighings and playing cards, recreate an opulent chapter of the Indian past.

Politically, King James would read proof of Roe's prowess in Jahangir's writ (now preserved in the British Museum).

Let your royal heart be as fresh as a sweet garden. The letter of love and friendship which you sent and the presents, tokens of your good affection toward me, I have received by the hands of your ambassador, Sir Thomas Roe (who well deserveth to be your trusted servant) . . . . I have given my general command to all the kingdoms and ports of my dominions to receive all the merchants of the English nation as the subjects of my friend, that in what place soever they choose to live they may have reception and residence to their own content and safety, and what goods soever they desire to sell or buy, they may have free liberty without any restraint . . . .

India's future had been prepared by one staunch diplomat—a man of good fire and quick pepper, highly intelligent and highly literate, rash only in the honor of king and country. Even the devious logic of a Mogul ruler and his son could be impressed by such straightforward virtues. Sir Thomas Roe had won a foothold in the realm.

CHAPTER

4

Kings Rise from Coffins

Toward the end of the year 1618, just before Sir Thomas Roe's departure, two significant events took place in India. One was the manifestation in the ecliptic between Scorpio and Libra of what seems to have been a supernova, which Jahangir's diary compared in shape to a porcupine or javelin. "Astrologers," he feared, "have written that it portends evil." Sixteen days later, in the same quarter of the sky, a comet with a long tail appeared. Superstitiously inclined, the Moguls linked these twin heavenly occurrences with a famine that had ravaged portions of Hindustan the preceding year; while a court scribe would later observe that "it was also through the effects of this phenomenon that a misunderstanding arose between His Majesty and the fortunate Prince Shah Jahan. The disturbances which thus originated lasted seven or eight years. What blood was shed in the country! And what families were ruined!"

The second event was the birth of a new son to Mumtaz Mahal, on October 24. England's ambassador had only recently taken leave of Jahangir in Gujarat province; the emperor now proceeded at a leisurely pace to Agra, with Shah Jahan and his family among the royal party. At the village of Dauhad, about three hundred miles northeast of today's Bombay, Muhiuddin Mohammed Aurangzeb made his squalling way into the world. Aurangzeb was the sixth child of Shah Jahan by Mumtaz Mahal, his sister Raushanara having been born the year before. Roe had been present for the death of one child at Ajmer, and six other offspring would die in infancy. But five of the royal septet destined to be major dramatis personae in the Mogul tragedy were already in evidence: Princess Jahanara, the four-year-old eldest sister; Prince Dara Shikoh, three years old; Prince Shuja, two years old; and Princess Raushanara and the newly born Prince Aurangzeb. Two more participants were yet to come: Prince Murad in 1624, and Princess Gauharara in 1631. A few days after Aurangzeb's birth, the roving court reached Ujjain, capital of Malwa province, where his nativity was celebrated with appropriate splendor. A handsome twenty-six-year-old Shah Jahan gazed down at the infant, but could not remotely have guessed the horror this son would visit upon him.

With Agra still in the throes of plague, the court lingered for a bit at Akbar's quasi-deserted stronghold of Fatehpur Sikri while Jahangir showed his son details of exotic sandstone palaces. Shah Jahan examined the imposing Victory Gate of Fatehpur, on which in 1602 Akbar had hauntingly inscribed: "The world is a bridge, pass over it, but do not build upon it. He who hopes for an hour may hope for eternity. The world is but an hour; spend it in devotion, the rest is unseen."

In April 1619, Shah Jahan's mother died; Jahangir condoled with him and took him to his palace. After a six months' stay in Agra, imperial father and son and court headed in the autumn for Kashmir, shooting antelope along the way. Kashmir was India's paradise, an alpine "Switzerland" for the Moguls; ancient Srinagar, its capital city on the Jhelum River, with nine bridges and waterways reminiscent of Venice, and an adjacent lake of moored houseboats and gondola-like *shikaras*, provided a lyric spring and summer interlude in 1620. Ringed by the Himalayas, the valley spread a carpet of bluebells and narcissi, pink and white almond blossoms, and flaming fields of mustard and poppy. This was Shah Jahan's first visit to Kashmir and Jahangir, impressed by his son's budding architectural zeal, confided the supervision of an enterprise to him: the creation of Shalimar Gardens, the "Abode of Love." In cool rustic surroundings, Mumtaz Mahal for once could relax from the rigors of childbirth on campaigns. And though we have no proof, even compulsively scheming Empress Nur Jahan perhaps stopped her intrigues long enough to enjoy the beauties of a nature as unchanging as Hinduism and the Hindus.

By autumn, alarming news interrupted the Kashmir interlude: war had broken out again in the Deccan. Shah Jahan's earlier success had been only a patched-up affair, a diplomatic truce; Deccan sultans of Bijapur and Golconda, together with the smaller state of Ahmadnagar, were besieging imperial forces once more. Intense guerrilla fighting now obliged the southern Mogul army to retreat to Burhanpur.

More than one historian observes that the brilliant military victories of Jahangir's reign—the submission of the Rajput state of Udaipur, and Deccan conquests—were really the achievement of Shah Jahan. With the emperor's other sons limited to rebellious Khusrau, drunken Parwiz, and adolescent Shahriyar, there could be no other choice. Once again, Jahangir ordered Shah Jahan to do battle for him. The prince agreed, but stipulated terms. Though outwardly heaped with honors, he knew that his position at court was less secure than it had been. By this time Nur Jahan's jealousy undoubtedly flourished in the open, and Jahangir's mercurial moods could hardly be relied upon. Combined factors—the emperor's failing health, a subtle shift of the scales toward imprisoned Khusrau, and rumors that Khusrau might actually enter into an alliance with the empress—all these made Shah Jahan cautious. Boldly he asked for Khusrau to accompany him as a formal hostage. Jahangir acquiesced; nor could Nur Jahan have deep-dyed reason to spike the request, since in spite of gossip she had already discarded the notion of Khusrau as a prospective son-in-law.

Military aspects of this new Deccan campaign need not concern us: by dint of Mogul strategy and force, Deccan princes would once again submit in the course of a year, ceding captured imperial territory and paying the usual tribute in glittering loot. It would be a new feather in Shah Jahan's cap; but he seemed restlessly eager to end matters and return to court, since Nur Jahan was not to be trusted in the event of a crisis.

In August of 1621, report, in fact, reached the Deccan that the emperor had suffered a serious asthma attack. Court doctors prescribed medicine, but Jahangir's memoirs reveal a stubborn patient: "I gave up all doctoring, and threw myself upon the mercy of the Universal Physician." Obviously alcohol and not Allah was meant; he started to drink by day, which only made matters worse. Desperate, Nur Jahan took over, gradually cutting down imperial intake of wine. The carcass was not yet in evidence, but vultures were already gathering. Prince Parwiz, pickled but resolute, hurried too quickly to court, insisting on making three turns round his father's sick bed. Jahangir recovered; Parwiz got labeled "a kind and dutiful son" in the royal diary but took raps on the knuckles (probably at Nur's instigation) and found himself sent back to govern his province.

Events now burst over Hindustan. The most significant and sinister was the death of Shah Jahan's hostage brother, Khusrau—quietly but ominously encompassed in a single sentence of Jahangir's daily record: "A letter from Khurram informed me that Khusrau died of colic." Whether Jahangir suspected the worst, there is no evidence. But for nobles at court and for Nur Jahan it could mean only one thing: Shah Jahan had removed the first of three fraternal obstacles to the throne.

Did Shah Jahan murder Khusrau, or arrange for his murder? Virtually every foreigner in the empire thought so; inland English employees of the East India Company would later write to their peers at Surat port that Shah Jahan had "cruelly murdered all other princes of the blood," more specifically repeating gossip that "by Sultan Khurram his brother's command he [Khusrau] was made away." Tavernier, a French jeweler in Mogul territory, would later concur; and even Mogul historian Mohammed Salih Kambu, writing in Shah Jahan's own lifetime, would relate that Jahangir "in an hour of drunkenness" had handed Khusrau over to Shah

Jahan, while Shah Jahan's advisers euphuistically urged him to shift Khusrau "from the ditch of prison to the plains of non-existence."

As usual, Dutchmen in Hindustan managed to furnish curiously specific details for their superiors in Amsterdam. Shah Jahan had hatched a plot with trusted nobles in the Deccan, providing himself an alibi by going off on a hunting expedition. The heart of the incriminating account is worth examining:

> He [Shah Jahan] called together Khan-i-Khanan and his most trusted *ommerauws* [nobles], leaving a slave named Riza in the palace with the order to go to Khusrau at night and strangle him to death. Following his order this slave with some of his associates went to Sultan Khusrau at night but found him asleep. They knocked at the door which was bolted inside, until the Prince awoke and cried, "Who are you that knock at my gate at this late hour?" The slave replied, "I am Riza Gholam of Shah Jahan. The King has sent a *saropa* or dress for you, which I have brought." Sultan Khusrau said, "Where is the hurry that you come so late in the night? I shall take the King's *saropa* and put it on next morning." But the more the Prince refused to open the door, the more did the slave Riza persist. Finally seeing that Sultan Khusrau would not open the door, he ordered it to be unhinged. They did so and entered the room. The Prince got up and groped for a sword, poniard or knife with which to kill the slave, but found only a water-pot which he threw . . . . The Prince was all alone and defenseless and there were six or seven of those wicked men. Although he made a great noise by shouting, and with his hands and feet, no one heard him. They threw him on the ground and sat on his chest. One of them took a cord and putting it round his neck, drew it tight till he was dead. They then lifted the body and laid it on the bed, as if he had died a sudden natural death. They then placed the door in position as before, closed it and went away.

The detail of the chamber pot is admittedly original.

Warming to its narrative, the Dutch account goes on to tell how Khusrau's wife ("who had slept in another room") found him cold and dead in the morning, shrieked, and summoned servants. Shah Jahan, fifteen or twenty miles away on his ostensible hunt, returned to Burhanpur and "summoned all his *ommerauws* and *mansabdars* [petty nobles] to bear witness to the letter that he wrote to the King concerning his brother's death that his hour had come and that he died suddenly. They all confirmed this with their seals or signatures. The corpse of Sultan Khusrau was taken out of the town, and buried in a garden." But according to the Dutch, one noble wrote Jahangir sufficient details to provoke a grief-stricken and angry imperial inquiry: did Khusrau die a natural death or was he murdered by someone? At Jahangir's orders, the corpse was exhumed and sent to Allahabad for burial in "his mother's garden"; Khusrau's widow and little son, Dawar Bakhsh, were to be returned to the emperor at Lahore.

Modern Indian scholars generally agree: Khusrau's death can be laid to Shah Jahan. But there are a few dissenters—notably Mountstuart Elphinstone, England's first great and classic historian of India in the early nineteenth century. "We ought not," Elphinstone rises to the moral occasion, "believe that a life not sullied by any other crime could be stained by one of so deep a dye." Many practical considerations will also occur to armchair detectives. If it were murder, Shah Jahan could hardly have chosen a more ill-advised moment when all suspicion would naturally gravitate to him, not to mention that Khusrau's wife might easily observe strangulation marks. Surely the poison so often employed at the time offered a better method, especially if administered at a more convenient moment and in another place. Dutch chronicles, often uncannily corroborated by unimpeachable sources, are also just as often in error as to date and fact. In addition, Khusrau had already spurned Nur Jahan's overtures for marriage with her daughter, and the empress had arranged another match before Shah Jahan even took his hostage to the fateful Deccan; Nur Jahan's daughter, in fact, married Shahriyar, Jahangir's youngest son, in April

1621, and news of the nuptials must surely have reached Shah Jahan before Khusrau's death. It would almost seem as though the annoyed empress deliberately nullified the importance of Khusrau as a pawn; certainly a disgraced and half-blind rebel constituted less of a rival to the throne than either young Shahriyar or even drunken Parwiz. The truth will never be known. But from that moment onward, Shah Jahan's motives were tinged with ambiguity.

Affairs at court had meanwhile been moving in new directions with unprecedented swiftness. Jahangir's illness alarmed Nur Jahan, and her plots now became wild. For all her masterful personality she emerges from subsequent events as an hysteric—the wicked stepmother flying into a rage over Shah Jahan's pride, ambition, and very obvious ability. Sometime during this same year of 1621 Nur's mother died, and a restraining influence was lost. Her father, old Itimad the prime minister, would also become a moribund entry in Jahangir's diary. Vainly pursuing lost health, Jahangir and the court were moving north again when Itimad fell ill. Prompted by the queen's anguish, the emperor went to visit Itimad at twilight but concurred in a negative prognosis. "He was at times insensible, and Nur Jahan, who was by my side, made signs and asked if I perceived [his critical state]. I stayed by his pillow two hours. Whenever he came to his senses, his words were intelligible and sensible. On the 17th of the month he died." It was now January 1622.

With the death of both mother and father, Nur Jahan lost her only objective advisers. The famous Persian junta was in pieces, with only her brother Asaf Khan remaining; and as Shah Jahan's father-in-law, he could hardly be persuaded to take an active role in his sister's revenge. For her scheme was now nothing less than a complete destruction of Shah Jahan's power. Over the years the prince had steadily advanced, ironically at her instigation, to an unprecedented control of cavalry; many important Mogul army officers were his intimate friends. In addition he held *jagirs* (crown lands and assigned provinces) which yielded handsome resources. Such funds had to be cut off; new army men had to be found to create a formidable counterweight. She could not worry for the moment about dissolute Prince Parwiz, who never really mattered anyway. And her son-in-law Shahriyar, the little boy who stood up to Jahangir's beatings without a whimper, had now become effeminate and soft, preferring harem dreams to power plays—a perfect puppet. The enemy was Shah Jahan, whom she now hated intractably.

It all seems madly obsessive; undoubtedly it was. If in retrospect the plot becomes at times almost hilariously naïve, we ought perhaps to refresh our memory of European monarchic machinations during the same period. Besides, there are so many offshoots in Mogul history—every Hindu Rajput or Moslem khan worth his name had an ax to grind, a reason to prevaricate or to rebel—that the actual sequence of events may have been a good deal more confused than the pattern which reconstructors seize upon. A further factor must be remembered: the Moguls were always highly emotional and impetuous—a heritage from rambunctious central Asia, so that moments of crisis inevitably triggered intrigue and counterintrigue.

At this point, Shah Jahan was not yet thirty. His whole career hung in the balance because of one woman, who had become his implacable enemy. Fuel had been heaped on the fires of his ambition from early childhood: Akbar said that Prince Khurram took after him; Jahangir had for years doted on Khurram and his military exploits, and always seemed to acknowledge him as heir apparent. Who else was there— rebel Khusrau (now dead), ineffectual Parwiz, or handsome and foolish Shahriyar? If Nur Jahan thought twice, she would have continued her support of Shah Jahan, accepting a neat back seat as powerful dowager queen on his accession to the throne. But with Shah Jahan's second victory in the Deccan, Jahangir heaped no fresh laurels on the hero and no drums were beaten. At Itimad's death, the emperor had assigned all of the prime minister's lands and wealth to Nur Jahan, and commanded that her drums and orchestra should play directly after his own. It was now the empress who presented robes of honor to forty-four nobles; like a legendary Amazon, she sat in the balcony of her palace while khans prostrated themselves before her. Coins were struck in her honor, with the superscription: "By order of the King Jahangir, gold has a hundred splendors added to it on receiving the impression of the name of Nur Jahan, the Queen Begum." Any firman that went out received not only Jahangir's signature, but the empress's as well. Jahangir was drunk night and day but Nur swilled from another cup—power, absolute and unlimited power.

In March 1622 came the crisis. Persia had taken advantage of Mogul preoccupation with the Deccan in order to besiege Kandahar fortress on the border of her own domains—Kandahar, in dispute ever since the time of Humayun. Orders went out for Shah Jahan to relieve the Kandahar garrison. It was not a bad ploy. If he fell for it, he would be losing his established hold on the Deccan, leaving an area he knew like the back of his hand for a remote and far-from-easy command. Jahangir had only to die (that he had lived this long was a miracle) and Nur Jahan could proclaim her son-in-law Shahriyar emperor in Shah Jahan's absence at Kandahar, thus robbing her proud enemy of what he now considered his birthright. Wielding impressive authority, she might easily sway key nobles to her side by promises of advancement, and fortify a new position with armed strength before her opponent could ever return to court.

At first Shah Jahan acceded to imperial demand, moving as far north as Mandu; then, invoking the late month and the state of his troops, he balked. He demanded absolute command of the Mogul army, governorship of the Punjab, and ownership of the fort at Ranthambor for his family. Granted these concessions, he would agree to go to Kandahar after the rainy season. Though sugarcoated, the terms were clear enough.

There is an element of farce in all this. Neither bitter opponent could come out in the open; each had to transmit his chess moves through a tipsy referee, and Jahangir could be wantonly fickle in his own right. Informed by letter of Shah

Jahan's demands, the emperor wrote mildly in his diary, "I was not at all pleased, or rather I was displeased." But it did not take much persuasion from Nur Jahan to convince Jahangir that sedition was at hand. Accordingly, the referee sent back a new imperial order: nobles and officers under Shah Jahan's command must return to Agra.

There was a further irritant. Having earlier applied for a certain acreage, Shah Jahan confidently sent his agent to take charge of it; but the queen had already won this contested property for her new son-in-law, Shahriyar. A nasty battle broke out between opposing pawns. Once again, the emperor sent a reprimand from Kashmir, this time ordering the entire army of the Deccan to return to court. At Nur's prompting, Jahangir appointed the hopeless Shahriyar to lead a Kandahar expedition, and the empress expressed delight by giving her drunken husband two Turkish pearls worth sixty thousand rupees. Further wheedling led to rejection of overtures by Shah Jahan's right-hand man, Afzal Khan, who arrived at court to plead on the prince's behalf. Little by little, Shah Jahan's territories in the Punjab and elsewhere in the north were now expropriated, while he made vain attempts to apologize and explain. Unwilling to rely on her brother Asaf Khan, who had good reason to support his son-in-law, the empress advanced a knight: onto the chessboard from nowhere came a man she had previously disliked—the greatest Mogul general of them all, Mahabat Khan, who had been languishing by her whim in Kabul in Afghanistan.* Mahabat Khan's bitter enemy, Asaf Khan, was then prudently sent off to bring a portion of royal treasure from Agra to finance the Kandahar operations.

Kandahar fell to the Persians, a blow to Mogul prestige. But a far more serious blow afflicted Jahangir: Shah Jahan had at last broken out into open rebellion, and was marching

---

* A minor historical fragment of the period maintains that Mahabat Khan had some time before remonstrated candidly with the emperor about the empress's domination over him. This alone would account for Nur's attitude.

from Mandu toward imperial Agra with part of the Deccan army. Civil war swept chessboard and referee to the floor.

Jahangir felt crushed. He himself had challenged his father Akbar; then Khusrau in turn had revolted against *him;* and now, for an unbearable second time, another beloved son was following in Khusrau's disastrous footsteps. Reduced to near idiocy by opium and alcohol, the emperor could hardly be expected to see the difference: Khusrau had voluntarily challenged for the crown, but Shah Jahan was defecting in desperation. Having lost all hope of justice so long as the empress really controlled the realm, a proud prince refused to be emasculated by an Amazon.

Jahangir's memoirs unleash a battery of feelings, castigating an "ungrateful" offspring who has "torn away the veil of decency." Shah Jahan becomes an "ill-starred son"; and finally, "I issued an order that from this time forth he should be called 'Wretch'."

More important than imprecations, rebellion focused on Agra—imperial Agra, seat of Mogul government and storehouse of the Mogul treasury. Once before, in revolt against Akbar, Jahangir himself in years past had tried to seize the capital and failed. Shah Jahan must be prevented from succeeding.

Jahangir's memoirs become totally unreliable at this juncture, because his actions were utterly dictated by the queen. Nur Jahan had spies everywhere. Acting through the emperor, she quickly set up the chessboard again, moving her pieces fast and (as it proved) effectively. Mahabat Khan now directed imperial affairs, commanding royal forces and flushing out traitors in league with Shah Jahan. Prince Parwiz and loyal Hindu Rajput chiefs from their desert strongholds of Amber, Jodhpur, and elsewhere, were summoned to support the imperialists. In February 1623, Jahangir and his queen moved to Delhi, intending further travel south to Mandu where they would supervise on-the-spot strategy. Meanwhile, an envoy from the emperor to Shah Jahan opened up time-saving negotiations.

Behind Shah Jahan were principal officers of the Deccan, and unquestionably some secret friends at court. The greatest was his father-in-law, Asaf Khan, whom Thomas Roe had long since assessed as a canny politician. During this whole period of rebellion we have to rely entirely on imagination in determining what Asaf Khan was really thinking and scheming; but the upshot would reveal the detailed extent of his operations. However taciturn and indifferent he seemed, did he remain consistently firm in his hidden support of the prince? If so, he managed to conceal his intentions from Jahangir and from his own shrewd sister. European gossip in the realm tells us that Asaf Khan was suspected of sedition and possibly imprisoned. But we then find him on the open road again, assigned to pick up imperial treasure at Agra or even to take part in a campaign against his own son-in-law! Knowing him as we do from Roe's journal, it may even be that Asaf Khan was finally loyal only to himself; *he* would survive and prosper, no matter *who* got the throne.

As a matter of fact, Asaf Khan never did pick up coin of the realm. The eunuch treasurer of Agra, Itibar Khan, refused to hand it over, probably suspecting that Shah Jahan's father-in-law had conveniently arranged for his own convoy to be sacked. Playing it both ways, Asaf Khan in any case was the first to inform Jahangir of Shah Jahan's rebellion— no betrayal of his son-in-law, since Nur Jahan's spies would quickly relay events to court.

What happened next seems curious. Though commanding many men and resources, Shah Jahan quite obviously avoided taking full advantage of the situation. It would almost seem that he recoiled in horror from the thought of any direct clash with his own father, and hadn't counted on Jahangir's advancing to meet him. Preliminary rebel dash wound down on reaching Fatehpur Sikri; only twenty miles beyond lay Agra, but Itibar Khan closed Agra's gates and now successfully repelled a strangely weak assault. Surely the brilliant Shah Jahan with Deccan forces and three great victories behind him could have done better than that. Yet he retired obligingly to the hills, suffering defeat at Bilochpur in

April 1623. One of his chief supporters fell in battle, and other nobles would soon defect over a period of months as his cause seemed to wane. Pursued by Prince Parwiz and Mahabat Khan, he retreated first to Burhanpur and then to the Deccan kingdom of Golconda. No longer seriously threatened, Jahangir even broke camp at Ajmer and started again for Kashmir in November. Under orders to bring Shah Jahan back a prisoner or drive him out of Mogul territory, Mahabat Khan rode hard. Shah Jahan swung east from the Deccan toward Orissa and Bengal, effectively rallying to seize these provinces as a base of operations for acquiring other provinces and imperial Agra itself. But for three years of war he would be countered by Mahabat Khan again and again, on occasion even fleeing for his life. At one moment during all the hubbub, Mumtaz Mahal was left in the fort at Rohtas, not far from holy Banaras on the Ganges, and gave birth to Prince Murad on August 29, 1624. Death and desertion ate away at the prince's ranks. Shah Jahan decided on unconditional surrender.

Surprisingly, the queen received his overtures. Terms came quickly from Jahangir: certain strongholds had to be relinquished, and the prince's two sons, ten-year-old Dara Shikoh and seven-year-old Aurangzeb, must go to court as hostages. Shah Jahan immediately complied, was forgiven, and appointed governor of a minor province. Three years of civil war had ended.

Further humiliation of the vanquished was spared by an unexpected turn of events. Nur Jahan's machinations began to hem her in. She found herself fighting a hydra; with one head chopped off, a new one surged up. Now it was Mogul general Mahabat Khan whose ambition threatened her—perhaps he had even been in collusion with Prince Parwiz who still coveted the crown. Well, that threat could be scotched: Parwiz and the general must be separated.

Mahabat Khan dutifully went to Bengal, the province of disgrace. But even that wasn't enough for Nur; he had to be ruined completely. Breathing a spark of life into the old Persian alliance, Nur Jahan again took up with her brother, Asaf

Khan, and between the two of them they concocted a grave stew: Mahabat Khan found himself summoned to court to answer to charges of embezzlement and disloyalty.

It was all too much. Accompanied by five thousand Hindu Rajputs and with honor and life at stake, a wary, infuriated Mahabat finally reached Jahangir's camp at Jhelum River. The court had come from Kashmir, heading for Kabul. A military coup was now at hand.

Taking advantage of the fact that most of the imperial army had already crossed the river, Mahabat Khan detached two thousand men to guard a bridge of boats, then proceeded into the royal camp where Jahangir remained with a handful of men. Eyewitness Mutamad Khan, a noble in charge of court ceremony and military recruiting, would later record the coup in his chronicle of Jahangir's reign. Mutamad had finished morning prayers and was on a round of inspection when he encountered the rebel general. "He addressed me by name and asked after His Majesty. I saw that he had with him about 100 Rajputs on foot, carrying spears and shields, and leading his horse in the midst of them." Mahabat Khan charged into the imperial tent, while Mutamad exclaimed, "This presumption and temerity is beyond all rule; if you will wait a minute, I will go on in and make a report." Jahangir, who had doubtless not recovered from the previous evening's debauch, was in the imperial bathroom. When informed of Mahabat Khan's presence, he came forth calmly.

Jahangir's camp now witnessed a weird scene: subservient but implacable, Mahabat was taking His Majesty prisoner in order to assure himself of regal protection! Armed Rajputs guarded the bridge and surrounded the imperial tent. Would the emperor allay fears and display himself to the public eye while being escorted to Mahabat Khan's camp? An elephant was brought forward, and Jahangir entered the howdah. The royal cup-bearer braved Rajput spears, scrambling up on the beast with wine cup and flagon! Solaced by his bottle, a royal pawn proceeded to the rebel camp; Prince Shahriyar also found himself detained.

Laying hands on the imperial personage was, of course, a capital offense, and Mahabat Khan was acting in a state of wild emotion. The chronicler saw him "so distracted . . . he neither knew what he said nor what he did." As it happened the nervous general forgot all about Nur Jahan, who thinking Jahangir had gone hunting was now safely across the river visiting her brother. Apprised of the coup, she called chief nobles and tongue-lashed them. Mutamad preserved the dialogue: "This," she said, "has all happened through your neglect and stupid arrangements. What never entered into the imagination of anyone has come to pass, and now you stand stricken with shame for your conduct before God and man. You must do your best to repair this evil."

Jahangir sent his signet ring across the river, advising his queen against precipitate action. Indomitable Nur Jahan, next morning with attending nobles, forded the river at the worst point. Everyone got separated and mixed up in the current. Asaf Khan and other grandees attended the queen's elephant, but found themselves blocked by a solid contingent of Mahabat Khan's Rajputs lining the river bank with an opposing elephant phalanx. Officers moved about willy-nilly, in total panic; horsemen and footmen, camels and carriages jammed the middle of the river, colliding with one another as they pushed shoreward. Arrows whizzed, men were killed, wounded, drowned, and blood turned the river red. In a sensational tableau Nur Jahan led the fray, with her elephant wounded and Shahriyar's baby daughter and nurse incongruously ensconced in the howdah. An arrow struck the nurse in the arm; Nur Jahan pulled it out and stained her garments with blood. Rajput horsemen waving swords pushed after the queen's retreating elephant, but had to turn back in deeper water. Nur's beast swam to the opposite bank in safety.

There is more than one way to cope with an adversary. Direct action failing, the queen now surrendered and shared Jahangir's restraint; Asaf Khan fled but later capitulated. Just what Mahabat Khan expected to gain by victory is not certain: he respected the emperor's inviolability, entertained no treasonable designs for the throne, and further action might lead to disastrous consequences for himself and all India. In effect he had achieved a limited military coup, static in its implications. He could only tread water, trying to squelch Nur Jahan's influence while holding administrative power with men in key positions. After several months, Jahangir and the court were allowed to proceed under Mahabat's escort to Kabul. Acting on the queen's instructions, Jahangir even feigned relief to be accorded a rebel general's protection. A Rajput contingent assigned to keep watch was reduced.

Nur Jahan laid her plans carefully. Taking advantage of Moslem dislike for Rajputs, she secretly began giving money and promises to Moslem camp followers, and thus was able to rally several thousand troops behind her. Returning from Kabul, the imperial retinue stopped near Rohtas fort. Jahangir wanted to make a review of his wife's Moslem troops, but would Mahabat Khan keep Hindu Rajputs at a distance to avoid friction? The rest proved easy: during the review Moslems closed ranks and left Rajputs out in the cold. A disenthralled emperor proceeded to safety.

Mahabat Khan's "reign of a hundred days" had ended, very likely with his own tacit complicity: what was the point of sustaining it? He took leave and dragged pusillanimous Asaf Khan along by way of hostage, but soon released him at the empress's furious command. Truce terms required the abruptly pardoned Mahabat to give chase to Shah Jahan, who had mysteriously turned up in the northwest bulge of Sind. Asaf Khan was meanwhile made prime minister of the realm. His sister would live to regret it.

During all these months of coup and countercoup, Shah Jahan had been cautiously moving northward; now he attempted to besiege Tatta, a port in Sind. Doubtless he had been informed of Mahabat Khan's uprising against the emperor, and with Prince Parwiz entrenched in the Deccan had decided on the northwest as a new springboard of operations—especially if the shah of Persia helped. But Mahabat Khan's coup had failed; Persia responded frostily, and a lonely siege of Sind was fast failing from lack of troops. Carried in a palanquin because of illness, Shah Jahan decided to return to the Deccan where Parwiz languished in the last stages of alcoholism. Thus Mahabat Khan missed his quarry in Sind; but since they would later join forces in mid-India, we can surmise that Asaf Khan may have been fostering plots of his own during that little hostage ride with his staunch enemy.

There comes a point when intriguers fall victim to their own monstrous egotism. In fact, Nur Jahan's power plays had become little more than absurd, and her empire was on the verge of falling apart by the sheer play of opposing centrifugal forces. The enemy surged up everywhere: Shah Jahan, Parwiz, Mahabat Khan. One moment she had made Mahabat Khan top dog; then he too fell from favor; now he was pardoned for his coup and sent once more against a newly menacing Shah Jahan. The hydra had become the battle of Laocoön.

Nur Jahan's downfall occurred suddenly, with brutal concatenation. Prince Parwiz died. He had been drinking suicidally in the Deccan, suffered stomach gripes, had to be cauterized in "five places on the head and forehead," and succumbed at the age of thirty-eight. Jahangir, once again in the paradise of Kashmir, was himself growing weaker, losing appetite, rejecting even opium after all these years, and tapering off on wine. Nur Jahan's son-in-law Shahriyar humiliatingly fell ill of "fox's disease," infected with morbid scab which made all his hair, whiskers and eyebrows fall off. He retreated to Lahore in shame.

A somber imperial camp started to follow in Shahriyar's wake. With Jahangir hardly able to breathe because of asthma, the queen wanted to winter in Lahore close to her chosen puppet. Briefly, Jahangir revived his love of sport, somehow finding the strength to command a final deer drive. Beaters drove an animal near the seated emperor; wanly he lifted his gun and fired. The stricken deer bounded off to its females, pursued by a royal beater who stumbled over a precipice and instantly got killed. For Jahangir, the incident became an omen of Azrael, the Moslem angel of death. It was the end at long last; he had seen the vision. Haunted and unable to sleep, he heroically survived several hallucinatory marches further to a place called Rajaur, where at sunset he called for a valedictory glass of wine. But with the cup held to his mouth, he could not swallow. Night came on; his condition grew rapidly worse, and at dawn the next day he died. It was October 29, 1627, the twenty-second year of his reign. Astonishingly, he had reached the age of sixty. The royal retinue would soon descend the mountains with his imperial corpse, for funeral rites in nearby Bhimbar and interment later at Lahore.

Nur Jahan's game was winding down at last, and she must have guessed it. She sent a message to scurf-ridden Shahriyar at Lahore in a last bid to crown him, but she knew the worst: as prime minister, her brother could win over important court nobles to his cause. Asaf Khan did exactly that. Acting in concert with one of the grandees, Iradat Khan, he immediately took steps to protect the throne in Shah Jahan's absence. Moguls fought for an emperor, not for abstract causes; the emperor had to be here and now, to rally sympathy and legalize action taken in his name. So Khusrau's little son, Dawar Bakhsh, affectionately dubbed "Bulaki" ("nose-ring"), was hauled out of confinement and became a sacrificial lamb—a stopgap or winter king. Mutamad Khan tells how the bewildered child "did not believe them, and placed no confidence in their proposals till they had bound themselves with stringent oaths. Then they placed him on horseback, raised the royal canopy, and proceeded toward the royal quarters. Nur Jahan Begum sent several persons to bring her brother to her; but he made excuses and did not go. Asaf Khan now sent off Banarasi, a swift runner, to Shah Jahan, with intelligence of the death of Jahangir; and as there was no time for writing, he sent his signet ring as a guarantee."

In Lahore, bald Shahriyar, scornfully called "fit for nothing" by later court chroniclers, declared himself king at the urging of his wife, Nur's daughter; seizing the royal treasure, he frantically began dispensing money left and right to gain support of troops. But he could not even fight: a son of Jahangir's dead brother Daniyal arrived to take command of Shahriyar's forces.

It was a mop-up. The Mogul army and Asaf Khan moved on Lahore by elephant, with little Dawar Bakhsh mounted beside him on another beast. Seven or eight miles from the city, Shahriyar's hastily assembled defenders broke and scattered at the sight of imperial forces. Instead of taking flight, Shahriyar retreated to Lahore, seeking refuge in the harem. A eunuch dragged him before Dawar Bakhsh; he was imprisoned and blinded several days later. By way of precaution, Asaf Khan also imprisoned Daniyal's two sons, both princes in their own right.

Mahabat Khan had meanwhile joined forces with Shah Jahan in the Deccan. The runner Banarasi arrived in twenty days, presenting the signet ring; Shah Jahan sent a message back to Asaf Khan (according to Mutamad's account) saying "it would be well if Dawar Bakhsh and [Shahriyar] the useless brother of Khusrau, and the sons of Prince Daniyal, were all sent out of the world"—a not so covert hint.

Nur Jahan had good reason to be stunned by her brother's treason: he had actually left her stranded in the imperial camp with Jahangir's corpse, rushing on to Bhimbar and Lahore with the little stopgap king. She had quickly followed with Jahangir's dead body and Mumtaz Mahal's three sons by her side: hostages Dara and Aurangzeb, together with Shuja, who had been attached to the imperial camp some time previously. Once Asaf Khan had won key nobles over to his side, he wrested control of Shah Jahan's children from his sister, sending Jahangir's body to Lahore for burial. Nur was now put under surveillance and kept incommunicado.

Shah Jahan's triumphal procession northward—through Gujarat and Rajputana, attended along the way by welcoming governors of provinces and gift-laden Rajput chieftains —has been recorded in detail by flattering court historians. But at least three Europeans—an East India Company employee named "honest" Peter Mundy, the French jeweler

Tavernier, and the important Italian adventurer, Niccolo Manucci—concur in a dramatic interpretation of events. Manucci begins the needlework: little Dawar Bakhsh had his supporters, who warned the frightened king of Bijapur not to allow Shah Jahan's exit from Deccan territories. Almost forcibly restrained, Shah Jahan had to simulate death, drinking goat's blood and then vomiting it up in front of the Bijapur king's envoys. "Then," Peter Mundy takes up the thread, "she [Mumtaz Mahal] desiring leave to carry her husband's body to be buried in his own country, it was granted her; and by that means, in a coffin covered with black," Shah Jahan got transported from the Deccan. The imperial party approached Agra incognito, where Asaf Khan met the weird procession and had the bier opened. "Shah Jahan raised himself," Tavernier completes the design, "and appeared standing before the eyes of all the army." Kings rise from coffins; for all its bizarreness, the account was obviously prevalent gossip in India at the time, and might just possibly be true.

However he got there, Shah Jahan reached Agra on Thursday, January 28, 1628, and waited twelve days until the date fixed by court astrologers for his coronation, not even formally entering the city until February 4. On that same date of Thursday, January 28, according to the chronicle of Mutamad Khan, the prisoners Dawar Bakhsh, and his brother Garshasp, and Prince Shahriyar, and the sons of Daniyal, were all put to death.* It was a gruesome precedent: Mogul sons had certainly rebelled in time past, but royal Mogul blood had never before been shed on an emperor's accession to the throne—not by Babur or Humayun or Akbar or Jahangir. Shah Jahan would reap the whirlwind by this single act.

Coronation day thrilled all imperial Agra. The invocational prayer for king and subjects was read in the name of

* There is historical disagreement about Dawar Bakhsh's fate. Some sources maintain that he escaped to Persia, and was seen there by Holstein ambassadors as late as 1633. Tavernier later claimed: "I had an opportunity of conversing with him during my travels in Persia, and drank and ate with him."

Shah Jahan the Magnificent at crowded mosques, while runners set out for every corner of the realm to proclaim his accession. Hundreds of sheikhs, Hindu Rajput chiefs, and Moslem khans converged for the occasion, streaming into the capital with attendant hordes of cavalry; eminent writers, astrologers, and sages were on hand. In public pageant and with kettledrums pounding, a cascade of precious gems flowed over Shah Jahan's head from enormous gold platters sent out by the royal harem. Standing on the traditional balcony where emperors matutinally greeted their subjects, the new symbol of Mogul power looked out upon a living sea of people. He had overcome those five obstacles of brothers and stepmother; he was absolute master of India.

From the Hall of Public Audience, Shah Jahan withdrew to zenana apartments, where the beloved Mumtaz Mahal, and fourteen-year-old Princess Royal Jahanara, and all the ladies of the court showered him with further ceremony. Everyone received rewards that day: for Mumtaz Mahal there were two hundred thousand gold pieces, six hundred thousand rupees, and a fixed annual allowance of a million more; Jahanara's endowment amounted to four hundred thousand rupees, with a yearly appanage of six hundred thousand; moneys were set apart for Crown Prince Dara Shikoh, for Prince Shuja, Prince Aurangzeb, little Murad, and Princess Raushanara. The office of prime minister naturally went to Asaf Khan, newly honored with the grand title of "Uncle" and a high cavalry rating. Mahabat Khan became commander-in-chief of the Mogul army—Khan Khanan of the realm. A host of loyal nobles earned promotions and confirmations; while a few others, not so trustworthy, found themselves quietly removed from posts.

But an even greater event capped three weeks of coronation festivities. On February 26, Asaf Khan brought the long-absent young princes back to Agra. In the afternoon they reached Akbar's mausoleum at suburban Sikandra, where Mumtaz Mahal met them in a tent set up for her reception. Passionately, she embraced her sons; how tall they had grown! Next day all the court nobles escorted Asaf Khan and the princes to the *jharoka* window of the Red Fort, where with Emperor Shah Jahan they looked out over Agra and that living sea of people. The boys scattered money over their father's head, to ward off evil influences. Dara received a daily allowance of a thousand rupees, and Aurangzeb five hundred. Asaf Khan was allowed the ultimate privilege of kissing Shah Jahan's feet, and the royal signet ring formally became entrusted to him.

In the middle of all this, a woman almost totally disappears from Mogul history—Empress Nur Jahan, barely ever to be mentioned again by official scriveners. For the record she was not treated badly, considering her machinations: Shah Jahan settled an annual allowance of two hundred thousand rupees on her. Proudly, she put on her white robes of widowhood and withdrew with her equally bereaved daughter to Lahore, avoiding public entertainments and devoting the rest of her life to prayer and good works.

Yet even in defeat the dowager empress's artistic taste triumphed, creating two imposing monuments to death. Across the Jumna River from Agra's Taj Mahal and Red Fort, more-than-casual sightseers can inspect the double-storied tomb she built for Itimad-ud-Daulah; a chastely delicate and personalized work, with snub minarets, square-cut dome, latticed windows, and strongly Persian flavor. As Nur Jahan's final intrigue, her father's tomb preempted architectural innovations wrongly attributed to Shah Jahan: hers was the first Mogul edifice in white marble, and also the first to employ inlay decoration of semiprecious stone.

Nur Jahan's other masterwork can be found on the banks of the Ravi River in the Shahdara Garden of Lahore, today the showpiece city of Pakistan. Jahangir's long, squat, gloomily imposing mausoleum, with rows of Saracen arches invoking the melancholy of a Di Chirico painting, unfortunately suffered some depredation when the Sikhs later used it as a quarry for their Golden Temple at Amritsar. Not far from him, in the elegant ruins of a summer pavilion, his consort lies buried. At least the fact of her death was recorded by Shah Jahan's chief court chronicler: "On the 29th Shawwal

1055 [December 8, 1645] died Nur Jahan Begum, widow of the late Emperor Jahangir. After her marriage with the Emperor, she obtained such an ascendancy over him, and exercised such absolute control over civil and revenue matters, that it would be unseemly to dilate upon it here."

Part II

FAMILY PORTRAIT

CHAPTER

5

Intermezzo at Agra

I N THE NEW ERA ushered in by Shah Jahan's coronation, Mogul Hindustan resembled nothing so much as a miracle patient convalescing from cholera. The unabated virulence of Nur Jahan's plottings had racked the subcontinent with six years of hectic political convulsions until Jahangir's death. Now, in 1628, the ruthless dowager queen found herself summarily relegated to obligatory seclusion at Lahore; by etiquette, the only person who could assume her vacated role in the hierarchy was Mumtaz Mahal, who thus became not only empress in name but the supreme feminine eminence at the Mogul court. Seemingly launched on a career of regal fulfillment, settled luxury, and happiness, the Lady of the Taj could not know that, in fact, she had barely three years left to live.

As Shah Jahan's trust swelled in measure, Hindustan's fecund empress had more than children to bear. He consulted her in both private matters and affairs of state, making her co-regent, adviser, and confidante of the realm. Supplicants came to her as once they had come to Nur Jahan, and she never turned a deaf ear to any worthy plea. At her intercession, the emperor forgave enemies or commuted death sentences. Widows, orphans, and other indigents visited Agra from all parts of India; she listened patiently. Yet however great her fame, Mumtaz Mahal still remained only a virtuous shadow in Mogul chronicles. Lacking the intrusive historical claims of her trouble-making predecessor, she did not make events but only quietly sustained them.

In humanitarian endeavors the new empress found herself assisted by a very able lady—Sati-un-Nissa ("lance head among women"), imperial secretary and companion. Sati was the daughter of a respectable Persian family of scholars and physicians, and her brother had been "Prince of Poets" under Jahangir. When her husband died in India, she had entered Mumtaz Mahal's service, winning the queenly heart by good speech, perfect conduct, and knowledge of medicine. A fine elocutionist, she could recite the Koran stirringly, together with Persian poetry and prose. Under her literary tutelage, young Princess Royal Jahanara learned holy suras and wrote Persian. Now entrusted with the empress's own seal, Sati acted as intermediary for charity to women, duly reporting cases of distress—perhaps the most typical were poverty-stricken virgins in need of marriage dowries.

Now, for almost two years until the court's journey to the Deccan where death waited, Shah Jahan and his family enjoyed a tranquil intermezzo of splendor in the Red Fort of Agra. Though Mumtaz Mahal and the children all maintained separate royal quarters, they were doubtless within palace purlieus; only later would the grown princes build themselves mansions along the Jumna, or ride off to govern distant provinces (except for the favorite, Crown Prince Dara Shikoh, who stayed at court).

Privately tutored, the four sons (Murad was already four, Aurangzeb ten, Shuja almost twelve, and Dara an adolescent of thirteen) took primary and secondary studies which by then had become stereotyped. They were taught the Koran and standard works of Persian poetry, and of course the history of their great ancestors—Babur, Humayun, Akbar the Great, and Jahangir. Calligraphy now received considerable attention as culture became more involuted: the princes had to write well and emulate a graceful epistolary style, best exemplified by Akbar's prime minister-scholar, Abul Fazl, whose ornate writings had become "the model and despair of the age."

Early aspects of the boys' characters and personal bents were readily apparent. Of the four, only Dara Shikoh took a keen esthetic interest in both music and painting; in time he would gather a priceless collection of Mogul miniatures for posterity. Under his mullah Abdul Latif, Dara also clearly favored speculative sciences—what we today would call metaphysics. Aristotle and Plato became his philosophical idols, and in Persian poetry he preferred the mystics. Unlike Shah Jahan (who significantly admired Alexander the Great) Dara thought history dull; he was fascinated, on the other hand, by the miracles of Sufi fakirs and saints, and for the rest of his life remained passionately preoccupied with mysticism and allegory. Fatally pursuing deeper insight, Dara was to find orthodox Mohammedanism narrowly intolerant and intellectually sterile, while Islamic jurisprudence frankly bored him. His search for the divine ground of being would ultimately engender a dangerous liberalism: Hindus might regard Prince Dara's spiritual quest as the reincarnation of Akbar's open-minded curiosity, but strictly orthodox Moslems were yet to recoil in growing horror at the spectacle of an "apostate" cohorting with Hindu mystics and Christian Catholic fathers. Still, for Dara truth remained subjective—a conviction held by other thinkers in other epochs, who knew that "the road to discovery leads through private places."

By sharp contrast, young Aurangzeb displayed a starkly literal religious concern. During these formative years he closely studied the Koran (later he would master it by heart); his life's correspondence would be strewn with sacred quotations and traditional sayings of Mohammed. In languages he applied himself to Arabic and Persian no less proficiently than his eldest brother. Though Hindustani had become the convenient medium of everyday life, Persian dominated the cultural scene. More practically, Aurangzeb would learn Turkish in later military campaigns at Balkh and Kandahar —a definite asset in dealing with a linguistically heterogeneous army. Then, or in early manhood, he began his lifelong pursuit of copying the Koran by hand, and also knitted skullcaps that were "doubtless bought up by the courtiers of Delhi with the same enthusiasm as was shown by the ladies of Moscow for Count Tolstoi's boots." The caps constituted religious manual therapy, since Mohammed himself had made it a precept that every Moslem should practice a trade. The holy earnings from these twin tasks would wistfully be salted away for payment of his death shroud and for posthumous distribution to holy men. Yet for all his knowledge of chapter and verse from the Koran or Persian moral analects, Aurangzeb was not really very fond of poetry. Curiously, he disliked history as much as his brother Dara did; but his specialty was Dara's anathema—Moslem jurisprudence, the canons of Islamic law. As for music, Aurangzeb had a tin ear; and he abominated painting (probably because Mogul portraits smacked of irreligion, since the Koran proscribed human delineation as an impious imitation of Allah the Creator).

Stubborn little Murad was at this moment too young for formal education, though he subsequently displayed no great talent in any direction—every large family has its black sheep. Prince Shuja seemed capable enough, but already betrayed signs of self-indulgence. Both would play important roles in the forthcoming Mogul cataclysm, yet the two main protagonists could only be Dara and Aurangzeb—mystic versus puritan, the unorthodox versus the orthodox. Radical differences in the characters and motivations of the four princes would profoundly deepen with ensuing years; this was merely the children's hour.

● ● ●

What did they look like? Rich visual evidence of royal Mogul children, along with grownups and the entire court, is uniquely offered by Mogul miniature paintings. Vermeer or Holbein had their Indian counterparts. Emperor, harem ladies, children, courtiers, dancers, colloquies with holy men, hunts and love affairs, flowers and birds—nothing is missing.

Exposure to these miniatures evokes a naïve wonder: so the Moguls were palpably real, the people and the world of their tragedy actually existed! Shah Jahan, Mumtaz Mahal, her father Asaf Khan, Emperor Jahangir, scheming Nur

Jahan, or princes Dara Shikoh and Aurangzeb have all been preserved like flies in amber, caught by a superlative art.

Again Persia set the tone of Mogul achievement, at least initially. Miniatures began with Persian teachers of the Herat school, and Babur brought early examples of Timurid art to India. But India soon developed its own style, with masters working so much in the same vein that even experts find it hard to distinguish differences. During Akbar's rule, human sketches were rare; but with Jahangir and Shah Jahan, emperor and nobles wanted likenesses in the best bourgeois manner of an English peer sitting for Reynolds or Gainsborough. "There are few courts," a connoisseur concludes, "one knows so well by portraiture as that of the Mogul emperors."

So we find dignitaries and military men, invariably standing in profile, hands across their stomachs according to the obeisant gesture adopted at durbar. Princes and younger grandees are brusquely good-looking with almond eyes and Persian beards, swords and shields adding an aggressive note. Later in Shah Jahan's reign, it was fashionable for painters to finish heads and only outline bodies. At first sight those Christian halos behind kingly Moslem heads seem startling, until the viewer remembers Akbar's insistence on monarchic divinity, and that flirtation with Christianity which continued under Jahangir and Shah Jahan. Marvelously, people grow old from painting to painting: three decades of rule take their toll, and handsome young Shah Jahan turns up as an aging emperor with a white beard and aureole, standing in jeweled half-robe and striped pantaloons while a spring garden blooms at his slippered feet. Mumtaz Mahal's father, Asaf Khan, is sleekly rapacious with that hawk on his gloved wrist; but he, too, becomes stout and white-bearded with the years. In group scenes we find Shah Jahan and his sons visiting a holy man, all kneeling before the wild patriarch's cave while retainers hold their horses in the foreground. Elsewhere, Jahangir embraces Shah Jahan on a raised pavilion, as noblemen and elephants crowd the durbar forecourt below them.

Few details of human character can be hidden from such realistic assessment. In remorseless closeups, Jahangir looks baggy-eyed and dissolute. Dara Shikoh shows a strikingly sensitive face; Aurangzeb reveals that of the complex puritan; Nur Jahan's ambition leaps through her beauty; and we would like to have known Mumtaz Mahal of the candid, bemused gaze. A few characters seem to escape: research discloses no portraits of Princess Jahanara and her sisters. The exclusiveness of purdah made Mogul royal women elusive subjects for court painters, and the several representations of "Great Empresses" are exceptions rather than the general rule.

By contrast, all of the princes can be traced almost from the outset. Capturing a moment in youthful time, one colorful miniature entitled "The Three Sons of Shah Jahan" depicts Shuja, Aurangzeb, and Murad; Murad looks about nine, with Aurangzeb an adolescent fifteen, and Shuja perhaps seventeen. They are prancing along a road on Arabian chargers, the two elder brothers holding spears. Careful scrutiny of the faces reveals Murad as a somewhat doltish, pugnacious boy; while Shuja is good-looking in an easy-going sensual way. Later, when we know them better, we can be impressed by the anonymous court artist's perspicacity. Aurangzeb here becomes a curious study, very different from those Mogul portraits of him as a sanctimonious old man; there is a thin set to his lips, and his self-contained mien already signals strange depths. He raises his young eyes heavenward, as though interceding with Allah for the painter: "Forgive him, Lord, for he knows not what he does when he makes images apeing the Creator."

For Dara Shikoh, the family album offers a breathtaking portrait which may have been executed at the same time as the group horseback picture of his three brothers, since he seems to be eighteen or nineteen. In profile, he wears a striped and feathered Mogul cap, together with rich silk garments and necklaces of pearls interlarded by precious stones. His mouth is delicate and dreamy, with the faintest suggestion of hauteur; his jet almond eyes and fine nose show elegant breeding. His is easily the most interesting face of all four brothers.

● ● ●

The lives of the young princesses remain tantalizingly fragmentary, hidden in the seclusion of the harem. Only later will they emerge in greater detail. In 1628 Jahanara had already turned fourteen, with Raushanara all of eleven, and Gauharara still to be born. We can guess their education and culture from Sati-un-Nissa's tutelage of Jahanara; and Jahanara will turn author in later years, writing poetry and biographies of Moslem holy men.

Perhaps the best general description of the girls' characters was volunteered long after they became women. Unreliable but inimitable, the Italian adventurer Niccolo Manucci had personal access to the Mogul court and claimed knowledge of his subject. Poor Gauharara gets rudely dismissed: "I have nothing to write about that princess," Manucci admits, "and may be excused from taking the trouble. I will only state that she was proud, very passionate, fancied herself clever, was envious, not generous, and furthermore not good-looking."

Manucci also found Raushanara not so good-looking, yet "very clever, capable of dissimulation, bright, mirthful, fond of jokes and amusement, much more so than her sister Begum Sahib [Jahanara]. But she did not enjoy equal rank . . . had not the same liberty, and was not so much confided in as Begum Sahib; nor had she the same authority, seeing that she lived within her father's harem. In spite of her power of concealment, she could not hide the fact that she was the declared enemy of Dara and of Begum Sahib."

Jahanara became Manucci's favorite. "The eldest of all, whom her father loved to an extraordinary degree," Manucci sums her up as "discreet, generous, open-minded, and charitable. She was adored by all."

Harem life of Mumtaz Mahal and her daughters must be pieced together from scant sources, supplemented by first-hand inspection—anyone can now wander freely through zenana apartments in the Red forts of Delhi and

Agra. In Delhi, the ladies' *mahal* or palace suffered final ignominy after 1857, when British rule turned it into a barracks. Despoiled, stripped bare, whitewashed, and ruined, it
yet suggests luxury in traces of silver ceiling inlay and a narrow marble channel where the perfumed Stream of Paradise
flowed, burbling out of a central fountain whose precious-
stone inlay was gouged out by callous soldiers of Queen Victoria. From this harem, visitors look down through marble
grillwork onto a plain below the fort, where Delhi's populace
gathered to view Shah Jahan at his adjacent *jharoka* window.

At imperial Agra, harem quarters have been much better
preserved: one *mahal* leads into another, all of them airily
perched above the Jumna River like an exotic eyrie and
affording a view in the distance of a shimmeringly illusory
Taj Mahal. Presumably built for Jahanara and Raushanara,
several choice white marble apartments are surmounted by
brass domes; scalloped archways have been prettily decorated with inset designs in amethyst and carnelian.

These inner palace apartments, completely void today,
were once furnished in cloying Moslem splendor on the testimony of patient scholars. Exquisitely chased, silver lamps
burned perfumed oil; myrrh and frankincense made the air
sweetly heavy. Garlands of fresh flowers coiled around marble pillars and bedsteads, while young begums traipsed from
mahal to *mahal*. We are given a picture of chief queens and
royal princesses surrounded by numerous servants as they
paced palace halls and adjoining apartments, dressed in di-
aphanous silks and adorned with precious jewels. Mumtaz
Mahal and Princess Jahanara had as many as a hundred female attendants for their smallest wants. The zenana opened
onto gardens of roses and jasmine, while at Agra there were
subterranean chambers where the ladies retreated at noon to
idle away sultry hours. A *shish mahal,* so called from tiny
mirrors imbedded in plaster walls and ceilings, afforded
bathing and dressing luxury for queens and princesses. Many
hanging lamps spangled a network of filigreed light, and fish
designs in the floors came alive as water flowed over them
from fountains playing inside the apartments.

Harem inmates were divided into small groups, each commanded by a woman selected for the purpose. All groups fell under a hierarchic matron who wielded great influence at court—more often than not she was the queen mother. Ladies of the highest rank inevitably maintained separate quarters; but everyone found employment, and with a population close to five thousand the harem resembled a busy beehive. Powerful sentinels were posted in and about the zenana, with staunch females fortifying the interior while eunuchs stood balefully at the outer gates. Indiscreet conduct was punishable by death.

A few salacious seraglio details are supplied by Manucci, who in later years in Mogul India became a self-styled medical quack and actually gained admittance to the harem for "treatment" of its ladies. Manucci creates a lavish swirl: princesses never wearing the same garments for more than a day; Kashmiri women guards and a string of eunuchs carrying messages to and fro; detailed inspection of anything going into the women's apartments, with seizure of opium, wine, nutmeg, and, of course, phallic vegetables such as cucumbers!

On his visits to the zenana the Italian had to play blindman's buff: with eyes covered, he was led in by a eunuch and taken out in the same manner. Boredom spawned lascivious thoughts, and some ladies only pretended to be sick in order to talk to the doctor or have their pulses taken. The doctor (Manucci speaks of himself) "stretches out his hand inside the curtain; they lay hold of it, kiss it, and softly bite it. Some, out of curiosity, apply it to their breast, which has happened to me several times; but I pretended not to notice, in order to conceal what was passing from the matrons and eunuchs then present, and not arouse their suspicions."

For Mogul princesses, life in the harem had one particularly unhappy drawback: they were forbidden to marry. This harshly arbitrary edict had begun with Akbar and would continue through Shah Jahan's reign. Ostensibly no man could be good enough for a Mogul emperor's daughter, but the real motive was obviously political: a married princess's husband might become a potential candidate of intrigue for the throne itself. Jahanara, Raushanara, and Gauharara were thus doomed to be spinsters; a bitterly insular fate, stirring up wild frustration and strangely incestuous attachments—ingrown loyalties to father or brothers in crisis to come.

• • •

In this frankly Ptolemaic system, everything revolved around Shah Jahan himself. Surrounded by stupendous luxury and adoration, what great Mogul could deny his kinship with the gods and his divine right to rule? The same fawning myrmidons had deified megalomania in Roman emperors and Stuart kings of England; in our own times, mystical autocracy infected gentle but heedless Nicholas and Alexandra of imperial Russia. Indeed, absolute sovereignty became easier with Islam: in Hindustan's theocracy, the emperor logically constituted Allah's representative on earth. Shah Jahan dressed for his role, richly clad in silk pantaloons and gold tunics; a jeweled dagger hung from his waist, and his person was forever embellished with gems valued at twenty million rupees (the aigrette of large rubies in the imperial turban alone would today assess at half a million dollars). Ministers, high military officials, and petty chiefs attended him day and night—great retinues trailing the royal presence like a comet's tail, waiting patiently outside whenever he retreated to the harem.

Yet for all this luxury, India's emperor maintained a grueling schedule during his thirty-year reign. Shah Jahan rose at four o'clock, and after ablutions and prayers appeared at the *jharoka* window to show himself to his subjects. This presentation ritual, called *darshan* from a Sanskrit word meaning "the viewing of an idol or saint," had begun with Akbar. When Shah Jahan was in residence at Agra or Delhi, huge crowds gathered expectantly on the plain below the palace. At his appearance three-quarters of an hour after sunrise, they bowed and returned the imperial salute. In fact, a whole class of servile people, *darshaniyas,* became a distinct sect of emperor worshippers—rather reminiscent of those guilds of Augustales in the Roman Empire. Shah Jahan's adorers would not think of beginning their day's work, or even eating breakfast until they had gazed on the emperor's auspicious morning face. Half an hour and more had to be spent on display in this public balcony, with affairs of state conducted in full view of the multitudes. It was an opportune hour for the oppressed to submit petitions, tying them to a chain let down and drawn up by court attendants; but in awe of majesty or fearful of retribution from circumvented court nobles, who dared to take advantage of imperial grace?

A review of cavalry was followed by durbar in the great Hall of Public Audience, which measured 600 feet long by 370 feet wide. Only nobles, chiefs, and officers gained entry beyond inner silver rails, but a subsidiary enclosure accommodated a throng of commanders below the rank of two hundred horse, together with archers, gunners, and retainers; behind them menial servants and foot soldiers gathered, while outer fort precincts bristled with elephants, horses, and camels.

From a door connected with the harem, Shah Jahan abruptly stepped out upon a high balcony abutting on the hall, taking his seat (by 1634) on the almost legendary Peacock Throne—an artisan's triumph of graven and enameled gold, encrusted with flashing diamonds, rubies, emeralds, and sapphires, topped by a pearl-fringed canopy supported by golden pillars wreathed with bands of studded gems. With new additions and alterations to the palace, ladies of the court now watched durbar proceedings from latticework windows on either side of the three-tiered marble gallery in which he sat. The imperial orchestra boomed, musicians sang, nautch girls danced, royal attendants sprinkled perfumed water on the throng and proffered trays of betel leaf to all; musk and ambergris hung in the air. Grandees and princes now placed right palms to their foreheads and bowed their heads: for all his love of luxury, Shah Jahan had banished ceremonial groveling. Once formalities began, strict silence reigned over palace and pageantry.

After durbar, Shah Jahan withdrew to his Hall of Private Audience and conferred with important nobles about confidential business of the realm. Important correspondence would always be written in his own hand, while lesser instructions to provincial governors were first drafted by ministers of various governmental departments. Every imperial directive required the Great Seal, kept in charge of Mumtaz Mahal (later it would be entrusted to Jahanara). Here in private audience, revenue officers reported finances; the head almoner brought needy cases to Shah Jahan's attention, and there would be time to inspect architectural plans for great buildings in progress—mosques, tombs, additional palaces.

By noon Shah Jahan entered the harem, performed midday prayer, took his meal and an hour's nap, then talked with Mumtaz and Sati-un-Nissa about petitions from widows, orphans, virgins, theologians, and scholars. Following afternoon prayers, there would be still further business; with luck, the work day ended around eight o'clock. Later, in the royal bedroom, narrators with good voices sat behind screens and read aloud from biographies of saints and prophets, or from histories of former kings. By ten or ten-thirty he fell asleep for six hours, and at four the schedule began anew. His routine was broken only by a special day set apart for judicial cases, or on Fridays (the Moslem sabbath) when no court was held. In effect, pomp operated within a rigid etiquette, as formal as the Japanese court of the mannered Heian period some six hundred years earlier.

Throughout Shah Jahan's three decades of rule there would, of course, be wars, but military pursuits were Mogul stock in trade. By and large, those thirty years now afforded internal peace for India, allowing the court to cultivate rarefied tastes in art and literature. Seeking royal patronage, many poets, philosophers, scholars, artisans, and even saints would flock to Agra and later to Delhi.

Aside from major pursuits, court life offered some charming minor pastimes: hunting, riding, fishing, polo, magic shows and acrobats, even the theater. Indoors, Shah Jahan and the ladies played cards or chess; outdoor parcheesi utilized living pawns, with harem minions scuttling up and down squares amid much laughter.* Palace environs glittered for Moslem festivals, fancy fairs, and gala weddings —costly affairs which taxed the wits of a paymaster responsible for finances. The high steward bustled as he supervised cooks and servants in imperial kitchens, from which an infinite variety of dishes came forth on gold and silver trays: kedgerees and meats, grains and vegetables, sweet and spicy dishes with cardamom and cinnamon. Palace pools reflected the wriggle of goldfish; stone floors submitted to soft Persian carpets; *mahals* were decorated with gorgeous tapestries, mirrors, exotic furniture, paintings, betel boxes, narcissus pots with gold engraving and precious-stone inlay, and even silver spittoons. By night, red and blue bowls with burning wicks illuminated the walls; divans, pillows, fans, dancing girls and story tellers rounded the waking dream.

● ● ●

This was Shah Jahan's court in all its excessive artifice. Now, three centuries later, sightseers walk a desolate Indian way through barren imperial apartments at Delhi and Agra. Yet for all their emptiness, these Mogul palaces are no suggestive, ruined Alhambra of legend and myth; boldly concrete expressions of a refined materialism, they insist on nothing less than recorded history to revive their past. Only in one edifice did Mogul architecture transcend history: at the mausoleum of the Taj, the dynasty attained spiritual heights in memory of one woman—Mumtaz Mahal.

---

* The great palace quadrangle at deserted Fatehpur Sikri still preserves light and dark stones of Akbar's alfresco parcheesi board.

CHAPTER

6

A Voice from the Womb

DURING THE HOT SUMMER night of June 7, 1631, Empress Mumtaz Mahal died abruptly in childbirth; not at imperial Agra, but hundreds of miles to the south in the Deccan city of Burhanpur. Shattering enough in itself, her death would now be ghoulishly surrounded by a ramifying nightmare of thousands of unimperial, unsingular deaths. The entire Mogul province of Gujarat, from the Arabian Sea almost as far inland as Burhanpur itself, had for some time been writhing in the coils of a black famine soon to be followed by an even blacker plague.

The incident which had prompted emperor and empress to set out in December of 1629 for this Deccan seat of administration was trivial, and might just as well have been left to subsidiary hands. Not quite two years after Shah Jahan's accession to the throne, a famous Mogul general, Khan Jahan Lodi, had defected with the seven thousand horse he commanded and fled southward. Apprehensive of a rebel coalition with the powerful southern ruler of independent Bijapur, Shah Jahan had felt obliged to manifest his personal presence. Crown Prince Dara Shikoh traveled with the imperial camp, but took no part in military action. As one of her final counsels, Mumtaz Mahal had proposed an appropriate royal match between Dara and the daughter of Shah Jahan's dead half-brother, Prince Parwiz. This particular piece of matchmaking was warmly endorsed by husband and son alike, and imperial orders were dispatched to Agra to set up grand-scale nuptials when calamity suddenly intervened.

An event of morbid grandiloquence only sparsely detailed by official Mogul documents, the death of the Lady of the Taj looms symbolically large through indirect testimony. At the same time as Mumtaz Mahal's death, "honest" Peter Mundy of the East India Company—now advanced from clerk to important commercial travel within the Mogul Empire—had undertaken a harrowing journey from Surat to Burhanpur and imperial Agra beyond. Mundy sets a fiendish scene for the empress's demise. "There was," he relates unflinchingly, "a great famine begun, causing the highways to be as it were unpassable for thieves and others who infested it, not so much for desire of riches as for grain." Whenever the English caravan passed through towns, rapacious Mogul governors demanded their usual absurd customs levees. Desolate villages looked "half burnt up and almost void of inhabitants, the most part fled, the rest dead, lying in the streets and on the tombs." Farther inland, Mundy found men and women desperately selling children for a few pennies, even giving them away "to any that would take them, with many thanks, that so they might preserve them alive, although they were sure never to see them again."

Sometimes Mundy's party could hardly make space to pitch tent for the night among the vast numbers of corpses scattered about. Their noses reeked with the stench of death; their own bodies at one point almost became infected with a noxious smell that was finally traced to a great pit full of decomposing men, women, and children—"a miserable and most undecent spectacle." Horrified, Peter Mundy watched people scraping in dunghills for food, poking at horse and ox excrement for undigested grain, and even coming to blows over it. The living already looked like skeletons; many were actually dying, or had just died. Highways were strewn with bodies, especially outside of towns where stark naked victims of all ages and both sexes had been dragged beyond the gates and obscenely abandoned.

[107]

Country folk in desperation now latched onto the English contingent like macabre children following a pied piper of hope—anywhere, so long as it was outside the compass of death. "As we passed their towns, they daily joined to us by multitudes, and likely so to continue until our arrival at Brampore [Burhanpur]."

When Peter Mundy arrived at Burhanpur, the charnel-house spectacle abruptly ended. Here a bazaar adjoined the provincial palace where Prince Parwiz had received Sir Thomas Roe sixteen years before. Shah Jahan was now in residence, and the market was well stored with a variety of provisions against the disaster that had befallen neighboring towns.

Beyond Burhanpur, Mundy's party would still come upon carcasses of beasts—elephants, camels, horses, buffalo, and oxen. But wheat fields showed green now; cotton flourished, fruits and herbs grew in gardens, and town bazaars were plentiful. Thousands of ox carts laden with grain, butter, and other victuals moved along the roads under the watchful eye of *Banjara,* the carrier or drover caste of Hindus; but none of this abundance found its way to famine-stricken areas, "it being all sent to Brampore to supply the King's army." Many months later, on returning to the English "factory" or trading station at Surat, Mundy found most of his friends of the East India Company dead of plague.

Others have left similar though less graphic accounts of the disaster. Even the emperor's official Mogul scribe candidly admitted: "Life was offered for a loaf, but none would buy; rank was to be sold for a cake, but none cared for it. . . . For a long time dog's flesh was sold for goat's flesh, and the pounded bones of the dead were mixed with flour and sold. . . . Destitution at length reached such a pitch that men began to devour each other, and the flesh of a son was preferred to his love."

But the chronicler goes on to enumerate Shah Jahan's response to the famine: His Majesty directed officials of Burhanpur, Ahmadabad, and the country of Surat to establish soup kitchens, or almshouses for the benefit of the poor and destitute. Every day, enough soup and bread were prepared to satisfy the wants of the hungry. Shah Jahan further ordered that so long as he remained at Burhanpur five thousand rupees should be distributed among the deserving poor every Monday. "Under the direction of the wise and generous Emperor, taxes were remitted by revenue officers"—who cynically ignored imperial directives whenever they could get away with it. From rural dishonesty would later come a proverb—"Delhi is distant."

It was against this stark spectacle that the life of Mumtaz Mahal, empress of India, suddenly ended. Vying with the extremes of famine and plague, kismet had ordained a positively eerie locus for her death: not Burhanpur itself, but the Deccan plateau of which it was a part might have seemed a gigantic catafalque of nature herself. Hugely enclosing this weird bier, westward mountains ran parallel to the Arabian Sea, while hundreds of miles of indiscriminate Vindhya ranges blocked access from the north. Close to Burhanpur, high Satpura regions abounded in forest-girt hills; southward, barren tablelands extended to endless rocky eyries studded by the forts of wiry Hindu Marathas who would one day successfully challenge Mogul supremacy. The Deccan, fateful now for Mumtaz Mahal and later for her last surviving son, was so historically vital that an eminent British historian would one day label it "the Dauphiné of the Mogul Empire." Politically, culturally, and geographically separate from the north, the area had developed into a festering abscess for Mogul rule. Akbar, Jahangir, and young Prince Shah Jahan had spent months there in often fruitless military campaigns; and as emperor, Shah Jahan had ominously returned—together with the woman who accompanied him everywhere and anywhere.

The rigors of these campaigns had unquestionably taken their toll during Mumtaz Mahal's endless pregnancies over the years. All thirteen previous children had been born to her in perpetual wandering, and seven had succumbed to the high infant mortality which even royalty could not escape. Six had survived, and another would now also survive. Yet for Mumtaz Mahal this fourteenth and last child was not birth, but death itself.

● ● ●

During the empress's thirty hours of delivery pain, Persian and Indian astrologers had been hovering about Burhanpur's Red Fort with astrolabes and charts. Planetary predictions for Gemini had already been drawn up, and the entire royal household became impatient for news of a princely birth so that drums could be beaten.

Death came brutally, three hours before dawn. Like a page torn from some gothic horror story, several stubborn but unsubstantiated accounts insist on a sinister prognostication: just before delivery Mumtaz Mahal heard her unborn child cry out—a long-drawn wail from prenatal darkness. Hearing the muffled howl, she shrieked; then she asked Princess Jahanara (now seventeen) to call Shah Jahan to her bedside. It was not a prince who emerged from the distended ring of birth; a final daughter, Gauharara Begum, was thrust forth, probably in a hemorrhage of blood. The emperor came quickly from an adjacent apartment. Mumtaz Mahal opened her eyes, conferred the safekeeping of her children upon him, said good-bye, and died. The event was swift; stunned, Shah Jahan burst into tears.

Only facts are recorded by court chronicles, which do not even mention the voice from the womb. But understandably desperate for every detail of despair and anguish, less reliable sources go even further: Mumtaz told the emperor of the omen, begging his forgiveness if she had committed any offense during their married life. Presumably she made two unverified requests, both of which he promised to keep "on his life and soul." First she begged him not to have children by another wife, fearful that the sons of different mothers would come to blows for accession to the throne. It seems unlikely that any dying person would be so vain as to preoccupy herself with the second request: the emperor must build over her a mausoleum the like of which might not be found anywhere else in the world.

Whatever the true version of those final moments, the

essential tragedy remained: Mumtaz Mahal was dead at the age of thirty-eight. In traditional rendering, the Moslem cavalier who comes from Paradise to visit cradles had lightly closed a mother's eyelids and led her into eternity. For the moment, the Lady of the Taj seemed condemned to the oblivion of funeral rites hastily arranged at Burhanpur; not until six months later would her corpse be transported hundreds of miles north to Agra, to the enduring glory of the most famous tomb in history.

Had there been time for last Moslem rites? If so, then most likely the "O Man" chapter of the Koran was read by her bedside at the moment of death. Its beautiful bleak verses promised that those who merited Paradise on the day of judgment would be happily employed and find themselves reclining on thrones in pleasant shade. Some authorities believe that according to Moslem tenets women have no entry into heaven; but this is disputable.* In any case, her face had already been turned toward Mecca.

As was usual for a great person's decease, announcement of the event to the royal household took the form of euphemisms. Surely everyone gathered, anguished and appalled. Ladies-in-waiting and slave women burst into sobs and lamentations, a funerary observance in direct defiance of Mohammed's commands.

The injunction of the Koran regarding quick burial was doubtless followed. Mumtaz Mahal's body reliably received a cold camphor-water bath by a professional female washer, before being wrapped in a customary shroud which for women consisted of five pieces of white cotton. Since ghosts were much dreaded, the corpse may very well have been removed from Burhanpur Palace through an opening in the wall—carried out head first to prevent the spirit from finding its way back in.

Funeral services perhaps took place at dawn in Burhanpur Mosque, with prayers recited by an imam and his

---

* As witness the chronogram on page 113.

high attendant. The bier was then carried by four near relatives to a building in the Zainabad garden on the banks of the Tapti River for transitory interment. Shah Jahan certainly followed the procession, pulling out his hair in grief. Mumtaz Mahal's rank demanded the tribute of insignia, flags, elephants, and cavalry. Her body was gently placed in the vault with its head pointing north and its face turned toward the Kaaba—the cubic shrine in the court of the Great Mosque at far-away Mecca that contained the famous black stone said to have been given by the Angel Gabriel to Abraham. These rituals must all have been duly observed, in spite of the interim nature of the burial. A few verses from the Koran were recited, and the tomb closed.

There followed a customary mourning period of forty days, during which the emperor succumbed to melancholia. For the entire week following Mumtaz Mahal's death, he refused to attend to any affairs of state whatsoever. He canceled his morning durbar; he even stopped appearing to the populace of Burhanpur at dawn from the palace balcony. By official opinion, Shah Jahan never again showed the same enthusiasm for administering the realm. He later said he would have become a total recluse if the duties of kingship had not stood so emphatically in the way.

In the middle of religious services at Mumtaz Mahal's temporary tomb on the Tuesday following her death, the emperor broke into convulsive weeping while reciting the necessary prayer for the dead. Every Friday, during subsequent months of the court's stay at Burhanpur and until the transfer of the corpse to Agra, he made nocturnal pilgrimages to her grave. His hair began to turn white.

This abnormal bereavement continued unabated for two years. Shah Jahan refused to be distracted or amused; on festival days he burst into tears when ladies of the harem assembled, and any visit to the zenana served only as a reminder of the queen's absence. For a longer than prescribed period, he refused to wear any colored or embroidered garments and appeared only in white—Islam's color of death. He abandoned music, a difficult renunciation for the passionate amateur who was now lavishing patronage on great Hindu musicians of the day. And he never again used the perfume to which he was greatly attached.

Bebadal Khan, one of the Moslem nobles of the court, composed a chronogram for the empress: "May Paradise be the abode of Mumtaz Mahal." Certain Persian letters of this inscription expressed the year of her death, 1040 A.H. But a better and briefer chronogram made use of only one word—"Sorrow."

In early December 1631, Mumtaz Mahal's body was disinterred and sent to imperial Agra, escorted in a solemn procession headed by fifteen-year-old Prince Shuja traveling with the family doctor, Wazir Khan, and faithful Sati-un-Nissa. As royal mourners, they and their attendants all wore white garments. Along the northward way, by order of Shah Jahan, enormous sums of silver were freely distributed in alms to masses lining the roadsides—the greater part of them not Moslems but anonymous Hindus. While the funeral party marched to Agra, crowds grew larger and larger. Not only alms but food was lavishly distributed to the poor, who fell on their knees and blessed this dead woman with all their hearts.

The cortege arrived at the capital three weeks later. Here the empress was interred anew on the banks of the Jumna River in a plot which Shah Jahan now acquired from the Hindu Rajah Jai Singh, at the nominal price of a magnificent palace. Over the tomb a provisional dome would be hastily constructed, in order to hide Mumtaz Mahal's remains from public view.

The spot became instantly sacred, and work on the Taj began almost at once. Sketches had already been submitted, discussed, and criticized by master architects of the empire; one final plan, approved by Shah Jahan, emerged in miniature wooden model. Foundations were now being cast for the masterwork which would take over twenty years and employ twenty thousand workmen living across from the site in a veritable city appropriately called Mumtazabad. White Makrana marble would be lugged from the quarries of Jodhpur state in Rajputana a hundred miles away. For the garden walls, the entry arch, and the great tomb's mosque and guest house, red sandstone had to be brought from Akbar's capital city of Fatehpur Sikri, which now stood totally abandoned to ghosts and birds wheeling endlessly in the blue sky. Precious-stone inlay work on the Taj would require turquoise from Tibet, lapis lazuli from Ceylon, jasper from Cambay, malachite from Russia, carnelian from Baghdad, and chrysolite from the Nile, together with agate, chalcedony, sardonyx, quartz, jade, amethyst, and black marble. Smiths were to fashion those silver doors for future looting; and there would be gold wall panels to invite vandals, and a canopy of ten thousand pearls, and diamonds, emeralds and other jewels from the far corners of the world. Construction would require an inclined road-ramp $2\frac{1}{2}$ miles long (as did the Pyramids of Egypt) to carry heavy slabs to a height of almost 250 feet. Master calligraphers, artisans carving undying flowers in stone, dome experts, pinnacle makers, and master masons must now come from Constantinople, Samarkand, Kandahar, and Baghdad, as well as from within the realm, and devote years of their lives to this edifice. All for a dead woman, all for Mumtaz Mahal.

● ● ●

Shah Jahan did not follow the corpse until three months later, when his entire retinue left Burhanpur in early April 1632. They arrived in Agra about mid-June, since the cumbersome court traveled more slowly than the funeral party which had preceded it.

Peter Mundy, stationed for some time at the Mogul capital, decided to witness the spectacle of the emperor's return. He and Sundar Das, a Hindu assistant, had trouble getting a vantage point outside of town, being "stopped and hindered by a great number of elephants, camels, carts and coaches" —an advance guard of the royal procession. Palanquins with thick bamboo handles lurched as each royal lady was borne homeward by six or eight men. Behind them came several hundred red-bedecked camels, carrying slave women, servants, attendants. A multitude of elephants and more camels laden with luggage, tents, chests and bedding brought up the rear. But was it the rear? There followed several hundred additional elephants, with closely covered howdahs secreting the emperor's and nobles' ladies.

"The face of the earth," Mundy noted, "was covered with people." Some hung in neem trees to get a better view of the procession. Now appeared troops on horseback, still more elephants, and innumerable flags "which made a most gallant show." Twenty of the emperor's coaches passed; thousands of horsemen followed. The parade stretched out to crack o' doom! Twenty great elephants of state lumbered along, covered with gold and velvet cloth, their mahouts displaying the Mogul banner on which a couchant lion sat with the rising sun behind him. The most imposing elephant of all glittered with gold and silver chains and bells. Officers with silver staves appeared on horseback and on foot, crying, "Make way!"

At last the widower Shah Jahan came into view, mounted on a dark gray horse; and side by side with him could only be the imposing Mahabat Khan, veteran commander-in-chief of the entire Mogul army. A little distance behind them rode Crown Prince Dara Shikoh—"all alone." A cluster of lords walked before, behind, and on either side of Dara. "Half a flight shot behind the King" clopped an armed retinue—multitudes of cavalry with lances glittering brightly against the sun. Even more elephants appeared, belonging to the nobles, each with five or six flags flying; and warrior elephants galumphed by, with two small field pieces mounted on their backs. Round and about the fantastic parade careened great wings of horsemen, majestic hordes circumvallating the plains.

Shah Jahan entered the cool shade of suburban Dehra Bagh Gardens. On the advice of court astrologers, he waited until midnight before proceeding two miles further to the Red Fort of Agra.

[115]

CHAPTER

7

The Smell of Apples

LESS THAN A YEAR AFTER Shah Jahan had returned a widower to the capital, ubiquitous Peter Mundy wrote in his journal: "The Great Mogul's or King's daughters are never suffered to marry (as I am informed), being an ancient custom. This Shah Jahan, among the rest, hath one named Chiminy Begum, a very beautiful creature by report, with whom (it was openly bruited and talked of in Agra) he committed incest, being very familiar with him many times in boy's apparel, in great favour and as great means allowed her." Chiminy or Chamani Begum, literally "Princess Flowerbed," was a new nickname for Jahanara.

The astonishing assertion of incest can be deferred for a moment. Mundy's fragment conjures up an evocative image: physical beauty, and saucy ease in wearing men's clothing—not a tomboy, but a spiritedly forthright personality. This is Jahanara in her late teens: the apple of her father's eye and shortly to become the darling of all her brothers—not merely Dara Shikoh's confidante but adviser for everyone, a center of involvement in political events to come. Already wealthy in her own right, Jahanara was at that very moment, in 1633, contributing great sums of money in preparation for Dara's and Shuja's weddings, and supervising details with the certain authority of a mother surrogate. Her riches would soon increase, augmented by a stream of costly gifts from every quarter; indeed, no future enterprise could prosper at the Mogul court without her influence. Yet never for a moment did she appear to be designing or spoiled; her character seemed closer to that of her dead mother—candid and warmly appealing. In court chronicles and in European letters and reports, Jahanara had become and would for many years remain the dominant female personality of all Mogul India—Begum Sahib or "elder sister," with an almost mystical respect attached to her role.

Maddeningly, the secrecy of Mogul purdah creates so many lamentable gaps with regard to Shah Jahan's two younger daughters: who was raising the new child Gauharara, and where is sixteen-year-old Raushanara in this greenhouse of seedling tragedy? We can only imagine Raushanara's (and later Gauharara's) spleen at having to play second fiddle to Jahanara. Raushanara exerts less influence, rates less privilege—not merely because she is younger, but because she is also less beautiful and less intelligent. By the time Raushanara emerges dramatically from Mogul history as more than a mere name, it is too late to find out *how* she evolved; in the climactic autumn of 1657 she will be forty years old, rigidly hardened into a scheming and ruthless virago determined to rule the Mogul harem. Not for nothing will she become Aurangzeb's ally: perpetually criticized or passed over in favor of their elders, they share the common ground of frustration.

Incest between Shah Jahan and Jahanara: admittedly, any such rapport was allegation—*bavardage* of the realm, since no official Mogul source would dare to mention it. Yet almost every other European in India at the time sustains Peter Mundy and repeats the story: over and over, incest crops up in the narrative of Tavernier the French jeweler, and in Dutch accounts, and in letters from diligent English factors at Agra or Surat assessing the scene for their East India Company superiors. European trade still depended on internal Mogul politics; even the slightest aspect of purported court intrigue became grist for the mill of speculation. Where scandal could not be certified, it could at least receive careful qualification—"some say," or "everyone believes," or the inevitable "by report."

[117]

Long afterward, when the French physician François Bernier reached a Hindustan already in full crisis, old-mint gossip about father and daughter would still be circulating as unimpeachable coin. "Begum Sahib, the elder daughter of Shah Jahan," Bernier expatiates on Mundy's fragment, "was very handsome, of lively parts, and passionately beloved by her father. Rumor has it that his attachment reached a point which it is difficult to believe, the justification of which he rested on the decision of the mullahs, or doctors of their law. According to them, it would have been unjust to deny the king the privilege of gathering fruit from the tree he had himself planted."

Rumor had it, but was incest true? No single ambiguity in Mogul history became more hotly debated at a given moment, though the argument now seems virtually antediluvian. Hardly endowed with the dispassionate insights of later depth psychology, Victorian and Edwardian scholars worked themselves into an emotional lather, venting staunch moral disapproval of those who had even dared to raise the issue in the first place. It was scandalous royal gossip; Jahanara's name would always "adorn the pages of history as a bright example of filial attachment, and heroic devotion to the dictates of duty." Even as late as the sophisticated 1930s, Shah Jahan's Indian biographer decided that only a "perverted imagination" could picture the emperor committing such an act.

But considerably more pertinent than these highly starched attitudes, the question is still there: what unquenchable source inspired all those imputations of incest? Was it merely common gossip, or could gossip have been based on something more than the mere knowledge of Jahanara's inordinate love for her father?

At least one English critic, Vincent Smith, invoked the displeasure of his stuffy peers after a brave investigation of Mogul texts: the "accusation against Shah Jahan and his daughter, even if it be not conclusively proved, certainly is not disproved." By adroit reasoning, Smith even managed to determine the moment in time when the disputed intimacy between Shah Jahan and Jahanara might first have occurred: *in the Deccan, immediately after the death of Mumtaz Mahal.*

However shocking, the deduction is humanly profound. Given the gloomy abnormality of a Mogul Empire where imperial princesses were doomed to remain unmarried, inbred love for father or brothers might more than logically find overt expression. Quite aside from her attachment to the emperor, the passion between Jahanara and her brother Dara Shikoh would also take on a strangely mystical quality at a later date—almost a supernatural identification. Far from being unimaginable, incest between father and daughter becomes all too imaginable: forbidden by royal taboo to marry, a seventeen-year-old incarnation of the dead Mumtaz Mahal comforts Shah Jahan in his extreme violent grief, and he seizes on equally extreme means of consolation. It is classic and relentless; European gossip cannot easily be dismissed, because it illuminates the events that follow. Jahanara remains no less remarkable a person whether seen in the light of persuasive aberration or prudery. In any case she will develop from a regally assured young princess to a spiritual and self-effacing woman, moving through moments of staggering drama with a high dignity.

● ● ●

Along with rumors of incest, those of fraternal hatred—more easily certifiable—would soon preoccupy both Mogul court and Europeans alike. The first indications of a deadly feud between Dara Shikoh and Aurangzeb had already manifested themselves, later to explode in a mushroom cloud of acrimony enveloping Murad and Shuja as well.

Behind the feud stretched a mist of legend: the smell of apples. As related by Manucci, the apple story antedates both the death of the empress and the emperor's coronation —taking place in the Deccan during one of Mumtaz Mahal's pregnancies when Prince Khurram was technical prisoner of the king of Bijapur. She longed for fruit out of season; Shah Jahan ventured forth to find it, meeting a fakir who gave him two apples along with a prediction. If ever he fell ill, he must smell his hands: "So long as they had the scent of apples,"

Manucci affirmed, "his illness would be neither dangerous nor mortal. When they ceased to smell of apples, it would be a warning that he had reached his term of life." Pressing for further revelation, Shah Jahan then wanted to know "which of his sons would be the destroyer of his race. The fakir answered that it would be Aurangzeb." The royal father had from that moment begun to rebuff his own child, labeling Aurangzeb "the White Snake" in mockery of his fair complexion. Shah Jahan even considered filicide; but, Manucci concluded, "Raushanara Begum always preserved [Aurangzeb], and God reserved him to be the chastisement of his father."

Legend can be discounted as hindsight, though like most legends it has a grain of truth: Shah Jahan did, in fact, come to mistrust Aurangzeb, inadvertently contributing to the growing hatred between his two sons.

Yet in the last analysis, no historian or historical document has ever satisfactorily explained the real basis of the Dara-Aurangzeb conflict. A family phenomenon, their hatred simply existed, begun perhaps in childhood from a natural antipathy of character. Only later would contention take on a religious significance, with Aurangzeb asserting himself as the champion of orthodox Islam against his brother's unorthodox "heresies." On the personal level, Aurangzeb's later correspondence would impute sustained mischief-making to Dara—years of presumably calculated plots intended to poison Shah Jahan's attitude and deliberately spike Aurangzeb's ambitions or denigrate his achievements. The accusation seems moot: Dara was far from being a vindictive personality as will be seen, whereas coming events would expose in a near-paranoid light Aurangzeb's well-known suspicious character, and his need for the most involuted self-justification.

Whatever its origin, hatred between the brothers was now very evident: isolated but significant moments of rising tension date from 1633, which began as Dara's year. Grief for Mumtaz Mahal was slowly fading away; the pageant of court life had revived again with preparations for the crown prince's marriage on February 1. His chosen bride was still his first cousin Nadira Begum, and elaborate preparations cut short in 1631 were now resumed under Jahanara's supervision, with the capable assistance of Sati-un-Nissa.

In deference to her dead mother, Jahanara went to great lengths to make the wedding as grand an affair as possible: nuptial costs exceeded three million rupees, of which the princess personally contributed half. Great celebrations enlivened the Red Fort, and Shah Jahan not only allowed music in the palace for the first time since Mumtaz Mahal's death, but appeared in festive apparel to preside at the wedding banquet. Seated on a magnificent horse, Dara was escorted by Murad, Shuja, and Aurangzeb from his mansion along the Jumna River to the Hall of Public Audience, where Shah Jahan put pearls around his neck and fastened on the groom's crown, even as his own crown had been fastened on by Jahangir on the night of his marriage to Mumtaz Mahal. After midnight, the official marriage ceremony took place. By one of those little ironies of history, the *qazi* who married the unorthodox Dara and Nadira Begum was a fanatically orthodox Moslem.

Business affairs brought Peter Mundy back to Agra in time to witness both Dara's wedding festivities and also those of Prince Shuja, which took place about three weeks later. On a strand by the river side, Mundy watched a display of fireworks that turned night into day—"Methought it made a brave and pleasant show."

Dara's love for his cousin Nadira Begum proved to be even more faithful than that of Shah Jahan for Mumtaz Mahal—for unlike his father, he never contracted any other marriage. Nadira Begum emerges from Mogul chronicles as no less beautiful than Mumtaz Mahal, and perhaps just as courageously loyal. Her fortunes were now bound to Dara's for the rest of their lives; she would bear him eight children, with two sons and a daughter surviving to play important minor roles in future events. Within two years, in 1635, handsome Sulaiman Shikoh would be born; another son, Sipihr Shikoh, would follow in 1644, and a daughter, Jahanzeb or Jani Begum, would appear some time afterward.

Four months after Dara's wedding, one of the few revealing incidents concerning young Aurangzeb took place: the famous elephant encounter of May 28, 1633. By Shah Jahan's command, several enormous beasts had been goaded to combat along the Jumna River bank near a mansion in which he had once lived as prince. In an unpredictable course of action, the two adversaries had shifted to a fresh arena directly beneath the *jharoka* balcony of Agra fort itself. Accompanied by Dara, Shuja, and fourteen-year-old Aurangzeb, the emperor now followed on horseback to witness the spectacle. Eager for a close-range view, Aurangzeb jockeyed his mount dangerously close to the enraged elephants. Momentarily disengaged and losing sight of its opponent, one of the animals turned on him, trumpeting wildly. With cool adolescent courage, the prince prevented his horse from turning away and launched his spear at the elephant's head. Panic ensued: bolting and tripping over one another, the assembled crowd fled in all directions. Khans and menials shouted, crude Saint Catherine's wheels were ignited to discourage attack, but the maddened behemoth charged horse and princely rider, knocking them down with a sweep of its long tusk. Aurangzeb scrambled to his feet, pulled his sword, and faced the fury—the history of India hung in the balance. Shuja pushed his charger through men and fireworks' smoke; galloping up to the elephant, he wounded it with his spear. But soon Shuja's horse reared, throwing him to the ground. Hindu Rajput to the rescue, Rajah Jai Singh now entered the fray, attacking while managing his own shying steed. Shah Jahan shouted to imperial guards for help.

With both princes in peril, help came from an unexpected quarter: the opposing elephant now returned for revenge. Harried by renewed assault, confused by spear-jabs and fireworks going off in its face, the maddened beast retreated with its determined rival following in full pursuit. By official Mogul report, Shah Jahan embraced Aurangzeb, praised his courage, bestowed on him the title of *bahadur* or hero, and showered him with presents. Court nobles decided that Aurangzeb had inherited his father's courage, recalling a hunting episode when the young Shah Jahan had attacked a wild tiger with only his sword while Emperor Jahangir watched.

But one old noble, Hamiduddin Khan, preserved Aurangzeb's peculiar dialogue after the event. When Shah Jahan lovingly reproached his son for displaying such rash courage, Aurangzeb replied, "If the fight ended fatally for me it would have been no matter for shame. Death drops the curtain even on emperors; that is not dishonor. The shame lay in what my brothers did!" The slap was mainly at Dara— an unfair accusation of cowardice, since Dara had actually been some distance away from both Shuja and Aurangzeb; in the flash of crisis and resolution, he could hardly have come to their assistance.

A conventional derring-do tidbit for Indian historians, this elephant encounter actually affords no little insight—indeed the only ominous glimpse we have—into the formation of Aurangzeb's character. Danger had arisen in the first place because of his insistence on watching wild-beast combat close at hand. Though aggression was characteristic of the Moguls, this compulsive adolescent fascination betrayed an excessive preoccupation with violence. The sly denigration of "my brothers" becomes more than the implication of "I was brave, they didn't come to my rescue." In fact Shuja was very much there, and Dara couldn't have been. By belittling them, Aurangzeb aggrandized himself. "Death drops the curtain even on emperors": did he already see himself in such a light, and vaunt his courage as meriting a crown? It needs no master psychologist to find the reverse side of braggadocio: hidden envy and rankling feelings of inferiority were already expressing themselves with the sanctimonious self-righteousness later to become Aurangzeb's virtual trademark of expression.

Three days after the elephant interlude, Aurangzeb turned fifteen, and Shah Jahan had him weighed against gold pieces in full court. The young hero's deeds were lauded by verses composed in Persian and Urdu; Shah Jahan's poet laureate even received five thousand rupees for a commemorative ode.

Glimpses of the young Aurangzeb now become infrequent. Toward the end of 1634 he became commander of ten thousand horse, and then assumed governorship of the Deccan in July 1636. He returned to Agra in 1637 at the age of nineteen for his marriage to Dilras Banu Begum, a daughter of the military noble Shahnawaz Khan. The following year, another of Shahnawaz Khan's daughters married Murad, then only fourteen. Shah Jahan's sons were growing up.

In due course Murad and Shuja also found themselves assigned to various provinces for war and government, winning periodic increases in rank along with Aurangzeb. But Crown Prince Dara Shikoh was obviously Shah Jahan's fixed choice of heir. In October 1633, Dara had become master of twelve thousand horse; within five years, his command increased to twenty thousand horse, and later increments lifted him beyond competition. By 1656, on the eve of Mogul crisis, Dara's cavalry rank would be larger than Shuja's and Aurangzeb's combined. Without question the emperor loved and favored his eldest son.

As usual, the court moved about perpetually in the decade following Mumtaz Mahal's death. The emperor found himself alternately in the Deccan and Kashmir, or sojourning in Kabul and Lahore when military attention focused on the northwest frontier of Hindustan. It was in Lahore on November 11, 1641 that Asaf Khan died.

Catching a forbidden last glimpse of Mumtaz Mahal's crafty father, a Portuguese Augustinian friar, Sebastien Manrique,* bore bizarre witness to a royal Mogul banquet: he

---

* Manrique's Indian journal later received the pope's *nihil obstat* for European publication, achieving modest success under the title *Itinerario*. But the author himself proved less fortunate: he was murdered in London in 1669 by his Portuguese servant, who put the body in a box and threw it into the Thames. English authorities traced and hanged the murderer.

and a companion had been hidden by a eunuch in a gallery of Asaf Khan's house at Lahore. There was an extra dividend for prying eyes: India's prime minister had invited Emperor Shah Jahan and Crown Prince Dara Shikoh to the feast. Below Manrique, the banquet hall was adorned with "rich carpets of silken, silver and golden embroidery, which covered the floor so as to form tables on the ground, as is the national custom." Manrique's eyes popped at the sight of five-tiered stands covered with gold vessels, silver braziers, and perfume holders; odors of ambergris, eagle-wood, and civet drifted up to him, and a seven-spouted hydra of silver spewed scented water into a trough.

Shah Jahan entered, "accompanied by a large bevy of gallant, handsome women" including Mumtaz Mahal's mother and Princess Jahanara. Among near relatives, purdah was not maintained. Behind them came Dara Shikoh with Asaf Khan. Manrique saw matrons waving fans over the emperor, while Asaf Khan's family made obeisances. Soft voices sang of Shah Jahan's victories, as four young ladies ("relations of Prince Asaf Khan and daughters of great noblemen") brought water for the washing of hands. One girl laid out a white satin cloth; another placed an inlaid gold vessel on it; a third held a ewer of water and poured for the emperor. Twelve more girls brought water for Dara's and Asaf Khan's ablutions.

Then the feast began. Manrique catalogued the "deafening sound of instruments . . . not unlike our trumpets, but of uncertain and mournful tone. Dinner was brought in rich golden dishes by eunuchs, richly attired in Hindustan style, with trousers of different colored silks and white coats of the finest transparent muslin. These coats served to cover their dark-brown skins, which disseminated the precious sweet-smelling unguents with which, on this festive occasion, they were anointed."

How could a secret sharer smell body unguents and scented water from the distance of a gallery? The good friar's details are suspicious; but no matter. Now he watched many different dishes being served, some in European style—especially pastries and cakes concocted by slaves who had been with the Portuguese. Shah Jahan commented on the cakes; when told they were made by *Farangis* (Franks or Europeans), he added that Europeans would be great people except that they were kaffirs, ate pork, and did not wash "that part from which replete Nature expels the superfluities of their corporeal bellies."

If we are to believe Manrique, the meal lasted over four hours; dancing girls accompanied dessert, along with three great gold vessels filled with diamonds, rubies, and other gems. The friar saw Shah Jahan so full of greed that "he paid scant attention to the dancing . . . spending all the time gazing at these jewels and letting them pass through his hands. . . . When the feast had reached this stage, our eunuch returned to fetch us, telling us it was time we left."

Papal imprimatur of his Indian journal notwithstanding, Manrique was hardly above embroidering details or lifting them wholesale from other sources; but he probably did witness this particular event. Asaf Khan died shortly after the banquet, and by imperial prerogative the emperor seized all his property—worth about $15 million.

The roving court returned to Agra, where another mishap occurred on March 26, 1644: Jahanara, now thirty, very nearly died. As she was proceeding from Shah Jahan's apartments to her own, her perfumed muslin garments caught fire from a candle; four ladies-in-waiting immediately threw themselves over the princess to smother the flames, but their own dresses caught fire as well. Before the blaze could be extinguished, Jahanara had suffered first-degree burns on her back, sides, and arms.

Anguished, Shah Jahan remained at his daughter's bedside for weeks, feeding her and putting medicine on the burns with his own hands. Daily durbar dwindled to a few moments; only urgent affairs of state were handled, and every healer in the realm found himself summoned to provide treatment. By way of atonement for any sins which may have provoked fate, great sums of money poured out to charity: every night a purse of a thousand rupees was placed under Jahanara's pillow before being dispensed to beggars the next morning. Bribing officials found themselves released from prison, their debts annulled in a wave of imperial compassion. Each evening the emperor went down on his knees, weeping and praying until midnight.

The princess royal's precarious state lasted four months. Her case seemed hopeless: two of the ladies-in-waiting had died of burns within a few weeks of the incident. Even a physician to the late king of Persia tried helplessly to combat Jahanara's fever. But then, "a slave named Arif prepared an ointment which entirely healed her sores in two months."

There is a certain mystique in these various accounts of the princess's illness: some of them take on an almost symbolic tinge. In one version she is cured by a Dr. Gabriel Boughton, an Englishman from the East India Company's Agra factory. For his reward, Boughton is said to have asked Shah Jahan to give the company a writ of trade for Bengal— "One of the many Englishmen who at all times have been content to spend themselves without reward for the sake of England," comments a popular writer of the Edwardian period!

Prompted by news of Jahanara's grave state, Murad and Aurangzeb hastened to Agra from their respective provinces. Aurangzeb arrived on May 2 and within three weeks he had suffered the humiliation of being summarily dismissed as governor of the Deccan and deprived of both rank and allowance. Deliberately obfuscating, the court historian squirmed for an explanation: "Prince Aurangzeb, under the influence of ill-advised, short-sighted companions, had determined to withdraw from worldly occupations and to pass his days in retirement. His Majesty disapproved of this."

Some scholars interpret the incident as meaning that Aurangzeb wanted to become a hermit in the religious sense; but the Persian phrase "turning recluse" more commonly meant a quiet resignation from military office. The best clue would come from a letter of Aurangzeb's to Jahanara, written ten years later in 1654, by which time Shah Jahan's intensive mistrust had become acute. Aurangzeb wrote bitterly:

If His Majesty wishes that of all his servants I alone
should pass my life in dishonor and at last perish in an
unbecoming manner, I have no recourse but to obey.
. . . But since it is hard to live and die without enjoying
his grace, I cannot, for the sake of perishable earthly
things, continue in pain and grief nor deliver myself up
into the hands of others. It is better for me to be released from the shame of such a life by His Majesty's
own command, thus avoiding any harm to the good of
the State and allowing [other] hearts to be composed
about the matter. Ten years ago I realized this fact; I
knew my life was a target [of rivals], and therefore I re-
signed my post . . . so that I might retire to a corner,
cause no uneasiness to anybody's heart, and be saved
from such harassment.

The meaning is clear enough: far from being dismissed
by the emperor, Aurangzeb had openly quit his Deccan governorship in 1644 by way of protest. Rightly or wrongly he
felt discriminated against by his father, and by inference his
guarded phraseology implies that he is the victim of Dara's
hostility. It speaks well for Jahanara's character that Aurangzeb would reveal himself to Dara's acknowledged partisan.
About the same time, in another letter, Aurangzeb quoted a
Persian couplet to his sister: "O rose, if thou wilt listen to the
murmur of the nightingale only, those who cannot open their
tongues in the garden shall be confronted with great difficulties."

By the end of November, Jahanara had completely recovered from her burns. Costly celebrations were in order. It
was a fortunate day for Aurangzeb: at her intercession, he
once more became persona grata.

A sinister anecdote survives from that same year of
1644, again attested by the gossipy old courtier, Hamiduddin
Khan. During the worst Agra heat, Dara Shikoh had invited
his three brothers and Shah Jahan to visit an underground
retreat in his princely mansion by the Jumna River. The
room, hung with full-length mirrors from Aleppo, afforded
only one door for entrance and exit. Everyone else entered

willingly, but Aurangzeb sat resolutely blocking the doorway. According to the narrative, Dara winked at Shah Jahan as much as to imply "Look where he is sitting." The emperor voiced mild rebuke to Aurangzeb: "My child, though I know you to be learned and hermit-like, yet it is also needful to maintain one's rank. There is a popular saying, 'If you do not maintain your rank, you are an atheist.' What necessity is there for you to sit down in the path by which people pass, and in a position below and behind your younger brother [Murad]?" Aurangzeb replied, "I shall afterwards tell you the reason of my sitting thus." After a while he rose on the plea of performing midday prayer, and went to his own house without royal permission.

As a result of this incident, Aurangzeb found himself barred from court for seven months. Shah Jahan presumably sent Jahanara to discover the meaning of such odd behavior. Aurangzeb confided in his sister: when they were all gathered in the underground room, Dara had continually passed to and fro through the single door while supervising entertainment; "I feared that he might shut the door, and then all would be over [with us]. If he acted thus through carelessness, it repeatedly struck me that I should do the work [of guarding the door] while he was inside the room."

Aurangzeb had acted as sentinel against possible assassination! No one, not even Dara Shikoh's critics, could conceivably believe the crown prince capable of murdering his father and brothers in an underground chamber. But if the story is true, it becomes a patent instance of projection: an ambiguous personality suspected others of secretly harboring his own unconscious thoughts—thoughts which would yet be father to actual deeds.

Whatever Jahanara's explanation to the emperor, her usual tact prevailed; Shah Jahan restored the disgraced prince to imperial favor, sending him off on February 16, 1645 as governor of Gujarat province—an appointment he would hold for less than two years. By now it was frankly impossible to keep him at court with Dara: the rivalry and hatred between them were too great. Later assignments would

find Aurangzeb in central Asia, and in the Deccan again—
anywhere out of Dara Shikoh's sight. Aurangzeb himself had
reportedly begged Sadullah Khan, the new prime minister:
"Send me away from court by any means that you can, as I
have lost my sleep and peace of mind."

CHAPTER

8

Martial Airs

ARLY IN 1645, Shah Jahan left imperial Agra to spend three years in the Punjab and in Afghanistan. A year and a half later he would still be hovering about Kabul, supervising campaigns on India's northwest frontier. These were the years of his main military exploits—grandiloquent efforts to annex Babur's and Timur's ancestral domains beyond the Oxus River, or repetitive tussles with Persia over Kandahar fortress. Accompanied by kettledrums and fifes, princes and nobles rode off on caparisoned elephants and horses for endless months of siege and countersiege. In a persistently medieval game of high ritual, lands and fortresses would be taken or lost—all subject to a complicated etiquette of coercions, withdrawals, booty, and on rare occasions the actual acquisition of territory.

But Shah Jahan, more than any of his predecessors, was determined to leave his cultural mark. Far more important to him than the unavoidable reality of war was a fantasy world of very special esthetics which he created and into which he later withdrew for consolation: never before had music, painting, literature, poetry, and particularly involuted architecture been held in such high Mogul esteem. Shah Jahan knew that art would endure, even as war would pass away.

Ironically, Indian experts have sometimes criticized him (and his father Jahangir as well) for their lack of aggressive initiative; both inherited Akbar's empire and both were content to accept it as it was, with only spasmodic attempts at military expansion. Implicitly, the argument assumes that war and imperialism are either admirable or necessary to the maintenance of a great power. In point of fact, it was Shah Jahan's genius that preserved a stable conglomeration of opposing forces in a Mogul Empire soon to reveal its latent instability under a very different ruler.

Akbar had actually endowed India with an anomalous and even paradoxical legacy of peace and war. By force he had unified two-thirds of the subcontinent and imposed order on it, with the cohesive strength of imperial personality now holding minority groups together in a liberal entente endorsing Hindu and particularly Rajput equality. But this peace was only temporary: Akbar's grandson had inherited his dream of bringing the entire subcontinent under Mogul rule, and in any case the peculiar military colossus guarding the realm could hardly be kept inactive—it thrived on war. Whether he liked it or not, Shah Jahan was virtually obliged to uphold Mogul prestige with intermittent attempts at expansion and acquisition.

More practically, in terms of potential military thrusts, he faced a ticklish problem—where to find a guarantee of victory and not humiliation? In the northwest, Persia loomed as a rival and limited his scope of activity. Besides, though they might squabble over possession of Kandahar, neither empire cared to indulge in really suicidal activities when both benefited from their joint control of the great Iranian plateau: Mogul India held its restless Afghan citizens in check and left Persia free to deal with a dangerous Ottoman Empire to her west, while Persia deterred nomadic invasion from central Asia, allowing the Moguls to look southward. But reluctant to tamper with powerful independent Moslem and Hindu states south of the Mogul Deccan, Shah Jahan manifestly tolerated their existence—a toleration which maintained a delicate center of gravity. In effect he had to cope with inherent contradiction—furnishing necessary exercise for restive troops, yet running the risk of all-out war with Persia if northwest Mogul designs became excessive, or inviting internal upheavals in the subcontinent itself if he seriously menaced a complete southern takeover.

Shah Jahan could never openly admit his dilemma. Like other empires, his had risen and would fall in terms of a classic concept—balance of power. So long as balance of power was maintained, Mogul India endured; once the balance became upset, Mogul India collapsed. It is to Shah Jahan's credit that Akbar's initial achievement of conquest remained intact for the greater part of the seventeenth century.

War and art: the emperor's twin pursuits preoccupied thousands of nobles and hundreds of thousands more from among the anonymous masses, but preeminent roles of authority were delegated to immediate members of the royal family. In art the field narrowed. Among the princesses, Jahanara alone became authoress and esthetic patron; and while Shah Jahan personally displayed architectural near-genius, the only prince with a wide range of artistic interests was Dara Shikoh. Since Dara was also heir apparent, he would inevitably be kept at court to promote the glories of Mogul culture. The remaining brothers, radically different from Dara and from one another in both temperament and character, thus formed an effective or ineffective martial trio for military events of the reign. If Adam had produced four sons, they could hardly have constituted a more psychologically disparate quadrumvirate than these four Mogul princes soon to be engulfed in a fratricidal blood bath.

● ● ●

Prince Mohammed Shuja, Shah Jahan's second son, was thirteen months younger than Dara Shikoh. From Mogul miniatures he emerges every inch a prince—almost too handsome, yet showing the faintest tinge of complacent fleshiness. Until the age of twelve Shuja had lived with his grandfather Jahangir, and though far less vivid in character he had obviously acquired a few of the same personality traits. By all accounts he was sharply intelligent, but inclined to sensuality and a life of comfort. One or two modern interpreters conceive of Shuja as a mixture of Aurangzeb and Dara—the competent soldier and realistic politician blended with sympathetic human and even esthetic qualities. But this is a synthetic composite that does not really jell. In spite of rare moments of galvanized tactical brilliance when his life depended on it, Shuja was, in fact, *not* a very competent soldier; and his willingness to make a deal revealed more of an indolent compromiser than any shrewd assessor of power plays. As for heart, he displayed no whit of Dara's empathy or sensitivity, merely a casual indifference. In art, Shuja's elegant tastes were those of a sybarite.

Dara was a genuine spiritual seeker, while Shuja couldn't have been less interested in spirit or religion. If he professed himself a follower of Persia's brand of Islam—a Shia, a disciple of Ali—it seems to have been merely a bid for loyalty from the considerable number of Shias and Persian nobles who sustained his provincial army.

In one of his letters, Aurangzeb quotes Shah Jahan as having remarked that Shuja "possessed no other quality than enjoying life"—the puritan brother passing judgment on healthy sensuality. Bernier, who never knew Shuja personally, would give a second-hand impression of the prince spending "whole days and nights in dancing, singing, and drinking wine." Others bolstered the conclusion that Shuja's harem indulgences ruined his career, that he was negligent and easy-going, that his practical talents shone by fits and starts or more often than not failed to shine at all. But if his administration of one particular province was lackadaisical, it was still efficient enough for his father to keep him there for eighteen long years. His main fault actually lay in a certain lack of awareness: "small things like the Chameli flower escaped his sight," as one Mogul of the time astutely commented.

Yet persistent examination reveals more than mediocrity in Shuja's makeup. Something in him (and this is what makes him likeable) really couldn't take it all seriously; those military prancings around the empire, and the game of assaulting enemy citadels and exacting tributes, apparently bored him.

If he retired to his zenana or got roaring drunk, it wasn't a retreat to unreality: the flesh was real, and so was the hangover.

In 1632, at the age of sixteen, Shuja failed to take an obscure Deccan fortress and gained the reputation of being an indifferent warrior. By 1639 Shah Jahan had discovered the perfect niche for him—Bengal—while the adjoining territory of Orissa was added to his governorship in 1642. In effect Shuja became uncrowned monarch of eastern India, largely left to his own devices and never subjected to the critical barrage of letters which would soon haunt Aurangzeb's career; from time to time the emperor even sent presents. Still, intermittent ripples stirred Shuja's surface of apparent indifference: like Aurangzeb and Murad, he too felt jealous of Dara's exalted position at court. Sooner or later, even a placid Shuja could be persuaded that the crown prince was actually intriguing against him.

In time Bengal would be dubbed, properly enough, the nursery of Shuja's ambition and the tomb of his energy. Watered by the Ganges and the Brahmaputra, this was a lushly riparian part of India with a long history of "peace, plenty, and pestilence." Calcutta had not yet been founded, but even the most disciplined Englishmen would one day wilt in its enervating summer heat. Slightly northeast of the unfounded city were the delta mouths of the Ganges, sucking sweetly at any will to action; while elsewhere in the province, alluvial plains radiated outward through mile after mile of hypnotic rice fields and languid coconut palms. Who after eighteen years in Bengal would not find rust on his sword, not to mention his ambitions? In the humid backwaters of Mogul history, Shuja had been left to rot. But in the forthcoming War of Succession he would defy all predictions by proving himself something more than anyone guessed—a man of hidden capabilities, with surprising resilience, stamina, and an innate sense of decency.

●●●

Mohammed Murad Bakhsh, whose name meant "Desire Attained," was the youngest of Mumtaz Mahal's sons, and even at the outbreak of crisis in 1657 he would still be barely thirty-three. Mogul sources, Europeans in the realm, or historians in general make short shrift of him: he is a black sheep, a political booby, an impetuous and belligerent mesomorph devoted to war and the hunt. He spears wolves and boars; he is a hard-drinking, fornicating fool. Turning a phrase somewhat more charitably, Victorian and Edwardian scholars make him "a gallant swashbuckler, brave as a lion," impelled with the "reckless valor of a soldier." Murad also becomes "frank and open as the day." But then, some critics challenge Murad's reputed candor, pointing to his private dickerings with court nobles and even a secret letter which he sent to Shah Jahan after the War of Succession had begun.

Yet there is little point in trying to improve his portrait. In a wily Mogul Empire even an ignoramus was bound to pick up a few tricks of deceit, while brute courage becomes a dubious virtue at best. Basically Murad was stupid, coarse, and not really very likeable. Only when the plot thickened would he achieve a kind of pathos—and then it would be too late.

Black sheep he certainly was. For all his aggression, Murad's soldierly achievements by Mogul or any other standards added up to a depressing zero. Now, in June 1646 at the age of twenty-two, he would be dispatched at the head of fifty thousand men on an expedition into the central Asian precincts of Balkh and Badakhshan—his big chance.

It was Shah Jahan's one moment of unprecedented military folly. Even Akbar had never attempted to exceed the natural geographical bounds of the Indian subcontinent. The hoofs of Mogul horses had not been heard on Babur's nomadic stamping grounds for a century and a half. Indeed, this whole trans-Oxus thrust of Mogul imperialism has a ring of madness. Prompted by tactical insanity, the emperor had committed himself to a megalomaniac endeavor which would cost the Moguls forty million rupees in two years and end in total disaster.

Timur's flash-in-the-pan Indian incursion in 1398 had come from beyond Afghanistan and the snowy Hindu Kush mountains; this time the Moguls had inaugurated a reversal with intent to stay: Balkh and Badakhshan were meant to be stepping-stones to Timur's ancient capital of Samarkand. Both provinces lay between the Hindu Kush range and the Oxus River—Badakhshan rather bleak, sparsely cultivated, and ringed by savage tribes, but Balkh somewhat more fertile.

Aside from his army of fifty thousand, Murad was solidly backed by a man of no mean ability—the Persian, Ali Mardan Khan, who less than a decade before (in 1638) had defected to Shah Jahan and handed over to him, lock, stock, and barrel, the important Kandahar Fortress on the border of Persia herself. The details of Murad's campaign are not important; he subdued and annexed Balkh and Badakhshan easily enough, seizing a little loot. But this was a temporary and deceptive victory. Murad next committed the inconceivable: restless and bored, he decided to go AWOL! Leaving the Mogul army leaderless (except for top-ranking nobles), he returned to India without permission.

Shah Jahan promptly castigated the errant prince by totally depriving him of rank and revenues and dismissing him from court. Murad's mercurial desertion has never been adequately explained; or rather, there could only be one explanation—crass stupidity, and the rashness of flouting paternal authority in this most idiotic of ways.

A trans-Oxus victory was by no means effected: the black sheep had left fifty thousand chestnuts in the fire by deserting his central Asian post. Still, Murad had a further career: forgiven two years afterward, he became viceroy of the Deccan. But again his ungovernable character and temper added insult to chaos; he soon picked a quarrel with his Deccan guardian and father-in-law, Shahnawaz Khan, turning Deccan administration into a shambles, and finding himself out in the cold for the second time. Then, once more pardoned, he became governor of Gujarat province in 1651, where a totally disabused emperor now appointed the most stalwart person available to stand behind his son as *eminence grise*, finance minister, and counselor—Ali Naqi, who would later represent the most important single occasion of Murad's progressive folly. For the interim, Murad presided over Gujarat and would do so until the outbreak of the War of Succession.

● ● ●

Someone had to salvage the abortive trans-Oxus venture, and it could only be the third member of the royal military triumvirate. In 1647 Aurangzeb responded to the emperor's call, meeting Shah Jahan in Lahore. During the interval since his disgrace in 1644 he had acquitted himself well in lawless Gujarat, checking robbers and rebels with a strong hand, and even receiving a promotion and an increase in revenue. Now the emperor appointed him governor and commander-in-chief of Balkh and Badakhshan, to replace the wayward Murad. In this final decade of preparation for tragedy, Shah Jahan had begun alternately to praise and punish Aurangzeb, to encourage and humiliate him.

At this time the prince was only twenty-nine, far from the absolutely astonishing historical personality he would become. But what to make of him at twenty-nine or eighty-nine? Coleridge described Shakespeare's Iago as a case of "motiveless malignancy," and it would be tempting to apply the description to Aurangzeb; yet he is not simply an evil monster. In any case, much more is known about Aurangzeb than Iago—not that knowing helps very much. Given all the details and every clue, Shah Jahan's third son remains ambiguous to the end.

Aurangzeb is inevitably described as being "first and last a stern puritan," but this was no Indian Savonarola as later history would show. It is really too facile to make him that most dangerous of all combinations—a hot head and a cold heart. From the moment of meeting Shah Jahan in Lahore in 1647, there will be no lack of detail, and yet the key is somehow missing. Now will come the spectacle of years of overwhelming compulsion: the relentless discipline of a fantastic soldier, together with aloofness, bigotry, reactionary vehemence, morbid suspicion and mistrust. Finally Aurangzeb will become an alienating despot, and clearly a man who cannot love. This is someone who should be pursued by the Furies—except that *he* is the pursuer. Now and later, he remains larger than the sum of his obsessions: others will submit to fate, he will impose it; others will be human, he will be transformed into an inhuman demigod. For many orthodox Moslems Aurangzeb is a hero to this day, for Hindus he was a villain and a catastrophe. From any point of view, he measures on a colossal scale.

Yet it would be a mistake to let him dwarf other impressive protagonists. However belatedly, Shah Jahan will rise to tragic grandeur, and at least three other personalities transcend the horrifying events to come—Dara Shikoh, his sister Jahanara, and the naked fakir Sarmad. Theirs will be a spiritual victory in defeat, while Aurangzeb's will be a victory at the expense of spirit. Lacking spirituality (for all of his excessive orthodoxy) he can only cling to the letter of religious law; his punishment, in the end, will be fear of divine judgment without divine love—a belated vision of the abyss.

But in 1647, the amplitude of this puzzling personality was still to be revealed. If Shah Jahan had already gauged its sinister potential, he was still utilizing that potential for his own military ends. Only later would a fearful Dara Shikoh persuade the emperor to hold Aurangzeb's aggressions positively in check.

Shah Jahan's growing apprehensions can be seen in, or may even have determined, his ambivalent treatment of Aurangzeb; their relationship was really a feud in its own way, but never so obvious as Aurangzeb's quarrel with Dara —at least not in the beginning. The emperor had always intended Aurangzeb for important military and administrative positions, since with Dara Shikoh kept at court as heir presumptive there was really no other choice: Aurangzeb's capabilities both as soldier and statesman far exceeded those of either Shuja or Murad. Alone of the trio, he had first been chosen governor of the Deccan, only to resign flatly in resentment against Dara's real or imagined machinations. Now, in 1647, after several years of languishing in Gujarat, Aurangzeb was again called up for active military service.

Since Murad's abandonment of central Asia, part of the Mogul forces had been recalled. Quite aside from lacking leadership except for some top-ranking nobles still stationed there, these central Asian provinces offered poor pickings for sustenance—neither Balkh nor Badakhshan could yield the salary of a third-rate Mogul peer, much less support an invading army. Those Mogul soldiers who remained were now threatened with concerted guerrilla tactics by Mongols, Turks, and Uzbeks representing a coalition—central Asia's rallying response to Shah Jahan's initial imperialistic success. The emperor was obliged to defend conquered territory in the most ridiculous way, with rearguard supplies and communications straggling over the formidable Hindu Kush mountains. Aurangzeb had inherited nothing less than a debacle.

But his ensuing and inevitable withdrawal highlights disciplined control of a harassed army. Nagged by guerrillas, Aurangzeb slowly withdrew Mogul troops in order to defend Balkh from fresh opposition rallied by the king of Bukhara. Hungry soldiers cooked food on the backs of moving elephants! In repeated engagements the prince managed to maintain superiority of muskets over arrows, consistently deterring his enemy. The enemy helpfully developed problems of its own: always less than fervent, a disparate assortment of Uzbeks and Turks subordinated patriotism to plunder; finding small loot, many wanted to go home—Turks had even gone so far as to sell their horses to the Moguls and break camp. The greatness of the Moguls was now reaffirmed in an astonishing spectacle. In the middle of a late day's battle the hour of Moslem devotion arrived, and Aurangzeb spread his prayer rug on the battlefield, kneeling and performing holy ritual oblivious of heavy fighting on all sides. The entire Bukhara army stood agape, while their king acknowledged that "to fight with such a man is to court one's ruin."

It was really a stalemate. With his army exhausted and sick of exile, nobody wanted to stay, and Aurangzeb advised the emperor of a proposed enemy settlement. Shah Jahan had virtually decided to relinquish conquered territory anyhow, but Mogul prestige required the king of Bukhara to offer submission and pardon. Afraid of treachery, the king sent his grandsons to Aurangzeb on the plea that he was ill. Imperial pride had to be content with grandsons: winter was coming on, and the mountain passes would soon be snowbound. Retreat became a sniping nightmare, with hill tribes taking over where Uzbeks left off. Mogul soldiers and mules fell over gelid precipices to their death; camels lay down in the snow and positively refused to get up. Elephants, horses, oxen, and ten thousand men died, and property was buried under snow or thrown into ravines. The following spring would find the path a litter of bones—the price of war beyond India's northwest frontiers. But it wasn't all a Pyrrhic victory: Aurangzeb had won the admiration of Mogul commanders, and cut hard spurs in ice.

His pursuit of glory rebuffed, Shah Jahan returned to Agra and the consolations of art and architecture. Prince Shuja had been summoned as far as Afghanistan during the disaster, but it was Aurangzeb who now found himself kept last in the area—until March 1648 and even later. Appointed governor of the northwestern Multan and Sind provinces between 1648 and 1652, he dealt with wild Afghan hill tribes and gained additional know-how. More importantly, these five years also afforded additional tactical experience in war: not against crude guerrillas, but against sophisticated Persian soldiers.

The three Mogul ventures at Kandahar (two under Aurangzeb and one under Dara Shikoh) are mainly of interest for the light they shed on three protagonists—Shah Jahan and his sons. Kandahar fortress, in southern Afghanistan, had always been strategically important as an entrepôt for overland trade. West of it lay Ispahan, beyond level but desolate country; southward were deserts; and though the Hindu Kush range loomed to the north, its foothills were insignificant enough in these regions to afford easy passage to trader caravans. Thousands of camels loped annually to and from Persia or central Asia, and merchants of India, Persia, and Turkey rubbed beards at Kandahar.

Kandahar could only be a bone of contention. Babur had first taken the fortress; then it had fallen to the Persians again in Akbar's time but Akbar had gotten it back. Jahangir had lost it, but Shah Jahan retrieved matters without firing a shot when the Persian, Ali Mardan Khan, surrendered Kandahar to the Moguls in 1638 and entered Mogul service. The place had by now become a shuttlecock of honor, and so toward the end of 1648 the Persians launched a new offensive. Significantly, Shah Jahan chose Aurangzeb (backed by Prime Minister Sadullah Khan) to relieve the defending Mogul garrison. But before their relief army even reached Kabul in Afghanistan, Kandahar had already fallen —in February 1649.

Shah Jahan now gave orders for Aurangzeb to conduct a countersiege before the Persians could entrench themselves, and he himself went to Kabul to act as rearguard commander. But the fall of Kandahar would prove a lasting blow to Mogul prestige, and no assault would ever win it back; though nobody admitted it, the Moguls feared Persia from that moment on.

Aurangzeb's first attempt at recovery was hampered from the outset: he had come only to reinforce, bringing no large cannon or artillery of consequence. The Persians, in their long wars with Turks, had by now become masters of gun and artillery. Between May and September 1649, all Mogul counterattacks proved vain. Three years later, in 1652, the prince commanded fifty or sixty thousand men in a second endeavor, and twenty million rupees went for expenses. Again the end was disaster; the walls of Kandahar could not be breached.

Now began the caustic correspondence from Shah Jahan that would shower Aurangzeb with acrimony for the next five years. The emperor wrote, "I greatly wonder how you could not capture the fort in spite of such vast preparations." Aurangzeb tried to justify himself, but a firm reply cut him off peremptorily: "I am not going to give up Kandahar. I will try every means to recover it." Aurangzeb begged to be allowed to stay in Afghanistan, and even asked for a subordinate role in the next assault—anything to redeem his military reputation. He would give up the viceroyalty of the Deccan (now offered to him) if only he could participate. Shah Jahan witheringly ordered him to the Deccan at once: "Had I considered you competent to take Kandahar, I would not have recalled your army. . . . Every man can perform some work. It is a wise saying that men of experience need no instruction." The prince replied with a subdued proverb, "Whosoever has a particle of sense can know his own good from his harm": he could not willfully have failed, knowing that it would displease the emperor.

Obviously something more was at stake than the failure to recapture Kandahar, something even more than the need for a scapegoat. Aurangzeb had actually been restricted during the entire 1652 siege, with Shah Jahan himself directing movements through Sadullah Khan. The prime minister ought to have taken the blame. But whatever the emperor's private reasons, it was too late: the prince had lost favor and confidence. To complete mortification, Dara Shikoh and Dara's partisans were certain to be scornful. A third siege of Kandahar, under Dara, would come later (and would reveal Shah Jahan's prejudice). For now, Aurangzeb suffered total defeat.

CHAPTER

9

The Mystic Prince

Without Dara Shikoh there would still have been a Mogul tragedy. With him, the tragedy becomes unique: he was an anomaly for any time and any age—a mystic. Dedicating his whole life to abstruse philosophy, Dara searched for an ultimate meaning in dangerous conflict with Islamic orthodoxy. If he had been born outside of the regal sphere, he might have lived and died as a saint; within it, he was doomed.

Whatever his personal flaws—princely vanity or flights of conceit—the marvel was Dara's passionate urge for transcendence struggling within the straitjacket of a largely materialistic Mogul house. Most Mogul princes were cut from a standard pattern: for a Murad or a Shuja, life consisted of the three w's (wine, women, and war) and adventures of the intellect or spirit remained outside their ken. Nor did Aurangzeb's religious obsession qualify him for higher pursuits, since his fanatically narrow vision precluded liberty of scope. Dara Shikoh alone was the exceptional prince in the entire history of the Moguls, an intellectual aristocrat and sacred seeker.

There is a haunted attractiveness about Dara. In the Mogul portrait gallery, he catches the discerning eye: a private face in a public place, handsome yet sensitive, betraying a refined sense of humor and a suggestive melancholy. He is a kind of theosophical Hamlet, filled with undefined predestinarian yearnings. Caught in the court of the Moguls, he makes a stab at coping with the practical details of statesmanship or war. But he is too naïve, too credulous; he is fine and ingenuous where others are coarse and cunning. He is highly emotional and candid in expressing his point of view. Worse, he is no real judge of men. This, coupled with an inborn fatalism, will surely do him in.

As a religious freethinker, Dara not surprisingly incurred the violent antipathy of orthodox Moslem contemporaries. Court chronicles written by Aurangzeb's partisans seethe with epithetical bile; Dara Shikoh is condemned as "unworthy and frivolous," guilty of "heretical tenets." Even in the twentieth century, eminent but inflexible Moslem historians categorically refuse any reconsideration of his case.

Quite aside from the still-fulminating religious issue, Dara's undeniable defects of character have been magnified out of all proportion. Here the unintentionally guilty party seems to have been François Bernier, whose biased pen sketch influenced virtually every later analysis of the crown prince. As a European in the Mogul realm, Bernier might be expected to have no orthodox Moslem ax to grind, and enjoyed the further advantage of knowing Dara personally— even though only from one encounter. The Frenchman's account begins sympathetically enough: Dara "was not deficient in good qualities: he was courteous in conversation, quick at repartee, polite, and extremely liberal." But another hand clearly guided Bernier's quill—behind him stood his Mogul court patron, Danishmand Khan, an ardent admirer of Aurangzeb. Abruptly, description turns sharp; Dara "entertained too exalted an opinion of himself; believed he could accomplish everything by the powers of his own mind, and imagined that there existed no man from whose counsel he could derive benefit. He spoke disdainfully of those who ventured to advise him, and thus deterred his sincerest friends from disclosing the secret machinations of his brothers. He was also very irascible; apt to menace; abusive and insulting even to the greatest [nobles]. . . ." Bernier concludes by accusing Dara of being "a Gentile with Gentiles, and a Christian with Christians"—in other words, a religious opportunist.

Accurate or not, this cameo of the crown prince would remain unchallenged by scholars and amateurs for almost three hundred years. Even aged Niccolo Manucci, writing his memoirs years later, plagiarizes his French rival blatantly. Is this the Manucci who loathed Aurangzeb and devoted three or four years to Dara's service? Surely he could have given us a more personalized portrait. But these accounts are by no means the last word.

Little is known of Dara Shikoh's childhood and early career, though his scholastic and spiritual interests manifested themselves from an early age. Then as now, India swarmed with mystics. In his youth he had come in contact with renowned Moslem and Hindu holy men, highly individual thinkers who found religious dogma oppressive to the soul searching for God; through them, Dara would develop his intuition and something far more dangerous—his love of free expression.

The mystic prince was playing with fire from the start. The liberal religious climate begun with Akbar and sustained through Jahangir's and Shah Jahan's reigns had deeply offended orthodox Moslems at court and throughout the realm. Before long, a "Counter-Reformation" would rally behind Aurangzeb, and Dara Shikoh would find himself embroiled in nothing less than an Islamic "Inquisition."

It is tragically ironic that Dara and his teachers were about to unleash religious controversy, when in point of fact they had done so much to hold intolerance in check. From the earliest Moslem conquerors, the problem in India had always been a reconciliation of Moslems and Hindus. Where bigotry had failed, idealism succeeded. Holy fakirs were a salve on religious wounds, promoting understanding and the beginning of unity between two disparate communities. They had been in the political arena since the time of Akbar, and Mogul monarchs held them in high esteem. Akbar himself had been devoted to a particular order of freethinkers, which

assured a tone of liberalism throughout Jahangir's and Shah
Jahan's reigns; liberalism had prevailed over orthodoxy, in
spite of occasional ambiguities and lapses. Credited with mir-
acle-working powers, Moslem saints charmed both Hindu
and Moslem multitudes, and a few of them exerted powerful
influence over the royal Mogul family—not least over Dara
Shikoh.

Dara's passion was Sufi mysticism, the occult flower of
Islam. Already many centuries old in its development
through Arab countries and Persia, Sufism now flourished in
an India which from time immemorial had evolved its own
Hindu mysticism. Two mystic streams inevitably blended;
indeed, they shared basic insights which even find expression
in the writings of great Christian introspectives—Saint John
of the Cross, or Meister Eckhart.

Like all mystics, Dara was seeking inward revelation
beyond rational thought. His goal was nothing less than
"cosmic" illumination, which could only be achieved after
years of unusual passive discipline. Profoundly religious
beyond Aurangzeb's rigid letter of the law, Dara looked inward for the Divinity; impressed by his more extreme Sufi
teachers, he probed for final ecstasy—total loss of his self or
ego by losing that self to God.

In Hindustan as elsewhere, Sufi fakirs belonged to particular orders. Important was the Qadiriya order, founded by
Abdul Qadir-al-Jilani in A.D. 1165; he preached with absolute compassion that the gates of Hell should be closed, and
the doors of Paradise opened to all mankind. Qadiriya rites
included the wearing of green turbans and the recital of the
blessing of the Prophet. In the nineteenth century, no less a
person than Sir Richard Burton received initiation into the
Qadiriya fraternity and won his diploma. Several hundred
years before Burton, two other persons had also become
members of the order, attracted by its philanthropy, humility, and aversion to fanaticism—Prince Dara Shikoh and his
sister Jahanara Begum.

Dara was no spiritual dilettante, in spite of vituperative
orthodox critics. His writings constitute a voluminous and by

no means superficial achievement for a man destined to die in his early forties. He translated sacred Hindu texts and the entire Hindu religious epic of the Bhagavad-Gita from Hindustani into Persian; his version of the epic, later rendered into German, intrigued Schopenhauer as one of the first Westerners to take up Eastern metaphysical thought. Dara Shikoh's original compositions in Persian include a biography of the Moslem saints; a handbook on the Qadiriya order which he and Jahanara had espoused; a volume instructing novices in the path of Sufism; and an ambitious foray into comparative religion. He also collected aphorisms of saints, and wrote mystical poetry and Persian quatrains.

Aside from literary pursuits, Dara was the artistic mainstay at his father's court. He patronized other poets and also painters. It is known that Shah Jahan delegated to the crown prince the supervision of both the royal Mogul library and the workshop for Mogul miniature painting. Indeed, Dara Shikoh almost single-handedly created "the cultural history of the reign of Shah Jahan," which might otherwise have been limited to architecture.

Dara's exposure to the Qadiriya order came very early, when he was only nineteen. He had married his cousin Nadira Begum in 1633, and within a year she bore him a daughter who died on March 21, 1634 while the court was traveling to Lahore in the Punjab. Dara fell so ill of grief that the family physician, Wazir Khan, had to be summoned from Agra to treat him. Conventional medicine apparently failed; only one person could offer proper consolation and spiritual guidance—the great Sufi mystic of Lahore, Mian Mir.

Shah Jahan himself regarded Mian Mir as one of the two saints he had met in his whole life who had "the knowledge of God." The crown prince now met destiny. "I was suffering," Dara relates in his handbook, "from a chronic disease; for four months the physicians had not been able to cure me. . . . [Shah Jahan] took me by the hand and with great humility and reverence entreated . . . [Mian Mir] to pray to God for my health. The saint took my hand into his

own, giving me a cup of water to drink. Results were immediate: within a week I recovered from the serious malady."

On his second visit to Mian Mir, Dara was full of humility. "On this occasion I went barefoot to his house and he
gave me a rosary; while he was talking to the King, he threw
out of his mouth chewed clove which I gathered and ate and
when the King left I lingered behind. I went up to him and
placing my head on his foot remained in that position for
some time."

Then, one evening, the relationship between saint and
new disciple became apocalyptic. In a mysterious ritual,
Mian Mir exposed both Dara's breast and his own. "Placing
his right nipple upon mine [he] remarked, 'It had been entrusted to me, take it away.' Thereafter such exuberating
lights emanating from his heart entered mine that eventually
I begged, 'It is enough, Sir, if you give me more my heart will
burst.' From that moment, I find my [soul] full of enlightenment and ecstasy."

There may have been homosexual undertones in this
mystical transmission of power; but whatever its interpretation, it paved the way for later states of trance. Mian Mir
died soon afterward (in 1635) without having had time to
make Dara his formal pupil, but his influence continued
beyond death. Toward dawn on an enigmatic night, the
prince now saw and heard hallucinatory phenomena—an experience not uncommon to some mystics. Dara recounts:

> I was sitting with my face turned toward the Kaaba,
> when a sudden restlessness of mind overtook me . . . .
> At dawn I saw a palace of grand structure, surrounded
> on all sides by gardens. As I thought, it was Mian Mir's
> mausoleum. He came out of the tomb and sat on a
> chair, and when he saw me he called me by his side and
> showed me every kindness. Afterwards he took me by
> the hand and said, "Come, I would teach you some-
> thing." He . . . placed his two index fingers in my ears,
> with the result that the Voice of Silence overpowered
> me; the sound affected me so much that after envel-

oping me . . . it threw me off the ground. I then lost consciousness and such a "state" overtook me as it is not possible for me either to describe or write . . . . I obtained what I sought . . . distance and nearness became alike.

The "Voice of Silence" which inundated Dara was metaphysical, heard only by mystics in states of illumination. Mohammed himself, when asked how inspiration came to him, had once commented that "he heard a sound like silvery bells or the beating of a drum." In Persian Sufi verse, the mystic poet Hafiz had written, "I hear the constant chime of bells."

For Dara the moment had been one of ineffable mystical awareness—impossible to "describe or write." Day by day, the veil was being lifted. He had not yet become an "apostate," because he still followed acceptable spiritual guides who avoided orthodox condemnation by saturating public utterances with reverence for Mohammed and his teachings. Ecstatic experiences were secrets of the mystical Sufi order, hidden behind veiled metaphors of love and wine. Ever since the martyrdom of the mystic Hallaj in A.D. 922, Sufis in the East had been wary of charges of heresy.

But Dara Shikoh would prove indiscreet. By a grave defect of character, he tended to reveal his most intimate spiritual thoughts in both writing and speech to intimates and enemies alike—this was candor, but not caution. By the time he was twenty-eight, he had begun openly to slough off orthodoxy; dangerously he wrote to an eminent contemporary saint: "Exoteric Islam has ceased to influence the mind of this fakir and the real esoteric 'infidelity' has shown its face." His soul was discarding the shell of dogma in its search for absolute truth.

The search could only lead to pantheism and a passionate interest in mystics of all religions. More extreme Sufi gurus now held Dara Shikoh in thrall: there was one named Mulla Shah, and on the verge of the War of Succession came Dara's fatal friendship with the incredible, naked mystic Sarmad. Both these saints threw caution to the winds, ignoring dogma and social convention in a weirdly ecstatic assertion of other-worldly values beyond the frontier of normal human experience.

We know little or nothing of the inner life of Dara's wife, Nadira Begum. But Jahanara soon joined Dara in mystical pursuit, and a strange spiritual incest sprang up: the mysterious and unholy union of brother and sister.

Of Jahanara's few literary works, a hitherto unknown tract has only recently come to light. In it she says revealingly, "I love my brother Dara Shikoh extremely both in form and spirit. We are, in fact, like one soul in two bodies and one spirit in two physical forms." Regarding Dara as the "perfect gnostic," Jahanara now entered the Qadiriya order. Already twenty-seven, she felt the pressing need to become a disciple of a perfect guide. During a visit to Kashmir with Shah Jahan, the princess had become an admirer of Mulla Shah on Dara's recommendation, and began exercises in meditation. Soon a haunting sense of fulfillment made her feel that she and Dara had found a unique path to God and the truth: "Of all the descendants of Timur, only we two, brother and sister, were fortunate to obtain this felicity." Yet she was still waiting for illumination. It came: in a tranceful vision, Jahanara beheld a conclave of Mohammed and great saints, including her preceptor Mulla Shah, who placed his head on Mohammed's feet; Mohammed then observed, "O Mulla Shah, thou hast illumined the Timurid lamp." Regaining consciousness, Jahanara was happy without bounds.

Dara Shikoh regarded Mulla Shah with awe. The saint had reached profound enlightenment through grueling years of breathing exercises, night vigils, fasts, and introspection. Yet now he had abandoned all these practices, and by willpower and personal magnetism revealed his holy knowledge. "Every moment I hold my own self in my arms," he recited to Dara. In Mulla Shah's house, all was poverty: no servants, no cooked meals, no lamps—he preferred darkness as "the light of the universal." Besides being a poet and scholar, he expressed ferociously anarchic opinions. His influence on Dara's religious and moral life was devastating.

Soon the hatefulness of dogma and orthodoxy began to color Dara's poetry as he indicted formal theologians: "In the city where a mullah resides, no wise man is ever found." For the strictly orthodox Aurangzeb and tight-minded but highly placed zealots, such words could only be insult and high theological treason. In other poems, Dara claimed that prophets and saints had suffered torment because of the viciousness of bigots and narrow-minded priests. It was true, of course; quite aside from Islam's "heretical" sufferers, a long line of Christian martyrs from Jesus Christ himself to victims of the Inquisition would have agreed.

Anything that now stood in the way of a direct vision of God became Dara's obstacle. The unitary flames of Sufism consumed him; convinced that the highest attainment of any human life was spiritual, he began to view penury as preferable to the court: "Kingship is easy, acquaint thyself with poverty. Why should a drop become a pearl when it can transform itself into an ocean?" His poetry even reveals a revulsion from the materialism of the world around him: "Hands soiled with gold begin to stink; how bad would be the plight of a soul soiled with gold!" Equally repulsive was the whole gamut of human selfishness and vanity: "Drive egoism away from you, for like conceit and arrogance it is also a burden." This was the haughty Dara Shikoh depicted by his denigrators.

"Apostasy" from Islam would soon be forthcoming. "With what name should one call Truth?" Dara asks; "Every name that exists is one of God's names." In answer to Aurangzeb he openly acknowledges in verse, "To revile me thou hast termed me an 'infidel.' I, too, consider thy talk as true: disgrace and glory have become alike to me." It was no surprise that doctrinaire minds found appalling heresy in the mystical solipsism of such startling statements as "Thou [i.e., Dara himself] verily art God," though other Moslem mystics had reached the same conclusion centuries earlier: Hallaj the martyr had said, "I am the Truth," and another Sufi indicated his clothing and observed, "There is nothing inside this coat except Allah." This was wild language for Aurangzeb and his fellow orthodox believers—"more 'rash' than anything ever said by Meister Eckhart." Yet, intoxicated by a sense of the divine unity of everything in the universe, how could a mystic properly distinguish between himself and God?

The religious die had been cast; Dara Shikoh had given Aurangzeb and the strict fanatics their justification to destroy him, and they would have many texts to quote from when the time was ripe. All the externals of Islam, except for Allah himself, and Mohammed and the Koran, had been sacrificed to Dara's overwhelming pursuit of truth. For liberals at court, Dara Shikoh had become an acknowledged scholar and master of Sufism; to Aurangzeb and orthodox mullahs, he seemed the Devil incarnate.

The Devil now turned an allegorical eye on the fifty-sixth chapter of the Koran: "Indeed there is a book, which is hidden. None shall touch it but the purified ones. It is a revelation by the Lord of the worlds." For Dara, this secret text could not be the Psalms or the Book of Moses or the New Testament; it must be Hindu, and he proceeded to translate with a vengeance. Meanwhile, he was fervently patronizing scholars of every religion: Moslem, Hindu, Jew, or Christian Jesuit. His studies in Sanskrit led him to Vedanta and Yoga philosophy, to Hindu ritual and mythology; he spent time in Banaras, talking with learned pandits and holy men. This was a renewal of Akbar's syncretism, but utterly devoid of political motive; Bernier or orthodox critics might think Dara a religious opportunist, yet, in fact, his fascination with Hinduism stemmed from a mystical pantheism determined to find a common ground between two religions which would yet split India in two. For almost a decade Dara studied Hinduism; from this study came his book, *The Mingling of Two Oceans.*

Even in a theologically sophisticated twentieth century, *The Mingling of Two Oceans* must be viewed as a highly altruistic endeavor to reconcile the spiritual doctrines of

Hinduism and Islam. For any serious student of comparative religion the work, in spite of its naïve cornerstone, remains a valiant probing beyond dogma for unifying truth. But orthodoxy would apply the letter and miss the spirit. For narrow-minded Moslem circles at the Mogul court, this was the literary work which would condemn Dara Shikoh. It burst on the Islamic scene, and Dara was denounced as a heretic, atheist, hypocrite, and opportunist.

Worse: he fraternized with Hindus on equal intellectual and religious terms. Aurangzeb's later court chronicler, Mohammed Kazim, would afterwards write scornfully: "He was constantly in the society of Brahmans, yogis and *sannyasis,* and he used to regard these worthless teachers of delusions as learned and true masters of wisdom. He considered their books . . . the word of God, and . . . employed them in translating. . . . He spent all his time in this unholy work." More specifically, Dara had taken up the Hindu name *Prabhu* [Lord] and inscribed it on rings which he wore; he had "given up the prayers, fasting and other obligations imposed by the law. . . . It became manifest that if Dara Shikoh obtained the throne and established his power, the foundations of the faith would be in danger and the precepts of Islam would be changed for the rant of infidelity and Judaism."

Today such polemics might evoke a smile; then, a man's life was at stake. Dara Shikoh would in due time be convicted of heresy. His long-standing vilification at the hands of European travelers and Mogul or later historians became an exquisite and almost enduring irony: a spiritual prince, devoted to promoting harmony between Moslem and Hindu, could be dismissed as "inordinately conceited, self-satisfied and an emancipated protagonist"—this in the words of a qualified Victorian scholar.

But Dara would be vindicated. In attempting to create brotherhood by bridging the gulf between two religions he had left his humanitarian mark. In the 1930s, a sympathetic biographer would find him the "central figure of a great religious and literary movement for the adaptation of Islam to the spiritual traditions of India"; Dara stood "unique among the Moslem thinkers of India as regards . . . moral courage and sincerity of conviction." And in the 1950s the spiritual educational center of Santiniketan (founded by Rabindranath Tagore) would produce a detailed study of Dara's writings, placing the prince in the tradition of great mystics.

●●●

Against the background of Dara Shikoh's astonishing spiritual life, his military involvements can only be viewed as nightmares—phantasmagoria thrust upon him by an accident of birth. Absurdly caught in a martial autocracy and incongruously favored by Shah Jahan, a dreamer-mystic son never meant to be a soldier nonetheless received unprecedented noble ranking and commanded more horse than anyone. Money poured in from provinces ruled in absentia; by military rank alone Dara had an income of over twenty million rupees a year. Yet during his entire official career before the War of Succession he had only been in three military engagements—two "holiday parades" and one weird siege of Kandahar in 1653, after Aurangzeb had twice failed to wrest the fortress from Persian control.

Dara has been judged harshly, even by objective critics, for his venture at Kandahar; he is seen in the "odious light of an incompetent braggart, almost insane with conceit, capricious, and childish." But Kandahar can now be viewed in its proper perspective—Dara's outing was really a hilarious mystical interlude, the equivalent of placing a guru in command at the battle of Sicily.

The enterprise was daft from the start. Hindustan's impractical mystic prince took more than an army to the northwest—shibboleth and the occult went with him. Still, the whole age reeked of superstition: even practical Aurangzeb would later be sewing mystical emblems in his armies' banners with his own hands.

Looking ahead to Kandahar from Kabul in Afghanistan, Dara entertained two Sufi mystics in his parlor. Heads buried in patched robes, they produced appropriate visions. One cried, "I am now witnessing the affairs of Persia; the Shah of Persia is dead." The other mystic went all the way:

"So too am I; but I will not come back till the coffin of the Shah is deposited in the earth." Gullibly, Dara added that he too had had a vision; he would not be "required to stay at Kandahar for more than seven days, and during these seven days the fort will be conquered."

More prudently, months had gone into practical preparations. Dara's mustered army numbered seventy thousand cavalry under Moslem and Rajput officers, together with archers, infantry, war elephants, diggers, stone cutters, water carriers, and more. Astrologers had selected February 11, 1653 for starting from Lahore. The emperor suggested a line of march and sent presents galore: jewels, arms, elephants, and horses for the crown prince, together with a hundred thousand gold coins and ten million rupees for his military chest.

Twice defeated at Kandahar, old army hands at court were no little annoyed at the wave of spiritual optimism which Dara had engendered among officers and men. His payroll included a number of "praying mullahs," and just to be on the safe side a few magicians in league with darker powers were engaged to provoke dissension in Persian ranks. How could a strong army, backed by both God and the Devil, fail to win?

But taking Kandahar—citadel, ramparts, fortifications and all—could be no easy matter. During opening months of fruitless Mogul siege, the Persians made nightly sneak attacks and beheaded Mogul soldiers in their trenches. Undaunted, Dara counted on his miracle workers. One holy man had forty genies at his bidding; another was a magician and hypnotist, and assured the prince that he could make Kandahar fall by magic. In addition, other mahatmas of the occult streamed into camp. A yogi arrived with forty disciples, volunteering special prayers to make the Persian garrison fall in twenty days. Several gurus from the Deccan also showed up; imaginative Indian forerunners of Count Zeppelin, they offered to build a "wonderful thing which could carry two or three persons with hand-grenades, and fly in the air without wings and feathers." Dara granted rations and rupees to all.

Aside from magic endeavors, Dara's officers had not been idle. Several dependent forts surrounding Kandahar had been captured, though the prize itself eluded their grasp. The master key was a hill of granite rock overlooking citadel and marketplace; but it could be taken only by tedious mining operations and bombardment, all of which entailed heavy cost in human life. Dara decided that a perpetual rocket discharge might frighten Persian guards away from their commanding towers. For two nights running, several thousand rockets were shot off but the results were unexpected: the delighted Persians "had never seen a more brilliant display of fireworks."

By August 21, Mogul mining operations had effected next to nothing, and Dara now opted for direct assault. Chief nobles were convoked to give their opinions, though one sent a message that he had taken a laxative and could not appear until the afternoon. Khans and rajahs pussyfooted and declined to comment on princely decision: "We are servants; we have nothing else to do except carry out your orders. Kings only can advise a king."

"Why don't you speak plainly?" Dara said bluntly; "you seem to think of returning home without capturing Kandahar." By various Mogul accounts, the prince selected the Hindu rajah, Jai Singh of Jaipur State, for lambasting. The alleged exchange is more than revealing:

> *Dara:* Your exertions in the Emperor's business have fallen short of expectation from the very start. . . . This is the third time that you have come to Kandahar. If you fail this time also . . . how will you show your face to the women of Hindustan?
>
> *Jai Singh:* I . . . obey your command.
>
> *Dara:* You must say plainly whether an assault is advisable or not. If you mean to keep yourself aloof from the affair, give it to me in writing.
>
> *Jai Singh:* I am prepared to give it in writing that I

am always in favor of an attack, and also ever ready to deliver it.

Dara: Your heart and tongue do not seem to agree. What is in your heart, your tongue does not give out, and whatever your tongue utters finds no echo in your heart. If they are in unison, why do you not say straight-way that you consider an assault to be advisable and that by a concerted effort you will capture the fort? Per-haps it has occurred to you that I shall return without conquering Kandahar. If I do so, how can I show my face to the Padshah [Shah Jahan]?"

Jai Singh: Your Highness is the very light of the Emperor's eyes. Whenever His Majesty's glance will fall upon your Highness's world-illuminating countenance, [you] will be quite welcome. But how shall we humble servants show *our* faces?

The argument is clear enough, and underlines the struc-tural weaknesses of despotic autocracy: nobody wanted to take the blame in case of failure. Being Shah Jahan's acting surrogate, Dara Shikoh as a prince of the blood had the right to give definitive orders. By stating their willingness to obey him, his officers could hardly be accused of insubordination; they might lose their lives in the assault, but if they made a wrong decision they would lose face, which was worse. Sens-ing Dara's uncertainty the nobles even became insolent, replying to him on equal terms. Disgusted, the prince wound up the meeting by saying: "Whether you agree to the pro-posal or not, I *command* you to make an assault, no matter whether you die or conquer the fort."

The assault, of course, failed. Defending Persians coolly held fire until they could see the whites of eyes, and then set Mogul elephants and horses into a stampeding panic. Top Mogul commanders proved indifferent or downright reluc-tant to the verge of scandal. After four hours of battle Mogul rout was complete, with a thousand men dead and a thou-sand wounded. Dara retreated to his tent while victory music struck up in Kandahar fort, and the Persians even sent out dancing girls to undulate in full sight of silent Mogul bat-teries.

This third and final debacle at Kandahar pointed up something more than the superiority of defense over attack in seventeenth-century siege warfare: it revealed a fatal flaw in Mogul strength. The Mogul army proved a weakly heterogeneous unit, with too many conflicting mercenaries of different nationalities and an irregular mass of troopers ready to turn tail as soon as difficulties arose. Inside of India, martial operations could take advantage of Hindu caste divisions and clan feuds, or Islamic fervor, or the colossal indifference of those to whom one conqueror could be no worse than another. But against Moslem Persians the weakness of Mogul arms was apparent, and had plagued Aurangzeb as well as Dara.

For Dara personally, Kandahar meant more than military rebuff—even Aurangzeb had twice suffered the same fate. But Aurangzeb knew how to play the game; lacking worldliness, Dara was already marked as a victim. He could not dissimulate; he alienated self-seeking nobles and lacked the cynical tact which underlay most if not all of Mogul history.

On the day after Christmas 1653, the defeated Dara was received in high court at the Mogul capital, together with his son Sulaiman Shikoh. According to Rajah Jai Singh's predictions, Shah Jahan embraced and kissed his son's "world-illuminating countenance." Nothing had changed: nothing could change the emperor's love, and the prince took refuge in his mystical studies once more. Fewer than the fingers of one hand, the years that were left to him for further pursuit of finer shadows would count off quickly and inexorably to the moment of final encounter with Aurangzeb on the plains below Agra.

CHAPTER 10

Puritan in Armor

IN AUGUST 1652, Aurangzeb's fortunes stood at their lowest ebb: over the preceding eight years he had first been stripped of rank for quitting his Deccan post, then forgiven and buried in western India, and finally resurrected for two disastrous campaigns involving central Asia and Kandahar —an up-and-down career subject to Shah Jahan's ambivalent praise and scorn. Now, at the bottom of imperial esteem and smarting with humiliation, he found himself reassigned to the Deccan, relegated to southernmost Mogul frontiers in perpetuation of his geographical isolation from the splendors of the emperor's court.

In effect, the prince had become a pariah. Neither incompetent Murad nor indolent Shuja had ever been the object of such prolonged paternal disapproval: Shuja had always enjoyed a free hand in Bengal, while Murad managed a lavish life in Gujarat in spite of his watchful guardian. But Aurangzeb remained the focal point of suspicion and reprimand. In the next five years he would come to feel like a leper; more than his entire preceding life, this hounded period would provide the impetus for his determination to seize the crown of Hindustan. At the outbreak of the War of Succession he would be forty, hammered and annealed into that strange personality whose power repelled yet commanded the respect of veteran Mogul army men.

With a little reflection, Shah Jahan might have foreseen

that continued repression and quarantine could only accelerate an already morbid situation. Inevitably, Aurangzeb was not going to stew in ostracism without casting about for release in action. Before long everyone at court, including the emperor and Dara Shikoh, would be embroiled in the alarming events of Deccan politics.

Personal psychology is scarcely unrelated to religious or political beliefs, and with Dara Shikoh and Aurangzeb such speculation becomes unavoidable. In religion, an absolute father on earth unquestionably determined each son's approach to an absolute Father in heaven. Dara received imperial love, Aurangzeb knew only imperial authority; Aurangzeb staked his salvation on the letter of Islamic orthodoxy, while Dara espoused the spirit of loving pantheism. In politics, Dara was pacifist and conciliatory, whereas Aurangzeb persecuted and made war. Across a hostile chasm, a puritan in armor glared at his mystic enemy. The only thing they might have claimed in common was a mutual attraction to other-worldly asceticism; but neither practiced what he preached, since the mystic never rejected worldly luxury and the puritan continued to pursue worldly power.

Yet curiously, a hidden denominator often links deadly opponents. For all their radical differences of outlook on God and life, the brothers seem to have shared a basic problem: both emerge from the pageant of Mogul history as profoundly displaced men, alone and estranged from the reality of the Mogul court. If so much had not been at stake they might ultimately have become reconciled or at least understood each other. But it would take Aurangzeb almost a lifetime to become impaled on black doubts about the meaning of his actions, whereas a pampered but vulnerable Dara had already glimpsed the void behind the veil of regal conceit.

Of the two, Aurangzeb emerges as the greater stranger—alienated even from the wives and concubines who shared his moments of passion. His marriage to one of the daughters of nobleman Shahnawaz Khan had in any case been more of a remote formality than a love match: Dilras Banu Begum proved proud beyond her station; though she bore him three daughters and two sons, there is no record that Aurangzeb displayed more than conventional grief when she died.

Other marriages were even less meaningful as Aurangzeb became increasingly unapproachable. Two secondary wives (though they produced five more children for him) seem still more remote for lack of detail. One, the daughter of a rajah, soon fell out of favor and spent years in isolation; the other was the vague Aurangabadi Mahal, who died of bubonic plague. Much later, a sensual concubine named Udipuri Mahal will garnish his old age. And we must somehow believe in a romance with an ill-starred slave girl named Zainabadi: at Burhanpur, in those same Zainabad Gardens where Mumtaz Mahal's body was first interred, Aurangzeb sees the girl jumping up to pluck a mango from a tree. Subsequently he takes her away with him, and she very nearly taunts him into drinking a cup of forbidden wine as a test of his love; but then, she dies young.

All of these women have the intangible quality of people in a dream, bearing no vital relationship to his life. Even Udipuri Mahal, with her animal abandon, is like some extraneous character in a play, invented to provide contrast or elicit dialogue from a man almost impervious to emotional attachments. A later European traveler who actually met Aurangzeb, the Italian lawyer Gemelli Careri, confirms what might have been suspected—Aurangzeb's puritan revulsion to sex. Dismissing harem adornments as "ostentation," Careri goes on to relate a backstairs anecdote in which Aurangzeb arranged to make love with a lady of the zenana, but "instead of going to bed, fell a reading the . . . [Koran] all night." When a eunuch came to announce that the morning bath was ready, the disappointed courtesan cried out that there could be no need of ablution because Aurangzeb "had not broke wind." Aurangzeb "never after look'd her in the face." For all its bawdy malice, the story underlines a point: imagination balks at the notion of Aurangzeb in all-too-human intimacy, physical or otherwise. Later, all his sons will fear him, and his daughters will become disaffected; he is really beyond the human pale.

•••

Licking his wounds in the early autumn of 1652, the prince proceeded southward to assume command of the Deccan. Defiant, he took his time, spending nine months in Burhanpur (now came the romance with Zainabadi) while stringent instructions from Shah Jahan ordered him to continue onward to Aurangabad, the official Deccan capital.

The Deccan, like the central squares of a chessboard, would actually determine the winner of all Hindustan. In princely days Shah Jahan had begun his career there, revolting against Jahangir from Deccan strongholds; when the time came, Aurangzeb would also challenge his father from the same vantage point. Ironically and certainly unconsciously, the emperor had given Aurangzeb a formidable advantage over Dara; with such wild hatred corroding his two sons, it could only be fatal politics.

Since the days of Akbar, when the north Deccan first submitted to Mogul rule, there had always remained a stubbornly resistant and independent south Deccan—smaller states, together with the two larger kingdoms of Bijapur and Golconda. Southward activities of the Mogul Empire languished during the pallid reign of Jahangir, with trusted imperial generals taking bribes from Deccan kings; Shah Jahan's own youthful strategies had soon come to nothing. But with his accession, the emperor embarked on an actively coercive policy marked by wars, rebellions, and treaties. Early in 1636, Shah Jahan personally outmatched the kings of Bijapur and Golconda by swallowing up the last of the smaller Deccan states. On that occasion, fearful Golconda succumbed to the status of an annually tributary sultanate under Mogul protection, while tougher Bijapur held out and conceded to a once-only but hefty settlement. Aurangzeb's initial appointment from 1636 to 1644 had thus been merely a nominal rule, restricted to mopping up local Deccan bandits and exacting indemnities here and there from defiant rajahs.

Aurangabad, where the prince now began a renewed sojourn as governor, lies 233 miles due east and slightly north
of Bombay—easily accessible today by plane or train, and a
convenient center for visiting the famous Ajanta and Ellora
caves nearby. Originally an insignificant village, Aurangzeb
had given his name to the place during his first viceroyalty
and metamorphosed it into an imposing city—an achievement which meant combating dry soil, creating a large water
tank four miles in circumference, building a palace for himself, and running an irrigation canal from a nearby river. Nobles and officers had duly received land for residence, and
when everything was ready Aurangzeb and his staff had
moved from the cramped fortress of nearby Daulatabad and
taken residence. In the intervening eight years, Aurangabad
had grown quickly as undisputed capital of the Mogul Deccan.

Its founder had also grown—into a restless, tormented
soul. Writing many years later to his grandson, Aurangzeb
volunteered a revealing retrospective description of his second Deccan tenure: "In my folly I used to ride about and
make forced marches, under the instigations of Satan and of
my own passions." For distraction he took to horseback and
hunted game, abundant in the vicinity: there were herds of
wild deer, nilgau or Indian antelope, tigers in the hills, and
flocks of lake herons to be brought down by trained hawks.
When hunting palled he toured the lakes of the district, made
pilgrimages to the tombs of Moslem saints, and admired the
caves of Ellora with their rock-hewn frescoes.

More significant than these pursuits, he gave vent to his
spleen in acts of religious bigotry. Some years before in Gujarat, Aurangzeb had desecrated holy "infidel" architecture
and even killed a sacred cow. The Deccan neighborhood
now provided a hilltop Hindu temple with an idolatrous
image linked to sacred prostitution. "By Allah's grace I demolished it," he admits, "and forbade the temple dancers to
ply their shameful profession." Islamic zeal might condone
an isolated act or two of religious iconoclasm, but it seemed
downright unwise to carry discrimination into the adminis-

trative sphere. When Aurangzeb began to abrade Hindu Rajputs under his aegis, Shah Jahan quickly communicated royal disapproval. The prince dissimulated by recommending a Rajput captain for a high post. But camouflage was belated: orthodox Deccan officers and mullahs had already beheaded a district Brahman tax collector for uttering "improper words with reference to the Prophet," and the victim's Hindu brothers now sought justice from the imperial capital. Aurangzeb sent an explanation to Prime Minister Sadullah Khan, reminding him that it was "proper for all Moslems to do their utmost to assert the rules of the Prophet's religion"; surely the prime minister would cut off "the road of complaint of this wretched tribe." Orthodoxy was already casting a long shadow.

For the moment, these incidents of friction manifestly reflected stifled ambition: the infernal aggression bottled up by his defeat at Kandahar seethed to find an outlet. Yet tasks at hand proved administrative rather than punitive. Agriculture had lapsed badly, and a hopeless regional deficit attested to the corrupt legacy of six temporary governors (including Murad). One ruthless viceroy had even been murdered, much to the joy of afflicted peasants around Burhanpur city. The plain fact of the matter was that the Deccan did not pay for itself. A large Mogul garrison had to be maintained in the area because of two great powers immediately bordering on the Mogul frontier. But this was poor soil compared to alluvial north or east India; land collections that had sagged as a result of capricious rains, indifferent harvests, and an alienated rural population—all made the Deccan a drain on other Mogul provinces. Shah Jahan now urged Aurangzeb to improve relations with the peasants, thereby increasing cultivation and revenue. Yet the problem (which had also cropped up during his first viceroyalty) was how to provide adequate revenue to *produce* revenue. His officers lost no time in complaining that they could not pay their soldiers on income from the poor lands assigned to them; they wanted and virtually demanded more productive crown lands in other parts of India, such as both they and he had formerly enjoyed.

It was the old story of Mogul greed. Akbar had worked out a fair revenue system a hundred years earlier, but in the Deccan no system existed at all. Years of extortion and wars had compounded the mess; overexploited peasants often fled and deserted entire villages, leaving cultivated land to lapse into jungle. Under his new revenue minister, Aurangzeb began setting about to improve matters: officers were shifted or dismissed, while the prince repeatedly put his head on the block to defend good men, maintain his army, and raise additional funds. Still, the bad administration of the past dogged him everywhere.

Argument with Shah Jahan now took a new turn in imperial correspondence: having apparently failed in the military sphere, Aurangzeb was being measured for an administrative dunce cap as well. "If Your Majesty wishes me to be honored with a great viceroyalty, give me the means worthy of it," he pleaded. Elliptically, Shah Jahan replied that the prince should exchange his own sterile lands for more productive ones in the hands of other officers. But Aurangzeb could hardly appropriate districts from important or competent khans, and when he curtailed the revenue of a few lazy or minor officials their complaints flew to court. In desperation he asked for cash payment as well as land. The emperor became so annoyed that he made withering references to his son in open court.

The financial wrangle soon reached a malevolent pitch. How could the emperor stop the drain of money to a deficit-ridden province if Aurangzeb kept asking for cash instead of resolving that deficit? Suspicious of revenue papers, Shah Jahan launched a barb where it would be sure to fester: "It is unworthy of a Moslem and an act of injustice to take all productive villages for yourself . . . and to assign only less productive lands to others." Back came the reply from a deeply wounded prince, protesting that "I have never in my life acted unjustly, but always tried to please God and His vice-regent on earth."

Debate rages in letter after letter. Why has Aurangzeb not yet improved the lot of the peasants and extended cultivation? Aurangzeb will do so, but needs time and men and money; how can he correct the results of war and maladministration overnight? No, the emperor replies, he is a failure as an administrator, and will lose his income if he doesn't bestir himself.

We have only Aurangzeb's evaluation of the controversy, with blame cycled back to Shah Jahan: the prince's enemies have undermined him, and the emperor does not appreciate Deccan difficulties. But apologia is useless: imperial suspicion, mistrust, and reprimands will continue. Now, for five long years Aurangzeb will not once be invited to court; and though his brothers send birthday or anniversary presents to the emperor, official records show him giving none. Dara Shikoh's sons receive jewels and money, while Aurangzeb's sons are neglected. Shah Jahan counters Aurangzeb's recommendations for posts and promotions, criticizes him openly, and even asks Shuja if he wants to take over command of the Deccan! Mogul envoys stationed in Bijapur and Golconda take their orders directly from the Mogul capital and not from Aurangzeb, though the Deccan is much nearer to them.

Finally the quarrel degenerates into picayune neurotic bickering. At one moment, Shah Jahan accuses Aurangzeb of receiving presents from the king of Golconda and not crediting their value against annual Golconda tribute. Aurangzeb replies that the presents were of little value; the jewels had flaws, and in any case they were a personal gift. Later, the emperor upbraids him for taking the best weavers in Burhanpur for himself, depriving the court of artisans. Later still, the Deccan revenue officer recommends a loan of fifty thousand rupees to enterprising peasants, and Aurangzeb refers the matter to court; when rebuked for not having advanced the money on his own authority he answers, "Little wonder I did not assume the responsibility . . . seeing that I have been taken to task for acts which I never did. In my first viceroyalty I did not wait for previous sanction in such matters. But now I have grown more cautious." At other moments Aurangzeb is even accused of diverting Deccan mangoes meant for the emperor. In a letter to Jahanara, the prince complains that after twenty years of service he receives less authority and trust than Dara's son, Sulaiman Shikoh.

If this was calculated torment, it could only prepare a ghoulish day of vengeance. Compulsive doubt of Aurangzeb had reached sadistic proportions. The victim might partly blame Dara Shikoh for such imperial treatment, but much more lay behind Shah Jahan's ambiguity. For the emperor, Aurangzeb seemed an incarnation of the guilty past: thirty years before, another prince had been ambitious to the point of rebellion against his father, and had gone so far as to commit oblique fratricide. Mistrust of Aurangzeb stemmed not from paranoia, but from instinctive recognition of the same determined core which once motivated young Prince Khurram. Young Prince Khurram had become old Shah Jahan, mellowed, not without a sense of justice, and certainly the most loved of all Mogul emperors. Yet among his sons only one loved him, two were indifferent, and the fourth made him afraid.

It was against this background of ominous psychological tension that Deccan politics now erupted, in 1656, with Aurangzeb's invasion of Golconda. The riches of Golconda: the phrase would even enter the English language. There below the Deccan it lay, with its capital city of Hyderabad famous as a seventeenth-century center of diamond trade for India and indeed the whole world. Golconda produced steel for Damascus blades; its lances, swords, and daggers got exported everywhere, and Golconda chintzes had already become famous in England and on the continent. Carpets emerged from Golconda, along with fish and wheat; herds of prized elephants roamed its forests; tobacco grew and palm trees flourished. Eastward, Golconda's port of Masulipatam afforded the best anchorage along the entire Bay of Bengal.

At the imperial Mogul capital, two factions watched the Golconda crisis with interest and acted according to their own lights: Dara Shikoh and Jahanara Begum of course lent their names and influence to the peace party; Sadullah Khan, the prime minister, favored war. Sadullah Khan was to die in

1656, but another aggressor already waited in the wings to take over his role. Shah Jahan, like a pendulum, vacillated between the attractions of martial spoils and his mistrust of Aurangzeb. For Aurangzeb himself, stirring up trouble in the Deccan by provoking war against two rich but weak sultanates held compound advantages: through strife and victory he could vindicate his earlier failure at Kandahar, at the same time providing himself with a valid excuse for attracting a formidable Mogul army to his command. All in all, the ploy afforded a fine opportunity to make bright the arrows, seduce officers, and exercise his pent-up energy as a preliminary to the scramble for the crown. After all, Shah Jahan was already in his sixties.

In preparation for war, Aurangzeb started to cross swords with the sultan of Golconda from 1653 onward. Golconda's annual tribute as a protectorate of the Moguls fell forever in arrears, and its ruler received peremptory demands: he must come up with laggard payment at once. But the situation quickly became complicated; the real gray eminence of Golconda, and plainly a man who would figure prominently in India's forthcoming War of Succession, was its powerful vizier—known to history as Mir Jumla.

Ever since 1636, when struggle with Mogul power ended in treaty and tribute, Moslem Bijapur and Golconda had turned their own hopes of expansion south to the narrowing proboscis of the subcontinent (almost too uncannily, India does resemble an elephant's trunk). Portugal held the enclave of Goa, but there were no end of petty Hindu principalities in the Carnatic to the southeast. Still, it wasn't so easy for lazy dragons to swallow quails' eggs: every one held a barb of Hindu defiance, and Bijapur and Golconda had spent long years in southward annexation. Most of Golconda's successful peninsular conquests had involved the ubiquitous Mir Jumla.

Mir Jumla was actually a Persian, the son of an Ispahan oil merchant. After the manner of other adventurers he had left Persia at an early age; being a schismatic Shia, he decided to seek fortune not with the Moguls (who were orthodox Sunnis) but with Deccan kings. Shrewder than any Mogul and a business genius to boot, he became incredibly rich as a diamond merchant. Mines were worked under feigned names to conceal his monopoly; his gems could be counted "by the sackful," or certainly amounted to $35\frac{1}{2}$ pounds at more exact estimate. But Golconda's vizier betrayed other talents far beyond the measure of any ordinarily cunning tradesman: he had also proved to be an equally impressive military and administrative genius, who went after power like a pig searching for truffles. Mir Jumla soon exerted his monopoly over civil and military matters, so that nothing reached Abdullah Qutb Shah—the sybaritic sultan of Golconda—without his prior seal of approval.

Backing an obvious winner, Qutb Shah had blissfully lent sanction and initial support to his vizier's Carnatic spearhead; where previous attempts had failed, Persian enterprise succeeded. Sustained by European artillery and a disciplined army, Mir Jumla even captured impregnable Hindu rock fortresses. Southern loot swelled his diamond-laden pockets (the usual pillaging of Hindu temples) and he became virtual ruler of a huge Carnatic province, maintaining his own army and cavalry there.

Favoritism soon changed to anxiety: Golconda's ruler began to worry that Mir Jumla was becoming more of a dangerous rival than a loyal subject. A quarrel followed about booty, and the sly vizier was summoned back to Hyderabad; he did, as a matter of fact, return briefly, but escaped when he found a plot under way to seize and blind him. It looked like open war between sultan and subordinate. But taking up the art of juggling, Mir Jumla considered defecting to Bijapur for protection and sent trial presents to its ruler; he also dickered with the shah of Persia for possible asylum, and—more important—began a flirtation with the Moguls. Aurangzeb eagerly entered into private correspondence through the Mogul envoy stationed in Golconda.

Mir Jumla was now playing games with three major powers, while Aurangzeb pressed Shah Jahan for assurance of protection and honors to such a valuable intriguer. Assurance arrived but the diamond merchant pussyfooted: would the Moguls give him a year to collect his property, keeping their little agreement secret till then? "I think," Aurangzeb wrote to the emperor with annoyance at the delay, "that Mir Jumla does not really wish to enter imperial service . . . so long as he can dexterously avert the hostility of two sultans."

Dexterity had its limits. Secret deals soon became no secret (it is tempting to think that Aurangzeb may deliberately have allowed a leak) and the kings of Golconda and Bijapur now agreed to combine and scotch a devious serpent. Urgently, Mir Jumla decided to seek immediate Mogul protection, but this time it was Aurangzeb who stalled: let the two Deccan powers take action against a man whom the Moguls guaranteed to protect, and he would have good reason for war.

The sultan of Golconda had not yet acted against his wayward vizier when crisis arose in an unexpected way. Mir Jumla's son, Mohammed Amin, acted as his father's deputy in Hyderabad; insolent in the knowledge of family power, he had become almost insulting to Qutb Shah in open court. The sultan swallowed abuse until November 21, 1655. On that day Mir Jumla's son came to court staggeringly drunk, fell asleep, and drooled vomit on the imperial carpet. It was the last straw. He and his family found themselves clapped into prison, their property confiscated.

Aurangzeb's occasion had been dumped in his lap. But no action could be taken without Shah Jahan's consent, and he now wrote asking for permission to go to war. Shah Jahan had meanwhile sent a robe of honor and a royal decree to Mir Jumla, appointing him commander of five thousand horse and making his vomiting son a peer as well; concomitantly, an imperial dispatch to the sultan of Golconda requested him not to detain the Jumla family or their property. As relay man, Aurangzeb remitted the letter to Golconda and threatened to send an army if the emperor's instructions were defied. In fact, he began mobilizing Mogul troops along Golconda's frontier in anticipation of Shah Jahan's approval.

Qutb Shah temporized—"under the influence of the

fumes of arrogance," as a high-flown court chronicle put it. By Christmas 1655 Shah Jahan belatedly received news of Mohammed Amin's imprisonment, and sent a stiff follow-up note to Golconda *commanding* release of Mir Jumla's family —by weird reasoning, the Jumlas had already become important Mogul servants. Almost simultaneously, a somewhat reluctant firman to Aurangzeb sanctioned a demonstration of force *if* Mir Jumla's son were not released—the "if" was to become crucial and required a little circumventing finesse. Both these imperial letters reached Aurangabad on January 7, 1656; but the emperor's new note to Golconda could easily suffer slow transmission in order to arrive *after* war had been declared!

Appointing his sixteen-year-old son, Mohammed Sultan, to lead the Moguls across Golconda's frontier, Aurangzeb opted for a cavalry dash to Hyderabad. He himself lingered behind, apprehensive that Bijapur's army (which had nervously assembled at the Deccan border) might intervene. When Bijapur faltered, father followed son.

According to plan, it was only after Aurangzeb's troops had entered Golconda territory that the sultan of Golconda received Shah Jahan's second letter. Fearfully and instantly, Qutb Shah released Mir Jumla's son and family, dispatching them with an appropriate statement of submission. Aurangzeb's son actually encountered the liberated pawns some twenty-four miles from Hyderabad, but found a reason to continue his father's invasion: Qutb Shah had not yet restored the Jumla family property. Mogul cavalry swept on to Hyderabad; the sultan beat a last-minute retreat to Golconda fortress (six or eight miles away) with his children and as much treasure as he could gather, leaving the capital to be defended by seventeen thousand soldiers. By taking flight he had unknowingly saved his life. Aurangzeb's secret orders to Mohammed Sultan were frank to say the least: "If you can manage it, lighten [Qutb-ul-Mulk's] neck of the burden of his head."

Invasion exposed the sultanate's vulnerable underbelly, with appeasement prevailing over resistance. From his Gol-

conda fortress, Abdullah Qutb Shah sent Mohammed Sultan
not one but fifty doves with olive branches. Daily envoys carried presents (two hundred caskets of jewels, two elephants
with silver howdahs, and four horses with gold trappings)
and all of Mir Jumla's property was restored. But nothing
could be done until Aurangzeb arrived, which he did on February 6 with his main Deccan army. They now spent the rest
of February and all of March besieging the fortress, while its
terrified occupant continued to transmit gifts and offers of
peace.

Why give quarter? Aurangzeb wrote to Shah Jahan and
appealed to his greed: "Such a money-yielding country, unmatched by imperial dominions, has fallen into this wretch's
hands!" Diamond and crystal mines were mentioned; Qutb-
ul-Mulk was a godless Shia, ungrateful for Mogul protection,
a ruler given over to vice and oppression of his people, an
ally of Persia, a heretic who must be punished by the orthodox Moslem ruler of India. Well aware of the peace party at
court headed by Dara Shikoh and Jahanara, Aurangzeb
begged the emperor not to heed pacific intercession nor to
reply to the sultan of Golconda's submissive letter. "I hope
Your Majesty will order annexation."

Representatives of the Deccan sultanates had been stationed at the Mogul court for some time; in desperation and
to Aurangzeb's fury, Golconda's official envoy now approached Dara Shikoh. Dara's peace party went to work—no
easy matter, since the emperor's sense of justice had been
corroded by Prime Minister Sadullah Khan working in con-
junction with Aurangzeb's belligerent persuasions. The argument can be imagined: was the emperor going to ruin the
sultan of Golconda simply for trying to bring Mir Jumla to
heel? What were Aurangzeb's intentions in pushing matters
so far? Shah Jahan reflected and then wrote Qutb Shah an
imperial pardon at the price of indemnity, dispatching it with
a robe of honor. But the letter was sent via Aurangzeb, who
withheld communication: the sultanate's queen mother herself was soliciting peace, proposing terms of heavy compen-
sation in cash and even in kin—a marriage could surely be

arranged between a princess of Golconda's house and Aurangzeb's eldest son. Shah Jahan, when informed that Aurangzeb had suppressed his letter, reacted with unexpected approval—the prince seemed to be employing sound strategy for further extortion! Distinctly, Dara Shikoh's peace party had not yet won out.

Aurangzeb's own sinister intentions exceeded the mere question of indemnity. "Qutb-ul-Mulk is now craving pardon," he wrote to Mir Jumla; "but I wish to send him to the wilderness of destruction." On second thought (and probably out of fear of exceeding imperial sanction) Aurangzeb decided to settle for a tribute of ten million rupees and the royal intermarriage. But before dickering could proceed further, abruptly contradictory orders came from Shah Jahan himself: the siege of Golconda fortress must stop. In a sharp setback, Aurangzeb found himself commanded to withdraw from conquered territory immediately.

It was a surprise defeat at the moment of victory, and the whole Mogul camp knew of it. Stunned, Aurangzeb left Golconda; on April 13, 1656 he remitted the emperor's pardon to Qutb Shah, together with the robe of honor and an agreement stamped with the impression of Shah Jahan's hand dipped in vermilion. By way of consolation, Mohammed Sultan did marry Golconda's princess, and a grateful Mir Jumla offered gifts to Aurangzeb. Mir Jumla then went off by summons to the Mogul court, where he gave Shah Jahan the incomparable Kohinoor diamond and promptly became Hindustan's prime minister!

How had Dara Shikoh's peace party managed to prevail at the final moment? The clue would be preserved in correspondence between Dara and Golconda's ruler. Dara acknowledges receipt of "three letters written by Your Highness to His Majesty, the Emperor, to my illustrious sister Jahanara Begum, and to me. I placed all three letters before His Majesty . . . who out of graciousness wrote a firman of favor to Your Highness . . . so that it may be made clear to you that the Emperor . . . *did not in fact sanction a siege of*

Golconda and the occupation of Your Highness's territory."*
Additionally, Golconda's envoy at the Mogul court had been
enabled to confront Shah Jahan with the full extent of Aurangzeb's machinations: Aurangzeb had tricked the sultan of
Golconda, almost killed him by treachery, withheld more
than one imperial firman, and sent back a false picture of
events. The result was Shah Jahan's otherwise puzzling
switch to righteous indignation.

Mir Jumla and Aurangzeb were birds of a feather. Even
before the Persian adventurer went off to court, they had
come to an agreement on future Deccan policy. By mid-July
1656, India's new prime minister successfully revived Shah
Jahan's cupidity with a dazzling display of diamonds, rubies,
and topazes. The emperor now dallied with the idea that perhaps Golconda and Bijapur were worth annexing after all,
especially with Bijapur's king almost on his deathbed. Besides, the Mogul Empire had acquired an invaluable servant
who knew the Deccan kingdoms inside out—an irresistible
wedge of intrigue. Dara Shikoh's peace party fell into the
background again.

The renewed phase of Deccan imperialism in 1656 and
1657 can only be described as sordid. On the side of outright
aggression were Aurangzeb and Mir Jumla; whirring their
dove wings, Dara Shikoh and Jahanara counseled against
force. Shah Jahan continued to vacillate, alternately swayed
to peace or inclined to sanction Mogul belligerence for the
sake of extortion. In correspondence to Mir Jumla, Aurangzeb mapped fresh strategy. Mogul India's new prime minister
must return to the Deccan: invasion of another sultanate was
imminent.

True to Shah Jahan's prediction, Bijapur's king died on
November 4, 1656. Aurangzeb promptly wrote to his father
that the newly crowned eighteen-year-old successor constituted no legitimate heir, being allegedly a bastard of obscure
parentage who had been brought up at Bijapur's court. Once

---

* The significant italics are by Dara's biographer.

more, in anticipation of imperial approval, aggressive Mogul troops massed along the Deccan frontier. Shockingly or cynically, Shah Jahan acquiesced by giving Aurangzeb permission to "settle the affair of Bijapur in any way he thought fit." Mir Jumla accordingly received orders to proceed with sustaining troops and officers to the Deccan; the most Dara Shikoh could effect was for the Jumla family to remain behind as "hostages" for the prime minister's loyalty.

The situation bristled with inherent danger. If the powerful combination of Aurangzeb and Mir Jumla took over Bijapur and went on to annex Golconda, then their potential threat to Shah Jahan and Dara Shikoh could only become enormous. Yet the emperor had given carte blanche.

Mir Jumla arrived at Aurangabad on January 18, 1657. With unprecedented speed, he and Aurangzeb set out on the very same day to invade Bijapur. But again imperial decision reversed itself: this time it was apparently Bijapur's envoy at court who had sought the intermediary of Dara Shikoh to persuade Shah Jahan for an end of hostilities. Peace negotiations began, with the usual indemnities agreed upon. Once more Aurangzeb had been contradicted—halted in opening months of war. His Mogul army now had to retreat, and several top-ranking imperial officers received mysterious orders to return to court with their contingents—the emperor had entered on a new phase of acute mistrust.

In effect, Aurangzeb's Deccan politics had been nullified after four years of aggressive exertion; stalemated, he smoldered with repressed volcanic hatred against Dara Shikoh and Shah Jahan. But only a short time remained before eruptive chaos and vengeance: India's War of Succession was due to break out in the autumn. When it did, Aurangzeb would become transformed into a demigod—in the opinion of his contemporaries.

Curiously, their opinion was justified. Hitherto at least partly approachable in psychological terms, Aurangzeb would soon surpass himself in a strange way. On the brink of crisis, his personal past could only feebly explain the implacable future. Connecting links were certainly all there: the youthful elephant encounter, antipathy to Dara Shikoh, the prayer rug in battle, central Asia and Kandahar, endless humiliations and disgraces, perpetual isolation from court, mockingly momentary victories. More than obvious was the disastrous relationship with an imperial father who had never approved of him and never given him love. But whence the demigod who spurned the whole battery of primary emotions? Even the most consuming hatred rarely if ever insists on such marvelous definition: this man is a darkly obsessed titan in a gargantuan royal drama. Opposed in polar magnificence to weakly human limitations, a new force will soon enough invest his life with superhuman powers. What force? Labels only simplify one of the most astounding personalities in all world history. Whatever motivated Muhiuddin Mohammed Aurangzeb, he relentlessly intended to drag a subcontinent in the wake of his spectacular destiny.

CHAPTER

I I

Paradise on Earth

DOOMSDAY WAS at hand. It had taken nearly three decades for a delayed fuse to ignite an imperial powder magazine; within the next three years, explosions of unbelievable violence would rock all India to its foundations.

Ironically, March 7, 1657 prompted elaborate terdecennial festivities to celebrate thirty Moslem years of Shah Jahan's reign. The date very nearly corresponded to Julius Caesar's fateful ides. Outwardly, the Mogul Empire had never been more flourishing and opulent.

In twenty-six years since Mumtaz Mahal's death, scrupulous court painters had reflected the passage of time with ineluctable Mogul miniatures. Eternal spring flowers still bloomed at his slippered feet, but Shah Jahan could now count sixty-five birthday weighings against gold and grain. Most of his children had reached middle age: Jahanara was forty-three, Dara Shikoh forty-two, Shuja forty-one, Raushanara forty, and Aurangzeb thirty-nine. Only impetuous Murad remained boisterously stupid at thirty-three, while his one-dimensional sister Gauharara Begum added up to an inchoate twenty-six.

The three princesses still remained unmarried by harsh Mogul law. Seemingly ciphers during these years, Gauharara and particularly Raushanara would soon come to the foreground with the outbreak of civil war. Jahanara's spiritual development had involved her deeply with Dara Shikoh, though she remained a bedrock of fidelity for Shah Jahan.

Fig. 1.   Shah Jahan

Fig. 2. Mumtaz Mahal

Fig. 3.   Jahangir

Fig. 4.   Nur Jahan

Fig. 5. Dara Shikoh

Fig. 6. Aurangzeb on his prayer rug

Fig. 8.   Akbar the Great

Fig. 7.   Aurangzeb reading from the Koran

Fig. 9.   Dara Shikoh hands hawk to Shah Jahan. Shuja stands at left.

Fig. 10.   Three of Shah Jahan's sons on horseback—Shuja, Aurangzeb, and Murad

Fig. 11.　Shah Jahan, his four sons, a courtier, and two attendants visit an ascetic outside a leaf hut. Murad is the small figure above the horse's tail.

Fig. 12.   Shah Jahan with child and women attendants

Fig. 13.   Shah Jahan presents a jewel to Dara Shikoh.

Fig. 14.   Shah Jahan in old age

Fig. 15.   The Red Fort of Delhi   Fig. 16.   The wall of Agra's Red Fort

Fig. 17.   Shah Jahan's Hall of Private Audience in the Red Fort, Delhi

Artistic and even architectural activities had brought her high cultural prominence, quite aside from her importance as first lady of the realm. All the brothers, including Aurangzeb, still regarded her as a confidante; in spite of her known pacifist stand, Aurangzeb continued to write to Begum Sahib during the present troubles and tensions of his second Deccan governorship. Dara Shikoh himself remained close to Shah Jahan, holding absentee viceroyalty of Allahabad, the Punjab, and Multan while pursuing his scholar's life. Indolent Shuja slept away his mornings in Bengal, while Murad hunted and caroused as viceroy of Malwa and Gujarat provinces, under the watchful eye of his finance minister Ali Naqi. Unified but already effectively quadrated among four sons, Hindustan was wrapped in unbearably static tension, like charged air before a summer storm. Flashes of heat lightning would periodically accompany long-range developments in the Dara-Aurangzeb feud, or distant sounds of thunder heralded Murad's and Shuja's growing discontent and Raushanara's cankerous envy.

Superstitious court nobles brooded over an omen: events had really begun to go amiss ever since 1648, when the emperor fatally relocated his capital at Delhi. Agra had been the enduring center of Moslem domination in India since 1504, before the Moguls ever arrived on the scene; Delhi had never brought good luck to any empire, and this switch of imperial capitals seemed to all a harbinger of disaster.

Hardly sudden, the move to Delhi reflected ten years of preparation: as early as 1638, Shah Jahan had wanted a more expansive imperial luxury than the confining Red Fort of Agra could provide. More than possibly, the constant sight of the Taj Mahal's seemingly endless construction stirred up painful memories. Whatever the reasons, Delhi had been chosen; and after a decade of plans and active labor, a district renamed Shahjahanabad emerged in transformation. Inspiring the artisans, imperial fantasy took shape: hidden behind the great sandstone walls of the Red Fort of Delhi, a rarefied ensemble of palaces represented an austere yet sensual culmination in white marble. By April 1648 these fresh *mahals* had become habitable, and inauguration ceremonies were held. In the city itself, construction of public edifices dominated the next few years. The imposing thoroughfare of the Chandni Chowk witnessed creation of Shah Jahan's great Friday Mosque; and Jahanara sponsored that impressive caravanserai for travelers which Bernier would later compare to the Palais royal. A modern age of gold had dawned, but Cassandras muttered at the horror of change.

Sure enough: within six months of the transfer to Delhi, hadn't Persian forces reoccupied Kandahar and obliged the honor of Mogul arms to do battle again? Abruptly called away, Shah Jahan had spent a year and a half in the Punjab and in Afghanistan supervising those three expensive campaigns under Aurangzeb and Dara Shikoh which in the end had failed to regain the fortress. Not until March 1650 did the emperor return to his new capital, consoling himself with the echo of temporal gaiety and cries of "Long live the King." Indeed, solace could henceforth be found only in his ornate dream world of art and artifice, in those palaces of sepulchral white marble where he sat on the gem-encrusted Peacock Throne transported from Agra.

"If there be paradise on earth, it is this, it is this, it is this": in letters of gold, the Persian inscription can be found repeated four times inside Shah Jahan's Hall of Private Audience at Delhi. As a static summation of bliss, the text seems infinitely melancholy. From 1628 to 1657, thirty years of beneficent rule had blended intricate esthetics with cloying hedonism; at a pitch of insular extravagance, the Mogul Empire was a cross between mannered Orientalism and the never-never sensuality of the *Arabian Nights.* Yet beyond the fairy tale, Shah Jahan's India seethed with poverty, suffering, and famine—the stark reality of anonymous Hindu and Moslem masses whose history found no narrative. Not that social judgment is relevant here—it was no French Revolution that lopped off Mogul heads. Thirty years of paradise were soon to be lost for purely inward reasons; millions might be involved and great numbers might die, but tragedy was precipitated by eight strange men and women invested with the sacrosanct prerogatives of absolute royalty.

The haunting question was, of course, why: why was the House of Timur about to commit familicide like a tree strangling itself with its own roots? Before the last Mogul protagonist died, John Dryden's rhymed couplets would be dramatizing the events of Hindustan for English audiences. For the Moguls or for Dryden, the answer was classic fate; for a more analytical twentieth century, fate becomes the instrument of unconscious motivation urged to fulfillment as inexorably as water seeking its own level. The motivation was death.

● ● ●

By no accident, the world's greatest monument to death now stood complete in this portentous springtime of 1657. In fact, the glorious Taj Mahal had been finished in 1652, though work on adjunctive features continued for several years more. Begun in one woman's memory, the mausoleum would now transcend her to cast its apocalyptic aura over a dynasty of doom.

No doubt about it: Shah Jahan's thirty years of rule left a testament of impressive art, and the architecture of Delhi and Agra alone conjures up an Islamic splendor to rank with the Alhambra of Granada. But the Taj, after twenty years of labor, represented something preciously spiritual, and was already being inspected with a reverent eye to its eternal upkeep. Rather wistfully, in 1652 Aurangzeb examined the premises and wrote a letter to his father: "The dome of the holy tomb leaked in two places . . . during the rainy season." Shah Jahan very likely took active steps to repair the damage.

Indeed, construction of the vast edifice represented a high ritual in itself. Even as early as 1632, on the first anniversary of Mumtaz Mahal's death, the courtyard of the mausoleum in progress had been adorned with superb tents, with the entire court assembled to pay homage—princes of the royal blood, grandees, and an assemblage of religious scholars including sheikhs, ulemma, and *hafizes* who knew the whole Koran by heart. Shah Jahan had graced the event with his presence; and as the empress's father, Asaf Khan was present by imperial request. A great banquet was spread before the then-nascent tomb, and guests partook of a variety of foods, sweetmeats, and fruits. Verses from the Koran filled the air, prayers were offered for the soul of the dead, and a hundred thousand rupees went in charity. In later years on other anniversary days, Shah Jahan attended memorials at the incomplete edifice whenever he was in Agra, formally accompanied by Jahanara and the harem. Inevitably, the ladies always occupied a central platform set up for the occasion, and remained concealed from public gaze by *kanats,* screens of red cloth and velvet. Noblemen gathered under pitched tents; and always, great sums in alms would be distributed to the poor.

Europeans in the realm watched the construction of the Taj. Peter Mundy early commented in his diary: "There is already about her tomb a rail of gold. The building is begun and goes on with excessive labor and cost, prosecuted with extraordinary diligence, gold and silver esteemed common metal, and marble but as ordinary stones. [Shah Jahan] intends, as some think, to remove all the city hither, causing hills to be made level because they might not hinder the prospect of it, [with] places appointed for streets [and] shops . . . ." The golden palisade which Mundy saw, studded with gems and valued at six hundred thousand rupees, would be removed in 1642 for fear of vandals; the suburban market, meant to provide revenue for the mausoleum, is long since gone.

Tavernier, the French jeweler, appraised all phases of construction during his repeated trips to India. "I witnessed," he writes, "the commencement and accomplishment of this great work, on which they have expended twenty-two years, during which twenty thousand men worked incessantly; this is sufficient to enable one to realize that the cost of it has been enormous . . . . Shah Jahan began to build his own tomb on the other side of the river . . . . An eunuch in command of two thousand men guards both the tomb of the Begum and the Tasimican [camp of the Taj] to which it is near at hand."

Manrique, the Portuguese friar, also saw work done on the tomb. In the 1640s it was "still incomplete, the greater part of it remaining to be done." On roads leading to Agra Manrique saw great blocks of marble, "of such unusual size and length that they drew the sweat of many powerful teams of oxen and of fierce-looking, big-horned buffaloes, which were dragging enormous, strongly made wagons . . . ." Manrique noted that "a thousand men were usually engaged, overseers, officials, and workmen: of these many were occupied in laying out ingenious gardens, others planting shady groves and ornamental avenues." It was the friar who would pull the pin of a historical grenade: *The architect of these works was a Venetian, by name Geronimo Veroneo.*

Shah Jahan's mysterious Taj Mahal attributed to Italian genius! Surely, Manrique must be mistaken. But no: "The Emperor . . . paid [Veroneo] a very high salary . . . . Fame, the swift conveyor of good and evil news, had spread the story that the Mogul summoned him and informed him of his desire to erect a great and sumptuous tomb for his dead wife, and he was required to draw up some designs for imperial inspection. The architect Veroneo carried out this order, and within a few days proved the great skill he had in his art by producing several models of the most beautiful architecture."

No other writer, no other source credits the Italian Veroneo with being the master mind behind the Taj Mahal; at best he is mentioned in passing as a jeweler or goldsmith, and not as an architect at all. Could the Portuguese friar be right? Inscrutable shadows were falling across Hindustan and its symbolic mausoleum. Ultimate answers would be provided for the twin enigma of empire and tomb, but not yet.

● ● ●

Aside from death-inspired Mogul architecture and politics, the seeds of India's future had been sprouting healthily over three decades of Shah Jahan's reign. Portuguese enterprise in Mogul territory had long since fallen on evil days, and as early as 1631 (the year of Mumtaz Mahal's death) the emperor had engaged in violent suppression of the troublesome Portuguese colony at Hughli in Bengal. But Portugal still remained a force in Goa. The English had by contrast prospered under Shah Jahan, who true to his word had been their protector ever since Sir Thomas Roe's embassy so many years ago. By 1647 the East India Company could count no less than twenty-three English employees. At Surat, a visiting Holstein nobleman named John Albert de Mandelslo found the foreign colony playing darts and enjoying an English table, while Peter Mundy had himself scribbled mention of wheat bread, beef, and mutton prepared by English cooks, and Indian delights of kedgeree and pickled mangoes. As an exotic touch, Englishmen wore turbans and white linen coats; but they pulled on Western breeches, belted their daggers, and always rode horseback. They watched; they did not consciously wait to seize an empire, but they felt confident of their power. They needed confidence, and one day in the not-too-distant future they would need something more than daggers: Moguls and Englishmen would yet cross swords.

● ● ●

Now, from 1652 onward, Shah Jahan remained almost constantly in Delhi. In January 1654, an attempt was made on his life in open court. But the would-be assassin reeled from a blow in the chest by police chief Naubat Khan's baton; and on trying again to ascend to the throne, he was hacked to pieces by a grandee's sword. That same year, Dara Shikoh's eldest son Sulaiman married a Rajput princess. Grandfather Shah Jahan might soon become a *great* grandfather!

More and more, the emperor relied on the crown prince. It was the interlude before chaos, a period during which Dara found himself uplifted to the highest regal honors. On Saturday, February 3, 1655, he appeared at durbar in a special robe of honor conferred by Shah Jahan: his vest was gold-embroidered, his collar studded with a fortune in diamonds, his sleeves and skirts sewn with endless pearls. The occasion actually coincided with the emperor's sixty-sixth lunar birthday; but after the imperial weighing, Shah Jahan formally removed a turban fillet set with a great ruby and two wide strings of seed pearls, and attached it to the prince's head. Pointedly he addressed Dara by a new title, Shah Buland Iqbala, which formerly had been bestowed upon Shah Jahan himself by Jahangir in days of princely glory. Dara was now requested to occupy a golden chair placed beside the Peacock Throne. Modestly, he hesitated; finally at Shah Jahan's insistence, he sat. In effect, Dara Shikoh had become co-ruler of all India.

Writing later to his spiritual adviser Mulla Shah, Dara recounted the dialogue: "His Majesty said, 'My child, I have made up my mind not to do any important business or decide on any great undertaking henceforth without your knowledge and without consulting you first . . . . I cannot sufficiently thank Allah for blessing me with a son like you."

For the final two years of Shah Jahan's reign Dara Shikoh was to exert preponderant influence on the administration of Mogul India, and only in matters of foreign policy would the emperor still take independent action. For better or worse the fated crown prince had become referee of the political arena; he was being groomed for a throne he would never sit upon. In an autocratic Mogul Empire, such unprecedented influence made Dara the cynosure of anybody and everybody with a need for imperial intercession. If Sir Thomas Roe had arrived in a later India, Dara Shikoh would have been the person to curry favor with; vassal princes and great nobles looked to the crown prince for help; Europeans came to him. Court factions and intrigues were inevitable.

To Dara's eternal credit, he tried to use his power for good ends. But as a philosophical and religious liberal, it stood to reason that he would seek a rapprochement with Hindu Rajputs and antagonize narrowly orthodox Moslems at court. Attempting to reconcile himself with Rajah Jai Singh after their abrasive argument at Kandahar, Dara had encouraged the recent political marriage of his son Sulaiman Shikoh to the rajah's niece. By way of prudent counterbalance, Shah Jahan would, two years later (in October 1656), take the initiative for a second marriage of Sulaiman to a daughter of a Moslem noble—a concession to the feelings of Moslem nobility in general.

Steeped in Hindu thought and translations during the important three years between 1654 and 1657, Dara extended more than a political marriage to the Rajputs: he actively displayed partiality. When Shah Jahan engaged in regional hostilities with the maharana of Udaipur, Dara's insistent mediation prevailed—much to the irritation of Prime Minister Sadullah Khan, who hoped to see the maharana's domains annexed to the Mogul Empire and who had even been sent at the head of a punitive army. Through Dara's intervention the maharana got off with cession of a few miserable land tracts, and was forgiven when he might easily have lost his life; furious, Sadullah Khan had to be content with a bit of demolishing mayhem before withdrawing from Rajput territory. In a letter to Rajput spokesman Jai Singh, Dara wrote: "The particular kindness and love which I bear toward [Hindus] has become manifest. . . . Let it be known to the whole Rajput race to what extent I wish well of them." A sentimentalist, Dara would soon discover how much certain Rajputs reciprocated such noble affections when selfish motives blinded them.

It was now, with Aurangzeb's distant but aggressive Deccan intrigues, that the animosity between Dara and Sadullah Khan became pronounced. Torn between the advice of son and vizier, Shah Jahan felt pained. Dara detested the prime minister's Sunni bigotry, not to mention his capability; rapier thrusts of mutual jealousy and verbal parryings, together with Dara's "arrogance," would soon be recorded in anecdotes told by the crown prince's enemies. When Sadullah Khan died in 1656, malicious gossips would even claim that Dara had poisoned him. Yet the obvious cause was stomach cancer: court chronicles diagnose four months of "painful colic," after which the victim was confined to his house in acute agony. Abrogating the sacred text, "When your time of death has arrived, see that ye defer not a moment, nor procrastinate," Sadullah stubbornly lingered before migrating "from this transitory sphere to the realms of immortality."

But Dara's enmity with the prime minister was far from being Shah Jahan's only pain. Before long the emperor would purportedly observe with unwonted critical acumen: "No doubt the Crown Prince possesses the resources, majesty and pomp of a king; but he appears to be inimical to honest people, being good to the bad, and bad to good men." The remark would go down to history at one remove in a letter of Aurangzeb's; but whoever said it had a point. Credulously, Dara interceded with the emperor to save dubious lives (though significantly he never used his influence to destroy anyone). For sensitive Dara, there could be no greater moral desideratum than the exercise of royal clemency; unable to resist tears, he rescued human crocodiles who took the shape of desperate insurgents and dismissed nobles. In the particular case of a petty noble condemned to death for rebellion, Dara had even intervened at the moment when the man lay splayed for execution on the public platform in front of Delhi's police prefecture. One day, that same man would show his gratitude: he would be Dara's death warrant.

As India headed for the abyss, court factions became more extreme in their struggle for the rudder: Dara and Jahanara steered for the shallows of peace, Aurangzeb and his partisans delighted in the unpredictable eddies of aggression. The course of empire proceeded toward an inevitable War of Succession. For their own dark reasons, Aurangzeb and many other persons in the realm wanted that war. And Dara Shikoh, pacifist and mystic dreamer, would soon be obliged to fight.

● ● ●

Dara could hardly fail to be aware of the powerful forces gathering to prevent his ultimate accession to the throne. But sustained by a mystical optimism that all would yet be well, he deferred practical military plans and alliances; in a philosophical trance he pursued rarefied colloquies with Hindu and Moslem holy men, consorting with strange der-

vishes and searching Hindu scriptures for the "Hidden
Book" alluded to in the Koran. More prosaic friends periodically reminded him of an actively growing entente among
Aurangzeb, Shuja, and Murad—three spiders weaving a
common web. But at best he would spasmodically rally to
use his influence with Shah Jahan for court politics aimed at
curtailing, in particular, Aurangzeb's deep intrigues. Dara
Shikoh was sadly lacking in foresight.

Equally out of touch with reality but in another way,
Shah Jahan indulged in more than the uncritical folly of
shifting responsibility to Dara without firmly guaranteeing
the crown prince's future safety. The emperor now opted for
a frankly escapist tertiary phase of life: little by little, he had
left both ambitious young Prince Khurram and authoritative
middle age behind him, and abandoned himself to strangely
hermetic pursuits. Outwardly he had mellowed with the
years, settling into what promised to be a luxurious old age—
imperial Delhi, summers in Kashmir, or birthday weighings
in gold. John Dryden later encompassed the conventional
decline of three decades in a single couplet:

> So he who in his youth for glory strove
> Would recompense his age with ease and love

—but there were certain facts that Dryden never knew, some
of which seemed more suited to latter-day, under-the-counter
novels than lofty heroic drama. Hindustan's ideal father
figure, benevolent and popular, had become an uncontrolled
hedonist, almost exclusively preoccupied by etiolated esthetic
fancies coupled with sexual indulgences that set tongues wag-
ging even at the sophisticated Mogul court. If burdens of
state interfered with royal pleasure, what could be easier than
a partitioning of imperial authority? Dara managed Delhi
and three other sons governed the major provinces of India,
even though all four had to be kept apart. Indeed, their separation may have been provoked less by the desire to delegate
responsibility and more out of fear: so long as an outburst
was kept at bay, the dread possibility of civil war, of unfilial

ambitions to contest the crown, might somehow never materialize. An aging ostrich buried his head in sands of sensuality.

How far did sensuality go? Keen for court rumors, Niccolo Manucci pens a cynically comic portrait of a licentious sovereign sleeping with whatever woman pleases him, including the wives of his own nobles. When these cuckolding ladies went to court, "mendicants called out in loud voices to Jafar Khan's wife: 'O Breakfast of Shah Jahan! Remember us!' And when the wife of Khalilullah Khan went by they shouted: 'O Luncheon of Shah Jahan! Succor us!' "

The emperor's excesses of concupiscence even included voyeurism: "For the greater satisfaction of his lusts, Shah Jahan ordered the erection of a large hall, twenty cubits long and eight cubits wide, adorned throughout with great mirrors . . . so that he might obscenely observe himself and his favorite women. It would seem as if the only thing Shah Jahan cared for was the search for women to serve his pleasure."

Lasciviousness now reached a frenetic pitch, together with an opulent imperial greed that took pleasure in subterranean gloatings over gold and precious gems. Even if much of European gossip is discounted, there remains the image of a voluptuary soon to have fire poured over his head.

Scattered events precede the climax. Early in 1655, we find Shah Jahan stopping for three days at Akbar's deserted city of Fatehpur Sikri. "The world is a bridge, pass over it, but do not build upon it"—did he read Akbar's inscription again? And he spends a day in Agra, visiting the Taj Mahal by boat. Then Delhi again, for a year. In December of 1656, a plague struck the capital, forcing emperor and court to withdraw to the hunting precincts of Garh Mukteshwar along the banks of the Ganges. But restlessness brought them back in less than a month; and with the plague still continuing, they migrated again along the Jumna River about a hundred miles north of Delhi. This was Mukhlispur, Shah Jahan's summer retreat in the foothills of the Sirmur range, but accessible by boat; he had long since built imperial pal-

aces here for Dara and himself, renaming the place Faizabad.

Now, in Faizabad, came the great terdecennial ceremony commemorating his thirty years of rule. Mogul court
chronicles, written at the emperor's command, yielded a volume devoted to each decade; three decades together constituted an epoch, numerically fortuitous. It was an important
and solemn event, summarizing a prosperous regency whose
wonders included the Peacock Throne, the Kohinoor diamond, and all those architectural masterworks in white marble. No other Oriental empire boasted such wealth; though
Shah Jahan's military ventures at Kandahar and in the trans-
Oxus had come to nothing, Mogul boundaries within the
subcontinent itself had extended beyond any previous emperor's domains. More important, India was internally at
peace, and even the pauper masses enjoyed relative protection from rapacious provincial governors. Competent nobles
augmented imperial judiciousness, and the court had become
a marvel of Eastern culture.

Yet an underlying note soured the occasion, a sense of
impending disaster that could not be shaken off. Partly it was
the sheer passage of time: the last act is always tragic, however happy the prelude. Prime Minister Sadullah Khan had
succumbed the year before; important grandees and old
friends were also disappearing. And now, in this very springtime of 1657, the first peer of the realm died—Persian noble
Ali Mardan Khan. Shah Jahan himself was in his sixty-sixth
year, and felt it. Though no one talked about the future, the
unspoken question was: what would happen when the emperor died? He himself had occasionally discussed the future
with intimates, and prognostications were gloomy. Friction
among four princes had been avoided only by their geographical separation; the bitter feud between Dara and
Aurangzeb still constituted the principal gossip of empire.
Private forebodings anticipated civil war.

The roving court returned to Delhi. Then came September 6, 1657—the date when all the years added up to a tragic
total.

Elliptically, Mogul court chronicles reported: "The Emperor was attacked with serious illness in the form of strangury." It is too vague; how can euphemism hide the truth? Scandal will out. "The Mogul," François Bernier's French candor asserts, "was seized with a disorder the nature of which it were unbecoming to describe. Suffice it to state that it was disgraceful to a man of his age, who, instead of wasting, ought to have been careful to preserve the remaining vigor of his constitution."

The colossal Mogul Empire, brought to crisis by Shah Jahan's sexual indulgence! Years later, the lawyer-traveler Gemelli Careri would dig up corroborative gossip: Shah Jahan became "desperately amorous of a Moorish young woman. His unruly passion prevailing, he gave himself up entirely to her, beyond what became his age . . ." But the sordid details could only be supplied by Niccolo Manucci, at that moment very much on the Delhi scene: "I was then in the service of Prince Dara. Shah Jahan brought this illness on himself . . . he wanted still to enjoy himself like a youth, and with this intent took different stimulating drugs. These brought on a retention of urine for three days, and he was almost at death's door." Shah Jahan the Magnificent, a victim of aphrodisiacs!

Strangury or retention of urine; and the court chronicles innocently add constipation and other symptoms. For a week the royal physicians work over him; his legs swell up, his palate and tongue grow dry, fever comes intermittently. He takes no food or nourishment, and medicine does not help. No one has access to him now except Dara Shikoh and a few officials. Shah Jahan is already given up for dead, but we know he will not die—not yet, not for nine years more, not until every last horror has been visited upon him. Somehow, on September 14, he rallies to show himself at the *jharoka* window to great crowds. But the damage has been done, Hindustan is already in full alarm. Lies and rumors are spreading like cancer: the emperor is supposedly dead; those appearances at the window are impersonations by an old eunuch; official dispatches from court to allay Murad, Shuja, and Aurangzeb are dismissed as forgeries or Dara's post-poning inventions.

No one can prevent the ghoulish conflict that will split an empire at the seams: demons or gods have been invoked, Krishna propels the war chariot and the crescent of Islam be-comes a scimitar. Abruptly the protagonists emerge from shadowy Mogul chronicle and innuendo, thrust into the glare of reality. This is India's War of Succession, without exagger-ation an almost Shakespearean tragedy: uncannily, Shah Jahan will now resemble King Lear howling half-demented on the heath; Aurangzeb will exceed Richard III; Dara Shi-koh will parallel Hamlet; Jahanara will become Cordelia; and Raushanara and Gauharara will take on the colors of Regan and Goneril. On and on the infernal machine will un-wind, through crisis after crisis of towering implication involving not only Shah Jahan and his children but their chil-dren and their children's children and millions of anonymous participants. When a concatenation of ruin begins, nothing can stop it.

Part III

THE WAR
OF SUCCESSION

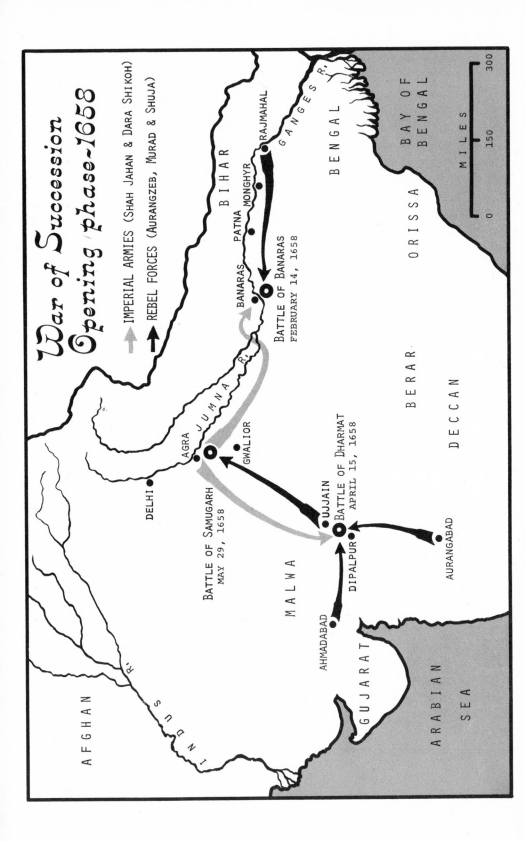

War of Succession
Opening phase~1658

→ IMPERIAL ARMIES (SHAH JAHAN & DARA SHIKOH)
→ REBEL FORCES (AURANGZEB, MURAD & SHUJA)

AFGHAN

INDUS R.

DELHI

AGRA

JUMNA R.

GWALIOR

BATTLE OF SAMUGARH
MAY 29, 1658

MALWA

AHMADABAD

GUJARAT

DIPALPUR

UJJAIN
BATTLE OF DHARMAT
APRIL 15, 1658

AURANGABAD

BERAR

DECCAN

ARABIAN
SEA

BIHAR

BANARAS
PATNA
MONGHYR
RAJMAHAL

BATTLE OF BANARAS
FEBRUARY 14, 1658

GANGES R.

BENGAL

ORISSA

BAY OF
BENGAL

MILES

0   150   300

CHAPTER 12

Reign or Die

LIKE OTHER AMBIGUOUS events in world history, India's great War of Succession has submitted to endless analysis over three centuries. What were the real causes of the disaster—political, psychological?

Most scholars lay heavy blame on Shah Jahan, insisting that he could have prevented or postponed the war if he had acted with authority immediately following his illness. Admittedly he succumbed to a weird inner paralysis while events swirled about him, and even seems to have unconsciously abetted the tragedy—men who live by power sooner or later reach that awful emasculating moment when judgment or grasp weakens, and downfall begins.

But more damaging than Shah Jahan's imminent transformation into King Lear were the fatal errors which no young Lear could have committed: the emperor had himself set up a classic situation of paternal favoritism. Shuja, Aurangzeb, and Murad had been given ample opportunity to choke on their spleen, watching Dara Shikoh heaped with robes of honor, privileges, and titles, sitting in a golden chair in their father's presence. Outcasts from the esthetics of the court, they had been relegated to distant territories and thankless campaigns, while Dara remained the pampered artistic prince at the superbly mannered court. Dara's military achievements had been negligible, yet he commanded more cavalry than all three of his brothers combined. To add insult to injury, Dara's sons also ranked high: twenty-two-year-old

Sulaiman Shikoh was now absentee viceroy of the Afghan province, and even thirteen-year-old Sipihr Shikoh enjoyed a command of horse exceeding Shuja's or Aurangzeb's eldest sons. Dara Shikoh was showered with jewels and elephants; Dara Shikoh's servants became noble khans; Dara Shikoh's galaxy of fakirs, poets, and musicians received the emperor's generous patronage.

Nevertheless, it is not entirely true that indiscriminate love of Dara was the major factor precipitating the War of Succession. Short of suicidally partitioning the empire to display equal love, any approach to the problem of a successor would have created difficulties for Shah Jahan: the slightest partiality in any direction could only have stirred up a hornet's nest of jealousy, hatred, and intrigue. Candidly the emperor had chosen the most lovable of four sons, who was also the eldest and therefore the logical heir to India's crown—a cultured aristocrat, openly tolerant of disparate religions, and liberal to a fault. In elevating Dara beyond competition, Shah Jahan had evidently intended to avoid posthumous civil war by stressing the succession of the crown prince as a virtual *fait accompli* and buttressing him with military strength.

The real trouble lay in the choice—Dara Shikoh was the right choice but for the wrong reasons. By the most charitable assessment, it seems doubtful whether an intellectual mystic, credulous and trusting, could ever have ruled seventeenth-century India: Dara's was a hopeless combination of talents in a vulgar world of force. Even so, his imperial qualifications certainly exceeded those of Murad or Shuja; and while Aurangzeb clearly possessed both military genius and administrative capability, his personal pathology was already casting a dark shadow over the Mogul Empire. Whatever his defects, Dara Shikoh would never have alienated a Hindu majority by turning back the clock of history and insisting on converting a polyreligious subcontinent into a rigidly Islamic state. Just possibly, Dara as emperor might even have inspired a religious fusion great enough to alter the entire future course of Indian history. No one will ever know.

[196]

In any event, the Moguls were now to become victims of their own created world. Behind Shah Jahan's actions, or the contrasting characters of his sons, or the partisanship of spinster sisters and Moslem and Hindu nobles, the extraordinary empire fashioned and vivified by Mogul genius had acquired unpredictable autonomy, and the power to turn masters into puppets. In effect, not so much the passive Indian masses (who had endured and would yet endure so much) but the privileged principals themselves were trapped in an insular nightmare that allowed little if any freedom of royal choice. Too much was arbitrary, too much inbred. Forbidden to marry, the three princesses had been impelled to those quasi-incestuous attachments which would soon dictate their loyalties; strict etiquette made Jahanara first lady of the realm, a position of prominence which had only provoked sisterly envy and added further fuel to conflict. As Mogul princes, Shah Jahan's four sons had every reason to expect that they would be favored with high rank and great provinces to govern, regardless of their capabilities or limitations; rank they had gotten and provinces they governed, but all subject to their father's rebuke or favoritism, while he himself was fearful of threats to his absolute power. Within the rigid framework of unquestioned regal absolutism, Moslem and Hindu nobles of the realm must now align themselves for political or religious motives; and though *they* at least were cynically free to switch sides at critical moments, even betrayals had long since been conditioned by the peculiarities of this very strange society.

Still, other despotic governments endured much longer; why was the Mogul Empire destined to collapse so soon? Pharaonic Egypt spanned millennia, and Turkey's Ottoman Empire would somehow survive until the twentieth century. The ultimate answer lay in India's heterogeneous peoples, since Hindus would yet challenge Moslem supremacy. But immediate disaster could only be triggered by the Moguls themselves: these conquerors had come from beyond the subcontinent, bringing a particular kind of Islamic monarchy

[197]

with them—the notoriously unstable inverted pyramid of Eastern absolutism.

The marvel was that the Mogul Empire had kept its balance for 131 long years, since in its essence the entire structure of autocracy rested on a single geometric point—the cult of the emperor himself. His death or mere absence from the *jharoka* window became a prelude to chaos. Worst of all, Islam had never established any rules for hereditary monarchy within its religious purlieus; there was no recognized primogeniture, no really clear-cut line of succession from Baghdad to Ispahan or Delhi. Usurpation or arbitration by the sword had plagued more than one Moslem dominion.

From their central Asian ancestors, Mogul princes in particular had inherited a turbulent spirit of rebellion and an implicit belief in the survival of the fittest—a fitness based in the last analysis on cunning, treachery, or sheer brute force. In a widening pattern of aggression, imperial sons turned on imperial fathers: Jahangir had revolted against Akbar, and both Khusrau and Shah Jahan had challenged Jahangir.

Yet in the struggle to reach the throne, no Mogul had actually murdered members of his own family until Shah Jahan set the black seal of precedent by disposing of all his collaterals. No one had forgotten the crime, least of all his sons. The bitter example of their own family history would sooner or later have driven Dara and Shuja and Aurangzeb and Murad to contend for the Peacock Throne with desperate fury. Court manners, outward etiquette, and the Persian veneer of culture had become more elaborate over the years, but blood was now no thicker than water in a ruthless scramble for power. The stake was more even than India, it was life itself—crown or coffin, no alternative existed. Beneath all the political and psychological complexities of the subcontinent, one thing was certain: the War of Succession would quickly degenerate into unavoidable fratricide. Four princes could only kill or be killed.

● ● ●

The immediate impact of Shah Jahan's illness was felt in Delhi. Daily durbar stopped abruptly, worshipping *darshan-*

iyas waited in vain for his dawn appearance on the balcony of the Red Fort, and all but a handful of trusted nobles found themselves denied entry to the palace. Speculation had the emperor dead already, with Dara suppressing the truth until he had secured the throne for himself. By Manucci's eye-witness report, "this confusion lasted in the city for three days and three nights, the shops remaining shut, and there being a scarcity of supplies." Manucci even claims that Shah Jahan ordered the Red Fort closed except for two wickets. Mistrusting Moslem khans, the emperor presumably placed thirty thousand Rajputs on guard under two Rajput nobles, Rajah Jaswant Singh of Jodhpur and Jai Singh's young son, Ram Singh of Jaipur State; only Dara and a retinue of ten nobles could enter twice a day, while even Jahanara and the servants had to swear their faith on the Koran to allay imperial fears of being poisoned.*

For Dara Shikoh, the emperor's prostration abruptly and belatedly crystallized the full reality of his peril. Now at last, the crown prince was frankly afraid and with obvious good reason: Shuja, Aurangzeb, and Murad were virtually independent sovereigns in powerful segments of the empire; they had armies behind them, they commanded considerable sources of revenue, and they were united by the most dangerous of all human emotions—jealousy. In a Mogul Empire where few intrigues could be kept secret, Dara and his supporters surely knew that five years ago the three princes had even informally agreed to a mutual defense pact against him; the beloved heir apparent constituted the enemy. It took no great deduction to pinpoint the active member of the conspiracy: Aurangzeb. In December 1652, Aurangzeb had openly met with Shuja when both were visiting Delhi; much to Shah Jahan's displeasure, each had entertained the other in his house for three days, cementing brotherly friendship by an intrafamilial betrothal of daughter and son. Later in

---

* His twentieth-century translator comments wittily: "Manucci's readiness to see poison everywhere may be attributed, perhaps, to his Italian origin."

the same month, Aurangzeb had contrived to meet with Murad while passing through Malwa province, on the threshold of the Deccan. Since then, the triumvirate had intermittently corresponded by letter.

Dara's initial response to the crisis of Shah Jahan's illness would prove revealing: quite simply he dreaded assuming authority; perhaps he had been dreading it for years. Militarily deficient, he had only the unsuccessful siege of Kandahar behind him; sheltered by Shah Jahan, Hindustan's mystical co-ruler had endlessly deferred the thought of what would happen when his father died. Reflecting obvious panic, his first act now became another form of deferral: he would prevent any news of the emperor from reaching his three brothers. Shuja, Aurangzeb, and Murad all had agents representing them at Delhi; wangling their pledge of silence pending the outcome of Shah Jahan's illness, Dara simultaneously clamped down on any letters or messengers destined for Bengal, Gujarat, or the Deccan.

Despite these precautions, rumor continued to spread like bush fire. Manucci tells us that the agents at court (apparently ignoring their pledges) "wrote . . . in haste to the princes about the King's illness, whereupon every one of the sons began to plan and prepare his army." Even Delhi's cautious moneylenders transmitted dire gossip through metaphoric correspondence: "Let it be known to your worship that the vessel of butter was filled to overflowing, and the butter in it was lost." Everyone believed Shah Jahan dead. Dara's censorship of news actually aggravated the situation, making Shuja, Aurangzeb, Murad, and all their attendant military nobles assume that the worst had already happened. With official news cut off, reports smuggled out of Delhi mingled truth with lies. Partisans of the three absent princes had good reason to exaggerate, hoping their favorite would take advantage of the crisis before it became too late: if Shah Jahan was not dead, he was surely dying. Now, for the first time, Mogul chronicles mention rapacious Raushanara Begum as "guarding" Aurangzeb's interests against Dara's; and it takes no great imagination to see her intriguing in the harem, putting her ear to marble grillwork, slipping a letter full of state secrets to some trusted eunuch. Gauharara likewise kept Murad abreast of events at court.

From a compendium of official Mogul reports, the damage seems to have become extensive within two months of Shah Jahan's collapse. By early November, most of India knew that a civil war was imminent which promised to exceed all Mogul revolts of the past. Aside from Aurangzeb's abiding hatred of Dara, there were practical indications of the intense struggle to come: never before had rival claimants enjoyed such power or commanded such resources; Jahangir's revolt against Akbar, or Shah Jahan's own bid for power against the machinations of Nur Jahan, seemed anemic by comparison.

With the central symbol of power apparently dead or dying, Mogul officers in distant provinces wondered what to do in the absence of orders. Iconoclasts had a field day, upheavals shook country districts, peasants balked over land assessments, tax collectors crossed swords with local governors, and even frontier incidents broke out in the northeast.

From the moment they received news of Shah Jahan's illness, the "triumvirate" burst into active penmanship. First Murad and Aurangzeb, in the middle of October, simultaneously revived their friendship by letter, each commenting guardedly on Shah Jahan's illness. These dispatches went by confidential messengers, and were augmented by oral communications that can only be guessed at. As early as October 19, Murad was writing to Shuja (via Aurangzeb) proposing an alliance; Aurangzeb added a plea of his own to the same effect, and sent both missives onward to Bengal.

Relay runners speeded the correspondence, some of which has been preserved for history. By the end of November, Murad had posted two men every ten miles from his provincial seat at Ahmadabad to the frontier of the Deccan. Aurangzeb's own relay took over from there, bringing documents to Aurangabad and then carrying on the chain of communication to the boundaries of Orissa, where Shuja's men transmitted material to Bengal. Aurangzeb's communiqués to both brothers show careful respect. In a letter to Shuja, he suggests an exchange of representatives: each of the three brothers should send confidential agents to the courts of the other two, thus helping to mesh their plans. A later message to Shuja (when matters were more in the open) specifically urged that "if the enemy attacks only one of us, the other two should try to prevent him." In a final note, Aurangzeb bluntly warned Shuja not to be taken in by any conciliatory offers from Dara.

Their entente with Shuja suffered from the great distance to Bengal and poor roads; but Aurangzeb and Murad communicated more effectively, and the exchange was indeed enlightening. Impatient by nature, Murad nonetheless looked to his elder brother for clues to action, but Aurangzeb in those first weeks continued to move with utmost caution. Action against Dara Shikoh must await clarification of the situation in Delhi; besides, another plot had to be fostered very discreetly: the gradual alienation of Murad from Shuja as well as from Dara. Early on, Aurangzeb sent his younger brother a secret code for future communiqués. Eager for a sense of direction, Murad rebuked every temporary silence: "Delay in correspondence at this juncture is improper." Later he became more persistent: "As the exchange of news is one condition of our pact, I beg you to let me know what you have learned from spiritual and temporal sources." Aurangzeb prudently replied, "I understand that the influence of the enemy in administration, transfers and appointments has attained undesirable proportions. He is now trying to collect treasure and an army . . . . We should be very cautious at this time, and not write anything undesirable in our letters."

The triumvirate plan emerges clearly enough, along with Aurangzeb's deeper strategy. When the time was ripe, Shuja was to lead his soldiers from Bengal, Murad was to link his Gujarat forces with Aurangzeb's army of the Deccan, and all three were to conjoin for a concerted march on the capital. With Shah Jahan dead, the justification of war against Dara

Shikoh could be religious: Dara was a heretic, an apostate from orthodox Islam who cohorted with Hindu mystics, Christians, and dangerously unorthodox Sufi fakirs; Dara wore rings with Hindu inscriptions, and his writings betrayed kaffir leanings. Hardly the most religious person in the Mogul Empire, Murad naïvely agreed to this smokescreen: "I am ready to advance," he wrote; "inform me of your wishes and I shall act accordingly." Aurangzeb's "wishes" were for irreligious Murad to pose as an orthodox Moslem and champion of Islam. Privately to Murad, he also denounced Shuja's heretical leanings: Shuja was a professed Shia, the hated Islamic sect of Persia.

Not entirely gullible, Murad seems to have had some suspicions of Aurangzeb's dissimulating intentions, and pressed for a clear and solemn pact. This was finally given in writing just before the two conjoined some months later for their famous march into north India. Linked with Murad against "idolatry and infidelity," Aurangzeb swore by "God and the Prophet as witnesses" that Murad would receive in booty the Punjab, Afghanistan, Kashmir, and Sind—in effect the whole western part of Mogul India.

● ● ●

Back in Delhi, Shah Jahan rallied somewhat after the first week of his illness, took mint-and-manna soup, and even pulled himself to the *jharoka* window on September 14 to prove to the swelling crowds that he was still alive. In gratitude to Allah the usual alms were distributed, prisoners were released, and Dara received promotions and rewards for his ministrations. Still very weak, the emperor did not appear again to the public for a full month—not until mid-October. But state papers flowed into his bedroom, and firmans went out in his name with the royal seal stamped on them.

Without a doubt, Dara Shikoh loved Shah Jahan: the French jeweler Tavernier would later depict a devoted crown prince sleeping beside the royal sick bed "on a carpet spread on the floor." Even prejudiced Mogul sources acknowledged that "Dara tended and nursed his father beyond the utmost limit of possibility." Obliged to manage state affairs, he still persisted in acting only as imperial proxy; he alone, of all four brothers, was not eager to assume the crown.

In spite of improvement, Shah Jahan felt decidedly moribund. Convoking confidential nobles and chief state officers, he now formally nominated Dara as his successor, instructing them to obey his eldest son "in everything, at all times, and in every place." Dara was counseled to strive to please God; the masses of India and the Mogul army were his to command.

Certainty of death turned the emperor's attention to death's monument: the Taj Mahal. His doctors had suggested a change of air; he would go now to Agra and die in sight of the tomb, rich in the memory of Mumtaz Mahal. By October 18 Shah Jahan was well enough to leave Delhi, proceeding by slow stages and reaching a place called Sami Ghat on the Jumna River six miles above Agra fort. It was now November 5, 1657. He felt so much better that he gave up medicine, waiting by the advice of astrologers until the auspicious twenty-sixth of the month for his entry into the old capital. A state barge carried him down river in a procession that could hardly have failed to move emperor and bystander alike. Three decades of rule over all India coalesced in great crowds of people lining the river banks for many miles, to gaze once more on their beloved ruler. Prayers and blessings filled the air with a buzz of benediction as he made his way to Dara's mansion. From there, nine days later, Shah Jahan entered Agra Fort and held durbar. He would never go back to Delhi, to Shahjahanabad with its white marble palaces and cusped arches, its inscriptions boasting "Paradise on earth." Agra was his last stop—its fort his confinement and purgatory, its mausoleum his hope of heaven. Wanly, he would start for Delhi in late April 1658, in springtime; but the journey would be aborted, and he would turn back to Agra for those final years of unremitting horror.

● ● ●

Even before Shah Jahan left Delhi, events had been

moving swiftly. From mid-September 1657 until May 1658, Dara Shikoh spent eight months attempting vainly to divert a tidal wave of disaster. By the time news of the emperor's recovery reached the three brothers in their provinces, it was already too late: both Shuja and Murad had proclaimed themselves emperor, though Aurangzeb significantly took no such precipitate action. Before mid-November, Shuja had stamped his name on coins of Bengal, announced that Dara had poisoned the emperor, and proceeded to march on Agra in spite of Shah Jahan's own letter assuring his good health. By December 5, Murad had also struck coins in his name at Ahmadabad, caused the bidding prayer to be recited in mosques in his honor, and assaulted and looted the lucrative port of Surat. Only Aurangzeb played an ominous waiting game. No amount of persuasion from court could convince the triumvirate that Shah Jahan's letters were other than suave forgeries—not even the pleas of Jahanara, who now tried desperately to make peace among her brothers. They declined an olive branch: they were ready for total war.

It would be easy to underscore Dara's lack of purpose during these critical months; holding the reins of government, he still needlessly consulted Shah Jahan. But Dara had also keenly foreseen a number of imperatives as early as mid-September, and did in fact take independent action. His actual weakness lay in his underlying panic, which prompted breach-the-hole tactics rather than a carefully planned strategy.

For one thing, every certain partisan or confidante of Aurangzeb had to be stalemated or recalled to the capital. In this context, the most dangerous focal point for intrigue was the new prime minister; unfortunately, in the aftermath of Aurangzeb's recent war with Bijapur, the devious Mir Jumla was actually in the Deccan at that very moment. No matter, he had to be removed from office; this Dara was able to effect by the end of September. Orders also went out from Dara to a slew of important nobles still in the Deccan under

Aurangzeb's nominal command: Mahabat Khan,* Rajput chiefs, Mir Jumla himself, and other outstanding veterans were ordered to return to court with the Moslem and Rajput troops they had taken to the Deccan as reinforcements for Aurangzeb's army. Mir Jumla did not return, for reasons which will soon enough become clear; but Mahabat Khan and others obeyed their summons, abandoned Aurangzeb without so much as a by-your-leave, and proceeded to Agra for an audience with Shah Jahan on December 20. Mahabat Khan received a robe of honor for his loyalty, and was made governor of the Afghan province of Kabul—his father's old stamping grounds.

Concomitant with these independent actions by Dara, Shah Jahan also promoted Dara's apparently loyal friends and followers. Khalilullah Khan (later to be a traitor) became governor of Delhi; and a certain Qasim Khan now came to the foreground, soon to be appointed to supersede Murad as governor of Gujarat. Bihar province (contiguous with Shuja's state of Bengal) was assigned to Dara Shikoh, and there was so much contemplated reshuffling of other territorial commands that rumors flew from court: even Malwa province would yet be taken away from Murad, while Aurangzeb would lose the district of Berar. Such news could hardly fail to alarm an already apprehensive triumvirate, and may well have impelled both Shuja and Murad to crown themselves prematurely.

With Shah Jahan recovered by mid-November, Dara confided the most urgent problem to his father: Shuja had invested himself with imperial prerogatives and was advancing from Bengal. The emperor agreed to send a deterring army led by Rajah Jai Singh of Jaipur State; but since only princes could negotiate with princes, Dara's eldest son, twenty-two-year-old Sulaiman Shikoh, accordingly had to be placed under Jai Singh's tutelage. Together with thousands of cavalrymen, the Rajput commander and his princely ward left

---

* Not to be confused with the Mahabat Khan of Jahangir's reign and Shah Jahan's early years of kingship, who had died of a fistula in 1633. This was his son.

Agra on November 30 (and would later encounter Shuja on Valentine's day 1658 near Banaras). Shah Jahan seemed not very worried: he considered the venture a military outing for Sulaiman; Dara, more emotional, unwisely deprived himself of some of his best officers to sustain his son.

Having barely dispatched the expedition against Shuja, emperor and crown prince now received the official news of Murad's self-crowning in Gujarat. A letter went out to Murad, ostensibly from Shah Jahan, immediately transferring him to Berar, which happened to be one of Aurangzeb's provinces. But complotters would not fall out so easily, and Murad defied imperial orders.

Dara remained agonizingly in the dark about Aurangzeb's intentions, since the viceroy of the Deccan had not yet committed any overt act of disloyalty nor made any known preparations for war. Further cloaking his intentions, Aurangzeb had effectively cut off any communication Dara might hope for from allies or friends in mid-India. But if the court was mystified by Aurangzeb, *he* followed Dara's every action through Raushanara Begum, and also had secret agents who managed to smuggle news across the Narmada River that separated the Deccan from the north. Yet for all of Aurangzeb's precautions, Dara knew that he was allied with Shuja and Murad, and was busily scheming with court nobles and military officers sympathetic to him. By early December, urgent imperial directives went out to the last remaining generals in the Deccan, summarily recalling them to court. Between December 18 and 26, two additional imperial armies were dispatched, this time in the direction of Malwa province: one force had orders to prevent Aurangzeb from marching northward, while the other received instructions to kick the defiant Murad out of Gujarat.

With no imperial prince to command them, it was far from easy to find leaders for either army. Most court nobles flatly declined: they would defend Shah Jahan or Dara in person and to the death, but froze in horror at the thought of shedding princely blood on their own responsibility. One Rajput, Jaswant Singh of Jodhpur, finally agreed to fight Aurangzeb and bring him back a prisoner. Accordingly Jaswant Singh was made governor of Malwa, replacing Malwa's present governor, Shaista Khan—who moreover had served under Aurangzeb in the Deccan and seemed too intimate with both Aurangzeb and Murad. The assessment proved accurate: Shaista Khan found himself recalled to court, where he secretly abetted Aurangzeb's cause. The second loyalist army fell to the command of Qasim Khan, who now indeed became governor of Gujarat to replace Murad. Both armies, like the one which had already gone on expedition against Shuja, received instructions to avoid shedding imperial blood; if the princes could not be persuaded to turn back then force might be used, but they were not to be killed except in dire emergency.

By January 1658, somewhat belatedly, Aurangzeb had shown his hand. He had arrested Prime Minister Mir Jumla in the Deccan, seizing his property, troops, and artillery! On the surface, Aurangzeb probably covered the gesture with a dispatch to court accusing Mir Jumla of treason, but Dara couldn't be fooled. As a matter of fact, Dara *could* be fooled: the Mir Jumla plot was deeper than that. In any event, further concealment of Aurangzeb's intent became impossible: his vanguard army had started to move on January 25, 1658.

Absurdly enough, all three rebel princes now invoked a ridiculous explanation for what was clearly a military assault. Jointly they insisted that their actions did not signify rebellion; they only wanted to see Shah Jahan with their own eyes, as proof that their father was still alive. Afterward, if he *were* alive, they would meekly return to their provinces. After all (it was Murad who had raised this argument in one of his letters) hadn't Murad and Aurangzeb come posthaste to the capital when Jahanara was burned? Everyone knew that Dara Shikoh could imitate Shah Jahan's handwriting, and Dara of course had access to the imperial seal. In further rationale, the brothers argued that either Shah Jahan was dead or else helpless—an invalid in Dara's power. As for reassuring letters from their own agents at court, who could believe such letters when the agents themselves had already been restrained and literally imprisoned? Whatever they now wrote could only be under compulsion and at Dara's dictation.

The camouflage was needless, and deceived no one. It becomes interesting only because of their need to justify what really constituted more than an attack on "apostate" Dara: they were engaged in the unholy battle of wresting power from their own father while he was still alive. Just how far obsessive self-justification would go will become evident in Aurangzeb's later weird epistolary duel with Shah Jahan himself.

Nothing could check the tide of disaster now—not Shah Jahan, not Jahanara, nobody. No diplomat could dicker with events; no intrigue or dissimulation could hold back the elemental hatred that spilled over like a cauldron of molten lead. It was too late. Only Mumtaz Mahal herself, the mother of the four sons, could possibly have stopped them; but she was dead and in her tomb. Destroy or be destroyed; from four corners of the empire, which now threatened to become the most gigantic mausoleum of all, four protagonists moved to meet their fate: sensualist, black sheep, puritan, and mystic. Three were doomed.

CHAPTER 13

An Invasion of Cobras

Several years before the War of Succession, a bizarre and disturbing incident had occurred in Shuja's province of Bengal. Outside of his capital city of Rajmahal, which was situated just above the delta of the Ganges, a mass of cobras suddenly appeared one morning at eight o'clock. By Manucci's report, this undulating army materialized in a plain a league and a half broad. Large and small specimens "covered the field and moved from west to east until four o'clock in the afternoon, looking like ripples on the ocean. In the greatest fright, the inhabitants of villages climbed upon the tops of their houses and upon trees. They beheld moving in the midst of the said cobras one of great size, which carried on its head another smaller one, entirely white. [The snakes] pursued their way without harming anyone."

When Shuja wrote to Shah Jahan about the phenomenon, the emperor's fatuous astrologers offered a sanguinely symbolic interpretation: "the wickedness of the empire was taking its departure, and . . . he would survive for many prosperous years." Somewhat more realistic but equally mistaken, Shuja's own stargazers predicted rebellion in the realm, with their patron becoming emperor. Obviously, they said, the small white cobra carried upon the head of the larger serpent was really king of the cobras; having come to the end of his reign, he was compelled to leave his old abode.

The real meaning of the cobras would become apparent.

Something autochthonous and implacable, spawned by India, was now on the move.

● ● ●

News of Shah Jahan's illness, together with the rumors of his death, had reached Mohammed Shuja in Rajmahal. This was a crisis important enough to rouse the prince from his habitual torpor; in fact he lost no time, being first of the rebel brothers to crown himself emperor under the bombastic title of "Abul Fauz Nasiruddin Mohammed, Timur III, Alexander II, Shah Shuja Bahadur Ghazi." The "Alexander" touch was not really megalomaniac: actual or presumptive Eastern potentates loved to string out compound names, as though the mere echo of past conquerors could enhance their aura and invoke power. Further legitimizing his intentions, Shuja had the bidding prayer read in his name in Bengal's mosques, and new coins were minted to celebrate the occasion. All that stood in the way of actuality were three brothers and a father!

Whether or not Shuja's self-crowning constituted a repudiation of his alliance with Aurangzeb and Murad is open to question. Some accounts assume that by declaring himself emperor he had in effect abrogated the triumvirate's entente, while others claim that he still acted in concert with his younger brothers. The few of their letters which escaped oblivion offer no clear-cut indication of just how far the triple alliance extended. But Shuja in any case was shrewd enough to realize that verbal or written agreement meant next to nothing when the issue was throne or tomb. Indeed, both his present and subsequent actions strongly indicate that he was only being practical, angling to make the best deal to spare his life.

An indolent Shuja could hardly have felt as strongly as Aurangzeb about Dara's exalted position at court; by the evidence, Shuja's attitude to the crown prince only became manifestly hostile when he decided that Dara was intriguing against him. For some time Shuja had wanted the contingent province of Bihar annexed to his Bengal domains, but Dara (probably on the advice of supporters) objected for two reasons: he had no wish to augment Shuja's strength, and even less enthusiasm to share a common frontier with him. When Dara received Bihar for his own governorship on the eve of the War of Succession, Shuja's antagonism flared into action. In frank retaliation he assembled his Bengal troops in November 1657 and sent them smartly westward into Bihar, where their advance could be coordinated with the dispatch of Bengalese war boats up the Ganges (these very likely transported artillery equipment "commanded by Portuguese in his service"). By Manucci's guess, Shuja had forty-five thousand cavalry and considerable infantry.

Shuja's army aimed at holy Banaras, situated on the left bank of the Ganges. Imperial troops invariably took an easy left-bank route between Allahabad and Banaras, where they were then obliged to cross the river and continue along a famous military road running via the rock fortress of Chunagarh to Patna and Shuja's Bengalese capital of Rajmahal. If he reached Banaras first, Shuja could stop his opponents cold simply by holding the river's right bank.

On this, his first campaign of any importance, Dara Shikoh's son Sulaiman was a fantastically handsome boy of twenty-two who happened to be intelligent as well as eager to show his youthful mettle. Sulaiman Shikoh commanded an army of twenty thousand horsemen, several thousand infantry, many elephants, and military supplies. But he was only nominally in command, and had to be duly respectful to his guardian Jai Singh, a Rajput of no little experience. It was an agonizing combination of tortoise and hare: Jai Singh and other high officers proceeded at best with dampened enthusiasm, hesitant to shed the blood of a rebel prince, while Sulaiman was all high spirits and expectant energy. Back in Agra, a dazed Shah Jahan (who still considered his imperial rescripts awesome enough to turn the trick) had cautioned his generals against killing Shuja. More emotional and more aware of real danger, Dara Shikoh had by contrast sanctioned fast, decisive action. Fearful of being damned if they did or didn't, old imperial veterans were cautious and deeply disturbed.

Shortly after the imperial forces began their march from Agra, Shuja had experimented by sending a letter to Shah Jahan and Dara—a vague step toward some kind of political reconciliation. He wanted the fortress of Monghyr in Bihar province; Dara responded with a willingness to concede, provided the fortress would be dismantled and that neither Shuja nor his sons would reside there. But Shuja then seemed to have ignored both Dara's offer and Shah Jahan's sentimental postscript of forgiveness, and followed up this diplomatic straw in the wind by perversely continuing his march.

Both Shuja and Murad seem to have adopted obsessively blind points of view in the Mogul civil war. It is hard to understand why Shuja repudiated an understanding with a father and elder brother far easier to deal with than an implacable Aurangzeb. It would even seem that blockheaded Murad might at some point have realized the extent to which he was being duped. But jealousy had obliterated all reasoning, or it may have been that no one (except perhaps Dara Shikoh) really knew Aurangzeb until it was too late. Shah Jahan himself had succumbed to the addled belief that he was still in authority, when in fact he had been discarded —a spectator castrated by events, swept aside in this suicidal battle for his throne. Sensing his futility, he now railed wrathfully through his mouthpiece, and Dara wrote Jai Singh, "His Majesty desires very much that the severed head of that unmannerly wretch [Shuja] should be brought to him." In case Jai Singh doubted whether the emperor had shifted from caution to blood, Dara added that Shah Jahan had instructed Jai Singh's own son to write to his father in the same vein. Dara's further letters, clearly meant to pep up the old rajah, offered encouraging Sufi visions and astrological forecasts that predicted "great victory."

In manifest disapproval of their joint task, Jai Singh maintained such a stiff and formal attitude to his ward that young Sulaiman Shikoh began to worry, even conveying to court his suspicion of the rajah's integrity. But Sulaiman was briskly rapped on the knuckles by both Shah Jahan and Dara, who affirmed their implicit trust in the rajah by insisting that future news dispatches come from *him*. Undaunted, Sulaiman kept chivvying Jai Singh to make haste; and after a forced march the imperial army reached Banaras, took exactly twenty-four hours to set up a bridge of boats across the Ganges, and promptly crossed to the other side. In the race for the holy city, they had won the first round.

Sulaiman and his army now camped for a week at a village just southeast of Banaras, where they were reinforced and considerably cheered by the arrival of a crackerjack Afghan noble named Dilir Khan. Rebel Prince Shuja had meanwhile turned up with his opposing army and fleet, sized up the situation, and chose an admirable position in a Ganges loop for entrenchment: from the front he was inaccessible (or seemed to be) because of thick jungles, and at his back he had the river itself, where his war flotilla was moored. The two opposing armies were separated by three miles.

Sulaiman Shikoh was all for goading Shuja's troops to fight, though Jai Singh advocated a defensive waiting game. For a few days both sides fitfully and distantly exchanged artillery, with occasional flare-ups between advance scouts. The Bengal army was well protected by its flotilla, and after a while grew somewhat lax. Unbelievably true to character, Shuja now became "inaccessible to man and mosquito alike," sleeping until midday on a couch under mosquito nets while his patrols waxed inattentive as officers failed to check them.

The actual engagement at Banaras proved nothing more than a lightning-fast, ignominious rout. Early in the morning of February 14, 1658, young Sulaiman set his troops moving with the ostensible intention of finding new camp grounds. We are never told how they bypassed those thick jungles, but abruptly Sulaiman's mail-clad cavalry descended on Shuja's somnolent army, and in a half-awake melee rebel Bengal soldiers fled in all directions. Surrounded by confusion and very likely wine-soused, Shuja staggered from his tent and mounted an elephant; he shouted for officers and troops, but only a few of his men stopped long enough to fight. In a rush of cavalry, high-spirited Sulaiman Shikoh and Dilir Khan were joined by Jai Singh. It was a hairbreadth escape: Shuja's mahout urged a beleaguered elephant to the Ganges under protection of rebel artillery guns which had now opened fire; and a few belatedly staunch Bengalese set up sufficient resistance to enable the prince to flee to the safety of his boats. Behind him, his deserted camp gave way to a riot of imperial plunder. Unlike modern loot of war, this was the booty of Mogul royalty and nobles, who like snails carried their houses on their backs: tents, jewels, gold and silver, horses, elephants, and precious objects. The spoils totaled twenty million rupees.

No defeat is funny, but this one did have farcical aspects. Shuja's boats headed ten miles down river, ignoring their own men who ran along the Ganges in panic. His main Bengalese army—ten to fifteen thousand soldiers—fled overland to Patna, so demoralized that they allowed themselves to be easily assaulted by small groups of villagers who promptly seized their money and property. Even modest village women turned Amazon, offering stragglers drinking water and then stealing the clothes off their backs with scarcely a murmur of protest from them. The whole road to Patna became a treasure hunt, a looter's delight of abandoned animals—camels, mules, horses, and elephants—together with precious items and sacks of coins newly minted in the name of "Timur III, Alexander II," Shah Shuja himself.

News of imperialist success reached Agra a month later, but though it was Sulaiman Shikoh's doing he won no credit for it: Shah Jahan and Dara praised Jai Singh, who received an absentee promotion in rank. Writing to the rajah in uncontrolled hyperbole, Dara began his letter with a Sanskrit incantation and concluded that "within the last hundred years such a victory was vouchsafed to none else."

Jai Singh replied in a dark, brooding mood: the valor of

a Rajput had been called into question by gossip. Was it true that the emperor gave credence to stories that the rajah had deliberately allowed Prince Shuja to escape? Shah Jahan hastened to reassure him by return messenger: "None intimated any such thing to me. My confidence in the loyalty of the Rajah is . . . great."

Shah Jahan's confidence was certainly not shared by Europeans on the scene, then or later. Almost reducing history to a matter of petty vanity, Manucci tells us that Dara had previously insulted Jai Singh by saying he "looked like a musician, an occupation much despised in Hindustan, because all such men act the part of buffoons." In revenge, the rajah allowed Shuja "to retreat and save himself." Manucci offers other motives: Shah Jahan had asked Jai Singh to avoid a battle; and besides, if Shuja were taken prisoner and later released by the emperor, the Rajput would merely have made another enemy. In confirmation, Bernier also asserts that Jai Singh "was too prudent to lay his hands on a prince of the blood."

Unquestionably, individual treachery played a crucial role in the War of Succession, and Jai Singh was not the only Mogul noble whose motives were suspect. But this was treachery of a different kind from latter-day definitions of the word. In the twentieth century, being a traitor always carries the abstract stigma of betraying one's country; in Mogul India, betrayal was strictly personal, just as loyalty represented an individual attachment to emperor or prince. Considerable ambiguity prevailed, and Jai Singh openly became a traitor only when events made it clear *who* would be winner; if his attitude was relative, pragmatic, and profoundly cynical, it could be no more so than that of royalty itself. The entire structure of Mogul government encouraged hunting with the hounds and running with the hare.

In the aftermath of his rout near Banaras, Shuja had meanwhile fled to Patna where he effected a patchwork rally of forces. We have a timed indication of just how dilatory Jai Singh was: it took Shuja five days to reach Patna, while "pursuing" imperial forces required twenty days. Young Sulaiman Shikoh's hands were tied, since this was unknown enemy country and he could not go it alone. Even Shah Jahan now commented in an imperial firman that ten days should have been ample to cover the distance. Withdrawing his wealth from Patna, Shuja retreated to Monghyr in Bihar province, determined to make a last stand. In a burst of energy he created a two-mile long rampart just outside the city limits, and reinforced it with trenches, stockades, and artillery.

Faced with this impasse, Sulaiman's imperial army camped fourteen miles west of Monghyr, and again Jai Singh seemed to be restraining his ward from taking precipitate action. Two precious months—March and April of 1658—went by, while urgent appeals from court advised fast resolution of the tussle with Shuja. Then came news of black disaster: Aurangzeb and Murad had united their rebel armies, pushed north from the Deccan, and on April 15 had defeated Jaswant Singh's opposing contingent at a place called Dharmat. They were now heading directly for Agra. Sulaiman Shikoh and Jai Singh were solicited by both the emperor and Dara to make a truce with Shuja—their army was needed to bolster Dara's forces for an imminent major confrontation.

Peace talks took a few days. Jai Singh could meanwhile only be secretly pleased that a hated Rajput rival, Jaswant Singh of Jodhpur, had been defeated by Aurangzeb and Murad; and if Manucci's allegations of piqued vanity can be taken seriously, the rajah must also have had mixed feelings about Dara Shikoh. Terms of agreement with Shuja were now concluded through Bengal's vizier and plenipotentiary: Bengal, Orissa, and Bihar were conceded to the rebel prince, but he must withdraw to his capital city of Rajmahal in Bengal and rule from there.

It was now May 7, 1658. Sulaiman and Jai Singh would have to ride hard to reach Agra in time for the vital engagement looming ahead. Unfortunately, the depressing news of imperial defeat at Dharmat had already infected their troops; and with the tide apparently turning in favor of Aurangzeb and Murad, there was considerable confusion and even disloyalty in Sulaiman's camp. Bravely, the ward kept marching in advance of his rajah, but dared not leave him altogether for fear that the whole army might fall apart.

The situation was crucial: Dara had deprived himself of key men to sustain his son, and now faced the greatest enemy of all. Ironically, in spite of mistaken early worries that enemy was not Shuja, who had obligingly accepted a status quo. As for Murad, he could not alone have commanded sufficient troops or nobles to matter a hill of beans. The real threat was Aurangzeb—master strategist of the Deccan, who had more military cunning than anyone in the Mogul Empire.

● ● ●

Murad Bakhsh had been presiding over Gujarat for some five years when word of Shah Jahan's expected demise filtered through to him. He lost no time in rustling up troops and summoning district officers to Ahmadabad for consultation. Then, probably in early October 1657, his unbridled emotions provoked the violent incident which would later cost him his life.

Gujarat's revenue minister, Ali Naqi, was that rare anomaly in Mogul history—a very able and honest man, but so stringently righteous that he was anathema to the oily backscratchers and corrupt drinking companions of Murad's court. They had all taken plenty of graft in their day and expected still more from the prince's stupidity and prodigality (Murad was indifferent to money, a virtue by default). But Ali Naqi handled the purse strings, and Ali Naqi had many enemies.

One arch foe happened to be among the provincial officers convoked by Murad; his name, Qutb-ud-din Khan, is not as important as the creakingly old-fashioned conspiracy he hatched with Murad's favorite eunuch. Together they forged a letter in Ali Naqi's handwriting and bearing his seal: addressed to Dara Shikoh, it proposed active support of Dara in the struggle for the crown. Rather cleverly, the fake document was then given to a courier who deliberately allowed himself to be intercepted by Murad's road patrol.

When the persuasive evidence was brought to Murad just before dawn, it found him in a black mood and probably with a hangover; wild with fury, he ordered Ali Naqi to be "dragged" into his presence. The finance minister had been reading his morning Koran, hastily put on court robes and rushed to the royal call. Murad sat glowering in a chair, holding a spear. With clenched teeth he asked, "If a man plans treason against his master, what should his punishment be?" Ali Naqi replied forthrightly, "Death." Murad then threw the letter in his face. Secure in his virtue, the minister dismissed the document as a forgery and rebuked the prince for being duped. By way of answer, Murad jumped up and jammed the spear straight through Ali Naqi, shouting at the top of his lungs, "In spite of all my favors you have turned such a traitor!" Attending eunuchs finished the job.*

It was a sordid murder, the killing of the voice of conscience. With the only honest official in Gujarat out of the way, Murad's flatterers and grafters now encouraged him to take extreme action. In need of money, he promptly sent one of his eunuchs, Shahbaz Khan, to loot Surat—that same Surat where Sir Thomas Roe had arrived in India forty years before and encountered young Shah Jahan's wily revenue officer. Clogged with British trade and rich in revenues, Surat had long since become Hindustan's most famous port. Imperial treasure (mainly customs levees) was kept in the city's fort together with the wealth of local merchants; on a sea promontory and fortified by guns, this stronghold could not be captured so easily. Failing to bribe the commandant, Shahbaz Khan finally blew up a good part of the defending wall by means of mined explosives laid with the help of Dutch intriguers. Murad's men took treasure and guns, along with a hefty loan extracted by force from Surat's mercantile community. Cash was sent to Ahmadabad by fast camel,

---

* In obvious prejudice, Mogul chronicles almost always depict eunuchs as villains compensating for the loss of their testicles with malice and spite. Now and later, we will find them doing the "hatchet" work at grim events.

while the prince privately crowned himself (four hours and twenty-four minutes after sunrise on November 20) and dispensed titles and money left and right to swell his troops. Coronation was publicly celebrated two weeks later, with district mosques proclaiming Murad under his modest new title of Maruwwajuddin; and an envoy was even sent off to Persia with gifts from the new "emperor."

By late January 1658, Murad's looting troops from Surat had joined him in Ahmadabad, and he felt ready for the march to Agra as soon as Aurangzeb sanctioned it. As a last act of cheerful pessimism Murad had even deposited his wives and children, together with those of his nobles, in the protecting fortress of Champanir. If he died in the struggle and his family became vulnerably exposed, the outcome could not be pleasant: widows inevitably went to the victor's harem, while children might find themselves confined in a state prison, withering away to imbecility on forced imbibings of opium juice. It was just as well to have a refuge for them, or for himself if the going got rough.

During all the adolescent bravado of these preliminaries, Murad had been consistently urging Aurangzeb to strike while the iron was hot; Aurangzeb had cautiously replied that they must temporize. Murad's notions of military tactics were bold and rudimentary: march north at once, attack Dara before he had time to consolidate imperial troops or to rally Mogul army commanders from disparate areas of the realm. Aurangzeb countered that the time for revolt had not yet come; they must continue to dissimulate, even keeping up a vapid correspondence with Dara until they knew whether Shah Jahan was dead or not, and it had been very rash of Murad to loot Surat and crown himself publicly. But Murad needed no convincing: the emperor was certainly dead, letters from their agents at court rang false, any news leaking through from Delhi or Agra had to be suspect. So it went—a relay of fire and ice between Gujarat and the Deccan, a contrast of hot Murad and cold Aurangzeb. "To wait for true news from court is to lose time and assist our enemy," Murad argued; "our enemy is growing stronger."

Actually, there is good reason to believe that Aurangzeb's slow opening moves did not all stem from deliberation or devious profundity. He could not feel so certain of defeating Shah Jahan and Dara Shikoh combined. Thus, at one moment, he even suggested to Murad that it might be a good idea to invite the Persians and Uzbeks to invade Afghanistan province and create a serious diversion for Dara's forces. Murad at first took this in dubious stride: Persians were old enemies and didn't have to be prompted to take revenge on the Moguls, not to mention that it seemed downright improper to *encourage* an invasion of India! But by the time of his December coronation he had taken up the idea and was requesting Persian aid. With diplomacy, Shah Abbas II professed friendship and boasted an army ready to intervene in India; he even promised reinforcements by sea, but did nothing—Persia would wait to see the outcome of events.

It was the moment for Aurangzeb to allay Murad's anxiety by sealing their pact with a formal document acknowledging that "the design of acquiring the throne has now been set on foot." In jointly pious aim the two brothers would "uproot the bramble of idolatry and infidelity from the realm of Islam and overwhelm and crush the idolatrous chief with his followers and strongholds, so that the dust of disturbance may be allayed in Hindustan." Aurangzeb's florid style was standard, but the contents of his agreement bristled with specifics: "Whereas my brother, dear as my own heart, has joined me in this holy enterprise . . . I shall keep my promise, and as previously settled I leave to him the Punjab, Afghanistan, Kashmir, and Sind. . . . Attesting the truth of this desire, I take Allah and the Prophet as witnesses!"

The die was cast, with its flaw of deception carefully hidden. Aurangzeb and his army now left Aurangabad early in February 1658, heading for the Narmada River that separated the Deccan from northern India; in a final letter, he suggested that Murad should time the movement of his own forces to effect an undelayed rendezvous.

● ● ●

From early October 1657 until this northward march, Aurangzeb had actually been far from coolly evaluating events. For him, these four months constituted an agonizing period of appraisal. The situation in northern India called for urgent action: Shuja and Murad were moving with or without him, and he had to enter the arena or lose everything. But his position in the Deccan was far from tenable, financially and otherwise.

Many factors hinged on his recent aggressions against Golconda and Bijapur; restrained from further Deccan aggrandizement by imperial command before Shah Jahan's illness of September 6, Aurangzeb had been left with a battery of unresolved problems. One particular sideplay of no little importance had cropped up during his brief Bijapur war: in the northwest of Bijapur, a young Hindu Maratha chief rose up in active challenge to Mogul supremacy—this was Shivaji, later destined to become a formidable hero in Indian history. At the moment Shivaji could only be a gnat stinging an iron bull, yet by ominous guerrilla tactics (while Aurangzeb and Mir Jumla were invading Bijapur) he had managed not merely to seize various Bijapuri fortresses on his own, but even to assault unguarded Mogul strongholds. Only when Bijapur seemed more or less defeated did Shivaji prudently make a truce with Aurangzeb. With Deccan politics about to be suspended, the Hindu brigand became a renewed imponderable; worse, obligatory Mogul retreat from Bijapur had been interpreted by Bijapur as a sign of weakness, and even pusillanimous Golconda was creating border troubles again. News of Shah Jahan's illness must soon filter through to both these kingdoms as well as to Shivaji. Obviously Aurangzeb could not remain in the Deccan: if he delayed his march north, Dara Shikoh as the emperor's surrogate would have time to recall top-ranking Deccan generals and rally Mogul officers and troops from other key provinces; anybody who was ambitious or selfish (which was everybody) would be won over to Dara's cause, thinking that a dilatory puritan stood little chance of becoming emperor. On the other hand, if Aurangzeb marched north at once and made an open bid to rule India, the combination of Shah Jahan's illness and civil war between his sons would make all imperial authority collapse throughout Hindustan; Bijapur, Golconda, and Shivaji would take advantage of the vacuum, and the fruit of two years of dogged Deccan strategy and war would go down the drain.

Autumnal letters to Mir Jumla reveal Aurangzeb's anxieties and plans. He hoped to utilize his present Deccan strength to collect a useful indemnity before Bijapur got wind of Shah Jahan's illness; then he would fight for India's throne. In this connection Mir Jumla had already been dispatched to take a fortress (promised by Bijapur treaty terms) and Aurangzeb had had long secret consultations with him; written messages now went to and fro. "I have no friend but you," Aurangzeb acknowledged. Simultaneously (in October) he was renewing contact with Murad: "You have not written to me for such a long time past. . . . I shall soon return to Aurangabad. You must have heard the news about the Imperial Court." He also wrote to Shuja in Bengal.

By mid-October Aurangzeb had begun to withdraw from Bijapur territory, heading for his Deccan capital. Putting a hopeless mask on retreat movements, he informed the sultan of Golconda that he had decided to end military occupation of Bijapur in order to reassure its populace. But no one could be fooled, and his enemies were delighted. En route to the north he now received conveniently gloomy news from Aurangabad: his principal wife, Dilras Banu Begum, had died in childbirth. It was a reminder of Mumtaz Mahal's death; and in his wife's memory, Aurangzeb would later build a copy of the Taj Mahal at Aurangabad—a curiously spiritless replica. But for now, Dilras Banu's death became a perfect alibi for returning to Aurangabad instead of staying put at the emperor's (or Dara Shikoh's) orders: he had to console his grief-stricken children. Actually he did not write to the imperial court for some weeks, though he continued to correspond with both Murad and Shuja.

During his progress to Aurangabad, Aurangzeb expected to hear at any moment of Shah Jahan's death—in which case he would have marched immediately to north India. But no news came from Delhi, or rather conflicting news: by October 21, report filtered through that the emperor was better; but the very next day word arrived that Dara had become all powerful at court and was daily taking steps to neutralize all potential threats. For the moment, Aurangzeb could only believe Shah Jahan to be dead or a helpless invalid. He contemplated sending his son with an army to Burhanpur, in order to clamp down on the ferry over the Tapti River and detain Mogul khans now returning northward. But this would be tantamount to open rebellion—a dangerous act if a sick father should by any miracle recover. Mir Jumla's opinion was solicited: he advised Aurangzeb against doing anything rash, and suggested that the prince's son might find better employment by being sent to help him acquire that promised fortress along with indemnity from Bijapur. But as time passed it became evident that even the master tactics of Mir Jumla were not going to effect a quick settlement.

Aurangzeb arrived in Aurangabad on November 11, 1657. His alliance with Murad was now definite, and there was at least a vague entente with Shuja regarding common action against Dara. Old Deccan hands and supporters looked to their prince: what was he going to do now? "After a year's hard campaigning, the army of this province has lost heart on hearing of the Emperor's illness, and has been unsettled in various ways," Aurangzeb wrote to Mir Jumla; "many of my officers want to return to the Emperor." Secretly, in code, he also opened his heart:

> The desires of my well-wishers can be realized only when . . . Shah Jahan's death is verified. . . . But I gather from my court agent's letter that it is impossible for the Emperor to recover from this disease; he has not strength enough left to pull him back to life. Most probably the affair has become past remedy. If in such circumstances I delay in equipping my army . . . in what hope will men consent to keep my company? If the officers here, seeing my negligence and indifference, re-

turn to the court, and Dara becomes aware of my condition, it will be impossible for me to attract other worldlings and seekers of rank.

For this reason, he hoped that Mir Jumla could enforce the Bijapur treaty terms and collect badly needed loot.

But a clarion command came from the imperial capital: Mir Jumla must return at once. Aurangzeb seemed profoundly depressed. "Friend," he wrote, "God assist you! What shall I write about my own troubled state or describe how the days pass over me? I have no remedy save patience."

By now Murad had reached fever pitch, dunning his brother to take action. In the light of Aurangzeb's later ruthless decisiveness, there is an almost curious wistfulness in his refusal to burst into open rebellion before knowing for certain that Shah Jahan was dead. Various Deccan generals had already gone off to court by request, his own army was small (for the moment) and he still hoped for funds from Bijapur. Or was he waiting for Dara to attack Murad and Shuja first, thus weakening himself by division?

In late November Aurangzeb learned that Dara had sent an army to stop Shuja's advance from Bengal, and December brought daily news of additional imperial strategies. There could be no mistake: Shah Jahan was in the background, dictating or approving every action so that even if he died Dara Shikoh would be safe. The reassignment of provinces could only be intended to split Murad and Aurangzeb, while two armies were being sent to prevent them from moving northward, and Aurangzeb's last Deccan generals were being recalled to court. Leaning on Mir Jumla, Aurangzeb wrote entreatingly: "Now is the time to display your devotion. . . . Come to me, so that with your advice I may engage in preparations for the work of gaining the crown."

Mir Jumla reached Aurangabad by the beginning of January 1658, ostensibly on his way to Agra at the emperor's command. With his family virtual hostages at the Mogul capital, he could not openly afford to help a rebel prince. The result was a staged scene. Pretending to be afraid of Aurangzeb he refused to see him, until Aurangzeb's son insisted that his father had an oral message to be transmitted to Shah Jahan. Mir Jumla then went to Aurangzeb and was immediately arrested as planned and imprisoned at Daulatabad fort, while his vast property, artillery, and army were all appropriated. For the Mogul court, Aurangzeb had a good political cover: suspicion that the wily Persian was in collusion with the rulers of Bijapur and Golconda, and had not sufficiently exerted himself to exact tribute from them! Under Aurangzeb, Mir Jumla would soon become the highest peer in the realm and take an active part in later stages of the War of Succession. But for now, he was on ice.

"Confiscated" artillery and European gunners would be of great value, but Aurangzeb still worked hard to improve his position even more before leaving the Deccan. Threat and conciliation finally resulted in partial payment of indemnities by Bijapur and Golconda, while at every moment he promoted intrigue with his friends at the Mogul court and high officers in contiguous Malwa province. Dara reported to Shah Jahan, "Aurangzeb is winning over nobles and pillars of the state. He is doing his work by means of secret epistles." Just how effective these deals and coercive communiqués were will be seen in the endless treasons and capitulations to follow. For all his unavoidable retreat from central Asia and outright failure at Kandahar, Aurangzeb had gained experience: it was *his* military exploits which had brought Golconda and Bijapur to their knees. Court nobles and army generals appraising the four sons of Shah Jahan found good reason to lay odds on the implacable puritan. Many officers had in fact remained in the Deccan to back him up: his revenue officer, his equerry, and even Rajput chiefs. Soldiers were now recruited with the lure of a month's pay in advance; lead and gunpowder were bought and stored. By the end of January Aurangzeb had thirty thousand crack men and Mir Jumla's European-backed artillery. He was ready.

Murad at last received the signal, and Aurangzeb dispatched his eldest son with a vanguard army toward Burhan-

[226]

pur. He himself left Aurangabad on February 5, handing out titles and rank as though he were already emperor. A month's halt was made in Burhanpur between mid-February and mid-March, while Murad wondered where his brother could be and imperial contingents sent to stop the rebels remained in suspense somewhere to the north. There is actually no explanation for this strange delay of a month; it seems to have been a final holding back from confrontation and catastrophe, a dread centered on the father about to be challenged and deposed. Significantly Aurangzeb wrote to Shah Jahan—asking about his health, wondering if the emperor were better and hoping for his recovery. The prince's personal agent now arrived from Agra with first-hand news: yes, Shah Jahan was improved but totally devoted to Dara Shikoh, who had in effect become ruler. Yet many nobles at court privately believed in their Deccan puritan and urged him to march on the capital: the imperial army might be large, but at heart gave no loyalty to a panicky crown prince.

This was the needed final encouragement. Aurangzeb had to move quickly now, to prevent advancing imperial opposition from consolidating its hold over all of Malwa and closing the northern road. On March 20 he left Burhanpur; shortly afterward he sent his eldest son back to arrest and imprison old Shahnawaz Khan: despite his being both Aurangzeb's and Murad's father-in-law, the veteran soldier had lingered behind. At least *one* noble in the Deccan didn't want to join in open rebellion, and he would become a prisoner for seven months.

CHAPTER 14

The Crystal Tower

MAHARAJAH JASWANT SINGH of Jodhpur had fallen into a total quandary. As commander of one of the twin armies dispatched by Shah Jahan and Dara Shikoh to confront Murad and Aurangzeb, he and his troops had arrived at the city of Ujjain (about a hundred miles north of the Narmada River delineating the Deccan frontier, and twice that distance east of Murad's Gujarat capital of Ahmadabad). His instructions had been to deter Aurangzeb from advancing northward, but the movements of both rebel princes were now frankly puzzling to the old Rajput.

For Murad to achieve the distinction of puzzling *anybody* could mean only one thing: he himself was puzzled. In effect, for the whole month of March 1658 he had heard nothing from his brother; their joint forces were to rendezvous at the Deccan border, yet Aurangzeb was nowhere to be seen. Obliged to mark time, Murad had indulged in a good deal of zigzagging and retreat—perpetually avoiding Jaswant's forces while still attempting to fall in with Aurangzeb's presumed path of advance. At first, rebel scouts had estimated only three or four thousand imperial cavalry; but after a premature sortie between the end of February and mid-March, Murad quickly learned that the opposition was actually much stronger than anticipated. This meant that Qasim Khan's royal contingent, whose original purpose had been to boot the black sheep out of Gujarat province, had evidently linked up with Jaswant Singh. Poised east of Gujarat and north of the Deccan, such a formidable massing of troops obviously intended to prevent any conjoining of the two troublemakers: Jaswant could move south to deter Aurangzeb as soon as the movements of the Deccan army became apparent, while Qasim Khan had only to head west in order to pin down Murad. Meanwhile, their double army occupied the vital center of a tactical chessboard.

But where were the advancing knights? As an old Mogul hand, it annoyed Jaswant to remain so totally in the dark about Aurangzeb's whereabouts. If the maharajah hoped for information from loyal imperial sources to the south, he would by now be acutely disappointed: all roads from the Deccan and every ferry crossing of the Narmada River were being watched by Aurangzeb's spies to make certain that no news of his troop movements filtered through. And though Murad had proved typically less prudent, so that the Rajput chief at least knew where *he* was, his evasive circlings boded ill: whenever imperial soldiers advanced, Murad simply withdrew and detoured. In fact, the mystery by now had become compound for everybody: spies from all three armies were all over the place, trying to make sense of one another's troop deployments. It remained imperative to Jaswant's strategy to keep the two rebel armies from uniting; but he was not the most adroit commander in the Mogul army.

Whatever the psychological reasons for Aurangzeb's inexplicable delay during the month of March, he suddenly loomed up from nowhere on April 3, 1658, crossing the Narmada River without encountering any opposition and heading due north toward the befuddled imperial army. By April 13 he had reached a village called Dipalpur about twenty-four miles southwest of Ujjain; there he discovered that Murad was due west of him and promptly sent off a messenger to announce his arrival. The following day the two brothers finally met near the lake of Dipalpur, and immediately pushed north with their combined armies to meet Jaswant Singh's forces which were a day's march away. Aurangzeb and Murad encamped at the village of Dharmat, some four-teen miles southwest of Ujjain; on adjoining terrain the bat-tle would be fought the next day.

Laggardly receiving only half the bad news—that Aurangzeb had outmaneuvered him by crossing the river border—a stunned Jaswant Singh reacted in momentary confusion and withdrew several miles to Ujjain. Here a Brah-man envoy advised him to go home to Jodhpur and let Au-rangzeb pass: the prince merely intended to visit his father, not to make war. Galvanized by a Rajput code of gallantry Jaswant apparently replied, "I must carry out the Emperor's orders. I cannot retrace my steps in disgrace." So forward he marched again, camping opposite Dharmat village to block Aurangzeb's path and discover the full truth in all its horror: Aurangzeb and Murad had already coalesced; the dilatory imperial forces would have to face a united rebel army.

The following morning, with his opponents already on the march, Jaswant Singh gave in to his fear and sent Au-rangzeb a messenger. Begging the prince's pardon, he didn't want to fight: "I have no power to show audacity to Your Highness. My wish is to visit and serve you. If you pardon me and give up your project of a fight, I shall go and wait on you." Aurangzeb sensed the advantage and refused to parlay, replying that if Jaswant Singh meant what he said then he should come alone to the rebel camp and ask for pardon.

Though afraid, Jaswant Singh was after all a Rajput: he could not submit, and now had to do battle. If he had had any notion that the mere show of imperial forces would stop the rebels, he was mistaken; they were headed invincibly for Agra. Again we find the fascinating dilemma of a Mogul general paralyzed by conflicting factors—a situation almost medievally Japanese in its stark opposition of honor and eti-quette. Jaswant's duty to the emperor required him to chal-lenge not one but two rebellious princes of the blood, both of whom were infinitely superior to him in the Mogul hierarchy —he was merely a petty noble, a commander of horse. At the same time, he had also received imperial orders not to lay hands on the princes or fight them except as a desperate last measure. To complicate the issue, the Hindu Rajput further had to share authority with a Moslem, Qasim Khan; though two ranks lower, Qasim was now Jaswant Singh's social equal as the newly appointed governor of Gujarat province. Jaswant commanded his own Rajputs, but it was Qasim Khan who gave orders to Moslem soldiers—a discordant army at best, since Moslems and Rajputs worked well together only if their commanding general had the authority to make them do so. In addition, certain Moslems in the imperial forces were secret friends of Aurangzeb or had already been won over to his cause.

In this curious aura of hierarchy and rigid rule, the Battle of Dharmat (and the subsequent stupendous engagement with Dara Shikoh himself) must be viewed as more of a ritual than any conventional clash of arms. By present-day notions of combat, these engagements seem weirdly archaic, and so they were. But then, any war is essentially an idiotic game of power.

The engagement at Dharmat would prove to be a classically mismatched affair: Rajput cavalry versus deadly artillery. Commanding Aurangzeb's larger weapons were both French and English gunners: Europeans had the know-how to handle Mogul cannon, and many foreign adventurers became involved in Mogul warfare. One account claims that Jaswant's chief officer warned him of an artillery threat the night before the battle, suggesting that a surprise midnight assault could kill enemy gunners and wipe out deadly opposition. But Jaswant nobly thought it was "inconsistent with manliness and Rajput usage to employ stratagem or make a night attack." He planned to skirt enemy artillery with his Rajput cavalry, engaging rebel troops directly.

Now and later, Rajputs would play a formidable background role in the War of Succession, mainly on Dara Shikoh's side for obvious religious reasons: Dara's liberalism offered more advantage to Hindus than Aurangzeb's orthodox Moslem views. It was Akbar who had first conciliated Rajputs with Mogul rule, and they still remained the only hereditary nobles in India. Their homeland, Rajputana or Rajasthan (literally, "the abode of kings"), had a history of heroism and chivalry dating back to legendary days of Indian epics. From deserts and hill ranges petty Rajput chiefs came, together with the grand rajahs of Jaipur State, Jodhpur, and Udaipur; all of them brought clansmen into battle with them. Recklessly courageous, proud, and with a high sense of honor, Rajputs fought against overwhelming odds. The men wore yellow robes of self-sacrifice, while their women often committed acts of suttee, dying in flames to avoid capture or disgrace. All of this was Jaswant Singh's background, and he could not easily forget it.

As luck would have it, the loyalist commanders could not have chosen a less ideal site for encounter. The fight would take place on narrow, uneven ground, with (in Murad's description) "ditches of water on all four sides [joined] to swamps." Far from affording a wide sweep for cavalry, the battlefield resembled a constricting island.

By fair estimate Aurangzeb had thirty thousand troops and Murad supplied perhaps ten thousand more. Opposing imperialists at least equalled and possibly surpassed them—Aurangzeb counted "thirty thousand horse and many infantry."

The night sky barely flushed dawn of April 15, 1658 when hostilities began. Long-range artillery opened fire; rockets flared. Paralyzed into defensive tactics, Jaswant Singh watched Aurangzeb's advancing troops and heard kettledrums boom and trumpets blare. Three hundred miles to the northeast, dawn also streaked red over the imperial Red Fort of Agra, where Shah Jahan, Dara Shikoh, and Jahanara Begum could not know that at that very moment their fate was being sealed with black wax.

● ● ●

The Battle of Dharmat can only be viewed as an Indian version of the Charge of the Light Brigade, and proved even more disastrous. It was Dara Shikoh's death warrant written in blood; indeed, for the imperialists, defeat represented a profound moral failure—the forerunner of wholesale defections and breathtakingly cynical treasons. Ironically, only

Hindu Rajputs fighting for a Moslem emperor (and not even all of them) emerged with anything resembling honor.

Hampered by impossible terrain, Rajput cavalrymen shouted their war cry of "Ram! Ram!" to invoke the Hindu god Rama, and galloped in suicidal waves to meet Aurangzeb's and Murad's combined army. Rebel bullets mowed them down but still they swept forward, killing Aurangzeb's chief of artillery and engaging his van in hand-to-hand combat. Swords and daggers ripped through human flesh until the battlefield was "dyed crimson with blood like a tulip-bed." Heroism became unorganized slaughter as disparate Rajput units fought in isolated clan groups, and Qasim Khan's imperial Moslem contingent (later suspected of collusion) made no great effort to come to their aid—even Jaswant Singh's cramped adherents found it hard to follow up the initial assault. Aurangzeb lost no time in closing his broken line of defense, cutting off Rajput retreat and quickly bringing reserve units forward. Rajput chiefs (six of them) died in frantic fighting, one with an arrow through his eye. French and English gunners had rallied after the first Rajput onslaught and now opened murderous fire from high ground on Jaswant Singh's central column crowded between ditches and swamps. A few Hindu leaders ignored inbred valor, deserting the scene and taking clansmen with them; two thousand braver souls stayed to die for Jaswant Singh, their Jodhpur commander. With Qasim Khan's Moslems also prepared to take flight, Jaswant Singh soon found himself alone and hemmed in on all sides. Twice wounded during the battle, he now prepared himself for certain death. But his ministers grabbed his horse's bridle and dragged him from the field: why should an eminent Rajput leader die for Mogul princes determined to kill one another in a family feud? Jaswant, together with what was left of his clan, withdrew in defeat to Jodhpur. The remnants of the imperial army also took to their heels, Hindus heading for Rajputana and Moslems for Agra. Behind them, distant strains of triumph from drums and clarion announced a rebel victory. Six thousand imperial soldiers—mostly Rajputs—lay dead on the field, including one entire family of six royal brothers. It was all over in less than eight hours.

Aurangzeb refused to allow pursuit on the grounds of pleasing Allah. But his real reasons were more practical: it was a hot April day, everyone was exhausted, and the abandoned enemy camp overflowed with loot—artillery, elephants, enemy treasure, and equipment. Two-thirds would go to Aurangzeb and a third to Murad (who also received a present of fifteen thousand gold pieces as "surgeons' fee for his wounded followers").

Nothing succeeds like success: the scales had tipped in Aurangzeb's favor, and wholesale defectors from the imperial army joined rebel forces the next day. Titles and promotions were distributed and, after a brief halt for several days more, the northward march of the two princes continued on April 20. Their next obstacle was the Chambal River, a tributary of the Jumna not quite forty miles south of Agra; here Dara Shikoh would be certain to dispute passage.

An interesting sidelight on Rajput notions of honor was provided by Jaswant Singh's wife, who welcomed him home by barring the gates of Jodhpur fortress against him. For her he had failed either to win the battle or to die in it, and was now in limbo—a coward and a disgrace to Rajput honor. She could neither be a live hero's wife nor immolate herself in an act of suttee. Details would later filter through to Europeans in the realm, and François Bernier has her ranting and raving against Jaswant in the grand manner: " 'The man is covered with infamy,' she said, 'and he shall not enter within these walls. I disown him for my husband, and these eyes can never again behold him.' . . . The next moment the temper of her mind took another turn. 'Prepare the funeral pile,' she exclaimed. 'The fire shall consume my body. I am deceived; my husband is certainly dead; it cannot possibly be otherwise.' " Presumably the lady's mother calmed her down with the consoling assurance that Jaswant would rally another army to fight Aurangzeb; though Manucci adds that she taunted her husband for his cowardice for years.

● ● ●

Agra was meanwhile in a total uproar. Four days before the Battle of Dharmat, the entire court had set out for Delhi: Shah Jahan had been at Agra since November, but with summer coming on his doctors advised a change of climate. They had almost reached Delhi when news of the disaster arrived on April 25, 1658, and the entire court turned back again to Agra. Jaswant Singh had been defeated, Qasim Khan was a probable traitor; nothing could stop Aurangzeb and Murad now but a concerted army led by Dara Shikoh himself.

Political affairs at Agra had actually been in a state of high confusion for some weeks prior to the debacle at Dharmat. Plots and counterplots abounded; aside from Raushanara Begum, Aurangzeb had secret adherents among court nobles who offered temporizing advice to both Dara Shikoh and Shah Jahan. Wanly, the emperor still believed that civil war could be avoided by diplomatic measures, and listened to anyone who volunteered suggestions as to how to avoid it. In a sisterly attempt at conciliation, Jahanara now sent a letter to Aurangzeb before he crossed the Chambal River. She wrote desperately:

> The Emperor has recovered and is himself administering the State and trying to remove the disorders that cropped up during his late illness. Your armed advance is therefore an act of war against your father. Even if it is directed against Dara it is no less sinful, since the eldest brother both by Canon Law and common usage stands in the position of the father. If you value your good name in this world and salvation in the next, you should obey your father and report your wishes to him in writing without advancing any further.

Aurangzeb's reply was bluntly self-justifying:

> Shah Jahan has lost all real power and control. Dara is doing everything himself and trying to ruin his younger brothers. Witness how he has crushed Shuja already. He also foiled my invasion of Bijapur when complete success was at hand, and he emboldened the Bijapuris to

[235]

defy me. He has poisoned the Emperor's ears . . . and taken away Berar from me for no fault whatever. Against such overt hostility I am bound to take up arms in self preservation. My wish, however, is only to go to Shah Jahan's presence and reveal everything to him personally. I shall not brook any obstacle to this loving design. See how Jaswant fared in making the attempt. Dara should therefore be sent away from the Imperial Court to his province of the Punjab, to avoid mischief.

But other correspondence offers even more revealing phrases. Writing directly to Shah Jahan, Aurangzeb accuses Dara of having "ever caused vexation to me, and attempted to close the doors of gain to me on every side." Dara is to blame for curtailing the income of the Deccan treasury "in order to ruin my army." Dara Shikoh is the enemy, depicted in the distorting mirror of vituperation.

● ● ●

Aside from imperial correspondence and Mogul chronicles, an ebullient European adolescent was vividly storing up first-hand impressions of Agra in crisis. His testimony has often been accused of being highly unreliable, since he wrote many years after events took place and was prone to exaggerate and embroider; still, he *was* an eyewitness and an active military participant in the War of Succession. For better or worse, it is time to meet Niccolo Manucci in more than transitory fashion.

Manucci was an Italian adventurer, of a breed familiar enough in the seventeenth century. In 1653 he had left his native Venice and a domineering father ("I had a passionate desire to see the world") and stowed away on a ship bound for Smyrna. True to romantic form, the fourteen-year-old boy found himself befriended by an English cavalier, a certain Lord Bellomont who was a refugee from Cromwell's dictatorship; Bellomont had orders from exiled Charles II (it was a mad restoration plot) to seek aid from the shah of Persia and later from India's Mogul. After spending time in Turkey and Persia, he and his ward had finally reached the royal road between Agra and Delhi when the Englishman died abruptly—apparently of plague. Manucci offers a flourishing account of the ambassador's gloomy death near a caravan-serai: thirst at evening, burial at dawn, Mogul impounding of effects (including Manucci's few possessions) and later appropriation of the same by two English rogues. From whom else would a young hero ("I vaulted lightly onto my horse") seek justice but from Shah Jahan himself? Duly the young Italian was received at Delhi durbar; the English rogues were punished, Manucci's two muskets, four pistols, clothes, and other trinkets were restored to him, and he was about to make his way back to Surat when a French artilleryman suggested that he seek employment with Prince Dara Shikoh.

Dara had already heard of the new European's arrival and expressed an interest in meeting him. By now fluent in Persian, Manucci was able to hold direct discourse with the crown prince. "At the end of this conversation Dara asked me if I wished to remain for a time in the Mogul country, to which I replied affirmatively. He said to me, with a smile on his face: 'Would you like to enter my service?' " Manucci would and did, starting at a salary of eighty rupees a month as an artilleryman. By the time of the Mogul crisis the Venetian runaway had been in India for several years, was now nineteen, and could speak not only Persian but Hindustani and Turkish too. He knew the Mogul court intimately and at first-hand, so that many of his anecdotes have persuasive verisimilitude. Whatever his defects (and they are enormous) Manucci personalizes Mogul history with the outrageous flare of a Baron Munchausen and the candor of a Pepys.

His account of Agra at this particular moment in 1658 is filled with intrigue. Thus, only a few weeks before the defeat at Dharmat, Dara Shikoh had confiscated inflammatory letters written to Aurangzeb by two grandees—Shaista Khan (Malwa's recalled governor), and Mir Jumla's son. "Thereupon [Dara] arrested these two nobles and confined them to a room of his palace," Manucci writes. "The whole court supposed that without a doubt he would order them to be beheaded, and the whole of that day I waited on in the court solely to learn the end of the business. At seven o'clock at night they were liberated on the prayer of Raushanara Begum and other princesses, who persuaded the King that the captured letters were forgeries."

How can we doubt the plausible touch of "I waited on in the court solely to learn the end of the business"? Yet if individual episodes seem believable, it is also unfortunately true that Manucci's interpretation of events in Hindustan is a mingled yarn that does not always jibe with official sources. But he is always colorful, refreshing even in his malice, and when he has actually participated in an event he is at least as trustworthy as biased Mogul chronicles also written long after the fact. More than likely Manucci was with the imperial retinue between Agra and Delhi when news of the rout at Dharmat reached Shah Jahan and Dara Shikoh, and he offers pertinent dialogue. An anguished emperor cries out, "O God! Thy will be done," and Dara Shikoh falls into such a passion that he stamps on the ground, wrings his hands, and curses both Qasim Khan and Mir Jumla as traitors—the one for fleeing and the other for allowing his Deccan army to be appropriated by Aurangzeb. Dara even turns on Shah Jahan, crying, "But this day our own arms are turned against us. If Your Majesty had only listened to my advice in the first instance, we should never have arrived at this plight."

The plight now called for a new imperial army to be assembled at once. Shah Jahan placed both the treasury and the arsenal of Agra fort at Dara's disposal, but writhed on the horns of dilemma: he was being forced by events to yield to war among his own sons, and at the same time he wanted desperately to avoid fratricidal confrontation. Alternately he would advise Dara on military matters, simultaneously dictating firmans urging Jai Singh (Sulaiman Shikoh's guardian) to patch up a truce with Prince Shuja and return at once. There was no lack of counsel for peace from court nobles with private reasons for appeasement; it would be easy, they argued, for the emperor to assert his awesome presence once Murad and Aurangzeb reached Agra. His mere word could cow rebel generals, and with the princes sheared of their military strength they would meekly go back to their provinces. Indiscreetly but not incorrectly, Dara accused peace advocates of being cowards or traitors; he had Hindu support from loyal Rajputs and didn't need the help of doubtful Moslems.

But Dara's new imperial army was a patchwork affair. Lacking some of his most trusted men who had been sent with Sulaiman Shikoh against Shuja, he now found himself obliged to summon lesser nobles and commanders from nearby provinces. Money poured out of Agra's treasury both for new recruits and to assure the adherence of mercenary khans; armor and weapons spilled from the Red Fort—guns, elephants, ammunition. Manucci offers a detailed picture of military activity:

> More than one hundred thousand horsemen assembled and more than twenty thousand infantry. There were one hundred pieces of field artillery . . . and over two hundred European artillerymen. There was no want of subordinates, of shopkeepers who furnish supplies for the sustenance of the whole realm and army, a large number of *sarrafos* who provide the cash required by the whole army, many majestic and well-armored elephants, and five hundred camels. . . . When on the march we covered the ground as far as the horizon, making a brave and splendid show.

But it was a dubiously brave and splendid show. Not a few commanders were carpet knights with little experience, and Manucci acknowledges that the greater number of soldiers were "butchers, barbers, blacksmiths, carpenters, tailors, and such-like." An aura of defeat already hovered over this vastly assembled army. Disturbed, the youthful Italian now asked a Jesuit priest of Agra, Father Buzeo, whether there could be any doubt of victory with so many men and so much treasure behind them. Father Buzeo took a dim view of the outcome: "he was much afraid that Dara would never become emperor, pointing out to me that the people of Hindustan were very malicious, that such a race required to be ruled by a more malignant king, and not by a good-natured man like Dara."

Full of apprehension, Shah Jahan still felt that it was his personal duty to set forth and confront the rebels in an attempt at parlay; but Dara resolutely opposed the notion, as did nobleman Shaista Khan for his own private reasons. Shaista Khan was more than erstwhile governor of Malwa: he was Mumtaz Mahal's brother, the maternal uncle of Shah Jahan's sons, and years of trust and favoritism allowed him latitude for deep intrigue. Convincingly making a case for Aurangzeb's good intentions, he had discouraged Shah Jahan from going out to meet Murad and Aurangzeb. But with later news of defeat at Dharmat, the emperor had become so angry with Shaista Khan that, according to Mogul sources, "he struck him on the breast with his staff, and refused to see him for some two or three days." Yet the brother-in-law was soon back in favor.

Dara's plan of action seemed straightforward enough: he intended to hold the Chambal River and prevent Aurangzeb's army from crossing either by ferry or on foot at any known fording point. More decisive action could be deferred until Sulaiman Shikoh's forces returned from Bengal. By May 9, 1658, an advance contingent of Dara's troops started for the town of Dholpur just north of the Chambal, to watch over ferry crossings and set up artillery batteries and earth embankments (forerunners of the modern pillboxes) at strategic points. Dara himself would start out on May 18 with his main army.

Agra's Red Fort was now the scene of a highly formal but anguished leave-taking, graphically described by both Mogul sources and Manucci. Manucci mentions that Dara said good-bye to his sister Jahanara as well as to Shah Jahan, and it must be assumed that she watched from behind grillwork as a moving pageant unfolded in the great quadrangle before the red sandstone Hall of Public Audience. The emperor's uncontrollable feelings made the occasion a kind of death. He presented Dara with ceremonial robes and ornaments, as well as arms, horses, elephants, and an auspicious chariot; he embraced Dara with trembling hands, holding him for an unconscionably long embrace as though they were not father and son but lovers. In a wild surge of emotion Shah Jahan turned to Mecca and raised his arms to Allah, blessing Dara's venture by reciting prescribed texts from the Koran. Even the orthodox Hindu prayer was invoked.

By special royal favor, Dara's presentation chariot had been brought to the bottom of the six steps leading up to the hall, and he entered the vehicle while kettledrums beat a departing tattoo. Imperial banners unfurled, displaying the Mogul lion against a rising sun; khans and officers surrounded Dara in order of precedence, while right and left of them as they issued from the Red Fort were clusters of captains, horsemen, footmen, retainers, spearmen and rocket-throwers. Dara left his chariot and mounted a great elephant named Fath Jang. "We began the march in such great order that it seemed as if sea and land were united," Manucci relates, rising to the occasion.

> Prince Dara amidst his squadron appeared like a crystal tower, resplendent as a sun shining over all the land. Around him rode many squadrons of Rajput cavalry whose armor glittered from afar, and their lance-heads with a tremulous motion sent forth rays of light. There were . . . ferocious elephants clad in shining steel with chains on their trunks, their tusks encrusted with gold and silver, and broad cutlasses affixed thereto by rings. . . . A marvellous thing was it to behold the march, which moved over the heights and through the vales like the waves of a stormy sea.

Behind the procession, inside of a dwindling Red Fort in the near-empty Hall of Forty Pillars, the emperor watched them out of sight. Shah Jahan was old now, his beard white and his body emaciated from illness; he leaned on his mace and stared into the distance for a long time after the cavalcade had left the palace quadrangle. Neither he nor Jahanara would ever see Dara Shikoh again.

Dara reached Dholpur, thirty-seven miles south of Agra and about a mile from the left bank of the Chambal River, on May 22. Guns had already been set up along the river's north bank, and every ford and ferry-crossing was seized and guarded. Any rebel attempt to cross the river under such circumstances would be sheer folly: the banks were steep and rocky, with approaches intersected by ravines. Here, Dara could hold Aurangzeb's advance and avoid an engagement until Sulaiman Shikoh's forces joined him. By Manucci's account the enemy "appeared afar off after three days," encamping on the opposite bank for a spell. Then a spate of nervous waiting culminated in the impossible: Aurangzeb had already outmaneuvered Dara by crossing the Chambal at a place forty miles east of Dholpur—those enemy tents with their token force across the river were a mere blind!

In their northward march of over a month, Aurangzeb and Murad had arrived on May 21 in the vicinity of the gloomy cliff fortress and state prison of Gwalior, some twenty miles south of the river. Advance scouts brought word of Dara's seizure of the Chambal. But an obliging local traitor informed Aurangzeb that forty miles east of Dholpur there was a little-known crossing only knee-deep; few travelers and no army had ever gone that way, and Dara had neglected to guard it—Aurangzeb, on the testimony of imperial scouts, was still some way from the river. A hefty division of the main rebel army staged a forced all-night march and crossed the Chambal the next morning; Aurangzeb and the rest of his men followed a day later. At least five thousand men died of thirst! But human loss had its military compensations: Dara's embankments and river batteries were now of no use whatsoever, and unless he wanted to be intercepted from the rear he had to fall rapidly back toward Agra. He chose retreat, abandoning heavy guns on the river bank and weakening his artillery for the major encounter soon to come.

The Jumna River flows in a southeasterly direction past

Agra's Red Fort and the unreal vision of the Taj Mahal. Only eight miles downstream from Mumtaz Mahal's mausoleum, Raipur ferry crossing leads over to the south-bank village of Imadpur and its landmarks: several of Shah Jahan's imperial hunting lodges. A mile or so eastward is another village, Samugarh, with the ruins of still another hunting lodge built by Jahangir. Beyond and below this village and extending all the way to a bend of the Jumna River, the great Plain of Samugarh now became the site of one of the most spectacular and significant battles in all world history. It took place on a day of appalling heat known only on the plains of India —a heat which would create a blazing hell for men in heavy armor. It was May 29, 1658.

CHAPTER

15

The Battle of Samugarh

IN RETREAT FROM the Chambal River, Dara's men had encamped eight miles east of Agra on the Plain of Samugarh. "We made use with great labor of pond water in open fields," Manucci says, adding that "the heat was stifling." After a lull of several days, Aurangzeb's advancing forces appeared on May 28. Dara marshaled his troops for combat, but then curiously held them back in a static parade of strength. Hour after hour, imperial cavalry created a tableau in a burning sun; horses restlessly pawed the sandy plain while soldiers in armor literally died from heat and thirst. Aurangzeb rode out to "a cannon-shot distance" and surveyed the scene but refused to take any offensive: his troops were worn out, and he decided to rest them until the following morning. By sunset, indecisive in the sight of both armies, Dara withdrew to his camp.

As an actual battle participant, Manucci attributed his master's hesitation to the advice of turncoats in the imperial ranks. "Dara wanted to commence action," he insists, "but the traitors intervened on astrological grounds by saying that neither the day nor the hour was favorable." Their perfidious motive was to give Aurangzeb time "to refresh his people and secure the arrival of guns." But the more likely and simpler truth is that Dara was afraid.

By Manucci's estimate the imperial army numbered 120,000 men, though official Mogul accounts revise this to somewhere between 60,000 and 80,000. Aurangzeb's opposition totaled forty thousand, with another ten thousand under Murad—by any total the rebels were vastly outnumbered. The vital difference lay in the makeup of the two armies, and in the characters of their royal commanders: between a credulous mystic philosopher whose life had been devoted to meditation and art, and an obsessive soldier with years of involuted intrigue and war behind him, there could be little doubt of the outcome. Defeat was already infecting imperial army morale.

Contemporary scribes would focus on the challenging princes and not on grandees of the empire, yet by suggestion and counsel the nobility played a decisive role in events. Of no little importance in the lineup of khans and rajahs was the ideological factor: if social and religious attitudes did not actually decide the military outcome at Samugarh, they profoundly affected it. Aurangzeb identified himself as a staunchly orthodox Moslem crusading against the supposed heresies of Dara Shikoh, and for convenience' sake an indifferent Murad also wrapped himself in the orthodox banner; by contrast, Dara represented a tradition of tolerance which had begun with Akbar and culminated in unprecedented rights for Hindus, the abolition of hateful religious taxes, and even open hostility to rigidly conventional Islam. Not unpredictably Aurangzeb's followers were largely Sunni Moslems, while Dara Shikoh's partisans emerged chiefly as Shia Moslems and Hindu Rajputs. Yet decisions were also dictated by other than religious factors: Moslem khans in particular tergiversated against an ambiguous pattern of kinship and matrimonial alliances, or their past personal devotion to a particular prince.

In the outcome of the impending battle, certain nobles would soon become famous as either great heroes or great traitors. Stung by accusations of Rajput cowardice because Jaswant Singh had fled the battle of Dharmat, the greatest Rajput generals of the age were now chafing to annihilate themselves for Dara Shikoh: their various clansmen would be led with fanatic bravery. One already legendary Deccan veteran, the Shia grandee, Rustam Khan, would also die for

Dara. The most spectacular traitor of the day hovered in Dara's shadow with his contingent of Uzbek horsemen: Khalilullah Khan, a noble of the first rank stationed at the imperial court. Surprisingly, another commander of horse whose loyalty was more than open to doubt would also participate with the loyalists; by necessity, Moslem Qasim Khan had to be forgiven for his flight from Dharmat.

During the restless night which now enveloped the plain, Aurangzeb ordered strict watch kept around his camp. One of his flowery scribes says that he harangued his officers to bolster their spirits: "Tomorrow will be a day of valiant deeds. My capital [Aurangabad] is very far from this place. You must attack the enemy with one heart."

Suspicious Manucci gives a deeper-dyed account of activity in the enemy bivouac. Three pieces of rebel artillery abruptly went off at midnight—a signal to traitors that Aurangzeb had made his dispositions for battle at daybreak. About one o'clock in the morning, Dara and a few cavalrymen left the imperial camp to inspect battle environs; "it was necessary to take down my tent to allow a passage for his exit," the Italian adds with his usual touch of verisimilitude.

As a high-spirited young European artilleryman on his first major military engagement, Niccolo Manucci was bursting with curiosity. A little while later he took his own horse and went out to survey the scene from a height adjoining an uninhabited village; though it was still dark, he discerned "many horsemen leave our army for that of Aurangzeb and never return"—defection had already begun!

Accuracy can hardly be expected from the memoirs of an old man looking back on a battle he participated in many years before. But by contrast with authoritative Mogul accounts there is a personalized excitement in Manucci's eagle's-eye view of what now took place: the stylized Indian battle formation of two cumbersome armies due to clash within hours. It was almost daybreak. "As the light grew clearer, I saw that Aurangzeb was advancing very leisurely with his whole army. It was formed into five divisions of cavalry."

Manucci spotted Aurangzeb in the middle of the first division, "seated on a large elephant, accompanied by 15,000 horsemen, well armed with lances, bows and arrows, and matchlocks." The rebel right wing boasted an equal number of cavalry under the joint command of high-ranking Bahadur Khan and Aurangzeb's son Mohammed Sultan. A third division buttressed this right wing, while Murad Bakhsh presided over a fourth division from the howdah of a lofty elephant in which he sat with his little son. To the extreme left of Murad came the remaining army—"of problematical value, made up of low-class men of unwarlike habits, in addition to baggage, carts, camels, and unloaded oxen." Even as Manucci watched, enemy artillery was being brought forward.

"I answer for all this with confidence," wrote the irrepressible European. But his positioning of Aurangzeb's troops varies considerably from Mogul assessment: Aurangzeb was indeed in the middle, yet well protected behind a van of cavalry; far from being on the right, his son preceded him. Distributed like chess rooks among the great mass of cavalry and infantry, armor-clad elephants bristled with body barbs and blades attached to their tusks.

Returning to his own side, Manucci saw that Dara had been busy arranging imperial forces in a lineup five miles wide! A front row of artillery carriages fluttered with scarlet pennons. Behind this facade of guns came twenty-five thousand musketeers, sustained by five hundred camels with swivel guns; a row of armor-clad pachyderms plodded next, followed by twenty-eight thousand cavalry. Dara commanded the extreme rear astride a massive elephant, followed by numerous other elephants carrying drums and drummers, trumpets and trumpeters, and an assortment of other instrumentalists. The crown prince's right wing consisted of fifteen thousand Rajputs, while to their extreme right Khalilullah Khan brought twice as many Uzbeks. The veteran general, Rustam Khan, headed Dara's left wing of fifteen thousand cavalry, and a far left flank contributed an equal body of horsemen—largely Rajputs. "All this array made a lovely sight," Manucci intrudes esthetically, "both by the beauty of arms and by the number of standards and pennons of so many colors." His description of the deployment of imperial troops (aside from exaggerated numbers) is more or less correct, except that the Rajputs mainly formed an advance cavalry, while Dara's fourteen-year-old son, Sipihr Shikoh, accompanied Rustam Khan's division as titular royal commander.

A curious unreality hovers over all Mogul battles, and Samugarh is no exception. It may be the florid Persian accounts of court chroniclers, but everything becomes marvelously static: the caparisoned elephants, the valiant princes and their baby sons in howdahs, the Rajputs in yellow robes of death and with faces smeared by turmeric, the prancing horses, the glittering lances and pikes, the arrows and the rockets—all seem to be frozen forever, like the figures on Keats's Grecian urn. At a given moment, everyone charges; and the next moment, everyone flees. But like Zeno's arrow, there has been no real movement between charge and flight, only a series of undynamic scenes representing action.

To belligerently sophisticated Europeans, Indian battle tactics seemed downright absurd. François Bernier would later comment keenly: "These immense armies frequently perform great feats; but when thrown into confusion it is impossible to restore them to discipline. They resemble an impetuous river which has burst its banks . . . . I could never see these soldiers . . . without reflecting upon the ease with which five-and-twenty thousand of our veterans from the army in Flanders, commanded by Prince Condé or Marshal Turenne, would overcome these armies, however numerous."

Manucci pinpoints the same weaknesses. "I saw in this action," he writes, "as in so many others where I was afterwards present, that the only soldiers who fought were those well to the front. Of those more to the rear, although holding their bare swords in their hands, the Moguls did nothing but shout 'Ba-kush! Ba-kush!' and the Indians 'Mar! Mar!'— that is to say, 'Kill! Kill!' If those in the front advanced, those behind followed the example, and if the former retired the others fled, a custom of Hindustan quite contrary to that of Europe."

Schooled in a deadly Western tradition of war, both Europeans missed the meaning. Mogul conflicts had long since become stylized, etiquette-laden games of hierarchical force which often stopped short of annihilation through submission, tribute, or conciliation. The difficulty in the War of Succession was that regal princes equal in rank could not easily submit; and the special hatred between Dara Shikoh and Aurangzeb turned ritual into chaos.

The Battle of Samugarh began with an inevitable artillery engagement. By Mogul clocks it was noon of May 29, 1658, but Manucci places the battle between nine and noon; at all events, the hugely cumbersome encounter quickly degenerated into confusion. Dara's gunners opened fire at too great a distance, doing little damage to Aurangzeb's troops. "I was much amazed," Manucci confesses, "at their making us work thus for nothing." In an atmosphere filled with cannon smoke and whizzing rockets, Aurangzeb's artillery replied briefly and then fell silent.

Both armies had been aligned for defensive action; but an emotional Dara now decided on direct assault, mistakenly assuming (or treacherously advised) that enemy fire had been effectively silenced by his own guns. Imperial kettledrums, trumpets, and exotic instruments struck up a weird martial overture, punctuated by musket fire and wildly blaring elephants as the twin hordes came together.

Obsessed with betrayal, Manucci flatly blames Khalilullah Khan for persuading Dara that Aurangzeb's guns had been put out of commission. The old veteran Rustam Khan more prudently advised defensive tactics, but dark urging prevailed: Dara ordered imperial artillery wagons to be unchained for the horses to pass.*

In a suicidal dash marked by curdling cries and drawn

---

* By rules of Indian fighting, cannon were linked with chains to prevent enemy cavalry from riding between artillery carriages and attacking the gunners.

sabers, the imperial left wing of at least ten thousand cavalry, heartened by Rustam Khan and Sipihr Shikoh on lumbering elephants, poured from behind their lines and charged a division of enemy artillery head on. Meeting a hail of cannon balls, Rustam Khan veered in search of Aurangzeb while rebel defenders moved forward to counter his assault. Men were now fighting hand to hand, with swords and daggers flailing. Rustam's cavalry seemed to make headway, wounding Bahadur Khan and killing two of his captains; but the imperial wedge was soon outnumbered. Wounded in the arm, Rustam abandoned his elephant for a horse and fought his way to the enemy center in a savage finale: his head was hacked off and tossed before Aurangzeb's elephant as a token of victory. Sipihr Shikoh and a remnant of Dara's left wing fell back.

Bullets, arrows, javelins, and pikes had by now inundated the general encounter of cavalry and infantry. In fact, the imperial infantry (by Manucci's more sordid account of events) "fell into confusion. Barbers, butchers, and all the rest turned right-about face, abandoning artillerymen and guns. Many made for the baggage train to plunder it, which they did, breaking open chests of gold and silver and carrying off whatever they could lay hands on."

As a perfunctory gesture, Khalilullah Khan's contingent of Uzbeks clopped forward and discharged a volley of arrows at Murad's division, but retreated into obscurity for the rest of the battle. Rajputs, taking over the assault on Murad, managed to separate his entire wing from Aurangzeb's main army. Even prejudiced Mogul accounts (including Aurangzeb's own court historian) praise Rajput chivalry. Maddened by opium and bhang, their faces an orange mask of turmeric, their robes dyed the brilliant yellow of the Hindu spring carnival, imperial Rajputs looked for an absolute bride: death. Rajah Ram Singh Rathor, with a string of pearls wound round his turban, dismounted with a group of his men and led a charge on Murad's elephant. The beast had already been wounded by arrows, spears, and battleaxes to such an extent that Murad had ordered its legs chained. Arrows bris-

tled from the howdah like porcupine quills.* Murad himself
suffered from three arrow wounds in the face. Manucci provides a bizarre momentary glimpse of Murad's restless infant
son, "so anxious to see what was going on that his father was
forced to cover him with his shield and place one foot over
his head." Rajputs now tried to slash loose the howdah and
bring Murad to the ground. Ram Singh called savagely to the
mahout, "Make the elephant kneel down!" Then he hurled
his javelin at Murad with a contemptuous shout: "*You* dare
to contest the throne with Dara Shikoh?" The javelin missed
its target; Murad responded by shooting an arrow into Ram
Singh's chest.

Decimated by arrows, bullets, and rockets, fallen Rajputs made the ground "as yellow as a field of saffron." Outnumbered, the remaining golden bridegrooms of death
pushed Murad and his wing still further backward with all
the fury of a suicide squad, even wildly gashing their way to
Aurangzeb himself and attacking his Moslem guards in a signal burst of hatred—"like ravening dogs," as Manucci puts
it. Many Rajput leaders were already dead; and Rajah Rup
Singh Rathor now joined them in a spectacular moment of
endeavor: jumping down from his horse, he slashed a ferocious path to Aurangzeb's elephant and tried to cut the
howdah girths. Impressed with such fanatic bravado, Aurangzeb called out vainly to his bodyguard to spare the
Rajput's life. But Rup Singh was already being hacked to
pieces.

In effect, both Dara's left and right cavalry wings had
been put out of commission. From the very opening of hostilities, Dara had urged his elephant forward through artillery
and aimed for Aurangzeb. For a later Mogul historian he
showed "great bravery," but by most other accounts the
move proved fatal: he had abdicated his center and could no
longer direct imperial forces. His own artillery was ob-

---

* Murad's arrow-studded howdah was preserved for years afterward in the storerooms of the Red Fort at Delhi as a testament of
valor.

structed from firing, while Aurangzeb's European gunners began a deadly volley.

Manucci offers a somewhat different view of events. Dara, rallying imperial troops, had penetrated the rebel line and put camels and infantry to such rout that Aurangzeb seemed in "great risk of being taken." At this point Aurangzeb ordered his elephant's legs chained, shouting, "O God! O God! In you is my trust! I will sooner die on this spot than give way."

It was the peak moment. Yet conflicting versions make it difficult to determine what now actually did happen. By Mogul assessment, Dara had been so battered by Aurangzeb's artillery and musketmen that he shied away to help Rajputs who were fighting Murad's contingent. Manucci recounts the exact opposite: Dara's heroics had destroyed Aurangzeb's center and scattered rebel reinforcements as well as Mohammed Sultan's troops before he veered to assist the attack on Murad. Yet if Dara really came so close to defeating Aurangzeb, why did he turn away? His maneuver against Murad seems bizarre: it entailed a long sweep from left to right across the entire battlefront. With men dropping from sunstroke in the heat, those who followed Dara's wheelings were soon more dead than alive.

Both contemporary Mogul historians and Manucci have axes to grind. As Dara's European sympathizer saw it, an almost victorious prince would now be betrayed by a stunning act of treason. To orthodox scribes faithful to Aurangzeb, Dara was in any case ready for the coup de grace: in extreme peril he saw newly created peers dying at the feet of his elephant, their heads or arms shot off by cannon balls while a rocket struck his howdah.

Whatever the circumstances, all descriptions agree: Dara dismounted from his elephant and shifted to a horse— the gesture would literally cost him a kingdom. According to Manucci, "this was as if he had quitted victory; for soldiers and commanders who in the midst of battle kept an eye on Dara, not seeing him on his elephant, assumed that he must already be dead. For this reason they were thrown into great confusion. I myself was in astonishment and in great dismay." Manucci blames the villain: Khalilullah Khan, having previously held aloof from the battle, galloped up to Dara and promised Aurangzeb's defeat; now was the moment to exchange a clumsy elephant for a horse, and lead imperial cavalry to victory with the support of Khalilullah's division (expressly held back for this purpose).

Khalilullah Khan's betrayal has always been dismissed by reputable Indian historians as mere bazaar gossip. Yet Manucci *did* participate in the Battle of Samugarh, and Bernier's later second-hand account also accuses the same noble. Manucci's version may be oversimplified but it cannot be far from the truth: Khalilullah Khan had certainly retired behind the lines with his Uzbek cavalry after a token volley of arrows in Murad's direction, depriving the imperial army of a whole contingent; additionally, his outright collusion with Aurangzeb would become apparent almost immediately after the battle.

In any event, it was all over. Rajputs and their chiefs lay dead on the battlefield; Rustam Khan had been decapitated, Sipihr Shikoh was weeping bitterly, and in a panorama of disaster men were dying of sunstroke and crying for water, while what was left of the imperial army broke up and fled from the field. Khalilullah Khan and his division were already well out of sight, and only a remnant of personal bodyguards surrounded Dara. A wind like a sirocco now sprang up. Determined attendants grabbed the bridles of Dara's and Sipihr Shikoh's horses, forcing them to take the road to Agra.

Four or five miles away, Dara stopped in the shade of a neem tree to take off his burning helmet, so exhausted and so profoundly depressed that even the approaching roll of enemy kettledrums made little difference. He is supposed to have cried out, "Whatever is destined to happen, let it happen now." Finally his shocked followers persuaded him to mount horse again.

Alerted of impending battle by advance reports from Dara's camp, both the royal court and populace of Agra had spent the day in fear and trembling. Beginning at noon, distant sounds of artillery fire could even be heard. Everyone, from Emperor Shah Jahan and Princess Royal Jahanara to the lowest citizen, was preoccupied: the outcome for Dara Shikoh and the imperial forces would be either victory or total disaster. As early as two o'clock in the afternoon, fugitives from the battlefield began to straggle in; but they were deserters able to confirm nothing. At nine o'clock in the evening, a dwindled group of horsemen without torches (Dara and his followers, many of them wounded) clattered past the Taj Mahal and bypassed the entry of the Red Fort on their way to Dara's mansion along the Jumna River. Shrieks and wails of disaster came from inside, and news spread throughout the city at once.

All Agra responded like Thebes after Oedipus had blinded himself. Inside the Red Fort, Shah Jahan and Jahanara burst violently into tears, with women of the harem sobbing a black chorus. After the initial shock had subsided, the emperor sent a eunuch to Dara with a bleak acknowledgment of kismet: "What has reduced you to such a state is only the decree of Fate. It is better for you now to come to the Fort and see me. After hearing what I have to say, you may go wherever Fate leads you. What is predestined for you will happen wherever you may be."

In its acceptance of defeat, the message was profoundly Moslem: the will of Allah. Dara received it writhing on the floor, completely broken in body and spirit. Two days of merciless sun had culminated in a heap of corpses; all India was lost, together with the two indispensable attributes of a Mogul prince conditioned by the century he lived in—pride and honor. Worse: he could blame no one but himself. Shah Jahan had been consistently opposed to a military clash, and had been prevented from personal parley with the rebel princes; an entire imperial army (larger than rebel forces) with imperial arms and imperial money had been given to Dara, and he had even left Agra with an exultant cry of "crown or coffin." Defeated but not dead, he could not bring himself to see his father or sister now.

Dara's reply to the emperor was simple to the point of

[254]

eloquence. "I cannot face Your Majesty in my present distress. And if I stay here longer, I will be dead. Do not ask to witness my shame, but permit me to go away. I beg your farewell prayer for a distracted and half-dead man in the long journey that he has before him."

For Shah Jahan this refusal was double sorrow, but immediate practical steps had to be taken for Dara's flight. Mules laden with gold coin were sent from the treasury, and orders were dispatched to the governor of Delhi to open the Red Fort with all its assets and matériel of war. There were still grounds for hope: Sulaiman Shikoh's army was momentarily expected from Bengal, and troops loyal to Dara would leave Agra to join him in Delhi. By Manucci's report, Jahanara also sent a eunuch messenger to Dara with valuable jewels: "She expressed her deep grief, telling him that she was even more discomfited than he; but she had not lost all hope of someday seeing him reign peacefully [and] would petition God in her prayers."

About three o'clock in the morning of May 30 Dara left Agra for Delhi, accompanied by his wife Nadira Begum, his son Sipihr Shikoh, his daughter Jani, his grandchildren, and a pitiable escort of a dozen horsemen—guards and servants. Loyal partisans straggling out of Agra over the next several days would raise his supporters to some five thousand men; Shah Jahan would continue to send money and supplies until Aurangzeb seized Agra and closed the Delhi road. Dara dispatched instructions to his son Sulaiman Shikoh to join him in Delhi at once. For the moment, other members of his household—musicians, slave girls and women of the harem —took refuge in Agra Fort with the emperor. The crown prince had managed to retrieve jewels and coin from his own house, but the rest—furniture, elephants and horses—would soon be looted.

Manucci's role in the War of Succession was by no means over. He writes:

Seeing our total defeat, I made in haste for the city of Agra, where I arrived at ten o'clock at night. The whole city was in an uproar, for a Portuguese called Antonio de Azevedo (who early in the battle had witnessed the plunder of the baggage) rode off at full speed. On arriving at . . . Agra at two o'clock in the afternoon, his horse fell dead at his door. Thus the news began to spread that Dara had lost the battle, and the confusion was increased by Dara's own arrival. The curiosity of everyone was aroused to know how defeat had happened, and men asked each passerby about the safety of their masters. This happened to me. An old woman asked me what had become of Khalilullah Khan. Owing to the rage I was in at his treachery, I replied at once that I was present when he was torn to pieces* . . . . On learning that Dara was resuming his journey and making for Delhi, I decided that very instant upon rejoining him. But my steed was so worn out that he could hardly stand, just as were those of everyone who reached the city that night. I decided to take a rest for twenty-four hours, and after that to start and go in search of Dara.

As it turned out, Manucci was delayed in following his sponsor, and thus became witness to events in Agra during the next few historic days.

Behind Dara, ten thousand imperial troops lay dead on the Plain of Samugarh, along with many hundreds of horses and transport animals. Nine high-ranking Rajput and nineteen eminent Moslem nobles had died for the loyalist cause. By dawn, all the way from Samugarh to Agra, the aftermath of war would be revealed in its full horror. Groups of wounded, dying, or dead soldiers stretched for miles along the roadside, which was also littered with the carcasses of oxen, mules, camels, horses, and elephants. In the city itself, dead men were piling up.

The battle of Samugarh has been compared to Waterloo. Heroic Rajputs had been as loyal as Napoleon's guards, while Aurangzeb had rivaled Wellington in cool defensive tactics; Dara's great army collapsed like Napoleon's, and the

---

* Wishful thinking: Khalilullah Khan remained very much alive.

imperialist cry of *nous sommes trahis* was leveled against Khalilullah Khan. But comparison quickly founders: Dara Shikoh was no Napoleon; on the contrary, the future dictator of Hindustan had won the day.

For India, Samugarh was perhaps the most decisive military engagement that had ever been fought and lost. Far from settling a petty family dispute over a crown, the disaster presaged three hundred years of vital events: British conquest, the ultimate division of Pakistan and India, Hindu-Moslem feuds, and endless bloodshed. Medieval Mogul splendor had ended; the so-called Age of Akbar, with its liberal coalition of Moslem and Hindu, its fused nationalism in politics and art, was gone forever. Aurangzeb would see to that.

For Dara Shikoh personally, defeat at Samugarh meant the agony of flight foredoomed. A new theme of hunter and hunted would preoccupy India for some time to come—a theme encompassing more than Dara. Murad had ironically accelerated his own imminent downfall, and events must now engulf Shah Jahan, Jahanara, Raushanara, Shuja, Sulaiman Shikoh, every person of royal blood, every noble, and every holy man. Brooding over the military blueprint of a subcontinent, Aurangzeb alone would dictate every subsequent move with relentless brilliance, only to find fate accumulated and waiting for him in a still-distant end. His strategy, though he couldn't have known it then, was really turned against himself.

CHAPTER

16

A Game of Finesse

AT THE MOMENT OF Dara Shikoh's flight from the Battle of
Samugarh, Aurangzeb got down from his elephant and
said his prayers—twice over, by Mogul accounts. Khalilullah
Khan immediately transferred himself and his Uzbek cavalry
to the winners, and Aurangzeb ordered kettledrums to be
struck up in token of victory. For a few days, until his openly
formal defection to the rebels on June 5, Khalilullah would
play the role of a useful inside man at Agra fort; Aurangzeb
now presented him to Murad as a "most faithful friend."

The victors moved in on Dara's deserted camp after first
making certain it had not been mined, but furniture and
treasure had already been cheerfully looted by imperial deserters. Aurangzeb modestly ascribed credit for the day's success to his younger brother, adding that Murad's "reign" had
already begun. Though terms of their treaty of alliance promised Murad nothing more than India's western provinces, the
puritan had outrageously been flattering the black sheep ever
since the conjoining of their two armies. Adopting a new outlook, Aurangzeb represented himself as a humble but pious
Moslem whose only desire was to squelch Dara's apostasy;
afterwards he would take up the life of a fakir, and Murad
could sit on a materialistic throne. By now he was even call-
ing Murad "His Majesty," while Murad deferred to Aurangzeb as "His Holiness." If this deception was not the public
play-acting they had privately agreed upon to lend a religious
sanction to their rebellion, then Murad was even more stupid

than history makes him out to be. Quite clearly, the man who dictated their every strategy had no intention of retiring from the political scene.

Murad's arrow wounds were now treated by army surgeons. Aurangzeb withdrew to his tent nearby to reward meritorious officers. The rebel camp at Samugarh settled down to a night of victory celebrations, illumined by the flames of myriad funeral pyres as Hindus cremated their dead from the field of battle.

Two days later, on June 1, the princes and their swollen rebel army camped two miles outside of Agra (not far from the Taj Mahal) where they remained for ten days. Panic prevailed in the city: despite Aurangzeb's strict disciplinary orders, Murad's soldiers indulged in the usual looting and mayhem. By June 3 Aurangzeb had to send his son Mohammed Sultan to restore order, and at least one report affirms that Agra's chief of police was executed and replaced by a rebel Tartar officer (Manucci's account makes Aurangzeb's son the chief of police in this new setup). Aurangzeb had meanwhile stationed cavalry at the western road to and from Agra, in order to prevent Dara's followers from joining him in Delhi. All of Agra came under rebel control except for the Red Fort, still in the hands of Shah Jahan and a loyal imperial guard.

Some of Dara's adherents, including a few Europeans, had managed to take the road to Delhi before the blockade. But Manucci waited too late until the morning after defeat at Samugarh. "I made a start," he explains, "riding my horse, followed by a loaded camel and some servants." Outside of Agra, five hundred cavalrymen stopped him. The commander "asked me lovingly where I was going. I replied without subterfuge that I was on my way to find my master, Dara. He took compassion on my youth and innocence, and said to me that if I followed his advice I should return home, for if I proceeded farther I ran great risk of losing my life. This captain was so generous that, to protect me, he escorted me safely to my house." The loving captain's soldiers were crestfallen at having been robbed of plunder, while Manucci received a warning to stay put, since "the government had already changed hands, and Aurangzeb was victor." He bided his time, waiting for "a safer opportunity to start in search of Dara, for whom I had a great affection."

Defection from the loyalist cause to Aurangzeb now became a virtual stampede. Imperial army officers, grandees, and khans flocked to the rebel camp to pay their respects and pledge allegiance. A few more enterprising opportunists had even left Agra the very day after the Battle of Samugarh in order to greet the rebel victors en route. First to shift alliance was Mir Jumla's son, Mohammed Amin, who promptly received a robe of honor and an increase in rank from Aurangzeb. Mumtaz Mahal's brother, Shaista Khan, after a few days of temporary imprisonment by Shah Jahan, went over to the rebels by June 5. Qasim Khan and a host of top-ranking nobles followed suit, while imperial troops unable or unwilling to follow Dara in his flight also joined the rebel army.

A few belated defectors were not so well received. Some days later (when the imperial cause had really dimmed) Jahanara's snobbish musician Dulera decided to cultivate new friends, and Manucci recounts the sordid outcome:

> He went to see several of Murad Bakhsh's commanders and was well received, for he could sing to perfection. Being in merry mood, the wine began to go round. Dulera, already heated, ran down the wine they gave him; he ordered his servants to fetch some more exquisite wine, such as he always drank. The officers noticed the grand ways of the musician; and when the wine arrived they found it was in bottles of gold and enamel, adorned with precious stones such as [they] themselves did not possess. Dulera exalted himself a good deal in his talk, assuming to be the equal of the officers. Seeing so much impudence and assumption, and also moved by the envy and resentment they felt towards Begum Sahib, they had him bound; and stripping him of his trousers, forced a lighted night-lamp into his anus, leaving it to burn until the musician begged pardon for his transgressions. They sent him off with blows and

kicks. This occurrence made him lower the lofty ideas
that he had, and retiring to his house he stayed there
until his death and never appeared again.

Observing other events in the city, Manucci gives a running description of Aurangzeb's strategy. A eunuch and
confidant named Fahim was dispatched to the Red Fort with
soft words and excuses: the Battle of Samugarh had been
precipitated by Dara's ambitions, it was all most unfortunate, but the rebel princes were delighted with the emperor's
improved health and waited upon his orders. Shah Jahan
found himself in a dilemma: he might be able to count on the
passive sympathy of Agra's citizens, but both his nobles and
the remnant of Dara's army had already gone over to Aurangzeb. He now decided "to play a game of finesse with Aurangzeb, a supreme master in that line."

With minor variations, European accounts substantially
corroborate Mogul narratives. By June 1, with Aurangzeb already at the gates of the city, Shah Jahan had sent him a
handwritten letter through two personal intermediaries—a
doddering old court chamberlain named Fazil Khan, and
Agra's chief Moslem justice, Sayyid Hidayatullah. The emperor longed to see his son and discuss matters of state; Aurangzeb tentatively agreed to a meeting. Twenty-four hours
later the ambassadors returned to the rebel camp with gifts
from the emperor, significantly presenting "His Holiness"
with the famous *Alamgir* or "World-Conqueror" sword. But
by now Aurangzeb had become suspicious: his nobles advised him that he would be in grave danger if he visited the
Red Fort. The disappointed old chamberlain paid a third
courtesy call on June 5, this time accompanied by Khalilullah Khan; Shah Jahan, appalled by his son's mistrust, begged
him to come to the fort and "see for himself the full extent of
his father's love and kindness." Khalilullah Khan winked
and received private audience with Aurangzeb: yes, it was an
assassination plot; the prince risked his life as long as Shah
Jahan remained at liberty. At last old Fazil Khan, who had
been cooling his heels outside, was informed that Khalilullah

Khan had been placed under arrest and that Aurangzeb declined to see the emperor. The chamberlain reported to Shah Jahan that "the matter had now gone beyond the stage of sending letters and messages."

Bernier and Manucci both confirm that, "without a shadow of a doubt," armed Tartar and Uzbek women in the harem would have murdered Aurangzeb as soon as he entered the fort. Rather exaggeratedly, Bernier depicts a bewildered Shah Jahan completely under Jahanara's control, with the princess royal dictating his every message and strategy; more restrained, Manucci admits that Jahanara would likely further Dara's cause as much as she could.

By any interpretation of events, both sides were obviously up to their eyes in intrigue. Diplomacy having failed, Shah Jahan now closed the gates of Agra fort and prepared for defense with a small band of loyal officers, a garrison of some fifteen hundred Turks and Abyssinians, and a few European artillerymen. The closing of the gates came none too soon—Aurangzeb abandoned pretense and opened siege that very night with a sneak attack by a rebel detachment. Formidable artillery was emplaced on Dara's mansion along the Jumna River and also on the terrace of the great mosque facing the west gate bastion of the Red Fort; continuous assault knocked out several fort guns and damaged upper stories of the palace. But Akbar had made Agra's stronghold virtually impregnable for its time: a deep moat and massive walls frustrated mining and assault tactics, while rebel cannon could effect only small damage. Crack imperial musketeers, shooting at bobbing heads and shadows, maintained defensive fire from the walls.

Impregnable yet vulnerable: with Agra under Aurangzeb's complete control, his troops found no difficulty in at least surrounding the Red Fort, taking cover behind trees and under fort eaves or inside of nearby houses. Manucci writes:

> Although already caught as in a cage, Shah Jahan never desisted from firing his guns and musketry to hold back

the investing force from nearer approach. But no damage was done, the enemy being safely under cover and without need to return fire. Guns were loaded and discharged for three days and three nights, making a great noise. At the end of that time artillerymen, headed by the Englishman Reuben Smith, began to . . . descend the walls by ropes. They had been bribed by Aurangzeb, who communicated with them by letting fly an arrow into the fort. The remainder of the garrison, when they saw the departure of the artillerymen, lost heart and also began to plan a means of flight.

For Aurangzeb it was a question of days and hours. Sustained assault on the Red Fort would detain his army in Agra, allowing Dara Shikoh time to rally effective support in Delhi. Most authorities agree that Aurangzeb was a master strategist, and yet there remains an unanswered puzzle: why did he allow Dara to escape from the Battle of Samugarh, when it would have been so easy to pursue him at once and capture or kill him before he ever left Agra? Practical motives could be invented: the immediate and outright murder of Dara (before Aurangzeb had consolidated his strength through the defection of nobles and the greater part of the imperial army) might have backfired and caused nobles to rally to Shah Jahan. Or Aurangzeb might have thought that a disgraced Dara would leave India without attempting any further military struggle. But such rationale seems weak in the light of Aurangzeb's hatred of Dara. The answer must be psychological: until Shah Jahan was completely neutralized, Aurangzeb's abiding fear of his father still seems to have prevailed. In the intense ambiguity surrounding their game of finesse, it is almost as though Aurangzeb were still wanly seeking some shred of proof that Shah Jahan loved him— anything rather than believe that the emperor would murder him for the sake of Dara Shikoh. Whatever the truth, Shah Jahan now had to be quickly robbed of all final power.

Still in his camp outside of the city, Aurangzeb held discussions with his chief military officers and decided on a plan to force submission of Agra fort in short order: he would cut off the water supply. A commando assault by a rebel detachment now gained control of the fort gate that opened on the Jumna River; protected from overhead rampart fire by the arch, they simply prevented water from being taken in by the garrison. It was a siege by thirst, since the palace had no other water supply aside from a few long-disused and brackish wells. Within twenty-four hours, imperial officers began to filter forth on the pretext of parleying with the enemy for water; overcome by June heat, the rest of the defenders wanted to capitulate.

Desperately, the old emperor wrote a letter in prose and verse to Aurangzeb, addressing him as "my son, my hero," and invoking sentimental Islamic metaphors. But there is a false ring in Shah Jahan's pleas at this moment: like a fake King Lear he still attitudinizes, and real suffering can only come later. "Why," he writes, "should I complain of the unkindness of fortune, seeing that not a leaf is shed by a tree without the will of Allah? Only yesterday I was master of nine hundred thousand troopers, and today I am in need of a pitcher of water! Praised be the Hindus . . . who offer water to their dead, while my devout Moslem son refuses water to the living."

The rebel's reply was crisp and unpoetic: "It is your own doing." After three days, with every tongue in the fort hanging out, Shah Jahan decided to yield. The doddering chamberlain delivered a capitulating letter full of starkly gloomy imprecations: no emperor had ever suffered such a fate; it might be God's will but it was also a Luciferian display of power by a son who had forgotten Koranic injunctions of filial piety. Besides, Aurangzeb ought not to ruin imperial Mogul family prestige.

A new phase of the Aurangzeb-Shah Jahan correspondence had begun with this shift of power from father to son: a relentless psychological castration by proxy. Now all the years of humiliation would be paid back in kind and without compunction; there would be no face-to-face encounter, only an epistolary duel of attrition. Aurangzeb had not seen his father in years, nor would he ever see him again. For the moment a cool etiquette still prevailed: he was not being disloyal, he stressed, but had been provoked by Dara's enmity. "Owing to certain occurrences," he wrote, "I am afraid to interview Your Majesty . . . . If Your Majesty surrenders the gates of the Fort to my men and gives them free ingress and egress, and thereby removes my suspicion, I shall go and wait on you, consent to whatever you wish, and do nothing displeasing or harmful to you."

On June 8, 1658, Shah Jahan opened the Red Fort of Agra to Aurangzeb's commanders. They took over lock, stock, and barrel, and dismissed the emperor's remaining nobles. Imperial treasure—jewels, robes, and furniture—was placed under lock and seal, and the entire arsenal fell to the rebels. In effect, the booty of three generations of Mogul emperors now belonged to Aurangzeb.

Bernier and Manucci offer a somewhat different version of the fall of Agra fort: far from submitting, the emperor had been defeated by treason. Aurangzeb's son, Mohammed Sultan, on the pretext of delivering a message from his father to the emperor, rushed in a contingent of his men to overcome guards stationed at the gate and quickly occupied the fort. Shah Jahan now tried a new ploy: if Mohammed Sultan would free him and help him, he would turn over the keys of the fort and all its treasures and make his grandson king of India. Mohammed Sultan declined the offer. "Few will believe," Bernier concludes with neat French cynicism, "that Mohammed Sultan was restrained by a sense of duty to his father . . . it is more likely that he doubted the sincerity of the King's promises, and felt all the danger of disputing the crown with a man endued with the mental energy and imposing talents of Aurangzeb."

Aurangzeb's eunuch, Itibar Khan, now became governor of the fort; Shah Jahan and Jahanara were confined in the harem with their retinue, while many of the gates were promptly walled up. Manucci notes that only one woman was allowed to leave—"Raushanara Begum, the beloved sister of Aurangzeb, who was despatched with great pomp."

She had served her purpose as rebel confidante, and would be duly rewarded. With fort gates and wickets closed, Shah Jahan was kept virtually incommunicado. A strong rebel guard inside and outside of the fort precluded any rescue plots; eunuchs and servants were carefully screened, and Aurangzeb appointed his own doctors to attend to the emperor's health.

On June 10, two days after Shah Jahan's submission, Jahanara decided to make a personal embassy to her brother in the hope of effecting terms for the emperor. The very fact that Aurangzeb received her (knowing that she was Dara's and Shah Jahan's partisan) shows the esteem in which she was held by all. Aurangzeb's official chronicler would suppress the purpose of her visit, but by independent accounts she brought a candid offer: the emperor was willing to divide the Mogul Empire among four princes, with Dara assigned to the Punjab, Murad to Gujarat and Shuja to Bengal; Aurangzeb's eldest son could be made governor of the Deccan, with Aurangzeb himself receiving the rest of the realm and full title to the throne.

The offer was rejected. Aurangzeb is supposed to have said: "Dara is an infidel to Islam and a friend of the Hindus. He must be extirpated for the sake of the true faith and the peace of the realm. I cannot visit the Emperor before concluding this business." After further discussion, Jahanara managed to elicit her brother's promise that he would visit Shah Jahan. The very next day he did in fact start out for the Red Fort, in a ceremonial procession with great crowds of cheering people lining the streets of Agra—the anonymous masses had proved no less fickle than grandees. En route, Mumtaz Mahal's brother and another noble clattered up on horseback, warning Aurangzeb that assassination lay in wait at the hands of Shah Jahan's harem women. The rebel stopped his elephant, while at that moment a slave conveniently arrived from the Red Fort with a secret letter which the emperor had entrusted to him for smuggling out to Dara. "Dara Shikoh!" the message read; "Stay . . . in Delhi. There is no lack of money and troops . . . . I will take care of matters here."

Such split-second melodrama seems unbelievable, even by old-fashioned seventeenth-century standards of intrigue. Manucci flatly insists that the letter was a forgery to allow for a calculated bit of play-acting: Aurangzeb had it read aloud, feigned consternation and terror, and even concluded that it might be a fake! But his nobles agreed: he must not visit Shah Jahan. An open petition of grievance was now written to the emperor, accusing him of sending mule-loads of gold coins to Dara (this by "indisputable authority") and prolonging civil war. Bernier adds that it was Raushanara Begum who informed Aurangzeb of the gold given to Dara, as well as of the assassination plot. Adducing further proof of dissimulation, Manucci goes on to say that Shah Jahan never received the petition of grievance: "Aurangzeb started these stories solely to the end of conciliating the people and excusing his deceptions. He wanted to place the culpability upon Shah Jahan and Dara, and to prove that all the tyranny employed against his father was amply justifiable."

In this Oriental maze of intrigue, one thing certainly becomes clear: everyone had his own self-justifying rationale, and Aurangzeb's was compulsively religious. From his camp outside of Agra the conqueror had written to the emperor after the Battle of Samugarh: "Obedience was my passion as long as power was vested in your venerable hands; and I never went beyond my limit, for which the all-knowing God is my witness. But owing to Your Majesty's illness the Prince [Dara], usurping all authority and bent upon propagating the religion of Hindus and idolators and suppressing the faith of the Prophet, had brought about chaos and anarchy throughout the Empire . . . . Consequently I started from Burhanpur, lest I should be held responsible in the next world for not providing a remedy for disorders . . . ."

In other correspondence Aurangzeb more categorically unfurls his religious banner: "I had no intention of ousting the King of Islam, and God is my witness that such a sinful and unholy thought never entered my mind . . . . [But] as Your Majesty, on account of prejudice and unmindful of political conditions, wanted the eldest Prince to propagate heresy, I determined to make a *jihad* [religious war] against him."

The tone is too sincerely self-righteous to be mere hypocrisy. For Manucci, who frankly disliked Aurangzeb, this religious attitude was a sham and a pose, a mask for a blatant power drive which would do anything to gain its end. But Aurangzeb is considerably more complex than that. True, all of his sanctimonious promises and religious assertions are inevitably followed by unreligious acts of imprisonment and murder. But this is not hypocrisy in the ordinary sense of the word. There is a certain persuasive fascination in Aurangzeb's insatiable need for religious justification: God, the ultimate father who is more absolute and more reliable than Shah Jahan, must be invoked—a metaphysical father sanctioning rebellion against an earthly one. "Not my will, O Lord, but thy will": when religious self-effacement welds together with an overwhelming compulsion to power, then the result becomes a personality as paradoxical as Aurangzeb's. The hypocrisy is little short of sublime.

Yet impure motives interfere with tragedy. Dara and Jahanara are consistent and hence authentically tragic; but between professional dissemblers—between Shah Jahan and Aurangzeb—the situation often becomes allied with farce. Shah Jahan had proved hypocritical and still devoted to Dara; Aurangzeb's own hypocrisy was now vindicated. False letter or true melodrama to the rescue, he had bypassed the Red Fort and a meeting with the emperor and proceeded to Dara's mansion in the city where he took up quarters.

Shah Jahan's imprisonment was now made even more strict, and all channels of communication with the outside world were cut off. Voluntarily, Jahanara shared her father's imprisonment. Aurangzeb became emperor in all but name; a grand durbar had already been held in his camp on June 10, and in Agra city on the eleventh and twelfth he made new appointments and distributed titles and rewards. Mumtaz

Mahal's brother, Shaista Khan, took over as governor of Agra; Aurangzeb and Murad, fortified by money from Agra's appropriated treasury, started out for Delhi on June 13 in pursuit of Dara Shikoh.

Disguising himself as a holy mendicant, a nineteen-year-old faithful mingled and marched along with the rebel army in the hope of reaching Dara and continuing in his service. Niccolo Manucci would thus become an on-the-spot witness to Aurangzeb's next move: Murad's downfall was at hand.

CHAPTER 17

A Lover's Farewell

B Y AN OVERWHELMING concordance of opinion, Murad's tragedy resulted from his excessive naïveté: like a sheep following the Judas goat he seemed determined to do himself in. Mogul assessments make him "stupid and ignorant"; or, more charitably, "simple-minded." Europeans in Hindustan were frankly baffled by such willful self-destruction: Bernier says that Murad seemed almost hypnotized by Aurangzeb, and even eyewitness Manucci watched him shrug off his advisers and invite disaster. For anyone but Murad, Aurangzeb's plot would have been too obvious.

By contrast, one historian proposes the novel theory that Murad's outward subservience to Aurangzeb might have been mere expedience—the black sheep may have intended to fool the puritan before getting caught in his brother's trap. Perhaps; but there could hardly be a more unlikely candidate to play Tartuffe.

In one doubtful version* of the first rebel days in Agra, Shah Jahan supposedly sent a secret letter to Murad suggesting Aurangzeb's assassination. A text is trotted out for credence: "I have conferred the sovereignty of the whole of India on my illustrious son Murad. I enjoin you to be most careful . . . and not to divulge this secret to anyone . . . . After a few days, invite your brother and his son to your

---

* Offered by Shuja's historian, Mohammed Masum, who lived in Bengal at the time and depended on "bazaar gossip" and hearsay.

camp on the plea of a banquet and see the last of them; and then have the *khutba* [bidding prayer] recited in your name, and assume the imperial title which I bestow upon you of my own free will. You should perform this task with the greatest caution." With the greatest caution Murad left the letter in a book; his librarian found it and sold the document to Aurangzeb. Exploring all avenues, Shah Jahan would write encouraging later missives to Shuja!

But the threat of secret plots against his life hardly constituted Aurangzeb's primary reason for wanting to put Murad out of the way: by a more pertinent and immutable law of physics, two kings could not occupy the same kingdom at the same time. Nursing his wounds from the Battle of Samugarh, Murad had taken an obligatory back seat after their arrival at Agra; yet even an idiot could see defecting imperial officers pledging exclusive allegiance to Aurangzeb. Agra fort had capitulated, and with every top-ranking noble paying his respects to Aurangzeb's sanctimonious genius, Murad's influence was negligible. Their brotherly treaty of alliance (giving him the western provinces of India) meant nothing unless Aurangzeb's oath on the Koran could be trusted.

Rather wistfully, Murad still entertained notions of sitting on the encrusted Peacock Throne. During all the weeks since leaving his provincial capital of Ahmadabad he had lugged his own less glamorous seat through two major battles, along with the golden umbrella and other symbols of sovereignty left over from his premature self-crowning. While hope dimmed daily, petty vanity and jealousy increased. Murad's more worldly advisers (including the eunuch Shahbaz Khan) were highly suspicious of Aurangzeb, and at first advised their prince to stay in Agra and let Aurangzeb pursue Dara Shikoh alone. Spurred to exercise a little deceit on his own, Murad now increased his army at Aurangzeb's expense by offering more pay to defecting imperial troops than his tightwad brother. With the lure of gold and an easy-going commander, mercenaries soon doubled Murad's forces to an impressive twenty thousand men. Openly apeing Aurangzeb he handed out titles and privileges, and finally decided that it was "beneath his dignity" to visit his elder brother. In a situation of ever-increasing friction, the black sheep's army offered a haven to a disparate assortment of malcontents.

The usual Mogul kaleidoscope of intrigue shifted daily to form new patterns. Reports of Dara Shikoh's revived military buildup were already filtering through to Aurangzeb, but pursuit posed problems: if Murad resorted to treachery and concluded a private agreement with Dara through intermediaries, Aurangzeb might find himself caught between crossfire. Even now he had little or no control over the lawlessness of Murad's soldiers, and with an all-out civil war the forces of anarchy would have a field day.

Manucci claims that the hordes of both rebel princes left Agra for Delhi simultaneously, with Murad trailing a mile or so behind his brother's army. By Mogul accounts it was Aurangzeb who started out first; but Murad's advisers quickly changed their minds, fearing that it would be easy for a wily puritan to crown himself emperor in Delhi if he arrived there alone. Whatever the circumstances, someone had to keep watch over "His Holiness."

Conjoint but separate armies thus marched along the banks of the Jumna, following a standard imperial route between the two cities. Disguised as a holy man, Manucci watched "a great number of Dara's men" join Murad's army —the count included deserters (both troops and officers) now arriving from Sulaiman Shikoh's loyalist forces in Bengal. Aurangzeb began a calculated attempt to charm the bird out of the tree and smooth its ruffled feathers. After several days' march from Agra he sent Murad 233 horses and two million rupees by way of belated booty, promising more. To Manucci the ruse seemed like the ceremony of wooing a bride: several times a day messengers brought fruit and flowers for Murad, while Aurangzeb made preparations for a "wedding" feast in a swirl of new tents and caparisoned elephants; sweetmeats and perfumes were dug out of army supplies, and dancing women and musicians remained on the alert.

The twin rebel contingents had by now reached the

Hindu town of Mathura, about thirty miles north of Agra and a conveniently historical site for betrayal. Presumed to be the birthplace of the Hindu god Krishna, Mathura represented accumulated centuries of art, monasteries, and violence, and in Jahangir's reign a Rajput chief had consummated regional holiness by building a Hindu temple so high that it was visible even from Agra. Aurangzeb already had his eye on the temple and would one day ordain its destruction; but for now, thoughts of destruction centered on Murad.

Manucci draws a neat contrast between the two armies. An aura of intrigue hung over Aurangzeb's camp, with soldiers talking in metaphors about their leader's scheme—"the tiger big with young will soon bring forth." But in the army of Murad Bakhsh "there was nothing but music, dancing, wine-bibbing, and revelry."

Almost all Murad's advisers (with the exception of a personal attendant who had been corrupted by Aurangzeb to allay suspicion) protested vehemently against the proposed visit to Aurangzeb's camp. But Murad refused to be dissuaded, and after demurring for a day or two he set out on horseback with his eunuch Shahbaz and a few other officers for Aurangzeb's tents. It was June 25, 1658. Manucci invokes a final warning from a khan who met the party en route and gently took the bridle of the prince's horse in an attempt to deflect him; when Murad flew into a rage and continued onward the would-be savior called out, "Your Majesty is on his way to prison." Murad responded by clapping his hand to his sword, retorting that he was braver than anyone. Even at the entrance to Aurangzeb's tent, a well-meaning mullah bowed and whispered, "With your feet you have come," but the implication was lost.

The usual protocol prevailed within Aurangzeb's compound. Murad's attendant officers were seated in an outside pavilion and entertained by their opposite numbers, while Aurangzeb's guardsmen occupied the forecourt. Attended only by his eunuch, the black sheep entered the royal tent. In an aura of unction and salaams, Aurangzeb flattered his brother and seemed pleased at his recovery. Rosewater was sprinkled and flower petals were scattered while musicians played and dancing girls performed. In the Eastern manner a sumptuous feast was spread, with Aurangzeb acting almost as maître d'hôtel while his officers poured wine from Shiraz and Kabul for Murad. As a pious teetotaler Aurangzeb sanctioned this breach of etiquette* by saying, "Drink in my presence. I long to see you supremely happy after so many adversities."

There are varying interpretations of what happened next. Naturally enough, Aurangzeb's official chronicle mentions the arrest of Murad ("an excellent stratagem") without giving details; independent Mogul sources make it clear that, after eating and drinking, Murad lay down at Aurangzeb's suggestion while Aurangzeb retired to his harem—both princes would have a nap and discuss campaign strategy later. Murad removed his sword and dagger and sprawled supine while his eunuch massaged his legs. A slave-girl entered, motioned the eunuch to retire, and continued to massage until the victim dozed off. Then she took away his weapons.

Manucci tells the story somewhat differently. Murad withdrew to an inner compartment where a beautiful concubine had been provided; but when he wanted to have intercourse with her the eunuch Shahbaz kicked her out and began to massage his master's feet, all the while watching the door. Aurangzeb later appeared at the entranceway and motioned to the eunuch, who stuck his head outside and was immediately strangled by four men—"they buried him without a sound." Aurangzeb then sent his five-year-old son Azam as an ambassador to the sleeping prince, first to drag away Murad's sword and later his dagger; for each visit the child received a jewel by way of bribe. "This was done," Manucci explains, "so that if Murad Bakhsh should wake he would see that he who had roused him was an innocent child, and would suspect no evil."

---

* It would normally be considered rude for Murad to tipple alone in the company of his elder brother.

Whatever the ruse, Murad, half drunk, was now awakened by a dozen of Aurangzeb's most trusted officers bursting into the room. He started up and felt for his weapons, then subsided with a comment: "This is the word and oath sworn to me on the Koran." Aurangzeb, who had been hidden behind a screen, answered with a long and pharisaical diatribe: Murad's recent actions had been provoked by bad advisers and were likely to make trouble; he had become proud and insolent and needed a cooling-off period, but there was no danger since a puritan promise would still be honored—"My brother's life is safe in the protection of God."

Golden handcuffs and manacles were now put on the prisoner's hands and feet; to cry out would have been suicide. Manucci says that Aurangzeb had musicians play to camouflage the coup, while two elephants with covered howdahs and two contingents of four thousand cavalry each were brought into the royal compound to escort the prisoner. Murad was placed (like a Mogul lady) in one of the two litters, and one elephant and its escort headed for Delhi while the other took the road to Agra—authentic and decoy convoys being intended to confound any rescue attempt. It was six o'clock in the evening. (By Mogul accounts the time was midnight, and there were four elephants instead of two.)

The rest of the "excellent stratagem" proved easy. Attendant officers found themselves restrained, with the suggestion that they enter Aurangzeb's pay and forget about a lost cause. By the time the elephants had ambled off with their escorts it was clear to Murad's camp that something was going on; Manucci recalls cavalry and foot criers who came from Aurangzeb's precincts shouting "Long live King Aurangzeb," and promising double pay to anyone enlisting in "His Holiness's" cause. By morning, Murad's entire army of twenty thousand men—officers, clerks, servants, and camp followers—had been summarily absorbed.

The elephant carrying the prisoner actually took the road to Delhi (Dara had fled on news of the advancing rebel army). Murad's immediate destination was Salimgarh fortress and state prison, built in time long past in the middle of the Jumna River and connected with Delhi's Red Fort by a great bridge. Later, his little son Izad Bakhsh would join him in captivity.

Manucci says that by Aurangzeb's orders the howdah was uncovered before the elephant and its escort proceeded into the city: "It was very pitiful to see poor Murad Bakhsh make this miserable entry into Delhi visible to all, his face dejected, wearing a blue turban ill put on; behind him an executioner with a naked sword in his hand, ready upon any attempt at rescue to cut off his head." Ominously the Italian adds, "it was ordered that poppywater be given him to drink to deprive him of his senses." Called *poust,* this decoction from the milky juice of the opium poppy had become a classic Mogul device, reserved for members of the royal family to avoid marks of outward violence. Drinking it produced a secret, lingering death, in which the victims became emaciated, torpid, and almost idiotic. But here Manucci seems to have been mistaken: Murad was politically too important for a secret death. He would not die so soon; when he did, $3\frac{1}{2}$ years later, death would be public. Even Aurangzeb could be generous in memory of an oath on the Koran.

● ● ●

Fate was no less grim for having been deferred. After seven months of incarceration at Salimgarh prison in Delhi, the captive found himself transferred in late January 1659 to the Mogul state prison at Gwalior. Some seventy-odd miles due south of Agra, Gwalior seemed the quintessence of a gothic horror story. Its approach led through weird sandstone ranges and indurated iron strata; there were no villages nearby, no vegetation, "not one redeeming quality."

Wildly medieval and isolated on a steeply gargantuan mass of sandstone, Gwalior fortress even in Mogul days had been in existence for a thousand years of Hindu, Rajput, and Moslem history. Its situation was formidable: a tabletop almost two miles long, half a mile wide at its thickest point, and well over three hundred feet high. Entering the great fort gate and making the ascent by elephant, more than one royal

Mogul prisoner caught a dizzying glimpse from his lurching howdah of the ramparts of his last place of confinement: this was Rajah Man Singh's palace, built between 1486 and 1516. Beneath the awesome architectural mass of the fortress, the town of Gwalior prostrated itself at the base of the sandstone cliff. In Shah Jahan's youth, Peter Mundy of the East India Company had commented on several caravanserais and tombs, and the ascent to the fort "with so many intricate walls, bulwarks, and fortifications that it is strange to behold." In the sides of Gwalior hill, Mundy saw caves or holes where fakirs lived a trapped, Mount Athos-like existence, "having their meat let down to them by a string." Battlements and turrets completed a scene more like ancient Rome than medieval India. This stronghold, under the Moguls, had become the official state prison for members of the royal family or high-ranking nobility.

Murad spent his three last years at Gwalior, and in spite of its prepossessing murk he seems to have asserted extroverted good spirits. In his free days he had showered money on his soldiers and gotten drunk with them; surprisingly, they now showed their loyalty. Popular poems and songs about the prince began to circulate in the bazaars of Delhi and Agra, and a small but persistent band of Mogul admirers even followed him to Gwalior—ekeing out an incognito existence at the foot of the fortress as fakirs, their food supplemented by half of Murad's prison allowance. Writing about these events many years later, the independent Mogul historian, Khafi Khan, tells how his father lived at Gwalior as part of Murad's supporting contingent which spent its time plotting his release. The scheme finally adopted called for a rope ladder to be dropped from the ramparts at a given time and place, with a saddled horse waiting below. But determined to prove that fate is character, Murad botched his own escape. As a sop to sexual appetite, his favorite concubine Sarsati Bai had been allowed to share his confinement. Unable to resist a midnight lover's farewell, the prince revealed the plot to her; he would do his best, he promised, to come back and rescue her another day! Breaking into wild laments the concubine unintentionally alerted guards, who came running with torches and soon discovered the ladder.

It was a poor bid for freedom, but meticulous Aurangzeb became annoyed or felt threatened; Murad had to be permanently put out of the way. Manucci again invokes opium: every month Aurangzeb "caused the Prince's portrait to be taken, to see if the opium-juice produced any change in his natural complexion, and his face gave any sign of approaching death. But finding Murad Bakhsh's natural robustness overcame the poisonous juice, he made a plan to take his life . . . ."

Compulsive rationale of course required a justification for Murad's death, and one was soon found. Who could forget that four years earlier, at the beginning of Shah Jahan's illness and the Mogul crisis, Murad had murdered his finance minister, Ali Naqi, in Ahmadabad? Ali Naqi's two sons were now prodded to lodge a belated complaint of murder in Moslem law courts; and though the eldest declined vengeance, the younger even pursued the issue to Gwalior. By Koranic law, Gwalior's presiding judge could settle a price on murder unless the nearest of kin demanded blood, in which case the death sentence became mandatory. Murad rose to the occasion and refused to face his accusers: "If he [Aurangzeb] is resolved to take my life, there is no good in listening to such low fellows as these. He has the power, and can do what he likes."

"Alas and alas! on some pretext they killed him": imbedded in the Persian chronogram was the date of Murad's royal death—Wednesday, December 4, 1661. A company of Aurangzeb's guard and two slaves arrived at Gwalior fortress; in the presence of the complainant and other witnesses Murad suffered decapitation. He was thirty-seven years old. The corpse received burial in the so-called "Traitors' Cemetery" of Gwalior. Another imperial body would keep it company in a matter of months.

Around the base of Gwalior fortress, colossal figures of Jain saints still stand in benediction—one of them fifty-seven feet high. In the old city at the foot of the cliff is an early

Moslem mosque and the revered tomb of Ghaus Mohammed, a holy man of repute. There is also the tomb of the
greatest of all exponents of Indian music: Tan Sen, a name
so legendary that musicians from all parts of India still visit
Gwalior to pay homage to his memory. But no one pays
homage to Murad Bakhsh, the youngest son of the Lady of
the Taj. Forty years after the prince's death, Aurangzeb as an
old man referred to Murad's grave in one of his letters without a shred of compassion or regret: kingship knows no kinship.

CHAPTER 18

Pursuit in the Punjab

WITH MURAD OUT of the way, Aurangzeb was by no means master of India. Two remaining royal brothers continued to pose a considerable threat: even in defeat Dara had formidable resources at his disposal, and Shuja (as a result of the patched-up truce with Dara's son Sulaiman Shikoh) still held Bengal and exercised nominal authority over adjoining states. In addition there was Sulaiman's own imperial army, presumably heading from Bengal to join forces with his father. The Rajput chief of Jodhpur, Jaswant Singh, had retired to his homeland after failing to hold back Aurangzeb and Murad at Dharmat; but he, too, could enter the picture again with faithful tribesmen, and there were other Rajputs who might well rally to Dara's side for obvious religious reasons. The great northern province of the Punjab was still in the hands of Dara's loyal deputy, while Afghan territories to the northwest also remained unsubdued; south of the Deccan, the sultanates of Bijapur and Golconda nurtured open hostility to Aurangzeb. An entente or actual coalition of any of these forces was certainly possible.

Possible, but not likely: parochial jealousy had always been India's weakness; disparate groups which together might have defeated their common enemy were morbidly suspicious of one another, ready to be conquered, to submit, or to betray. A master soldier and fiendish strategist, Aurangzeb would now pursue his advantage relentlessly and well. Wherever time was of the essence, he would personally push forced marches against one or the other adversary; and since he could not be in two places at once he would make cunning use of stopgap tactics in those areas beyond his immediate control. The certain defeat of Dara and Shuja, the step-by-step coercion of Rajputs and independent Moslem khans inimical to Aurangzeb's interests—all this was predictable, and everyone would succumb either to unremitting force or to endless dissimulation compounded of ruses, threats, lies, and false letters. Nor would Aurangzeb lack for companions in deceit: many grandees in the empire were ready to astonish even hardened misanthropes. No scheming Medici, no Spanish Inquisition, no Byzantine plot of poisoned Eucharist wafers to kill kneeling popes in church, no aspect of world history ever excelled the nastiness and cupidity of Mogul intrigue. It all seemed designed to disillusion angels, to prove that human beings were really beyond the pale of redemption.

The obvious thing would have been for Dara and Shuja to unite: if Dara had advised his son Sulaiman to coalesce with Shuja's army for a concerted eastern attack from Bengal while he himself raised an army in the Punjab and moved from the west, Aurangzeb might have been caught in a pincer movement. There may also have been other possible joint military moves. But Dara Shikoh was emotional and impulsive; his every decision for the remainder of the War of Succession would be curiously suicidal.

After fleeing from Samugarh, Dara had traveled 120 miles northward and reached the environs of Delhi on June 5, 1658. Within the next several days some five thousand soldiers managed to rejoin him in straggling bands, until complete rebel takeover of Agra blocked all city exits and made further exodus impossible. Very temporarily (as it turned out) Dara established new headquarters at a small ruined fort in old Delhi. Shah Jahan had done what he could: in addition to urging his own adherents to join the crown prince's cause, he had provided massive coin from Agra's treasury and sanctioned access to all war matériel in the Red Fort of Delhi. Dara promptly took over arms and munitions, horses and elephants, expecting that he would have time to rally a new army while waiting for Sulaiman Shikoh's troops from Bengal—they had been instructed to return to Delhi along the east bank of the Jumna River, in order to bypass Aurangzeb's forces at Agra. Feverish imperial correspondence now went off in a dozen different directions to grandees and officers in an attempt to enlist additional aid. Momentarily, it even remained possible to maintain secret contact with Shah Jahan.

But events moved with unprecedented speed. Within three days of Dara's arrival in Delhi, Agra fort had capitulated to Aurangzeb and tight security measures isolated an impotent emperor. News soon filtered through to Dara that the rebels were already preparing to advance. Meanwhile, there was no sign of Sulaiman Shikoh; without him, a ragtag assembly of soldiers (at least half of whom had already been defeated) could hardly offer much resistance to Aurangzeb's swollen army, while the monsoon season would soon inundate escape roads leading to the Punjab. Renewed flight seemed inevitable, and it could only be in one of two directions: either north to the Punjab's capital city of Lahore, or east to the Ganges. Eastward Dara might conceivably join up with Sulaiman Shikoh's twenty-two thousand imperial troops; together father and son could make their way south to Allahabad at the junction of Jumna and Ganges, where Dara's officers still held a virtually impregnable fortress. If Shuja agreed to a coalition, their combined armies could then meet Aurangzeb.

Decision wavered in a failure of nerve. Utter loss at Samugarh had left Dara incapable of bold strokes or of looking ahead to the consequences of present action. Obligatorily he would seek a renewed confrontation with Aurangzeb sooner or later: no Mogul prince had ever shown the white feather. But by Dara's hasty reasoning, Shuja had been a part of the rebel triumvirate and could not now be trusted; if a naïve crown prince moved southeast to Allahabad, he might easily find himself wedged between two enemies. By contrast, the province of the Punjab and its neighboring Afghan territory offered mercenaries for the asking. Indeed, the Punjab was Dara's own viceroyalty, and its imperial fortress at Lahore could provide military supplies and at least ten million rupees in cash. Fatally, Dara opted for Lahore. Aurangzeb gained the advantage of being able to pick off his enemies one by one.

On June 12, Dara left Delhi for the Punjab with an army which had doubled in a week—there were now ten thousand men. He could not know that in a matter of days Murad would become Aurangzeb's prisoner, which might have tipped the scales in favor of trusting Shuja. An offer of coalition would come later, but too late. In the interim, Aurangzeb's network of scouts would be busy watching the movements of both his brothers—and of his nephew Sulaiman Shikoh as well.

● ● ●

Handsome Sulaiman was meanwhile inundated with troubles. Only titular head of those troops dispatched in December to stop Shuja's advance, he had consistently been held back by the real man in command—Rajput veteran Jai Singh. After Shuja's defeat and flight from Banaras, Sulaiman and Jai Singh had pursued the rebel prince along the Ganges to the border of Bengal; it was here, between the Kharagpur hills and the holy river, that they had received news of Jaswant's defeat at Dharmat by Aurangzeb and Murad. Shah Jahan and Dara had urged a quick truce with Shuja, since Sulaiman's army was desperately needed in Agra.

Dara Shikoh's modern biographer observes sourly that "had Jai Singh shown half as much zeal and generalship in the pursuit of Shuja as he afterwards displayed in chasing the fugitive Dara . . . the issue of the War of Succession would have been totally reversed." The judgment seems justified: even Jai Singh's dickering with Shuja's plenipotentiary had been agonizingly slow, and a peace treaty had not been formally signed until May 7, 1658. By riding with light kit, imperial forces could still have made it back to Agra in time for the Battle of Samugarh; but Jai Singh was in no hurry to save

Dara's neck. Sulaiman impatiently pushed several stages ahead of the Rajput chief in an endeavor to spur him on, though loose unity of their troops remained essential to preclude total dissolution. By June 2 they were almost halfway between Allahabad and Agra when messengers brought the news of Dara's colossal defeat at Samugarh. An accompanying letter from Shah Jahan urged Jai Singh and his ward to join up with the crown prince at Delhi, and Dara had written his trusted officers to the same effect. But these imperial rescripts only augmented panic: Aurangzeb and Murad had won two major battles. Sulaiman's entire army went into a dither, Delhi was a good three hundred miles away, and the imperial cause could only be lost anyway. Jai Singh prepared himself to change horses in midstream.

An inexperienced Salaiman now asked for advice as to what to do. Jai Singh suggested that the young prince could make a forced march to Delhi to join Dara, or else retreat to Allahabad and wait for further news; in any case, the rajah candidly intended to take his own clansmen and join Aurangzeb's side. Sulaiman solicited further counsel from Dilir Khan, the Afghan hero. Chivalrous Dilir agreed to accompany him if their combined troops withdrew to Allahabad and crossed the Ganges, whence they could head northeast and recruit an army from the Afghan colony living near the border of Nepal. By June 4 Sulaiman had agreed to this strategy; but Jai Singh meanwhile persuaded Dilir Khan and several lesser officers to defect along with him.

Nor was other persuasion lacking. Aurangzeb had been busily writing letters to "every viceroy and governor in the empire" since the rebel victory at Samugarh. A neatly coercive communiqué to both Jai Singh and Dilir Khan informed them that Dara had not only lost the Battle of Samugarh but his entire army had submitted; he was in solitary flight but would be captured, Shah Jahan lingered on the threshold of death, and men of good judgment who wanted to be Aurangzeb's friends knew which course to adopt—a course that included taking Sulaiman Shikoh prisoner. Once again, Jai Singh felt too prudent to lay hands on a prince of the blood:

there was always the possibility of retribution if a freak of fortune turned the tables in favor of Shah Jahan and Dara. Cannily the rajah showed Aurangzeb's letter to Sulaiman, advising his ward that most of the imperial officers were traitors and suggesting that the Prince seek refuge in the northwest mountains of Srinagar.*

Jai Singh's treason might at first seem understandable: with Dara already defeated, Jaipur State could easily be invaded by Aurangzeb in retaliation for any continued support of a lost imperial cause. But the rajah's easy desertion suggests more unpleasant motives than mere self-preservation. He had served with Aurangzeb at Balkh, and may always have sympathized with the rebel princes. He brooded over insults and nursed grievances, just as they did. Anyone else might forget what happened five long years ago, when Jai Singh's oily refusal to make a clear-cut military judgment at Kandahar had incited Dara to humiliate him publicly. But Jai Singh remembered. Rajput without honor, he could now indulge in double revenge by repudiating both Dara Shikoh and Dara's vulnerable son; and others could be vigorously seduced to abandon young Sulaiman as well. Within two or three weeks the new defectors would all join Aurangzeb, with Jai Singh becoming a zealous high priest of future calculated treacheries. This was only the first of a series of impressive betrayals.

Sulaiman now found himself abandoned not only by Jai Singh and Dilir Khan, but by a whole slew of imperial commanders and troops whose homes were not far distant. Out of twenty-two thousand men, only six thousand elected to follow their bewildered prince in retreat to Allahabad under the aegis of one of Dara's few trustworthy and long-time officers, Baqi Beg.

Situated at the important confluence of the Ganges and Jumna, the city of Allahabad could look back to uninter-

---

* Not to be confused with Srinagar in Kashmir. Sulaiman Shikoh's proposed sanctuary was savagely precipitous country, the home of Garhwal rajahs in the pocket of India between Tibet and Nepal.

rupted strategic history: the almost legendary Gupta emperors had made it one of their capitals well over a thousand years before the Moguls, while Akbar himself had built its fort in 1583. Sulaiman spent a distracted week in these surroundings, trying vainly in his inexperience to jell some feasible plan of action. An unintentionally comic note of Oriental opulence in the middle of his dilemma was the staggering amount of baggage, human and otherwise, with which he found himself burdened. As a novice prince on his first military campaign, he had been inundated with gifts by Shah Jahan and Dara. All through the campaign against Shuja and now in retreat at Allahabad, princely kinetics had turned into a slow-motion nightmare of harem women and "furniture and articles of pomp beyond imagination"—gold palanquins and gold couches, silver and gold chairs, jewels and gold plate and costly fabrics. Whatever decision he made, it was high time to cast ballast!

There was no lack of counsel from his aides. A few aggressive strategists plumped in favor of taking over the territory between Allahabad and Patna to the east, creating an autonomous pocket of resistance against Aurangzeb; others suggested linking up with Shuja (which would actually have been Sulaiman's best alternative). But Dara's more persuasive followers preferred a scheme which presciently paralleled the suggestion Dara himself was about to relay to his son: if Sulaiman crossed over to the north bank of the Ganges here at Allahabad, he could give a wide berth to both Agra and Delhi by marching through the middle Doab (the fertile alluvial tract between the Ganges and Jumna); it would then be feasible to double back across the two rivers at the foothills of the Himalayas, and join his father in the Punjab without ever once having to encounter Aurangzeb's army.

Reluctantly, Sulaiman Shikoh left gilded pomp and supernumerary harem attendants at Allahabad fort, crossed the Ganges, and moved northward through the Doab past Lucknow. Hordes of soldiers continued to desert him daily. In a final gesture of sleazy contempt Jai Singh and Dilir Khan had already plundered some of his baggage, including several elephants laden with jewelry and gold mohurs.* All along the route "the villagers assassinated or stripped his people." Farther north, despite the maneuverability of a dwindled army, the prince now found it impossible to retraverse the Ganges: officials in charge of ferry crossings bristled with hostility, and boats withdrew to the other side of the river at the mere appearance of his troops. At last approaching the territory of Srinagar, he made a fatal halt for several days and sent an officer to the local rajah for help.

Aurangzeb had meanwhile been keeping track of his nephew's movements. By mid-July he sent a rebel army division north under Mumtaz Mahal's brother, Shaista Khan, to prevent Sulaiman from recrossing the holy river; a further contingent was dispatched to guard the Jumna. It was at this point in the game of hounds and hare that a newly promoted rebel officer took fifty cavalrymen and spurted ahead in an excess of zeal, riding 160 miles in a single day to a place called Hardwar. Here the Ganges first entered the Indian plain country from adjacent mountains, a topographical event which made the district a sacred source of pilgrimage for Hindus seeking the purifying bath. Sulaiman had been on the verge of crossing the river at Hardwar when Aurangzeb's eager cavalry van arrived; fearful that a larger army was in their immediate wake, he withdrew at once to nearby Swalik hills for asylum. Misfortunes began to compound: almost simultaneously, his faithful old guardian Baqi Beg died abruptly, triggering further defections among even loyal men. In black melancholy, the young prince found himself swallowed up by the bleak mountain fastnesses of Srinagar with only two thousand men left.

It was a sinister withdrawal into wild upland country. Srinagar's offputting environs of rough, stony terrain and impassable mountains afforded a perfect stronghold, and had

---

* A gold coin equal to fifteen rupees.

even defeated Shah Jahan some years before when an invading Mogul army of cavalry and foot soldiers had either been killed or had their noses cut off—the rajah of Srinagar feared nobody. Travel was by foot or on yak in much of his domain; the yawning ravines were passable only in baskets pulled across by ropes.

On the frontier, appropriate representatives now met Sulaiman and escorted him inland. The rajah himself even came out some four marches from his capital, and agreed to sanctuary on one condition: Sulaiman could bring into Srinagar only his immediate family and servants, but had to send away the entire remaining army, horses and elephants (presumably roads were bad and the country too poor to sustain a horde). The young prince spent a week weighing an offer more like an ultimatum, since it left him totally vulnerable to a virtually unknown protector. But there was no choice: three divisions of Aurangzeb's army controlled the Ganges, the Jumna, and the middle Doab; there could be no crossing of rivers, no reunion with Dara in Lahore. Sulaiman decided to accept the rajah's offer.

A last twist of the knife of deception was still to be given. Many imperial retainers now longed to desert, but the rajah's men guarded Srinagar's hills. Feverishly, Sulaiman's advisers hatched a scheme: he could not trust the rajah, he must return to Allahabad. By way of persuasion they hauled out a forged letter (this advice becomes ridiculous in Mogul history) apparently written by Allahabad's commander and cheerfully implying that Shuja had arrived there with a great army. Sulaiman fell into the trap, thanked the rajah for his kind offer of sanctuary and gave him obligatory gifts before descending from the mountains. At lower altitude he promptly found himself abandoned wholesale by all except seven hundred men. Total despair left no alternative except to return to Srinagar; but the next morning every camel driver, almost every mahout, and most of the servants also took flight. There were now barely two hundred persons left in the party, with virtually no transport for numerous harem ladies. Aurangzeb's human bloodhounds pressed hard at their heels. The bulk of concubines had to be given away to anyone who would have them; horrified, "ladies of spotless honor" who "had so long been kept in seclusion with care became frantic with grief, pulling out their hair and slapping their own cheeks." It was a winnowing moment of disaster: some women went to new masters, many were frankly abandoned, and only Sulaiman, his wife, and a few high-ranking harem beauties, together with a foster brother and seventeen followers, entered the hills on the few remaining elephants whose mahouts had not bolted. Their flight soon became frantic, with rebel pursuers less than a day behind.

For the rajah of Srinagar, Sulaiman Shikoh's return in extremis became an occasion of social hobnobbing and snobbery beyond his wildest dreams. A true prince of the Mogul house seeking asylum with him was worth any danger he might incur. The dilapidated palace of his ancestors was repaired in a flurry of joy, and he gave his daughter in marriage to this fugitive guest: Srinagar blood would mix with genuine blue blood of the imperial house of Delhi! It could only be "divine grace, because no such event had ever happened to his dynasty before." Now, in August 1658, Dara's fantastically handsome eldest son had found a haven out of Aurangzeb's reach. But Sulaiman's tragedy was merely deferred.

●●●

Much had happened in almost four weeks since the Battle of Samugarh; it was imperative for Aurangzeb to call a halt and digest the situation. Rebel soldiers needed a breather, India had become a political and administrative shambles, and the military situation wanted assessing.

In terms of strategy, Murad had been completely neutralized. Dara was on the run in the Punjab, already pursued by one unit, and Aurangzeb now sent off an additional contingent of men under the command of a newly appointed governor of the Punjab—the venomous Khalilullah Khan. In anticipation of possible aggression by Shuja, another force also went southeast to capture Allahabad fortress and to protect the eastern approaches to Agra. But threat from Bengal seemed remote. Shuja remained temporarily out of commission as a result of his earlier defeat by imperial forces; for the moment, holding action could be restricted to a blandishing letter spiked with promises and offering territory as soon as Dara was crushed. The movements of Dara's son Sulaiman had remained only briefly obscure; Aurangzeb, correctly divining that his nephew was headed north to join Dara, had promptly dispatched troops to block the Ganges and Jumna crossings.

By now it had become vital to set up a whole new Mogul administration in place of the crushed and splintered machinery of government. Centralized control needed to be quickly reaffirmed in provinces which had fallen into anarchic disorder since the outbreak of civil war; new army and territorial officers were required, and all sorts of mandates and regulations were necessary to restore public services. In addition, those troops moving into the Punjab against Dara Shikoh would have to be sustained by munitions, supplies, and the whole lifeline of war.

But all these actions fell corollary and contingent to one inevitable step: the master dissimulator must crown himself and formalize his rule over India. It was ludicrous to go on with an outworn charade, pretending to be an orthodox knight in armor who had waged a holy war to free Shah Jahan from the thrall of apostatic Dara. "Free" Shah Jahan was quite obviously imprisoned, the old government had collapsed, and only by proclaiming himself emperor could Aurangzeb resolve any dilemma of conflicting authority and lend weight to appointments and decisions. It was a moment of global contrast: in far-away England the dictator Cromwell was dead or dying and would soon be replaced by a monarch; in India, a quasi-liberal monarch was being supplanted by a rigidly orthodox dictator.

Like all his family, Aurangzeb believed in the stars. He bowed to Oriental superstition and relied on astrology for setting the date of his coronation; stargazers accordingly consulted their charts and came up with July 21. In any case, the event was preliminary and makeshift; grand celebrations would have to be reserved for later, when a troubled usurper felt more secure in his power. No bunting or velvet decorated this occasion of rude brevity as India's new ruler assumed his imperial halo in a garden setting eight miles northwest of Delhi. In Aurangzeb's day, the locale represented a kind of minor Versailles with a number of handsome buildings. Here he now took the title of *Alamgir* or "World Conqueror," after the sword which Shah Jahan had sent him by way of diplomatic sop when the rebel armies camped outside of Agra. But *Alamgir* could hardly stop for long; within six days he would be on his way to the Punjab in pursuit of Dara Shikoh.

● ● ●

Someone else was looking for Dara, not in pursuit but to volunteer further service. Still indefatigably picaresque, nineteen-year-old Niccolo Manucci, metamorphosed from artilleryman at Samugarh into an unlikely holy man, had reached Delhi incognito with Aurangzeb's army. "There I remained some fifteen days," he relates, "awaiting the assembling of more travellers. For villagers and thieves were plundering on the highways, and created a good deal of tribulation."

Soon to leave Delhi with an assortment of itinerant civilians, the Italian was in for some hairbreadth adventures. At one moment he even found himself left behind by the group when a diarrheal cart driver ("overcome by his necessities") went off to find a suburban ditch by way of latrine and fell asleep! Outraged, Manucci "fell upon him in a great rage and gave him a sound beating." But destiny profited by nature's delay: some hours later, when the two were proceeding through a wood, they

> . . . beheld with terror the greater number of our party heaped together, either decapitated or wounded, and all plundered and ruined; the few who survived were stripped naked. The cart-man, frightened to death at the spectacle, wanted to drive off . . . across the jungle without attending the dead and wounded lying on the road. I told him to go slowly, that there was nothing to be afraid of, for the danger had passed (although I was a good deal frightened myself). I found one poor crea-

ture lying in the middle of the road with a spear thrust through him, who raising his hands to heaven prayed me to help him.

The victim would have to take intent of aid for actual deed: Christian charity had no chance of prevailing over a panicky driver who only urged his bullocks at double speed.

The Punjab, Dara's chosen retreat and Manucci's objective for rendezvous, was perhaps the most famous part of Hindustan. North and somewhat west of Delhi, it constituted a hugely triangular tract of territory which boasted Lahore as its capital. The very name Punjab meant "Five Waters," referring to five rivers flowing down through the district from the Himalayas and Kashmir. Travelers from Delhi to Lahore had to cross two of these streams, the Sutlej and Beas; Lahore itself bordered the Ravi, while beyond lay the Chenab and Jhelum. All five were navigable tributaries, converging with the mighty Indus which then snaked down through Sind, formed a delta, and culminated at the Arabian Sea. West of the Indus River beyond a mountain barrier lay Afghanistan and Persia; while to the northwest, four uterine passes (the most famous being the Khyber) led through the Hindu Kush range into the Punjab. By this route over millennia India had received immigrants from the west, and the Punjab in particular had become a kind of ethnological womb, pooling the genes of many conquerors and their cultures.

At the first Punjab river crossing, Manucci found a guardian contingent—artillery, cavalry, and infantry—of Dara's army under the leadership of an officer named Daud Khan. "I presented myself to him; and as he recognized me, he treated me with much honor and granted me a passport for my onward journey. Without such no one could go on to the city of Lahore."

It was an intimate historical moment.

There [in Lahore] I arrived at four o'clock in the afternoon when Prince Dara was actually seated giving audience. Quitting the cart, I threw my small wallet across my shoulder, and taking in my hands my bow and seven arrows I entered the palace. When my commander Barcandaz Khan saw me, he advanced to greet me, and after embracing me with great affection . . . led me joyfully to the presence of the Prince. . . . There I performed the usual obeisances, and he [Dara] with exceeding gladness exclaimed in a loud voice, "*Shabash! Shabash!*"—that is to say, "Bravo! Bravo!" His eyes brimming over with tears, he turned to his officers and said in a troubled tone: "See, you others, the fidelity of this European lad, who, although neither of my religion nor of my race, nor for long an eater of my salt, having only entered my service when these wars began, came after me with such loyalty through the midst of such dangers; while those maintained by me for so long, and getting immense payments, with base ingratitude and utter disloyalty abandoned me when I had need of them. . . ."

Hopeful, Dara now asked Manucci whether other Europeans had accompanied him. "To this I answered that the hardships of the road hindered many . . . but as they found a chance they would come. Dara ordered a horse to be given to me, which was at once brought. Not liking the look of it, he directed them to give me another and better one. He increased my pay [from] eighty rupees [to] one hundred and fifty rupees every month." Manucci received a further gift of five hundred rupees and a ceremonial robe, and then "put up at a house where several of my European friends were staying; they had got away from Agra before it was invested, and with them I dwelt."

● ● ●

Lahore was an old and very beautiful city, founded in the misty past of Hindu myth and enduring through centuries of invasion and conquest. Under Akbar, Jahangir, and Shah Jahan the town had risen in importance to become a magnificent urban tapestry of royal fort, palaces, mosques, and gardens—the Shahdara planted by Jahangir and the

Shalimar by Shah Jahan himself. But for Dara there were gloomy childhood memories: Jahangir's mausoleum seemed a hollow echo of mortality, and the imperious Nur Jahan who once had held both Dara and Aurangzeb as hostages now lay rotting in her tomb nearby. Here in Lahore, Shah Jahan's brother Prince Shahriyar had made his hopeless bid for the Mogul crown until he was blinded and put to death by Mumtaz Mahal's father, Asaf Khan.

Briefly, for six weeks in Lahore, things went somewhat better for Dara. A flurry of enlistment resulted in twenty thousand new troops under his standard—neighboring tribesmen sniffing gold; mohurs poured out of Lahore's treasury and titles were distributed. A few imperial commanders even managed to rejoin him after long separation, and he was now able to try his hand at diplomacy by writing persuasive letters to Rajput chiefs and even to Aurangzeb's own officers. Belatedly making a bid to Shuja in Bengal, he suggested that an eastern front be opened against Aurangzeb and offered a division of empire after the defeat of their joint enemy.

But it was all a depressingly false dawn. Typical and even symbolic, one of the nobles who established fresh contact from ambiguous motives was Rajah Rajrup of the Jammu Hills; the rajah volunteered to recruit a cavalry host of hill Rajputs if only Dara would give him financial backing. Dara's life had been spent in bridging the gap between Hindu and Moslem, and in studying the Hindu religion to find comparative spiritual grounds with Islam; Rajputs were brave, Rajputs were faithful, Rajputs could be relied upon. Dara's wife Nadira Begum even summoned Rajah Rajrup to the harem. Placing a valuable string of pearls around his neck, she then bound his loyalty in a bizarre ritual: having no milk in her breasts, she washed them with water and gave him the liquid to drink, thus making him a proxy son to her —the Rajah would replace her eldest son Sulaiman Shikoh, whose fate was then unknown. Rajrup drank the sacred breast water and swore to be true, and Dara promptly gave him a million rupees. Then the Rajput returned to his own country; he would come back soon, he promised, with that great cavalry host. Partly true to his word, he did turn up a year later but as an officer in Aurangzeb's army; indeed, the rajah soured Nadira Begum's milk by delivering the military coup de grace to Dara with a sneak attack from the rear in a final battle yet to be fought. Rajrup would not be alone: appalling betrayals were only beginning.

In order to delay rebel pursuit, Dara had ordered the destruction of all ferry boats within range along the Sutlej River. He had posted his chief general Daud Khan at a major Sutlej crossing, and was now sustaining him with additional men and supplies recruited at Lahore. The monsoon season would quickly make the Punjab a quagmire of muddy roads; the barrier of rivers would also give Dara time for reorganization. It was also hoped that Aurangzeb's army would be exhausted after coming all the way from the Deccan and engaging in two major conflicts.

But Aurangzeb had over the years developed an extravagantly disciplined persistence and endurance. By the end of the first week of August (barely a month after Dara had settled in the Punjab) two units of the rebel army reached the Sutlej River within two days of each other. The van even carried portable boats on wagons—the "World Conqueror" had anticipated every possible need! Assessing this imposing phalanx, Daud Khan felt unequal to direct encounter. Reluctantly he retreated to the second Punjab water barrier, the Beas; he would conduct holding operations from its west bank at the main ferry crossing. Fourteen-year-old Sipihr Shikoh was soon to be sent out from Lahore with reinforcements and specific instructions to engage the enemy. But the enemy intended to decline engagement until the arrival of further rebel divisions.

Dara had counted on holding out in the Punjab until Shuja opened an eastern front; and there was also the possibility that Jaswant Singh of Jodhpur would stage a sympathetic revolt from neighboring Rajputana and force the rebel army to quit the Punjab. But Dara's defeat at Samugarh had implanted a psychological cancer which had begun to grow inside him; slowly but surely he was being consumed by anguish. For one Mogul chronicler, the moment turned to Hamlet-like indecision: "the Prince began to waver in mind to be or not to be at Lahore." Daud Khan, evidently summoned fifty miles from the defensive front for consultation, had earlier reminded Dara that despair was condemned by the Koran as a form of infidelity. By Daud's counsel, the crown prince ought to stay in Lahore and send his son Sipihr as nominal commander-in-chief of the forces now facing Aurangzeb's two advance divisions. Yet to complicate the issue Dara's wife had had a temporary lapse of her otherwise remarkable courage and hysterically refused to allow Sipihr Shikoh out of her sight. Her eldest son Sulaiman was now presumed to be dead, and she didn't want to lose her remaining one. By the time she regained her poise and consented, it was militarily too late: Aurangzeb himself had reached the Sutlej with a huge army. His new commanders included both Jai Singh and Dilir Khan, who had lost no time in joining him after abruptly abandoning Sulaiman.

It is a commonplace that failure feeds on dark thoughts. The palace and fort at Lahore took on the tincture of doom; Dara had already judged himself a lost cause, and to his intimates he now admitted with shocking candor, "I cannot resist Aurangzeb. If it had been anyone else, I would have fought him here." Aurangzeb had already won two major battles against all odds since leaving the Deccan, and his pack of seasoned veterans had almost reached Lahore. Against them, Dara's army could be weighed and found wanting—green and greedy Punjab recruits, depressed fugitives from the battle of Samugarh, doubtful mercenaries who would desert in a moment, and traitors ready to stick the knife at any turning. Only the supreme confidence of a Napoleon or an Aurangzeb could galvanize the lot of them—not a mystic, not a dreamer, not a Mogul Hamlet, not an open and vulnerable heart, not a Dara Shikoh. In the ruthless game of power Dara was lost—and any animal can smell fear.

Inevitably, dejection spread through the city like a virus. With predictable alacrity, the majority of newly raised troops deserted and went off to join Aurangzeb's forces. A number of Dara's officers had received persuasive letters and also abandoned their posts. Even the trusted Daud Khan fell under suspicion: in a ploy to undermine Dara's confidence, Aurangzeb had sent Daud a phony document of pretended collusion and made certain it would be intercepted by imperial patrols. Lahore was in turmoil.

Probably at his wife's insistence, Dara now recalled Sipihr Shikoh to the city. Aurangzeb had already dispatched both Jai Singh and Dilir Khan across the Sutlej to buttress his advance divisions at the Beas, thus creating an invincible union of four top-ranking generals (Bahadur Khan and Khalilullah Khan commanded the two vans). Daud Khan received orders to burn all boats at the second river barrier, and to fall back when the rebel army could not be retained any longer.

On August 18, 1658, Dara Shikoh fled from Lahore with his family, taking ten million rupees from the imperial treasury together with government stores and artillery left over from the last abortive siege of Kandahar. These stores went down the Ravi River by boat, while fourteen thousand cavalry accompanied the fugitive Prince—"attracted by his hoard of gold," as the Mogul chronicles put it. His immediate destination was the city of Multan, about two hundred miles below Lahore in the western Punjab.

There remains a considerable mystery: why did Dara reject a much more attractive escape route—a northwest passage from Lahore toward Kabul, now governed by Mahabat Khan? No friend of Aurangzeb, Mahabat had dutifully returned to court from the Deccan during the first stages of the War of Succession, and had received grateful imperial appointment as governor of Kabul. Early on in his confinement, Shah Jahan had even secretly written to the veteran commander: "Dara Shikoh is proceeding to Lahore. There is no want of money in Lahore, there is abundance of men and horse in Kabul, and no one equal to Mahabat Khan in valor and generalship. The Khan ought therefore to hasten with his army to Lahore; and, having there joined Dara Shikoh, they might march against the two undutiful sons* to inflict upon them the due reward of their misconduct and to release the Emperor . . . from prison."

For the fugitive Dara, Kabul represented an ideal retreat affording hardy Afghan troops and also the easy possibility of escape to either Persia or the Uzbek domains of central Asia. A puzzled François Bernier (soon to arrive in Hindustan) would later apply his French acumen to discover that Dara had actually been advised to proceed to Afghanistan—"his reasons for refusing such sage counsel must always be enigmatical." Equally puzzling was the fact that Mahabat Khan did not come to Dara's aid in Lahore.

The clue would be offered by Manucci: Dara had indeed contacted Mahabat Khan and requested passage through Afghan territory to Persia; but Mahabat suspected that the crown prince planned to seize Kabul as a base of operations, and moreover bore a grudge for a long-past incident—years before, one of Dara's soldiers had been killed by a trooper of Mahabat's, and Dara had made the issue personal until Shah Jahan intervened. Reply from Kabul to Lahore now proved significantly cool: Dara had "better choose another road, because no reliance could be placed upon the Pathan [tribes] in the hills." No alternative remained, except to head southwest for Multan.

Flight came none too soon: within a week an advance rebel contingent entered Lahore to prevent looting, and by August 29 Khalilullah Khan arrived on the scene and headed immediately south in hot chase. For three weeks Aurangzeb himself remained bogged down at the Sutlej, shuttling his cumbersome army across river; but on reaching the Beas he found a boat bridge already set up by advance troops. Khalilullah Khan meanwhile sent back a message revealing familiar problems of hierarchy: "It is expected that Dara will

---

* Shah Jahan did not know that Murad's arrest had been effected or was imminent.

make a firm stand at Multan. The pursuing forces have no general high enough to encounter a prince of the blood and to secure the obedience of the entire army. If a battle is precipitated now, a disaster may befall [us]. So, we have slackened our pursuit." Aurangzeb now decided to lead the rebel bloodhounds himself; sending most of his soldiers and heavy baggage on to Lahore, he veered south with a chosen body of men at a speed of 14 to 22 miles per day.

All the way down the vast reaches of the Punjab from Lahore to Multan, Dara witnessed the snowballing spectacle of desertion (including that of his own paymaster). Niccolo Manucci remained in the Punjab capital for three days after Dara's departure—"owing to some business," he tells us mysteriously—but caught up with retreating imperialists before they reached Multan on September 5. They would remain there barely eight days. A strategic city on the road to Sind province, Multan had been an important entrepôt of spices and drugs in days before the Portuguese wrested control of Arabian Sea traffic from Arab hands. During their short stay, Manucci witnessed Dara's unflagging mystical credulity as the prince made a final religious bid for protective orisons. Under a huge dome of blue tiles, the greatly venerated tomb of a thirteenth-century Moslem saint dominated the middle of town. Dara summoned this saint's descendants (very likely the tomb caretakers) and made gifts of twenty-five thousand rupees in addition to an expensive cloth covering for the catafalque, exhorting the holy men to supplicate Mohammed on his behalf. Results were depressing: "The following day," Manucci says, "Dara took care to have them called so as to know the results of their prayers. They appeared (as this sort of knave knows so well how to do) with downcast faces, and told him that all night long they had been in the presence of Mohammed, but were unable to speak to him because Aurangzeb was in conversation with him!"

About a hundred miles southwest of Multan, the splayed-finger network of Punjab tributaries conjoined with an impressive Indus River to create a wide, swift, and treacherous current which plunged through Sind to the Arabian Sea. Still another hundred miles below this juncture, the great fortress of Bhakkar loomed on an island in midstream and lent confidence to townships on both sides of the river. The fortress now became Dara's next point of retreat. From Multan he sent 507 boats laden with treasure, munitions, and "food requisite for a beleaguered citadel." In charge of the boats was a trusted eunuch, Basant, whose name encouragingly meant "Springtime." But autumnal chill prevailed as Dara's troops dwindled to half the number which had left Lahore.

The distance between fugitive and pursuers was also perpetually dwindling. Advance rebel troops under Khalilullah Khan had been twelve days behind Dara when he fled Lahore; they entered Multan eight days after his departure; and now, near Bhakkar, they were only four days away. On October 13 Dara reached Bhakkar, halting at a town on the west bank of the Indus just opposite the island citadel. Several thousand men were selected to comprise a defending fortress garrison under the eunuch Basant, and among the twenty-two European gunners assigned to the task was Manucci; Dara would leave munitions, stores, many of his harem ladies, and much treasure here, while he himself continued south along the right bank of the Indus by hacking a way through Sind jungle.

Manucci felt heartbroken. "I presented myself before Dara," he writes, "and urgently besought him to [let me accompany] him. With words of exceeding love and tenderness, he replied that he longed to take every one of us. . . . But it was of the greatest importance to him to make sure of the . . . stronghold; and for this reason he left us in it, having such great reliance upon our valor and fidelity." Manucci wept; Dara appointed him captain of the Europeans, doubled his pay, and promised that the Italian would become a noble of the Mogul Empire if ever Allah made an emperor out of a refugee crown prince.

Daud Khan, still under a cloud of suspicion, had reportedly murdered the ladies of his own harem in order to free himself of earthly ties and concentrate on devotion to Dara. But Dara now dismissed the veteran soldier by formal written command, authorizing him "to serve whom he pleases." Having doggedly followed his prince at a distance all the way from Multan, Daud broke down and howled with grief. For Manucci the spectacle seemed pitiful; in fact it was hair-raising as the man withdrew from the precincts like some unwilling Cassandra, uttering wild imprecations that "evil fortune dogged Dara's footsteps." Yet he, too, could be seduced: Aurangzeb would later offer high nobility rank to Daud, who accepted on condition that he would not be ordered to take up arms against his former master.

Even in Mogul India human motivations were not all black, and men had other reasons for defection than opportunism or cynical appraisal of Dara's winnowing chances. Many followers were frankly dismayed to learn that Dara had refused to make a stand at Bhakkar fortress; with such a leader their cause seemed truly hopeless. Dara Shikoh had lost more than his ship of state: every withdrawal since Agra had been compounded by further withdrawal, while pleas of strategy could no longer hide transparent cowardice. He was falling into a pit of fear, and it would become a pit of stark terror as time went on. Shakespeare might have understood, but never a professional soldier.

With less than three thousand men left, Dara now headed south from Bhakkar fortress for some fifty miles. It was the geographical and psychological moment to take the road to Kandahar and Persia, as his ancestor Humayun had done (and Humayun had returned to reconquer India). Correspondence had actually been opened with Persia's king, who prudently refused to enter the Punjab though he was nonetheless willing to offer asylum to a crown prince. Dara might have accepted the offer, but his entire retinue—harem and servants alike—mistrusted Persians. Fate led south: through jungle and sand into Sind, into the quicksands and salt lagoons of the Rann of Kutch, and through the Great Indian Desert.

Aurangzeb meanwhile reached Multan on September

25, joining up with advance rebel forces. Even before he arrived he had received word of Dara's further flight to Bhakkar, and knew that Dara's army was rapidly dwindling. But within five days, the obsessed new emperor of Hindustan would have to relinquish his role of personal bloodhound and leave pursuit of the fugitive to divisional commanders: alarming news made it imperative for him to turn back toward Delhi. Indolent Prince Shuja, in a surprising display of energy, had rallied a formidable army to the east and was now marching from Bengal to Agra. The "second front" had opened at last.

CHAPTER

19

Enigma in Arakan

DARA SHIKOH'S MISFORTUNES had in effect given Shuja a breather in a desperate moment: no longer pursued by imperial troops, he had won a truce treaty affirming his possession of Bengal and adjoining provinces. A dissimulating letter from the victorious Aurangzeb merely confirmed this status. "As you had often before begged the Emperor for the province of Bihar," Aurangzeb wrote from Delhi before setting off toward Lahore, "I now add it to your viceroyalty. Pass some time peacefully in administering it and repairing your broken power. When I return after disposing of the affair of Dara, I will try to gratify your other wishes. Like a true brother I will not refuse anything you desire, be it land or money." The "true" brother had already imprisoned Shah Jahan and rewarded Murad by incarcerating him at Salimgarh prison. Shuja was no fool: he sent back a hollow statement of gratitude while assessing his chances.

In the welter of conflicting accounts of the War of Succession, there can be no determining just how far Shuja would have been willing to go in any rapprochement with Dara. If he responded formally to the crown prince's belated overtures from the Punjab inviting him to open a second front against Aurangzeb, no written record exists; aggressive action seems to have been taken independently. With Aurangzeb and most of his army away in pursuit of Dara, it was in any case an ideal moment to attempt an assault on Agra and Delhi. Shuja is supposed to have countered his hesitant advisers by saying, "Aurangzeb has left . . . no general strong enough to oppose me. If Prince Mohammed Sultan bars my path I can win him over, and by a quick movement secure the person of Shah Jahan and restore the old government. And then I will stay at court as my father's obedient servant." The modesty of adopting a role as Shah Jahan's liberator may have been more than a feigned attitude intended to win support from the imprisoned emperor's sympathizers: Shuja seems never to have been politically very devious, and was incapable of sustaining vendetta or treachery. The simple possibility is that he might well have had sobering second-thoughts in the wake of Aurangzeb's usurpation of power; better to restore a peaceful Mogul Empire than to continue a power struggle which could only destroy everyone.

At Patna, the capital of Bihar province, Shuja restored his shattered forces. By the end of October 1658 he had assembled twenty-five thousand cavalry, considerable artillery under European gunners, and a protecting flotilla to sail up the Ganges. His initial advance toward Agra was even promising: by Dara's orders a series of forts along the route surrendered, Banaras welcomed him, and the commander of Allahabad sent a message of submission. Persuaded by a little arm-twisting, even the bankers of Banaras came through with a forced loan of three hundred thousand rupees. By the time Shuja had reached Allahabad at the strategic junction of the Ganges and Jumna, his strength provoked a retreat of the rebel division which Aurangzeb had sent to besiege the fortress some time before.

It was only beginner's luck. At the end of December, halfway between Allahabad and Agra, Shuja's hordes came to an abrupt halt: his path was now blocked by Aurangzeb's eldest son, Mohammed Sultan, who astonishingly appeared with an opposing force. Three days later—on January 2, 1659—soldiers in both armies were astonished to see Aurangzeb himself arrive out of nowhere to take command of his son's troops. A major battle was imminent!

For Shuja, his brother's materialization seemed almost

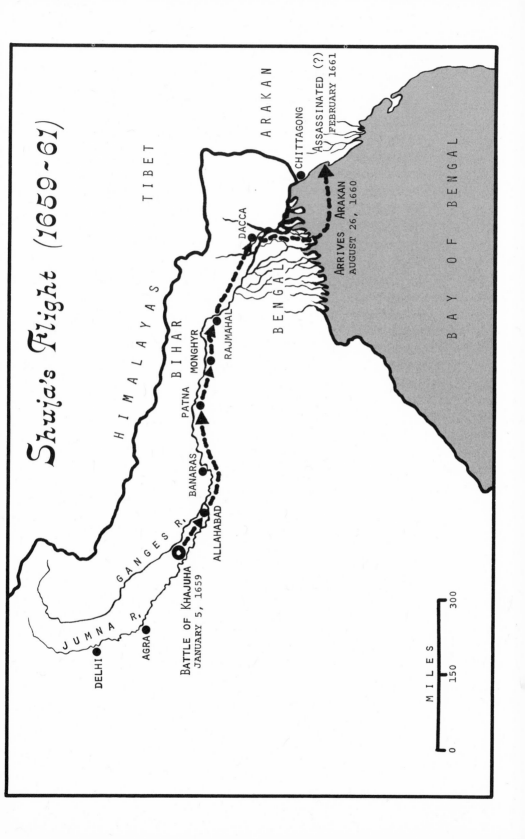

Shuja's Flight (1659~61)

DELHI

AGRA

JUMNA R.

GANGES R.

BATTLE OF KHAJUHA
JANUARY 5, 1659

ALLAHABAD

BANARAS

PATNA

MONGHYR

RAJMAHAL

HIMALAYAS

TIBET

BIHAR

BENGAL

DACCA

ARAKAN

CHITTAGONG

ASSASSINATED (?)
FEBRUARY 1661

ARRIVES ARAKAN
AUGUST 26, 1660

BAY OF BENGAL

MILES

0   150   300

unbelievable. It was almost four hundred miles from the middle of the Punjab to Delhi, over difficult routes; and another three hundred miles separated Delhi from this encounter. With as much apparent ease as though he had been skating across a winter pond, Aurangzeb had spanned a good part of India. Abandoning a diminishing threat in the Punjab for an emergent danger from Bengal, he had effected a military maneuver of impressive stamina within three months—including a stopover in Delhi to issue orders, dispatch armies, and dictate strategy.

Aurangzeb had actually been keeping eyes in the back of his head while pursuing Dara. Shuja remained a disturbing potential, and a network of eastern spies continued to report every suspicious movement through a relay of bhang-intoxicated runners who could link Bengal and the Punjab in a matter of days. Logically (after the defeat of his army by Dara's son) Shuja should have made a neatly chastened withdrawal to his Bengalese capital at Rajmahal near the delta of the Ganges, burying his head in the harem. But he refused to stay put, and his maneuvers had been transmitted to Aurangzeb some months earlier. If a master strategist continued to chase Dara it was for one reason only—he held Shuja cheaply. The easy-going and indolent viceroy of Bengal was no military genius, and would be slow to formulate plans and slow to move.

Yet Dara could not be captured so soon, while Shuja proved not so lethargic or incompetent after all. By the end of September, Aurangzeb had been obliged to turn back from Multan toward Delhi. Traveling with a crack cavalry escort, he managed two laps a day instead of one. In Manucci's estimate, "so great was the terror of Aurangzeb lest Shah Shuja might arrive first at Agra city . . . that he went on in advance of his army two or three leagues, followed by very few men and sometimes quite alone. His object was to make his men follow with greater quickness. He rested beneath trees, his head supported on his shield, until some men overtook him and formed a retinue."

It took about seven weeks for Aurangzeb to reach Delhi

(on November 20) from the Punjab. By the twenty-third he had already dispatched an impressive army and artillery from Agra under his son Mohammed Sultan, intending to reinforce the division at Allahabad and block Shuja's advance; other contingents—Rajputs and Punjab veterans—followed soon after. Shuja had not even left Banaras before these steps had been taken, and by the time he reached Allahabad the road to Agra was closed forever. Aurangzeb's son could not be won over—not yet—and in a whirlwind climax Aurangzeb himself reached the scene.

One other person also arrived in time for battle, coincidentally on the same day as Aurangzeb. Making forced marches from the Deccan, the wily old master of intrigue, Mir Jumla himself, now assumed his title as Aurangzeb's right-hand man. His wife and family had been freed from hostage with Dara's defeat and the fall of Agra. No further purpose was served in playing a game of detainment, and Aurangzeb had sent instructions to the Deccan for Mir Jumla's "release" from Daulatabad fort. In fact, between the lines of official Mogul historians, it was clear that Aurangzeb felt the need of keen counsel and help in fighting Shuja; and so Mir Jumla's "zeal" had "urged him to make a quick journey," fortuitously turning up with military supplies.

Shuja's army had encamped at a large artificial pond or reservoir midway between the Ganges and Jumna (both of which were only ten miles distant). An adjoining village called Khajuha, with clumps of palm trees growing about, seemed more like an oasis. Aurangzeb's forces elected for the banks of a small stream several miles away. Between the two opponents were level plains—the site of what would later be called the Battle of Khajuha.

● ● ●

Through the reversed telescope of three hundred years, the engagement seems like a Victorian child's game of tin soldiers. On this particular morning of January 4, 1659, an unbelievable ninety thousand horses paraded before Aurangzeb, who at eight o'clock lurched forth on a great elephant to inspect his troops and raise their morale. By three in the afternoon his advancing hordes came within a mile of the enemy position. Shuja bided his time, and the rest of the day passed with desultory artillery exchanges from both sides. At twilight Shuja's artillerymen withdrew from their vanguard position to maintain contact with his army; Mir Jumla quickly hauled Aurangzeb's own cannon to the vacated spot, which happened to be on high ground overlooking Shuja's camp. Aurangzeb decided to provoke action the next day, obliging his soldiers to sleep in their armor with their horses still saddled. While he himself ensconced in a field tent, chief officers kept watch over their divisions and Mir Jumla made keen rounds to inspect the entire assemblage.

Astoundingly enough, one of the commanders in Aurangzeb's army was Jaswant Singh, rajah of Jodhpur. Apparently annoyed by his wife's vehement sarcasm after his desertion from the Battle of Dharmat (when he failed to stop the advance of Aurangzeb and Murad from the Deccan), the rajah had latterly spited her by sending his representatives to Aurangzeb and asking forgiveness for his offenses. His apology had been accepted; he had gone on to a reception in Delhi and had accepted gifts and a confirmation of rank. But these were only surface gestures of submission. Whatever the Rajah's real underlying motives, a complicated double-cross was now about to take place.

At that moment, Niccolo Manucci was hundreds of miles away in the Punjab with Dara's defending garrison at Bhakkar; nevertheless, he tells the story of Jaswant Singh in his narrative (presumably he collected details from eyewitnesses at a later date). On the eve of the battle with Shuja, Aurangzeb was being carried about his royal compound in a sedan chair. Manucci relates:

> Then came Rajah Jaswant Singh from his tent and met [Aurangzeb], and after the usual obeisances . . . took hold of the chair with one hand, and with a disturbed face walked alongside for some steps, making inquiries about the post appointed for him to occupy. . . . Aurangzeb (who was delighted to remove the Rajah to

some distance, not liking the action he had adopted and suspecting him of some treachery) ordered him to take charge of the rear-guard. Thereupon the Rajah mounted his horse and went off energetically. Aurangzeb remarked: "Great are the courage and boldness of this Rajah; I like him not."

It was now just before dawn. In his tent, Aurangzeb recited Moslem prayers for the last watch of the night. A confused babble of noise began in the vanguard of his army and then encompassed the entire camp in an overlapping chaos of yells, cries of agony, stampeding animals, and the sound of retreating cavalry. The disturbance immediately sparked a general uproar of looting and plundering by scavenging camp followers. In the midst of total tumult, messengers brought the news to Aurangzeb's tent: Rajah Jaswant Singh had precipitated an overwhelming act of treachery—so overwhelming that even the master of deceit himself was shocked. Aurangzeb would later write in a letter to Jai Singh that "the behavior of Jaswant Singh at the battle of Khajuha was such as could not be expected even from the meanest of mean soldiers, not to mention the chief of [a] Rajput tribe."

Later Mogul accounts would be frankly at a loss to explain Jaswant's motives, imputing them to wounded Hindu pride brooding over some insult or other. But clearly the rajah had sent a message through enemy lines, promising a sneak attack on Aurangzeb's army; if Shuja took advantage of the confusion, his brother's defeat was certain. Assembling his fourteen thousand Rajput cavalry troops, Jaswant then bolted forth from Aurangzeb's right wing. He and his Rajputs galloped headlong through the sleeping division commanded by Mohammed Sultan, killing men left and right and making off through camp with whatever could readily be plundered. Aroused by the disorder, confused soldiers (concluding that Shuja was making a night attack) began to load booty on horses and camels prior to fleeing; Rajputs swept away these conveniently ready treasures, along with cash and general army stores. In a wild concatenation of looting, Aurangzeb's camp now fell utterly apart as distorted rumors of catastrophe swept over cavalry and infantry alike. Many fled with the Rajputs or shifted over to Shuja, while even commanders left their post in panic and rushed about in search of private property. Dawn would reveal that half of the World Conqueror's army—at least forty thousand men—had been irretrievably dispersed!

In the deepest irony of the entire War of Succession, Shuja never profited from the situation. Though he had received Jaswant's message and heard of the rioting, he refused to make a night attack: Aurangzeb was a past master of deceit (violating holy oaths sworn on the Koran and writing false letters) and surely had colluded with Jaswant Singh in order to persuade Shuja to walk into a trap!

Disturbed at prayer by news of Jaswant's coup and flight, Aurangzeb responded with theatrical cool-headedness: imperiously silent, he made a gesture of disdain implying "Good riddance to bad rubbish," and then deliberately finished his orisons. Afterwards he announced from a sedan chair to his military grandees, "This incident is a mercy from God. If the infidel had betrayed us in the middle of battle, everything would have been lost."

Orderlies were now sent around the field to division commanders: no rider, no elephant, no horse was to budge, and anyone not at his post would be dragged in humiliation to Aurangzeb himself. New right wing commanders were rustled up, and the rest of the night passed without incident.

By dawn Aurangzeb was reconnoitering on an elephant, in order to assess the extent of disaster. Half the army had been dispersed, but a few sheepish officers realized their mistake and now slipped back into the ranks. There were still fifty thousand men to Shuja's twenty-five thousand—though Aurangzeb's historian preferred to emphasize "trust in God and the escort of angelic legions."

It was a foregone conclusion that Shuja would lose the battle, but the surprise is that he almost didn't. For once in his life he displayed near military genius, abandoning conventional formation (which would have dwindled his front in the face of a numerically superior enemy) for a single long line of force behind an artillery shield. Three maddened elephants with iron chains in their trunks were promptly goaded forward, to provoke a confused stampede. Compounding the previous night's disaster, a weird rumor of Aurangzeb's death swept through his forces and triggered another mass flight of "even veterans of the Deccan." All along the road to Agra, Jaswant Singh and retreating Rajputs already created the impression that Aurangzeb had been defeated and taken prisoner by Shuja; a new wave of deserters confirmed for a certainty that Shuja was on his way to release Shah Jahan from imprisonment. Aurangzeb's modern biographer comments: "Agra then must have resembled Brussels just after Waterloo!"

On the battlefield, Shuja's forces seemed momentarily about to justify rumor: barely two thousand troops remained to defend Aurangzeb, and one of those enraged enemy elephants had already approached his sacrosanct howdah. Given the slightest sign of retreat, his entire army would disperse. As a static symbol of fortitude his own elephant's legs were now chained to prevent withdrawal, while Aurangzeb furiously commanded guards to shoot the attacking mahout. In a split-second rally, a neutralizing circle of loyal pachyderms surrounded the maddened beast; with a wild leap, a new rider clambered on its back and diverted it from the scene.

A significant byplay now illustrated the vulnerability of royal command over an entire Indian army. Aurangzeb's right wing had fallen into danger; but if he led his center forces to assist the right, then the whole army might think he was fleeing the field of battle! With no little presence of mind he first sent orderlies to front-line officers and informed them of what he was doing. Soon the reinforced right made a countercharge; and Shuja's army, which had acquitted itself well up to that point, began to fall back in a hail of artillery, rockets, and bullets. Heads, arms, and pieces of torsos were lopped off by cannon balls. Shuja left his exposed elephant and mounted a horse.

Immediately, as with the defeat of Dara at Samugarh, it was all over: Shuja's empty howdah became a signal for mass retreat. His officers looked around and saw themselves abandoned; hopelessly Shuja shouted that he wasn't dead, but some of his men had already rushed to embrace the opposition. There was nothing for it but to flee the field with his sons, high officers, and a remnant of his army. Among the plunder of his camp, the victors would appropriate eleven fine Bengal elephants.

● ● ●

Fearful of a revolution in Agra, Aurangzeb was obliged to return immediately in the wake of the unpredictable Jaswant Singh. But this time he allowed no respite before pursuing a defeated brother: Mohammed Sultan was sent after Shuja the same afternoon. Shortly afterward, reinforcements (and friction) followed in the person of Mir Jumla; he and Aurangzeb's son would lead thirty thousand men against Shuja, though Indian involutions of the plot were bound to present themselves—court gossip even gave rise to the notion that Aurangzeb sent the ambitious duo to Bengal simply to get rid of them.

Four days later, Shuja crossed the Ganges and looked for sanctuary at Allahabad fort; but Dara's commander was not going to offer suicidal asylum to a loser, and peremptorily shut the gates on him. Aurangzeb's men would be invited to take over Allahabad on January 12.

Now began a considerably different game of hare and hounds, leading into tricky territory which Shuja knew inside out—Bengal. His flotilla of ships on the Ganges east of Banaras afforded him the advantage of crossing the holy stream as he pleased, whereas Aurangzeb's forces would find themselves hard pressed to obtain boats and find fording places. Keeping to the south bank of the river, Shuja stopped at Patna—an idiotic delay to marry off one of his sons to the daughter of a retired old army officer who might conceivably be of help. When pursuers came within twenty miles of town, it seemed time for the hare to flee again.

Eastward beyond Patna was the strategic city where

Shuja had made his last defensive stand and treaty with Dara's forces a year before—Monghyr, in Bihar province. Though small, this "key to Bengal" occupied a narrow defile only $2\frac{1}{2}$ miles wide, through which ran the main road from Patna to Bengal. Above the defile flowed the Ganges, while below it lay Kharagpur hills. Any invader coming along the south bank of the Ganges could be summarily blocked at Monghyr, or else obliged to take a circuitous unpopulated route through bleak hills and jungles infested with tiger, rhinoceros, and wild buffalo. By either route, the objective was Shuja's capital city of Rajmahal in West Bengal.

Shuja managed to stay a little over two weeks in Monghyr, bringing artillery ashore and even contemplating taking something of a stand against his pursuers. In addition to escapees from Khajuha, he had (with a good reputation for liberality) enlisted new men from the provinces of various rajahs living north and south of the Ganges all along his line of retreat. But there would be no blockade: nearing Monghyr city in early March 1659, Mir Jumla quickly appraised a long siege and decided it was more worthwhile to detour and come out in Bengal at Shuja's rear. As provincial governor, a local rajah had faithfully promised Shuja that he would guard the hills; but with cheerful promptitude he accepted a bribe from Aurangzeb's forces and now became their guide. On hearing the news, Shuja continued to retreat.

Further along the Ganges at a place called Sahibganj, he again tried the same defensive tactics—blocking the road to Bengal while enlisting the aid of local governors to seal off the south. But again bribery effected hill passage, and Aurangzeb's troops threatened to outflank their fugitive. At this moment a flabbergasting piece of news reached the pursuers: Dara Shikoh had presumably rallied a new army and routed Aurangzeb at Ajmer, sending him in flight to the Deccan! It was of course a totally false rumor, but threw Mir Jumla's camp into bizarre speculation: everyone concluded that Mir Jumla had been moving his soldiers through the hills not to attack Shuja's rear, but with intent to retreat by a southern route to the Deccan and Aurangzeb!

Rajputs in Aurangzeb's service became particularly moody. They believed that their ruling rajahs had prematurely deserted the imperial cause, and a newly ascendant Dara might easily decide to hurl thunderbolts of retribution at Rajputana; it seemed wise to head west and patch up a truce. Abruptly four thousand of them fell behind and took not French but Rajput leave, dwindling Mir Jumla's and Mohammed Sultan's resources to twenty-five thousand men —still double the force of Shuja, but time had been lost and every moment counted in the move to cut off fugitive retreat.

Shuja had meanwhile withdrawn as far as his Bengal capital of Rajmahal (just past the sharp southward bend of the Ganges). He now decided to quit the right bank of the river entirely. The plan was to ferry his army across the river below Rajmahal; with his family safely deposited in the delta stronghold of Tand, he would pit a delta-based flotilla against Mir Jumla's land forces. But for his followers, retreat into the delta clearly preluded a cul-de-sac, with an unwinding ribbon of escape ending at the outlying delta city of Dacca or worse: beyond Dacca lay ambiguous pirate territory.

It was time for sensible men to defect—defection, the farcical refrain of Mogul history. This time chief chafer-at-the-bit would be Shuja's right-hand man, a noble named Alawardi Khan who had been governor of Bihar province until Shah Jahan's illness, and then joined Shuja's standard in the contest for the throne. Shuja had often called Alawardi "my noble brother." Desertion tactics were becoming increasingly elementary: Alawardi and other malcontents intended to wait until Shuja crossed the Ganges at the ferry junction below Rajmahal, after which they would simply slip away to Mir Jumla.

Unfortunately for the conspirators, a storm prevented Shuja from crossing river on April 1 and during the delay he discovered their intent. The following morning, the prince rode ten miles to Rajmahal and stopped at his garden in the outskirts of the capital. Insensate with rage, he kept sending a stream of officers to bring Alawardi Khan to justice; troops

surrounded Alawardi's house and forced capitulation. Alawardi and his son were escorted to Shuja, then handcuffed
and paraded into the city on elephant back. Together with
two other nobles who had taken part in the conspiracy, they
were publicly beheaded in front of Shuja's palace.

The bulk of a chastened army now crossed over into
delta territory, under front guard from Shuja's flotilla. But
several thousand troops had to surrender to pursuers: Mir
Jumla had at last completed his circuitous march through
southern hills. From Shuja's capital westward, the entire
south bank of the Ganges now fell to Aurangzeb.

Bengal's delta constituted strange scenery for the last act
of Shuja's tragedy. Here below the turn of the Ganges, the
river and its tributaries break up like streams of mercury, and
become softly capricious forces of nature with no fixed channel. Much of the delta area is in effect little more than a shifting network of rivulets or hollow sandy beds which the river
like a sleepwalker has abandoned. In the north delta, the
principal Ganges artery receives various lesser veins; southward, the original holy river slithers its way down to Calcutta
and the sea (though the great city did not exist in Shuja's
time). But another quite separate and really main body of
water still presses inexorably eastward, where it merges with
the descending Brahmaputra to form a wide flow called the
Padma, situated below the city of Dacca (itself on a separate
artery). Beyond the Padma, exotic jigsaw streams of this eastern delta converge toward Chittagong and the Bay of Bengal.

During the rainy season, the entire delta valley becomes
a flooded nightmare; and when the rains at last subside they
leave a fickle labyrinth of lakes and watercourses behind
them. Not all these streams flow off into Bengal's river complex; many become stagnant dead ends, spawning slime
pools and swampy morasses until the hot summer makes dry
land again. Yet even the dry land is never the same, any
more than the river pattern is: through endless eons, the eerie
delta perdures yet alters. Symbolic and disturbing, it seems
an alluvial version of Shiva dancing—the endless creation

and destruction of a Hindu illusion called the Mouths of the Ganges.

This was to become Shuja's final arena of struggle against Aurangzeb. On any other terrain the quarry would have been immediately doomed; but the rainy season was close at hand, and Shuja had his flotilla. These Bengalese war proas were an inadvertent gift from Shah Jahan himself: as governor of Bengal province, Shuja had always had a liberal revenue allowance for boats. In a forbidding land of waterways, boats alone could patrol the river network as troops maintained order and kept Chittagong marauders to a minimum of destructive activity. Shuja also had artillery, augmented now with cannon brought by Portuguese of the district. Ousted from Ceylon and the Coromandel coast by the Dutch, the indefatigable Portuguese had long since migrated to Bengal's delta, and there were now about eight thousand families of Europeans and half-castes in the area. In the past Shuja had conciliated them (give or take an act of piracy now and again), and they were willing to help—for a price.

By contrast, Mir Jumla remained frustratingly land-locked. He had no vessels, and Shuja in retreat had made sure there would be none by scuttling all private craft in the area. Mir Jumla could stand on the south bank and look across the Ganges, but to invade delta territory was another matter: all he had were cavalry and infantry. Against these, Shuja commanded both men and boats—an effective floating army with mobile artillery, though their numbers were insufficient to launch anything more than limited guerrilla warfare. Neatly, the situation paralleled a Bengali nursery story of a duel between the alligator and the tiger.

Shuja now entrenched himself along the entire eastern bank of the Ganges; Mir Jumla managed to scrounge up a few boats, and so it went. Shuja's artillery peppered Moguls on the western bank; Mir Jumla's men retaliated by capturing an island in midstream, and after commandeering more boats actually made a commando raid on the east bank of the river. But a second commando raid suffered ambush, with the loss by drowning or slaying of "the very pick of the imperial army." Such a mortifying blow to Mir Jumla's vanity made him cautious for the remainder of the Bengal campaign.

June 8 brought further mortification by a stunning turn of events: Aurangzeb's son, Mohammed Sultan, defected and fled to Shuja! There can really be no satisfactory historical explanation for this switch to the obviously losing side. Official Mogul sources make much of young Mohammed Sultan's jealousy of Mir Jumla, who had been named commander of Aurangzeb's army with the power to appoint military nobles. Mohammed Sultan was presumably vain and swollen with conceit because he had captured Agra fort from Shah Jahan, and had also acquitted himself better than anyone else at the battle of Khajuha. In secret correspondence, Shuja made use of "letters and presents, and the arts which gain the feelings of young, inexperienced men." The "arts" included an offer of the throne of India, and Shuja's daughter in marriage. As early as December 1652, Aurangzeb and Shuja had met in Agra and agreed to an informal alliance against Dara, sealing it by engaging Mohammed Sultan to Shuja's daughter Gulrukh Banu (Lady Rose-cheek). Aurangzeb's son had been barely thirteen at the time, but the marriage of first cousins had never been consummated because of the outbreak of the War of Succession and the subsequent falling out of their two fathers.

In any case, the defection took place. On a drizzling June night at the beginning of the rainy season, Mohammed Sultan crossed the Ganges along with two nobles (his go-betweens), some eunuchs and servants, and as much treasure as he could manage. Shuja sent his son Buland with boats and porters to conduct the prince into delta territory. When the news leaked out, it shook the morale of Aurangzeb's army to its foundations. Mir Jumla rode horse the next morning from Rajmahal to Mohammed Sultan's leaderless camp a few miles away, where he rallied spirits and restored order with strong talk. By one succinct Mogul account, the pursuers had "lost only one man—the Prince."

[318]

The rainy season began in earnest; now came the torrential rains of Bengal which would flood streams, mire roads, and mildew spirits. The entire environs of Rajmahal soon became a swampy lake all the way up to the approaching hills: the city became a temporal Venice with boats literally plying to and fro. Much of the army was forced to retreat to posts on higher ground; Mir Jumla himself had withdrawn a good seventy miles away, but important officers and troops continued to hold the flooded capital. With Aurangzeb's split-up army separated by quagmires, it seemed an ideal moment for Shuja to become aggressive. Local rajahs were soon bribed to prevent grain from reaching Rajmahal; red rice and lentils soared in price, cattle and horses began to die, and men gnawed at weeds. Imperial officers started to quarrel, making the city vulnerable to water raids; in fact they soon pulled out entirely, and Shuja's flotilla reclaimed the capital.

Fortified by a new batch of men, Shuja waited for the end of the rainy season and then launched a full-scale attack on Mir Jumla. With superior artillery, he made such headway that the opposing troops were beginning to show signs of capitulation.

But help was coming. Aurangzeb himself, alarmed by his son's defection and the failing stamina of Mir Jumla's contingent, had proceeded as far as Allahabad to be close at hand if the situation deteriorated any further. In addition, he sent another division (under Daud Khan) from Patna as early as May 13, 1659, to march along the north bank of the Ganges and beard Shuja in his den. Rains, flooded rivers, and enemy entrenchments had delayed this division; but by December of 1659 it pushed past Shuja's outer perimeter of defenses and headed straight for his delta stronghold. Reinforcements of money and war matériel (artillery, seven hundred rockets and over a million rupees) also reached Mir Jumla.

Shuja retreated toward Rajmahal, hoping to cross the Ganges at the ferry junction and withdraw from both north and south banks entirely. But he was in a tactical bind: with Mir Jumla breathing down his neck, how could he take his men across river? If Shuja went first, troops would surely desert; if he went last, he risked being captured. Desperately he dug a moat around his position, set up defensive artillery, and then transported his entire army across on a bridge of boats. It was January 9, 1660.

Mir Jumla now reoccupied Rajmahal; Daud Khan's division arrived on the left bank of the river with 160 boats; and an Afghan contingent of twenty-five hundred men arrived to bolster right-bank forces. Shuja was outnumbered five to one. This time, there could be no slip-up: Mir Jumla crossed river above Rajmahal and joined Daud for a combined drive to encircle Shuja in his delta stronghold. The net was closing fast.

Pursuit narrowed down to a swamp chase without bloodhounds. For a while the fugitive put up stubborn resistance along the banks of secondary rivers, but Aurangzeb's forces hacked their way through jungles and waded streams. A detachment even moved south to cut off Shuja's line of retreat.

●●●

It was time for Mohammed Sultan to switch sides again! On February 8 Aurangzeb's son returned secretly to the Mogul camp a few miles below Rajmahal—not without a little derring-do as Shuja's men opened fire on defecting boats.

Even for Mogul India with its farcically Pelion-on-Ossa intrigues, the whole episode had been impossibly bizarre; but Bernier would later provide what may well be the only explanation: "Many persons have told me that all this strange conduct of Mohammed Sultan was planned by Aurangzeb, who was very willing to see his son engage in any enterprise, however hazardous, which had for its object the ruin of Sultan Shuja. Whatever the event might be, he hoped to gain some specious pretext for having Mohammed Sultan conveyed to a place of security." In less circuitous idiom, Aurangzeb had effected an impressive double play of deception: by infiltrating his son behind Shuja's lines to operate as a lone fifth column, he had also provided himself with a valid public excuse for imprisoning Mohammed Sultan afterward —the boy's ambitions were becoming a threat to him.

Once again, the gloomy closed howdah with its royal prisoner would lurch up the steep path to Gwalior. Over the years Aurangzeb would send artists to draw his incarcerated son's portrait, thus keeping tabs on Mohammed Sultan's health (Manucci says the victim was fed opium juice "until his mind was destroyed"). But still far from idiocy after twelve years at Gwalior, Mohammed Sultan enjoyed a more lenient transfer to Salimgarh fortress in Delhi, and was even granted an interview with his emperor-father. Aurangzeb had plans for this pawn of fortune: though still kept in prison, he was finally married off to Murad's daughter and to several other ladies; his title and allowances were restored. Yet imperial grace could only be temporary—one of His Holiness's little strategies to impress another son in line for succession and make him behave. On December 3, 1676, Mohammed Sultan mysteriously died at the age of thirty-seven; he had very likely been poisoned. Royalty at least received royal interment: the body was unceremoniously dumped in the echoing amplitude of ancestor Humayun's tomb.

● ● ●

Shuja was now being relentlessly pursued. The rest of February and March 1660 passed in marches and countermarches through a maze of delta waterways. Determined not to spend another rainy season in Bengal, Mir Jumla urged his troops forward and crossed another river at a terrific loss of lives. A thousand men in armor drowned, and an obligatory day had to be spent dredging for corpses and giving them a decent burial. It was the one day Shuja needed in order to escape from Aurangzeb: April 5, 1660.

The fugitive prince now bolted for the delta stronghold of Tanda (where he had left his family during endless months of skirmishing). Aurangzeb's forces were only eleven miles behind; he had to move fast. At dawn on April 6 Shuja reached Tanda in panic: harem ladies had no time to change costume, and treasure and stores were hastily loaded into several boats. Accompanying the fleeing party were Shuja's two sons, his faithful chiefs of staff, and a handful of soldiers, eunuchs, and servants—three hundred people in sixty boats. Years of splendor in Bengal, together with the panorama of capital cities and great armies, had dwindled to this moment of chaos.

It was a hairbreadth escape. Mir Jumla arrived at Tanda only hours afterward, where abandoned soldiers were looting left and right—vulnerable treasure on six elephants and twelve camels had been brought to the riverside in the custody of a bewildered eunuch. Such valuable property of course needed to be relooted for Aurangzeb's imperial government; guards must be placed around the harem to protect women reluctantly left behind. A detachment of troops set off immediately to harass Shuja, and promptly captured both treasure boats and half of his flotilla. Mir Jumla himself would be obliged to stay in the precincts of Tanda for twelve days to restore order, before starting off toward Dacca in further pursuit.

The delta city of Dacca in Lower Bengal bordered the Buriganga River, just above where the Brahmaputra and Ganges married to form the wide Padma. From 1608 onward it had become a logical bureaucratic base for the Mogul province of Bengal, and had even been named Jahangirnagar in honor of Shah Jahan's father. Dacca was effectively the last stopping place in Bengal and the Mogul Empire: from here down river through a hundred miles or so of interlocking jigsaw pieces, the mouths of the Ganges emerged at the non-Mogul port of Chittagong on the Bay of Bengal. From Chittagong the seacoast straggled down to Burma. Shuja reached Dacca on April 12, literally bankrupt and by now persona non grata to every district officer in Bengal territory. He had no other choice but to seek asylum with the pirate king of neighboring Arakan.

Even for lawless Mogul days, Arakan was a wild kingdom with a wilder reputation—the land of the Maghs. On today's map it appears as a strip along the lower Burmese coast leading down to Rangoon; but its absorption by Burma was not to come until 1784, and it existed as an independent maritime kingdom extending up to and including Chittagong. Arakan had become a kind of barbaric catchall, inhabited by pirates and the offscourings of Portuguese and other foreign contingents, all mixed together with half-castes, Malays, and escaped criminals. Most of this human offal had entered the service of Arakan's ruling rajah, though their chief occupation was to be predators of lower Bengal. In this they were aided and abetted by the Arakanese themselves, and piracy operating out of Chittagong in the Bengal River network had left its mark of terror: entire districts in the coastal jigsaw from Chittagong to Dacca had been deserted because of ferocious raids.

Ironically, many of the pirates were Christians. Manucci sums them up finely:

> These inhabitants inflicted great damage on the lands of Bengal, and, penetrating with their boats into all parts of that province, carried off men, women and children, gold and silver, and when they could get them they did not hesitate to carry off babes at the breast along with their mothers. When these cried at night, they would, with unheard of cruelty, snatch them from their mothers' arms and throw them into the sea. . . . I say in one word all that need be said: they were unworthy not merely of the names of Christians, but of men.

As for the rajah of Arakan and his Arakanese, they were singularly lacking in any religion or caste; they ate unclean animals, and were so barbaric looking that everyone in Bengal—Hindu and Moslem alike—held them in terrified loathing. Predictably, nobody knew the country of Arakan except the Arakanese and a few European traders, and Manucci echoes the general fears of the time when he says that "no one can enter this territory with an army, the ground being marshy, with impenetrable jungles and mighty rivers full of alligators." Grandiloquent Mogul conquest had always stopped short of Arakan.

This was to be Shuja's fate: exile in Arakan, with the

vague possibility of getting from there to Mecca. He had already asked through his son for help from Arakan's ruler, but no word was forthcoming as Mir Jumla closed in on Dacca. Resolutely, Shuja left Dacca on May 6, proceeding by boat down river. By Manucci's colorful account, the confusion of escape became so great that many women in Shuja's harem remained shockingly without veils in one of the boats leaving Dacca—a polluting exposure to public gaze which left the humiliated prince no choice but to have the boat sunk with everyone on board.

At every stop Shuja now found himself deserted like someone infected with bubonic plague—soldiers and boatmen fled, and even the last inner circle of nobles withdrew. On May 8 the pitiful party encountered fifty-one boats manned by Portuguese and Arakanese: these had been sent by Chittagong's governor at the command of the rajah of Arakan. Shuja still wanted to capture one of the Mogul forts along the river in a last bid to avoid exile. But three additional ships soon arrived with an Arakanese general, who refused to counsel any such half-baked endeavor: "Our king," Shuja was told in no uncertain terms, "ordered us to help you fight if you had any chance of success or held a single fort. But you . . . had better start at once in our ships for Arakan, or we will abandon you."

Arakan was preferable to Aurangzeb. With Shah Jahan immured at Agra fort, Murad incarcerated in Gwalior, Dara's fate darkly obscure, and Sulaiman Shikoh a fugitive in Srinagar, anywhere offered more hope than India. On May 12, 1660, Shuja left Bengal forever. He had ruled the province for twenty years, was now forty-three years old, and had less than forty people left with him. Among the refugees, a handful of nobles remained faithful to the last: twelve Moguls and ten Sayyids of Barha—Indian grandees whose Moslem roots extended for generations into the past, and who under Akbar had won the hereditary right to fight in the forefront of any Mogul emperor's battle line. Shuja was their emperor; they would stand by him to the end.

● ● ●

One brother had succeeded in evading Aurangzeb; one brother had held out and fought to the last river crossing. For all his early years of indolence and indifference, Shuja had put up a brave show—stubbornly resisting where a more sensitive Dara would have fled, and always too straightforward to yield to despair. Shuja had escaped.

Now, almost appropriately, his flight trailed off into nowhere. Mir Jumla's pursuit ended at Dacca, and Aurangzeb would never have the satisfaction of tracing Shuja to any definite conclusion. Eleven years later, in 1671, a Mogul historian would grudgingly admit, "Up to this time no one knows anything about Shuja's fate in Arakan. It is utterly unknown in what country he is and what he is doing, or whether he has died."

For Aurangzeb the unfinished mystery became intolerable, plaguing him for a long time to come. Was Shuja really dead? Alarming rumors perpetually circulated in Delhi, and after several years François Bernier (then actually at Aurangzeb's court) found that the vanished Shuja had become positively ubiquitous:

> It was reported, at one time, that . . . the kings of Golconda and Bijapur engaged to support his cause with all their forces. It was confidently said, at another period, that he had passed within sight of Surat, with two ships flying red colors, with which he had been presented by the King of Pegu [Burma] or of Siam. Again, we were told that the Prince was in Persia; that he had been seen in Shiraz, and soon afterwards in Kandahar, ready to invade the kingdom of Kabul. Aurangzeb once observed, perhaps by way of joke, that Sultan Shuja was become at last a *hajji* or pilgrim; insinuating that he had visited Mecca; and even at this day, there are a great many persons fully persuaded that he is returned to Persia from Constantinople, having obtained large supplies of money in that city.

Bernier himself would leave India in 1666, but counterfeit Shujas continued to spring up like dragons' teeth: two uprisings in 1669 and 1674 were led by impostors.

There was only one way for Aurangzeb to know what had happened to Shuja with any certainty: invade Arakan. But Mir Jumla, the new viceroy of Bengal and a logical choice for further sleuthing, had been temporarily busy leading a Mogul expedition northward against Assam. The Assam probe was a successful piece of operative surgery, snipping out bits for the Mogul Empire, but in this case the "doctor" died: during his arduous return from Assam to Dacca, wily old Mir Jumla succumbed in January 1663. His successor would be Mumtaz Mahal's brother, Shaista Khan, who, as a matter of fact, did succeed in taking at least Chittagong port from the Arakanese; but Chittagong provided no information about Shuja.

Nobody loves a mystery unless it is cleared up, and a few sources did know Shuja's fate—or seemed to. Arakan might be out of bounds to Moguls, but not to European traders—the English and the Dutch. Stories of Shuja's denouement now began to circulate in Delhi through resident Dutch merchants, and Aurangzeb became curious. By Manucci's testimony, "he ordered all the factors . . . to be sent for—namely, the English and the Dutch—also several others, private merchants and priests. All were examined in much detail as to the case and circumstances of Prince Shuja. They all replied that Shuja and his son were dead."

As pieced together by Manucci, Bernier, and the official Dutch register kept in the East Indies and later published in The Hague, Shuja's end was grisly. Fugitive but clinging to his dignity, he arrived in Arakan and received all due honors but declined an invitation to a royal feast, sending his son Buland in his stead. Buland regarded the main dish with horror: a basin of raw buffalo blood which Arakan's rajah swizzled with great relish. Shuja now waited impatiently for the monsoon season, when prevailing winds might take him to Persia or Mecca. But the barbaric pirate ruler detained him unconscionably, and finally suggested a wedding between his son and Shuja's daughter. Appalled and fearful of violence, Shuja hatched a plot of escape: his own armed guard had dwindled to minuscule proportions, but there were a few Moguls and Afghans in Arakan with good intentions. Together they would assassinate the rajah, take over the kingdom, and make it a base for a new assault on Bengal; or Shuja might withdraw to Persia as a last resort. Arakan's ruler learned of these intentions and decided to kill the prince and all his followers.

In Manucci's lurid version of events, the rajah's guards staged a dawn attack on Shuja's residence, shouting "Slay those traitorous Moguls who fled here from Bengal." Running with a few aides into the jungle, Shuja scattered retarding bags of jewels in his wake; but the Maghs "pursued the poor Prince like famishing wolves, cutting his body into pieces, stripping it bare, and plundering all his valuables." His son was later beheaded with a hatchet, while Mogul women were first taken into the Rajah's harem but later expelled to end their days as castaways.

Less gory, Bernier simply says that Shuja was pursued while trying to escape to Burma, and even holds out a wan note of hope: "It is said that he reached the hills, accompanied by an eunuch, a woman, and two other persons; that he received a wound on the head from a stone, which brought him to the ground; that the eunuch having bound up the Prince's head with his own turban, he arose again and escaped into the woods." Later in Bengal, Bernier would personally meet one of Shuja's eunuchs and his former artillery commander; "both assured me that their master was dead, although they were reluctant to communicate any further information." But like Manucci, Bernier gives Shuja's son the ax, though harem women come to a more dignified end—confined to their apartments to starve to death.

In the 1661 volume of the Dutch "Dagh" Register at Batavia, there is a note that Shuja arrived in Arakan on August 26, 1660; Arakanese allegedly surrounded the prince's house on February 7, 1661, and he set fire to it and escaped with his family and followers. His sons were captured; but even the Dutch admit that "there can be no certainty" Shuja was killed. The only speculation they had from Voorburg, their resident in Arakan, was that Shuja's corpse had been mutilated beyond recognition by the Arakanese in order to facilitate appropriation of his treasures and jewels. Mir Jumla had meanwhile sent a letter to both Arakan's rajah and the Dutch resident, Voorburg, asking for Shuja's sons to be given up to him; but the Arakanese were busily melting down Shuja's gold and silver to carry it to their ruler's treasure house.

Aurangzeb listened to the Dutch narrative as told by Jan Tak, a Dutch factor then in Delhi, who ended by producing a substantiating letter from Holland's resident in Arakan. After the letter had been translated into Persian, Aurangzeb raised his hands to heaven and commented, "Pride is chastised in the end; humility is prized even in heaven." He then, by Manucci's account, "ordered grand funeral obsequies, and gave alms, principally to those learned in the faith, praying them to supplicate God for that Prince dying in the realm of Arakan, within a heathen and idolatrous land. Similar obsequies were ordered to be performed in all principal cities of the empire. The cunning fellow made these demonstrations of piety, not for his love to the deceased Prince, but to make known to all the people that Shah Shuja was dead."

But though Shuja was indeed probably dead in the jungles of Arakan, he still had his posthumous triumph: Aurangzeb could never know for certain.

Cockcrow in Rajputana

IT HAD TAKEN a year and a half to hound Shuja out of India to a macabre end in Arakan, and the undertaking had been left entirely to veteran Mir Jumla. In the interim, Aurangzeb had been involved with other events of the War of Succession; crises mounted with a cumulative density which would be hard to match elsewhere in world history.

For the briefest moment after Shuja's initial flight from the field of Khajuha, Mogul destiny had hung in the balance: Agra city, the political Achilles' heel of Aurangzeb's new rebel government, teetered on the brink of revolution. Taking the road to Agra, the unpredictable Jaswant Singh of Jodhpur and his Rajput cavalry of fourteen thousand men had dispersed half of Aurangzeb's army in their sensational midnight defection. A few hours afterward a new wave of Aurangzeb's men—fugitives from the opening phase of the battle with Shuja—were also streaming along the same route ready to confirm the wildest news: Aurangzeb had been defeated, he and Mir Jumla were in shackles, and Shuja was advancing on Agra at the head of a victorious army. Shah Jahan would be liberated and avenged.

Partisan Mogul historians conveniently repress details at this point, so that the moment can be reconstructed only through the indirect testimony of a Bernier or a Manucci (neither of whom were actually on the spot). As governor of Agra, Mumtaz Mahal's brother Shaista Khan had a seizure of wild fright when he saw Jaswant's legions approaching the gates of the city. In a last-act gesture inspired by imperial Rome he took up a cup of poison; but (Bernier comments) "was prevented, however, from swallowing it by the promptitude of his women, who threw themselves upon him and dashed the cup to the ground." The commandant of Agra fortress also fell into a tremor, ready at the least coercion or threat to release Shah Jahan from prison. With the entire populace of Agra in passive sympathy, a coup would hardly have been difficult.

But Jaswant Singh knew the truth: Shuja had been wary of Rajput offers to create rearguard havoc, and Aurangzeb had not been defeated. The puzzling maharajah of Jodhpur now hesitated to compound extremities, and retreated toward his sand-bound stronghold in Rajasthan. Considering the courage it had taken him to wreak so much damage, it was a strange moment to be diffident. "Two days elapsed before the inhabitants of Agra were undeceived," Bernier sums up, "and it is not doubted that the Rajah would have succeeded in releasing Shah Jahan from confinement had he acted with vigor and decision; had he threatened with boldness, and promised with liberality. But as he was acquainted with the actual state of affairs, he would neither venture to prolong his stay in the capital, nor to undertake any daring enterprise; he merely marched through the town, and proceeded homeward. . . ." Jaswant's peculiar involutions were not yet at an end.

Aurangzeb had meanwhile stopped over in Khajuha for the night following his victory over Shuja. He was candidly embarrassed because even *he* had been plundered of all his property in the Rajput predawn raid, and new horses, munitions, and clothing had to be recruited for him from imperial supplies. For the moment, only Mohammed Sultan and a single pursuing column went in chase of Shuja; Mir Jumla and reinforcements would follow later, but might be needed temporarily near at hand. Fully expecting to hear of an insurrection in the city and deeply troubled over Jaswant's actions, Aurangzeb took the bulk of his army back to Agra. In addition to pursuing two fugitive brothers, he was now

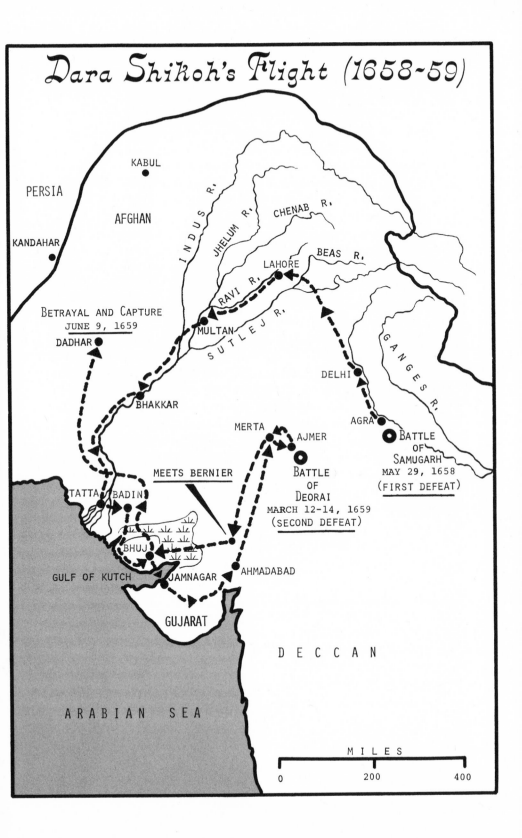

Dara Shikoh's Flight (1658~59)

KABUL

PERSIA

AFGHAN

KANDAHAR

INDUS R.

JHELUM R.

CHENAB R.

BEAS R.

LAHORE

RAVI R.

Betrayal and Capture
JUNE 9, 1659

DADHAR

MULTAN

SUTLEJ R.

GANGES R.

DELHI

BHAKKAR

AGRA

MERTA

AJMER

Battle
of
Samugarh
MAY 29, 1658
(FIRST DEFEAT)

MEETS BERNIER

Battle
of
Deorai
MARCH 12-14, 1659
(SECOND DEFEAT)

TATTA

BADIN

BHUJ

GULF OF KUTCH

JAMNAGAR

AHMADABAD

GUJARAT

DECCAN

ARABIAN SEA

MILES

0   200   400

obliged for the sake of discipline to deal with the treason of a high-ranking rajah. Between the lines, a typically deadpan Mogul chronicle offers a lesson in how to play one Rajput off against another: "Aurangzeb appointed Amir Khan with ten thousand horses to punish the traitor Rajah Jaswant. He also joined to this force Rai Singh Rathor, a nephew of Rajah Jaswant, who had a family feud with his uncle. This chief was honored with the title of rajah and many presents. Hopes also were held out to him of a grant of Jodhpur, his native country."

While embroiled in these arrangements, Aurangzeb received a preliminary report from his son Mohammed Sultan —imperial officers had surrendered Allahabad fortress and Shuja was withdrawing to Bengal. The new rule of India lapsed into momentary quiescence, soon to be broken by intelligence reports that Dara Shikoh had risen like a phoenix from its ashes. Miraculously rallying from desperate straits, he had achieved the impossible.

● ● ●

Dara's flight in the Punjab had led him south from Lahore to Multan and then to the island fortress of Bhakkar in the middle of the Indus River, where young Niccolo Manucci had been left as part of a defending garrison. From there, with Aurangzeb's forces in hot pursuit, he headed further south into historic Sind. This was the great valley below the point where Punjab water veins conjoined with the Indus artery. The monumental terrain had witnessed the birth and collapse of a brilliant civilization at Mohenjo Daro three thousand years before Christ. Later came the navy of Alexander the Great, floating down the Indus as his army tramped along its banks to the apex of the delta. Sind province was larger than England, and Dara would traverse much of it.

At Multan, Aurangzeb had personally given up pursuing his brother in order to turn back toward Delhi and Agra and a military encounter with Shuja. But he had left two generals and fifteen thousand men to sustain the chase; so many men, in fact, that they had divided into two units and were now tracking Dara through jungle and briar along both banks of the Indus River. Army oxen bogged down and died; camp followers were so exhausted that tents and stores often fell behind the troops. At Bhakkar fortress the huntsmen found their quarry gone already, but continued south after leaving a token force to besiege Dara's garrison.

It was a lopsided pursuit, with the left-bank rebel army several days in advance of its right-bank counterpart. The left-bank commander now received a message (on October 30, 1658) from the chief officer of Sehwan fortress a hundred miles below Bhakkar: Dara was nearing those precincts by land while his treasure boats were coming down river; with a little haste, rebel units could overtake him. Responding to the challenge, a thousand musket cavalry (backed by rockets and fourteen swivel guns on camel back) immediately set out on a forced march, outdistancing Dara's boats and entrenching a mile below Sehwan. Here the river narrowed, and passage could be vigorously disputed. Aurangzeb's left-bank commander himself soon arrived, having outstripped Dara's army as it marched along the farther shore. The crown prince's entire flotilla could now be glimpsed hugging the right bank, behind which a part of his land force appeared— a thousand cavalry, ten elephants, and banners.

The chase had now reached a moment of real crisis. Outnumbered five to one, Dara seemed caught between Scylla and Charybdis: to his rear, right-bank pursuers were only several days behind him, while hostile Sehwan fort blocked his forward path; across the river Aurangzeb's speedier rebel division had settled in for ambush, and Dara's flotilla would have to run a murderous gauntlet between left-bank artillery and gunfire from Sehwan fort.

One loophole remained: the Indus was still wide and swift, and Aurangzeb's left-bank commander had been obliged to leave rebel boats behind during his rapid advance —boats which were now kept at bay by Dara's own flotilla. An effective blockade of the fugitives could be effected only with the help of Sehwan fort, and word to that effect was now sent across river: Aurangzeb's forces needed transportation to shuttle over to the right bank and cross swords with Dara. Also, would the fort commander kindly dispatch men from his garrison to hold a narrow defile through which enemy troops would have to pass? And would he kindly keep a weather eye on the Indus, in order to open up full blast with guns and muskets if Dara's boats tried to sneak along the right bank in the shadow of the fort?

Sehwan's commander quickly revealed himself as a pusillanimous soul caught in a bind. How could his tiny garrison hold back Dara's land troops without support from Aurangzeb's men? And how could he possibly send his few boats across river to obtain that support? They would be sunk by Dara's vastly superior flotilla. In any case, he reported, the river was shallow near Sehwan fortress; Dara's boats would obligatorily have to proceed down the left stream, thus being exposed to Aurangzeb's entrenched artillery. The left-bank commander had to remain satisfied with this answer. Two days passed; in a matter of quick time, right-bank pursuers would descend on Dara's rear.

It was now or never. On November 2, at nine o'clock in the morning, a dust cloud rose from the right bank: Dara's army was on the move. And so was his flotilla, perversely hugging the right bank near Sehwan fort—the water proved not so shallow after all. Impotently out of range, left-bank rebel artillery opened fire. As for Sehwan's fort commander, he made no dent in history: only two of Dara's boats were damaged while the rest moved triumphantly down river; fugitive land forces passed unchallenged through that narrow defile, continuing on into the Indus delta and reaching the city of Tatta on November 13, 1658.

Dara was now not more than sixty-odd miles from the Arabian Sea. No port of Karachi existed then, and Tatta in Sind (together with its cheek-by-jowl river sister of Lahribandar) had early become famous for seventeenth-century trade—muslins and indigo arrived from Lahore via Punjab waterways, while ocean-going vessels descended to the sea. Yet the Indus River mouth had gradually been sanding up, and Tatta was now in decline. All that remained was its colorful and sleazy maritime reputation. Dara's contemporary, the Portuguese friar Sebastien Manrique, found the place "a sink of iniquity" with "the unmentionable vice so common that catamites dressed and adorned like women parade the streets, soliciting others as abandoned as themselves. These men also take part in their barbarian festivals and weddings, instead of women dancers. Moreover, they receive such good salaries that it enables them to obtain all the feminine finery and trinkets required on such occasions."

In addition to homosexual drag queens there were prostitutes; from Tatta all the way up to the sandy wastes of Jaisalmer on the edge of the Great Indian Desert, the shocked priest found people "so given up to sensuality, especially the female sex, that the stranger is aghast at the large bands of whores, who . . . live wholly by singing and dancing at festivals and entertainments, and visit the caravanserais to prostitute themselves to the large number of travellers who are always there met with."

Manrique could never have known it, but a very remarkable person both in Dara's life and Indian history had already made a fateful sojourn at Tatta some years before—the naked Moslem saint, Sarmad. But Sarmad's great moment in the War of Succession was yet to come. In any case, Dara's troops found little time to enjoy such a delightfully salacious environment: they were to be in Tatta only three days.

Discovering that their quarry had escaped, Aurangzeb's left-bank pursuers continued along the Indus for several days in hopes of keeping track; before long right-bank forces caught up with them, and the two armies blended for a concerted assault on Tatta. By November 17 advance rebel scouts entered the city, exchanging sniper fire with a few of Dara's men who had not yet traversed the Indus River— Dara himself had already crossed on the preceding day. Within forty-eight hours the invaders took possession of Tatta and of Dara's abandoned property there; by the twenty-third they set up a boat bridge across the Indus and continued in renewed pursuit.

But Dara was nowhere to be found; he had disappeared

from Sind entirely. Before the trail could be picked up again, Aurangzeb sent urgent orders to his fifteen thousand human bloodhounds: they were to abandon chase at once and return to court, since he needed them to take part in the campaign against Shuja's invading army from Bengal.

Every man jack was only too glad to relinquish an exhausting game of hunter and hunted. Rebel infantry were worn out from weeks of hacking through Sind jungle and tramping across hot sand; too many oxen and spare horses had died. On December 5 they and their commanders turned back, honored and not entirely unsuccessful. The three-month chase from Lahore may have come to a dead end; but wherever Dara Shikoh was he had no army to speak of and little hope of survival: east of Tatta lay the Great Indian Desert, while southward loomed the Rann of Kutch. Either would be purgatory.

●●●

Even on the map the Great Rann of Kutch looks sinister. Bordering the Tropic of Cancer, its ominous saline marshes form a two-hundred-mile wide paludal barrier between Sind and the boot of Gujarat province to the south. In places it is fifty miles across, or even a hundred toward its eastern boundary, where it merges with the Little Rann in a further inimical extension of nature. The *rann* is really a salt lagoon filled with quicksands, and there is no drinking water at all. But neither was there any choice between Aurangzeb's pursuers and this hellish terrain.

In flight from Tatta, Dara had spearheaded inland to a place called Badin, some fifty-five miles to the east. From there he turned south, straggling for three days along the northern edge of the *rann* in a parched nightmare. There had been little rainfall that year, and every water tank along the way was bone dry; a scattering of wells offered an inch or two of mud water. Transport animals collapsed in paroxysms of thirst, with soldiers crack-lipped and feverish. It was impossible to turn back, and like demented lemmings the entire party (including Dara's wife, harem, and daughters) entered the *rann* on November 27, 1658.

[337]

In a ghoulish journey they somehow managed to cross the Greater or Western Rann to the village of Luna, in northwest Kutch. Here the salt lagoon yielded to desert, and a few friendly regional officers led the way across bleak sands and along the coast of the Arabian Sea. No one had ever taken the route before, but it led finally to Bhuj, the capital of Kutch.

Through hell to guardian angels: exotic but hospitable Hindu rulers governed these outlandish geographical extremities of India. One of them, the rao of Kutch, prudently adjusted himself to the contradictions of God and Mammon and publicly worshipped both Hindu gods and Allah; in his royal family household even the cooks were Moslem, and religion certainly offered small barrier to a suitable matrimonial alliance. The rao now opened his palace to Dara. It was a great honor to receive a prince from the Imperial house of Delhi, not to mention that the prince's son, fourteen-year-old Sipihr Shikoh, made a perfect match for the rao's little daughter. In this respite from purgatory, the children became engaged. Of course Dara's new Hindu friend would (and did) help in every way he could.

For Dara, the reception seemed a good omen. Fortified and once more full of faith in humanity, he crossed the Gulf of Kutch to no less bizarre Kathiawar Peninsula, where the Hindu ruler—the jam of Nawanagar—prostrated himself before his royal guest in a flurry of gifts, welcome provisions, and practical means of transportation. From a hopeless fugitive Dara had now become strong enough to march into Gujarat, his army daily improving with the addition of sometimes unwilling provincial khans.

These great western tracts of Gujarat had been Murad's domains, and they were rich: Surat port yielded formidable customs dues from European traders, while the prosperity of the glorious capital city of Ahmadabad was said to hang on three threads—silk, cotton, and gold. Akbar himself had annexed Gujarat to the Mogul Empire after an independent sultanate's downfall, and young Shah Jahan had enjoyed its tenure and revenues. In spite of the shake-up of the War of

Succession, much of Gujarat still remained in the actual possession of Murad's top-ranking officers, who simmered with fury over Aurangzeb's treatment of their master. Aurangzeb's choice of a new governor for Gujarat, the nobleman Shahnawaz Khan, seemed a curious lumping of malcontent with malcontents. Shahnawaz apparently represented an adroit political choice, since the veteran general was father-in-law to both Aurangzeb and Murad. But Shahnawaz had also suffered seven months' imprisonment at Burhanpur for refusing to join Aurangzeb's rebellion against Shah Jahan, and the wound still festered. Besides, his daughter, Dilras Banu Begum, was now dead, and Aurangzeb was no longer a son-in-law to command family loyalty.

More practically, Shahnawaz Khan's appointment had been so recent that he exerted no real control over Mogul officers and army detachments in Gujarat, not to mention that his own military backing amounted at this point to nothing. Dara decided to besiege Ahmadabad in spite of a pitifully small force of only three thousand men, but was now in for a surprise: Shahnawaz Khan warmly welcomed him outside the gates of the city. Whatever the old veteran's motives (Bernier describes him as "a man of no military reputation, but accomplished, polite, and addicted to pleasure") he threw open Ahmadabad fort on January 9, 1659. Access to the treasury yielded a million rupees—part of Murad's cache.

Gujarat now became a whirlwind center for new military endeavor. Within five weeks and with rupees to burn, Dara expanded his army to twenty-two thousand men. Surat yielded gracefully, volunteering customs revenues as well as ammunition and artillery. Still deferring to an imprisoned Shah Jahan, Dara refused to assume a crown and titles, though Shahnawaz Khan nagged him into appearing at the *jharoka* window each morning.

Even without the perspective of historical hindsight, it was all an obviously false new dawn. There is something obstinately futile in Dara's last efforts to turn the tide of fortune and recapture India from Aurangzeb. Given the progressive disillusionment of his flight from Lahore with wholesale abandonment by troops and officers alike, it seems odd that he did not withdraw from India entirely (in spite of his harem's objections to seeking asylum in Persia). But with Shah Jahan and Jahanara prisoners in Agra fort, redemption of both them and himself from an intolerable fate had become a kind of melancholy monomania. Basic human pride can be stronger than fear—sooner or later, every decent man in extremity has to stop running and face his nemesis. Dara had stopped running; he would challenge Aurangzeb once more. A colossal second defeat, total terror and further insane flight awaited him. The destruction of a finely-tuned, sensitive prince was now at hand—the degraded spectacle of a human soul robbed of all dignity. Yet Dara would still find partial salvation: beyond degradation, beyond cowardice, beyond all moral failure, those years of spiritual quest had been preparing a benediction for the last striated hours of his life. Fulfillment would come, at the price of terrible martyrdom.

For the moment, a final practical rally had to be effected. He had a new army, munitions, and money. Fleetingly he thought of the Deccan: the kings of both Bijapur and Golconda owed their sovereignty to his peaceful intercession in 1656 and again in 1657, when he had prevented Aurangzeb from carrying through aggressive invasion and annexation. It might be possible to effect an entente with them against a common enemy. But by now the news of Dara's phoenix-like revival in Gujarat had spread; Aurangzeb's sixteen-year-old son, Prince Muazzam, was quickly forewarned as governor of Aurangabad to oppose any southern thrust.

In any event the thrust would be in the opposite direction: spreading like bushfire, a rumor swept through Hindustan that Shuja had defeated Aurangzeb's army and Jaswant Singh was returning to Rajputana with Aurangzeb's loot. Dara decided to move north, where he could link up with triumphant Rajputs for a massive attack on Agra. On February 14, 1659 he started out from Ahmadabad for Ajmer; in tow with his army were Shahnawaz Khan, along with Murad's servants, children, and wives. Truth caught up with rumor after three days of marching: far from being defeated, Aurangzeb had routed Shuja at Khajuha well over a month before. But there was compensating hope as Jaswant Singh sent one of his trusted Rajput officers to Dara with a letter of assurance. If Dara pushed on to Ajmer he would find Jaswant's forces and many Hindus from other clans—all of them ready and waiting to unite in a vast Rajput host of cavalry behind the crown prince. Shah Jahan would yet be freed.

It was a moment of high emotion. Dara Shikoh had been born at Ajmer, and was now coming back to his birthplace. As a young prince, Emperor Shah Jahan had cut his spurs in military expeditions emanating from Ajmer—the "Gibraltar of India," as an Anglican bishop would later call it. More accurately, for the Moguls (and for the later English) the city was the very pulse of Rajputana, equidistant from those great princely states of Jaipur, Jodhpur, and Udaipur; in all compass directions, Rajput territory extended northwest to Jodhpur and the Great Indian Desert, south to Udaipur, and southeast to the smaller Rajput state of Bundi—each area with its strongholds and tribes, its legends of heroism and glory. For Dara, Ajmer would be a perfect rallying point to coalesce his Hindu friends, whose religion he respected and whose true integration with India's Moslem empire had always been his dream.

Pushing rapidly on to Merta, some thirty-seven miles northwest of Ajmer and only three days' march from Jodhpur, Dara waited for Jaswant Singh and those great Rajput armies. He would wait in vain: it was the gorgeously contemptuous collapse of all Rajput honor.

Jaswant Singh's deceit seems mindboggling at first. Aurangzeb's modern biographer writes emphatically: "A Rajput of the highest rank and fame had turned false to his word. Of all the actors in the drama of the War of Succession, Jaswant emerges from it with the worst reputation: he had run away from a fight [i.e., Dharmat] where he commanded in chief, he had treacherously attacked an unsuspecting friend [Aurangzeb at Khajuha], and now he abandoned an ally whom he

had plighted his word to support and whom he had lured
into danger by his promises. Unhappy was the man who put
faith in Maharajah Jaswant Singh, lord of [Jodhpur]. . . ."

The judgment is staunchly Edwardian and somewhat
less than analytical. Jaswant may deserve exile to Coventry,
but he can still be understood as a paradox of crossed motivations. At Dharmat, the maharajah had been hampered by
Shah Jahan's orders to avoid a clash with Murad and Aurangzeb if at all possible. His "treachery" against Aurangzeb
at Khajuha clearly represented a deliberate fifth-column attempt to unseat a usurper and restore the throne to Shah
Jahan (in this case through helping Shuja). Now he had
offered assistance to Dara only to withdraw it—yet once
again the explanation lay deeper than mere perversity.

In actual fact, the Rajput chief succumbed to devastating psychological pressure. After the battle of Khajuha, Jaswant had retired to Rajputana determined to hold out
against Aurangzeb; with the best intent, he gathered his
forces and pledged allegiance to Dara. But Aurangzeb meanwhile dispatched an army of ten thousand men to invade the
maharajah's domains; at the same time, he invoked diplomatic coercion in a final (and successful) attempt to keep Jaswant from siding with Dara. There was no better diplomat
than another Rajput—Jai Singh of Amber, who had abandoned Sulaiman Shikoh and promptly entered Aurangzeb's
service. Jai Singh now wrote a persuasive letter to Jaswant,
the fair gist of which would be transmitted to Bernier some
time later:

> What can be your inducement . . . to endeavour to sus-
> tain the falling fortunes of this Prince? Perseverance in
> such an undertaking must inevitably bring ruin upon
> you and your family, without advancing the interests of
> the wretched Dara. From Aurangzeb you will never ob-
> tain forgiveness. I, who am also a rajah, conjure you to
> spare the blood of Rajputs. Do not buoy yourself up
> with the hope of drawing other rajahs to your party; for
> I have means to counteract any such attempt . . . . If,

on the other hand, you leave Dara to his own resources, Aurangzeb will bury all the past in oblivion; will not reclaim the money you obtained at Khajuha, but will at once nominate you to the government of Gujarat. You can easily appreciate the advantage of ruling a province so contiguous to your own territories: there you will remain in perfect quiet and security, and I hereby offer you my guarantee for the exact fulfillment of all I have mentioned.

It was inspired strategy: with Aurangzeb's troops closing in for the kill, Jaswant could either obtain full pardon and reinstatement for the second time, or subscribe to Dara's losing cause without a shred of hope for other Hindu support. High Rajput valor and honor wavered between self-preservation and political suicide. Jaswant was simply not up to such moral courage; clinching the only deal which would save his neck, he withdrew his cavalry to Jodhpur.

In agonized limbo, Dara now sent a Hindu messenger to remind Jaswant that he was waiting. Shockingly, Jaswant temporized with the reply that he expected additional adherents to their cause but would join Dara at Ajmer. But from Ajmer Dara again contacted him, and even put princely pride in his pocket in a third and final attempt: Sipihr Shikoh was humiliatingly sent to Jodhpur to hold a mirror up to Rajput honor and the sanctity of a Rajput's promise. Three days of courtesy and oiled words ended in disappointment.

Dara had meanwhile been contacting other Rajput chiefs with the same polite rebuff. It was a black lesson in human gratitude to a liberal prince who had every reason to expect Rajput backing: no one in the Mogul Empire had been a better friend to them. One of Dara's poignant appeals has even been preserved in the archives of the city of Udaipur. Three years before, he had personally intervened to save Udaipur principality when Shah Jahan wanted to send a punitive army against the Maharana Raj Singh. Surely the spiritual leader of all the Rajput clans had not forgotten? Baring his heart, Dara now wrote: "We have entrusted our honor to the keeping of the Rajputs, and we have indeed come as a guest of the whole Rajput race. Maharajah Jaswant Singh is also preparing to join us. You are the head of the Rajputs, and we have recently learned that your son has come away from Aurangzeb's side. Such being the case, we hope that the worthiest of worthy rajahs will come to our help in liberating Emperor Shah Jahan."

The worthiest of worthy rajahs proved no different from any other Hindu chief—politically myopic, and downright blind when it came to identifying with anything beyond his own narrow sphere of interests. Forgetting that he owed the very existence of his principality to Dara, he was still brooding over a few scattered acres which Shah Jahan had confiscated at the price of pardon. A master in the understanding of mean motives, Aurangzeb had even been playing on Raj Singh's petty feelings since the outbreak of the War of Succession: before marching north from the Deccan he had written to Udaipur, promising restoration of territory. And afterward, India's new master had contemptuously thrown a few more bones to the Hindu dog, granting minor purlieus to bribe "the custodian of the interests of the Hindu race."

The cock had crowed; Rajputs had betrayed. Dara Shikoh found himself abandoned by Jaswant Singh and every other Hindu chief of Rajputana. In the interval of waiting for their help he had also lost time: Aurangzeb was now advancing on Ajmer with a formidable host.

Bernier writes: "Willingly would he [Dara] have conducted the army back to Ahmadabad, but how could he hope to effect this . . . in the midst of the hot season, and during the drought that then prevails; having a march of five-and-thirty days to accomplish through the territories of rajahs, friends or allies of Jaswant Singh, and closely pressed by the eager Aurangzeb at the head of a fresh and numerous army?"

There could be no further retreat; there was no choice but to fight. In the face of an overwhelmingly superior enemy, Dara withdrew his troops to the narrow pass of Deorai four and a half miles south of Ajmer.

[344]

● ● ●

Fought from the twelfth to the fourteenth of March 1659, the Battle of Deorai was predictably hopeless from the outset. Dara's only advantage would be his position, in an upland defile protected on both sides by hill ranges—he hoped to lure the enemy into adopting storm-the-ridge tactics. By March 11, Aurangzeb's army halted about a mile from Deorai; on the twelfth, a four-hour pitched battle was fought for possession of a mound. With enemy artillery dragged forward under cover of fighting, Dara's men drew back. Then, from sunset of the twelfth until midafternoon of the thirteenth, a violent artillery duel blackened the air with gunpowder smoke. Bravely, two thousand of Dara's cavalry poured forth from behind their defenses and fought hand-to-hand with Aurangzeb's troops until sunset.

Direct assault on Dara's entrenchments could lead only to useless loss of lives, human and otherwise—in the final count, 115 elephants died on both sides. During the night of March thirteenth Aurangzeb gathered his generals, lambasted the lot of them for incompetence, and invited a discussion of strategy. Quick with a plan was Dara's erstwhile friend Rajah Rajrup, who had solemnly accepted Nadira Begum's breast-water in Lahore and disappeared with a million rupees. He now offered to deliver a neat and literal stab in the back, since his Rajputs were expert mountaineers and had discovered a hill route leading to the rear of Dara's left flank (commanded by Shahnawaz Khan).

Late the next afternoon, a body of Rajrup's men started on their sneak ascent, while he himself stormed Shahnawaz in a violent frontal attack which was not without support: virtually every other general serving under Aurangzeb (and smarting from rebuke) swept into the fray. Their names were blatantly recognizable as chief defectors from Dara or Shah Jahan—Dilir Khan and his Afghans, Mumtaz Mahal's brother, Shaista Khan, and of course Jai Singh of Amber. It was an impassioned cavalry assault of betrayers, and Dara's men fought back with desperate bravery. But by now the surprise sneak contingent of Rajputs began to crown twilit heights from behind. Abruptly Shahnawaz Khan's body was blown away by a cannon ball; Dara's left flank had been wiped out. Night fell in more ways than one, and flight began.*

During the engagement Dara had been watching from rear center, dispatching support to hard-pressed segments of defense and bolstering spirits in general. But with the dramatic collapse of his left flank, much of the remaining army began to bolt under cover of darkness.

Now began his own disorganized terror. Though some right-flank officers would continue to fight on until nine o'clock in the evening, Dara himself seems to have lost complete control. Together with his son Sipihr Shikoh, one general, and a dozen men, he set off in wild fright toward Ahmadabad.

Several more charitable Mogul sources include his wife and daughter in the fleeing party; but another account of withdrawal is relentlessly sordid. By this version, Dara had anticipated defeat, appointing troop escorts and eunuchs to keep guard over his harem and treasure some five miles away on the shores of Ana Sagar Lake. But in the insensate panic of escape, he succumbed to such a total frenzy of self-preservation that the ladies were abandoned without warning. They had been waiting since noon on elephant, camels, and mules, assaulted by heat and in an agony of suspense. Before their eyes, five marble lake pavilions built by Shah Jahan created a wan esthetic counterpoint. There had been artillery fire in the morning, then a lull, then sounds of wild fighting by late afternoon. Gunsmoke hung over the horizon, and now at sunset the first groups of deserters could be seen fleeing. Cacophonous sounds of sacking came from Dara's camp, and clusters of Aurangzeb's soldiers could also be seen advancing in a swath of slaughter and robbery. No message

---

* European sources claim that Shahnawaz Khan was a traitor to Dara's cause. Far from dying in battle, Shahnawaz was beheaded by Dara (Bernier) or was shot to death with arrows launched by Dilir Khan (Manucci)!

had come from Dara, but it was clear what had happened. The eunuchs exerted themselves and somehow led their wards to safety.

There was worse to come. Ten or twelve miles away, loyal troop escorts promptly fell on vulnerable property and fought one another in frenzy. Dara's women found themselves thoroughly stripped of jewels, while coin and other valuables were piled onto camels and mules. The plunderers made off into desert hills, leaving frightened servants, women, and elephants. Only a few faithful eunuchs were concerned with Mogul honor: the ladies could not be left for Aurangzeb, and so howdahs lurched as they led elephants in track of Dara through the desert. It would be a night and a day before they overtook him.

The entire environs of Ajmer meanwhile writhed in orgastic spasms of greed. True to vulturine form, camp followers of both armies were inevitably looting whatever they could loot. In addition, thousands of Rajputs on horseback roamed the precincts like jackals; they had gathered in preceding days to help Dara Shikoh but, with Jaswant breaking covenant, had done no fighting. In the aftermath of battle, by night and on the following morning, Rajput valor now displayed its predatory mettle. It was, as a matter of fact, a party of Ajmer Rajputs who had volunteered to keep watch over Dara's harem and treasure, and were now miles away with bags of gold on mule back. Others less fortunate had to compete with sapient sutlers and servants—a concerted swarm of human piranha picking Dara's entire camp clean. Government and military stores vanished; wounded soldiers were stripped naked and left to wander the hills bleating in agony. And there was at least one European casualty: a clerk of the Dutch East Indies Company, Willem Verstegen, had become a mercenary in Dara's cause, but was now compensated with a fatal shower of arrows when his fleeing carriage encountered bandit-soldiers.

Aside from the one general who accompanied Dara, all of his high-ranking officers had lingered behind for good reason—their wives and property were in Ajmer. With daylight they capitulated to Aurangzeb and joined his ranks.

Aurangzeb himself would remain in Ajmer only briefly, returning to Delhi for a grand victory parade into the city and an official coronation whose pomp would surpass Shah Jahan's. There could be no further dispute as to who was India's master. Shuja had been defeated at Khajuha and was being pursued in Bengal; Dara Shikoh had made his last stand. Aurangzeb now assigned an army of twenty thousand men with instructions to bring back the crown prince dead or alive. Chief pursuers would be Bahadur Khan and Rajah Jai Singh; a few days later, as a turn-of-the-screw afterthought, he ordered a third officer to join the final hunt: Maharajah Jaswant Singh of Jodhpur.

For Dara, it was the cul-de-sac. Retreat to Delhi and Lahore after defeat at Samugarh had at least been a withdrawal respectable in its hopes of rallying an army and staging a counterattack. Aurangzeb's timing had interrupted his efforts, and hasty Punjab recruits had dribbled away in further retreat through Sind. Gujarat's momentary stroke of fortune had provided twenty thousand men; but they hadn't been enough, and Rajputs had deserted their crown prince in his hour of need. There could be no third chance, no final hope. This was not even flight again; it was the dregs of flight—the closing in on a beast at bay.

Utter fear is shocking, but it is still a human emotion; Dara's breakdown can be understood by any sensitive human being. For certain of his pursuers, and especially for the man whose apostolary kiss would deliver him to death, there can be no such understanding: monsters always repudiate human definition.

CHAPTER

21

Judas in Afghanistan

THE HISTORY OF the Moguls was fast approaching a climax of corpses and retribution. For sheer horror, Dara Shikoh's murder and its aftermath would rival Elizabethan tragedy—not Shakespearean, but the starker, unrelieved melodrama of a John Webster obsessed with death, betrayal, and human evil in all its glittering malevolence. Chronologically, neither Murad nor Shuja was yet dead: Murad languished in Gwalior state prison, and Shuja was still being hounded in Bengal by Mir Jumla. Shah Jahan and Jahanara remained confined within Agra fort, and Dara's son Sulaiman had found temporary asylum in the mountains of Srinagar. Dara would thus be the first member of the royal family to die.

His hysterical flight from the battle of Ajmer had continued all through the night of March 14, 1659 and the entire next day without a break. On other roads but with no less panic, harem ladies and eunuchs made their wild way, until both parties merged on the evening of the fifteenth and reached Merta—midway between Ajmer and Jodhpur but slightly to the north. From here they would snake south through Rajasthan, aiming for Ahmadabad city where Dara had left one of his officers in charge.

Hordes of Dara's soldiers had also dispersed from Ajmer in all directions, and about two thousand of these opted to leave Merta with him. It would take Aurangzeb's bloodhounds six days to get an accurate compass reading, but at every stopping place rumor made the pursuers seem much closer, and flight to the south soon degenerated into a pell-mell affair.

The province of Rajputana extends for close to 125,000 square miles of rugged terrain—vast expanses of rocky land and sandy desert occasionally interspersed with forests and fertile tracts. In abject misery, the fugitives traveled over thirty miles a day. All baggage and tents had been left behind at Ajmer, while necessities and even treasure were daily being abandoned for lack of servants to carry them. Though it was only March, the heat had already become unbearable and clouds of choking dust rose along the desert route—if it could be called a route at all. Wild bands of Koli tribesmen (who lived openly by robbery) now began to hound the party day and night, assassinating stragglers.

By March 20, Jai Singh had picked up Dara's trail at Merta and promptly dispatched a round robin of letters to every provincial governor or nobleman within a radius of hundreds of miles. Throughout all Rajputana, Kathiawar Peninsula, Kutch, Sind, and Gujarat, an imperial mandate circulated: stop Dara Shikoh. In Jodhpur, Jaswant Singh also received a letter from Aurangzeb himself, ordering Dara's arrest if he set foot in Jodhpur State. Though Dara had already left Jodhpur far behind, Jaswant obediently set out in pursuit and soon joined forces with Jai Singh for the chase into Gujarat.

This time Aurangzeb had left no loophole for discreet slackers: Dara must be captured, dead or alive. One or two observers might later claim that Jai Singh's pursuit of Dara now became deliberately dilatory to allow the prince to escape. But by way of dissent, Dara's modern biographer reiterates his categorically black view of Rajput chivalry: "The military genius, energy and forethought displayed by Jai Singh during the pursuit of Dara . . . stand in glaring contrast with the same Rajah's slackness and ill-concealed indifference to the chase of Shuja . . . . In fact, Jai Singh entered into this inglorious work with some ardor and zeal, and not without betraying a deep personal hatred. Far from conniving at Dara's escape, he spread a network of diplomacy to entrap the unhappy Prince."

Fleeing but not yet trapped, Dara had meanwhile annexed an unexpected and most welcome addition to his party. Indeed, on March 26, 1659, by one of the most unusual accidental encounters of world record, he was now with the man who would ensure his immortality. A weird fluke of fate had plunged a certain European traveler into the midst of the climactic closing incidents of India's War of Succession. "I had now," that European writes, "been three days with Dara, whom I met on the road by the strangest chance imaginable; and being destitute of any medical attendant, he compelled me to accompany him in the capacity of physician." No less a personage than François Bernier—French, highly intelligent, and beautifully literate—had appeared on the Indian subcontinent as a personal witness to Dara's flight. Later in Delhi, Bernier would also be on hand to watch the most stunning scenes of the Mogul tragedy. It was tantamount to finding a Saint Simon or Boswell for Indian history.

●●●

At the time of his arrival in Mogul India, François Bernier was not quite thirty-nine. Born in Anjou of leasehold farmers, he had grown up in the France of Louis XIII and come of age when Louis XIV ascended the throne. He seems to have succumbed to wanderlust early, and by his late twenties had already traveled widely in northern Germany, Poland, Switzerland, and Italy. At first a student of physiology, Bernier matriculated late at the University of Montpellier but finally received his degree as a doctor of medicine in 1652, at the age of thirty-two. Renewed wandering took him to Palestine and Syria; in Egypt he came down with the plague at Rosetta, recovered and went on to live in Cairo. Still eager to see the world, and intending to explore "the Red Sea from one end to the other," he embarked at last in a galley from Suez, intending to visit Ethiopia. But Ethiopia was too barbaric: "Catholics were not safe in that country," and so he went on through the Red Sea and beyond the straits of Bab el Mandel. Three weeks later he found himself at the port of Surat in India; it was probably the beginning of 1659.

Bernier's contemporary and friend, the French jeweler Tavernier, provides a glowing account in his own travel narrative of how Bernier met Dara.

> As [Dara] approached Ahmadabad, Monsieur Bernier, a French physician, who was on his way to Agra to visit the court of the Great Mogul, and who is well known to all the world, as much by his personal merits as by the charming accounts of his travels, was of great assistance to one of the wives of this Prince who was attacked with erysipelas in one leg. Dara Shikoh, having learned that an accomplished European physician was at hand, sent immediately for him, and Monsieur Bernier went to his tent, where he saw this lady and examined into her ailment, for which he gave a remedy and quick relief. This poor Prince, being much pleased with Monsieur Bernier, strongly pressed him to remain in his service.

Tavernier is somewhat less than accurate. The "wife" (doubtless a harem favorite) was not suffering from erysipelas but from a bad leg wound. In addition, the crown prince's extremity would soon make it impossible for Bernier to continue in his retinue. Bernier would go on to Agra and Delhi, to become a kind of resident philosopher in the home of Danishmand Khan, an important nobleman of the court who was himself a physician. Significantly, Danishmand was one of the few Mogul nobles who had not rushed to pay homage to Aurangzeb when Agra had fallen, but had stayed at home and declared his neutrality.

Bernier's *Travels in the Mogul Empire* is a classic of travel literature. He is a wandering Montaigne: analytical, skeptical yet humane, logical but passionately partisan to the institutions of a monarchic France. Very likely dependent on Danishmand Khan for those details of the War of Succession which he did not personally witness, his narrative is full of flaws, bias, and misinterpretation; it is also frequently astonishingly precise, and always a masterwork of prose style. English translations of the French text would appear by 1671 and with impressive results—no less a master than John Dryden based his historical tragedy, *Aureng-Zebe,* on Bernier's account of Mogul Hindustan. In the spring of 1675, with Aurangzeb still very much alive in India, Dryden's tragedy was performed in London. A century later, Dr. Johnson vouchsafed a few inimitably anfractuous comments: while it was disturbing for any dramatic work to be based on the actions of a living sovereign, Johnson also thought it fortunate that Aurangzeb's "dominion was over nations not likely to employ their critics upon the transactions of the English stage." Otherwise, "if he had known and disliked his own character, our trade was not in those times secure from his resentment." There was really no need for Dr. Johnson to worry: taking extreme poetic license, Dryden turned the ambiguously usurping Aurangzeb into a virtual hero.

● ● ●

For the moment, though he had barely entered India, Francois Bernier found himself in the thick of events—a hapless addition to Dara Shikoh's fugitive retinue. On March 29, Dara's party halted some forty-eight miles from Ahmadabad, with a scout proceeding ahead to assess their likely reception at the fort. But Jai Singh's coercive letters were already having an effect. Ahmadabad's civil and military authorities, deciding on allegiance to Aurangzeb, had arrested Dara's resident representative and taken possession of town and fort. The scout now returned with a warning from the new governor: Dara would encounter resistance if he attempted to enter the city. Bleakly philosophical, Bernier noted that "the hopes of the vanquished and unfortunate are seldom realized."

This depressing news reached the party at dawn. Grimly recording their state of mind, the Frenchman writes:

> The day preceding that on which he [Dara] received the governor's communication, he expressed his fear lest I should be murdered by the Kolis, and insisted upon my

passing the night in the caravanserai where he then was. The cords of the *kanates*, or screens, which concealed his wife and women (for he was without even a tent) were fastened to the wheels of the carriage wherein I reposed. This may appear almost incredible to those who know how extremely jealous the great men of Hindustan are of their wives, and I mention the circumstance as a proof of the low condition to which the fortunes of the Prince were reduced. It was at break of day that the governor's message was delivered, and the shrieks of the females drew tears from every eye. We were all overwhelmed with confusion and dismay, gazing in speechless horror at each other, at a loss what plan to recommend, and ignorant of the fate which perhaps awaited us from hour to hour. We observed Dara stepping out, more dead than alive, speaking now to one, then to another; stopping and consulting even the commonest soldier. He saw consternation depicted in every countenance, and felt assured that he should be left without a single follower; but what was to become of him? whither must he go? to delay his departure was to accelerate his ruin.

It was, as a matter of fact, the end of a brief friendship for Bernier. Dara could not advance to Ahmadabad, while flight to the north or east was equally impossible. His only road lay westward to purgatory again—the salt marshes of the Little Rann of Kutch. The entire retinue was falling apart at the seams. By Bernier's account, they had

> . . . marched, nearly without intermission, day and night; and so insupportable was the heat, and so suffocating the dust, that of the three large oxen of Gujarat which drew my carriage, one had died, another was in a dying state, and the third was unable to proceed from fatigue. Dara felt anxious to retain me in his service . . . yet neither his threats nor entreaties could procure for me a single horse, ox, or camel; so totally destitute of power and influence had he become! I remained behind, therefore, because of the absolute impossibility of

continuing the journey, and could not but weep when I beheld the Prince depart with a force diminished to four or five hundred horsemen.

Bernier would see Dara once more from a distance, as a prisoner in Delhi. For the moment, the Frenchman had to think about saving his own skin: he sat forty-eight miles from Ahmadabad in a miserable caravanserai surrounded by Koli robbers, and it would be no mean trick to solicit their compassion and hold onto his valuables.

> I made a grand display of my professional skill; my two servants, who experienced the same terror as myself, declared I was the most eminent physician in the world, and that Dara's soldiers had used me extremely ill, depriving me of everything valuable. It was fortunate for me that we succeeded in creating in these people an interest in my favour; for after detaining me seven or eight days, they attached a bullock to my carriage, and conducted me within view of the minarets of Ahmadabad. In this city I met with a [noble] who was proceeding to Delhi, and I travelled under his protection. On the road our eyes were too often offended with the sight of dead men, elephants, oxen, horses, and camels; the wrecks of poor Dara's army.

Dara had meanwhile struck due west. As a wry commentary on human nature, he was escorted to the boundaries of Kutch by the bandit chief of the Kolis himself—a Hindu version of Robin Hood somewhat more reliable than the Rajputs. En route the fugitives were joined by Dara's appointee in Surat, who materialized with fifty horses and two hundred foot soldiers.

A lamentable party now entered the waterless wasteland of the Little Rann. Dara had been reduced to a cheap linen tunic and shoes worth a fraction of a rupee, and had taken to shaking uncontrollably in spastic seizures of fear. Aside from the soldiers' beasts, his own personal transport animals amounted to one horse, a bullock cart, five camels for the women, and several pack camels.

This time the ruler of Kutch proved somewhat less hospitable: he had been intimidated by Jai Singh's threatening letters. In response to Dara's request for sanctuary, the rao allowed two days of grace; but Aurangzeb's huntsmen were headed for Kutch, and Dara must surely understand that it would be best for him to leave at once. However, the rao would go so far as to provide an escort to the border of the Greater Rann.

"Nearly the whole of the men, and many of the women, did perish; some dying of thirst, hunger, or fatigue," Bernier sums up Dara's recrossing of the great salt marsh. For the quarry it was very nearly the end: Aurangzeb's trap had begun to close on him. Once out of the *rann,* the party found that a thousand hostile troops held Badin village to the north. Khalilullah Khan, the new governor of the Punjab, had come down from Multan as far as Bhakkar Fortress (where Dara's besieged island garrison, including Manucci, still held out heroically); the upper delta was thus blocked, and Khalilullah had already dispatched other soldiers to seal off eastern approaches to Jaisalmer on the borders of Rajputana. Throughout all lower Sind province, Mogul officers kept on the alert; while behind the fugitives, Jai Singh had indefatigably tramped eighty miles across the *rann* by moonlight and by torch flares when the moon went down. Dara's only hope would be to head slightly northwest and attempt a crossing of the Indus into Baluchistan; then, with further luck, he could strike for Kandahar and Persia beyond. At this point the sole general who had accompanied him from Ajmer deserted to Aurangzeb—India ended at the Indus River, and he was homesick.

If Dara's party suffered, Jai Singh's pursuing army of twenty thousand men suffered even more. Horses and oxen needed water and fodder, and it had been a drought year in Gujarat; animals collapsed in the forced march, while men were sustained only by salary in cash. At times the host was obliged to split up into three divisions, and much time was lost in getting together again. When they reached Kutch, the rao prudently came out to offer his personal greetings to Jai

Singh, and to assure him that Dara had fled. But in a final gesture to endear himself to history, the rao also balked at supplying Dara's pursuers with a guide across the salt lagoon.

It was now that Jai Singh made his crossing by night; miraculously, no one was swallowed up in quicksand, though it was a desiccated horde of men and animals that staggered into the northshore village of Rahman. Wild with thirst, they attacked water sources with such frenzy that mud was quickly stirred up, and they found themselves lapping bitter draughts. By now, in the merciless summer heat on the other side of the *rann,* animals began to drop dead left and right. Jai Singh's personal escort was four thousand cavalry, but three thousand quickly became foot soldiers as their horses collapsed under them. At last (on June 11) the Rajput veteran reached the Indus, only to find that Dara had already crossed into forbidding territory; with the help of local tribesmen, he was headed for Kandahar.

Even for twenty thousand soldiers, to go beyond the Indus without a lifeline of supplies and into a labyrinth of endless desert hills was madness. Indeed, to take a Mogul army out of India went beyond the call of duty. With the sun of Sind so strong it could "turn a white man black," Jai Singh now sat down and wrote a letter asking to be recalled. He reminded Aurangzeb:

> When appointing me to this service, Your Majesty told me that so long as Dara was not captured or killed, or did not quit the empire, I should not withdraw my hand from him. I have left no means untried to accomplish the first two alternatives. At no place, however hard and difficult to traverse, did I take thought of the scarcity of water and grain or of the predominance of lawless men. But Allah ordains everything, and so the third alternative has come to pass. Since Your Majesty has now been freed from the mischief of that [enemy], and in view of the extreme privations borne by the army and the weakness of the horses and transport cattle, which have not strength enough to move more than six or eight miles a day, I beg to submit that I should be recalled to court.

Jai Singh did not know it, but Allah had already ordained a fourth alternative—Dara Shikoh's capture and martyrdom. Even as the exhausted troops moved slowly up the Indus toward the Punjab, surprising news now reached their Rajput commander: Dara had already been taken prisoner on June 9, and Jai Singh was obliged to escort him to Delhi.

●●●

There could hardly be a more savage enclave than Baluchistan, conquered late by Akbar and only nominally a part of the Mogul Empire. Northwest of India beyond the Kirthar Range, ominously barren hills led up to desolate Bolan Pass and on through even bleaker terrain to Kandahar in Afghanistan and to Persia beyond. Baluchistan's hill tribes were a lawless and savage assortment of Chandis and Makashis—a tough trans-Indus hodgepodge of cutthroats perpetually at war with one another, and never for a moment acknowledging the supremacy of either Persia or the Moguls.

In the river country of lower Sind, Dara had barely been able to effect passage—citizens with boats had fled to the farther shore at his approach. Finally crossing the Indus by rafts, his vulnerable and further-shrunken contingent had promptly been attacked by Chandi guerrillas and narrowly escaped with their lives. But at last the fugitives were befriended by Makashi tribesmen, whose chief offered escort to the Kandahar frontier twelve days' march away. It was Dara's last shred of hope, and it would be denied him— "Dara seemed doomed never to succeed in any enterprise," wrote Bernier.

By modern interpretation the prince had already unconsciously sealed his own fate with masochistic certainty, though outward coercion was certainly not wanting. Raising their former objections, the ladies of Dara's harem voiced opposition to quitting India outright. Sinister Baluch tribes swarmed in the territory they would have to cross; even if Persia could be reached, the Iranian shah's reputation for licentiousness equalled his capacity for drink, and they might ignominiously end up in his harem. More persuasively,

Dara's wife Nadira Begum was now dangerously ill with dysentery: the hardships of a journey through the Bolan Pass and over burning hill ranges to Kandahar would surely be her death warrant. The entire party, for that matter, had reached a state of extreme debilitation after two and a half months of breakneck flight through Rajputana deserts and across the salt lagoons of the *rann*—all in blistering summer heat. They needed sanctuary close at hand.

Under duress, Dara's evil genius had also apparently pushed him into one final and desperate gamble for the Peacock Throne. If he could find a reliable ally among trans-Indus tribes, it might just be possible to raise an army sufficient to relieve Manucci and the garrison at the Bhakkar island fortress on the Indus River. Then, leaving his women and remaining treasure there, he could push north to Kabul and perhaps persuade Mahabat Khan the younger to take up the cause of freeing Shah Jahan. With a redoubtable army of Afghan recruits pushing back into India through the Khyber Pass, there might yet be a victory over Aurangzeb.

Casting about in his mind for an absolute friend in the vicinity, Dara unwittingly selected his Judas. Some fifteen miles southeast of Bolan Pass was the fortress castle of Dadhar, and its castellan was the man whose life he had once saved—the Afghan chief Malik Jiwan. Years before, Malik Jiwan had been arrested by the governor of Multan and sent in chains to Delhi for a crime against the state; on Shah Jahan's orders, punishment was to be torture and trampling to death under the feet of an elephant. Weeping bitterly, one of Malik's friends had submitted the facts of the case to Dara; tender-hearted Dara interceded for pardon, and through his kindness Malik Jiwan found himself restored to honor. Surely Malik would now reciprocate to a friend in need? Malik would and did, even sending a servant to guide the party to Dadhar. Dara took leave of the Makashi tribesmen who had offered to take him to Kandahar.

It was June 6, 1659. Aggravated by dysentery and heartbreak (believing her son Sulaiman to be a victim of Aurang-

zeb), Nadira Banu Begum died as the party neared Malik
Jiwan's fortress. Dara immediately collapsed in an agony of
grief. It was the end now, nothing mattered any more: he had
already been destroyed. Allah had taken everything from
him. For twenty-seven years Nadira Begum had been far
more than a wife and consort; she had been companion,
counselor, disciple, a substitute mother filling the gap of
Mumtaz Mahal's early death. Nadira was the daughter of
Shah Jahan's half-brother Prince Parwiz; indeed, both her
parents had been royal, thus making her doubly the grand-
daughter of Akbar the Great. Dara had made no other marriage, and Nadira alone had given him his children: his two
daughters, Jani Begum and another scarcely mentioned in
history, together with his two sons Sulaiman and Sipihr Shikoh. Several offspring had died in infancy, and it was after
the death of their first daughter that Nadira and Dara had
sought spiritual consolation and enlightenment at the feet of
the Sufi mystic and saint, Mian Mir, in Lahore, so many
years ago. Since the War of Succession began, through long
months of reversal and crisis, Nadira Banu had been constantly with Dara—a symbol of royal sustenance and hope,
parallel to Mumtaz Mahal's devotion to the young Shah
Jahan in his own struggles for the crown. But Mumtaz Mahal
had at least lived to see Shah Jahan on the throne; with Nadira Begum dead, Dara lost heart.

The outskirts of Dadhar constituted a particularly hellish place for death. Trapped between barren, rocky hills,
Dara's party was assaulted by a summer heat which even
sober geographers acknowledge as "greater than that of any
other place in the world in the same parallel of latitude."
Malik Jiwan, who had come several miles from his castel-
lated stronghold to welcome the fugitive Prince with all due
honors, found himself greeting a funeral party. Sipihr Shikoh
and a few faithful followers were now apparently full of foreboding: what if Malik had already been coerced by letters
from Jai Singh or another of Aurangzeb's generals in Sind?
With Nadira Begum dead there could be no further obstacle
to asylum in Persia, and it would be better to leave at once.

But Dara was numbly putting on white mourning clothes; he would spend three customary days of grief in Malik Jiwan's stronghold before deciding what to do. The Afghan chief owed Dara his life, and could not possibly betray him.

Malik Jiwan, or Jiwan Khan in his proper title of petty Mogul nobility, was a representative Pathan tribesman from the no-man's-land between India and Afghanistan. Hardly generic, the term "Pathan" merely meant that he had been fostered by one of the various nomadic tribes of the district. Obscure spawn of Turkish and central Asian blood, these Afghan frontiersmen lived on the memory of their ancestor Sher Shah, who had shown a moment of rough genius by unseating the Mogul Emperor Humayun and becoming ruler of India during the interim of Humayun's exile. Less gloriously, the Pathans also made periodic raids into India as a form of legitimate banditry; a crudely bellicose lot never quite trusted by the Moguls, they nevertheless played a role in Delhi's court as crackerjack soldiers. Regarded in India even today as regional Shylocks, not a few Pathans became shrewd money-lenders. Malik Jiwan reflected every possible facet of frontier psychology: he was proud, he was ferocious, and his cupidity was naturally worth more than thirty pieces of silver.

Nobody loves a Judas. Even Mogul sources critical of Dara refer to Malik Jiwan as "evil," a "destroying angel," and "guest-murdering host." By Manucci's appraisal, the Pathan chieftain quite simply hoped for reward from Aurangzeb. Bernier, more aware of human complexity, strikes a qualifying note and adds that "it is still doubtful whether he [Malik] had been tampered with by Aurangzeb, or whether he were suddenly tempted to the commission of this monstrous crime." Whatever the motive, the imminent betrayer sized up an ingenuous victim in narrow straits: Dara's guard had dwindled to two or three hundred soldiers, while for treasure the women still had some jewels and there may have been a mule-load or two of gold coins. Malik curiously bided his time; indeed, his later actions would even indicate that he may have been bothered by a faint uneasiness of conscience.

Nadira Begum's corpse was now carried to Dadhar stronghold, where Dara and his immediate family and servants found themselves treated with respect and cordiality; his soldiers billeted among the villagers. The dead princess had either expressed a final wish to be buried in Hindustan, or had left a will to that effect. She would get her wish: two days later, her coffin was sent by Dara to Lahore, there to be interred within the tomb precincts of the Sufi saint, Mian Mir. With incredible naïveté Dara now provided Nadira a death escort of seventy-odd soldiers (or, by one account, all that were left to him) together with his last devoted officer; they would supervise funeral rites. Though ostensibly intending to seek exile in Persia, he was actually closing his life's ledger, and there is something apathetically beautiful in the passive despair of his final magnanimous gesture: gathering his remaining followers, he offered them a free alternative—they could have safe passage to India with the funeral party, or they could accompany him to the Persian unknown. But no person would be obliged to become an outcast, or to seek further danger for his sake. Everyone left. Aside from a finger-count of eunuchs and menials, Dara and his son Sipihr Shikoh were alone—dependent now on the honor of an Afghan.

The following morning, June 9, 1659, Dara and his son and their last followers left Malik Jiwan's Dadhar stronghold, heading for Bolan Pass; beyond lay Kandahar and Persia. Malik now went through his crisis of conscience, for there was an unaccountable time lag. The fugitives had even reached the head of the road before betrayal galvanized its black parishioner; then, swooping down on the party with a group of clansmen, the Pathan chief surrounded his victims. Dara seems to have made no resistance at all: Nadira's death had reduced him to a somnambule of sorrow, and in any case this was the world's last betrayal, the world's martyrdom. Fourteen-year-old Sipihr Shikoh seemed less willing to succumb, flailing out against his attackers until they subdued him and tied his hands behind his back. The prisoners were dragged back to Malik's stronghold. Immediately, he

sent out two of his fastest riding horsemen to Jai Singh's encampment on the Indus River. In the soporific nightmare of
midsummer Sind and with a simoom whirling up an inferno
of yellow dust, Aurangzeb's army received the news: Dara
Shikoh had been captured.

Time was to add legend and lore to a betrayal which
would be greeted with horror by the populace of Delhi. Thus
in Tavernier's account, Dara cried out to Malik Jiwan in the
stiltedly grand seventeenth-century manner: "Finish, finish,
ungrateful and infamous wretch that thou art, finish that
which thou hast commenced; we are the victims of evil fortune and the unjust passion of Aurangzeb, but remember
that I do not merit death except for having saved thy life, and
remember that a prince of the royal blood never had his
hands tied behind his back." It was true of course, and the
humiliated traitor promptly ordered Sipihr Shikoh's hands
untied. In the starker mode of ancient Greek tragedy, both
Manucci and Bernier insist that Nadira Begum was alive at
the time of Dara's betrayal, and ended her life by taking poison either in Malik Jiwan's house or at Lahore. What is certain is that Nadira Begum died, and Dara and his son
suffered arrest. With the psychology of a born Judas, Malik
Jiwan now itched to get the victims out of his contaminated
hands and delivered up to Aurangzeb—for what he hoped
would be a handsome reward.

Leaving camp and military baggage behind, the two
generals, Jai Singh and Bahadur Khan, pushed north with a
contingent of men to receive their royal prisoners, everyone
wrapped in the choking yellow dust of the simoom. Near the
invested fortress of Bhakkar on June 20, they crossed the
Indus and proceeded to meet Malik Jiwan. In manifest re-
pugnance of the task, both Jai Singh and Bahadur Khan
moved slowly at the rear of their advance detachment. By
June 23 Dara, together with his two daughters and Sipihr
Shikoh, was formally delivered up to Bahadur Khan by
Malik Jiwan, and the long march to Delhi began. In payment
for his betrayal, Malik Jiwan would receive a robe of honor
and be made commander of a thousand horse in the Mogul

peerage; he had also to accompany the prisoners back to the capital, in order to receive additional honors. Dara's legs were chained and his wrists manacled, and he and his children were sequestered in howdahs—each elephant escorted (according to Manucci) by three thousand horsemen armed with swords and spears.

● ● ●

During all the months since Dara's flight from the Punjab, his garrison at the Bhakkar Island fortress had been putting up stiff resistance—"under continual assaults, defending ourselves boldly," said Manucci. Frustrated in the use of arms, Aurangzeb's soldiers had by now adopted strategies to persuade European artillerymen inside the fort to defect. "To this end," Manucci relates, "they shot arrows to which letters were attached. These invited us to abandon the service of Dara and evacuate the place. One of these arrows hit me on the shoulder when I was sitting in my bastion at eight o'clock at night. Withdrawing the arrow, I went with it at once wounded as I was, to the eunuch [Basant, the fort commander]. He gave me a robe and some bottles of rose water in recognition of my fidelity."

Basant displayed a grimly brave sense of humor. In response to Khalilullah Khan's endless letters written from Multan suggesting capitulation, he finally agreed to come to terms if Khalilullah would personally appear on the scene. Aurangzeb's general duly arrived, and expectantly pitched his tent opposite the island fort. The eunuch now sent for Manucci, "and ordered me to load with horns and old shoes the cannon nearest to the garden where Khalilullah Khan had encamped. It was charged thus up to the very muzzle." While the cannon was being loaded with rubbish, a boat set out with a letter to Khalilullah Khan from the eunuch: "I hope to supply your want, having been all your life a pimp and used to shoe-beatings from women. Herewith what you deserve; I offer you a present proportioned to your merits." Basant allowed time for the letter to reach shore, and estimated when Khalilullah would be reading it; then he "ordered us to fire off the cannon, and we covered Khalilullah Khan's tent with the charge it contained."

Furious at the insult, Khalilullah responded with violent artillery fire the following night. Basant waited a day and launched a return salvo of bombs and musket fire, just to prove that the garrison had by no means run out of ammunition; in a dazzling show of bravado, he even illuminated the fort with Bengal lights as a midnight token of defiance. The humiliated Khalilullah withdrew toward Lahore, leaving his army of besiegers to continue their seemingly endless battle of attrition.

But the end was in fact in sight. Manucci writes:

> Forty days after the departure of Khalilullah Khan, we saw one morning a numerous force pass over the river from west to east at some distance from the fortress. Our artillery began to pound them as hard as it could. At this moment a horseman appeared on the river bank displaying a small white flag. Immediately the eunuch gave an order for a small boat to fetch the horseman. Upon entering the fortress, he handed the eunuch a letter, and proclaimed loudly thus: "I demand on behalf of Aurangzeb that you surrender this stronghold, since we are carrying with us in this army the Prince Dara, whom we have a prisoner." Hearing this sad and unexpected news, we were all cast down and dropped our arms.

The eunuch Basant was still not convinced; he would yield Bhakkar fort only at the personal command of Prince Dara Shikoh. Aurangzeb's generals had no difficulty obtaining assent: listlessly silent in the several days since quitting Malik Jiwan's territory, Dara had fallen into a kind of daze and agreed to whatever his captors suggested. Manucci describes the dismal finale:

> Seeing how resolute we were, Bahadur Khan repaired to Prince Dara and requested him to order the eunuch to surrender the stronghold; since the garrison was firm in

its resistance, the lot of us would in all probability come to a miserable end within the fortress. On hearing this Dara had compassion upon his eunuch and upon us, and wrote a note with his own hand, stating: "Unfortunate is the one for whom you fought. I now request and require you to deliver up the place."

When the eunuch Primavera [Basant] saw the letter, he recognized the writing and began to weep bitterly. He wrote to Bahadur Khan that we demanded to come out with our baggage, and if he did not consent we would fling cannon and treasure into the river and fight to the death with all desperation. Bahadur Khan sent back assurance that we could leave with our baggage, but must make over the treasure . . . and all matériel appertaining to the fortress. One condition was imposed: we must cross over to the west of the river, then eight days after he had marched we could take the road for Delhi. He made this condition because he feared we might enter his camp, and do our utmost to rescue Dara. After three days we issued from the fort in which we had endured so much. For two days before the evacuation I bought two calves for 600 rupees, and paid 1 rupee for every ounce of butter. Without exaggerating, I bought one chicken for 13 rupees.

Inflation may have set in, but clearly no one in the fort was starving.

Bahadur Khan's army moved on out of sight of Bhakkar fortress, with the royal prisoner under formidable guard. Faithful Niccolo Manucci was never to see Dara again, though his voluminous memoirs would piece together from bazaar gossip and court friends the distressing details of Dara's fate. Surrendered along with the fort were several of Dara's grandchildren who had been deposited there for safety—"the little sons of Sulaiman Shikoh," Manucci says, "of whom nothing more was ever heard, and it seems as if by order of Aurangzeb they were got rid of. . . ."

● ● ●

Manucci himself by no means disappeared from Indian history. After his usual picaresque escapades he arrived in

Delhi for presentation to Aurangzeb along with other Europeans. Impressed by the valor of Dara's artillerymen, Aurangzeb "was very anxious for us to enter his service," and offered four rupees a day to every man—five rupees to Manucci. He tells us:

> My companions accepted but I did not wish to do so, through the antipathy I had to him, and the point of honor I cherished of not serving under the murderer of my master. I communicated to the King my non-acceptance of employment. He caused me to be sent for once more, and asked why I did not accept service with him; did I want higher pay than he offered? I replied to him that I would willingly enter into his employ, but I longed to return to my native land, years having elapsed in absence from it; and thus he allowed me to leave.

It was a lie: Manucci never left India—not for the rest of his long life. He abandoned the career of artilleryman and turned up in Lahore as a self-styled doctor. There he won immediate renown by prescribing an enema for his first case, the constipated wife of a local police commissioner. His enema brew was a dubious concoction of mallows, wild endive, herbs, bran, black sugar, salt, and olive oil; the home-made clyster (from a cow's udder and a hookah tube) would have appalled even Molière. But it started the physician on his way. Some of Manucci's remedies seem ghoulish: red-hot iron rings to cure cholera or to induce birth; and of course there was plenty of popular seventeenth-century bloodletting. But in the country of the blind the one-eyed man is king; Niccolo Manucci continued to prosper. There would of course be inevitable medical intrigues. On one occasion the Italian narrowly escaped Moslem justice when authorities investigated him for receiving 504 ounces of human fat taken from a corpulent Mohammedan who had been beheaded. But Manucci assured them that the fat was not for internal use, merely for an ointment efficacious in nervous disorders! Later, in front of astonished nobles at the court of Golconda, he would successfully bleed a stout Georgian woman by striking a vein where others had failed; blood spurted up abundantly, and made the King "desirous of being bled also."

Throughout Aurangzeb's long reign, Manucci criss-crossed India from one end to the other. In Portuguese Goa he would witness nasty events of the Inquisition; he would turn up in Delhi and Agra again, and even become private physician in the retinue of one of Aurangzeb's sons. Finally, in Madras at the late age of forty-seven, he married an English girl born in India; "I had a son," he tells us, "but God chose rather to make him an angel in Paradise than leave him to suffer in this world." Between bouts as a physician, Manucci would also be negotiator, mediator, and ambassador for both the Portuguese and the British, perpetually embroiled in the intricacies of Indian politics. What other European had so many Mogul contacts? Who could rival his fluency in Turkish, Persian, and Hindi? At Fort St. George in Madras, even the eminent British governor Thomas Pitt would employ Manucci between 1698 and 1709; though when told that the Italian was writing his memoirs the governor later commented acidly, "It will be a history of Tom Thumb."

Pitt could not have been more wrong. Niccolo Manucci finally died in 1717 as an octogenarian, but his four-volume memoirs earned him an immortality which the governor might well have envied.

CHAPTER

22

Day of Vengeance

FROM JUNE 23, WHEN Malik Jiwan handed Dara over to Aurangzeb's generals, it took exactly two months for a return march to Delhi. Crossing the rain-swollen five rivers of the Punjab, the black escort and its dismal prisoners reached the capital on August 23, 1659.

Delhi had just rounded out eleven weeks of festivities in honor of Aurangzeb's second and formal coronation. After defeating both Shuja and Dara at the battles of Khajuha and Ajmer, the new emperor had made his triumphal entry into the city on May 12 in a regal din of kettledrums, tambourines, brass tympani, and trumpets. There was the usual fantastic parade of elephants caparisoned in gold and silver, with velvet-embroidered howdahs, imperial standards, cavalry and foot soldiers, and glittering gems and lances. Surrounded by a bee swarm of court nobles and grandees, Aurangzeb sat on a gold throne lashed to the back of the most imposing elephant in the royal stables. He was now just over forty, no pudgy and self-indulgent oriental potentate but more of a lean Iago crossed with Napoleon. His face had become angular; not yet the autocratic ghoul of later Mogul miniatures—nose and chin like knife-blades, cheeks hollow, brows beetling, and beard gray—but already revealing the inhuman palace of ice he had carved inside of himself. The eyes told all: implacable and piercing, their gaze took him beyond even the Nietzschean pale. Behind and on either side of that sea of encompassing nobles, ranks of his veteran army marched. The populace of Delhi looked on with awe. These were the Deccan veterans who had cowed Bijapur and Golconda, smashed the great armies of Shuja and Dara, brought Agra to its knees, and unseated Shah Jahan. It was an almost Roman display of power. Aurangzeb ordered sprays of silver and gold coins to be flung from elephant backs as the procession moved through the bazaar and entered the Red Fort.

Sunday, June 5 was the stargazers' choice for official coronation day. Shah Jahan had created the splendors of this new conglomeration of white marble palaces, and puritan Aurangzeb made no protest against the opulence of an event marking his assumption of absolute power. Ceilings and halls had been ornamented to the pitch of wildest fantasy. Surrounded by a gold railing, the Peacock Throne blazed with diamonds and rubies; there were canopies of state with gemencrusted columns, strings of pearls, and gold benches displaying the Fabergé-like artifacts of three generations—jeweled swords, studded ceremonial shields and spears. Velvet awnings covered the great courtyard below the Hall of Public Audience, with Persian carpets spread thick underfoot.

With nervous astrologers watching clepsydras and hourglasses, Aurangzeb's actual moment of ascension came exactly three hours and fifteen minutes after sunrise. On signal, in full attire from behind a screen, he entered the Hall of Public Audience and sat on his Peacock Throne. The precincts vibrated to the sound of kettledrums; and nautch girls with kohl-rimmed eyes assumed the erotic postures of consort Shakti winding her limbs around the Hindu god Shiva in perpetual sexual intercourse to all eternity. Only later would come Aurangzeb's rigorous edicts and the gradual squelching of all pleasures; for now, everyone enjoyed this full sensual spectacle.

A chanter called out the bidding prayer: by Allah and the Prophet, in the glorious wake of Genghis Khan and Timur, in the wake of Babur and Humayun and Akbar and Jahangir and Shah Jahan, the Emperor Aurangzeb had begun his mighty reign. Now came the trays of gold rupees

Fig. 18. The Victory Gate, Fatehpur Sikri

Fig. 19. Shah Jahan's Friday Mosque, Delhi

Fig. 20.   Gwalior fortress

Fig. 22.   Jahanara's tomb

Fig. 21.   Aurangzeb's tomb

Fig. 23.   Akbar's tomb

Fig. 24.   Dara Shikoh's tomb

Fig. 25.   Humayun's tomb

Fig. 26.   The Taj in its garden setting

Fig. 27.   Sir Thomas Roe

Fig. 28.   Niccolo Manucci

Fig. 29. Presumed portrait of
François Bernier

Fig. 30.   Sulaiman Shikoh (detail)

Fig. 31.   Asaf Khan, father of
Mumtaz Mahal

Fig. 32.   Dara Shikoh's Sufi mentors,
Mulla Shah and Mian Mir

Fig. 33.   Mir Jumla

Fig. 34.   Mogul battle scene depicts Murad fighting from the back of an elephant.

Fig. 35.   Jaswant Singh, maharajah of Jodhpur, with Hindu attendants

Fig. 36.   Elephants in combat

Fig. 37.   Gold coin shows Jahangir with wine-cup.

Fig. 38.   Gold coin depicts Mogul lion couchant.

Fig. 39.   Inscription on Mogul coin

and jewels—a ravishing shower over the heads of attending nobles. In the midst of robes of honor, betel leaf, burning incense and aloes, musk, ambergris, and the heavy smell of attar of roses, everyone shouted "Long live the Caliph of the Age!"

But there was a change in rupees minted for the occasion: henceforth there would be no inscription of Moslem articles of faith on one face of the coins, since Aurangzeb did not want holy text defiled by the touch of Hindu infidels. In place of religious epithets a Persian couplet stood out in relief—"This coin has been stamped on earth like the shining full moon, by King Aurangzeb, the Conqueror of the World"—and the verso simply bore the name of the mint-city, the year of reign and the emperor's full title. In further foreshadowing of coming events, the new emperor appointed censors of public morals to cope with a catalogue of vices offensive to Islam; at the top of the proscribed list was wine-drinking.

Formal letters of Aurangzeb's accession went out to all provinces of Hindustan, and of course there were harem celebrations. For Aurangzeb's sister, Raushanara Begum, his partisan and court spy during the events of the War of Succession, reward amounted to half a million rupees; emoluments were fixed on his daughters as well. Raushanara seethed with vindictive joy: her eldest sister, Jahanara, was a dishonored prisoner in Agra fort, ministering to a senile fool who had received his comeuppance and was no longer master of India.

Coronation festivities continued for weeks more. Grandees and rulers of fiefs presented gifts, and were baptized with a reciprocal cascade of titles, promotions, robes of honor, and tokens ranging from elephants to jeweled pen-cases. The Jumna River stood illuminated by night, with musicians in lamp-strung boats playing to crowds lining the banks. Appropriately enough, the Imperial Artillery Department provided a display of fireworks on the river plain below the fort as Aurangzeb looked on. It was in the midst of these celebrations, on July 2, that the great new Mogul received

the hasty but happy word: Dara Shikoh had been taken prisoner. By July fifteenth the report had been confirmed. Further rejoicing was ordered, especially "to inform the public,
who were still skeptical about Dara's capture."

● ● ●

Dara Shikoh, too, would have his coronation procession: defeat must receive its crown of thorns. Bahadur Khan
and the traitor Malik Jiwan had turned Dara and Sipihr Shikoh over to a hunchbacked slave named Nazar Beg, who had
been appointed by Aurangzeb to handle the contaminating
task of confinement. For the time being the prisoners were
placed under heavy guard in a building in the village of
Khawaspura, three miles south of Delhi. Two days later
Nazar was summoned to the imperial presence to report on
the condition of his miserable wards.

In private session with his grandees, Aurangzeb now invited pro and con arguments. For the moment it seemed that
Dara would be taken to Gwalior state prison, but debate centered on the question of whether or not there should be a
humiliating parade through Delhi's streets. A few nobles
counseled caution: it could only spatter mud on the royal
family to make a degraded spectacle of the prince, and there
was even the possibility of a riot or rescue attempt. The
opposition countered with blunt insistence: Dara had to be
exposed to public gaze in order to terrify the mob with the reality of Aurangzeb's power; besides, only seeing was believing, and nothing less than an open display could make it
quite clear that Dara was incontrovertibly a prisoner. Aurangzeb finally decided that future fake Daras must be
prevented from stirring up trouble. Dara and his son Sipihr
Shikoh would be dragged in squalor under military guard
through the main thoroughfares of central Delhi, for every
Indian to see.

There would be a European eyewitness to this excruci-
ating event, which took place on August 29, 1659. François
Bernier had now settled in Delhi, a keen observer among the
anonymous masses of Moslems and Hindus thronging the
streets. Bernier records:

[372]

The wretched prisoner was therefore secured on an elephant, his young son, Sipihr Shikoh, placed at his side, and behind them . . . was seated Bahadur Khan. This was not one of the majestic elephants of Pegu or Ceylon, which Dara had been in the habit of mounting, pompously caparisoned, the harness gilt, and trappings decorated with figured work; and carrying a beautifully painted howdah, inlaid with gold, and a magnificent canopy to shelter the Prince from the sun: Dara was now seen seated on a miserable and worn-out animal, covered with filth; he no longer wore the necklace of large pearls which distinguish the princes of Hindustan, nor the rich turban and embroidered coat; he and his son were now habited in dirty cloth of the coarsest texture, and his sorry turban was wrapped round with a Kashmir shawl or scarf, resembling that worn by the meanest of the people.

Such was the appearance of Dara when led through the bazaars and every quarter of the city. I could not divest myself of the idea that some dreadful execution was about to take place, and felt surprise that government should have the hardihood to commit all these indignities upon a Prince confessedly popular among the lower orders. . . . The people had for some time inveighed bitterly against the unnatural conduct of Aurangzeb: the imprisonment of his father, of his son Mohammed Sultan, and of his brother Murad Bakhsh, filled every bosom with horror and disgust. The crowd assembled upon this disgraceful occasion was immense; and everywhere I observed the people weeping, and lamenting the fate of Dara in the most touching language. I took my station in one of the most conspicuous parts of the city, in the midst of the largest bazaar; was mounted on a good horse, and accompanied by two servants and two intimate friends. From every quarter I heard piercing and distressing shrieks, for the Indian people have a very tender heart; men, women and children wailing as if some mighty calamity had happened to themselves. [Malik Jiwan] rode near the wretched Dara; and the abusive and indignant cries vociferated as the traitor moved along were absolutely deafening. I

[373]

observed some fakirs and several poor people throw stones at the infamous Pathan; but not a single movement was made, no one offered to draw his sword, with a view of delivering the beloved and compassionated Prince.

In fact, Delhi rocked on the verge of riot. In the blazing August sun, Dara's feet were chained as the parade mockingly followed a public route he had known in times of glory and splendor. Close to the prisoners, the hunchback Nazar Beg sat with an unsheathed sword; squadrons of mail-clad cavalry clopped along in a protecting body, also with drawn swords, and a contingent of mounted archers with bows and arrows at the ready sustained an aura of violence. Dara kept his head bowed in profound humiliation. Near the Red Fort a poverty-stricken fakir is said to have shouted to him, "O Dara! when you were master you always gave me alms; today I know well thou hast naught to give me." The Prince responded immediately; raising his hand to his shoulder and pulling off a dark, dingy-colored shawl, he threw it to the holy man. Bahadur Khan promptly ordered the shawl to be confiscated: a prisoner had no right to bestow anything. Unafraid, the fakir launched a torrent of abuse against Malik Jiwan when he passed by.

The procession followed a defined route, entering the walled metropolis by its Lahore Gate and passing down the famous Chandni Chowk* all the way to the Red Fort on the Jumna River, where it continued outward to the suburbs of the old city. At that time the heart of Delhi was the Red Fort, from which the town radiated outward in three different directions. In a warren of arcaded lanes, airy, set-back houses for the more fortunate citizens mingled with thatched clusters of huts, while crude camps afforded squalid lodgings for workers and soldiers. A canal ran westward from the Jumna near the fort; and the cries of Kashmiri boatmen could be heard as they plied gondolas for the Mogul emperor, as well

---

* Literally, "Silver Street."

as for the nobles whose villas commanded the choicer and more open parts of the city along the river banks. As for the Chandni Chowk, it bore no resemblance to today's narrow and degraded thoroughfare: "the richest street in the world" still boasts Shah Jahan's monumental Friday Mosque, but to Bernier's eye it also constituted a wide thoroughfare. It was replete with watercourses, while at the entrance to what are now the Queen's Gardens stood the sumptuous caravanserai of Princess Jahanara Begum—a building compared by the Frenchman to the Palais royal, because of its arcades and superposed gallery. This was the scene of Dara's martyred pilgrimage.

Opposite the entrance to the Red Fort, the mortifying parade halted for two hours in a brutal midday sun. Manucci, who despised Aurangzeb, asserts that the new emperor wanted to make Dara descend from the elephant and be dragged before him in chains; but Mumtaz Mahal's brother advised against this. After a while, the captives were taken back to their suburban prison under even stronger guard.

● ● ●

Contrary to expectation, the intention of the procession failed outright. Far from inspiring fear in the populace of Delhi or making Dara an object of ridicule, Aurangzeb had only increased popular grief and indignation to dangerous proportions. In fact, alarmed by the possibility of a general insurrection, the new emperor hastily convoked a secret assortment of grandees and mullahs in the Hall of Private Audience that very evening. It might be best to put Dara Shikoh to death at once, rather than risk transporting him to Gwalior prison. A moderating faction of nobles suggested that there could be no danger if a strong escort were provided to Gwalior. Persuasively arguing for Dara's life was Bernier's patron, Danishmand Khan—a creditable gesture, since he and Dara had been on bad terms for a long time. But other nobles were less kindly disposed; Khalilullah Khan, Bahadur Khan, and Mumtaz Mahal's brother recommended immediate execution "for the good of church and state." Dara's sister Raushanara Begum, unashamedly out for blood, tipped the scales in a wild outburst of malignance. As Aurangzeb's champion, she had simmered a brew of mean and mixed motives over the years: her elder sister Jahanara had been Shah Jahan's favorite and Dara's intimate. Filled with loathing, Raushanara insisted on her revenge—*kill Dara now.*

Orthodox zealots muttered approval: the ulema passed judgment like croaking ravens. Strict Moslem theologians had no reason to love Dara, who in his ascendancy had publicly mocked them—"Paradise is where no mullah abides," he had written in mystical contempt for those who applied the letter of the Koran yet missed the spirit of God. But Dara was not the first victim of ulemic wrath: liberal Moslems had been falling out with bigoted theologians since the time of Akbar. Schismatic in their influence on the state, the ulema rejected all honest difference of opinion in religious matters. They bristled at the slightest offence to their pride, and fought for ascendancy with virulence—not a few freethinkers had been executed on formal charges of heresy or rotted in dungeons or lived in exile. It stood to reason that if the ulema disliked liberal Moslems, their hatred of Hindus knew no bounds; Dara Shikoh had been both a liberal Moslem *and* a friend of Hindus. Once before, under Akbar, the ulema had found their priestly power brutally curbed: playing one lawmaker off against another, the great Mogul had forced the passing of an Act of Supremacy which made the emperor the supreme power of law. Giving vent to his own highly liberal attitudes, Akbar had gone so far as to exile starkly reactionary mullahs and shaikhs, even tabooing the Koran and enjoining fire and sun worship in an attempt to promote his own "Divine Faith"—a weirdly eclectic hash of Hindu and Zoroastrian ritual, though like a true son of the Renaissance he had remained a tolerant synthesist with hopes of composite religious unity for India. But Akbar's liberal tradition had gone too far with his great-grandson Dara Shikoh. It was the moment the ulema had been waiting for, and unanimously they now sanctioned or actually signed a decree: Dara merited death as an apostate from orthodox Islam.

Bernier mentions a grandee named Takarrub Khan—"a wretched parasite recently raised to the rank of . . . [noble], and formerly a physician"—who summed up in a violent harangue for government and mosque. " 'Dara ought not to live,' he exclaimed; 'the safety of the state depends upon his immediate execution; and I feel the less reluctant to recommend his being put to death, because he has long since ceased to be a Mussulman, and become a *kaffir*. If it be sinful to shed the blood of such a person, may the sin be visited upon my own head!' " Divine justice could hardly overlook such an imprecation: Takarrub Khan would soon find himself disgraced and sentenced to death.

The decree constituted political murder pure and simple. But Aurangzeb had found secular and, more importantly for his puritan conscience, sacred rationale. Dara's court agent, apparently still allowed to function, made a desperate last bid to find a mediator who might intercede for pardon, but his efforts were in vain. A final appeal would come from the crown prince himself, who now in prison was going through the last stages of spiritual anguish. He wrote:

> My brother and my king,
> I have no further thought of sovereignty. I only wish it may be auspicious to you and to your descendants. My execution is an unnecessary preoccupation for your lofty mind. Grant me a house to live in, and a maid from my former retinue to attend to my needs, and I will devote my life in retreat to praying for your good.

Aurangzeb sent the missive back to the prisoner with a verse written in Arabic on the margin: "You usurped authority, and you were seditious."

Pardon was unthinkable: no one and nothing could stop revenge. Behind the moment of fratricide were years of emotional blight: Dara Shikoh had been bathed in Shah Jahan's love; Dara Shikoh had plotted and schemed from Delhi, urging Shah Jahan to write acrimonious letters to the Deccan; Dara Shikoh had been a corrupting dove of peace spreading

[377]

his wings to protect Bijapur and Golconda from Aurangzeb's wars, which had been sanctioned by Shah Jahan himself; Dara gave patronage to enemies, Dara's sons had been preferred over Aurangzeb's. Murad was still alive at Gwalior prison, and Shuja might yet escape vengeance in Bengal. But Dara would be the first brother to be murdered, and it would happen sooner than anyone thought.

The humiliating parade of August 29 was succeeded by a riot on the next day—which unexpectedly became the day of Dara's death. In the morning, Aurangzeb held durbar to show proper appreciation for Malik Jiwan's dark services. The entire population of Delhi had already spotted Dara's traitor during the previous day's events, but a protecting ring of cavalry had held public protest to curses and a flung stone or two. With his new title of Bakhtyar Khan and rank of a thousand horse, Malik Jiwan now entered the city and passed through the bazaar on his way to court amid a cluster of Afghan followers. Soon the mob began to gather: a swelling, inciting, heterogeneous phalanx of every stratum of society—workmen, fakirs, friends of Dara Shikoh, beggars, riffraff, sweetmeat vendors, and dancing girls. Malik Jiwan and his contingent were abused and cursed. The crowd picked up anything at hand, and began bombarding the Afghans with stones, chunks of earth, rubbish, and sticks. Afghan shields formed a protective umbrella over their frontier Judas as ashes and pots brimming with urine and human stool got dumped from the roofs of houses. One independent Mogul chronicler, Khafi Khan, would later comment: "the disturbance on this day was so great that it bordered on rebellion." By now bystanders were being injured in the melee, a few of Jiwan's men had been knocked off their horses and killed, and many of the rest were bleeding. A total massacre was prevented only by the arrival of Delhi's chief of police and his armed men, who managed to shepherd Malik Jiwan through the crowd and into the Red Fort.*

---

* Despite the protection, Malik Jiwan's days were numbered; Aurangzeb would soon have him put out of the way. Thus Bernier:

Ironically, it was mob protest that catapulted Dara Shikoh toward his end. Within hours of this incident, Aurangzeb signed an order for Dara's immediate execution, to be carried out by Nazar Beg and other slaves under the supervision of a minor nobleman. The executioners arrived at Khizirabad Gardens about seven o'clock in the evening.

There are several versions of Dara's death, all of them ghastly and with only minor contradictions of detail. The most startling assertion (made by Manucci) was that Dara had reached a point of radical religious conversion: in his final hours he had repeatedly begged his guards to bring the Jesuit priest, Father Buzeo, or any other European priest to him. The request was denied. Dara now walked up and down his prison quarter in anguish, saying over and over, "Mohammed kills me, and the Son of God gives me life." In Tatta in Sind, he had apparently told a European friar that "if any faith in the world was true, it was that taught by European priests." Later, Manucci would ascertain through the jailers ("from whom I made inquiries with great eagerness and minuteness") that the crown prince "had a great desire to become a Christian."

The story seems dubious to modern Indian historians; and in any case, Dara would die a Moslem. Bernier and Mogul sources claim that Dara and his son Sipihr Shikoh, afraid of being poisoned, were boiling their own lentils when the executioners arrived. Starting back violently, Dara said, "You have been sent to kill us." Aurangzeb's henchmen shilly-shallied: "At present we do not know anything about killing anybody. It has been ordered that your son should be separated from you and kept in custody somewhere else. We have come to take him away." Sipihr Shikoh was sitting knee

---

"Malik Jiwan was summoned before the council, and then dismissed from Delhi with a few presents. He did not escape the fate, however, which he merited, being waylaid and assassinated in a forest within a few leagues of his own territory. This barbarian had not sufficiently reflected that though tyrants appear to countenance the blackest crimes while they conduce to their interest . . . they yet hold the perpetrators in abhorrence. . . ."

to knee with his father. The hunchback Nazar glared at the boy and said, "Get up." Sipihr began to cry, clinging to Dara's legs; hugging him closely, Dara broke down completely. The slaves now moved toward Sipihr: "Get up or we'll drag you away," and they started to pull at him. Dara wiped away his tears and said, "Go and tell my brother to leave his innocent nephew here." The slaves replied, "We cannot be anybody's messenger. We have to carry out orders." In a sudden rush, they tore the boy from Dara and took him into an adjoining room.

Dara grabbed a penknife he had hidden in his pillow. Turning to one of the slaves who advanced on him, he drove the knife into the man's side with such force that it stuck in his rib bone and couldn't be pulled out again. He threw himself at the assassins and began to flail out wildly with his fists, until they all fell on him in a mass assault. From the next room, Dara could hear Sipihr Shikoh's spasmodic sobbing. Then daggers hacked at his neck and the room grew silent. The hunchback severed Dara's head. Leaving the corpse in a welter of its own blood, the assassins hurried to Aurangzeb with the head.

Aurangzeb ordered the grisly relic to be placed in a basin and washed clean of blood. By one Mogul account, after a brief cursory glance he said, "Since I did not look at this infidel's face in his lifetime, I do not wish to do so now." Bernier, however, has Aurangzeb shedding tears and crying out, "Ah wretched one! let this shocking sight no more offend my eyes." But an English clerk named J. Cambell would write that when the trophy was brought to the Red Fort Aurangzeb stamped on its face; and "the head laughed a long ha, ha, ha! in the hearing of all, I, J. Cambell, present."

The following morning (August 31, 1659) Dara's headless corpse was placed on an elephant for a second parade through the bazaars and lanes of Delhi. Bystanders wept at the gruesome spectacle. Afterward the body was buried in a vault of Humayun's tomb. There were no formal funeral rites—no washing, no shroud, no honored procession. At the same time, Delhi's chief of police was investigating the riot and attack on Malik Jiwan. The instigator was alleged to be a gentleman trooper of the guards named Haibat, and he was sentenced by Aurangzeb to be sawn alive into halves.

The fate of Dara's severed head would be more obscure. Contemporary Mogul chroniclers insist that it was later joined to his trunk before burial in Humayun's tomb. But Manucci records the ultimate horror—a ghoulish yet curiously believable story, compounded perhaps from his palace friends or from bazaar gossip:

> When Aurangzeb learned that the head of Dara had arrived, he ordered it to be brought to him in the garden on a dish, with the face cleaned of surface blood and a turban on the [crown]. He called for lights to be brought so that he might see the mark borne by the Prince on his forehead, and might make sure that it was Dara's head and not that of another person. After he had satisfied himself he told them to put it on the ground, and gave it three thrusts in the face with the sword he carried by way of staff, saying, "Behold the face of a would-be king and emperor of all the Mogul realms. Take him out of my sight."
>
> He gave secret orders to place the head in a box, to be sent by runners to the eunuch Itibar Khan, who had charge of Shah Jahan's prison, with orders to deliver it to [the deposed emperor] when seated at table. It was to be offered in his name as a *plât*. This was planned by Aurangzeb with great glee, to avenge himself for the love lavished on Dara and the little account made of himself. It was as if he said: "Now has your love come to an end; he that was despised is lord of the empire, and the favorite gone down into death." After the head had been sent off, Aurangzeb ordered the interment of Prince Dara's body in the sepulchre of the Emperor Humayun. On that night Raushanara Begum gave a great feast.
>
> On receipt of Aurangzeb's orders, Itibar Khan, to comply with them, waited until the hour when Shah Jahan had sat down to dinner. When he had begun to

eat, Itibar Khan entered with the box and laid it before the unhappy father, saying: "King Aurangzeb, your son, sends this *plât* to Your Majesty, to let him see that he does not forget him." The old Emperor said: "Blessed be God that my son still remembers me." The box having been placed upon the table, he ordered it with great eagerness to be opened. Suddenly, on withdrawing the lid, he discovered the face of Prince Dara. Horrified, he uttered one cry and fell on his hands and face upon the table; and striking against the golden vessels, broke some of his teeth and lay there apparently lifeless. Begum Sahib [Jahanara] and the other women present began to wail, beat their breasts, tear their hair, break their ornaments, and rend their garments.

Then Itibar Khan removed the head. When the old man recovered consciousness, he began to pluck out his beard till it was all bleeding, and to beat his face; then, dissolving into a flood of tears, he raised both hands to heaven and said these words: *"Khuda! teri riza"*—that is to say, "My God, Thy will be done." At this time there came in various women and carried off Begum Sahib, who had swooned. . . .

Following the orders of Aurangzeb, Itibar Khan *then sent the head of Dara to be buried in the sepulchre of Taj Mahal, his mother. . . .** [The Queen's death] was one of the greatest sorrows endured by the Emperor Shah Jahan in his entire life, as many a time he had declared to the nobles. That is why he built this mausoleum opposite to his palace, thinking by sight of the tomb to dissipate the pain he felt. . . . But after the head of his beloved son was buried in the same place his sorrows were redoubled, and became so poignant that in a short space his life came to an end. The eunuch Itibar Khan made a report to King Aurangzeb of what had passed, with all the details, whereby he and Raushanara Begum received great delight.

Manucci's account has been rejected as historically in-

---

* Author's italics.

authentic—not because it is out of keeping with Aurangzeb's character, but because no other source (European or Indian) corroborates it. Still, the Italian was unwittingly invoking suggestive motivations. Why would Aurangzeb relegate Dara's severed head to separate entombment in the Taj, and splash his mother's sacred monument with blood? If it was Shah Jahan on whom spite centered, then why dump this beloved son's head in Mumtaz Mahal's lap? Whatever the implications of royal fratricide, it had culminated in an eerie manner. Dara's dissected body must be forever divided by the haunted hundred and twenty miles between Delhi and Agra, those twin cities of Mogul glory and doom.

●●●

Dara's modern biographer Qanungo was left to write his epitaph: "A martyr to love, human and divine, a heroic soul that stood for peace and concord among mankind, and the emancipation of the human intellect from the shackles of blind authority and dogma, Dara Shikoh merely justified in life and death the inscrutable ways of God to man."

Less inscrutable, the Hindu law of karma remained to work itself out for surviving family members—including the murderer himself. With Dara Shikoh's death, the sun behind a couchant Mogul lion had suffered eclipse; the twilight of the Moguls, which most scholars defer beyond Aurangzeb, had already begun.

Part IV

FALL OF THE
HOUSE OF TIMUR

CHAPTER

23

Fate of the Innocents

MANUCCI WRITES, "The death of . . . brothers and of so many other people was not enough to assuage Aurangzeb's thirst for the blood of his relations." Beyond the imperative of brotherly revenge, absolute power was now beginning to corrupt absolutely. And there were practical reasons for a continued dragnet of India to harry small fry to their doom: Aurangzeb had usurped the Peacock Throne, but it was an uncomfortable seat so long as the possibility of challenge existed.

At this moment, one other member of the Mogul royal family constituted the most dangerous threat: Sulaiman Shikoh, Dara's eldest son, who still remained at large. The best-loved of Shah Jahan's grandchildren, Sulaiman was more capable of action than his tragic, Hamlet-like father; Sulaiman had to be murdered.

Since the beginning of August 1658, the young prince had found sanctuary in the Garhwal hills bordering Nepal and Greater Tibet. He had been unable to reach Dara in the Punjab; with several of Aurangzeb's divisions at his heels, he had accepted the hospitality of the old Rajah of Srinagar, Prithwi Singh, and contracted a marriage alliance with the Rajah's daughter. For almost a year Aurangzeb had been too busy concentrating on the defeat of Dara and Shuja to take decisive action in regard to Sulaiman. There is no detailed record of Sulaiman's year of grace in Srinagar, though it obviously must have been a rustic letdown for a sophisticated and pampered prince who had known the luxury of the court at Delhi. Aurangzeb had made advance threats to Prithwi Singh: harboring a fugitive could only bring ruin on the house of Srinagar. The old rajah dissimulated by implying that Sulaiman had taken refuge in an adjoining mountain province. But by the end of July 1659 Aurangzeb felt free to concentrate on capturing his nephew, since Shuja was on the run in Bengal and Dara had become a prisoner on his way to Delhi. On July 27 Rajah Rajrup (the traitor who had turned against Dara after drinking Nadira Banu's breast-water) was delegated to employ a contingent of troops in an effort to dislodge the political fugitive. The upshot would be another year's grace for Sulaiman: unlike other Rajputs, the old rajah of Srinagar proved a tough nut to crack, and in stubborn gratitude to the memory of Dara Shikoh (who had rendered him service in 1656) he continued to hold out in his mountains. By October 1660 Aurangzeb was obliged to send musketeers and artillery reinforcement for his Mogul campaign against this two-by-four Himalayan enclave.

If war is the failure of diplomacy, the corollary is also true. With force of arms clearly getting nowhere, Aurangzeb invoked the perfect intermediary: Jai Singh of Jaipur State. The Rajput began with his usual epistolary intrigues: by surrendering a fugitive from Mogul justice, the rajah of Srinagar would cement a friendship with all-powerful Aurangzeb; Sulaiman Shikoh had no hope of ever recouping his fortunes, since Dara had already been beheaded; a word to the wise was sufficient, especially when Aurangzeb commanded the means for an all-out attack on Srinagar; and of course Jai Singh was writing this letter as one Hindu ruler and friend to another.

The rajah of Srinagar could not be so easily coerced. Many thanks to Jai Singh for his advice, but the house of Srinagar had not given sanctuary to a hapless young prince in order to turn him over to his enemy. As for Mogul power and friendship, Aurangzeb was not so impressive; surely Jai Singh remembered when Shah Jahan had sent thirty thousand cavalry and a hundred thousand infantry against Srinagar? Mogul noses had been cut off on that occasion, but if Aurangzeb persisted then a few Mogul heads could now be lopped off as well.

Prithwi Singh was adamant, and Jai Singh decided to dicker with the powerful Brahman minister of Srinagar: how would he like to sit on the rajah's throne in return for doing Sulaiman Shikoh in? The minister readily agreed—what the fugitive prince needed was a bracing tonic in the form of deadly poison. But this Borgia-like plot quickly collapsed: Sulaiman became suspicious and fed the tonic to a cat; when the cat died he informed the old rajah, who responded by having his minister beheaded.

By this time Jai Singh felt desperate. Insistent notes came from Aurangzeb: why not send presents and promises to the rajahs of contiguous hill states, inciting them to make war on Srinagar? Mogul troops had already blocked off Srinagar's access to the plains, and it could not be so difficult for mountaineering Rajputs to annex the territory. Indeed, Jai Singh himself would receive more territory from Aurangzeb "if only he could compel the Rajah of Srinagar to surrender Prince Sulaiman Shikoh"—the words are Manucci's.

Jai Singh abruptly resolved his dilemma. If the rajah of Srinagar had proved a doddering idealist, at least his son Medini Singh was realistic: a few favors from the Moguls would encourage his speedy succession before the old fool's stubborn politics lost the principality outright. Medini Singh now opened secret negotiations with Jai Singh, promising to deliver up Srinagar's long-disputed guest. Accordingly, Jai Singh's son, Kumar Ram Singh, left Delhi on December 12, 1660, headed for the foot of the Garhwal hills—an imperial prisoner always needed proper escort.

Medini Singh had more than overruled his father; by now he had almost imprisoned him. In Manucci's account, "Prince Sulaiman Shikoh heard of this plot of the Rajah's son, and resolved to absent himself from Srinagar. He seized an occasion of going out shooting, as he ordinarily did, with the intention of making off into Tibet. . . . When his departure was reported to the Rajah's son, he started after him with a sufficient number of men, giving no information of the project to the Rajah his father. Overtaking Sulaiman Shikoh, he seized him, put irons on his feet and handcuffs on his wrists. . . ."

Sulaiman Shikoh had indeed intended a kind of Shangri-la escape over the snow to Ladakh. But his capture proved less easy than Manucci implies: considerable resistance was put up, the prince's foster brother and a few companions were murdered, and Sulaiman himself was wounded in the struggle. On December 27, 1660 he was taken down from the mountains and given over to Jai Singh's son. Within two days runners brought Aurangzeb the news, and the emperor showed his pleasure by presenting Jai Singh with a jeweled artifact.

During the night of January 2, Kumar Ram Singh and a trio of Mogul generals and other nobles swept into Delhi with their royal captive. For the moment, Sulaiman Shikoh shared quarters in Salimgarh prison with another imperial victim: Mohammed Sultan, who had already been languishing ten months in the citadel fortress for having defected to his uncle Shuja. Aurangzeb's son had just turned twenty-one, and Dara's son would soon be twenty-six; doubtless they had much to say to each other.

On January 5 the new prisoner was brought into the presence of his fearsome uncle in the Hall of Private Audience at Delhi. This had been Shah Jahan's famous *Diwan-i-Khas,* a chastely refined creation with scalloped arches open to the Indian day, and massive interior pillars inlaid with precious-stone flowers in amethyst and carnelian. Interlaced giltwork adorned both ceiling and pillars, and repeated four times about the hall was the golden inscription, "If there be paradise on earth, it is this, it is this, it is this." Aurangzeb sat at the rear center of the hall, his Peacock Throne ensconced in a marble dais, while behind him were lattice-work marble windows with a view to the plain below. Shah Jahan had provided this Hall of Private Audience with a concatenation of marble doors and passageways, beyond which were the imperial private chapel and sleeping room, the *jharoka* window and the harem quarters. All these interior buildings of the fort were of pure white marble, in contrast to the massive red sandstone of the outer Hall of Public Audience, outer barracks, and towering defensive walls. White marble had been Shah Jahan's private inner world, now usurped by Aurangzeb. Sulaiman Shikoh had many times stood in these precincts in the honor of regal rites; today he stood in chains.

Once more, François Bernier would be personal witness to one of the great scenes of Mogul history: the interrogation of a captive prince by a tyrant. This is Bernier's description (it must be remembered that Aurangzeb had not seen Sulaiman Shikoh for many years, if indeed he had ever seen him):

> Aurangzeb acted upon this occasion as he had done in the case of Dara. That Sulaiman Shikoh's identity might be established, the King commanded that he should be brought into the presence of all the courtiers. I could not repress my curiosity, and witnessed the whole of this dismal scene. The fetters were taken from the Prince's feet before he entered the chamber wherein the [nobles] were assembled, but the chains, which were gilt, remained about his hands. [Manucci maliciously insists that the manacles were made of brass.] Many of the courtiers shed tears at the sight of this interesting young man, who was tall and extremely handsome. The principal ladies of the court had permission to be present, concealed behind a latticework, and were also greatly moved. Aurangzeb, too, affected to deplore the fate of his nephew, and spoke to him with apparent kindness. "Be comforted," the King told him; "no harm shall befall you. You shall be treated with tenderness. God is great, and you should put your trust in him. Dara, your father, was not permitted to live only because he had become a *kaffir*, a man devoid of all religion." Whereupon the Prince made a salaam, or sign of grateful acknowledgement, lowering his hands to the ground, and lifting them, as well as he was able, to his head, according to the custom of the country. He then told the King, with much self-possession, that if it were intended to give him the *poust* to drink, he begged he

might be immediately put to death. Aurangzeb promised in a solemn manner, and in a loud voice, that this drink should most certainly not be administered, and that his mind might be perfectly easy. The Prince was then required to make a second salaam; and when a few questions had been put to him, by the King's desire, concerning the elephant laden with golden rupees, which had been taken from him during his retreat to Srinagar, he was taken out of the chamber. . . .

As usual, Aurangzeb had lied. Ten days later on January 15, Sulaiman was conducted to the gloomy gothic fortress of Gwalior where his worst fears were now realized—his fate was to be not immediate execution, but slow, horrific death brought on by an elixir of opium seeds. Early each morning, a large cup of the beverage would be brought to him, and until it was swallowed the captive received no food —death would be either by starvation, or by gradual reduction to imbecility. Over a period of many months, for more than a year, handsome Sulaiman Shikoh slipped further and further into torpidity and senselessness; day by day he became emaciated, his strength and intellect ebbing in exquisite degrees of slow torment. Perhaps because of his youth and determined vitality, he held out surprisingly long—until May 1662. Murad, also at Gwalior, had been executed five or six months before; now it was Sulaiman's turn. Annoyed by his nephew's refusal to die of opium poisoning, Aurangzeb finally gave orders for the resistant prisoner to be strangled to death. The twenty-seven-year-old prince was buried on Gwalior hill close to another victim. Both were unhonored, but their juxtaposition added posthumous insult: Sulaiman Shikoh, the sensitive son of a sensitive prince, had been dumped next to his father's enemy—coarse uncle Murad.

● ● ●

For the briefest moment the bloodbath abated. Perpetual imprisonment seemed a safe enough fate for the remaining children of Dara and Murad, and even the children of Sulaiman Shikoh. As royal offspring, they would turn up

[392]

from time to time in Mogul chronicles; Aurangzeb had spilled family blood, but later on he would decide to mix it in a startling reversal of the Mogul edict forbidding emperors' daughters to marry.

Torn from Dara's final embrace, fourteen-year-old Sipihr Shikoh had been regarded by his tyrannical uncle as too young to murder. Shortly after his father's death, he was sent to Gwalior fortress, where he remained imprisoned for twelve years. Then by Aurangzeb's instructions he was transferred to Salimgarh prison at Delhi on December 8, 1672; eight days later he was presented to the emperor and must have made a favorable impression, since on January 30, 1673 Sipihr married his twenty-one-year-old first cousin, Aurangzeb's daughter, Zubdat-un-Nissa. A son named Ali Tabar was born of this ironic wedlock in 1676, but he died within six months—his death almost symbolic of the fast-withering Mogul vine. After that Sipihr Shikoh disappears from Mogul history—his years of imprisonment were so anonymous that Bernier thought he had long since been done to death at Gwalior with poppy juice.

Dara's two daughters, Jani Begum and her anonymous sister, had been taken prisoner along with their father, and on arrival in Delhi had been placed in the protective custody of Aurangzeb's harem. But at the entreaty of Shah Jahan and Jahanara the two girls were finally sent to Agra fort. Manucci observes interestingly:

> Aurangzeb ordered his men to bring into the palace lovely Jani Begum, daughter of Dara. . . . When the unfortunate young lady saw the throne of his murderer placed in the palaces where her father had sat, she began to distill tokens of grief from her eyes with such deep feeling that her life began to waste away. She was badly treated by Raushanara Begum, who incessantly recalled to her memories of the dead. When Aurangzeb found that the girl was wasting away, he forwarded her to the fortress of Agra to be made over to King Shah Jahan and Begum Sahib. By beholding her the old Em-

peror's sorrows were in part alleviated; Begum Sahib was pleased with Jani Begum's beauty, a reproduction of lost originals; and she herself was delighted at finding herself free from the sight of him who had killed her father, and out of the hands of a cruel enemy, Raushanara Begum.

Indeed, under the tutelage of her beloved aunt Jahanara, Dara's daughter Jani would grow up to be a remarkably beautiful and cultured woman; and she too would marry a first cousin—Aurangzeb's son, Mohammed Azam, in 1669.

There would be still further fraternal mingling of the tyrant's blood with that of his murdered brothers. Aurangzeb's imprisoned son Mohammed Sultan had already married Shuja's daughter in 1659, and later added a second wife to his harem—one of Murad's daughters in 1672. Even Murad's young son, Izad Bakhsh, would marry one of Aurangzeb's daughters, Mihr-un-nissa, when the girl was barely eleven.

Of Sulaiman Shikoh's two daughters, one named Salima Begum would be adopted and reared by Aurangzeb's sister, Gauharara Begum. There is something irritatingly elusive about Gauharara: youngest of Shah Jahan's three daughters by Mumtaz Mahal, she stands out in Mogul history by virtue of having caused her mother's death in childbirth; but aside from this she offers almost no scope for portraiture. Vaguely the evidence indicates that she was Murad's partisan in the War of Succession, but her role could hardly have been very active or she would have suffered imprisonment along with Shah Jahan and Jahanara. Her personality seems totally nebulous; yet she had adopted Sulaiman's daughter Salima, and in 1672 Salima would in turn marry one of Aurangzeb's sons, Mohammed Akbar. Once more and much later, Gauharara will significantly turn up at the end of the family story; but to the end she remains a nonentity, living quietly in the palace and enjoying her regal pension.

●●●

With the capture and death of Sulaiman Shikoh, Aurangzeb's reign might now have seemed reasonably secure:

two brothers had been murdered, one had been hounded to his death in Arakan, and the only nephew of consequence had been strangled. But unnecessary blood had still to be shed. Quite aside from those who "touched the sceptre" (and he dared not kill Shah Jahan or Jahanara) there would be at least one other immediate victim of Aurangzeb's puritanical frenzy. The problem of Aurangzeb's imprisoned father and sister at Agra fort was yet to be resolved, and favored Raushanara was headed for catastrophe. But one man still represented an open threat to the reign of the tyrant; one man defied censorship and had to be silenced; one man's martyrdom would rival and excel even Dara Shikoh's. Dara's fantastic friend and spiritual confidant was about to step forward—a formidable force, with no sword except his tongue and no army except for the invisible angelic hosts which had already blessed him and made him a mystical king of fakirs who commanded multitudes. The enigmatic person known to history only as Sarmad was now ready to write his name in blood.

A naked homosexual saint, a bizarrely personal Sufi ecstatic pitted against the puritanical dictator of the age—no fiction could have invented a more striking contrast. Dara Shikoh's death would be vindicated; Dara would be glorified, and Aurangzeb would go down in spiritual defeat at Sarmad's hands without even knowing it. Knowledge would only come later, at the very end of Aurangzeb's life—too late for him and for all of India.

CHAPTER

24

Naked to His Enemies

THE MAN CALLED Sarmad was unquestionably a saint—one of those profoundly disturbing mystics whom only the East could produce and perhaps only India could tolerate. Though not native to India he found his fulfillment and martyrdom there, and can really only be understood against the background of Indian religious thought, both Hindu and Moslem. Born a Jew, transformed by his homosexual fate into a fakir, he became not merely a great Sufi mystic poet but a dynamic spiritual legend whose force can be felt across a chasm of centuries. Yet very little is actually known of his life, and even that is contradictory.

India's tolerance of extremes is well known, stemming perhaps from its harsh conditions of life which over millennia encouraged the most incredible withdrawal of spirit from body. Only in India has God been wooed to such limits of self-abnegation and inward contemplation. Occasionally the Western world produces a mystic as unusual as Saint John of the Cross, whereas India produces many mystics and fakirs. In a West enamored of its own technology and scientific control over inimical forces of nature, the spiritual answers of India have sometimes been held cheaply, and not a few Westerners are even frankly repulsed by what seems to be a negation spawned of unbearable poverty. Yet, indicting the attitude of Western skeptics, the great modern Indologist Heinrich Zimmer states boldly: "We of the Occident are

about to arrive at a crossroads that was reached by the thinkers of India some seven hundred years before Christ."

Long before Sarmad and Sufi mysticism had penetrated
the Indian scene, Hinduism had evolved the caste system and
then provided an escape from its own straitjacket by conceiv-
ing of four life-stages. Hindu caste rigidly limited a man: in
the divine social order, he belonged to his family, his guild,
and his group, and each category made demands on him. But
to define was to limit, and an ideal life course passed through
four stages. First, as pupil of some guru, the individual went
through an apprenticeship of chastity, sacrificing youthful
sensuality to the spirit which would one day be set free. In
the second stage, he accepted his role in life—marriage, children, a profession. But later in the human cycle, a man found
his children grown and could begin to discard the social
mask which had previously defined him; breaking away from
preoccupations with money, desire or anxiety, he then entered the third stage of his life—"departure to the forest," or
the real quest for the self. In a fourth and final life phase, the
ideal person even became a wandering holy beggar—unfet-
tered by time and place, unattached to the body, indifferent
to karma or fate, and identified in his mind with the Holy
Power of God. It was in this last stage that men became
divine renegades, wearing the rags of Buddhist monks or
walking stark naked like some Jaina saint "clothed in space"
—nakedness was a deliberate mark of not belonging. The
spiritual iconoclast had now reached a point of total release
—nauseated and unconcerned with the illusion of reality.
Saints reached this stage sooner than other men; Sarmad was
one of them.

● ● ●

Aurangzeb's contemporary historians are silent about
Sarmad's execution, and do not dare to disturb the equanim-
ity of their emperor-dictator. But various writers of the period make reference to him, and a patchwork biography of
sorts emerges.

Sarmad (the name means "everlasting") was born at

Kashan, an important business center of Persia, sometime during the reign of Shah Abbas the Great. His family was well-to-do—Armenian Jews with an eminent rabbinical background. By prevalent Jewish custom, the boy (whose real name is unknown) began his education by studying Jewish theology: He committed the Torah to memory and qualified himself to become a rabbi. In order to widen his religious views, Sarmad studied the New Testament and other books on Christianity; still thirsting for knowledge, he mastered Islamic science and metaphysics under the tutelage of renowned scholars, and becoming a Moslem took the name of Mohammed Said. Sarmad's Moslem teachers apparently influenced him to turn away from Judaism and embrace Islam; but since the teachers were only lukewarm orthodox and inclined to Buddhism and Zoroastrianism, it was inevitable that their pupil would become unorthodox. In any case, certain Persian quatrains written to Mohammed by Sarmad would indicate that he converted to Islam before arriving in India. A brilliant scholar, Sarmad had not only assimilated the threads of Judaic, Christian, and Islamic thought; he had also mastered Arabic and Persian, with "very few among his contemporaries as his equal."

For a Sarmad or a Dara Shikoh, the formal dogma of Islam was unimportant; for Aurangzeb, reaffirming the letter of the law became a driving concern. Three liberal Mogul emperors—Akbar, Jahangir, and Shah Jahan—had long since discarded Moslem puritanism, but Aurangzeb would now restore it. Dara Shikoh's kind of liberalism, in the opinion of the orthodox, had become a cancer attacking the vital organs of empire. Sarmad and Dara, imbued with Sufi passion, sought God intuitively. Indeed, since the tenth century Sufi mystics had been the chief exponents of a doctrine of inner light—the "cult of the heart"—as opposed to formal scripture and its tenets. Free souls, they cast off the crushing weight of dogma, sometimes paying with their lives by making unguarded statements in politically repressive climates. For Sufi mystics, the individual was sanctified; religion became a question of heart and intuition, not reason and dogma, and even the ethical seemed sometimes abandoned for the transcendental. From childhood, Dara Shikoh had been exposed to Sufi and Hindu mystics, and his sensitive nature made him particularly susceptible to the "cult of the heart." Sarmad's background was more complex: the Jew and the rationalist needed a radical conversion. He would find it in India.

Just what Sarmad did for a living before arriving in the subcontinent is unclear. Completing his education and becoming a Moslem, he probably went into trade; then, prompted by greater gain, he moved to the port of Tatta in Sind. By a coincidence, his date of arrival is known to be 1631—the year in which Mumtaz Mahal died and the construction of the Taj began.

It was not unusual for Sarmad to migrate to India. With Persia economically and culturally linked to the Mogul Empire, traders moved freely between both countries. Jews in any case had been in India for many centuries before the Moguls; Beni Israelites are today found in Bombay and its vicinity, and there are White and Black Jews of Cochin. By the time of Akbar, the children of Israel had made settlements in Portuguese Goa and in Surat port, and Akbar himself included Hebraic recognition in a tolerant religious decree he issued in 1594: "If any of the infidels choose to build a church, or a *synagogue*, or an idol temple, or a Parsee tower of silence, no one is to hinder him." Inland, Jews could be found in Lahore, Delhi, Agra, and Kashmir; Persian Jews, in particular, were always on the move.*

---

* Thus a modern Jewish scholar, Walter Fischel, observes in his interesting monograph on Jews at the court of the Mogul emperors: "Persia, throughout the ages, served as a springboard for the Jewish diaspora in Central Asia, as a reservoir from which flowed continuously streams of wanderers to the East and to the West, to the North and to the South. The Persian Jews who wandered into India were mainly merchants, agents and jewellers, but not bankers or money-lenders, these occupations being monopoly of the Indians. In Monserrate's *Commentary* we read: 'for those Jews that live in Lahore deal in rubbish, cast-off clothes, iron-mongery, shoes, armlets, bolts and bars, and all manner of second-hand goods.' "

Though a convert to Islam, Sarmad would forever retain the discriminating label—historical sources inevitably refer to him as "Sarmad the Jew," or "the Jewish mystic" and "the Hebrew atheist." Indeed, the Jewish aspect of Sarmad's later martyrdom was scarcely irrelevant: Aurangzeb's orthodox scribe would categorize Dara Shikoh as an apostate from Islam who wanted to introduce the "rant of infidelity and Judaism." In Tatta, Sarmad settled into trade—an itinerant Jewish merchant soon to be transformed into a hypnotic mystic. His catalyst was love—the time-honored vehicle of Sufi ecstasy and enlightenment.

Shortly after arriving in Tatta, Sarmad became insanely infatuated with a Hindu boy of Banyan or merchant caste named Abhai Chand, the son of a rajah or landlord of Sind. Infatuation or love barely describe his feelings, seized as he was with *jazbaa* (rapture). By conventional psychological definition, Sarmad would be considered homosexual. But Sarmad goes far beyond conventional definition, and the platonic zeal of his attachment can hardly be understood as homosexual even in terms of the pure idealism of ancient Greece. For Sufi mystics of medieval times, beauty in any form constituted a transcendent embodiment of God the Creator. Abhai Chand now became a Hindu Apollo, a symbol of the godhead; and in the Sufi trance which makes no distinction between God and what God has created, Sarmad worshipped the boy as holiness incarnate. Soon he would apostrophize in a couplet:

> In this great monastery old and round,
> Is Abhai Chand my God? Whom have I found?

Other love fragments of Sarmad to Abhai Chand have been preserved across three centuries. "I am madly in love with those curly locks," he writes; "I did not wish it, it is Fate's doing." Indeed, the attachment went beyond Fate to become divine phototropism: "The source of light is in someone else's hands; I merely observe the attachment between moth and candle."

Sarmad's attachment to Abhai Chand may have been pure, but the boy's father was a tiresomely conventional man. Fearing scandal, he reported the matter to Mohammed Beg, the military governor and chronicler of Tatta; then he consigned his son to a secret retreat. The removal of the boy had a devastating effect on Sarmad: distracted to the point of madness, he abruptly gave away all his material possessions, including his clothes, and began to wander naked in the streets.

In the Western world he would promptly have been confined to an asylum; in India he became a holy man. Even the military governor felt moved to verse, and sent Sarmad a message:

> If the treasures of Heaven were at my door,
> I would give not money but stars for the poor.

Sarmad replied with an impassioned quatrain:

> O breeze, convey this message to the wise
> Whose power indeed controls the very skies:
> If he can offer stars by way of coin,
> In pity let him bid my "sun" arise.

The extremity of Sarmad's love for Abhai Chand now touched the father. Sarmad's morbid earnestness and the unearthly purity of his attachment could no longer be doubted, and he was allowed to visit his beloved's house. Abhai Chand, who at first had shown no great inclination to reciprocate Sarmad's love, became so attached to Sarmad that he too could not bear separation. He abandoned his family and became Sarmad's disciple; in a distracted and restless love of God, the two men left Tatta to wander the length and breadth of India together.

In lofty Sufi purity, Sarmad's rapport with the boy became that of father to son, or guru to disciple (it seems doubtful whether physical passion played any part in their love). Under Sarmad's tutelage, Abhai Chand learned the science and literature of the times; together they read the

[401]

Pentateuch and the Psalms, and Abhai even made a Persian translation of the opening chapter of Genesis—a translation that is still extant. Abhai also wrote verse; and the single couplet which has survived reflects the pantheism of his guru:

I am all things, a child of heaven and hell:
Monk, priest and rabbi, Moslem, and infidel.

As early as 1634, only three years after the two men left Tatta, Sarmad began to attract the attention of Mogul nobility. In Lahore, the new Sufi poet and mystic became highly popular, holding forth to a heterogeneous assembly including courtiers of high position. Dara Shikoh did not yet know the saint. But one of Shah Jahan's nobles, Mutamad Khan, tells how he "traced the whereabouts of Sarmad in a garden and went to visit him there. I found him naked, covered with thick crisped hair all over his body, and with long fingernails. He talked too much and uttered verses. He spoke correct Persian and was a poet."

A dozen years later, in 1646 or 1647, Sarmad and his Hindu disciple turned up in Hyderabad in Golconda. More than likely he had not yet visited Delhi or Agra: he would certainly have attracted Dara Shikoh's interest, yet Dara makes no mention of Sarmad in the several biographies of Moslem saints he completed during this period. In Hyderabad, Sarmad soon won the respect of Qutb Shah, the sybaritic ruler of Golconda, as well as of Shaikh Mohammed Khan, the chief minister. People of all walks of life now flocked to the naked prophet for mystical exhortation, blessings, and divination. For Mir Jumla, Sarmad predicted high position; sure enough, Mir Jumla became prime minister under Shah Jahan and governor of Bengal under Aurangzeb. But Sarmad could also offer somber predictions: the chief minister of Golconda was warned of his approaching death. Mystically inclined, the shaikh took the warning to heart; with so little time left he decided to make a pilgrimage to Mecca, but in a storm off the Arabian coast his ship sank and he drowned!

● ● ●

In Golconda, Sarmad was now reciting his own Persian verse extemporaneously, fascinating the town's poets and mystics. The Persian quatrain has become famous to English readers through Edward Fitzgerald's inspired translation of the *Rubaiyat* of Omar Khayyam. This form had in Sarmad's day become the chief vehicle for Sufistic expression, and every Sufi mystic tried his hand at writing quatrains. Few displayed any genius—even Omar Khayyam was regarded in Persia as second-rate. Yet the fame of Sarmad began to spread far beyond Golconda. In both conscious and ecstatic states, he poured forth poetry which stressed the immanence of God, unity in diversity, and divine illumination coming like a lightning flash—all typical themes of the mystic. Renunciation of the world, he felt, was essential, and there is a monotonous condemnation of worldly ties in his quatrains. "I am a disciple of Khayyam," he admitted, "but I have tasted little of the wine he offered."

Ironically, it was Aurangzeb who would give the poet immortality. As the instrument of Sarmad's martyrdom, Aurangzeb would also unwittingly serve the cause of mystics and mystical poetry in general. The story of Sarmad's execution and his lofty forbearance and fortitude would later sweep over the Mogul Empire. Sarmad's verses, especially the quatrains, were treated as the sacred relics of a great martyr.

As recently as 1950, an English version of Sarmad's *Rubaiyat* by a scholar named Asiri was published in India at Rabindranath Tagore's spiritual center of Santiniketan. The fairly literal and unrhymed text reveals a genius in fine Sufi tradition. Like other Sufi poets, Sarmad's youthful poetry was at first erotic and only later mystical. A few stray verses and about three hundred quatrains have somehow survived the ravages of time.

Comparison with Omar Khayyam seems inevitable; yet Omar was a philosopher and Sarmad a mystic. Sarmad, like Omar, believed in the transitory nature of worldly things, and echoed an Eastern conviction of predestination. But Omar's answer to life seemed to embody a refined hedonism:

live for the moment and let the future take care of itself. Whereas Sarmad felt that the best passport to eternity would be to seek union with God in this life: it was important for a man to attain knowledge of truth before he died.

Memorable lines stand out from Sarmad's quatrains. "A tree without foliage is no shelter against the sun," he writes; or again, "We grow old, but not our desires." Yet always, "Real greatness lies in humility." The mystic's negative anguish in his search for God comes through again and again: "How long wilt Thou keep Thyself concealed?" and "Come out of the Veil and be visible!" But in another more hopeful vein, he finds that "Thou art invisible and visible everywhere," while "Only my intuition led me to Thy abode." For Sarmad, social intercourse represented contamination: "Adopt solitude and give up everything," he advises. Yet his search for the absolute was haunted by the relative: "If you say I seek this world and that world at times, you are right: I am looking for both of them." He concludes grimly that "This house has been in ruins since eternity." A greater poet than Omar Khayyam, Sarmad still today awaits his Edward Fitzgerald.

• • •

In an aura of widening fame, India's naked Nostradamus now made his way to the heart of the Mogul Empire. It is not known exactly when Sarmad came to Delhi—at the very latest, certainly a year or two prior to Shah Jahan's illness. Sarmad's fame as a poet and mystical prophet had already preceded him, and great crowds of people surrounded him on his arrival in the Mogul capital. His sanctity and supernatural powers had long since silenced resentment against the strange figure who walked about *in partibus naturalibus*. Cultured society in the provincial capital of Lahore was doubtless shocked, since Sarmad professed to be a Moslem and few Moslems behaved so outrageously; but indifferent to what people thought, he had now been naked since his ecstatic first seizure of love for Abhai Chand more than twenty years before. At most, if he cared to justify himself, he would point out that Isaiah had gone naked in his old age. One European staunchly disapproved: for all his intellect, François Bernier's relentlessly French logic could make little of Eastern mysticism, and the great Sarmad is relegated to a sentence or two in the *Travels:* "I was for a long time disgusted," Bernier says, "with a celebrated Fakir, named Sarmad, who paraded the streets of Delhi as naked as when he came into the world."

Bernier's opinion rested on cultural misunderstanding and bias, but it echoed the sentiments of rigid Moslems. Sarmad was a heterodox Sufi mystic, dangerously powerful in his influence on the religious mind of the people. Yet he could not be silenced; he had now won the friendship of Prince Dara Shikoh, a friendship which would seal both their dooms. Scornfully, an orthodox author of the period described the encounter between Shah Jahan's son and the naked homosexual fakir: "Since Sultan Dara Shikoh had a liking for lunatics, he invited Sarmad to his court and enjoyed his discourses for a considerable time."

Enthusiastically, Dara wanted to present Sarmad to Shah Jahan himself, who in the liberal climate prevailing since Akbar was highly respectful of mystics and Sufi saints. The emperor obligingly sent a nobleman, Inayat Khan, to verify Sarmad's supernatural powers. Inayat proved less than credulous; he remained unimpressed with Sarmad's outward appearance, while the saint's alleged wonder-workings seemed merely the fantastic imaginings of Sufi lovers. Inayat now summed up his findings in a witty couplet to the emperor:

> Sarmad's famous miracles work by fits and starts:
> The only revelation is of his private parts!

Shah Jahan found the report flip and prejudiced; "A piece of rough cloth could silence scandalous tongues," he replied. As a matter of fact, out of deference Sarmad had already adopted a loin cloth to be worn in Dara's presence. Whether or not Shah Jahan himself ever received Sarmad at court is not known, but scandalous tongues could do no great harm to the naked saint for the moment: the emperor was tolerant for Dara's sake, and narrow-minded court nobles fell silent.

In spite of tacit orthodox disapproval, Dara's friendship with Sarmad now persisted both in and out of court; enthusiastically the two Sufi adherents exchanged visits and letters, and held frequent colloquy on intricate and controversial aspects of spiritual problems. Unfortunately, only one letter of Dara's to Sarmad has been preserved for history, together with the saint's reply. Addressing Sarmad as "my guide and preceptor," Dara wrote after an apparent period of neglect: "Every day I resolve to pay my respects to you; but the resolve remains unaccomplished. If I am really myself, why are my intentions defeated? If I am not myself, then who is responsible for the lapse?" With complex Islamic references, Dara's letter goes on to inquire into the paradox of human versus divine action. Mentioning the historical murder of a certain holy man, the prince almost foresees his own doom by asking Sarmad whether that murder was the will of God: "If it was not the Divine Will, then what is the meaning of the phrase, 'God does whatever He wills, and commands whatever He intends'?" Even when the Prophet Mohammed went out to do battle with infidels, the army of Islam sometimes met defeat. Orthodox scholars called it discipline; but for a perfect man like Mohammed, what discipline was necessary?

Unlike Dara, Sarmad had long since gone beyond hair-splitting academic query. He replied epigrammatically with a couplet:

> Dear friend,
> We have forgotten all the books we read:
> Only the text of love rings in our head.

It is not clear whether Sarmad's "text of love" refers to the Koran or whether he is simply invoking a pantheistic principle of love as the only meaning of life. But the exchange clearly suggested what prince and fakir discussed in their frequent meetings: Dara was raising ultimate and disturbing

[406]

questions about God and responsibility, human and divine. Conventional Moslems would have been silent, since this kind of probing led to distressing answers conceivably outside the pale of *shariah* or Islamic religious law. No bigoted ulema of the time could tolerate a free spirit of inquiry, any more than Western dogma of the time could countenance Galileo. With naïve courage, Dara and Sarmad approached truth by an unforgivably wayward path; but then, Dara's retinue seethed with such mystics and such discussions. The orthodox faithful bided their scandalized time. Let the crown prince be heedless of consequences, but he would pay dearly one day for his intellectual candor.

● ● ●

Heretic: Aurangzeb's ulema had set the black seal on Dara, and Sarmad would be next. To a rigidly orthodox tyrant like Aurangzeb, the naked homosexual mystic could only be anathema. Dara had been put to death and the public response of sympathy had infuriated the usurper. "After the death of Prince Dara," Manucci noted, "the common people composed a song about the fickle evanescence of Fortune's glories, it having placed Aurangzeb on the throne, made Shah Jahan a prisoner, and decapitated Prince Dara. The words ran: 'Fate turned the fakir's [Aurangzeb's] cowl into a crown, and took a prince's head away.' When Aurangzeb heard about this ballad, he ordained by public proclamation that anyone caught singing it would have his tongue cut out. But the song was so pitiful that almost everybody sang it in private."

Sarmad was not the only religious partisan of Dara to fall under Aurangzeb's scrutiny: the crown prince's death had precipitated a wholesale roundup of Sufi mystics. As a saint of wide intellectual outlook, Mulla Shah, who lived in quiet hermitage in Kashmir and had initiated Dara's sister Jahanara into the Qadiriya order, now received a court summons to answer certain charges made against him by orthodox theologians. Though his head was spared, he retreated to Lahore and "lived there in great distress and fear till his death; but all the while thanked God that his life ended as it had begun—in poverty." Others, less fortunate, suffered summary trial and punishment.

Sarmad of all Sufi mystics had been flamboyantly indiscreet by prophesying that Dara would become king. Annoyed, Aurangzeb at first resorted to indirect measures: the saint would be called to account for his nakedness. An initial interrogation took place before Aurangzeb's favorite courtier and teacher, Itimad Khan Mulla Qavi, who preened himself in aloof theological splendor. Puffed up with vanity, he regarded the naked saint with a jaundiced eye: Sarmad's influence over people high and low was too great. The Qavi now cross-examined Sarmad and asked him to explain his peculiar habits. Sarmad, shrugging, resorted to a play on words: the Devil was powerful, but so was his inquisitor. Elliptically he recited a quatrain suggesting that God had reduced him to nudity—"A strange thief has stripped me of my garments." To the Qavi the answers were insolent and disrespectful. He duly reported his displeasure to Aurangzeb, and the emperor made his decision: Sarmad would be arrested and brought to durbar to answer formal charges before the ulema.

Aurangzeb now faced "the saint of insanity" in person. So: Sarmad had predicted that Dara Shikoh would succeed Shah Jahan on the imperial throne of Delhi; but where was his beloved prince now? Sarmad replied with eloquence, "God hath given him eternal sovereignty and my prophecy has not proved false." According to Manucci, the mystic also added bluntly, "But you cannot see him, for you tyrannize over those of your own blood; and in order to usurp the kingdom, you took away the life of your brothers and committed other barbarities." Aurangzeb is said to have ordered Sarmad's immediate execution.

More subtle accounts, however, indicate that there was due process of law, prejudiced as it may have been. The formal charge against Sarmad was apostasy, to which he pleaded not guilty. Three counts were now raised by the ulema to justify their assertion: Sarmad went about naked, which was not allowed by Islamic religious law; also, in re-

citing the *kalima* ("There is no God but Allah, and Mohammed is his prophet") he never got farther than the words
"There is no God," which evidently suggested a denial of
God's existence; lastly, Sarmad denied the bodily ascension
of the Prophet Mohammed to heaven. Had he not even written a blasphemous quatrain?

> The mullahs say, "Mohammed rose to the skies,"
> But I say, "God came to him"—the rest is lies.

Orthodox arguments were hair-splitting and shaky at
best. If nudity or criticism of Islamic religious law constituted an effrontery which might encourage ignorant followers to become *kaffirs* themselves, then there were plenty of
naked fakirs wandering the lanes of Delhi uttering blasphe-
mies. But others had not been intimately associated with
Prince Dara. Sarmad's indictment subordinated God to politics.

With true Socratic courage, the accused presented a brilliant verbal defense. Nudity, he observed, could not be totally forbidden, since the Prophet Isaiah (venerated by Islam)
had gone about naked in his old age. Resorting to another
quatrain, Sarmad further observed that God gave sinners
dress to hide their sins, but to the immaculate he gave garments of nudity.

Aurangzeb and the mullahs frowned. Very well then;
but why did he stop the *kalima* short, truncating its holy
words to an atheistic "There is no God"? Sarmad was candid: "I am absorbed in the negative, and have not yet arrived
at the positive. Why should I tell a lie?" He had not realized
complete truth and still felt in the dark about God's existence; hence "There is no God" was as far as he had gotten.
He would certainly recite the whole *kalima* after he had seen
God with his own eyes, but to admit God's existence without
tangible proof was tantamount to giving false evidence. If
people chose to call him "Sarmad the atheist," that was their
concern.

And what about Sarmad's charge that Mohammed had

not ascended to heaven in the flesh? Sarmad's reply has been lost to history, but it could be invented for him: to a Sufi, truth resided everywhere and in everything, and Mohammed's literal or allegorical ascension into heaven meant pretty much the same thing; why should the Prophet have to rise to heaven in order to see a God who existed everywhere, without limitations of time and space?

According to one source, Aurangzeb himself had guided the ecclesiastical inquisition. He reminded the ulema that a man was not liable to execution for mere nudity, but should be required to pronounce the whole of the Islamic creed. This Sarmad refused to do. His defense had not been convincing; he was found guilty of apostasy and sentenced to death—by the Qavi, by all of the ulema, and by Aurangzeb.

It would be a spectacular execution for the Sufi martyr of Delhi: not strangling or beheading in a dark cell but death in public, in the blaze of noon, as a warning to anyone who dared to go against the state-cum-religion. A platform had been erected for the occasion, outside the main gate of Delhi's huge Friday Mosque. Shah Jahan had laid its foundation stone on October 6, 1650; within, flights of pigeons appropriated the great central quadrangle, with a very imposing three-domed edifice looming up in red sandstone. Marble inlay made white-striped minarets seem like exclamation points to the infinite, and scalloped entry arches boasted Arabic shields. It was the largest mosque in all India.

This was the site of Sarmad's execution in 1661 or possibly early in 1662—the exact date is unknown. Years earlier he had written, "In this wilderness death is hard in pursuit of you"; and now in the wilderness of Delhi his moment had come. Guarded by armed soldiers and surrounded by a great crowd, the saint marched in an ecstasy of self-annihilation from the Red Fort to his place of death. He was reciting extempore a series of beautiful quatrains, though the verses may also have been composed in the brief interval between trial by council and the grim event now awaiting him. Sarmad had often spoken poetry in company or alone, and the *Rubaiyat* on this occasion became his final pearls cast to the multitude. Indeed, he had gone beyond them, and could now say: "In my imagination I saw the whole world, and attained peace for my own self." By now the crowd had become so dense it was difficult to pass through it; somewhere in that sea of faces was Abhai Chand, Sarmad's beloved Hindu boy, the catalyst of his rapture, sainthood, and doom.

At the execution platform, the man assigned for beheading turned out to be low-caste, of sweeper class. Approaching with unsheathed sword, he proposed according to custom to cover Sarmad's face. But Sarmad made a gesture that it was not necessary, smiled, and addressed his killer in verse:

> My sweetheart is here and his sword is bare;
> I know him whatever disguise he may wear.

The crowd listened hushed as Sarmad continued:

> We opened our eyes from eternal sleep, awakened by the din;
> But it was still an evil night, and so we slept again.

For the assembled populace of Delhi this could not be death, only a soaring martyrdom; not beheading but beatitude. Sarmad was a saint, and he was being murdered for having loved Dara Shikoh. But Sarmad transcended Aurangzeb and death; Sarmad spilled over with so much divine love that Aurangzeb and the judges of the ulema and the executioner, and the whole universe including the victim himself— all became one and the same manifestation of God. His soul would now merge with unutterable mystery, with everything. He had already lost consciousness of individual life.

Aurangzeb's own court chronicler (Aqil Khan Razi) would later observe that, just before the executioner struck, Sarmad recited a final couplet:

> Love's path was blocked by this naked body a bit,
> But now the sword has cut my head from it.

A more sardonic version made the homosexual martyr say:

[411]

A flirt was my companion, and chopped my head from off its body;
I might have got a headache if he'd been a trifle shoddy.

In the moment before execution, one of Sarmad's friends named Shah Asadullah made a last bid to save the ecstatic saint from death. "Look," he is said to have reasoned, "there's still time to escape this hopeless tribulation. Do cover your nakedness, and utter the whole of the *kalima*, and I am sure you will be let off." Sarmad looked up, made no direct reply but resorted to verse again:

How many Sufi martyrs linger on people's breath?
Let me remind the world that there are instruments of death.

Then he added, "Sarmad died valiantly." The executioner decapitated him.

Sarmad was immediately canonized as a saint by the people at large. As his severed head rolled from the block onto the platform, it purportedly opened its lips and recited the whole of the *kalima:* "There is no God but Allah, and Mohammed is his prophet." The miracle would be duly recorded on the authority of those who heard it with their own ears, and after three centuries the story is still told in Delhi. Even more staggering, the decapitated body now got to its feet and picked up its own head; holding the head aloft, Sarmad carried it up the steps of the Friday Mosque shouting *"Anā'l Haqq!"* ("I am God!"). Stupefied by the supernatural happening, the crowd burst into eerie howls of grief.

Nothing is known about the fate of Sarmad's lover. Abhai Chand disappeared, swallowed up by the vastness of Mogul India.

CHAPTER 25

A La Tour Abolie

SHAH JAHAN'S CONFINEMENT in the Red Fort of Agra lasted 7½ years, until his death. For the Great Mogul it was a period of radical transition, with stages of change marked by anger, frustration, bitterness, humiliation, the gelding of pride and, finally, religious resignation. A dramatist might give his eyeteeth for a scene in which a deposed monarch faced his usurping son, but in point of historical fact no such meeting ever occurred: Shah Jahan would never see Aurangzeb again. Aurangzeb rejected repeated demands for an encounter, on the grounds that under the influence of destiny his father had lost all self-control.

From the moment of his capitulation on June 8, 1658, the old emperor had found himself restricted by massive fort walls, and with time his liberty manifestly dwindled to harem precincts. A Mogul King Lear could shout his impotence from the ramparts, but that was all. In place of Cordelia there was Jahanara—not exactly a voluntary prisoner herself, by the testimony of Jean Baptiste Tavernier. The French jeweler had been in Hindustan during the War of Succession and its aftermath, and would later have personal dealings with Aurangzeb. Tavernier now observed that Aurangzeb "also caused his sister Begum Sahib to be confined in the fortress, in order to keep company with the king whom she dearly loved. And he also took possession of all the wealth which she had received from her father's liberality." In addition to Jahanara there was a final passive retinue of harem women and eunuchs. The only person missing to King Lear was his fool.

First months of imprisonment proved particularly humiliating. Shah Jahan had lived to see every Mogul noble desert him flatly; and after relinquishing the fort in order to obtain drinking water, he had been surrounded by both a heavy guard and by spies inside the palace who reported his every move to Aurangzeb. In the first week or two of confinement one or two letters had been smuggled out to Dara Shikoh, but all later correspondence was rudely intercepted. Aurangzeb's biographer concludes: "A great Mogul who could not himself ride to battle and had no faithful noble to fight for him was a superfluity in Nature's economy. He must retire from the stage. This stern law Shah Jahan was slow to admit."

Every new wile of the old emperor was nipped in the bud. First (on Bernier's and Manucci's authority) came those overtures on the part of Shah Jahan to Aurangzeb's son Mohammed Sultan, with a promise of the throne in return for liberation. But Mohammed Sultan had been an honest jail warden and could not be tempted—a fact somewhat surprising in the light of his later defection to Shuja. In any event, the young prince had also become a prisoner early in 1660.

A swirl of further alleged plots likewise fizzled out. Shah Jahan's plan to have Aurangzeb assassinated in the harem by loyal Tartar women had backfired at the last moment: forewarned, the usurper had turned his elephant back from an intended visit to Agra Fort and never attempted to see his father again. Indefatigable, Shah Jahan presumably even wrote to Murad in an effort to turn one rebel prince against another; but by leaving the letter in a book, Murad stupidly ensured himself a one-way passage to Gwalior. One final bid for freedom had coincided with reports that Shuja was marching from Bengal to seize Agra. Hopeful, Shah Jahan made efforts to dispatch secret letters urging those who were loyal to the crown to support Shuja; Shuja himself received an encouraging message written in Hindi by his captive father. But then Shuja was defeated at Khajuha, and fled to Bengal.

It is debatable whether all these machinations actually took place, but if they did they were doomed from the outset. Immediately after the fall of Agra fort, Aurangzeb had ordered the warden Mohammed Sultan to move in with his prisoner. As a further precaution, mansions adjacent to the Red Fort were confiscated and given over to officers of the guard, "so that they might . . . be present at all hours." Mohammed Sultan would later be replaced. The guard undoubtedly rotated with the years; nevertheless Shah Jahan remained under tight surveillance to the end of his long imprisonment.

Chief henchman of nastiness inside the fort was the eunuch Itibar Khan, formerly in Shah Jahan's employ. Early on in the emperor's confinement, Itibar had bricked up fort gates and wickets, and by Manucci's account had posted "harsh women guardians in such a way that Shah Jahan could neither speak nor write to any stranger, nor come out from the door of his harem to enjoy a stroll in his garden without the eunuch's leave." Later, Manucci would see with his own eyes just how strict Shah Jahan's confinement continued to be. After the fall of Bhakkar fortress, the young Italian had rejected Aurangzeb's offer of employment, which less ethical European artillerymen accepted (these were promptly assigned to bolster the fort garrison of Agra). In December 1662 Aurangzeb went off to Kashmir in high pomp, while Manucci lingered in Mogul territory to say good-bye to friends in the twin imperial cities. European cohorts now pressed him to enter service with them at Agra fort; but "finding I would not listen to their words," he says, "they went and spoke to Itibar Khan, fancying that he could persuade me. Itibar Khan sent for me, and on visiting him I presented a cup of crystal." The eunuch seemed pleased: if Manucci chose to stay, he would be made captain of the Christians and receive a salary commensurate with his earnings under Prince Dara. Manucci refused, not only because of his aversion to Aurangzeb but also because "the face of Itibar Khan displeased me—in fact, to speak properly, he looked like a baboon. To me it seemed that from one with a face like that no good deed could proceed." Itibar Khan persisted, affording Manucci the opportunity of visiting Agra fort on several occasions and witnessing the petty persecution of Shah Jahan.

The Italian writes:

> I noted that Shah Jahan's imprisonment was closer than can be expressed. Not a day went by, while I and others were in conversation with the governor [Itibar], that there did not come under-eunuchs to whisper into his ear an account of all the acts and words of Shah Jahan, and even what passed among the wives, ladies, and slave-girls. Sometimes, smiling at what the eunuchs had told him, he would confide to the company what was going on inside, adding some foul expressions in disparagement of Shah Jahan. Not even content with this, he allowed it to be seen that he treated [the emperor] as a miserable slave."

Manucci now watched the chief eunuch's niggardliness at work. An under-eunuch came and whispered that Shah Jahan needed new *babouches* (heelless Moslem slippers). Itibar summoned a tradesman who displayed his wares: embroidered velvet slippers cost eight rupees, plain velvet somewhat less, and plain leather only half a rupee. Itibar chose the plain leather for the old emperor. "He smiled over it as if he had done some great deed; and it was a great deed, being after the nature of his friend Aurangzeb, who knew from this eunuch's physiognomy the vileness of his soul, and selected him to receive charge of his greatest enemy in the world, his father, so that by force of ill-treatment the wretched old man might die."

Manucci responded with no little emotion. "I felt it much," he says; "I knew the dignity with which Shah Jahan had lived when he was free and emperor of Hindustan." The prisoner was made to suffer other trivial cruelties: he sent out two violins to be restrung, but Itibar ignored the request. "Three days afterwards, Shah Jahan sent to inquire whether they were mended. At this the eunuch flew into a rage, and with a vinegary face sent them off to be repaired."

But then, Itibar Khan had a vindictive nature. He demonstrated it when his aged and poverty-stricken parents appeared in Agra during one of his audiences ("I was there myself," Manucci insists). Itibar Khan exploded: "How do you have the great temerity to come into my presence after having consumed the price of my body; and having been the cause, by emasculating me, of depriving me of the greatest pleasures attainable in this world?" The parents were ordered to receive fifty lashes. Manucci drew a Biblical parallel: hadn't the Christian God made use of the cruelty of Joseph's brothers to raise him to the highest dignity in Egypt; hadn't Itibar's parents unwittingly ennobled him? Calming down, the eunuch proved charitable: he would give his parents a hundred rupees, but if they ever appeared in Agra again they would be killed on his orders. Manucci had reason to be proud of his own persuasive powers, especially since "this eunuch was such a close-fisted fellow that it soon came to his selling the dung of his elephants and horses, whereby he made ten thousand rupees."

Itibar Khan's insults were only a small aspect of the old emperor's humiliation. Little by little, Aurangzeb now subjected his father to the same treatment. Shah Jahan must stop writing letters to people outside of Agra fort; it tended to "raise tumults and increase disorder in the realm." Informed of the proscription, the prisoner became furious: "Am I his son that I should obey his orders?" No, he would be intransigent. Very well then, the eunuchs who smuggled these missives out of the palace must be punished. By further orders, Aurangzeb soon decided to withhold writing materials entirely. Shah Jahan could dictate all future correspondence to a eunuch-clerk, and every letter would remain unsealed until his jailers had inspected it and given their *nihil obstat*.

These censors would soon be treated to a sordid epistolary wrangle between father and son for possession of certain crown jewels still worn by Shah Jahan or kept for safety in Agra fort. The prisoner balked: captive or not, he owned the jewels and a usurping son had no moral right to take them from him. The usurper claimed loftily that he was now ruler of India, and crown property belonged to him. Shah Jahan had lost material privileges; besides, since he was an emperor in retirement and presumably leading a life of religious meditation, it was out of keeping for him to wear jewels on his person.

The Peacock Throne itself would be taken away—Aurangzeb needed it for his second official coronation. Shah Jahan, who had been unable to resist a final inspection of the jeweled masterpiece, removed two panels set with diamonds and rubies but later relinquished them out of fear.

There was still more to be given up. In flight from Agra, Dara Shikoh had left jewels worth almost three million rupees belonging to his wife and daughters in the harem vault. Aurangzeb insisted on confiscating this property, and after much argument the prisoner agreed. Furthermore: the old emperor had a diamond thumb-ring, and also a Moslem rosary of one hundred round pearls; both seemed ostentatious for a royal recluse. Reluctantly, Shah Jahan gave up the ring but clutched the rosary: "I use [it] in saying my prayers. I shall give it up only after pounding the pearls in a mortar!"

Neither the sensualist father nor his puritan son emerged with any dignity. But the quarrel went on—sleazily observed by Europeans in the realm, and even filling the pages of state histories.

Dara had left not only gems but various members of his royal household at Agra fort—including women singers. Though he would later outlaw music at court, Aurangzeb now requested these ladies by arguing that "there is no skilled songstress with me whose music may soothe my heart, and you have no liking for songs these days." In reply to Shah Jahan's predictable outrage, Aurangzeb added in another letter: "If your objection is due to their being Dara's concubines, well, other persons of the same class have been taken into my house. What harm is there if his servants live with me?"

It wanted no great insight to discover unconscious motives behind all this tug of war over material possessions. The pariah had come to power; and if it was too late to win love, he was at least appropriating whatever his father and brother esteemed most. In addition, what better stratagem could remind a deposed emperor of his very real impotence? From the moment Agra fort capitulated, Aurangzeb had immediately ordered the closure of entire rooms full of royal furniture, plate, wearing apparel, jewels, and other treasures. Locked and sealed with triple seals, these worldly symbols of lost power became less and less accessible to Shah Jahan as time went on. Though first allowed to look at them by Mohammed Sultan, the old man later found himself confined to the boundaries of the harem; and when Itibar Khan became master of the fort, there was no longer any pretext of consideration for a former emperor's feelings. Thus, when the wardrobe keeper died, imperial clothing remained locked up for more than a few days until a new minion was appointed; it was only with considerable difficulty and delay that Shah Jahan obtained so much as a change of clothing.

Far more revealing than arguments over jewels and singers, other sharply acrimonious correspondence passed between father and son during the first year of Shah Jahan's captivity. Eight letters from Aurangzeb have survived for historical inspection, but none from Shah Jahan—though ample inference makes it clear that only a battery of harsh accusations could prompt such self-justifying replies. Immediately after his triumph at the Battle of Samugarh, Aurangzeb had written to the emperor from rebel encampment outside of Agra, insisting on the holy aspect of war against Dara Shikoh, the apostate. Aurangzeb further rationalized: Allah forbid that he should ever be regarded as a rebel; on the contrary, this fratricidal war had been unleashed by Shah Jahan's blind favoritism to an infidel eldest son, and by the calculated hatred which had been instilled in Aurangzeb's

[419]

two other brothers. "Although I heard that disturbances were being raised and [my] affairs were being thrown into confusion at your instigation," Aurangzeb wrote, "and that my brothers acted under your orders, I refused to lend credence to hearsay and remained loyal to you . . . *till I knew for certain that you did not love me but were trying to place some other son in power.*" * In scornful denigration of Dara he concludes: "If you had not helped in every way by elevating your eldest son to a trusted position—and his ability and God-fearing character are probably manifest to you now—and if, out of regard for him, you had not failed to make provision for the safety of your other sons, then all the brothers could have lived together peacefully and the fire of civil war would never have been ignited."

The tone is so insidious that Aurangzeb's biographer accuses him of the "affected humility of a Pharisee." But what a morbid hunger gnawed at the Pharisee's heart—*"till I knew for certain that you did not love me."* Pursuing his warped logic, Aurangzeb continues: Hindustan could never have become peaceful until Dara and Shuja had been driven into exile or taken prisoner along with Murad. Reluctantly the Pharisee had appropriated certain imperial prerogatives, recruiting nobles and dispensing titles in order to fulfill "the work of God and the people." The awful final step, taking up "the perilous weight of the crown," had been forced on him by "sheer necessity and not from free choice, in order to restore peace and the rules of Islam in the realm." Only thus could he answer to Allah on the Day of Reckoning, by "saving the people from destruction and the affairs of my ancestral kingdom from confusion."

It was a beautifully unassailable apologia: personal ambition and strange emotions had been wrapped in the cloak of God. In reproach of his deposed father's sensuality, Aurangzeb now invoked his own ascetic ideals: "Kingship means protection of the realm and guardianship [of the peo-

---

* Author's italics.

ple], not the enjoyment of bodily repose or lusts of the flesh." Manucci lists Aurangzeb's specific grievances: Shah Jahan had been unjust to his subjects, negligent to his ministers, a corrupter of other men's wives, a spendthrift who squandered money to indulge himself in sexual orgies reflected in his famous Hall of Mirrors, and a profligate who kept a public dancer in his palace. Aurangzeb, by contrast, devoted many hours to public audience, heard complaints and suppressed wrongdoing in the empire. Shah Jahan replied that:

> . . . a man who rebelled against his father, treated his brothers cruelly, and drank so much blood, not sparing even his own sons, would never be able to do useful work for others. As for praising himself on account of sitting many hours daily in audience, what more patent sign could there be that the kingdom was badly administered? For when he [Shah Jahan] directed the empire, officials walked so uprightly that, in spite of the daily beating of the big drum to call into his presence [those persons] wanting to complain of having received an injustice, months and months would pass without anyone coming to lodge a petition.

Aurangzeb retaliated that he had been crowned by God —his cause was just, and Allah had sustained him against all odds: "If God had not approved of my enterprise, how could I have gained victories which are only the gift of God?" It was the old argument of might equals right, especially when sanctified.

The windup of this compulsive correspondence now strained to a smugly hypocritical interpretation of kismet: "Nothing can happen without the will of Allah," Aurangzeb drummed at Shah Jahan; "Therefore this great event is not due to any mortal power or will. You are a wise man; why do you consider another as the author of God's intention? Submit to the will of Allah, and your sorrows and tribulations will turn into peace and contentment. If you consider [the matter] with justice, you have no cause for complaint: I have relieved you of such a heavy burden and taken it on my own shoulders, and made my free mind the slave of a thousand afflictions and fatigues."

Even by prevailing standards of acceptable Mogul cunning, no Mogul emperor had ever carried self-deception to such extremes of orthodoxy. Shah Jahan replied witheringly that true Moslems did not rob other people's property. Aurangzeb responded coolly: "You have written that it is contrary to Moslem faith to seize another's property. But royal property and treasures exist for the good of the people. . . . A kingdom is not hereditary private property. The king is merely God's elected custodian and trustee of His money for the benefit of all citizens of the realm."

It was time for Aurangzeb to end the tiresome duel with a neat stab to his father's heart. Shah Jahan had been deeply offended by Aurangzeb's scathing epithets with regard to Dara and Shuja,* but Aurangzeb now parried: "How do *you* still regard the memory of [your brothers] Khusrau and Parwiz, whom you did to death before your accession and who had threatened no injury to you?"

The thrust was less than true. Though Shah Jahan had probably been implicated in Khusrau's mysterious death by colic, Parwiz had actually died of alcoholism. But why quibble? There were other deaths on the old emperor's conscience: in his ascent to the throne and by his own tacit approval, at least four of his collaterals (his nephews Dawar Bakhsh and Garshasp, his half-brother Shahriyar, and two first cousins) had been put to death. Shah Jahan had been the first Mogul emperor to spill royal blood. He had set the precedent for Aurangzeb's fratricide.

Stunned and subdued, the prisoner could only taper off with a chastened warning: a harsh usurper ought to remember that *his* sons might one day accord him similar treatment. Aurangzeb responded with a shrug: "Well, nothing happens

---

* Even in Aurangzeb's official court chronicle, there is a consistent and malicious perversion of his brothers' names: Dara Shikoh is called "Be-Shikoh" ("the undignified") and Shuja becomes "Na-Shuja" ("the unvaliant").

without the will of Allah. The fate you mention overtook [my] ancestors as well. How can I escape the dispensations of Providence? Everyone gets from God a return according to his own intentions; since my intentions are good, I believe that I shall not get anything but good [from my sons]."

It was an irritating parting shot of pharisaical self-righteousness. And if Allah did not bring retribution, the laws of human psychology would: Shah Jahan had effectively predicted Aurangzeb's fate.

For Aurangzeb, their correspondence had simply reached a caustic impasse. Out of deference he had been writing to his father in his own handwriting; now he turned the matter over to his secretaries, and before long he lapsed into total silence—"to close the path of receiving and responding to [such taunts]." There would be no more personal contact with the prisoner.

● ● ●

Shah Jahan now began gradually to accept the inevitable. The will of Allah continued to manifest itself as horror after horror filtered in from the outside world: Dara Shikoh's beheading; Shuja's assassination in Arakan; Murad's execution at Gwalior; even the opium-induced idiocy and final murder of Dara's son, Sulaiman Shikoh. Little or nothing is known of the deposed emperor's response to these atrocities, though when he heard of Sulaiman's death he is supposed to have exclaimed with unintentional comedy, "What, will the wretch leave no one to avenge me on him?" There could be no more hope of revenge: three sons and a grandson had been murdered one by one, leaving Aurangzeb in supreme command of India.

Accounts of these years of imprisonment vary, depending on the source. As a partisan of Aurangzeb, Danishmand Khan persuaded Bernier that (aside from close confinement) "the deposed monarch was otherwise treated with indulgence and respect." Bernier presents the tolerable picture of Shah Jahan enjoying the palatial apartments of Agra fort, with the society of Jahanara and an entire harem which included singing and dancing women as well as cooks. "No request was ever denied him," the reader is assured; "and as the old man became wondrously devout, certain mullahs were allowed to enter his apartment and read the Koran. He possessed also the privilege of sending for all kinds of animals, horses of state, hawks of different kinds, and tame antelopes, which last were made to fight before him. Indeed, Aurangzeb's behavior was throughout kind and respectful, and he paid attention to his aged parent in every possible way. He loaded him with presents, consulted him as an oracle, and the frequent letters of the son to the father were expressive of duty and submission."

A more sinister though perhaps equally credulous appraisal of the old man's later years of imprisonment is offered by Manucci. Though prone to exaggeration, the Italian had undeniably visited Agra fort in the early stages of Shah Jahan's sequestration, and from European friends in the fort garrison he now gleaned inside facts of the denouement; he even goes so far as to suggest that Aurangzeb made repeated attempts at parricide. Thus, between May and August 1662, Aurangzeb fell ill of the fever from which he almost died. Court doctors recommended convalescence in Kashmir. Manucci relates:

> But the existence of Shah Jahan was like a thorn piercing his heart, hindering him from resting or taking the recreation demanded by nature. Therefore he now displayed no increase of gentleness to his father; on the contrary, he decided to aggravate the old man more and more. Of a truth, this was never the inspiration of the angel during his illness nor the teaching of God, but was arrived at from the perversity of his own nature. In order to bring his father's life quickly to an end, [Aurangzeb] sent orders to make his imprisonment more severe. He ordered the bricking up of a window looking towards the river, where Shah Jahan sat for recreation. A company of musketeers was posted below Agra palace with orders by firing to disturb the old man, and to shoot him if he appeared at the window. Further to increase his despondency, the greater part of the accumu-

lation of gold and silver money was carried away, with
as much noise as possible. . . . But Shah Jahan, too,
played a game of finesse, and made out that he saw
nothing: responding to cries, noise, and musket-shots
by music, dancing, and entertainments, and carrying on
a joyous life with his wives and women. Itibar Khan,
who knew everything that went on in the palace, wrote
it all to the court, so that Aurangzeb decided to take
Shah Jahan's life by poison.

The first alleged poisoning attempt backfired. A lethal
dose with a letter of instructions was presumably sent to Mukarram Khan, Shah Jahan's doctor, suggesting that the royal
patient be disposed of if the physician valued his own life.
Mukarram responded with the ethics of a man under the
Hippocratic oath: he committed suicide by taking poison
himself. Aurangzeb issued fresh injunctions to Itibar Khan to
guard Shah Jahan with renewed caution, and went off to
Kashmir anyway.

On his return from the north, he presumably decided on
a second poisoning attempt and sent a new doctor—a European—to Shah Jahan. Manucci hastens to assure us that the
doctor in question was certainly not Monsieur Bernier—"a
great friend of mine, nor while in the Mogul country did he
practise as a physician." In any case Shah Jahan rejected the
services of the anonymous European, "suspecting what was
sure to happen if he did accept." Manucci relates that Aurangzeb then made use of the unscrupulous doctor for another purpose: to poison Khalilullah Khan. "Aurangzeb was
already tired of seeing this traitor still alive," the Italian continues, "and ordered the aforesaid European, in whom Khalilullah Khan trusted, to dispatch him to another world
through some cordial. The poison was very slow, and Khalilullah Khan was many days in great pain; when he died, his
lips, hands, and feet were all black as coal. For this fine action, Aurangzeb made the European a noble, raising him
every month to double the pay he already had."

Khalilullah Khan may conceivably have been poisoned,

but Manucci's memory proved faulty: the veteran grandee's death actually took place in February 1662, almost ten months before Aurangzeb left for Kashmir. More than likely, all these outlandish Borgia-inspired plottings represent a rehash of public gossip stemming from strong popular disapproval of Aurangzeb. "Talk against Aurangzeb once more prevailed," the Italian acknowledges, "on account of the barbarities with which he was treating the old man." Citizens argued in the bazaars: Aurangzeb had killed his brothers and had no further competition; he should beg his father's forgiveness. What was Shah Jahan's crime, that he was "so hated by him he had created?" Criticized and slandered openly and fearing rebellion, Aurangzeb now sent Shah Jahan presents and made conciliatory gestures.

The poisoning attempts can all be dismissed as fantasy, though they are by no means unrepresentative of the age. Yet by a blending of details from Manucci, Bernier, Mogul sources, and even on-the-spot inspection, a fair idea of the deposed emperor's captive life can be arrived at.

It is difficult to say for certain just where Shah Jahan's prison boundaries began and ended within fort precincts. Certainly he was not allowed the run of a vast architectural complex which had aggregated since its beginnings under Akbar in 1565. With one side facing the Jumna River, the semicircular Red Fort of Agra has a circuit of a mile and a half, and even a superficial tour of the place takes several hours. Modern visitors ogle its massive double sandstone walls—the outer wall some forty feet high, and the inner one towering seventy feet. Double ditches further ensured an emperor's isolation, though only the inner chasm exists today. Beyond outer and inner gates lie spacious courtyards, where the great Hall of Public Audience and edifice after edifice stand remarkably preserved: there are a Hindu-influenced residence built by Akbar, and a so-called Fish Palace with its marble tanks of goldfish long since gone; there are white marble additions created by Shah Jahan, ranging from the Pearl Mosque and Hall of Private Audience to the pavilions of his sumptuous private quarters, and his Palace of Mirrors; and underground chambers, and gardens, and the octagonal "Jasmine" Tower. Very likely this latter was the captive emperor's confining center, a theory which derives unique support from a privy in the immediate neighborhood: Mogul esthetic sense would hardly permit construction of toilet facilities near such an impressive structure unless the exigency of the occasion required it!

All sources agree that the old voluptuary still had his harem women, and the company of his daughter Jahanara. The memory of former pomp and luxury perhaps lingered, but Shah Jahan focused more and more on less earthly things. To Jahanara, who served as both nurse and companion, he spoke frequently of his approaching death. He spent time reading the Koran and repeating Islamic prayers at prescribed hours; a marvelous patience descended on him, and even gratitude to God for this enforced retreat from the world.

Aside from his daughter Shah Jahan had another equally constant companion: Syed Mohammed of Kanauj, who piously served the function of chaplain, lector, and almoner. Duly this holy man held forth about the Koran and the Prophet's traditions, officiated at court prayers and carried Shah Jahan's gifts to the swarming poor outside of Agra fort's walls. Soon the old emperor was consumed with God and orisons—making copies of Koranic verses and listening with rapture to sacred texts.

Jahanara had aged: she was in her early fifties now, a far cry from the beautiful young tomboy who had worn male apparel and enjoyed her father's fawning indulgence so many years ago. When Dara was alive he had persuaded her to become a disciple of the Sufi saint, Mian Mir, and now she had gone further—metamorphosed into a kind of blessed spinster and nun. Solace of the harem and ministering angel of the fort, she watched over Shah Jahan; like the wings of the dove she sheltered the daughters of Dara and Murad, superintending their upbringing and education.

All this was a curious transformation for Shah Jahan,

one which a dead Dara and ecstatic Sarmad could not but have approved. The cloying materialism of money, jewels, banquets, and panoplied durbars had dwindled to the simplicity of an austere spiritual bubble, to a tiny compass of confinement that separated soul from meaningless substance like wheat from chaff. Paradoxically for Shah Jahan, imprisonment had become final freedom: the real prison had always been the outside world, and a greedy, irrelevant concern with power and pomp. Now he had no more heart left to be tormented; his heart had long ago been pulverized by fate, just as he had once threatened to grind the world's jewels to dust in a gesture of spite against a tyrant offspring. Beyond pain and beyond horror, he waited for death.

In January 1666 the former emperor became very weak. Clearly he was failing; his hands and feet trembled. On January 7, after rubbing himself with medicated oil, he fell ill with high fever. Symptoms began to compound rapidly: retention of urine, stomach gripes. One of the royal surgeons succeeded in eliminating the bladder obstruction, but weakness only increased. It was midwinter, and the palace was cold. The old man's lips and tongue were parched from sucking cold sherbet to relieve his thirst; no diet, no medicine could save him now.

On Monday, January 22, the invalid lay on the balcony of Agra fort's octagonal eyrie, looking out across the Jumna River toward a mile-distant Taj Mahal; the setting sun was turning death's white marble symbol to gold. This part of the palace complex had originally been the work of Jahangir's imperious consort Nur Jahan, and still bore the stamp of her artistic refinement. Its open gallery was framed with pillars and a low marble parapet, where carnelian, lapis lazuli, and other semiprecious stones created an inlaid tracery of some lost Persian summer; behind and beyond lay private rooms —all airy, all perched high on the castle walls. Nur Jahan's female slaves had faithfully executed her architectural designs; and she had spent her gloomy days of widowhood here before marrying Jahangir, watching the endlessly wheeling kite birds which now circled the Taj before a dying man's eyes.

For Shah Jahan was dying, fully conscious. His struggle with "the last enemy" would be duly recorded by Aurangzeb's scribe. Aloud, the old man turned his thoughts to God; in an audible voice he gave thanks for a thousand gifts, and then begged forgiveness for a thousand sins. He murmured the Moslem confession of faith, adding a prayer: "O God! Make my condition good in this world and the next, and save me from the torments of hell-fire." Jahanara and the ladies of the harem were sobbing violently. No, he admonished, they must accept the will of Allah. Jahanara must look after the women and arrange for his funeral as he instructed; and there were keepsakes and presents to be bestowed. Could the Koran be read now?

The verses were droned, but it was growing dark. It was the end of a long life, almost as long as that of another great ruler of India—an English queen whom he would never know. Shah Jahan had just turned seventy-five on January 5. He could look back down a dwindling corridor of time to himself as a child, sitting by the deathbed of grandfather Akbar, who had virtually founded the Mogul Empire (at least geographically). He had witnessed his father Jahangir's accession and reign; he had seen his own thirty years of rule go by, followed by the murder of three sons and Aurangzeb's triumph. How much longer would the Mogul Empire last? Its tomb was in front of his eyes: the Taj Mahal, in whose crypt Mumtaz Mahal had long since decomposed inside a floral-inlaid marble box dedicated by his love to what?—to eternity? His hands had stopped smelling of apples: the warning of death given by a Bijapuri fakir to young Prince Khurram almost forty years before. It was time now to die; it was a quarter past seven in the evening.

● ● ●

The body lay in the Octagonal Tower, in full view of the Taj. But it was night, and the tomb could no longer be seen. Dying, he had asked his daughter to bury him beside Mumtaz Mahal. Jahanara now summoned Radandaz Khan, the commander of Agra fort, together with the eunuch Bahlol: would they please present themselves in the *ghuslkhana* or harem quarters? The wicket in the fort gate was opened, and messengers were sent into the city to find the two men who alone could prepare the corpse for burial: Shah Jahan's chaplain Syed Mohammed, and *qazi* Kurban, the chief theologian of Agra. These two holy representatives arrived at midnight, and immediately imposed a stiff financial assessment on the dead man by way of atonement for his lapses in observing traditional rites of Islam. In a belated attempt at orthodox whitewashing, Aurangzeb's official chronicle would acknowledge the money but not the lapse: "Although His Majesty, since he had attained the age of discretion, had never missed a single prayer of the prescribed five times daily prayer, or a single fast of the month of Ramadan, atonement for them was given in a large sum of money which was set aside for the purpose." The priests now made their way to the tower, bowed low, and paid their respects to Jahanara. Then the body was removed to the adjoining hall; the ritual of death had begun.

Shah Jahan must have been pious: only the pious sustained speech and consciousness to the end, and before dying he had managed to recite the whole of the Creed. Sherbet may have been poured down his throat at the last moment to help his soul on its way, since Satan's last temptation would be to welcome the thirsty spirit with a cup of sweets as it left its earthly body. During the whole of the emperor's life, angels had been sitting on his shoulders recording his deeds—the angel on the right shoulder wrote down good deeds, and the one on the left took note of the evil he had done. Each night of his life, while he slept, those angels had flown up to Heaven and transcribed Shah Jahan's daily acts on his personal leaf attached to the tree of life. That leaf had fallen from the tree to earth just before he died; swiftly, the recording angels had carried it off to Azrael, the Moslem angel of death; and Azrael had sent them and a third angel back to the dying emperor. He died peacefully while they held his life

[430]

account up before his eyes; the scales had tipped toward the good.

Immediate burial was the Moslem rule, and Shah Jahan's would be at sunrise. Washing of the corpse had begun with pure water and then camphor water, gently used since the body was still warm and susceptible to pain. During washing, the holy men kept intoning, "I bear witness that there is no God but God, Who is One and has no co-equal; and I bear witness that Mohammed is His servant and is sent from Him." Then the corpse was dried in a clean white sheet, and wrapped in its shroud—three pieces of cloth for a man. The recitation continued: "Say, God is One! Say, I seek the protection of the Lord of Daybreak! Say, I seek the protection of the Lord of Men!"

Shah Jahan lay now in a sandalwood coffin. He would be buried in the Taj Mahal by his own wish, next to the woman he had loved. But it was almost dawn and Jahanara wanted a solemn procession, with due pomp accorded to a once-great emperor. She envisioned the details: "officers of state carrying the coffin on their shoulders; all the rich men and nobles of Agra and its environs, and all the scholars, theologians and popular leaders of the capital, walking beside the bier with bare heads and feet; the common people in their tens of thousands forming the rear of the procession; gold and silver being scattered on both sides every now and then as they moved."

There would be no such funeral: Begum Sahib was a prisoner herself, she had no power to command. Only Aurangzeb could command; and though he had been informed that Shah Jahan was dying, he remained aloof for the moment in Delhi. No authorization had come, no instructions. Aurangzeb's proxy, his son Prince Muazzam, still dawdled somewhere along that royal road between Delhi and Agra, and would arrive too late. Shah Jahan's life had seen a series of dazzling processions, always with thousands of spectators lining roads and river banks; death had reduced him to a handful of eunuchs for pallbearers.

By dawn the soldiers of Agra fort smashed open the

door at the bottom of the tower stairs—it had been bricked up for $7\frac{1}{2}$ years. Head first, the corpse in its coffin was brought out of the fort enclosure and carried down to the river bank: all Agra could witness a procession by land, but few if any would pay attention to several insignificant boats on the Jumna at dawn. Humiliation was kept from being absolute by Hoshdar Khan, viceroy of Agra, who now joined the small funeral party by the riverside and brought a few local officers with him.

Mogul sources make it clear that Aurangzeb was not present at the funeral: he was still in Delhi thirteen days after his father's death. But secret interment would infuriate the gossips of Agra's bazaars. Credulously, Manucci recorded that Aurangzeb became suspicious: could Shah Jahan really be dead, or was this a final subterfuge for escape? "Aurangzeb sent a trusty man," the Italian supplies fiendish details, "to pass a heated rod over his father's feet; and if the body did not stir, then to pierce the skull down to the throat and make quite certain. . . ." In Manucci's version, Aurangzeb deferred burial until his arrival, traveling quickly along the Jumna River from Delhi to Agra and putting up at the mausoleum of the Taj Mahal to await his father's corpse. Begum Sahib meanwhile "sent two thousand gold coins to be given to the poor; but the guards seized the whole, saying that prisoners could not give away anything. On arrival of the corpse at the tomb, Aurangzeb prayed and showed much devoutness, wiping his eyes as if he wept."

But the reality proved less dramatic: Aurangzeb was not there; it was just a quiet funeral by dawn with boats carrying the body, the weeping Jahanara, and a few officers and holy men down river—somewhat over a mile to the great white marble sepulchre. By some Mogul reports there was even a respectable assemblage of theologians, scholars, and nobles. Prayer readers included Shah Jahan's chaplain, the *qazi*, and others. At noon the temporary sandalwood box and its corpse were brought inside the Taj and taken down into the crypt to be placed next to Mumtaz Mahal's elaborate coffin; later, there would be a second stone sarcophagus like hers, with Persian floral inlay. And perhaps by way of expiating sins, an unesthetic Aurangzeb would even relax his hold on imperial purse strings long enough to enclose the cenotaph tombs of both mother and father with that delicately carved marble screen admired by connoisseurs as a masterwork of Mogul art.

There was an improbable romantic afternote to Shah Jahan's funeral: his favorite elephant, Khaliqdad, began to grieve. Manucci tells us:

> Hearing a great noise being made in the tomb of Taj Mahal in preparation for the burial of his master, the elephant grew fierce and restless. The mahout who had charge of him came up and said, "Unhappy Khaliqdad! What will become of thee now that he who was thy master is dead? What is there for thee now but to die too? for no one will take the trouble to look after thee!" On hearing these words, the elephant began to gather dust with his trunk and throw it on his head. Then, with groans and cries, he fell on the ground and died. . . .

Public grief over Shah Jahan's death would be widespread. Most loved of all the Mogul emperors, he had on the whole steered a liberal course over three decades—continuing the Hindu-Moslem accord begun with Akbar, controlling rapacious land-tax collectors and unscrupulous provincial governors, creating employment through massive architectural undertakings, and maintaining the glamour of a sumptuous court which even the poor enjoyed by proxy at public processions and celebrations. Official court sources acknowledge that "the cry of lamentation rose up from every house, in the lanes and market-places alike."

Thousands of miles away, in an England which was not yet ruler of India, other important events coincided with the demise and interment of Shah Jahan the Magnificent: London would know commoner agonies through the Great Plague and the Great Fire. Delhi's white marble Hall of Private Audience still bore its Persian verse inscription—"If there be paradise on earth, it is this, it is this, it is this"; but by way of irony, within a year of the Great Mogul's death, all of literate London would be reading John Milton's *Paradise Lost*.

Two Sisters

SINNER HAD TRIUMPHED over saint. Emotionally they had always been poles apart at the imperial court, but Jahanara and Raushanara now stood in even more striking contrast: the pious spinster who had shared her father's captivity seemed doomed to oblivion, while Aurangzeb's hard-bitten and scheming ally had risen to occupy the position of first lady of the realm. But a reversal was coming. Raushanara had already overplayed her hand, and even before Shah Jahan's death found herself sinking in Aurangzeb's esteem; once again, and unpredictably, her envied elder sister Jahanara would rise like a phoenix to live out her final years in grace.

After the War of Succession, Raushanara Begum had enjoyed considerably more than a brief moment of vindictive glory. Politically, this was her payoff as intriguer and spy inside of Agra's harem: in the crisis of 1657 and 1658, she had aided and abetted Aurangzeb's cause by signaling Dara's and Shah Jahan's movements and reporting on Jahanara and untrustworthy nobles until the capitulation of the Red Fort. Aurangzeb's victory could only be hers; her years of obscurity had ended. On her brother's official coronation in June 1659, Raushanara received half a million rupees—greater than the appanage accorded to his own daughters—and for several years she enjoyed complete ascendancy over the royal harem.

Her position had been dictated as much by peculiar

court etiquette as by Aurangzeb's gratitude. In the Mogul hierarchy, first lady of the kingdom was always the queen mother or the princess royal and never the empress herself— Nur Jahan and Mumtaz Mahal had been exceptions rather than the rule. Commenting on this oblique Oriental setup, Hindu historian Sir Jadunath Sarkar explains:

> Natural bashfulness would keep an empress from ordering . . . the general establishment of the harem, regulating marriages and other ceremonies in the family, or presiding over female society of the capital. But the death of her husband would at once raise her to the dignity of a widow and the influence of a queen mother, and remove from her even the possibility of any younger and fairer rival supplanting her in her husband's favor and hurling her from her seat of honor and influence. Social decorum prevented an emperor from placing his wife above his mother, his elder sister, or his paternal aunt. Thus it was that dowagers and old maids ruled the ladies' world in the Delhi palace.

With Shah Jahan's accession, imperious Nur Jahan had suffered obligatory downfall as his enemy, retreating to Lahore and vacating the role of first lady for Mumtaz Mahal. But within four years Mumtaz Mahal had died, and as eldest princess it was Jahanara who ruled the harem for twenty-seven years under the title of Begum Sahib, "Princess par excellence." The deposing of Shah Jahan in turn toppled his eldest daughter; she shared his eight years of disgrace and captivity. Raushanara had thus become supreme, and had every reason to believe that her new status was permanent.

No Mogul chronicle could ever admit a princess's indiscretions. One of the official histories of Aurangzeb's reign offers a vague, saccharine portrait of Raushanara: "She had noble qualities and admirable traits, and greatly loved her brother [the emperor]." But another Raushanara emerges from the uncensored pages of Bernier and Manucci: a sex-starved virago, hell-bent for power.

Raushanara hoped for sexual freedom. Though Aurangzeb would later be persuaded by a Moslem fakir and Mohammed's own example to rescind the weird Mogul law dooming royal princesses to be spinsters, it was too late for Raushanara—she was in her forties now. Her appetite fed on frustration and she wanted lovers. When Shah Jahan ruled as emperor at Delhi, Jahanara had enjoyed the unsupervised liberty of her own palace outside the confines of Delhi's Red Fort. Seeking equal rights, Raushanara now petitioned Aurangzeb: would he grant her the palace formerly occupied by her elder sister?

No, Manucci relates, he would not:

> Aurangzeb knew plainly enough the meaning of the request, but intentionally concealed [his awareness] and replied to her: "Raushanara Begum, my beloved sister! Most gladly would I concede what you ask, but my love for you will not allow me to live deprived of your society; and it being the custom for the king's daughters not to live outside their father's palace, my daughters would also resent being deprived of you. Thus it is fitting, for many reasons, that you live with them and train them in the habits of royal princesses. By any chance, is there anything deficient in the palace where you reside? Or do you enjoy less state than was maintained by your sister, Begum Sahib? You know perfectly well that all my empire and the wealth of the Moguls are yours."

Dangerously, Raushanara now resorted to indiscretion within the zenana itself. Both Manucci and Bernier shared the same sources of gossip, and an almost identical story of sex and murder would be related by the credulous Italian and the shrewd Frenchman. Sub-eunuchs in the harem reported to Aurangzeb's chief eunuch that two young men had been seen entering Raushanara Begum's apartments. The chief eunuch dissembled but posted guards, with the result that several days later the romantics were apprehended in the palace gardens. A budding Messalina, Raushanara Begum had "just dismissed [them] after they had complied with her will." Presented before Aurangzeb, the young lovers gallantly admitted nothing. How had they found their way into the seraglio? Well, one had wandered in through the gate and the other had climbed over the garden wall. Fine; they would go out the same way, and the less fortunate of the two now paid for his athletic lie: the chief eunuch had him bodily thrown over the garden wall to his death. "Aurangzeb was much disturbed at the eunuch's act," Manucci concludes the episode, "because he held it expedient to conceal a matter so greatly affecting the Princess's good name. Therefore the eunuch was removed from office for some days, the reason given being that he was too severe to servants working in the palace. Thus the eunuch had to take upon himself the sins of Raushanara Begum, but the Princess began to lose some of the esteem that Aurangzeb had for her. . . ."

She would soon lose a good deal more. At the beginning of the fifth year of his reign—on May 12, 1662—Aurangzeb fell violently ill of fever. His physical collapse seemed aggravated by what was rapidly becoming a devouring mania for work and religious austerity. Ramadan, the month of Moslem Lent, had just ended in the shimmering heat of an early Delhi summer; in a blind cocoon of overwork, Aurangzeb was holding durbar twice a day, fasting except for a meager midnight meal, and manipulating his rosary until dawn. Fever came on in the afternoon, and by May 13 his temperature had soared. In the therapeutic fashion of the period, royal doctors opened his veins and bled him to the point of insensibility. The harem became an uproar of sobbing women: surely the emperor was going to die.

For five days Aurangzeb failed to appear in public; once again, Delhi lapsed into a state of total confusion. "Rumors were current that the King was already dead," Manucci wrote, "wherefore everyone made preparations for doing what best suited his own affairs." Bazaars buzzed with gossip: Raushanara Begum was concealing Aurangzeb's death for her own ends; Jaswant Singh had massed his Rajputs to release Shah Jahan from Agra fort; and other liberators were on the way, including Mahabat Khan the younger with a contingent of cavalry from Afghanistan.

Intrigues of succession quickly encircled Aurangzeb's four sons (a fifth was still to be born). Completely out of the picture, Mohammed Sultan languished in jail; of three remaining sons, Azam aged nine and Akbar not yet five were offspring of the emperor's dead principal wife, Shahnawaz Khan's daughter, Dilras Banu Begum, while nineteen-year-old Muazzam had been conceived by Nawab Bai, a lady of noble Kashmiri Rajput stock. With Aurangzeb lying ill in the harem, his sister Raushanara Begum had the upper hand and could exclude or admit whom she pleased. Her best bet would be to opt for one of the younger sons, and thus set herself up as regent of India. "Believing that there was no hope of her brother surviving," Manucci says, "Raushanara Begum took away the royal [privy] seal and wrote to many rajahs and generals on behalf of Sultan Azam, then nine years of age and actually living in the harem." Bernier, a resident witness in Delhi and a first-hand source of palace information (via his patron Danishmand Khan) sustains Manucci in plot if not detail: by the French physician's account the little pawn would be five-year-old Akbar, with Raushanara's supporters limited to several noblemen and Aurangzeb's foster brother.

Annoyed by Raushanara's insolent takeover, Aurangzeb's Rajput wife decided to protest—especially since her own son Muazzam was being ignored. Manucci conjures up a wonderfully wild moment: ". . . she told Raushanara Begum that it was wrong to rouse the empire and stir up confusion and disquiet while the king was still alive and there was hope of his recovery. Having said this [the Rajput queen] proceeded to the King's bedside, but Raushanara Begum boldly seized her by the hair and ejected her from the royal chamber."

Raushanara allowed no one to see Aurangzeb except one eunuch belonging to her own faction. Frustrated young Muazzam, living outside the Red Fort in Dara's former Delhi mansion, now presumably paid a midnight call in disguise to Rajah Jai Singh, enlisting his aid to find out whether Aurangzeb was dead or not. Bribing one of the palace eunuchs, Jai Singh ascertained that Aurangzeb had not died and advised Muazzam to sit tight. But if Aurangzeb *should* die, Muazzam pursued, wouldn't it be best to go to Agra and fall at Shah Jahan's feet in order to enlist the old emperor's aid? Jai Singh hedged, as did other nobles; "they were aware," Bernier observes, "that to open [Shah Jahan's] prison would be to unchain an enraged lion." It seemed better to dissemble and wait; Jai Singh would back Muazzam in the event of a showdown.

There would be no showdown. After five days of unabated fever, Aurangzeb exerted superhuman force and displayed himself briefly at evening durbar—only his actual appearance could squelch bazaar rumors and satisfy court nobles that he was still alive. By the seventh day of his illness he was decidedly better: a quartet of high grandees assembled at his bedside for audience, public orders started to go out again, and at Agra the eunuch Itibar Khan breathed easier on receiving instructions to continue keeping Shah Jahan under heavy guard. Soon Aurangzeb was even sitting for short intervals on his throne in the Hall of Private Audience. On Friday May 22 he piously had himself carried in a royal litter to the great mosque of Delhi for public prayer; and he again began to show himself every morning on the *jharoka* balcony.

With the first renewed dispatch of letters and instructions, Aurangzeb called for his great seal of state—enclosed in a small bag and "placed under Raushanara Begum's care," Bernier says. Seal required counterseal, and was invariably "impressed with a signet which he always kept fastened to his arm." Bernier's description is most accurate: contemporary portraits of Mogul emperors display the signet or counterseal fastened underneath the royal right armpit (by contrast to an amulet, which would be worn under the left arm). It was now that Aurangzeb became suspicious: the counterseal could not be found.

"He asked Raushanara Begum where his signet ring was," Manucci writes. "The Princess replied that one day when he swooned it fell off his finger; since then she had

taken charge of it, keeping it beneath her pillow." Aurangzeb
dissembled, but decided to investigate when he was fully recovered. He still, indeed, suffered from a palsied tongue that
made it difficult to speak. In later weeks, court eunuchs
would fill in the gaps for him: Raushanara Begum had written letters to viceroys, governors, and generals to solicit their
support for the child-prince Azam, and then sealed these letters with the royal seal. Raushanara's hair-pulling of the reti-
cent queen would also be revealed. In short, "Raushanara
Begum lost much of the love that Aurangzeb had borne her,
he being now angered at her behavior."

Such low-down scheming would necessarily be suppressed in official court chronicles, and appears only in the
pages of Bernier and Manucci. Meanwhile, Aurangzeb's fantastic willpower and ability to cope with plots from the fifth
day of his illness onward now elicited admiration from Bernier's patron, Danishmand Khan: "I was present when my
agah became acquainted with all these particulars, and heard
him exclaim, 'What strength of mind! What invincible courage! Heaven reserve thee, Aurangzeb, for greater achievements! Thou art not yet destined to die.' "

True to prediction, the emperor had made a complete
recovery by the last week in June and took a ceremonial bath
to prove it. In the general rejoicing, nervous Raushanara
Begum tried to make amends by arranging a grand recupera-
tion feast.

In spite of her serious faux pas in sex and politics,
Raushanara Begum somehow continued to enjoy harem supremacy for a while. Under her influence, Aurangzeb even
allowed himself to be finally persuaded to visit Kashmir. For
Bernier, the Princess was "anxious to inhale a purer air than
that of the seraglio, and to appear in her turn amid a pomp-
ous and magnificent army, as her sister Begum Sahib had
done during the reign of Shah Jahan." Aurangzeb obligingly
started off for the Mogul Switzerland, attended by such a
horde of cavalry and so much artillery that the citizens of
Delhi felt certain he intended to besiege Persian-held Kandahar.

Bernier belatedly accompanied the royal procession at the insistence of his eager pupil Danishmand Khan, who "can no more dispense with his philosophical studies in the afternoon than avoid devoting the morning to his weighty duties as Secretary of State for Foreign Affairs and Grand Master of the Horse. Astronomy, geography, and anatomy are his favorite pursuits, and he reads with avidity the works of . . . Descartes."

Hastening to catch up with the army, the Frenchman had no choice but to travel in state:

> With one hundred and fifty crowns per month, I am expected to keep two good Turkoman horses, and I also take with me a powerful Persian camel and driver, a groom for my horses, a cook and a servant to go before my horse with a flagon of water in his hand, according to the custom of the country. I am also provided with every useful article, such as a tent of moderate size, a carpet, a portable bed made of four very strong but light canes, a pillow, a couple of coverlets . . . some few napkins of dyed cloth, three small bags with culinary utensils. . . . I have taken care to lay in a stock of excellent rice for five or six days' consumption, of sweet biscuits flavored with anise, of limes and sugar.

He also had a linen bag and hook for making *dahl* (curdled milk).

Goggle-eyed, Bernier now recorded the staggering pomp of a Mogul outing which conservatively dragged between its van and wake as many as two or three hundred thousand people. There were: two traveling tented cities, one "metropolis" always set up in advance of the other to spare the emperor any discomfort; red imperial tents lined with velvets and silks; a rotating guard of nobles surrounding the royal precincts; tents full of harnesses, brocades, sweetmeats and fruits, Ganges water for drinking, and betel leaf; kitchen tents, officers' tents, eunuchs' tents; tents for horses and elephants, for hunting dogs, and for hunting leopards. Aurangzeb moved in a worshiping cloud of alertly vertical khans and rajahs; though when not directly in his train they promptly became horizontal, carried supine in palanquins and attended by mace bearers, cymbal and trumpet players, and silver standards of "balances, fishes and other mystical objects."

Raushanara Begum had won her moment of ultimate splendor, with female slaves waving peacock feathers to brush dust and flies away. In a gorgeous procession, ladies of the seraglio went by on elephants with embroidered trappings and bells of silver. Bernier wrote:

> These lovely and distinguished females . . . are thus elevated above the earth like so many superior beings borne along through the middle region of the air. . . . Stretch imagination to its utmost limits, and you can conceive no exhibition more grand and imposing than when Raushanara Begum, mounted on a stupendous Pegu elephant, and seated in a *mekdambar** blazing with gold and azure, is followed by five or six other elephants with *mekdambars* nearly as resplendent as her own, and filled with ladies attached to her household. Close to the Princess are the chief eunuchs, richly adorned and finely mounted, each with a wand of office in his hand; and surrounding her elephant, a troop of female servants, Tartars and Kashmiris, fantastically attired and riding pad-horses.

Also accompanying the princess's assemblage were sub-eunuchs on horseback and swarms of foot-lackeys with large canes to clear the road of intruders, while other principal ladies of the court followed with their own numerous attendants. For Bernier, sixty and more loping elephants decked out in regal trappings seemed the quintessence of Oriental bedazzlement; "and if I had not regarded this display of magnificence with a sort of philosophical indifference, I should have been apt to be carried away by such flights of

---

* A kind of howdah.

[443]

imagination as inspire most of the Indian poets, when they represent the elephants as conveying so many goddesses concealed from the vulgar gaze."

It was probably Raushanara's first and certainly her last glimpse of Kashmir: Aurangzeb decided never to visit the alpine paradise again, as the result of "a strange accident [which] cast a gloom over these scenes and dampened all our pleasure." An elephant became frightened as the entourage crossed the awesome Pir Panjal Pass at an altitude of 11,400 feet; and in a concatenation of clashing bodies, a number of beasts and women fell down the precipice and were killed. "Two days afterward we passed that way," Bernier relates, "and I observed that some of the poor elephants still moved their trunks."

This accident was an omen. With the return of the court to Delhi and with Shah Jahan's subsequent death, Raushanara Begum would soon fall to the background and witness her elder sister Jahanara reinstated as first lady of the realm. "Thereafter we hear nothing more about Raushanara," writes Sarkar, dismissing her from history.

But there was more. From 1666 until 1671, the embittered lady turned with abandon to the only avenue left to her—sex. By 1669 her nieces and nephews were intermarrying, but she took no joy in it: these were Dara's or Murad's brats, reared by sentimental Jahanara or Gauharara, but not by her. Manucci comments:

> If this year was a joyful one for these marriages, it was a
> sad one through what occurred in the apartments of
> Raushanara Begum. She kept there nine youths in se-
> cret for her diversion. The discoverer of this noble con-
> duct was Fakhr-un-Nissa, the daughter of Aurangzeb.*
> This lady, although not desirous of marriage, had no in-
> tention of being deprived of her satisfaction. Therefore
> she asked her aunt to make over to her at least one out
> of the nine. Raushanara Begum declined the request in

---

* No such name exists. Manucci probably means Badr-un-Nissa.

spite of her niece's importunity. Moved by envy, the young girl revealed to her father what there was hidden in the apartments of Raushanara Begum. By diligent search they caught the young men, who were well-clothed and good-looking. [The lovers] were made over to the criminal authorities, being announced to the world as thieves; and following the orders he had received, the *kotwal* [police commissioner] Sidi Fulad destroyed them in less than a month by various secret tortures. Already angered at the misconduct of his sister, Aurangzeb shortened her life by poison. Thus, in spite of all she had done to get her brother made king, she herself experienced his cruelty, dying swollen out like a hogshead and leaving behind her a name of great lasciviousness.

Scholars reject Manucci's account—mere bazaar talk, not lifting the veil of purdah but tearing it to shreds, and, of course, finding no corroboration in "sober" history. Yet mysteriously, Aurangzeb's unsatisfied young daughter Badrun-Nissa died at twenty-three—in April 1670. Raushanara Begum's own no-less-mysterious death occurred a year later on September 11, 1671; she was fifty-six.

In cardboard Mogul chronicles Raushanara is nothing; at the hands of Bernier and Manucci she becomes a bold character in history—instantly recognizable as a fiendishly vindictive Salome demanding Dara's blood, gloating over her father's imprisonment, choking with hatred of her eldest sister, and indulging in a furious hair-pulling contest with Aurangzeb's wife. Surely Raushanara Begum herself, if given the choice of a pen portrait for posterity, would choose unreliable gossip over scant reference in insipid state papers: dimensions of evil at least give her a place in the sun.

●●●

In an almost day-and-night contrast of virtue, Jahanara's remarkable rise from disgrace to restored grace can only be explained in terms of unbelievably noble self-effacement. Of all characters in the Mogul tragedy, she alone emerges with unassailable dignity—more than a Cordelia or

Antigone, she becomes almost a reincarnated Mumtaz Mahal, a mother image who loves and forgives everybody. Like Priam blessing Achilles for slaying Hector and reaching out to touch the face of his own son's murderer, Jahanara would now offer unqualified pardon to Aurangzeb, who had killed her beloved Dara and reduced Shah Jahan to ignominy.

At the moment of Shah Jahan's death, Aurangzeb's proxy, Prince Muazzam, had been encamped about twenty miles from Agra. The news reached him the same night; and though he arrived in Agra the next day too late for the funeral, he soon paid his respects to Jahanara and other female members of the royal family. With proper etiquette, Muazzam ordered the entire Koran to be read by "pious and learned men," and ordained a distribution of money in alms to the needy.

Back in Delhi, Aurangzeb reacted to his father's death with fascinating ambiguity in a violent seizure of grief. His tears could hardly have been all play-acting: official report made him weep so bitterly that even "courtiers and nobles . . . were shocked." As prescribed by custom, he and the two young princes royal, together with harem ladies, put on white mourning clothes. The Mogul chronicle would claim that the emperor had wanted to be present at Shah Jahan's death, in order to receive benediction from his father. But spontaneous grief was now followed by dilatory action: the prisoner had died on January 22, and Aurangzeb did not start for Agra by river until early February, taking a week to make the journey. Thus almost a month tardy, he was met several miles from Agra by the city viceroy and other nobles. Following obeisances, Aurangzeb and the royal party continued their water journey to Agra, where he put up temporarily at Dara Shikoh's former mansion. The following day he visited the Taj Mahal with its twin coffins in the crypt, wept again, recited the Moslem prayer of the dead, and distributed twelve thousand rupees in alms; he performed his afternoon prayers in the adjoining mosque of the mausoleum. He would, as a matter of fact, go to the Taj daily during this stay in Agra, which coincided with the celebration of the Prophet's birth.

There was a twenty-four-hour delay from Aurangzeb's arrival until his important reunion with Jahanara in the Red Fort. It had been almost eight years since they last met, when she visited his camp outside of Agra in a desperate mission to stop a war of fratricide and arrange terms of peace. Her embassy had failed. Candidly rebuking both Aurangzeb and Murad for immoral rebellion, she had then chosen imprisonment instead of the money and liberty which would surely have attended defection to the winning side. Yet, though never making any secret of her partisanship for Dara or her passionate attachment to Shah Jahan, she had also been Aurangzeb's confidante in time out of mind, even interceding for his pardon some two decades earlier when he mysteriously fell from favor and found himself dismissed from his first viceroyalty of the Deccan. The moment was full of high emotion for both brother and sister.

It was more than high emotion, it was high drama. During her years of imprisonment, Jahanara had accomplished more than Aurangzeb could possibly guess. Nurse to Shah Jahan, tutor and guardian to her nieces, and a dedicated author who even in confinement had completed a biography of the Moslem saints of Kashmir, she was also nothing short of a saint. The years of somber restriction had filled her with compassion rather than bitterness, and on more than one occasion she broached the impossible: Shah Jahan must forgive Aurangzeb. The old man had refused, appalled; then, not long before his death, he yielded to gentleness. Jahanara now held in her possession a signed pardon—absolution to the religious fanatic and dictator for every sin he had committed against his father-emperor. It was a devastating spiritual trump.

For such a historic meeting, she prepared the Red Fort with all due honor. The Pearl Mosque submitted to embellishing tapestries of rich brocades, and carpets and bunting marked the spot where Aurangzeb would step down from his elephant before entering the Red Fort. On his arrival at the women's apartments in the seraglio, she now greeted him in a touching ritual, presenting a large gold basin heaped full of gems: her own jewels, and those which had belonged to Shah Jahan. It was a munificent symbol of love long denied, buttressed by the formal pardon which she now presented to him after the etiquette of obsequies. Bernier writes obliquely: "Moved by the magnificence of his reception, and the affectionate protestations of his sister, Aurangzeb forgave her former conduct and has since treated her with kindness and liberality."

In ensuing weeks, Aurangzeb made repeated visits to Jahanara. He instructed the nobles of Agra to present themselves at Agra fort, where they proffered salaams and gifts—both of which were conveyed through the intermediary of eunuchs to the invisible great lady of the seraglio. Aurangzeb had ordained that observance of his coronation day should henceforth coincide with the beginning of Moslem Lent, which this year fell on March 27; Jahanara received 100,000 gold pieces and an annual pension of 1,700,000 rupees. For the rest of her life she would bear the title of Padishah Begum ("Empress of Princesses").

The harem at Agra fort was now disbanded. Aurangzeb allowed those female servants and ladies who had not been wives of Shah Jahan to marry freely; widows found comfortable retirement in the so-called *suhagpura* (the "Hamlet of Happy Wives") which functioned as a division of the royal establishment.

In October of the same year, 1666, the reinstituted first lady herself moved back to imperial Delhi. Hauntingly, Tavernier would encompass the event in a one-line entry in his journal: "I saw the elephant pass upon which she was mounted when she left Agra with the court, as I was entering it on my return from Bengal."

In Delhi, Jahanara took up residence in the grand mansion of the dead Persian noble, Ali Mardan Khan. Once again she became the emperor's confidante. Bernier's patron, Danishmand Khan, would receive orders in December 1669 to "go to her and, standing in her outer drawing room, to inform her that he was present there to do any service in which she might command him." Presiding anew over social functions, Jahanara now arranged a lavish ceremony in her house to mark the marriage of Dara's daughter Jani to Aurangzeb's third son Azam. On hand for the occasion, Manucci gives these nuptials passing mention: "Begum Sahib . . . to the seed-pearls which issued from her eyes at thus losing her beloved niece, added lovely pearls and handsome jewels as a marriage present."

Jahanara's exalted position allowed her to criticize Aurangzeb where anyone else would have been afraid. Brief glimpses of her political activities show a witty as well as a holy woman. Little by little, she had watched the picayune dictates of her brother manifest themselves in the name of orthodox Islam. The censor of public morals prohibited alcoholic beverages, bhang, gambling, illicit sex, heretical opinions, blasphemy, and beards longer than "four finger-breadths." Restrictions had reached ludicrous proportions: court music, astrologers, and the office of poet laureate were outlawed; imperial clerks found silver inkpots exchanged for porcelain ones; planting of rose-beds in imperial gardens was frowned upon. Aurangzeb had also given up idolatrous morning display at the *jharoka* window, and vented his fury at effeteness by personally trimming a courtier's cloak which fell below the ankles. Women could hardly escape moral edicts, especially with narrow-minded mullahs egging the emperor on. Jahanara decided that it was time to take up the banner of emancipation.

Her methods delighted Manucci. Tartly, she assessed those proscripts which had already been railroaded into law: women could not wear tight masculine trousers but only loose ones; women, too, had to give up drinking, along with nutmeg. Jahanara retaliated by inviting the wives of theologians and orthodox grandees to her mansion, where she plied them with wine. Manucci concludes:

> Aurangzeb came to her palace and referred to the restrictions under which he had placed women. He made excuses, saying that he was under an obligation to uphold [Moslem] law. She replied that she had never heard

about such things being entered in the book of Law, but Aurangzeb told her it was the opinion of all the learned. Whereupon [Jahanara] invited the King behind the purdah, where he saw all the learned men's wives lying drunk and in disorder, with tight trousers on their legs! . . . [Jahanara] said to him that if such things were part of the Faith, then the learned should not allow their wives and daughters to go about clothed in this fashion, nor should they permit them to drink intoxicating [liquor]. Instead of issuing laws for others, they [should be] required to regulate their own households. Thus was appeased the storm that had been raised against women.

But comic anecdote turned tragic as Jahanara attempted to stem her brother's renewal of Islamic severity toward Hindus. From the very beginning of his reign, Aurangzeb had made it clear that he was prohibited by Islam from sanctioning the building of new Hindu temples; nor could old temples be repaired. In isolated incidents, shrines venerated all over India by devout Hindus had already succumbed to Islamic wrath. Now, on April 2, 1679, Aurangzeb issued formal orders reimposing the hated *jaziya*, the religious tax on unbelievers. By ruthlessly strict interpretation of Moslem theory, an infidel was an infidel and he must either convert or pay tribute. Akbar the Great had boldly abolished religious taxation outright in 1579; exactly one century later, his great-grandson was fatally reviving it.

Making a last bid for sanity, Jahanara visited her brother and begged him to reconsider an act of such devastating regression. India represented an "ocean" sustaining the "ship" of the Mogul royal family; what emperor could tax "the sea on which he sails"? Predicting widespread rebellion, she ended by trying to throw herself at Aurangzeb's feet. Unmoved, he invoked the justification of Mohammed and the Koran, and then (by Manucci's account) "bade her goodbye and turned his back upon her, a movement that cut the Princess to the very quick."

Hindu Delhi responded as Jahanara feared. Mobs gathered under the *jharoka* balcony of the Red Fort with prayers and wails, but Aurangzeb refused to acknowledge their presence. On the following Friday, thousands of Hindu supplicants thronged the entire route from the Red Fort to the great mosque: money changers, fabric sellers, shopkeepers from the Urdu bazaar, mechanics, and artisans—everyone had abandoned work for a massive demonstration, knowing that the emperor and his equipage of grandees must pass on their way to public prayer. Orders went out to force passage through the crowd, which stubbornly refused to disperse. Aurangzeb and his nobles fumed for an hour, after which another order went out: bring on imperial elephants and trample a path to the mosque. In a Macedonian phalanx of elephants and horses, many Hindus were crushed to death. The crowds continued to protest for some days more but it was hopeless; afterward, they would submit and pay *jaziya*. Puritanism had triumphed—at the price of alienating the Hindu Atlas that bore the weight of the Mogul Empire on its shoulders.

For the princess royal, the further political madness of her brother was more than she could bear: she predicted her end. At the same time as his new edict against Hindus, Aurangzeb inaugurated fresh military campaigns; he took leave of his sister to invade Rajputana, in a widening strategy of conquest which could only lead south to the Deccan. With the foresight of a dying woman, Jahanara guessed that he would never return to Delhi or Agra.

Once again, Manucci was on hand to record a somber event: the death of Begum Sahib. The irrepressible Italian, down on his luck, had decided to accept employment in Mogul domains as doctor to the household of Aurangzeb's son Muazzam—"thus, unwilling as I was to serve Aurangzeb, I became the servant of his son." Reluctant or unable to accompany a suicidal court, Jahanara witnessed Aurangzeb's departure with apprehension. Manucci was with the bivouacking horde which filtrated south:

The women . . . moved with us, except Begum Sahib or Padishah Begum, who being . . . old desired to remain in Agra. During this march to the Deccan, we heard that she had ended her life in fulfillment of her own prophecy. For before Aurangzeb left Agra, this Princess tried to prevent the King beginning hostilities against [Rajput states]. She told him the undertaking was very difficult if not impossible; and that it was very probable they would never meet again, as turned out to be the case. At the time of her death this Princess divided her property and jewels among her nieces. . . . Nor did she overlook her beloved Jani Begum, to whom she bequeathed her finest gems and a greater share of the money. Upon this news reaching the camp, we halted for three days at Aurangzeb's wish, and he showed himself touched by the death of a Princess of good ability who . . . left behind her . . . the name and fame of a wise woman.

Jahanara Begum died on September 6, 1681, at the age of sixty-seven. Aurangzeb commanded that in future she should be referred to in court documents as Sahibat-uz-zamani ("Mistress of the Age"). In a final gesture of love, the emperor's sister had offered one last pacifist counsel; but it had been rejected. Driven by unquenchable aggression, her brother was dragging himself and all of Hindustan to ruin.

CHAPTER 27

The Mountain Rats

IT WOULD BE easy to accept the superficial definition applied to Aurangzeb by his enemies: he was simply a Moslem fanatic. But blame can hardly be laid to Islam itself —every religion has had its persecuting henchmen, including Christianity. Like Aurangzeb whom he so much resembled, Cromwell also praised the Lord for delivering into his hands enemies for "execution." Yet whatever their personal motives, Cromwell and Aurangzeb both had made themselves the tool of an implacable God.

And the Hindu law of karma was ineluctable: actions determined ends. Indeed, in a subcontinent of heterogeneous races and religions, Aurangzeb's rigid orthodoxy amounted to a form of suicide. With the end of the War of Succession and the death of his father, brothers, and nephew, what could possibly threaten the stability of a usurped empire— except the usurper himself? Palpably and inexorably Aurangzeb was master of India, and could insist on policy regardless of holy mullahs and the Grand Sharif of Mecca. Akbar, the genius, had flouted Islam in the interests of national unity; an easy-going Jahangir and a tolerant Shah Jahan had been worldly men, willing to compromise or conciliate for the sake of a functioning Mogul autocracy. Though Moslems were still a tiny minority in a predominantly Hindu country, Hindu and Rajput subjects might well have continued to adjust to equable rule if the liberal tradition had continued to prevail. Aurangzeb, at the age of forty and with full knowledge of India, had inflexibly chosen another path.

Fanaticism provoked counterfanaticism, inevitably. As early as 1668 (a decade before Aurangzeb's reimposition of the hateful religious tax) sturdy Jat peasants in the district around Agra revolted against his initial oppression. In unequal encounters, villagers killed their own women to protect them from dishonor, and then threw themselves on Mogul troops in suicide squadrons. During a grisly debacle, twenty thousand Jats under a leader named Gokla were slaughtered; Gokla's arms and legs were hacked off piecemeal on a platform in front of the police station at Agra. Still the Jats fought on, looting Akbar's tomb at Sikandra in 1681 and dragging out his bones to be burned—what uncontrolled Jat mob could be told that they were desecrating the memory of a liberal genius who had himself hated Moslem bigotry?

Then came the almost supernatural revolt of Satnami fakirs in May 1672, which sent a current of fear through imperial Delhi. An agricultural Hindu sect who shaved all the hair from their heads including their eyebrows, Satnamis had monasteries all over upper India but were concentrated in a district seventy-five miles southwest of Delhi. Inspired by a toothless old Joan of Arc who claimed that her magic would make Satnamis invulnerable to enemy bullets and capable of multiplying like dragons' teeth, the sect soon had thousands of men under arms. They pressed toward Delhi, plundering villages and defeating small Mogul forces. Aurangzeb countered with ten thousand men, artillery, and even a detachment of his own imperial guard; to neutralize Satnami power, he wrote prayers and drew esoteric designs on paper talismans which were then sewn into Mogul army banners. In a distinctly unsupernatural finale which soon became high massacre, Satnami martyrs fell in cascades of blood.

The torch of revolt quickly passed to Sikhs of the Punjab. Originally of Hindu faith, Sikhs had formed a peaceful offshoot religion of their own at the end of the fifteenth century; rejecting caste and creed, they believed that God alone was love. Dara Shikoh had received Sikh blessing while fleeing; but Aurangzeb was cursed. These angels of God soon turned from love to war, and in their struggle against Moguls they became formidably disciplined soldiers. Brave Sikhs would continue throughout the eighteenth century until they carved an independent state out of the Punjab.

Clearly Aurangzeb intended to subdue an entire subcontinent and make it over into his image of a sovereign Moslem state. Quite aside from pogroms against isolated groups of Hindus, the first half of his long rule had already witnessed one expansive struggle after another—first the conquest of Assam and Chittagong, and then the coercion of Tibet. For most of the 1670s, Aurangzeb had provoked war with virtually every border clan of Afghanistan; men and money went down the drain in endless clashes. In a belated and "very imperfect settlement," the emperor at last submitted to paying subsidies to keep Afghan peace, at the same time fostering intramural friction between clans—"breaking two bones by knocking them together," as he put it. But in the meantime those northwest ventures had ruined Mogul finances, and may well have been one of the reasons for his levying a Hindu head tax. Quelling savage frontiersmen at the price of dividing them proved even more disastrous for Aurangzeb's own ends: Afghans could henceforth be of no use in his aggressive plans; he must seek assistance by pulling troops out of the Deccan. Every action seemed calculated to destroy the balance of India, as though a madman were deliberately setting the stage for his Mogul *Götterdämmerung*. No Akbar, no Jahangir or Shah Jahan, had ever carried military dictatorship to such fatal extremes. An empire fed on war would now choke on war and die by war.

● ● ●

Aurangzeb's self-destructive passion had led him, heedless of Jahanara's protest, to the fatal invasion of Hindu Rajputana in 1679. Grimly appropriate, the provocation for hostilities was troublesome Jaswant Singh, maharajah of Jodhpur. He died on December 10, 1678, with no immediate heir except for an inconsequent grandnephew at the Mogul court. The opportunity seemed almost too perfect: Aurangzeb could take belated revenge on an old traitor, at the same time making certain that there would be no centralized opposition to his repressive measures against Hindus. By seizing Jaswant's Rajput state, he literally planned to split Rajputana in half—effectively isolating southern Udaipur from its northern Rajput allies.

But not all of Jodhpur's royal widows had consigned themselves to the Rajput funeral pyre in acts of suttee: two ladies now gave birth to Jaswant Singh's posthumous sons at Lahore, and one of the infants managed to live. Aurangzeb proceeded with his invasion, while Jodhpur's ministers spirited the newborn ruler to a place of concealment—his name would become a rallying cry for Rajput legitimists.

Resorting to his usual dissimulation, Aurangzeb claimed that Jaswant's posthumous son was an impostor. But Rajputs were in no mood to play games: the capital of Jodhpur had fallen, and its Hindu temples and idols were smashed. All Rajputana united against Mogul aggression.

Significantly now, the Rajputs gained an ally, if indeed he had not been on their side from the beginning. Under rebuke for his supposed incompetence in combat against both Udaipur and Jodhpur states, Aurangzeb's favorite son, Prince Akbar, held discussions with the enemy: his father's bigotry would ruin not only Rajputs but the whole Mogul empire; now was the time, with Rajput backing, to seize the throne of Delhi and restore the conciliatory policies of Akbar the Great and Shah Jahan.

The coup d'etat almost worked. Preoccupied with invasion, Aurangzeb had moved to Ajmer to direct strategy himself; young Akbar dangerously commanded the main Mogul army, while the princes Muazzam and Azam had also been summoned from the Deccan and Bengal at the head of additional troops but were now far afield. The emperor remained vulnerable with a retinue of less than a thousand men—clerks, eunuchs, attendants, and a weak body of soldiers. Muazzam had dutifully given warning that Akbar was busy intriguing, only to be censured by Aurangzeb for stirring up false suspicion. But now the favored son's rebellion became the talk of a panicky imperial camp; Akbar was on his way with seventy thousand men, a combined force of Moslems and Rajputs. Aurangzeb faced the truth: "I am defenseless. The young hero has got a fine opportunity. Why is he delaying his attack?"

Why indeed? Inexplicably laggard, Akbar took two weeks to cover a mere 120 miles. In the interim, imperial messengers rode in every direction to recall loyal officers and troops, including the forces of Muazzam and Azam. When Akbar arrived for the showdown, Mogul officers had already begun to desert him in panic; encouraging further defection, Aurangzeb resorted to the hopelessly mildewed but effective ruse which he had employed a thousand times before—he sent his son a false letter, implying that Rajput allies had been led into a trap. At dawn on the day of the intended battle, Akbar woke to find himself in solitary opposition. Worldly hope had turned to ashes, and Omar Khayyám's simile of snow vanishing from the desert's dusty face had come into its own—an entire army had disappeared with the night, leaving only a few retainers and about 350 horses. Akbar fled in the wake of his Rajputs.

Before long, both parties discovered that they had been duped. Obligingly, Rajputs escorted the fugitive prince by a zigzag escape route through Rajputana and into the Deccan.

Unexpected involutions are often touched off whenever great powers interfere with smaller ones. In endlessly ironic ramifications, Aurangzeb's aggressive Rajputana policy would prove a giant failure. By insisting on a religious poll tax and interfering with the dignity of sovereign Rajput states, he had literally cut off the right arm of the Mogul Empire. The deserts of Rajputana swallowed up more than men and money: imperial prestige itself had been lost in an unresolved war. A few Rajput soldiers from loyal Jaipur State might fight for Mogul Hindustan in the future, but the rest had been alienated forever.

● ● ●

The Mogul family tragedy would end as it began—in the fateful Deccan. From this middle zone of India, Shah Jahan had revolted against Jahangir; and Aurangzeb had marched from Aurangabad to rebel against Shah Jahan and usurp the Peacock Throne. Now, in crushing fulfillment of Shah Jahan's prediction, one of Aurangzeb's own sons had completed the grand design, luring a demoniac father to the Deccan after him. Aurangzeb would remain in the south for twenty-five agonized years; every success would turn, Janus-faced, to display a profile of defeat.

By June 1681, the emperor began to divert his enormous Mogul war machine southward; by mid-November, all military resources of the empire had been concentrated in the Deccan under Aurangzeb himself, together with three of his sons (Muazzam, Azam, and young Kam Bakhsh) and all of his best generals. Strategically located in Aurangabad by March 22, 1682, the emperor settled in for an ominous period of watch and wait which puzzled both court and European observers alike.

Much had happened in the Deccan since his departure in 1658 to contest the throne, yet the basic situation had remained unaltered: the independent Moslem sultanates of Bijapur and Golconda were afraid of Mogul expansion, and every intrigue stemmed from that fear. Over the years, both had degenerated into near-total corruption, yet both clung to existence for a variety of reasons. Golconda was rich and still paid Mogul tribute; Bijapur was still strong enough to deter a limited Mogul invasion. Also, bribery-prone Mogul generals had up till now pursued only a languid policy of aggression: these Deccan kingdoms provided employment for Hindustan's soldiers, and what military Mogul fool would willfully destroy a complex balance of power that required the constant presence of imperial troops in the south? Deccan geese laid such golden eggs.

But most important, Mogul troops had been hampered by a distracting third power. Gallingly for Aurangzeb, that power was Hindu. Taking advantage of his twenty-five-year absence from the Deccan, Hindu Maratha guerrillas had gradually multiplied until they constituted a formidable conglomerate; though still without an organized kingdom to speak of, they commanded a sizeable no-man's-land west of Bijapur and south of the Mogul frontier. Aurangzeb could no longer regard the Marathas as insignificant irritants; in fact, his rebel son Akbar had now taken refuge among them.

Like the Incas of Peru, Marathas were the spawn of inaccessible uplands. Early Moslem conquest had literally pushed their ancestors into the isolated valleys and mountains of the western Deccan plateau, where they lived under petty chieftains and enjoyed local autonomy. It was a Spartan existence, and it developed a Spartan race—wiry, self-reliant, independent, clever. The Marathas thrived on war: nature had conveniently provided them with natural mountain fortresses; and though their caste status was low, their chiefs claimed to be *kshatriyas*—the warrior breed of Hindus. "War brought out their dormant capacities," says one historian, "and their daggers soon cut their name deep in the annals of India." It would be a very different signature from that of Hindu Rajputs: Rajputs cherished abstract notions of honor at the price of victory, whereas Marathas showed intense pragmatism and employed any and every means to attain their ends. Rajputs were noble and Marathas were vulgar. Perpetually resilient, their vulgarity would plague not only the Moguls but, later, the British as well.

The Marathas had early decided upon a guerrilla identity for themselves. Even in Shah Jahan's reign, small bands alternately flirted or fought with Deccan Mogul outposts. But flirtation ceased: in return for hefty backing from Bijapur, Marathas decided to become the Moguls' enemies—and Bijapur gained an ally against Mogul imperialism.

As Deccan viceroy in 1657, Aurangzeb had been plagued by the banditry of the Maratha leader, Shivaji. Shivaji took indecent advantage of the struggle between Mogul troops and Bijapur by stealing from both of them. Then he cunningly followed through with a truce offer when Aurangzeb went north for the War of Succession—a convenient interim allowing further Maratha nest-feathering at Bijapur's expense. In desperation Bijapur momentarily decided that matters had gone too far, and a leading general was sent out to assassinate Shivaji; but when they embraced in fatal parley, the wily Maratha tore open his enemy's bowels with a pair of hidden steel "tiger's claws." From then on Shivaji plundered and took new forts, extending his dominion all the way down India's western coastline to Portuguese Goa, and eastward to a width of sometimes a hundred miles. But Bijapur was reluctant to fight a useful foe, and Shivaji soon inaugurated fresh forays into Mogul territory—the gnat was still stinging the iron bull. In 1659, Aurangzeb's uncle, Shaista Khan, was assigned the governorship of the Deccan. Cheerfully impudent, Shivaji led a midnight attack on Shaista Khan's winter quarters at Poona, reached the viceroy's bedroom and cut off his thumb! Damnable Shivaji seemed an incarnation of the Devil, capable of appearing anywhere. By 1665, no less a professional than Rajput Jai Singh was delegated to put down this petty chieftain who in less than ten years had become powerful enough to challenge the southern forces of the Mogul Empire.

Intensive Mogul effort produced results: after five months of seizing Maratha forts, Jai Singh forced Shivaji to negotiations. The Maratha chief must surrender most of his strongholds and become a Mogul vassal; Aurangzeb would make him a commander of horse in an imperial rite to be held at the Mogul court. Accordingly, on May 9, 1666—less than four months after Shah Jahan's death—the "Mountain Rat" arrived outside Agra (where Aurangzeb had temporarily established residence) and a few days later attended royal durbar.

In the most important single mistake of his life, Aurangzeb decided to put an upstart Hindu in his place. The crude upland chief was a military genius and, properly treated, he would have been an indispensable ally in the Deccan. But Shivaji was also Hindu, a low-class bandit. After making salaams and proffering gifts, the Maratha was led to a place among third-rank officers, where he stood ignored as durbar continued—no title had been bestowed on him, no presents had been offered by way of reciprocation. Reluctantly, Jai Singh's son admitted in a whisper that Shivaji had been placed among the commanders of five thousand horse. "What?" the novitiate expostulated. His seven-year-old son had been created commander of five thousand horse without even appearing before Aurangzeb; his own servant held such a rank. Furious, Shivaji committed a serious breach of court etiquette by raising his voice loudly: he would commit suicide rather than be humiliated in this way! In a sudden excess of mortification he fainted on the spot. Grandees murmured; Aurangzeb asked what the matter was? Jai Singh's son replied diplomatically, "The tiger is a wild beast of the forest. He feels oppressed by heat in a place like this, and has been taken ill." The emperor must forgive Shivaji's rude conduct; he was a Deccani unused to courts and fine manners. Taken to an anteroom, the tiger was sprinkled with rose water; reviving, he received permission to leave durbar.

Still railing against Aurangzeb's insult, Shivaji complained so bitterly in the house assigned to him that he soon found himself forbidden from court and worse—he became virtually a prisoner with a guard around his residence. But he and his son Shambhuji escaped by hiding in baskets of sweetmeats intended for Brahmans and fakirs, and after devious travels returned to the Deccan by the end of 1666. Many years later, Aurangzeb's last will and testament would comment: "Even a minute's negligence results in shame for long years. See, the flight of the wretch Shivaji was due to carelessness, but it has involved me in all these distracting campaigns to the end of my days."

The comment was appropriate in a last will and testament. It would take time, but with renewed energy and endless warfare, persistent Maratha gnats intended to achieve the impossible: they would sting the iron bull to death.

These were Aurangzeb's enemies, more on hand than ever to greet his return to the Deccan. Only one thing had changed: the Maratha leader Shivaji had died—on March 24, 1680, in the midst of intrigue. Manucci concluded that "by rushing hither and thither he tired himself out, and died vomiting blood." A Mogul chronogram, "An infidel went to Hell," incorporated in its Persian alphabet the date of Shivaji's death at the age of not quite fifty-three. "Infidel" brigand or not, his exploits had made him a savior, protector of the *tilak,* the ritual paint mark on Hindu foreheads. Magnetic and shrewd, Shivaji had blown life into Maratha clay—inspiring his people to become a nation, rallying Hindus to a sense of their own worth and power. His prodigal son Shambhuji—cruel, ruthless, and capricious—duly assumed Maratha leadership. It was with Shambhuji that Aurangzeb's rebel son Akbar sought refuge, in June 1681.

For the Marathas, Akbar represented more than a mere ally: the Mogul emperor's defected offspring was a powerful prestige symbol. But any real merger with Shambhuji would prove impossible—the new Maratha chief had his own problems, and would later become downright indifferent to Akbar's cause. Bending like willows in the wind, Marathas adapted to quasi-guerrilla tactics; they shied away from proposals of a joint attack against Aurangzeb. It seemed best to them to wear down a formidable opponent by snapping at his heels rather than meeting him head on.

Prince Akbar curiously fizzles out of Indian history between 1681 and 1686. At first he helps Shambhuji in irrelevant sieges; but the Maratha chief has, as English traders at Surat comment, "too many irons in the fire." In Akbar's opinion, the thing to do is to launch a full-scale attack on one of the chief Mogul divisions at Aurangabad or Burhanpur, and open a wedge for massive appropriation of Mogul territory; if Shambhuji will only give money and men to such an enterprise, Akbar can return north and rally waiting Rajputs and dissident Hindus to overthrow Aurangzeb. The Maratha chief demurs: why exchange Deccan hills and jungles for the open plains of northern India? Why send the pick of Maratha manhood to foster Akbar's designs, when it would leave Maratha home ground undefended? Finally disgusted, Akbar sees Bijapur fall to the Moguls in September 1686; he loses all hope and sails away to Persia to wait for his father to die. Aurangzeb responds with a wry smile—"Let us see who dies first, he or I"—and invokes a Persian quatrain in which a potter wonders whether Fate will break him before it breaks a china cup he has made. The cup breaks first: later, upon hearing of Akbar's death, Aurangzeb will comment, "The great troubler of India's peace is gone."

● ● ●

Even greater troublers of India's peace were the Marathas who had given Akbar refuge. At the end of July 1682, the English at Surat observed Aurangzeb's fury: "He is so inveterate against the Rajah [Shambhuji] that he hath thrown off his *pagri* [turban] and sworn never to put it on again, till he hath either killed, taken, or routed him out of his country." But after a few fitful months of Mogul attacks on Maratha fortresses, Aurangzeb abruptly recalled all imperial divisions to Aurangabad; so that on April 10, 1683 the Surat council took note: "All his forces that were against his son Akbar . . . he hath withdrawn." By June 1683 the English had decided that "The Mogul is grown very crazy and his mind continually alters"; and in October they would still say that "he is extraordinarily peevish and uneasy because of Sultan Akbar." Anyone suspected of having aided Akbar— Prince Azam, or Jani Begum, or grandees—ran the risk of being demoted; as the British thought, "all persons of quality stand on ticklish terms."

It was a strange and watchful interlude, marked by highly contradictory actions. The English frankly considered that Aurangzeb was in his dotage—"he will in all likelihood not live much longer." But he was then only in his sixties; he would rule India for another twenty years and more.

Yet something was at long last beginning to make inroads on Aurangzeb's hitherto unassailable will power. In spite of all his precautions, two sons had revolted: first there was Mohammed Sultan's brief defection to Shuja during the War of Succession; and now Akbar's stunning rebellion had shaken the emperor to the depths of his strange being. Henceforth, no son could be trusted, no relative or faithful khan. History must not repeat itself again. The emperor had three sons left.

Prince Muazzam, the eldest, managed somehow to preserve a core of quizzical humanity and fundamental decency in the midst of the aggression raging around him. Prone to concession and conciliation, he often felt loath to carry his father's relentless policies to their extremes. Ironically, Aurangzeb found such decency suspect: it might be a mask, however subtle, for ambition. His wrath would yet descend on the prince's head.

Azam (who had married Dara Shikoh's beautiful daughter Jani) was a problem package of conceit, pride, and ungovernable temper. Subject to paroxysms of fury he often rolled up his sleeves, and on occasion even dared to explode in the face of his father. Aurangzeb had been obliged (by Manucci's testimony) to put Azam in prison for a year to cure him of alcoholism. For the moment he seemed to be acquitting himself well as a good soldier. If he continued to behave, he might even be allowed to sit at Aurangzeb's right hand for imperial functions. But such an honor had first to wait on his elder brother Muazzam's fall from grace; and even when it was bestowed, it would not be for long. Play son against son; let the two brothers almost come to blows (in a mosque!) over royal prerogatives, and temperamental Azam could then be cowed by an interview with his father "at a lonely place." Azam must have the fear of God put into him; Azam must be made to tremble openly for the rest of his life whenever he read a letter from his father.

The youngest son of all, Kam Bakhsh, had been born in 1667; presenting the least threat, he counted on his father's shelter. But in December 1698, even Kam Bakhsh would be sentenced by Aurangzeb to six months in jail for "misconduct."

Most tragic of Aurangzeb's daughters was the eldest, Zeb-un-Nissa—a gifted poetess and literary patron who wrote under the pen-name of Makhfi, the "Concealed One." Echoing Jahanara's support of Dara Shikoh, Zeb-un-Nissa had offered fidelity to her young brother Akbar and sent self-incriminating letters to him during his abortive rebellion. Unfortunately Aurangzeb's spies had discovered this correspondence; and Zeb-un-Nissa was imprisoned at Salimgarh fortress. The poetess indicted her father in a bleak verse couplet like an epitaph:

I have experienced such cruelty and harshness in this
land of Hind,
I shall go and make myself a home in some other land.

Others might have wished to migrate with her. Afraid of the tyrant but equally afraid of the anarchy which would inevitably follow his death, courtiers and officers had no choice but to accept his dictates. He intended to keep a whole imperial retinue and a vast Mogul army forever in exile from Delhi and Agra, plunged into war after gloomy war.

So far, two years of a game of tag with the elusive Maratha enemy had gotten the Moguls nowhere. It didn't matter that Shambhuji, the Maratha chief, bothered to assert himself only spasmodically. (The Dutch factors observed that Shambhuji "is not in very good odor with his officers. He diverts himself far too much with women and drink.") His father Shivaji had already galvanized the Maratha nation, turning unorganized peasants into organized bandits devoted to plunder and fired by their hatred of Moslems. More and more frequently, disparate Maratha hordes operated independently but with the same end in view. To Deccan countryfolk they were Hindu Robin Hoods—even the blackmail and assessments they levied were less odious than Aurangzeb's discriminatory religious poll tax. A disaffected Mogul citizenry willingly became Maratha eyes and ears, reporting on imperial troop movements and warning bandit friends of impending danger. This was a struggle of giant and pygmy, with ponderous Mogul cavalry stung by Lilliputian assault. Marathas under attack would scatter to hills or woods, only to return later in sniping attacks on unguarded imperial flanks; convoys would be plundered, and their booty carried off to Ghat strongholds. No matter if Mogul armies took enemy mountain forts—other mountains and other forts afforded fresh retreat.

A new imperial strategy emerged, if indeed it had not always been at the back of Aurangzeb's mind. Shambhuji and Maratha hordes thrived on the heavy tribute of Bijapur and Golconda. If these troublesome southern twin sultanates were once and for all incorporated into the Mogul Empire, it followed that a sizable source of Maratha revenue would automatically end. The "mountain rats" could then be exterminated. Bijapur and Golconda hung like overripe fruit from Deccan boughs—ready to be plucked and squashed, oozing with the sweet sap of internal corruption and sensuality. They might indeed have been destroyed years ago, if Dara Shikoh and his peace party had not intervened. But now the deed would be accomplished.

On the surface, Aurangzeb's plan seemed logical; but Dara Shikoh and the peace party had not been wrong. There was a virtue in decadence which a puritan emperor would discover: two weak Moslem Babylons had paradoxically been nothing less than powerful dams, holding back a mounting Hindu torrent of wrath.

CHAPTER 28

"This Stupendous Caravan of Sin"

THE STRONGER OF the Deccan twins, Bijapur, had to fall first. Sublimely hypocritical, Aurangzeb prepared for the kill: Bijapur candidly refused to cooperate with the Mogul Empire in squelching Hindu bandits; therefore Bijapur would immediately be condemned to death for refusing to sign her own death warrant!

Bijapur meanwhile mustered her internal military might, while Golconda and the Marathas helped by sending belated troops in August and December 1685. Aurangzeb early retaliated to the first sign of hostile coalition by openly breaking off diplomatic relations with Golconda, and dispatched an auxiliary army (under Prince Muazzam) toward Hyderabad —both Deccan sultanates having suffered invasion, the dispersal of Mogul forces would entail no little delay in the conquest of Bijapur itself.

In June 1685 the siege of Bijapur city began. On the Golconda front, Muazzam occupied Hyderabad and forced the sultan to retreat to his fortress. Pending actual takeover of Golconda, Aurangzeb accepted a letter of submission from its ruler along with tribute.

One year later, in June 1686, the siege of Bijapur's capital still raged apace: the city was well protected by its moat and walls. Resolute citizens bravely wiped out Mogul trenches and repelled commando units. "I had hoped," Aurangzeb confided to a Moslem holy man, "that one of my sons would take the fort; but it is not to be. So I want to go there myself, in order to see what kind of barrier is this Bijapur that it has not been forced for so long."

By early July the emperor, now almost sixty-eight, arrived on the scene. A deputation of Bijapuri mullahs came forth to plead with him: "You are an orthodox believer . . . doing nothing without the warrant of the Koran and the decrees of theologians. Tell us how you justify this unholy war against brother Moslems like us?" Aurangzeb's reply was artful: "I do not covet your territory. But the infidel son of the infernal infidel [Shambhuji, son of Shivaji] stands at your elbow. . . . He is troubling Moslems from here to the gates of Delhi, and their complaints reach me day and night. Surrender him to me and the next moment I shall raise the siege."

The moat around Bijapur's walls had been gradually filling up. Laborers received a fraction of a rupee for every basket of clay or earth they flung into the yawning divide, but their pay increased to a rupee and finally to a gold coin as they ran a murderous gauntlet of enemy sniper fire from the walls. The moat would soon be even fuller: according to one Mogul historian, godless workers "threw living men and women into the ditch and took away their money!"

Then, abruptly, Bijapur fell—not by assault but in capitulation. There could be no point in going on. The adolescent ruler Sikandar was just a pawn of selfish courtiers; outside help from Golconda and Marathas had vanished, and Bijapuri generals scarcely relished the idea of slow suicide. Sunday, September 12, 1686 marked the end of the long Bijapur monarchy. A tearful populace lined the streets to watch their final ruler come out of his palace at one o'clock in the afternoon, accompanied by an enemy escort. He looked back, poignantly, then passed through the open gate of the citadel; as khans led him to the emperor's great tent, music of mocking triumph was struck up.

Within, grandees and military elite stood to stiff attention. Sikandar, dazzlingly handsome, bowed in defeat before Aurangzeb. Even the tyrant of India now spoke softly: "God's grace be on you! You have acted wisely. . . . I shall exalt you with many favors and gifts. Be composed in mind."

Sikandar had need of composure: Aurangzeb's "gifts" to him included confinement to a few rooms in Daulatabad state prison, after which he was dragged about as a royal captive. In 1700 he died at the age of thirty-two; by his own request he was buried in the sepulcher of his spiritual Moslem guide at Bijapur city. When Sikandar's coffin was paraded into Bijapur, women wept and broke their bracelets in grief.

The collapse of Bijapur was quickly followed by the collapse of Golconda. Spared during three decades of Shah Jahan's reign, Golconda had miraculously survived for almost three decades more, leaving its ruler free to enjoy his dancing girls and "ingenious forms of sensuality." Golconda, cheerfully given over to any and all vice, had by now become India's Babylon. Some twenty thousand dancer-prostitutes made Hyderabad a merry place: there were mass bacchanales performed for the king in a public square on Fridays, and fermented palm juice flowed in raucous taverns. Degeneration and art went hand in hand; Hyderabad's skilled craftsmen produced exquisite artifacts admired throughout the subcontinent.

Six miles west of Hyderabad city on the summit of a cone-shaped hill, the fortress of Golconda stood encircled by a crenellated granite wall that boasted seventy-six bastions— each bastion fifty or sixty feet high, and composed of granite blocks weighing more than a ton apiece. This was the impregnable stronghold of the Deccan, with cannon surrounding the walls and a fifty-foot moat. Within the inmost citadel, enterprising medieval kings had constructed a two-storied palace that afforded an unbroken view for miles around. From here, Sultan Abul Hassan could watch the approach of Mogul forces.

By the end of January 1687, Aurangzeb himself was on hand for the $7\frac{1}{2}$-month siege of Golconda. In his own camp, sharp conflict raged over proper Mogul policy. Prince Muazzam's easy-going nature balked at reducing a Moslem sovereign to dust; Muazzam constituted Abul Hassan's only hope, and an exchange of envoys and letters began. It was a dangerous game to play twice (he had already secretly tried to help Bijapur) and this time it backfired: informed of intrigue, Aurangzeb arrested Muazzam and his entire family, confiscated his property, gave his troops to other commanders, and tortured his eunuchs for secrets. Muazzam's protestations of innocence only exacerbated his father, who now forbade the Prince to cut his hair, pare his nails, or to have fine food and drink. Muazzam would remain a prisoner for seven years.

Little by little, Aurangzeb had been cutting himself off from every son and daughter. Mohammed Sultan had died in prison in December 1676; Zeb-un-Nissa, because she had helped rebel Akbar, remained a lifelong captive; and now another prince had been locked up. With the arrest of Muazzam, Aurangzeb withdrew to his wife Aurangabadi Mahal, slapping his knees in anguish as he cried, "Alas! Alas! I have razed to the ground what I had been rearing up for the last forty years."

It was not only Muazzam who opposed the emperor's extremist policies: many Shia nobles disliked the idea of exterminating the last Shia kingdom in India, and even orthodox Sunnis disapproved. In their view, an unprovoked war between Moslems was sinful. The chief justice of the realm, Shaikh-ul-Islam, had advised Aurangzeb against storming Bijapur and Golconda. His successor now pleaded that Golconda be spared, but was summarily dismissed from camp. Mistrusting sons, family, imperial nobles, and holy men of Islam, Aurangzeb resolutely pursued his campaign of destruction as the siege went on.

As in the case of Bijapur, the damnable moat had to be filled up. Ceremonially washing and praying, Aurangzeb stitched together the first cotton bag to be filled with earth and thrown into the ditch. Following months brought gruesome famine, and outright epic deaths of several thousand Mogul soldiers caught in countermined explosions intended to breach Golconda's walls.

Aurangzeb refused to give up. If the walls of Golconda

could not be breached or stormed, there was another way: starve the garrison into surrendering. Fantastically, a gargantuan wood-and-earth barricade was now constructed around the entire Golconda fortress—a citadel enclosing a citadel! Guards watched over the doors of this new enclosure. By imperial proclamation the entire kingdom of Golconda was annexed.

Then, on September 21, 1687, the mighty Golconda citadel fell. An Afghan soldier of fortune whose cheerfully fickle military record already included desertion from Bijapur to the Moguls and subsequent desertion of the Moguls for service in Golconda, was eager to crown his career by selling out again. Having risen to become one of the two highest officers inside the stronghold, he blithely opened the impregnable doors. At three o'clock in the morning a party of armed Moguls who had been invited to be present crept through a postern gate, entrenching their position while imperial hordes poured into the fort. By the time Prince Azam arrived with still further Mogul support, victory music had struck up.

Inside Golconda fortress itself, cries of street fighting reached Abul Hassan, the final sultan of the dynasty. Sensual, cowardly, and sybaritic, he seemed the unlikeliest person in the world to play a dignified closing scene; but he did. Consoling his wives and asking their pardon, Abul entered his audience chamber, sat on his throne and waited for the Moguls to arrive. He ordered breakfast, and greeted the entrance of a Mogul officer and his party with a cheerful "Good morning." Would they join him in the meal? After breakfast, the sultan allowed himself to be conducted by Mogul officers to Azam's tent. There he placed a rope of pearls around the prince's neck, received condolences for his deposed state and was later presented to Aurangzeb.

According to one Mogul source, dancing girls and musicians amused Abul Hassan to the very end until the enemy burst in. When the alarmed girls stopped performing he cried out, "Go on dancing. Every minute that I can spend in pleasure is a great gain."

Whatever the curtain line, the play was over. After some

time, the sultan of Golconda found himself sent to Daulata-bad prison-fortress to join the deposed sultan of Bijapur. There, in those precipitous and windswept quarters, the Herod of the Deccan lived on for a few years more.

The great dynasties of Bijapur and Golconda had come to grief—twin Babylons fallen and annexed to the far greater Mogul Empire. But the Mogul boa constrictor had swallowed more than it could possibly digest.

● ● ●

The consuming energy of one man had carried Mogul imperialism as far as it could go. Bijapur and Golconda were Aurangzeb's; his armies marched east and south to claim the forts and provinces of a vast conquered territory, since both defunct sultanates had been expanding into the Carnatic over decades. All except the extreme southern tip of India had yielded or would yield to Aurangzeb.

But all this conquest would prove hollow quickly enough. Ostensibly master of the Deccan, Aurangzeb had unwittingly helped the Marathas instead of cutting off their source of strength. The social and political vacuum created by the collapse of Bijapur and Golconda would soon be filled by something far more insidious than Mogul troops vainly attempting to take over such vast territory. Many displaced soldiers of Bijapur and Golconda (especially Hindus) would now elect to join Maratha tribesmen or become free-looting marauders on their own. Governors of conquered territory had ample time either to form their own pockets of rebellion, or to become "patrons of anarchy" in the Maratha cause. The Mogul hierarchy itself was rotten at the core, and would soon come to terms with its Hindu adversaries.

But danger signals were not immediately discernible. Aurangzeb appointed a Mogul governor for Bijapur in the aftermath of its capitulation, and also dispatched competent generals to scurry for Bijapuri fortresses and revenue. He himself remained in Golconda until late January 1688, trying to set up a new government.

On his return to Bijapur, a macabre plague broke out. In Bijapur city and in the Mogul camp itself, buboes began appearing under people's armpits or in the groin—preludes to high fever and unconsciousness; those who did not die suffered brain disorders or the loss of faculties. Among the hundred thousand victims was the emperor's wife, Aurangabadi Mahal. But Aurangzeb refused to be delayed even by bubonic plague. The troublesome Deccan sultanates had been annihilated, and it was time for a new campaign against Shambhuji. Yet Mogul troops would get no farther than eighty-five miles north of Bijapur (in January 1689) before hearing unexpectedly good news: the "infidel son of the infernal infidel" had already been captured.

During the Mogul onslaughts against Bijapur and Golconda, Shambhuji had done precious little to prevent the death of either sultanate. Giving himself over to pleasure, he withdrew to Samgameshwar (about 120 miles south of Bombay) whose wonderful mansions and gardens had been created by his right-hand man, Kavi-kulesh. Shambhu's escort was small. A crack Mogul division crossed the Western Ghats and jungles, and after clashing with Maratha guards they cornered a double prize: both the Maratha rajah and his minister had taken refuge in a hole in the floor of the minister's house. Shambhuji and Kavi-kulesh were unceremoniously dragged out by their long hair. Heavily chained, they were paraded along Deccan roads lined by hundreds of thousands of spectators eager to catch a glimpse of them.

Moguls responded with insane joy: the Maratha devil had been caught, and there would be no more disorder in the Deccan. Garbed for public ridicule, both the devil and his advocate had been transformed into buffoons with fool's caps and bells on their heads; twin jesters mounted on camels, they now found themselves ushered into the imperial camp to the blare of victory music. Aurangzeb received these formidable enemies at full durbar. He descended from his throne and knelt on a carpet to thank Allah.

Various accounts indicate that Shambhuji might at least have saved his own life—either by revealing where Maratha treasure was hidden, or by naming names of corrupt Mogul officers. But enraged to the point of madness over the public parade, he screamed obscenities at his royal captor and blasphemed against the Prophet as well. That night he was blinded, and the following day his minister's tongue was cut out. Two weeks of subsequent torture culminated on March 11, 1689 in a horrendous death: their arms and legs were hacked off one by one and their flesh thrown to dogs. The decapitated heads were stuffed with straw and sent on a tour of Deccan cities, to the tune of trumpet and drum.

For a year afterward the Marathas, temporarily disorganized, yielded fort after fort to Aurangzeb. But by 1690 they were rallying in the southeast and in the west. Trouble seemed relatively minor at first: having been virtually crushed, how could these people possibly rise up again?

● ● ●

India was sick, and those with vested interests in her began to be alarmed. Even Englishmen now felt strong enough to enter into open dispute with Moguls. They might still be petty foreign traders, but they refused to be victimized by the turbulent internal politics of Hindustan.

Enterprisingly adjusting to curry and cholera, the East India Company had continued to flourish over the years of both Shah Jahan's and Aurangzeb's rule, and English warehouses sprang up in every direction of the compass. English trading stations at Surat port and in Agra had been followed by a solid establishment at Fort St. George in Madras; by 1651, under Shuja's lenient governorship of Bengal, an English factory had opened twenty-four miles north of the place which would one day be called Calcutta. True, the first English ledgers more often than not showed only small profit and sometimes even heavy losses in saltpeter and indigo, raw silks and taffetas; the War of Succession had unsettled everything for a while. But then, after 1668, the company's Bengal trade expanded rapidly: the value of exported goods rose to a dramatic £100 thousand in 1677 and £150 thousand by 1680. As for the west coast of the subcontinent, operations at Bombay island at first seemed likely to get nowhere—the place was cut off by creeks, swamps, and mountains. Originally a Portuguese enclave, Bombay had been ceded in 1661 as part of

Catherine of Braganza's dowry when she married Charles II; in 1668, Charles transferred such an unpromising possession to the East India Company for an annual rent of £10! But by 1687, Bombay had become important enough to supersede Surat port as company headquarters for all India.

Yet it was Bengal which now became the focal point of contention. Harassed by corrupt local khans who disregarded Aurangzeb's trade agreements and assessed and humiliated as they pleased, a small force of Englishmen sacked a Bengal port late in 1686. The following year, Shaista Khan tried to retaliate. In the midst of several smart Mogul defeats and negotiations, the city of Calcutta began to materialize out of malarial swampland. These events filtered through to Aurangzeb, still enmeshed in the siege of Golconda. By 1688 and 1689 trouble had shifted to the Bombay coast, and the emperor felt constrained to order the arrest of all Englishmen, the takeover of their warehouses in Mogul dominions, and prohibition of foreign trade. But England controlled the seas; England could stop pilgrim ships from going to Mecca, and foreign trade provided customs revenue to the Mogul Empire. By 1690 Aurangzeb had come to terms with the English, and trade continued.

But European pirates (including Captain Kidd) had begun to plague the seas, sailing under English colors; the East India Company soon found itself in fresh disgrace for pirate acts beyond its power to control, and Englishmen again found themselves in Mogul jails. Desperately a new ambassador arrived in 1701 in the very belated wake of Sir Thomas Roe's embassy to Jahangir—Sir William Norris now waited on Aurangzeb at the imperial Mogul camp in the Deccan. Results were fruitless for the moment: English, Dutch, and French traders must first clear the seas of pirates.

Despite the manifest limitations of their trading operations, the English were able to impress at least one Mogul with their potential power. The eminent historian Khafi Khan "had the misfortune of seeing the English of Bombay" while acting as go-between for Aurangzeb's Surat governor. Seeking convoy protection for an expensive shipment of

Mogul goods, the Moslem writer entered the British fort at Bombay and witnessed a formidable display of military power—a foreshadowing of things to come. "Every step I advanced," he recorded, "young men with sprouting beards, handsome and well clothed, with fine muskets in their hands, were visible on every side. . . . I saw some English children, handsome, and wearing pearls on the borders of their hats. . . . I found drawn up in ranks on both sides nearly 7,000 musketeers, dressed and accoutred as for a review."

Khafi Khan braved the peppery repartee of a high company official. Why, the Britisher bluntly wanted to know, did Moguls imprison English factors? Well, the guarded reply emerged from beneath Oriental euphuisms, British pirates seized the Moguls' pilgrim ships. "How do you know that this deed was the work of my men?" the company spokesman asked. Khafi Khan presented dubious evidence: personal acquaintances on one of the unfortunate vessels had informed him that the pirates "had the looks of Englishmen." This was greeted with loud laughter: "It is true they may have said so." Stressing the moral of recent history, an annoyed Khafi Khan wound up: "You must recall to mind that the hereditary kings of Bijapur and [Golconda] and the good-for-nothing [Shambhuji] have not escaped the hands of King Aurangzeb. Is the island of Bombay a sure refuge?" Moreover, weren't the British rebellious in coining their own rupees? The Englishman replied: "The coins of Hindustan are of short weight, and much debased; in the course of buying and selling them, great disputes arise. Consequently we have placed our own names on the coins, and have made them current in our own jurisdiction." In the end, Mogul India's historian felt "glad to escape."

Even a fanatically stubborn Aurangzeb knew what the upshot must be: he was as helpless at sea as every other Mogul emperor had been, and those twin exigencies of maritime pilgrimage and commerce once and for all demanded unconditional surrender to Europeans. Englishmen were in India to stay.

● ● ●

Meanwhile, the Marathas had revived in earnest. Now began the people's war—a war impossible to end because there was no central Maratha government or main army to overthrow. A Mogul general was captured and his camp looted; by autumn 1690, large Mogul forces had been diverted to the Madras Carnatic to fight there. By 1692 imperial troops were stalemated in the west; and in the east two more generals had been captured. Incessant Maratha partisan raids were making a mockery of cyclopean Mogul power.

By 1695 even the emperor had begun to realize what was happening. Nothing had been gained through the conquest of Bijapur and Golconda except the formal annexation of territories that still had to be digested. These Marathas were no longer mere bandits, but a catalytic, elusive enemy capable of rallying all the disaffected of the Mogul Empire. Mogul generals, harassed everywhere, made private deals with their Hindu opponents—after all, it was easier to accept bribes than to fight. In effect the authority of Mogul administration had given way, and the framework of an empire was sustained now only by the presence of a superannuated fanatic and his troops. Doggedly, Aurangzeb led his armies on an obsessive treadmill; endless moneys and men went into ridiculous ventures. Hill forts were wrested from Marathas, then recovered by Marathas, and then assaulted anew!

A near-demented specter tilted against Maratha windmills. On into and through his eighties, Aurangzeb would drag hordes of soldiers and camp followers through mud and across rivers, while transport animals died and food became scarcer and scarcer. Mogul officers became bored with this labor of Sisyphus, but the least dissent provoked a storm of imperial wrath: they were cowards, they were effeminate lovers of ease. In any case the old generals and nobles had all died, replaced by coteries of cowed myrmidons who hardly dared speak the unspeakable truth. Anarchy engulfed the Mogul camp: sniping Maratha guerrillas lay in wait wherever the emperor marched or halted.

By Manucci's estimate, warfare in the Deccan was now taking the toll of a hundred thousand men a year, not to mention a third of a million horses, elephants, camels, or oxen. Imperial tents were wrapped in a diurnal aura of flies and excrement. The Deccan had become a desert—no trees, no crops, only the bones of dead men. "The country," the Italian concluded, "was so entirely desolated and depopulated that neither fire nor light could be found in the course of a three or four days' journey." There was no longer any local revenue, and nothing remained to be looted. Between 1702 and 1704, drought and plague would kill an additional two million men and impel starving peasants to become bandits in the Maratha cause.

The Mogul Empire was bankrupt. There had been no breathing space between wars, and even a Spartan realm could not live by war alone. Customs, duties, rents, excise and Hindu poll taxes had all gone in support of troops; the accumulated treasures of Agra and Delhi, by Aurangzeb's orders, had been squandered on the Deccan. Mogul salaries, both military and civil, fell in arrears. Everyone was sick of war; Aurangzeb would now write to Prince Muazzam, "Owing to my marching through deserts and forests, my officers long for my death." When even the grand vizier suggested returning to Delhi after the conquest of Bijapur and Golconda, Aurangzeb snarled, "So long as a single breath remains in this mortal life, there is no release from labor." A whole generation of Moguls had been born and brought up in pitched Deccan tents without ever knowing Delhi or Agra! Such Rajputs as were left with the imperial army complained that their race would die out. One desperate grandee even offered the emperor a hundred thousand rupees in return for a transfer back to Delhi. Northern India participated in this chain reaction of despair; as resources poured off to support slaughter in the Deccan, weak northern governors succumbed to local uprisings. Indian arts and intellectual pursuits had been on the decline for decades, and inevitable moral disintegration of aristocracy and commoner alike began.

At the center of all this was Aurangzeb, no catalyst but disaster incarnate: the strange personal motivations of a single dictator-emperor had determined the fate of a hundred million people. But what secret impelled him? Did his alienation of Rajputs and Hindus stem from hatred of Dara Shikoh, and hence of liberalism in general? Had he killed his own brothers, not from the imperative to rule, but from an overwhelming need to destroy all rivals for his father's love? That love had never been given him; and he in turn had denied it to his own sons. Once at Kandahar, Shah Jahan had dismissed Aurangzeb as an incompetent soldier, and even the shah of Persia had accused him of not being a man. "You style yourself a world conqueror," the shah mocked in a cheeky letter sent after the War of Succession, "while you have only conquered your father [and murdered] your brothers. . . . You have failed in every undertaking requiring manliness." Could the reason for insensate aggression as Aurangzeb's be absurdly simple—a fiendish campaign to prove himself?

A curious, almost photographic description of Aurangzeb as an old man in the midst of his Deccan campaigns was now to be recorded by a Neapolitan traveler who gained an audience with him at the Mogul camp in Galgala. Giovanni Gemelli Careri, an Italian doctor of civil law and a well-heeled vagabond, had embarked on a five-year tour of the world in the course of which he would not only be received by Aurangzeb, but by the shah of Persia and by the emperor of China as well—few travelers of the period could boast as much. In March 1695 Careri arrived at the Mogul camp, which he later described as being, staggeringly, thirty miles in circumference. He estimated that there were half a million people in these military environs, including 60,000 cavalry, 100,000 infantry, "sutlers, merchants and artificers," 50,000 camels, 3,000 elephants, and 250 bazaars. The royal compound alone was "three miles in compass" and defended by palisades, ditches, and 500 pieces of light ordnance. Clearly, the emperor still moved in style.

On Monday, March 21, 1695, Careri won his private audience. Passing through regal precincts, the Italian glimpsed tents full of kettledrums and trumpets and gold Mogul ensigns. The walls of Aurangzeb's imperial apartments were

hung with silk and gold cloth. Informally receiving his Neapolitan guest, the seventy-seven-year-old emperor sat "after
the country manner, on rich carpets and pillars [pillows] embroidered with gold." Obeisance was followed by polite
kingly inquiry: Aurangzeb wanted to know which kingdom
of Europe Careri came from; where he had been, where he
was going to, and if he would serve Mogul India. Careri answered that he was a Neapolitan; he had been traveling for
two years, through Egypt, Turkey, and Persia, and had now
come out of curiosity to see "the greatest monarch in Asia."
It would indeed be a great honor to serve Aurangzeb; unfortunately, for business reasons, he had to return home after
seeing China.

After the interview, Careri withdrew to the great open
tent used for public durbar—a riot of red cloth and taffetas,
silver poles, and a giltwood throne with silver footstool.
Leaning on a forked staff and preceded by the usual swarm
of nobles and attendants, Aurangzeb entered. The Mogul
emperor was wearing a white robe tied under the right arm,
with silk sash and Indian dagger; his gold-webbed turban
flashed the green of an enormous emerald surrounded by
four smaller gems. Careri wrote:

His shoes were after the Moorish fashion, and his legs
naked without hose. Two servants put away the flies
with long white horsetails; another at the same time
keeping off the sun with a green umbrella. He was of a
low stature—slender, stooping with age, and with a
large nose. The whiteness of his round beard was more
visible on his olive-colored skin. When he was seated
they gave him his scimitar and buckler, which he laid
down on his left side within the throne. Then he made a
sign with his hand for those that had business to draw
near; who being come up, two standing secretaries took
their petitions and delivered them to the King while telling him the contents. I admired seeing him endorse
them with his own hand, without spectacles, and by his
cheerful smiling countenance he seemed to be pleased
with the employment.

The picture of Aurangzeb which Careri drew could only be a mask: the great Mogul emperor, simple in his dignity and pleasantly occupied with tasks of state. The real Aurangzeb was a man of fantastic and fanatic energy, a combination of Napoleon and a secretary-desk. But even then, the emperor's fate was closing in on him. "The art of reigning," Aurangzeb had told Prince Muazzam, "is so delicate that a king must be jealous of his own shadow." It was the shadow which would now overwhelm him.

In 1705, a decade after Careri's visit, Aurangzeb wound up his last military campaign with the siege of an insignificant fortress called Wagingera not far from Bijapur city. Three months of very minor struggle had exposed the fatal weakness of the Mogul Empire, and even with all the resources of India at his command Aurangzeb could not boast total victory. This was not even a Maratha stronghold, only a locus of Hindu opposition by people of low-caste status united with a few Maratha families inside the fort. Thousands of Mogul troops found themselves hard pressed by guerrilla tactics. The outcome was dubious: Wagingera fell but its chieftain escaped.

Aurangzeb was eighty-seven years old. It was time to return to Delhi, but he would never reach the capital. Retreating northward, the emperor and his great Mogul army were followed by a horde of at least fifty thousand exultant Marathas who persistently attacked stragglers, cut off supply convoys, and even threatened to invade the Mogul camp itself. No longer disparate bands of hit-and-run marauders, they were now the real rulers of the Deccan. A year before, Manucci had observed that "[Maratha] leaders and their followers operate in these days with much confidence, because they have cowed Mogul commanders and inspired them with fear. . . . They are equipped and travel about just like [Aurangzeb's] armies. . . . They move like conquerors, showing no fear of any Mogul troops."

By April 1705 Aurangzeb reached the quiet green village of Devapur, on the Krishna River in Bijapur province. Here, used up and worn out, he fell violently ill. Despair seized the

entire Mogul camp. For better or worse, a battered scare-
crow was all that held the Mogul Empire together; even Marathas respected Aurangzeb enough not to raid the royal
camp precincts. If he died, the symbol of autocratic power
that controlled all India would die with him, and the Deccan
army could expect rapid extinction at the hands of its enemies. The entire camp speculated on Aurangzeb's death: either there would be a war of succession among his sons, or
else some ambitious general would seize power.

But, after ten or twelve days, the invalid began to rally.
Recuperating in body but not in spirit, he brooded over a
stark quatrain written by a certain Sheikh Ganja:

> When you have counted eighty years and more,
> Time and Fate will batter in the door;
> But if you should survive to be a hundred,
> Your life will already be death to the very core.

Bravely, a noble in attendance at the sickbed commented,
"Peace be on Your Majesty! Sheikh Ganja composed those
verses merely as an introduction to the following couplet:

> 'In such a state lift up your heart: remember
> The thought of God lights up a dying ember.' "

Aurangzeb was fascinated. He commanded that the couplet
be recited over and over, and then had it written down for
him. By morning he was out of bed; "the people got back
their lives."

In October 1705 the camp at Devapur broke up. With
the emperor traveling northward in a palanquin by easy
stages and stops, the imperial retinue reached journey's end
on January 20, 1706. This was the city of Ahmadnagar, about
120 miles due east of Bombay, where Aurangzeb would
spend a final agonized year.

He was utterly alone now, a phantom surrounded by
phantoms. Court newsletters afforded glimpses of an obsessed Methuselah commanding the screen of his bedroom

tent to be drawn aside so that he might inspect officers and cavalry. All the old nobles were dead, and the young were liars and afraid. If the emperor's puritan austerity had made him a living saint for orthodox Moslems, it had also made him unapproachable. He was not a man, he was a dreadnaught impervious to human weakness, and therefore beyond human sympathy. Men might respect or fear him, but who could love him? Love was a product of humanity, of compassion, of everything incompatible with power. He had chosen power absolutely, and this was the end of power: control of the world meant alienation from the world. He had for companionship only a spinster daughter, Zinat-un-Nissa, and his last wife Udipuri Mahal—reputedly a Georgian slave girl appropriated from Dara Shikoh's ménage, a once-beautiful animal now given to freakish bouts of drunkenness which Aurangzeb saw fit to forgive.

Death was everywhere. Aurangzeb's daughter-in-law Jani Begum had died in Gujarat in March 1705; his rebel son Akbar had died in Persia in 1704; his poetess daughter Zeb-un-Nissa had died in Samugarh prison in 1702. Now, in 1706, came news of the death of Gauharara Begum—the last of all his brothers and sisters. It was Gauharara's birth years ago, in 1631 at Burhanpur, which had killed their mother and caused the immortal Taj Mahal to be built. Aurangzeb kept repeating, "She and I alone were left among Shah Jahan's children." Other deaths filled the year 1706: his daughter Mihr-un-Nissa and her husband Izad Bakhsh (Murad's son); and even his grandchildren were dying.

Behind him, in the Deccan, anarchy and desolation wove a black winding sheet. Maratha armies had to be driven away at staggering cost; Gujarat flared up in arms; even Aurangabad stood threatened, and Bijapur languished under shaky Mogul control.

Since it could not be long before the emperor died, his sons were already jockeying for position. Prince Muazzam had been assigned to the north, but by Aurangzeb's reluctant permission the ambitiously hot-tempered Azam arrived at Ahmadnagar on March 25, 1706. Backed by men and money from his province of Gujarat, he considered himself the heir apparent: Muazzam had been stationed far away; and though young Kam Bakhsh was kept protectively close to Aurangzeb, he could easily be disposed of at the proper time. As soon as the old man died, Azam planned to seize treasure and troops in the imperial camp—he had already won backing from the Prime Minister and other nobles. Aware of the danger to Kam Bakhsh's life, Aurangzeb appointed a strong bodyguard for his youngest son. Azam would have to wait.

Early in February 1707, the emperor again had a bad spell but recovered for the second time. Still, it could not be for long. Ever more fearful for the safety of Kam Bakhsh, Aurangzeb assigned him the governorship of Bijapur and sent him off with a large army: at least the sparrow would be separated from its brother hawk and given a fighting chance. Aurangzeb wept. Embracing the "Benjamin of his old age," he watched Kam Bakhsh ride out of sight while the imperial band played at the gate of the royal compound. A few days later, Azam was dispatched to Malwa as governor. Send them all away, isolate them from one another, stave off disaster. Cunningly, Azam proceeded slowly—a man almost ninety years old had to die soon, and it seemed wise for an eager pallbearer not to be too far away.

Four days after the last prince had gone, Aurangzeb was smitten with fever. For three days more, five times a day, he continued with public prayer and even held court. A new couplet of time and doom filled his dragging hours:

> A moment, a minute, a breath can deform,
> And the shape of the world assumes a new form.

Seeing death stamped on his face, the nobles now presented a petition on the advice of astrologers: would the emperor give away an elephant and a valuable diamond to ward off evil influences? True to character, Aurangzeb wrote down his reply: elephant offerings were the practice of Hindus and star-worshippers; let the court send four thousand rupees (the price of the beast) to the chief *qazi* for distribution to the poor. Grimly practical, he added in a postscript: "Carry this creature of dust quickly to the first burial place, and consign him to the earth without any useless coffin."

On the threshold of death, Aurangzeb dictated two final agonized communiqués to Azam and to Kam Bakhsh. For sheer horror, these last letters are unmatched in the annals of power stripped bare to itself.

To Azam, he wrote:

> I came alone and I go as a stranger. I do not know who I am, nor what I have been doing. The instant which has passed in power has left only sorrow behind it. I have not been the guardian and protector of the empire. Life, so valuable, has been squandered in vain. God was in my heart, but I could not see Him. Life is transient, the past is gone and there is no hope for the future. . . . The whole imperial army is like me: bewildered, perturbed, separated from God, quaking like quicksilver. . . . I fear for my salvation, I fear my punishment. I believe in God's bounty and mercy, but I am afraid because of what I have done. . . .

Kam Bakhsh received an even more anguished cry: "Soul of my soul. . . . I am going alone. I grieve for your helplessness, but what is the use? Every torment I have inflicted, every sin I have committed, every wrong I have done, I carry the consequences with me. Strange, that I came into the world with nothing, and now I am going away with this stupendous caravan of sin! . . . Wherever I look, I see only God . . . I have sinned terribly, and I do not know what punishment awaits me. . . ."

Full as they are with an avalanche of sin and visions of damnation, the letters also entreat brotherly love: "The guardianship of a people is the trust by God committed to my sons. . . . Be cautious that none of the faithful are slain." Later, a purported last testament found under Aurangzeb's pillow would reiterate a desire he had already made known in his lifetime: the partitioning of India among his sons to

·avoid "fighting between armies and . . . slaughter of man-kind." In another version of the will, four rupees and two annas (the price of the caps he had sewn in his lifetime) were to be spent on his death shroud, while the 305 rupees he had earned copying the Koran would be distributed to fakirs. He asked to be buried bareheaded—the coffin covered with white cloth, but no canopy and no musicians. One segment of the testament reflected Aurangzeb's bitterness to the end: "Never trust your sons, nor treat them during your lifetime in an intimate manner; because, if Emperor Shah Jahan had not [favored] Dara Shikoh, his affairs would not have come to such a sorry pass. Ever keep in view the saying, 'The word of a king is barren.' "

After morning prayers on Friday, February 21, 1707, Aurangzeb returned to his sleeping quarters and fell into a trance of compulsive prayer. The World Conqueror was dying, caught between the moment and eternity. His stiffen-ing fingers continued with the mechanical click of rosary beads; automatically, the creed issued from moribund lips. At eight o'clock the rosary fell silent as God answered his prayers: he had always wanted to die on a Friday, the Mos-lem sabbath.

While holy men prepared for royal funeral rites, the corpse lay in its bedroom apartment pending the arrival of Prince Azam, who was only fifty or sixty miles away. Surpris-ingly, Azam went through extreme paroxysms of grief, and at final obsequies on the Monday could barely manage to help carry his father's coffin through the Hall of Justice before breaking down so completely that the procession had to go on without him.

Aurangzeb's grave had been completed during his life-time. It was set within the venerated precincts of a Moslem saint's own tomb, in the village of Khuldabad about twenty miles outside Aurangabad. No Taj Mahal, no imposing mau-soleum had been ordered by the stern puritan. A red stone slab—three yards long, two yards wide, and a few inches deep—marks the spot, and is hollowed out in the shape of an amulet-receptacle for earth and herbs. The *sabza,* a small shrub sacred to Moslems, grows nearby; though once, in botanical mockery, the no-less-sacred Tulsi-tree of the Hindus found root room in a brickwork crevice and flourished there. The slab itself bears no inscription whatsoever: tabula rasa for the last of the Great Moguls.

Epilogue

WITH THE FOREBODING of some Old Testament prophet, Niccolo Manucci terminated his prodigious memoirs: "At the time the king [Aurangzeb] died a whirlwind arose, so fierce that it blew down all the tents standing in the encampment. Many persons and animals were killed, being choked by the dust. The day became so dark that men ran into each other, unable to see where they were going; villages were destroyed, and trees overthrown." The eighteenth century, India's period of "The Great Anarchy," had begun.

In a ruthless historical denouement, the Mogul Empire —and with it all of Hindustan—rapidly fell into chaos. Aurangzeb's three sons fought their own war of succession, in which Azam and Kam Bakhsh were killed; the brief rule of the victor, Muazzam, was followed by a ghoulish spate of puppet kings and assassinations. One tenacious sybarite, Mohammed Shah, somehow managed to outwit intriguers for three decades; but his reign virtually ended when renascent Persia's warrior-genius, Nadir Shah, sacked Delhi in 1739 and dragged away the Peacock Throne itself. Whole provinces seceded: Sikhs, Rajputs, and Jats continued in open revolt.

Just fifty-three years after Aurangzeb's death, imperial Delhi was a phantom capital. Even the Mogul emperor, threatened by an inimical vizier, had fled—the beginning of a long period of wandering. Great suburban tracts were desolate; and now, in the eerie twilight of the Mogul Empire, any traveler approaching the capital had to make his way through miles of forsaken gardens and tombs.

A no less brutal fate attended Aurangzeb's nemesis, the Hindu Marathas, who wound up their phase of expansion and tribute-taking with an outright bid for empire. But they no longer inspired a disaffected India. On January 6, 1761— alone and without allies—several hundred thousand Marathas confronted an agglomerate Afghan host on the Plains of Panipat where Babur had begun the Mogul Dynasty. The Marathas' dreams of dominion were washed away in a river of blood that flowed outward from the battlefield. Yet, ironically, a triumphant Moslem coalition dispersed as unpaid soldiers returned home, leaving an absent Mogul emperor with a crown that nobody wanted.

India had exhausted herself. She was ready for a new conqueror: the East India Company. Almost concomitant with the Maratha-Afghan struggle, the English now significantly defeated the French at Pondicherry and eliminated their last foreign rival in India. Robert Clive (once a £5-a-week clerk) had already seized on the "black hole" incident of Calcutta as a valid excuse to move northward and crush Bengal's independent ruler at the crucial battle of Plassey. Clive promptly nominated his own stooge as nawab of Bengal, received a gigantic booty of £234,100, and established a neat precedent. The British found no difficulty settling mercantile armies in the provinces of Indian "rulers" whose protectors they had effectively become.

Clive, later censured by England's parliament for Indian "malpractice," would slit his throat in November 1774; but Wellesley the Younger would defeat the remaining Marathas (and also Napoleon at Waterloo), while his aggressive older brother as governor-general of India would give up all pretext of nonintervention in Indian politics. Wellesley the Elder would be recalled in 1805 by annoyed company directors, but by then only Sind and the Punjab remained outside British control. "The imperialist answer, represented by Lord Wellesley, was an unhesitating 'March.' "

It was all, of course, inevitable: Europe was technically superior to India and Asia. The British raj had arrived with all its faults and virtues, and with a complex history of its own.

Shah Alam, the wandering Mogul emperor, had meanwhile ended his spasmodic feuds with the English and become their pensioner once and for all. But on his final return to Delhi, an Afghan madman picked out his eyes with a dagger. Lord Lake rescued the eyeless old man in September 1803. The emperor's domains had by now shrunk to so little that a wicked popular couplet summed them up:

> From Delhi to Palam*
> Is the realm of Shah Alam.

If anything, the poem overstated the extent of effective imperial authority.

By British courtesy, the Mogul title and pension would continue for another half century. But it was a court of chilling poverty into which Reginald Heber, the Bishop of Calcutta, was received by the Mogul emperor at Delhi in 1824. From the moment he entered the Red Fort, Heber found himself besieged by "a . . . swarm of miserable beggars, the wives and children of the stable servants." The palace complex was "full of . . . broken palanquins . . . and the throne so covered with pigeons' dung that its ornaments were hardly discernible." Somberly the Bishop contemplated Shah Jahan's inscription—"If there be paradise on earth, it is this, it is this, it is this"—and concluded that all was indeed vanity of vanities: "The spider hangs her tapestry in the palace of the Caesars."

Bishop Heber might well have been appalled by more than architectural ruin. The Mogul emperor's favorite son

---

* The locus of Delhi's modern airport.

was somewhere in the palace, drinking himself to death with Hoffmann's cherry brandy and commenting cynically, "This . . . is really the only liquor that you Englishmen have worth drinking."

"The King's realm and the Company's rule" both came to grief with the "Mutiny" of 1857. Abruptly, a doddering octogenarian monarch found himself triumphantly hoisted on the shoulders of revolutionary sepoys as the symbol of an ill-defined cause—India's "last convulsive protest against the coming of the West." When British troops at last recaptured Delhi from the insurgents, the aged emperor and three princes sought refuge at Humayun's tomb. Within a few days they were hunted down by Lieutenant Hodson, who forced the king's capitulation and murdered the princes. In the midst of inflamed emotions, Hodson received congratulations, though later British accounts would condemn him as a "tiger unsubdued by any feelings of human compassion."

Dara Shikoh's headless body had been paraded through Delhi's streets by Aurangzeb; and now the bodies of the last legitimate Mogul princes lay on display in front of Delhi's police station.

In the aftermath, the huge East India Company was liquidated in favor of direct British sovereignty. The English subjected the Mogul emperor to a forty-two day trial, during which he fainted once. He was found guilty of all charges and exiled to Rangoon; he died there in 1862, at the age of eighty-seven. The monumental House of Timur, begun in 1526, died with him.

Two alien masters, the Moguls and the British—bluntly linked by power—had imposed their successive integrations on a heterogeneous subcontinent, initiating the historical ironies that led to Gandhi, to Indian nationalism, to Nehru. Westerners departed. But for many millions of Moslems there could be no departure: India was as much a country for them as it was for the Hindus they had conquered centuries before. The rub was that Moslems and Hindus, despite a common fusion of culture and thought, were still poles apart;

for religion and other complex reasons, their joint freedom led to the agonies of partition and renewed strife. The enduring nightmare of Aurangzeb's schismatic intent had triumphed over Akbar's and Dara Shikoh's dreams of unity.

● ● ●

In Delhi there is a cynosure of reverence for Moslems—the tomb of Nizam uddin Aulia, a Sufi saint from Akbar's time. On this holy man's anniversary day, vending stalls outside his sacred shrine are always heaped with flowers, bottles of rose water, and piles of sugared anise seeds. Great crowds swarm about: beggars hope for alms, bearded patriarchs with goatskin bags scatter water to keep down the dust, naked children sleep in the arcades, and a few men can be seen taking purifying baths in a tank of glaucous green water.

Numerous dead cluster in the shadow of the Sufi saint. One of them is important, but sadly neglected. A small filigreed partition surrounds the almost anonymous resting place of a woman who by rights should be buried in the Taj Mahal—Jahanara Begum, daughter of Shah Jahan. A few blades of determined grass struggle up through the parched earth set within a hollow of her marble coffin, inlaid with a single Kashmir lily in green jade. Persian verses attributed to the princess herself adorn the headstone:

Let green grass only conceal my grave:
Grass is the best covering of the grave of the meek.

From Jahanara's burial site it is only a short distance to Emperor Humayun's mausoleum, where kite vultures wheel endlessly over the quadripartite garden. All about the vast tomb, a series of Saracen arches encompass sixty-four vaults; each contains a member of Mogul royalty, though many inscriptions have long since been effaced and most of the dead are unknown to us.

On the upper surrounding platform, a particular sarcophagus is presumed to be Dara Shikoh's—because of a trisection symbolic of dismemberment. Dara seemingly keeps watch over several children's stone coffins adjacent to his.

Epilogue

Across the modern city, a third grave is inextricably linked to those of the royal brother and sister. Along the Chandni Chowk, through which Dara was paraded as a prisoner, Shah Jahan's Friday Mosque suddenly looms up, with a bustling "thieves' market" at the bottom of its steps. Just beyond the market, on an equally busy cross street, stands a crude shrine with red-painted wooden canopy. A little oil lamp burns perpetually in a niche over the cloth-covered tomb of Sarmad—naked martyr, homosexual, and saint. Astonishingly, a thousand pilgrims still flock in remembrance every Thursday, to pay their homage and strew marigolds. The caretaker (like all his predecessors) bears the family name of Sarmadi, and proudly offers booklets of the Sufi poet's *Rubaiyat* in Hindustani.

A hundred and twenty miles south from this modest trinity of the dead, Akbar's deserted capital of Fatehpur Sikri mocks the harem laughter of a vanished imperial summer. Presiding over a regal conglomerate of sandstone palaces is his towering Victory Gate, surmounted by warrior-hat cupolas from some dim Asian past and inscribed with the epitaph: "The world is a bridge, pass over it, but do not build upon it. He who hopes for an hour may hope for eternity. The world is but an hour; spend it in devotion, the rest is unseen."

Yet in Agra, at the Taj Mahal, even the unseen becomes manifest. Allah views the marvel with a celestial eye; eastward by rail, travelers look back, as Ernest Havell did at the turn of the century, to see a masterwork "in all its glory . . . floating like the mirage of some wondrous fairy palace." Who could lend a moment's credence to those ridiculous assertions that the mausoleum had been designed by Europeans? Legend insists on laurels for the Italian Veroneo or Austin of Bordeaux, simply because they had been jewelers and goldsmiths to the Mogul court. Obscure Eastern builders—the mythical Ustad Isa and others—are credited with impossible genius.

But the obvious architect of the Taj was Shah Jahan. The Moguls alone could have created such a vision; or rather, the Moguls and India, the only real home they ever had. Mumtaz Mahal's tomb expanded to become their final refuge: Shah Jahan's anguish, Dara Shikoh's doomed spiritual quest, Aurangzeb's obsession, and Jahanara's haunting unfulfillment—all found shelter, all were embraced in the perfect architectonics of death.

ACKNOWLEDGMENTS

Five years were spent in researching and writing this book; many individuals and institutions in America, England, and India unstintingly lent their help.

Chief khan of all was my mentor and editor, Steven M. L. Aronson, whose intuition, judgment, and awesome perseverance contributed beyond measure to the final form and content. Without him, a massive prose elephant would have lost its way—sans mahout and howdah.

In India, Shanti Kumar acted as an enthusiastic liaison to key people; O. P. Sharma, assistant director of the Government of India Tourist Office in Delhi, led me on a detective hunt for important but obscure sites; S. D. Balooja, escutcheon agent, freely rendered service; R. D. Garg, of Jaipur, shared with me his intimate knowledge of Rajasthan; and the Maharajah of Udaipur's comptroller proved to be an inexhaustible source of stories about Rajput family history. In New York City, Ibrahim Chowdry of the Pakistani Consulate, and Arun K. Guha and the staff of the Indian Government Tourist Office located relevant material and information. Dr. Roland Figueredo added to my understanding of Gujarat; Benoy Paul and Shyam Parikh discussed important aspects of Indian history with me at an early stage in the project.

I relied on the kindness of the staff of the New York Public Library—Walter J. Zervas was of special assistance. The Rare Book Division kindly permitted me to consult a number of volumes, including the *Travels* of Robert Coverte and the original Mandelslo-Olearius opus. Sanford Kadet unearthed important material at Columbia University's Butler Library. The staff of a number of world museums and libraries—notably those mentioned by name in the illustration credits—provided photographs of Mogul minia-tures. Both Pauline Harrold of the India Office, London, and Enid Furlonger of London and New York, helped a great deal with pic-ture research.

Dr. William F. Morton, of York College of the City University of New York, made a number of pertinent suggestions, as did Paul J. Sanfaçon of the American Museum of Natural History.

Friends who gave moral or concrete support include: Richard Astor, John Proctor Cole, Natalie de Gendron, Carl Preston Green, Dorothy Heller, Edward Maisel, C. Eugene Oakes, Edward Sager, Albert Scarpetti, Cecile Weissman, and my brothers Harry and David Hansen. I owe particular gratitude to my literary agent, Blanche C. Gregory. Ever encouraging, Henrietta Buckmaster be-came nothing less than indispensable in the final stages of en-deavor.

Special thanks must go to Robert S. Howseman, who created the maps with scrupulous attention to detail and with full aware-ness of their dramatic potential in highlighting the text; he also composed the end-paper genealogy.

For my many trips to India over a decade and more, I am indebted to Thos. Cook & Son, under whose aegis I have often lec-tured; of particular help were the late Eugene C. Kelley, and Har-old R. Weston.

My obligation to Mogul scholars past and present is limitless —especially to the late Sir Jadunath Sarkar. Dr. Fazl Mahmud Asiri in West Pakistan and Dr. Bikrama Jit Hasrat in the Punjab both generously allowed me to make extensive use of their work. Of course, neither they nor anyone else can be held responsible for er-rors of fact or for my interpretation of Mogul history.

Lastly, the dedication to my English mother is appropriate in more than the personal sense: at her knee I learned to count in Hindustani.

New York City

Waldemar Hansen

NOTES

These notes primarily identify sources of quotations, here and there clarifying some odd or disputed point of Mogul history. For reasons of space, I have not documented generally accepted historical facts or background details. With regard to quotations from Mogul sources in particular, zealous seekers of chapter and verse might notice that I do not always conform word for word with existing translations: these are sometimes stilted, or larded with Persian metaphors and obscure Islamic references. In the interests of both lucidity and style I have not hesitated to make minor alterations—never, I hope, distorting fact or essential meaning.

Abbreviations

A	Aurangzeb
Adab	Aurangzeb's letters in the collection *Adab-i-Alamgiri*
AN	Mohammed Kazim's *Alamgir-nama*
BB	Beveridge translation of *Babur-nama*
DS	Dara Shikoh
Dutch	Broecke's *Contemporary Chronicle of Mughal India*
E & D	Elliot and Dowson
JRB	Jahangir's *Memoirs*, Rogers-Beveridge translation
JED	Jahangir's *Memoirs*, Elliot and Dowson translation
KK	Khafi Khan's *Muntakhab-ul-Lubab*
Kambu	Mohammed Salih Kambu's *Amal-i-Salih*
MA	Mohammed Saki Mustaidd Khan's *Maasir-i-Alamgiri*
MKED	Mutamad Khan, *Iqbal-nama*, in Elliot and Dowson
PN	*Padshah-nama*, followed by the particular historian's name (Lahori, Kazwini, or Waris)
SAB	Jadunath Sarkar's five-volume biography of Aurangzeb
SJ	Shah Jahan

Notes

Authors whose names are not abbreviated are cited by surname (or in the case of Moguls, by first name and appellative) as listed in the "Bibliography." In the case of authors of multiple works, a foreshortened title is included. Mogul anthologies of correspondence are indicated by key first words of their titles, also geared to the "Bibliography." Boldface italic type identifies quotations; boldface roman type refers to general aspects of text.

Prologue: The Taj Mahal
PAGE

2 ***Born in 1592:*** The date is in error, though often cited by modern writers. Mogul sources state that Mumtaz Mahal was born on April 5, 1593 [14 Rajab 1001 H.] and died at the age of thirty-eight (Kambu and PN Lahori; discussed in Chaghtai *Taj,* p. 40, and Chowdhuri, pp. 373–74).

3 ***Conceived by titans and finished by jewellers:*** A popular misquoting of Heber, p. 50: "These Pathans [Moguls] built like giants and finished their work like jewellers."

4 **Twin Taj intended by Shah Jahan:** Tavernier, p. 110.

5 **Gandhi saw Taj as symbol of oppression:** "The Taj Mahal made him think of all the forced labor that had gone into its building. His aesthetic sense only broke free in the presence of impersonal splendours." (Geoffrey Ashe. *Gandhi.* New York: Stein and Day, 1968, p. 258.)

5 ***Die tomorrow to have such a tomb over me:*** Sleeman, vol. II, p. 32.

Chapter 1: The Standard of Revolt

11 ***So long as there is one breath:*** PN Kazwini, cited in Saksena, p. 7.

12 ***He was not my friend:*** JED, vol. VI, p. 288. ***No one left but you:*** Dutch, p. 30.

13 ***You have paid no attention:*** ibid., p. 31.

15 ***The time will come:*** Roe, vol. II, p. 283.

16 ***Spear-high:*** BB, vol. II, p. 445.

16 **Strong homosexual tendencies:** Babur's random pejoratives about "catamites" and "pederasty" were aimed at over-indulgent khans. His own amorous indifference to women is an acknowledged fact. Married at sixteen, he admits that he only went to his wife once a month, im-

pelled by his mother's "driving and driving, dunnings and worryings." The wife had a rival:

> I maddened and afflicted myself for a boy in the camp-bazar, his very name, Baburi, fitting in. Up till then I had had no inclination for any-one, indeed of love and desire, either by hear-say or experience, I had not heard, I had not talked. At that time I composed Persian couplets, one or two at a time. From time to time, Baburi used to come to my presence but out of modesty and bashfulness, I could never look straight at him; how then could I make conversation and recital? In my joy and agitation I could not thank him [for coming]; how was it possible for me to reproach him with going away? . . . In that frothing up of desire and passion . . . I used to wander, bare-head, bare-foot, through street and lane, orchard and vineyard. . . . My wandering was not of my choice, not I decided whether to go or stay. (BB, vol. II, p. 120.)

17 *Ducks' eggs after hens:* Woodruff, p. 37.
18 **Son of a bitch:** Abul Fazl, *Akbar-nama*, E & D, vol. VI, p. 27.
20 **Hundred million subjects under Mogul hegemony:** Thapar (p. 27) estimates the population of seventeenth-century India at 110 million.
23 **Eighteen thousand Mogul rupees the equivalent of $60 thousand:** Sarkar (*Anecdotes*, p. 157) observes: "A rupee of that time was worth 2s. 3d., but its purchasing power was about seven times that of today." Sarkar wrote this in 1912, when two shillings and three pence represented approximately fifty cents; simple arithmetic thus brings the effective value of the Mogul rupee close to $3.50. By these figures, the Taj Mahal could not be duplicated today for less than $140 million!
26 **Prefer an old Hell to a new Heaven:** Foster, *Early Travels*, p. ix, quoting anonymous Englishman of 1675.
27 **Barbaric pearl and gold:**
Or where the gorgeous East with richest hand
Showers on her kings barbaric pearl and gold.
                    Milton, *Paradise Lost* ii, 3–4.
27 **Plundered all sweetmeat shops:** Dutch, p. 36.
28 **King personally went to see:** *ibid.*, pp. 38–39. Cf. Mundy, 104.

28 *For the sake of good government:* JRB, vol. I, p. 69.

Chapter 2: Henna and Intrigue

33 *Not so commendable:* Mundy, p. 216. *Dauncing wenches: ibid.,* p. 216. *Selling their maidenheads: ibid.,* p. 216.

38 **Mumtaz Mahal's alleged anti-Christian pique:** Manucci makes her responsible for Shah Jahan's harsh punishment of the Portuguese at Hughli in 1632. During his phase of rebellion against Jahangir, the prince "passed near to [Hughli], in the territory of [Bengal], a village that the King Jahangir had given to the Portuguese. . . . Some Portuguese sallied forth and seized two beloved female slaves of the Princess Taigemahal [Mumtaz Mahal]. . . . This lady sent word to them that it would be better to help a prince then seeking refuge in flight than to attempt to rob him. Therefore she urgently prayed them to send her the two slave girls, but the Portuguese paid no heed to her request, an act which cost them dear." (Manucci, vol. I, pp. 175–176.) In the upshot, "Finding himself undisputed King of Hindustan, Shah Jahan was compelled to make war against the Portuguese of [Hughli], for this was demanded by Taigemahal, from whom the Portuguese had carried off two slave girls." (*Ibid.,* vol. I, p. 182.)

Manucci is being somewhat fanciful: Mumtaz Mahal was dead at the time of Shah Jahan's reprisals, which were dictated by other factors than his own earlier humiliation at Portuguese hands—the Portuguese at Hughli had become oppressive and high-handed. PN Lahori (E & D, vol. VII, pp. 31–35) gives an account of the massacre at Hughli.

38 *Black plaited hair, soft black eyes:* Chowdhuri, p. 375, citing Maharani Suniti Devi's book, *The Beautiful Mogul Princesses.*

39 *Played their parts admirably well:* Chowdhuri, p. 376.

39–40 **Alcohol and opium quotations:** JED, vol. VI, pp. 342–343.

40 *Saint Paul's 'what does it matter?':* Cf. Romans 2:26–29.

41 **Enjoyed the sight of lions clawing out human guts:** Hawkins narrative, in Foster's *Early Travels,* pp. 110–111.

41   *Because they shivered in winter:* JRB, vol. I, pp. xii. *Entirely my own idea: ibid.,* vol. I, p. xii.

41   **Jahangir eats pork and refuses Ramadan fast:** Manucci, vol. I, p. 153. **Shoots wooden arrows at physician:** *ibid.,* vol. I, pp. 156–157.

41–42   *Dropped his head . . . defiled himself: ibid.,* vol. I, p. 156.

42   *Every evening went by water:* Dutch, p. 42.

43   *That vicious woman: ibid.,* p. 90.

43   **Nur Jahan possible murderess:** Sleeman, vol. II, p. 47.

44   *Two watches of the night had passed:* JRB, vol. I, p. 282.

Chapter 3: A Foothold in the Realm

46   *If he were unseen one day:* Roe, vol. I, p. 108.

46   *He drinketh five cupfuls:* Hawkins narrative, in Foster's *Early Travels,* p. 116.

46   *Liberty of traffic and privileges: ibid.,* p. 61. **Letter addressed to Akbar by mistake:** Woodruff, p. 27.

46   *King of Fishermen:* Hawkins, in Foster's *Early Travels,* p. 74.

47   **The English musicians, virginals, and cornet:** Foster, *Early Travels,* editor's text pp. 189–190, and Withington narrative pp. 200–204.

49   *Necessary correction:* In his introduction to Manucci, vol. I, p. lxx, William Irvine contrasts European observers of the Mogul scene with "official" chroniclers: "Oriental history, as tricked out by venal and fulsome pens, tells us little or nothing of the real character of the actors in it, or of the inner cause of events; and a writer like Manucci supplies us with the necessary corrective of lifelike, if at times sordid detail."

50   *The trade will in time be profitable:* Roe, vol. I, p. 120.

50   *They fear the Portugal: ibid.,* vol. I, p. 120.

51   *We bought ill-velvet of the Chinese: ibid.,* vol. I, p. 67.

51–52   *When I entered within the first rail: ibid.,* vol. I, p. 108.

52   *Sent a gentleman for my commission: ibid.,* vol. I, p. 109.

52   *In an outward room: ibid.,* vol. I, p. 127. *If his greatness: ibid.,* vol. I, p. 127.

52   *His pride may teach Lucifer: ibid.,* vol. II, p. 424.

52   *He asked if I had any more: ibid.,* vol. II, p. 299.

Notes

53 *He begged everything:* ibid., vol. I, pp. 161–162.

53 *Too poor of value:* Roe letter, January 1, 1616, to William Keeling of the East India Company; cited Roe, vol. I, p. xvii fn.

53 *At one side in a window:* Roe, vol. II, p. 321.

53 **A knife and a bottle of** *strong waters:* ibid., vol. I, p. 142 fn. Roe's financial accounts mention the "strong waters."

54–55 **Quotations for evening scene at Jahangir's court:** *ibid.,* vol. I, pp. 146–147.

55 *A lady that with her plate:* ibid., vol. I, p. 145. *Some whores did sing and dance:* ibid., vol. I, p. 145. *Pictures of the King of England, the Queen:* ibid., vol. I, p. 143.

56 **Bengal the province of disgrace:** In the course of the seventeenth century, Bengal came to be regarded by Mogul officers as sheer punishment; or, in Aurangzeb's later words, "a hell well stocked with bread." SAB, vol. IV, p. 51.

58 *Outcried cannons:* Roe, vol. II, p. 321.

58–59 *The watch was set:* ibid., vol. II, pp. 328–329.

60 *Would make his proud heart know:* ibid., vol. II, pp. 339–340.

60 *Articles of treaty on equal terms; A meaner agent:* Roe letter, November 24, 1616, to East India Company; cited Roe, vol. II, pp. 342–352.

61–62 *My son hath taken your goods:* Roe, vol. II, p. 381.

62 *Am I a king?:* ibid., vol. II, p. 382.

63 **Quotations re Jahangir's birthday weighing:** *ibid.,* vol. II, pp. 412–413.

63 *Sat to be worshipped:* ibid., vol. II, p. 424.

64 *Held it fit to give freely:* ibid., vol. II, p. 458.

65 *The King sat in a hat all night:* ibid., vol. II, p. 459.

65 *You can never expect to trade here:* Roe letter, February 14, 1617–[18], to East India Company; cited Roe, vol. II, p. 469.

65 **Englishman's** *protector and procurator:* Roe, vol. II, p. 458.

65 *Infinitely weary of this employment:* ibid., vol. I, p. xl.

66 *Let your royal heart:* Jahangir letter to King James, text from a copy in Roe's handwriting (British Museum additional ms. 4155), cited Roe, vol. II, pp. 557–558.

Chapter 4: Kings Rise from Coffins

67   *Astrologers have written:* JED, vol. VI, p. 363.

67   *Also through effects of this phenomenon:* MKED, vol. VI, p. 407.

68   *The world is a bridge:* Translations in Festing, p. 228; Mazumdar, p. 181.

70   *I gave up all doctoring:* JED, vol. VI, p. 381.

70   *A kind and dutiful son: ibid.,* vol. VI, p. 381.

70   *A letter from Khurram: ibid.,* vol. VI, p. 383.

70   *Cruelly murdered all other princes of the blood:* Letter from Agra factors to Surat council; text in Foster, *English Factors,* p. 240.

70   *By Sultan Khurram he was made away:* Mundy, p. 105. For identical gossip, cf. Tavernier, pp. 335–336 and Della Valle, p. 58.

70–71   *In an hour of drunkenness; From the ditch of prison:* Kambu, cited in Saksena, p. 35.

71–72   **Khusrau murder quotes:** Dutch, p. 54.

72   *In his mother's garden: ibid.,* p. 54.

72   *We ought not believe:* Elphinstone, p. 492.

73   *He was at times insensible:* JED, vol. VI, p. 382.

75   *By order of Jahangir, gold has splendors:* MKED, vol. VI, p. 405. In Jahangir's reign, Mogul coins were struck with Persian couplets inscribed on them. Court poets manipulated euphuistic verses extolling emperor or empress, or the glories of the reign: "To Shah Jahangir belongs the whirligig of Time"; "So long as the heavens revolve, current be/In the name of Shah Jahangir the money of Lahore," etc. Mogul emperors also used images on their coins: Akbar began with falcons, ducks, crowned archers, and a woman drawing back her veil! In the sixth year of his reign, Jahangir daringly put his own image on gold coins (see Fig. 37). The verso of coins inevitably depicted the Mogul lion with the sun behind it. (Cf. Lane-Poole, *Coins,* pp. lxviii–lxxxv.)

76   *I was not at all pleased:* JED, vol. VI, p. 383.

76   **Fn. minor historical fragment:** *Intikhab-i-Jahangir-Shahi,*

written by an anonymous associate of Jahangir's; excerpt in E & D, vol. VI, pp. 451–452.

77 *Ungrateful* **offspring;** *torn away veil of decency; ill-starred son; I issued an order:* JED, vol. VI, pp. 384–385.

80 **Accompanied by five thousand Rajputs:** Though Moslem, Mahabat Khan nonetheless commanded the fidelity of Hindu Rajput troops, and became so associated with Rajputs that some authorities wrongly speak of him as a converted Hindu. His biographical details are in *Maasir-ul-Umara*, E & D, vol. VIII, p. 190.

80 *He addressed me by name:* MKED, vol. VI, p. 421.

80 *This presumption beyond all rule: ibid.,* vol. VI, p. 421.

81 *So distracted he neither knew what he said nor did: ibid.,* vol. VI, p. 424.

81 *This has all happened through your neglect: ibid.,* vol. VI, p. 424.

82 *Reign of a hundred days:* Srivastava, p. 289.

83 **Cauterized in** *five places:* MKED, vol. VI, p. 429. *Fox's disease: ibid.,* vol. VI, p. 435.

84 *Did not believe them: ibid.,* vol. VI, pp. 435–436.

84 **Shahriyar called** *fit for nothing: ibid.,* vol. VI, p. 438; also PN Lahori, E & D, vol. VII, p. 5.

85 *Were all sent out of the world:* MKED, vol. VI, p. 438.

86 **Manucci begins needlework:** Manucci, vol. I, pp. 174–175.

86 *Leave to carry her husband's body:* Mundy, p. 213.

86 *Shah Jahan raised himself:* Tavernier, p. 339.

86 **Fn. re Dawar Bakhsh's fate:** Manucci (vol. I, p. 175) claims that he escaped to Persia. Elphinstone (p. 503) cites Olearius (see Mandelslo in "Bibliography") to the effect that Holstein ambassadors saw the fugitive Dawar in Persia. *I had an opportunity of conversing with him:* Tavernier, p. 339.

88 **Nur Jahan's other masterwork:** Some authorities attribute Jahangir's tomb to Shah Jahan. But it was six years after Jahangir's death before Shah Jahan even visited Lahore, and work on the tomb must certainly have begun earlier. It seems likely that construction was entrusted to Nur Jahan by way of "occupational therapy." Jaffar (p. 206) refers to the "mausoleum which she had raised over the grave of her husband."

Notes

88–89 *Died Nur Jahan Begum:* PN Lahori, E & D, vol. VII, pp. 69–70.

Chapter 5: Intermezzo at Agra

94 *Lance head among women:* Sarkar, *Anecdotes*, pp. 151–156, offers a biographical sketch of Sati derived from PN Lahori.

94 *The model and despair of the age:* Qanungo, p. 5.

95 *Road to discovery:* The quotation is from William James.

95–96 *Doubtless bought by the courtiers:* Lane-Poole, *Aurangzeb*, p. 65.

97 *There are few courts one knows so well:* Martin, vol. I, p. 82.

99 *Nothing to write about that princess:* Manucci, vol. I, pp. 218–219. In fact, Manucci mistakenly attributes Gauharara's loyalty to Shuja, whereas she was actually Murad's partisan.

99 *Very clever, capable of dissimulation: ibid.*, vol. I, p. 230.

99 *The eldest, whom her father loved: ibid.*, vol. I, p. 208.

101 *Stretches out his hand: ibid.*, vol. II, p. 329.

103 **The Peacock Throne:** Description in PN Lahori, E & D, vol. VII, pp. 45–46; also Mathur, p. 25, and Saksena, p. 246.

Chapter 6: A Voice from the Womb

106 **Khan Jahan Lodi fled:** He and his sons were later speared to death in an impasse effected by Mogul troops. PN Lahori, E & D, vol. VII, pp. 20–22.

107 *A great famine begun:* Mundy, p. 39. *Half burnt up and almost void: ibid.*, p. 40. *To any that would take them: ibid.*, p. 42. *Miserable and undecent spectacle: ibid.*, p. 44.

108 *As we passed their towns: ibid.*, pp. 45–46. *It being all sent to Brampore: ibid.*, p. 56.

108 *Life was offered for a loaf:* PN Lahori, E & D, vol. VII, p. 24.

109 *Under the direction of the Emperor: ibid.*, p. 25.

109 *Delhi is distant:* "*Dilli dur ast,*" an old Deccan proverb.

109 *The Dauphiné of the Mogul Empire:* Lane-Poole, *Medieval*, p. 344.

110 **Stubborn but unsubstantiated accounts:** The unborn child's cry from the womb is mentioned in the obscure Persian autobiography of Kasim Ali Afridi (1771–1827) as well as in a ms. treatise on the Taj; both cited by Sarkar, *Studies,* pp. 28–29.

110 *On his life and soul;* **Deathbed requests for mausoleum and no rival wife's children:** Sarkar, *Anecdotes,* p. 147, citing Afridi.

111 **"O Man" chapter of the Koran:** Koran 76. Pickthall (pp. 423–424) offers a translation.

113 *May Paradise be the abode; Sorrow:* cited Chaghtai, *Taj,* p. 46. In these and other chronogram poems, letters of the Persian alphabet had a numerical value assigned to them; words in a particular verse added up to a given Moslem date. For an interesting discussion of the device, see E & D, vol. VIII, pp. 441–444.

114 *Stopped and hindered by elephants:* Mundy, p. 188.

115 *The face of the earth was covered: ibid.,* p. 192. *Made a most gallant show: ibid.,* p. 192. *All alone: ibid.,* 194. *Half a flight shot behind: ibid.,* p. 194.

Chapter 7: The Smell of Apples

116 *Great Mogul's daughters never suffered: ibid.,* pp. 202–203.

118 *Passionately beloved by her father:* Bernier, p. 11.

118 *Adorn the pages of history:* Beale, p. 190.

118 *Perverted imagination:* Saksena, p. 341.

118 *Accusation . . . not disproved:* Smith, *Indian Antiquary,* pp. 240–244.

119–120 **Apple anecdote quotations:** Manucci, vol. I, p. 173.

121 *Methought it made a brave show:* Mundy, p. 202.

122 **Crude Saint-Catherine's wheels:** These were called *charkhi.* Coverte (p. 60) offers a description of royal elephants "clad in cloth of gold and silver, with drums, fifes and trumpets, whereof some fight one with another, wounding one another very deadly, and cannot be parted but with Rackets of wilde fier, made round like hoopes, and so run the same in their faces."

123 *If the fight ended fatally:* Hamiduddin, cited in Sarkar, *Anecdotes,* pp. 34–35; also SAB, vol. I, pp. 9–12.

125–126 **The banquet in Asaf Khan's house:** quotations from Manrique, vol. II, pp. 213–220.

127 *A slave named Arif:* PN Lahori; cited SAB, vol. I, p. 75.

127 *One of the many Englishmen:* Festing, p. 289.

127 *Under the influence of ill-advised companions:* PN Lahori, E & D, vol. VII, p. 69.

128 *If His Majesty wishes:* Adab, cited SAB, vol. I, p. 77.

128 *O rose, if thou wilt listen:* cited Moinul Haq, p. 37. Mogul source not given.

129 **Underground room incident and aftermath:** quotations from Hamiduddin; cited in Sarkar, *Anecdotes*, pp. 36–37.

Chapter 8: Martial Airs

134 *No other quality than enjoying life:* Adab; cited Qanungo, p. 226.

134 *Whole days and nights dancing:* Bernier, p. 8.

134 *Small things like the Chameli flower:* cited SAB, vol. II, p. 129 and Qanungo, pp. 226–227. Mogul source not given.

135 *Peace, plenty, and pestilence:* Qanungo, p. 226.

136 *Gallant swashbuckler:* Lane-Poole, *Aurangzeb*, p. 24.

136 *Reckless valor of a soldier:* SAB, vol. I, p. 319.

136 *Frank and open as the day:* Lane-Poole, *Aurangzeb*, pp. 24–25.

136 **Critics challenge Murad's reputed candor:** notably Ghauri, pp. 44–45.

138 *Motiveless malignancy:* Samuel Taylor Coleridge, in *Lectures on Shakespeare and Milton (1811–1812)*, speaks of "Iago's soliloquy, the motive-hunting of a motiveless malignity—how awful it is!"

138 *First and last a stern puritan:* Lane-Poole, *Aurangzeb*, p. 64.

138 **Hot head and cold heart:** Keene, p. 220.

140 *To fight with such a man:* Bakhtawar Khan, *Mirat-i-Alam*, E & D, vol. VII, p. 161; also PN Lahori; both cited SAB, vol. I, p. 107.

142 *I greatly wonder:* Adab; cited SAB, vol. I, p. 163, and Ghauri, p. 51.

143 *I am not going to give up:* ibid.; cited SAB, vol. I, p. 163 and Ghauri, p. 51.

143 *Had I considered you competent:* ibid.; cited SAB, vol. I, p. 164 and Ghauri, p. 51.

143 *Whosoever has a particle of sense:* ibid.; cited SAB, vol. I, p. 164.

Notes

Chapter 9: The Mystic Prince

145 *Unworthy and frivolous; Heretical tenets:* AN, cited E & D, vol. VII, pp. 178–179.

145 *Not deficient in good qualities:* Bernier, p. 6. *Entertained too exalted an opinion: ibid.,* pp. 6–7.

146 *A Gentile with Gentiles: ibid.,* p. 7.

146 **Manucci plagiarizes Bernier:** In scarcely altered phraseology, Manucci's Dara Shikoh is also "polite in conversation, ready and gracious of speech, of most extraordinary liberality, kindly and compassionate, but over-confident in his opinion of himself, considering himself competent in all things and having no need of advisers. He despised those who gave him counsel. Thus it was that his dearest friends never ventured to inform him of the most essential things." (Manucci, vol. I, p. 221.)

148 **Dara supervised royal library and workshop for Mogul miniatures:** Bassagli, p. 109.

148 *The cultural history of the reign:* Qanungo, p. 387.

148 *The knowledge of God:* DS, *Sakinat;* cited in Hasrat, p. 77.

148–149 *I was suffering from a chronic disease: ibid.;* in Hasrat, p. 77.

149 *On this occasion I went barefoot: ibid.;* in Hasrat, pp. 77–78.

149 *Placing his right nipple upon mine: ibid.;* in Hasrat, p. 78.

149–150 *Face turned toward the Kaaba: ibid.;* in Hasrat, pp. 78–79.

150 *Voice of Silence:* "The 'internal sound' known in the mystic phraseology as the Voice of Silence." (Hasrat, p. 73.)

150 *Heard a sound like silvery bells:* Hasrat, p. 74 and James, p. 374.

150 *I hear the constant chime:* Hafiz verse, quoted Hasrat, p. 74.

150 **Impossible to** *describe or write:* DS, *Sakinat;* in Hasrat, p. 79.

150 *Exoteric Islam has ceased to influence . . . this fakir:* DS to Shah Dilruba, the fourth of six letters in *Faiyyaz;* cited Hasrat, p. 65, and Qanungo, p. 119.

151 *I love my brother:* Jahanara Begum in *Sahabiya,* a tract on the life of Mulla Shah; cited Hasrat, p. 84.

151   The *perfect gnostic: ibid.*; cited Hasrat, p. 84.

151   *Of all the descendants of Timur: ibid.*; cited Hasrat, p. 84.

151   *O Mulla Shah, thou hast illumined: ibid.*; cited Hasrat, p. 85.

151   *Every moment I hold my own self:* DS, *Sakinat*; cited Hasrat, p. 87.

151   *The light of the universal: ibid.*; cited Hasrat, p. 87.

152   *In the city where a mullah:* Poem from DS, *Diwan*; cited Hasrat, p. 139.

152   *Kingship is easy: ibid.*; cited Hasrat, p. 142.

152   *Hands soiled with gold: ibid.*; cited Hasrat, p. 142.

152   *Drive egoism away from you: ibid.*; cited Hasrat, p. 143.

152   *With what name should one call Truth?:* Last half of a quatrain by DS; cited Hasrat, p. 145.

152   *To revile me:* Last three lines of a quatrain by DS; cited Hasrat, p. 146.

152   *Thou verily art God:* Part of second line of a quatrain by DS; cited Hasrat, p. 148.

152   *I am the truth:* Stace, p. 202, citing Hallaj.

153   *There is nothing inside this coat except Allah:* Stace, p. 202, citing unidentified Sufi mystic.

153   *More rash than . . . Meister Eckhart:* Stace, p. 201.

153   *Indeed there is a book:* Koran 56:78–80. The translation here is from Hasrat (p. 8); other versions in Pickthall, p. 386, and Qanungo, p. 148.

154   *Constantly in the society of Brahmans:* AN, E & D, vol. VII, p. 179.

154   *Given up the prayers: ibid.*; E & D, vol. VII, p. 179.

154   *Inordinately conceited:* Lane-Poole, *Aurangzeb*, pp. 22–23.

154–155   *Central figure of a great religious and literary movement:* Qanungo, p. x. *Unique among Moslem thinkers of India: ibid.*, p. 401.

155   *Holiday parades:* Ghauri, p. 33.

155   *Odious light of an incompetent braggart:* SAB, vol. I, p. 300.

155–156   *Witnessing the affairs of Persia:* Rashid Khan, *Latif*; cited Qanungo, p. 36. *So too am I: ibid.*; cited Qanungo, p. 36.

156   Not *required to stay at Kandahar: ibid.*; cited Qanungo, p. 37.

156 *Praying mullahs:* Qanungo, p. 42.
156–157 *A wonderful thing which could fly:* Rashid Khan; cited Qanungo, p. 55.
157 *Brilliant display of fireworks:* Qanungo, p. 62.
157 *We are servants:* Rashid Khan; cited Qanungo, p. 71. *Why don't you speak plainly?:* ibid.; cited Qanungo, p. 71.
157–158 DS-Jai Singh dialogue: *ibid.*; cited Qanungo, pp. 72–75.
158 *Whether you agree:* ibid.; cited Qanungo, p. 75.
159 *World-illuminating countenance:* ibid.; cited Qanungo, p. 75.

Chapter 10: Puritan in Armor
162 *Instead of going to bed:* Careri; in Sen, p. 236. *Had not broke wind:* ibid.; in Sen, p. 236. *Never after looked her in the face:* ibid.; in Sen, p. 236.
164 *In my folly: Kalimat*; cited SAB, vol. I, p. 172. *By Allah's grace I demolished it:* ibjd.; cited SAB, vol. I, p. 171.
165 *Improper words with reference to the Prophet:* A to Prime Minister Sadullah Khan, *Adab*; cited SAB, vol. I, pp. 173–174.
165 *Proper for all Moslems; The road of complaint:* ibid.; cited SAB, vol. I, p. 174.
166 *If Your Majesty wishes:* A to SJ, *Adab*; cited SAB, vol. I, p. 184. *Unworthy of a Moslem:* SJ to A, ibid.; cited SAB vol. I, p. 186. *Never . . . acted unjustly:* A to SJ, ibid.; cited SAB, vol. I, p. 187.
167 *Little wonder:* A to SJ, ibid.; cited SAB, vol. I, pp. 204–205.
170 *By the sackful:* Bernier, p. 17. **35½ pounds at more exact estimate:** Thevenot, in Sen, pp. 144–145, says "twenty *mans*" or "four hundred and eight pounds of Hollands weight," calculated in Bernier, p. 17 fn. at 35½ pounds.
171 *I think that Mir Jumla: Adab*; cited SAB, vol. I, p. 224.
171–172 *Fumes of arrogance:* Inayat Khan, *Shah Jahan-nama*, E & D, vol. VII, p. 110.
172 *If you can manage it: Adab*; cited SAB, vol. I, p. 230.
173 *Such a money-yielding country; I hope Your Majesty:* ibid.; cited SAB, vol. I, p. 236.
174 *Qutb-ul-Mulk is now craving:* ibid.; cited SAB, vol. I, p. 238 fn.

Notes

174–175 *Three letters written by Your Highness:* DS to Abdullah Qutb Shah, *Golconda Letters*; quoted Qanungo, pp. 189–190.

176 *Settle the affair of Bijapur:* PN Waris, also *Adab*; both cited SAB, vol. I, p. 262.

Chapter 11: Paradise on Earth

180 *If there be paradise:* The Persian inscription runs: *"Gar Fiardaus bar rue zamin ast, Hamin ast, Hamin ast, wa Hamin ast"* (Mathur, p. 15).

181 *The dome . . . leaked:* Cited in Vats, p. 5.

182 *There is already about her tomb:* Mundy, p. 212.

182–183 *I witnessed the commencement:* Tavernier, p. 110.

183 **Manrique re Taj:** All quotes from Manrique, vol. II, pp. 171–173.

185 **His Majesty said, 'My child':** Faiyyaz; quoted Qanungo, pp. 174–175.

186 *The particular kindness and love: Jaipur Records*; quoted Qanungo, p. 172.

186–187 *Painful colic; When your time of death; From this transitory sphere:* Inayat Khan, *Shah Jahan-nama,* E & D, vol. VII, p. 118.

187 *No doubt the Crown Prince: Adab*; cited Qanungo, p. 178.

188 *So he who in his youth:* Dryden, *Aureng-Zebe,* Act II, lines 86–87.

189 *Mendicants called out:* Manucci, vol. I, pp. 186–187.

189 *For the greater satisfaction: ibid.,* vol. I, p. 188.

189 *The world is a bridge:* See note for p. 68.

191 *The Emperor was attacked:* Kambu, E & D, vol. VII, p. 128. Cf. KK, E & D, vol. VII, pp. 213–214.

191 *The Mogul was seized with a disorder:* Bernier, p. 24.

191 *Desperately amorous of a Moorish young woman:* Careri, in Sen, p. 222. Sen observes in his notes (p. 368) that this is a "fantastic story," but cites "similar scandals" recorded by Manucci, Bernier, Manrique, Mundy, and Tavernier.

191 *I was then in the service of Prince Dara. Shah Jahan . . . took different stimulating drugs:* Manucci, vol. I, p. 231. Same gossip repeated by Tavernier, p. 325.

Notes

Chapter 12: Reign or Die

198 **Crown or coffin:** Jaffar, p. 256; Manucci, vol. I, p. 232, makes this "throne or tomb," and claims it was a proverb current among princes laying claim to the crown.

199 *This confusion lasted . . . three days:* Manucci, vol. I, p. 232. Cf. Bernier, p. 25.

199 **Fn.** *Manucci's readiness to see poison:* William Irvine, Manucci, vol. I, p. lxxii.

200 *Wrote in haste to the princes:* Manucci, vol. I, p. 232. *Let it be known to your worship: ibid.,* vol. I, p. 232.

200 **Raushanara Begum "guarding" Aurangzeb's interests:** AN, cited SAB, vol. I, p. 314; Qanungo, p. 219; SAB, vol. III, p. 66; Bernier, pp. 14, 65; Manucci, vol. I, p. 230.

202 *If the enemy attacks only one of us: Inayet-nama;* cited Saksena, p. 325.

202 *Delay in correspondence . . . is improper; As the exchange of news:* Jami-ul-Insha, cited Saksena, p. 325.

202 *I understand that the influence of the enemy: Inayet-nama;* cited Saksena, p. 325.

203 *I am ready to advance:* Faiyyaz; cited SAB, vol. I, p. 328.

203 **Against** *idolatry and infidelity;* **by** *God and the Prophet:* The pact is given in *Adab;* cited SAB, vol. I, pp. 335–337.

203 *On a carpet:* Tavernier, p. 327.

203–204 *Dara tended and nursed his father:* Kambu; cited SAB, vol. I, p. 305 and Qanungo, p. 222.

204 *In everything, at all times: ibid.;* cited SAB, vol. I, p. 306 and Qanungo, p. 223.

Chapter 13: An Invasion of Cobras

210 *Covered the field:* Manucci, vol. I, p. 219. *The wickedness of the empire: ibid.,* vol. I, p. 219.

212 *Commanded by Portuguese: ibid.,* vol. I, p. 232.

213 *His Majesty desires . . . the severed head:* Jaipur Records; cited Qanungo, p. 230.

213 *Great victory: ibid.;* cited Qanungo, p. 231.

213 *Inaccessible to man and mosquito:* Qanungo, p. 235.

215 **Shuja wine-soused:** KK, in E & D, vol. VII, p. 215.

215 **Dara's Sanskrit incantation:** *"Satchidanand,"* a vedantic formula meaning being-consciousness-bliss (Zimmer, p. 425).

215 *Within the last hundred years: Jaipur Records*; cited Qanungo, p. 238.

216 *None intimated any such thing: ibid.*; cited Qanungo, p.
238.

216 *Looked like a musician:* Manucci, vol. I, p. 217.

216 *To retreat and save himself:* vol. I, p. 236.

216 *Too prudent to lay his hands on a prince:* Bernier, p. 35.

219 *Dragged* into his presence: SAB, vol. I, p. 321.

219 *If a man plans treason:* KK, cited SAB, vol. I, p. 321. *In
spite of all my favors: ibid.*; cited SAB, vol. I, p. 322.

220 *To wait for true news: Adab*; cited SAB, vol. I, p. 333.

221 *The design of acquiring the throne: ibid.*; cited SAB, vol. I,
p. 335.

221 *Uproot the bramble: ibid.*; cited SAB, vol. I, pp. 335–336.

221 *Whereas my brother has joined me: ibid.*; cited SAB, vol.
I, pp. 335–336.

223 *I have no friend but you: ibid.*; cited SAB, vol. I, pp. 345–
346.

223. *You have not written to me for such a long time: ibid.*;
cited SAB, vol. I, p. 347.

223 **Copy of the Taj Mahal:** This is the "bastard" Taj, the
Bibi-ka-Maqbara, completed in 1679 at Aurangzeb's
command (with construction entrusted to his son,
Azam). Mogul architecture had by then deteriorated so
rapidly that the new tomb proved worse than mediocre:
in the words of Fergusson, it "narrowly escapes vulgarity
and bad taste." (Fergusson, vol. II, p. 312 ff.)

224–225 *After a year's hard campaigning: Adab*; cited SAB, vol I,
p. 357.

225 *Friend, God assist you: ibid.*; cited SAB, vol. I, p. 358.

225 *Now is the time to display your devotion: ibid.*; cited SAB,
vol. I, p. 361.

225–226 **Staged scene between Aurangzeb and Mir Jumla:** Bernier, pp. 28–30.

226 *Aurangzeb is winning over nobles:* Aqil Khan, *Zafar-
nama*; cited SAB, vol. I, p. 370.

Chapter 14: The Crystal Tower

230 *I must carry out the Emperor's orders:* cited SAB, vol. II,
p. 3, with multiple Mogul sources—AN, Aqil, Isardas,

Masum. Cf. KK in E & D, vol. VII, p. 218, who claims that Jaswant sent A an "impertinent answer."

230 *No power to show audacity: ibid.*, vol. II, p. 3, same sources.

231 *Inconsistent with manliness:* Isardas; cited SAB, vol. II, p. 9.

232 *Ditches of water on all four sides: Faiyyaz*; cited in SAB, vol. II, p. 10, fn.

232 *Thirty thousand horse and many infantry: Adab*; cited SAB, vol. II, p. 11.

233 *Dyed crimson with blood:* AN; cited SAB, vol. II, p. 16.

234 *Surgeons' fee for his wounded followers:* AN and KK; both cited SAB, vol. II, p. 24.

234 *The man is covered with infamy:* Bernier, pp. 40–41.

235 *The Emperor has recovered: Faiyyaz* and Kambu; both cited SAB, vol. II, p. 73. Saksena (p. 329) gives a slightly different version of this letter, translated from *Jami-ul-Insha.*

235–236 *Shah Jahan has lost all real power: Faiyyaz* and Kambu; both cited SAB, vol. II, pp. 73–74.

236 *Ever caused vexation to me; In order to ruin my army: Jami-ul-Insha*, cited Saksena, p. 329. This may actually not be a separate letter to SJ, since it closely parallels A's reply to Jahanara. Anthologies of Mogul correspondence often include variant texts of the same correspondence; and Mogul historians (Kambu and others) offer their own synopses as well.

236 *I had a passionate desire to see the world:* Manucci, vol. I, p. 5.

237 *I vaulted lightly onto my horse: ibid.*, vol. I, p. 91.

237 *At the end of this conversation Dara asked me: ibid.*, vol. I, p. 94.

237–238 *Thereupon [Dara] arrested these two nobles: ibid.*, vol. I, p. 245.

238 *O God! Thy will be done: ibid.*, vol. I, p. 251. For verisimilitude, Manucci even puts it in Persian—*"Ya Allah! teri raza!"*

238 *But this day our own arms: ibid.*, vol. I, p. 251.

239 *More than one hundred thousand horsemen: ibid.*, vol. I, p. 254.

239 *Butchers, barbers, blacksmiths: ibid.*, vol. I, p. 255.

Notes

239–240 *He was much afraid that Dara: ibid.*, vol. I, pp. 254–255.
240 *Struck him on the breast:* KK, in E & D, vol. VII, p. 220.
242 *We began the march; Prince Dara amidst his squadron:* Manucci, vol. I, pp. 256–257.
242 *Appeared afar off after three days: ibid.*, vol. I, p. 257.

Chapter 15: The Battle of Samugarh
244 *We made use of pond water: ibid.*, vol. I, p. 260.
244 *A cannon-shot distance:* KK, in E & D, vol. VII, p. 221.
244 *Dara wanted to commence action:* Manucci, vol. I, p. 260.
246 *Tomorrow will be a day:* Aqil Khan; cited SAB, vol. II, pp. 39–40.
246 *Necessary to take down my tent:* Manucci, vol. I, p. 262.
246–248 *Many horsemen leave our army: ibid.*, vol. I, p. 262. *As the light grew clearer: ibid.*, vol. I, p. 262. *Seated on a large elephant: ibid.*, vol. I, p. 262. *Of problematical value: ibid.*, vol. I, p. 263. *I answer . . . with confidence: ibid.*, vol. I, p. 263. *All this array: ibid.*, vol. I, p. 264.
248 *These immense armies:* Bernier, p. 55.
248–249 *I saw in this action:* Manucci, vol. I, p. 266.
249–251 *I was much amazed: ibid.*, vol. I, p. 264. *Fell into confusion: ibid.*, vol. I, p. 265. *So anxious to see: ibid.*, vol. I, p. 268.
251 *Make the elephant kneel:* KK, in E & D, vol. VII, p. 222.
251 *You dare to contest: ibid.*, in E & D, vol. VII, p. 222.
251 *Yellow as a field of saffron: ibid.*, in E & D, vol. VII, p. 223.
251 *Like ravening dogs:* Manucci, vol. I, p. 268.
251 *Great bravery:* KK, in E & D, vol. VII, p. 222.
252 *Great risk of being taken:* Manucci, vol. I, p. 267. *O God! In you is my trust!: ibid.*, vol. I, p. 267.
252–254 *This was as if he had quitted victory: ibid.*, vol. I, p. 269.
253 *Whatever is destined:* Masum; cited Qanungo, p. 260.
254 *What has reduced you:* Masum; cited SAB, vol. II, pp. 66–67.
254 *Crown or coffin:* See note for p. 198. In this particular instance, Manucci (vol I, p. 256) resorted to another Persian phrase for Dara: "To the humble, pardon; to the haughty, death (*Gharib mu'af, maghrur marg*).

[515]

255 *I cannot face Your Majesty:* Masum; cited Qanungo, p. 261, and SAB, vol. II, pp. 67–68.

255 *She expressed her deep grief:* Manucci, vol. I, p. 275.

255–256 *Seeing our total defeat: ibid.,* vol. I, pp. 275–276.

Chapter 16: A Game of Finesse

258 *Most faithful friend:* Manucci, vol. I, p. 270. Cf. Bernier, p. 56.

259–260 **Quotes re Manucci's attempt to leave Agra:** Manucci, vol. I, pp. 276–277.

260–261 **Quote re Dulera's fate:** *ibid.,* vol. I, p. 284.

261 *To play a game of finesse: ibid.,* vol. I, p. 278.

261 *See for himself . . . his father's love:* Kambu, AN, Aqil; cited SAB, vol. II, p. 76.

262 *Beyond letters and messages:* Same sources; cited SAB, vol. II, p. 76.

262 *Without a shadow of a doubt:* Manucci, vol. I, p. 278; Bernier, p. 61.

262–263 *Although already caught:* Manucci, vol. I, pp. 279–280.

264 *My son, my hero; Why should I complain:* SJ to A, *Adab;* cited in all its Persian floridity in SAB, vol. II, pp. 80–81.

264 *It is your own doing:* A to SJ, *ibid.;* cited SAB, vol. II, p. 81.

265 *Owing to certain occurrences:* A to SJ, *ibid.;* cited SAB, vol. II, p. 82.

265 *Few will believe:* Bernier, p. 63.

265 *Raushanara Begum was dispatched:* Manucci, vol. I, p. 282.

266 *Dara is an infidel:* Aqil Khan; cited SAB, vol. II, p. 84.

266–267 *Dara Shikoh! Stay in Delhi:* Aqil Khan; cited SAB, vol. II, p. 85. Cf. Bernier, p. 65, and Manucci, vol. I, pp. 282–283.

267 *Indisputable authority:* The authority was, of course, Raushanara Begum. Bernier, pp. 64–65.

267 *Aurangzeb started these stories:* Manucci, vol. I, pp. 283–284.

267 *Obedience was my passion: Adab;* cited Jaffar, p. 262. Cf. KK in E & D, vol. VII, pp. 252–253, for similar correspondence by Aurangzeb.

267–268 *I had no intention: Adab;* cited Jaffar, p. 262.

268 *Not my will, O Lord, but thy will:* Matthew 26:39; Mark 14:36; Luke 22:42.

Notes

Chapter 17: A Lover's Farewell

270   *Stupid and ignorant:* AN, in E & D, vol, VII, p. 228, fn.
      Simple-minded: KK, in E & D, vol. VII, p. 228.

270–271   *I have conferred the sovereignty:* Masum; cited Jaffar, p. 264.

272   *Beneath his dignity:* SAB, vol. II, p. 90.

272–273   *A great number of Dara's men:* Manucci, vol. I, p. 285.
      The tiger big with young: ibid., vol. I, p. 285. *There was nothing but music:* ibid., vol. I, p. 285. *Your Majesty is on his way to prison:* ibid., vol. I, p. 287. *With your feet you have come:* ibid., vol. I, p. 287.

274   *Drink in my presence:* SAB, vol. II, p. 93, Mogul source unidentified.

274   *An excellent stratagem:* AN; cited SAB, vol. II, p. 96.

274   *They buried him without a sound:* Manucci, vol. I, p. 289. *This was done so that if Murad . . . should wake:* ibid., vol. I, p. 289 (cf. Bernier, pp. 67–68).

275   *This is the word and oath:* Manucci, vol. I, p. 290.

275   *My brother's life is safe:* Masum and Isardas; cited SAB, vol. II, p. 95.

275   *Long live King Aurangzeb:* Manucci, vol. I, p. 291.

276   *It was very pitiful:* ibid., vol. I, pp. 291–292. *It was ordered that poppywater:* ibid., vol. I, p. 292.

276   *Not one redeeming quality:* Sleeman, vol. I, p. 340.

277   *With so many intricate walls:* Mundy, p. 61. *Having their meat let down:* ibid., p. 61.

278   *Caused the Prince's portrait:* Manucci, vol. I, p. 361.

278   *If he is resolved:* Kambu, in E & D, vol. VII, p. 132. *Alas and alas! on some pretext:* KK, in E & D, vol. VII, p. 267.

Chapter 18: Pursuit in the Punjab

283   **Had Jai Singh shown half as much zeal:** Qanungo, p. 240.

284   **Every viceroy and governor:** Manucci, I, p. 271.

284   **Jai Singh too prudent:** Bernier, p. 58.

286   **Furniture and articles:** Masum; cited SAB, vol. II, p. 223.

287   **The villagers assassinated:** Manucci, vol. I, p. 274.

289   **Ladies of spotless honor:** Masum; cited SAB, vol. II, p. 229.

289   **Divine grace:** Masum; cited SAB, vol. II, p. 230.

291–293   **Manucci seeks and finds Dara:** All quotations in Manucci, vol. I, pp. 292–295.

Notes

296 *To be or not to be at Lahore:* Masum; cited Qanungo, p. 267.

296 *I cannot resist Aurangzeb:* Masum; cited SAB, vol. II, p. 111.

297 *Attracted by his hoard of gold:* AN; cited SAB, vol. II, p. 114.

297–298 *Dara Shikoh is proceeding to Lahore:* KK, in E & D, vol. VII, p. 228.

298 *His reasons for refusing such counsel:* Bernier, p. 70.

298 *Better choose another road:* Manucci, vol I, p. 297.

298–301 *Expected Dara will make a stand:* AN; cited SAB, vol. II, p. 115.

299 *Owing to some business:* Manucci, vol. I, p. 297.

299–301 **All quotations re Multan and Bhakkar:** Manucci, vol. I, pp. 301–303.

Chapter 19: Enigma in Arakan

303 *As you had often begged the Emperor:* AN; cited SAB, vol. II, pp. 137–138.

304 *Aurangzeb has left no general:* Masum and AN; cited SAB, vol. II, p. 138.

307 *So great was the terror:* Manucci, vol. I, p. 304.

308 *Zeal urged him:* KK, in E & D, vol. VII, p. 233.

309–310 *Then came Rajah Jaswant:* Manucci, vol. I, p. 312.

310 *The behavior of Jaswant was such:* Dispatches of Jai Singh to A, Bibliothèque Nationale, Paris; cited Ghauri, p. 148 fn.

311 *This incident is a mercy:* AN; cited SAB, vol. II, p. 148.

311 *Trust in God and the escort:* AN; cited SAB, vol. II, p. 150.

312 *Even veterans of the Deccan:* Aqil; cited SAB, vol. II, p. 154.

312 *Agra resembled Brussels after Waterloo:* SAB, vol. II, p. 154.

315 *My noble brother:* The phrase is *Khan Bai.* AN and Masum describe Alawardi's attempted desertion; treated in SAB, vol. II, pp. 246–248.

318 *The very pick of the imperial army:* Masum; cited SAB, vol. II, p. 259.

318 *Letters and presents:* KK, in E & D, vol. VII, p. 249.

318 *Lost only one man—the Prince:* Aqil; cited SAB, vol. II, p. 262.

320 *Many persons have told me:* Bernier, p. 83.

321 *Until his mind was destroyed:* Manucci, vol. I, p. 321.

323 *These inhabitants inflicted: ibid.,* vol. I, p. 351.

323 *No one can enter with an army: ibid.,* vol. I, p. 352.

324 *Our king ordered us:* AN; cited SAB, vol. II, p. 283.

325 *Up to this time no one knows:* Kambu; cited SAB, vol. II, p. 286 and in E & D, vol. VII, p. 254 fn. KK also admitted that "no one ascertained what became of him" (KK, in E & D, vol. VII, p. 254).

325 *It was reported:* Bernier, pp. 112–113.

326 *He ordered all the factors:* Manucci, vol. I, p. 356.

327 *Slay those traitorous Moguls: ibid.,* vol. I, p. 355. *Pursued the poor prince: ibid.,* vol. I, p. 355.

327 *It is said that he reached the hills:* Bernier, p. 112. *Both assured me their master was dead: ibid.,* p. 113.

327 *There can be no certainty: Dagh Register, Casteel Batavia, anno 1661,* J. A. van der Chijs, The Hague, 1889, pp. 520–521.

328 *Pride is chastised in the end:* Manucci, vol. I, p. 357. *Ordered grand funeral obsequies: ibid.,* vol. I, p. 357.

Chapter 20: Cockcrow in Rajputana

330 *Was prevented from swallowing it:* Bernier, p. 78. *Two days elapsed: ibid.,* p. 78.

333 *Aurangzeb appointed Amir Khan:* KK, in E & D, vol. VII, p. 237.

336 *A sink of iniquity:* Manrique, vol. II, p. 240. *So given up to sensuality: ibid.,* vol. II, p. 242.

339 *A man of no military reputation:* Bernier, pp. 73–74.

341 *The Gibraltar of India:* The phrase is from Bishop Heber. Cited in *The Handbook of India* (October, 1966) p. 59; published by the Government of India, Ministry of Transport and Communication.

341–342 *A Rajput of the highest rank had turned false:* SAB, vol. II, pp. 170–171.

342–343 *What can be your inducement:* Bernier, p. 86.

343–344 *We have entrusted our honor:* DS to Maharana of Udaipur, *Udaipur Archives*; cited Qanungo, pp. 279–280.

344 *The custodian of the interests of the Hindu race:* A in a letter to Maharana Raj Singh, *ibid.;* cited Qanungo, p. 282.

344 *Willingly would he have conducted the army back:* Bernier, p. 87.

Chapter 21: Judas in Afghanistan

350–351 *The military genius, energy and forethought:* Qanungo, p. 295.

351 *I had now been three days with Dara:* Bernier, p. 89.

351 *The Red Sea from one end to the other: ibid.,* p. 1. *Catholics were not safe: ibid.,* p. 2.

352 *As Dara approached Ahmadabad:* Tavernier, p. 349.

353 *Dominion was over nations:* Dr. Johnson, cited by Constable in Bernier, pp. x–xi.

353–355 *The hopes of the vanquished:* Bernier, p. 89. *The day preceding: ibid.,* pp. 89–90. *Marched, nearly without intermission: ibid.,* pp. 90–91. *I made a grand display: ibid.,* p. 92.

356 *Nearly the whole of the men: ibid.,* p. 91.

357 *Turn a white man black:* The full Afghan proverb runs: "The sun of Sind will turn a white man black, and is sufficiently powerful to roast an egg." Postans' *Sindh,* pp. 357–358. *When appointing me to this service:* Dispatch of Jai Singh to A during pursuit of DS after battle of Ajmer, Bibliothèque Nationale ms.; cited SAB, vol. II, p. 202.

358 *Dara seemed doomed:* Bernier, p. 94.

360 *Heat of Dadhar greater than . . . any other place: ibid.,* p. 95, editor's fn.

361 *Evil; destroying angel; guest-murdering host:* notably KK, in E & D, vol. VII, p. 244.

361 *It is still doubtful:* Bernier, p. 96.

363 *Finish, finish:* Tavernier, p. 351.

364–366 **All quotes re resistance and capitulation of Bhakkar fortress:** Manucci, vol. I, pp. 333–336.

366 *The little sons of Sulaiman: ibid.,* vol. I, p. 343.

367 *Very anxious for us to enter his service: ibid.,* vol. I, p. 349. *My companions accepted but I did not: ibid.,* vol. I, p. 349.

368 *Desirous of being bled also: ibid.,* vol. II, p. 273.

368 *I had a son: ibid.,* vol. II, p. 279.

368 *It will be a history of Tom Thumb:* Governor Pitt to Mr. Wooley, Secretary at the India House (October 19, 1701)

in Yule's "Diary of Sir W. Hedges," pp. ii, cclxviii, n. 3. Cited by Irvine in Manucci, vol. I, p. lxx.

Chapter 22: Day of Vengeance

371   **Long Live the Caliph:** SAB, vol. II, p. 297.

371   **This coin has been stamped:** *ibid.,* vol. II, p. 297.

372   **To inform the public:** AN; cited SAB, vol. II, p. 211. Cf. KK, in E & D, vol. VII, p. 245, who says Dara's capture was made public "by beat of drum." Also Bernier (p. 98) states that both nobles and populace "still entertained doubts of Dara's captivity."

373–374   **The wretched prisoner:** Bernier, pp. 98–100.

374   **O Dara! When you were master:** Manucci, vol. I, p. 336.

375   **The richest street in the world:** Cited in *The Handbook of India* (October, 1966) p. 79; published by the Government of India, Ministry of Transport and Communications. The Chandni Chowk runs from Delhi's Red Fort to the Fatehpuri Mosque, and is still today the center for jewelers, goldsmiths, and silversmiths.

375   **For the good of church and state:** SAB, vol. II, p. 213. Bernier (p. 100) names the nobles who demanded Dara's death, and emphatically stresses Raushanara's "enmity against her hapless brother."

376   **Paradise is where no mullah:** DS, *Diwan;* cited Hasrat, p. 139.

376   **Mullahs sanctioned or signed a decree condemning Dara to death:** Ghauri, pp. 157–159, denies that the ulema were responsible for any written decree of Dara's death. The argument is hair-splitting: whether or not they actually signed a decree, the theologians certainly sanctioned Dara's death. Thus Aurangzeb's own official history, the *Alamgir-nama,* writes: "The pillars of the Canonical Law and Faith apprehended many kinds of disturbance from his [Dara's] life. So the Emperor, both out of necessity to protect the Faith and Holy Law, and also for reasons of State, considered it unlawful to allow Dara to remain alive any longer as a destroyer of the public peace." (AN; cited SAB, vol. II, p. 214.) KK, in E & D, vol. VII, p. 246, says Dara was put to death "under a *legal* opinion of the lawyers."

377   *A wretched parasite:* Bernier, p. 100. ***Dara ought not to live:*** *ibid.*, p. 101.

377   *My brother and my king:* Rukaat; cited Hasrat, p. 104.

377   *You usurped authority:* *ibid.*; cited Hasrat, p. 104.

378   *Disturbance bordered on rebellion:* KK, in E & D, vol. VII, p. 246.

378   *Malik Jiwan was summoned:* Bernier, p. 104.

379   *Mohammed kills me:* Manucci, vol. I, p. 338. ***If any faith in the world was true:*** *ibid.*, vol. I, p. 339. ***From whom I made inquiries:*** *ibid.*, vol. I, p. 339. ***Had a great desire to become a Christian:*** *ibid.*, vol. I, p. 339.

379   *You have been sent to kill us:* Masum; cited interrogative form by Qanungo, p. 316. Cf. Bernier, p. 102: "My dear son, these men are come to murder us!"

379   *At present we do not know anything:* Masum; cited Qanungo, pp. 316–317.

380   *Get up; Get up or we'll drag you away; Go and tell my brother:* *ibid.*, cited Qanungo, p. 317. ***We cannot be anybody's messenger:*** *ibid.*, cited SAB, vol. II, p. 218. ***Since I did not look at this infidel's face:*** *ibid.*, cited SAB, vol. II, p. 219 fn.

380   *Ah wretched one! Let this shocking sight:* Bernier, p. 103.

380   *The head laughed a long ha, ha:* Sloane ms. no. 811, fol. 14a; cited by Irvine in Manucci, vol. I, p. 340 fn.

381–382   *When Aurangzeb learned that the head of Dara:* Manucci, vol. I, pp. 340–342.

383   *A martyr to love:* Qanungo, p. 321.

Chapter 23: Fate of the Innocents

387   *The death of . . . brothers:* Manucci, vol. I, p. 358.

389   *If only he could compel the Rajah:* *ibid.*, vol. I, p. 359.

389–390   *Prince Sulaiman heard of this plot:* *ibid.*, vol. I, p. 359.

391–392   *Aurangzeb acted upon this occasion:* Bernier, pp. 105–106.

393–394   *Ordered his men to bring Jani Begum:* Manucci, vol. I, p. 342.

395   Those who *touched the sceptre:* Spear, *History*, p. 55.

Chapter 24: Naked to his Enemies

396–397   *We of the Occident:* Zimmer, p. 1.

397   *Departure to the forest:* *ibid.*, p. 157. ***Clothed in space:*** *ibid.*, p. 158.

398 *Very few . . . his equal:* Asiri, p. iii.

398 *Cult of the heart:* Yusuf Khan, *Dara Shikuh*, p. 167.

399 *If any of the infidels choose:* Badauni, *Muntakhab-ul-Ta-warikh* (An orthodox sunni's independent history of Akbar), vol. 2, p. 406. Tr. W. H. Lowe. Calcutta: 1924, Bibliotheca Indica, vol. 97.

399 *Fn. Persia, throughout the ages:* Fischel, p. 154.

400 *Sarmad the Jew; the Jewish mystic: ibid.,* p. 160. *The Hebrew atheist:* Manucci, vol. I, pp. 215 and 363.

400 *Rant of infidelity and Judaism:* AN, in E & D, vol. VII, p. 179.

400 *In this great monastery:* Author's rhymed version, A literal translation cited in Asiri, p. vi; also Wali, p. 112.

400 *I am madly in love:* cited in Asiri, p. 34.

400 *The source of light:* cited *ibid.,* p. 36.

401 *If the treasures of heaven:* Author's rhymed version. Literal translation in Asiri, p. v.

401 *O breeze, convey this message:* Author's rhymed version. Literal translation in Asiri, p. 57.

402 *I am all things:* Author's rhymed version. Literal translation in Asiri, p. vii fn.; also in Wali, p. 112.

402 *Traced the whereabouts of Sarmad:* This was the same Mutamad who, as a noble under Jahangir, wrote the *Iqbal-nama.* Mutamad's account here is from another ms., *Majma'ul Afkar;* cited in Asiri, p. v.

403 *I am a disciple of Khayyam:* cited in Asiri, p. 39.

404 *A tree without foliage:* cited *ibid.,* p. 5. *We grow old, but not our desires:* cited *ibid.,* p. 42. *Real greatness lies in humility:* cited *ibid.,* p. 4. *How long wilt Thou keep Thyself concealed?:* cited *ibid.,* p. 1. *Come out of the Veil:* cited *ibid.,* p. 1. *Thou art invisible and visible:* cited *ibid.,* p. 2. *Only my intuition led me:* cited *ibid.,* p. 2. *Adopt solitude:* cited *ibid.,* p. 12. *If you say I seek this world and that:* cited *ibid.,* p. 33. *This house . . . in ruins:* cited *ibid.,* p. 34.

405 *I was for a long time disgusted:* Bernier, p. 317.

405 *Since Sultan Dara Shikoh had a liking for lunatics:* Sher Khan Lodhi, in *Mir'at-ul-Khayal;* cited Asiri, p. x fn.; also Hasrat, p. 101.

405 *Sarmad's famous miracles:* Author's rhymed version. Literal translation in Asiri, p. x; also in Wali, p. 113.

405 *A piece of rough cloth:* cited in Asiri, p. xi.

405 **Sarmad adopted loin cloth for Dara:** Manucci, vol. I, p. 223.

406 *My guide and preceptor; Every day I resolve; If it was not the divine will:* This letter of DS to Sarmad appears in variant translations in Asiri, p. xi; Hasrat, p. 102; Wali, p. 118. The version here is author's composite.

406 *Dear friend, we have forgotten:* Author's rhymed version; literal translation in Asiri, p. xi; also Wali, p. 118.

407 *After the death of Prince Dara:* Manucci, vol. I, p. 343.

407–408 *Lived there in great distress and fear: Tarikh-i-Kashmiri*, a "provincial history" in Persian by Azam; cited Qanungo, pp. 357–358.

408 **The Devil was powerful, but so was his inquisitor:** In Persian, *Shaitan qavi ast*, with the double meaning "Satan is powerful" and "Itimad Khan Mulla Qavi is Satan." Original source for this repartee is *Massir-ul-Umara*, a seventeenth-century "Peerage" of the Mogul Empire; cited Wali, p. 113; also Asiri, p. xiv.

408 *A strange thief has stripped me:* cited Asiri, p. 4; also Wali, p. 114.

408 *The saint of insanity:* Hasrat, p. 103.

408 *God hath given him eternal sovereignty:* Walih of Daghistan, *Riyad ush Shu'ara* (a contemporary who knew Sarmad); cited Wali, p. 116; also Hasrat, p. 103.

408 *But you cannot see him:* Manucci, vol. I, p. 384.

409 *There is no God but Allah:* The *kalima* or Creed is in the Koran, 3:2–3. Islam's five primary duties are (1) Bearing witness to the Creed, (2) Reciting daily prayers, (3) Giving alms, (4) Observing Ramadan, and (5) Making a pilgrimage to Mecca during one's lifetime.

409 *The mullahs say, "Mohammed rose":* Author's rhymed version. Literal translation in Asiri, p. 22; Wali, p. 114. These are only the last two lines of the quatrain.

409 *I am absorbed in the negative:* cited Qanungo, p. 369; also Wali, p. 114; also Asiri, p. xv, who expatiates on Sarmad's logic.

410 *In this wilderness death is in pursuit:* cited Asiri, p. 3.

411 *In my imagination I saw the whole world:* cited Asiri, p. 39.

411 *My sweetheart is here:* Author's rhymed version. Literal version in Hasrat, p. 103; Asiri, p. xvi; Wali, p. 115; SAB, vol. III, p. 113. (Hasrat uses "sweetheart," other three use "friend.")

411 *We opened our eyes:* Author's rhymed version. Literal text in Asiri, p. xvii; Qanungo, p. 370; Wali, p. 115.

411 *Love's path was blocked:* Author's rhymed version. Literal text in Asiri, p. 24.

412 *A flirt was my companion:* Author's rhymed version. Literal text in Asiri, p. xvii; also Wali, p. 115.

412 *Look, there's still time:* cited Asiri, p. xvii; also Wali, p. 115.

412 *How many Sufi martyrs:* Author's rhymed version. Literal text in Asiri, p. xvii; also Wali, p. 116, who adds the phrase "Sarmad died valiantly."

412 *Anā'l Haqq!:* Ezekiel, p. 29, makes this "Awa-ul-Huq." But authoritative Cyprian Rice uses the spelling I have used, and observes (p. 20): "A hard-headed, matter of fact Westerner is often put off or irritated by the wilfully extravagant exclamations of bold spirits such as . . . Hallaj . . . when they cry: Anā'l Haqq [I am God]. . . . Such things, however, are explained to us as having their origin in the fact that these men had been led to transcend their own personalities and to become conscious only of HIM. . . ." Sarmad's posthumous ecstasy is merely a supernatural extension of this.

Chapter 25: A La Tour Abolie

413 **Chapter title:** From Gérard de Nerval's sonnet: *"Le prince d'Aquitaine à la tour abolie."*

413 *Also caused his sister to be confined:* Tavernier, vol. I, p. 342.

414 *A great Mogul who could not . . . ride to battle:* SAB, vol. III, p. 140.

415 *So that they might be present at all hours: Adab;* cited SAB, vol. III, p. 144.

415 *Harsh women guardians:* Manucci, vol. I, p. 282.

415 *Finding I would not listen: ibid.,* vol. II, p. 70.

415–416 *The face of Itibar Khan displeased me: ibid.,* vol. II, p. 71.

416 *I noted that Shah Jahan's imprisonment: ibid.,* vol. II, p. 71. *He smiled over it: ibid.,* vol. II, pp. 71–72. *I felt it much: ibid.,* vol. II, p. 72.

417　*Three days afterwards: ibid.*, vol. II, p. 72. *I was there my-self: ibid.*, vol. II, p. 72. *How do you have the temerity: ibid.*, vol. II, pp. 72–73. *This eunuch was such a close-fisted fellow: ibid.*, vol. II, p. 73.

417　*Raise tumults and increase disorder: Adab;* cited SAB, vol. III, p. 144. *Am I his son that I should obey: ibid.*, cited SAB, vol. III, pp. 144–145.

418　*I use it in saying my prayers:* KK, cited SAB, vol. III, pp. 147–148. Cf. Tavernier, p. 371; Manucci, vol. II, p. 17; and Bernier, p. 127.

418　*There is no skilled songstress: Adab;* cited SAB, vol. III, p. 148.

418–419　*If your objection: ibid.;* cited SAB, vol. III, p. 148.

420　*Although I heard that disturbances: ibid.;* cited SAB, vol. III, p. 152. *If you had not helped: ibid.;* cited SAB, vol. III, pp. 152–153.

420　*Affected humility of a Pharisee:* SAB, vol. III, p. 151.

420　*The work of God; The perilous weight; Sheer necessity; Saving the people; Kingship means protection: Adab;* cited SAB, vol. III, p. 153.

421　*A man who rebelled against his father:* Manucci, vol. II, pp. 16–17.

421　*If God had not approved; Nothing can happen without the will of Allah: Adab;* cited SAB, vol. III, p. 154.

422　*You have written that it is contrary to Moslem faith: ibid.*, cited SAB, vol. III, p. 155. *How do you still regard the memory of Khusrau and Parwiz: ibid.*, cited SAB, vol. III, p. 155.

422　**Fn. Malicious perversion of names:** AN, in E & D, vol. VII, p. 177.

423　*Well, nothing happens: Adab;* cited SAB, vol. III, pp. 155–156. *To close the path: ibid.;* cited SAB, vol. III, p. 157.

423　*What, will the wretch leave no one to avenge me?:* cited SAB, vol. III, p. 157 fn., "on doubtful authority."

423　*The deposed monarch treated with respect:* Bernier, p. 166.

424　*No request ever denied him: ibid.*, p. 166.

424–425　*But the existence of Shah Jahan was like a thorn:* Ma-nucci, vol. II, pp. 58–59.

425　*A great friend of mine: ibid.*, vol. II, p. 101. *Suspecting what was sure to happen: ibid.*, vol. II, p. 101. *Aurangzeb was already tired of seeing this traitor:* ibid., vol. II, pp. 101–102.

426 *Talk against Aurangzeb once more prevailed:* ibid., vol. II, p. 107. *So hated by him he had created:* ibid., vol. II, p. 107.

429 *The last enemy:* AN, long extract cited Latif, *Agra Historical*, p. 38.

429 *O God! Make my condition good:* Kambu; cited SAB, vol. III, p. 161.

430 *Although His Majesty had never missed:* AN; cited Latif, p. 38.

431 *I bear witness that there is no God but God:* This is the "word of testimony" (*kalimatu-sh-shahadat*) recited whenever water is poured during the washing of the corpse (Crooke, *Herklots' Islam*, pp. 92–93).

431 *Say, God is One!:* After the body has been shrouded, the *Fatiha* (Chapter 1) of the Koran is recited—the Moslem equivalent of the Lord's Prayer; this is followed by the Qul texts (Qul means "say"), which are Chapters 112, 113, and 114 of the Koran. The quotation here is the first verse of each of the three chapters comprising the Qul. (Crooke, pp. 95–96.)

431 *Officers of state carrying the coffin:* Kambu; cited SAB, vol. III, p. 162; also in Mazumdar, pp. 100–101.

432 *Aurangzeb sent a trusty man:* Manucci, vol. II, p. 117. *Sent two thousand gold coins:* ibid., vol. II, p. 117.

433 *Hearing a great noise:* ibid., vol. II, p. 118.

433 *The cry of lamentation rose up:* Kambu; cited SAB, vol. III, p. 164.

Chapter 26: Two Sisters

436 *Natural bashfulness would keep an empress:* SAB, vol. III, p. 65.

436 *She had noble qualities:* MA; cited SAB, vol. III, p. 68.

437 *Aurangzeb knew plainly enough:* Manucci, vol. II, pp. 30–31.

437 *Sex and murder:* Manucci, vol. II, pp. 31–32; Bernier, pp. 132–133.

437–438 *Just dismissed them:* Manucci, vol. II, p. 31. *Aurangzeb was much disturbed:* ibid., vol. II, p. 31.

438 *Rumors were current:* ibid., vol. II, p. 50.

439   *Believing that there was no hope: ibid.*, vol. II, p. 50.
439   *She told Raushanara Begum: ibid.*, vol. II, p. 50.
440   *They were aware that . . . to unchain an enraged lion:* Bernier, p. 124.
440   *Placed under Raushanara Begum's care: ibid.*, p. 125. *Impressed with a signet: ibid.*, p. 125.
440–441 *He asked . . . where his signet ring was; The Princess replied:* Manucci, vol. II, p. 54. *Raushanara Begum lost much of the love: ibid.*, vol. II, p. 55.
441   *I was present when my* agah: Bernier, pp. 125–126.
441   *Anxious to inhale a purer air: ibid.*, p. 351.
442   *Can no more dispense with his philosophical studies: ibid.*, pp. 352–353.
442   *One hundred and fifty crowns per month: ibid.*, p. 353.
443   *Balances, fishes and other mystical objects: ibid.*, p. 371.
443   *These lovely and distinguished females: ibid.*, p. 372.
443–444 *If I had not regarded this display: ibid.*, p. 373. *A strange accident: ibid.*, p. 407. *Two days afterward we passed that way: ibid.*, p. 408.
444   *Thereafter we hear nothing more:* SAB, vol. III, p. 67.
444–445 *If this year was a joyful one:* Manucci, vol. II, p. 177.
446   *Pious and learned men:* AN; cited Latif, p. 39.
446   *Courtiers and nobles were shocked: ibid.*; cited Latif, p. 39.
448   *Moved by the magnificence of his reception:* Bernier, p. 199.
448   *I saw the elephant pass:* Tavernier, vol. I, p. 344.
448–449 *Go to her and stand in her drawing room:* SAB, vol. III, p. 64.
449   *Begum Sahib to the seed-pearls from her eyes:* Manucci, vol. II, p. 175.
449   *Four finger-breadths: ibid.*, vol. II, p. 5.
449–450 *Aurangzeb came to her palace: ibid.*, vol. II, pp. 139–140.
450   *Tax the sea on which he sails: ibid.*, vol. III, p. 275. *Bade her goodbye: ibid.*, vol. III, p. 276.
451   *Thus, unwilling as I was: ibid.*, vol. II, p. 215.
452   *The women moved with us: ibid.*, vol. II, p. 239–240.

Chapter 27: The Mountain Rats
455   *Very imperfect settlement:* Elphinstone, p. 557.
455   *Breaking two bones: Kalimat*; cited SAB, vol. III, p. 279.
457   *I am defenseless:* MA; cited SAB, vol. III, p. 408.

459 *War brought out their capacities:* Lane-Poole, *Medieval,* p. 389.

460 *Tiger's claws:* Elphinstone, p. 546; Bhattacharya, p. 775. The Persian word is *baghnakh.* These claws were concealed in Shivaji's left hand and fastened to his fingers by a pair of rings; he also carried a thin, sharp dagger called a scorpion. See Srivastava, p. 380.

461 *The tiger is a wild beast:* cited SAB, vol. IV, p. 86. Mogul source not identified. There are a number of European and Persian accounts of the Shivaji incident: cf. Bernier, p. 190; Manucci, vol. II, pp. 127–130; KK, in E & D, vol. VII, pp. 276–281.

461 *Even a minute's negligence:* There are several alleged last wills of Aurangzeb. The quotation here is from Hamiduddin; cited SAB, vol. IV, p. 94, and SAB, vol. V, p. 267.

461 *By rushing hither and thither:* Manucci, vol. II, p. 217.

461 *An infidel went to Hell: Kafir ba jahannum raft* is the Persian. Cited Manucci, vol. II, p. 217 fn.; also KK, in E & D, vol. VII, p. 305, takes credit for having discovered the chronogram.

462 *Too many irons in the fire:* Surat factors, December 1683; cited SAB, vol. IV, p. 281.

462 *Let us see who dies first* **and Persian quatrain:** *Rukaat;* cited SAB, vol. III, p. 60.

463 *The great troubler of India's peace is gone:* MA; cited SAB, vol. III, p. 60.

463 *He is so inveterate against [Shambhuji]:* Foreign Records of Surat, Karwar Occurrences, July 30, 1682; cited SAB, vol. IV, p. 258.

463 *All his forces that were against his son:* F.R. Surat; cited SAB, vol. IV, p. 262. *The Mogul is grown very crazy: ibid.;* cited SAB, vol. IV, p. 262. *He is extraordinarily peevish: ibid.;* cited SAB, vol. IV, p. 263. *All persons of quality: ibid.;* cited SAB, vol. IV, p. 263. *He will in all likelihood: ibid.;* cited SAB, vol. IV, p. 262.

464 *At a lonely place:* SAB, vol. III, p. 58. *Misconduct: ibid.,* vol. III, p. 60.

465 *I have experienced such cruelty:* cited by Ali, p. 517.

465 *Is not in very good odor: Dutch Records;* cited SAB, vol. IV, p. 296.

466 The *mountain rats:* Lane-Poole, *Medieval,* p. 390, cites the phrase in quotes, indicating long usage. Perhaps Aurangzeb invented it by way of opprobrium.

Chapter 28: "This Stupendous Caravan of Sin"

467–468 *I had hoped that one of my sons:* MA; cited SAB, vol. IV, p. 319.

468 *You are an orthodox believer: Basatin-i-Salatin,* a history of Bijapur, by Mirza Ibrahim Zubairi; cited SAB, vol. IV, p. 321.

468 *I do not covet your territory: ibid.;* cited SAB, vol. IV, p. 322.

468 *Threw living men and women into the ditch:* Isardas; cited SAB, vol. IV, p. 322.

468–469 *God's grace be on you!:* MA; cited SAB, vol. IV, p. 325.

469 *Ingenious forms of sensuality:* Tavernier, vol. I, p. 158.

470 *Alas! Alas! I have razed:* MA; cited SAB, vol. IV, p. 365.

471 **Abul Hassan greets Moguls with *Good morning* and dignified closing scene:** KK, in E & D, vol. VII, p. 333.

471 *Go on dancing:* Isardas; cited SAB, vol. IV, pp. 385–386 fn.

472 *Patrons of anarchy:* Elphinstone, p. 575.

473 *Infidel son of the infernal infidel:* Aurangzeb's inevitable epithet for Shambhuji; a milder imperial imprecation was reserved for Prince Akbar, the "disturber of India." See SAB, vol. IV, p. 11.

475 *Had the misfortune of seeing the English:* KK; in E & D, vol. VII, p. 351.

476 **All quotations re KK's visit to English at Bombay:** *ibid.,* E & D, vol. VII, pp. 352–354.

478 *The country was so entirely desolated:* Manucci, vol. IV, p. 252.

478 *Owing to my marching through deserts:* cited Sarkar, *Anecdotes,* § 11.

478 *So long as a single breath:* Hamiduddin; cited SAB, vol. V, p. 450.

479 *You style yourself a world conqueror:* Tavernier, vol. I, p. 375, offers a version of this; the full letter is in *Faiyyaz,* cited SAB, vol. III, pp. 126–127.

479 *Sutlers, merchants and artificers:* Careri (in Sen, p. 218). *Three miles in compass: ibid.* (in Sen, p. 217).

Notes

480 *After the country manner: ibid.* (in Sen, p. 219). ***The greatest monarch in Asia: ibid.*** (in Sen, p. 220).

480 *His shoes were after the Moorish: ibid.* (in Sen, pp. 220–221).

481 *The art of reigning is so delicate:* Cited Lane-Poole, *Medieval,* p. 405, Mogul source not given.

481 *Maratha leaders and their followers operate with confidence:* Manucci, vol. III, p. 480.

482 *When you have counted eighty years:* Author's rhymed version; from MA; cited in Sarkar, *Anecdotes,* p. 25.

482 *Peace be on Your Majesty:* Author's rhymed version of the couplet. Quote is from MA; cited SAB, vol. V, p. 246. *The people got back their lives: ibid.;* cited SAB, vol. V, p. 247.

483 *She and I alone were left:* MA; cited SAB, vol. V, p. 250.

484 *A moment, a minute, a breath:* Author's rhymed version; MA, cited in Sarkar, *Anecdotes,* p. 25.

485 *Carry this creature of dust:* KK, in E & D, vol. VII, p. 386.

485 *I came alone and I go as a stranger: Rukaat;* author's composite of extant translations. For versions of this letter see: *Rukaat,* Bilimoria tr., Letter LXXII, pp. 70–72; E & D, vol. VII, p. 562; Lane-Poole, *Medieval,* pp. 407–408; SAB, vol. V, pp. 259–260.

485 *Soul of my soul, I am going alone: Rukaat;* author's composite of extant translations. For versions of this letter see: *Rukaat,* Bilimoria tr., Letter LXXIII, pp. 73–74; E & D, vol. VII, pp. 563–564; Lane-Poole, *Medieval,* pp. 408–409; SAB, vol. V, pp. 260–262.

485 *The guardianship of a people: Rukaat,* from A's last letter to Kam Bakhsh; the translation is from E & D, vol. VII, pp. 563–564.

486 *Fighting between armies and . . . slaughter of mankind:* From A's alleged will in India Office Library, ms. 1344, f. 49b; translation in SAB, vol. V, p. 262.

486 *Never trust your sons:* From A's alleged will as recounted by Hamiduddin; translation in SAB, vol. V, pp. 266–267; also in Sarkar, *Anecdotes,* pp. 51–55.

Notes

Epilogue

488 *At the time the king died:* Manucci, vol. IV, p. 398.

490 *The imperialist answer:* Spear, *History*, p. 113.

490 *From Delhi to Palam:* ibid., p. 15.

490 **Heber's impressions on visiting Delhi fort:** all quotations from Heber, pp. 40–46.

491 *This is really the only liquor:* The remark was made to Sleeman (see Bibliography under Sleeman); cited in Spear, *Twilight*, p. 64.

491 *The King's realm and the Company's rule:* Until 1857, the East India Company technically ruled India—divested of its trading monopoly, but still acting as executive agent for the British crown. Out of respect for the titular Mogul emperor, all proclamations were worded "The King's realm and the Company's rule."

491 *Last convulsive protest:* Spear, *History*, p. 143.

491 *A tiger unsubdued:* John William Kaye, *A History of the Sepoy War in India 1857–1858.* 3 vols. London: W. H. Allen & Co., 1877, vol. III, p. 642. Hodson emerges in a harrowing light from Kaye's narrative and from his own posthumously published letters (*Twelve Years of a Soldier's Life in India.* Boston: Ticknor & Fields, 1860). Prior to the Mutiny, he had been dismissed from political employment in the Punjab and "pronounced wholly unfit ever to exercise any . . . power" (Kaye, p. 643). Hodson's murder of the last Mogul princes was thus a sinister and personalized vendetta.

492 *Let green grass only conceal my grave:* English translation in Fanshawe, p. 239.

493 *The world is a bridge:* See note for p. 68.

493 *In all its glory:* Havell, p. 85.

BIBLIOGRAPHY

A vast bibliography exists for the Mogul period. Both primary and general sources are by no means exhausted in this selected list, which is limited to those authorities who are either cited in the Notes or proved invaluable. Primary works have here been divided into two categories: first, there are translated Mogul documents (originally written in Persian or, in the case of Babur, in Turki)— official court chronicles, imperial memoirs, independent histories, anthologies of Mogul correspondence, and literary tracts; secondly, there are the accounts of contemporary European travelers who spent time in Hindustan. For the first category I have relied on translations which vary considerably in scope: some key manuscripts from the Mogul storehouse have been completely rendered into English; others have been sizeably excerpted, or are represented by significant citations in the works of modern scholars. A number of biographies and histories listed under the general sources are thus "primary" material in themselves.

Primary Sources

Persian and Turki (in translation)

ABDUL HAMID LAHORI. *Padshah-nama.* Extracts in Elliot and Dowson, vol. VII, pp. 3–72. (Cited in the Notes as Lahori.)
    Lahori was one of Shah Jahan's official historians, and his work covers the first twenty years of the reign. Detailed and authoritative, it drew on state papers, news sheets, and other official documents.

ABUL FAZL. *Akbar-nama.* Extracts in Elliot and Dowson, vol. VI, pp. 1–102.

"Prince of Poets" and prime minister to Akbar, Abul Fazl wrote the history of his patron's reign until 1602. His famous Persian style made him virtually the Dr. Johnson of Mogul letters.

————. *Ain-i-Akbari.* Translated by Heinrich Blochmann and H. S. Jarrett. 3 vols. Calcutta: Asiatic Society of Bengal, 1873–1894.

A staggering gazeteer of Akbar's India, embracing every conceivable subject—coinage, precious gems, methods of refining gold, kitchen recipes, the harem, encampments, arsenals, illuminations, perfumes, elephant stables, officers, nobles, and even camel food.

AQIL KHAN RAZI. *Zafar-nama.* Frequent quotations in the works of modern scholars, chiefly Sarkar's five-volume biography of Aurangzeb.

Aqil Khan was Aurangzeb's equerry. His short independent history (sometimes unflattering to his master) covers a period from the 1657 Mogul invasion of Bijapur to the death of Mir Jumla.

AURANGZEB. *Adab-i-Alamgiri.* Extensive quotations in the works of all modern scholars. Also translated by Jonathan Scott in *Tales, Anecdotes and Letters.* Shrewsbury: 1800, pp. 345–466.

A collection of Aurangzeb's letters written between 1650 and 1658, the last ones being addressed to Shah Jahan about two months after the emperor became a prisoner in Agra fort. The correspondence was written on Aurangzeb's behalf by his secretary, Qabil Khan.

————. *Rukaat-i-Alamgiri.* ("Letters of Aurungzeb.") Translated by J. H. Bilimoria. London: Luzac, 1908.

A selection of Aurangzeb's later letters, primarily those to his sons. Other translations are extant: the two final communiqués to Azam and Kam Bakhsh appear in Elliot and Dowson, vol. VII, pp. 562–564 in a rendering by Jonathan Scott.

BABUR. *The Babur-nama.* Translated from the Turki by Annette Beveridge. 2 vols. London: Luzac, 1922.

Babur's extensive memoirs embrace his whole life from adolescence almost to the year of his death. This is generally regarded as one of the world's most candid royal autobiographies.

BAKHTAWAR KHAN. *Mirat-i-Alam.* Extracts in Elliot and Dowson, vol. VII, pp. 145–165.

The presumed author was a eunuch-nobleman of Aurangzeb's court, though this history has been ascribed to others. It
covers the first ten years of Aurangzeb's reign, cataloguing his
rigorous anti-Hindu measures and rigid application of Islamic
orthodoxy.

DARA SHIKOH. *Sakinat-ul-Awliya.* Extracts in Hasrat, pp. 64–104.

This was Dara's biography of Moslem saints of the Qadiri
order, filled with personal anecdotes and letters detailing his
relationship with Mian Mir and Mulla Shah.

———. *Quatrains.* Translations in Hasrat, pp. 129–157.

Dara's quatrains are in the classic Rubaiyat form, and
have been culled from various of his works. Hasrat's is the first
English translation ever to appear.

———. *Diwan.* Translations in Hasrat, pp. 129–157.

The *Diwan* consists of didactic poems and quatrains;
hitherto regarded as lost, it has only recently been rediscov-
ered.

ELLIOT, H.M., AND DOWSON, J. *The History of India As Told by Its
Own Historians.* 8 vols. Allahabad: Kitab Mahal (Wholesale)
Private Ltd., 1964 (a reprint of the original 1867–1877 edition).

A monument in the field, with translations by the editors
and others. Vol. III offers extracts from Timur's purported
memoirs, including his sacking of Delhi; Vol. IV deals with
Babur; Vol. V covers Humayun and part of Akbar's reign;
Vol. VI is divided between Akbar and Jahangir; Vol. VII includes Shah Jahan, Aurangzeb, and later Moguls; and Vol.
VIII continues Indian history into the nineteenth century.

FAIYYAZ-UL-QAWANIN. Quotations in Sarkar's biography of Aurangzeb and Qanungo's biography of Dara Shikoh.

The *Faiyyaz* is a massive anthology of Mogul correspondence, some taken from official annals. Compiled by Nawab
Mohammed Ali Hassan in A.D. 1723, it includes letters written
by Akbar, Jahangir, Shah Jahan, Aurangzeb, Jahanara, Dara
Shikoh, Shuja, Murad, Jai Singh, and the sultans of Bijapur
and Golconda.

HAMIDUDDIN KHAN. *Akham-i-Alamgiri.* Partial English translation
in Sarkar's *Anecdotes of Aurangzib.*

Gossipy memoirs ascribed to an old courtier who was Aurangzeb's partisan. Hamiduddin relates the elephant encounter in Aurangzeb's childhood, and the supposed reason behind
Aurangzeb's 1644 dismissal as governor of the Deccan.

INAYAT KHAN. *Shah Jahan-nama.* Extracts in Elliot and Dowson, vol. VII, pp. 73–120.

The author was a witty and urbane nobleman, born when Shah Jahan ascended the throne. Toward the end of the emperor's reign, Inayat became superintendent of the Royal Library and decided to simplify the florid chronicles of Lahori and others—his work is in the nature of a clarifying abridgment. He narrates the Balkh and Kandahar campaigns, Shah Jahan's favoritism to Dara, and Mir Jumla's and Aurangzeb's joint strategies in the Deccan.

INAYET-NAMA. Quotations in Saksena's biography of Shah Jahan.

This is another collection of contemporary Mogul correspondence; compiled by Inayet Khan Rasikh, a minor Mogul noble of the seventeenth century. It contains significant letters of Aurangzeb, Murad, and Shuja, written during the early phases of the War of Succession.

ISARDAS (ISHWARDAS NAGAR). *Futuhat-i-Alamgiri.* Passing mention in Elliot and Dowson, vol. VII, p. 198; frequent citation in Sarkar's biography of Aurangzeb.

The author was a Brahman of Gujarat, and his history covers a period from 1657–1698. He deals with the War of Succession, including Dara Shikoh's last stand at Deorai.

JAHANGIR. *Tuzuk-i-Jahangiri.* ("Memoirs of Jahangir" from the first to the twelfth year of his reign.) Translated by Alexander Rogers, edited by Henry Beveridge. 2 vols.; Oriental Translation Fund, N.S. XIX and XXII. London: Royal Asiatic Society, 1909–1914.

———. *Wakiat-i-Jahangiri.* ("Memoirs of Jahangir" from the first to the nineteenth year of his reign.) Extracts in Elliot and Dowson, vol. VI, pp. 276–391.

This translation, by Elliot and other hands, extends seven years beyond the Rogers-Beveridge version. Jahangir's continuator, Mohammed Hadi, transcribed the later portions of the emperor's memoirs at a much later date (they were probably suppressed during Shah Jahan's reign because of unflattering references to his rebellion).

JAIPUR DARBAR ARCHIVES. *Letters.* Quotations in Qanungo's biography of Dara Shikoh, pp. 169, 229–332.

These archives contain imperial firmans and correspondence which passed between Jai Singh, Dara Shikoh, and Shah

Bibliography

Jahan at the time of Sulaiman Shikoh's campaign against Shuja in the War of Succession.

JAMI-UL-INSHA. Quotations by Saksena in his biography of Shah Jahan, pp. 327–332.

Compiled by Jalaluddin Tabatabai, this is one of the numerous collections of contemporary Mogul correspondence. Important letters of Aurangzeb, Murad, and Shuja throw light on their triumvirate intentions in the War of Succession.

MOHAMMED AMIN KAZWINI. *Padshah-nama.* Mentioned with no excerpts in Elliot and Dowson, vol. VII, pp. 1–2; quotations in Saksena and others. (Cited in the Notes as Kazwini.)

Kazwini was court historian to Shah Jahan until the jealousy of his rivals displaced him. His work covers the first ten years of the reign. It is a useful source for Shah Jahan's education, his rebellion against Jahangir, and his struggle with Nur Jahan.

KALIMAT-I-TAYYIBAT. Quotations in Sarkar's biography of Aurangzeb.

A potpourri of dictation scraps, bits of verse, and Arabic texts which Aurangzeb intended to include in formal letters. Compiled in 1719 by his last and favorite secretary, Inayetullah Khan.

KHAFI KHAN. *Muntakhab-ul-Lubab.* Extensive extracts in Elliot and Dowson, vol. VII, pp. 207–533; also cited profusely in the works of modern scholars.

Khafi Khan is the unquestioned dean of Mogul historians—the best of them all. His father was one of Murad's officers, but after Murad's death went over to Aurangzeb's employ; Khafi himself held political and military posts under Aurangzeb. His monumental private history, written despite imperial veto of such endeavors, spans the House of Timur from its inception until its eighteenth-century decline. From the middle of Aurangzeb's reign onward, Khafi Khan wrote from personal knowledge and scrupulously consulted others for eyewitness verification of important Mogul events.

MOHAMMED KAZIM. *Alamgir-nama.* Extracts in Elliot and Dowson, vol. VII, pp. 174–180; also extensive quotations in the works of Sarkar, Qanungo, Latif, and others.

The official history of the first ten years of Aurangzeb's reign was written on imperial command; thereafter, Aurangzeb proscribed any and all chronicles. As might be expected from a court scribe, Kazim's narrative is flowery, fawning, and viciously abusive of Dara and Shuja. But its details make it important beyond bias, since Khafi Khan and all later historians borrowed from it freely.

MOHAMMED MASUM. *Tarikh-i-Shah-Shujai.* Described, without excerpts, in Elliot and Dowson, vol. VII, p. 198; frequently quoted by Sarkar and Qanungo. (Cited in the Notes as Masum.)

Masum was a minor noble in Shuja's service. His history provides details of Dara Shikoh's murder, Shuja's flight, and many other Mogul incidents from Shah Jahan's Trans-Oxiana campaigns onward. Since Masum lived in Bengal, he might be considered unreliable for events beyond Shuja's sphere; yet many of his particulars curiously parallel Manucci, as though both shared common informants.

MOHAMMED SAKI MUSTAIDD KHAN. *Maasir-i-Alamgiri.* Excerpts in Elliot and Dowson, vol. VII, pp. 181–197; also frequent quotations by Sarkar and others.

Written shortly after Aurangzeb's reign, this history is the work of a scribe who had observed court events over a forty-year period. It is less detailed than Mohammed Kazim's account, but is useful for many facts: Aurangzeb's campaign against Rajputana, his treatment of his sons, and his death. Though partial to Aurangzeb, it is not fulsome.

MOHAMMED SALIH KAMBU. *Amal-i-Salih.* Extracts in Elliot and Dowson, vol. VII, pp. 123–132; also important quotations in the works of modern scholars.

Kambu was a court scribe under Shah Jahan, employed in the Imperial Records Department; his respectable history of the emperor's reign spills beyond it to include the War of Succession in brief. He was partial to Shah Jahan, critical of Dara Shikoh, and candid about Murad's murder and Sulaiman Shikoh's fate.

MOHAMMED WARIS. *Padshah-nama.* Mentioned, with only a brief extract, in Elliot and Dowson, vol. VII, pp. 121–122; occasional quotation by modern Mogul scholars. (Cited in the Notes as Waris.)

Abdul Hamid Lahori's pupil and assistant, Waris completed his master's opus with a chronicle embracing the final decade of Shah Jahan's rule.

Bibliography

MUTAMAD KHAN. *Iqbal-nama-i-Jahangiri.* Extracts in Elliot and Dowson, vol. VI, pp. 400–438.

    Mutamad Khan was a Persian who became Jahangir's paymaster and later one of his scribes. By Jahangir's orders he wrote this history (really an abridgment of imperial memoirs for the first nineteen years of the reign, and thereafter original). Mutamad's account has more than naïve charm: he provides signal details of Shah Jahan's rebellion, Mahabat Khan's coup, and the final intrigue in which Shah Jahan obtained the crown.

RASHID KHAN. *Latif-ul-Akhbar.* Substantial quotations in Qanungo's biography of Dara Shikoh.

    Attributed to a nobleman in the service of Mahabat Khan the Younger, this is a first-hand diary of Dara Shikoh's Kandahar campaign.

SARMAD. *Rubaiyat.* Complete translation in Asiri (see Asiri under heading "General Sources").

European Travelers in Mogul India

BERNIER, FRANÇOIS. *Travels in the Mogul Empire A.D. 1656–1668.* Translated by Archibald Constable, 2nd ed. revised by Vincent A. Smith. London: Oxford University Press, 1914.

[BROECKE, PIETER VAN DEN.] *A Contemporary Dutch Chronicle of Mughal India.* Translated and edited by Brij Narain and Sri Ram Sharma. Calcutta: Susil Gupta (India) Ltd., 1957.

COVERTE, ROBERT. *Travels of Captain Robert Coverte.* Edited by Boies Penrose. Philadelphia: privately printed, 1931.

DELLA VALLE, PIETRO. *Travels of Pietro Della Valle in India.* Edited by Edward Grey, from the old English translation of 1664 by G. Havers. 2 vols. London: The Hakluyt Society, 1892.

FOSTER, WILLIAM (Ed.). *Early Travels in India 1583–1619.* (An anthology of accounts written by Ralph Fitch, John Mildenhall, William Hawkins, William Finch, Nicholas Withington, Thomas Coryat, and Edward Terry.) London: Humphrey Milford and Oxford University Press, 1921.

——— (Ed.). *The English Factories in India 1624–1629.* A Calendar of Documents in the India Office. Oxford: Clarendon Press, 1909.

HEBER, REGINALD, BISHOP OF CALCUTTA. *Heber's Indian Journal.* A selection, with an introduction, by P. R. Krishnaswami. London: Humphrey Milford and Oxford University Press, 1923.

Bibliography

MANDELSLO, JOHN ALBERT DE. *The Travels of John Albert de Mandelslo.* (In Olearius, A., *Voyages and Travels of the Holstein Ambassadors,* . . .) Translated by John Davies. London: Starkey & Basset, 1669.

MANRIQUE, SEBASTIEN. *Travels of Fray Sebastien Manrique.* Translated by C. Eckford Luard and H. Hosten. 2 vols. Oxford: The Hakluyt Society, 1927.

MANUCCI, NICCOLO. *Storia do Mogor.* Translated by William Irvine. 4 vols. First 3 vols. Calcutta: Editions Indian, 1965–1966 (a reprint of the 1907 edition); vol. 4, London: John Murray, 1908.

MUNDY, PETER. *The Travels of Peter Mundy.* Vol. II, *Travels in Asia 1628–1634.* Edited by Richard Carnac Temple. London: The Hakluyt Society, 1914.

PELSAERT, FRANCISCO. *The Remonstratie.* ("Jahangir's India") Translated from the Dutch by W. H. Moreland and P. Geyl. Cambridge: W. Heffer & Sons Ltd., 1925.

ROE, SIR THOMAS. *The Embassy of Sir Thomas Roe to the Court of the Great Mogul 1615–1619.* Edited by W. Foster. 2 vols. London: The Hakluyt Society, 1899.

SEN, SURENDRA NATH (Ed.). *Indian Travels of Thevenot and Careri.* Delhi: Indian Record Series, National Archives of India, 1949.

TAVERNIER, JEAN BAPTISTE. *Travels in India.* Translated by V. Ball. London: Macmillan, 1889.

General Sources

ALI, SYED AMEER. "Islamic Culture under the Moguls." *Islamic Culture* (October 1927), pp. 499–521.

ASIRI, FAZL MAHMUD (Ed. and translator). *Rubaiyat-i-Sarmad.* Santiniketan: Visva-Bharati University Publications, 1950.

BASSAGLI, MARIO. *Indian Miniatures.* London: Hamlyn, 1969.

BHATTACHARYYA, SUHINDRA NATH. "Rebellion of Shah Jahan." *Indian Historical Quarterly* (1934), vol. 10, pp. 671–722.

BOUVIER, RENÉ. *Le Dernier des Grands Mogols: Vie d'Aurengzeb.* Paris: A. Michel, 1947.

CHAGHTAI, MUHAMMAD ABDULLA. *Le Taj Mahal d'Agra (Inde); Histoire et Description.* Brussels: Editions de la Connaissance, 1938.

———. "A Family of Great Mughal Architects." *Islamic Culture* (April 1937), pp. 200–209.

CHOPRA, PRAN NATH. *Some Aspects of Social Life During the Mughal*

Age (1526–1707). Jaipur: Shiva Lal Agarwala & Co. Ltd., 1963.

CHOWDHURI, JOGINDRA NATH. "Mumtaz Mahall (1593–1631)." *Islamic Culture* (July 1937), pp. 373–381.

DASGUPTA, JOGENDRA NATHA. *India in the Seventeenth Century as Depicted by European Travellers*. Calcutta: University of Calcutta Publications, 1916.

DOLISY, LOUIS-LAURENT, COMTE DE MODAVE, CHEVALIER DE ST. LOUIS. "The Delhi Empire a Century after Bernier." Translated from the French by Jadunath Sarkar. *Islamic Culture* (July 1937), pp. 382–392.

DRYDEN, JOHN. *Aureng-zebe, a Tragedy*. In *Four Tragedies*, edited by L. A. Beaurline and Fredson Bowers. Chicago: University of Chicago Press, 1967.

EDWARDES, STEPHEN MEREDYTH. *Babur: Diarist and Despot*. London: A. M. Philpot, n.d.

———. *Mughal Rule in India*. London: Oxford University Press, 1930.

ELPHINSTONE, MOUNTSTUART. *The History of India, the Hindu and Mahometan Periods*. Allahabad: Kitab Mahal (Wholesale) Private Ltd., 1966. (A reprint of the 1843 edition.)

EZEKIEL, I. A. *Sarmad*. Punjab, India: Radha Soami Satsang Beas, 1966.

FANSHAWE, HERBERT CHARLES. *Delhi, Past and Present*. London: John Murray, 1902.

FERGUSSON, JAMES. *History of Indian and Eastern Architecture*. 2 vols. Delhi: Munshiram Manoharlal, Oriental Publishers, 1967. (A reprint of the revised 1910 edition.)

FESTING, GABRIELLE. *When Kings Rode to Delhi*. Edinburgh and London: William Blackwood and Sons, 1912.

FISCHEL, WALTER J. "Jews and Judaism at the Court of the Moghul Emperors in Medieval India." *Proceedings of the American Academy for Jewish Research*, vol. XVIII (1948–1949), pp. 137–177.

GHAURI, IFTIKHAR AHMAD. *War of Succession between the Sons of Shah Jahan*. Lahore: Publishers United Ltd., 1964.

GOSWAMI, A. *Glimpses of Mughal Architecture*. Introduction with historical analysis by Jadunath Sarkar; text by S. K. Saraswati. Calcutta: Sri L. C. Roy at Gossain & Co., in cooperation with the Government of India and the Government of West Bengal, 1953.

[541]

Bibliography

GUILLAUME, ALFRED. *Islam.* Baltimore: Penguin Books, 1954.

HASHMI, B. A. "Sarmad." *Islamic Culture* (October 1933), pp. 663–672.

HASHMI, SYED. "The Real Alamgir." *Islamic Culture* (1928), vol. 2, pp. 183–203, 622–633.

HASRAT, BIKRAMA JIT. *Dara Shikuh: Life and Works.* Santiniketan: Visva-Bharati University Publications, 1953.

HASSAN, IBN. *Central Structure of the Mughal Empire.* London: Oxford University Press, 1936.

HAVELL, ERNEST BINFIELD. *A Handbook to Agra and the Taj, Sikandra, Fatehpur Sikri, and the Neighbourhood.* 2nd ed. London: Longmans, Green, 1912.

HOLDEN, EDWARD SINGLETON. *The Mogul Emperors of Hindustan.* New York: Scribner's, 1895.

HOSTEN, H. "Who Planned the Taj?" *Royal Asiatic Society of Bengal Journal and Proceedings*, Calcutta, N.S. vol. 6, no. 6 (June 1910), pp. 281–288.

JAFFAR, S. M. *The Mughal Empire from Babar to Aurangzeb.* Peshawar: S. Muhammad Sadiq Khan Kissa Khani, 1936.

JAMES, WILLIAM. *The Varieties of Religious Experience.* New York: Collier Books, 1961.

KEENE, HENRY GEORGE. *A Sketch of the History of Hindustan, from the First Muslim Conquest to the Fall of the Mughol Empire.* London: W. H. Allen & Co., 1885.

KHAN, SHAFAAT AHMAD. "The East India Company's War with Aurangzeb." *Journal of Indian History* (1921), vol. 1, pp. 70–91.

KHAN, YUSUF HUSSAIN. "Dara Shikuh: A Mystic Prince." *Prabuddha Bharata*, vol. XLIV (April 1939), pp. 166–174.

———— (Ed.). *Selected Documents of Shah Jahan's Reign.* Hyderabad, Deccan: Daftar-i-Diwani, 1950.

LAL, KANWAR. *The Taj.* Delhi: R. & K. Publishing House, 1965.

LANE-POOLE, STANLEY. *Aurangzib.* London: Clarendon Press, 1893.

————. *Babar.* Delhi: S. Chand & Co., 1964 (reprint).

————. *The History of the Moghul Emperors of Hindustan Illustrated by Their Coins.* London: Archibald Constable for the India Office, 1892.

————. *Medieval India Under Mohammedan Rule.* Delhi: Universal Book & Stationery Co., 1963 (reprint of 1903 edition).

LATIF, SYAD MUHAMMAD, KHAN BAHADUR. *Agra, Historical and Descriptive.* Calcutta: Calcutta Central Press Co. Ltd., 1896.

Bibliography

MCWHIRTER, WILLIAM A. "Its Beauty Veils a Mogul's Ruthless Whim." Article on the Taj Mahal in *Life* magazine (November 3, 1967), pp. 60–63.

MARTIN, FREDRIK ROBERT. *The Miniature Painting and Painters of Persia, India and Turkey from the Eighth to the Eighteenth Century.* 2 vols. London: Bernard Quaritch, 1912.

MATHUR, N. L. *Red Fort and Mughal Life.* Delhi: Dr. N. L. Mathur, National Museum, New Delhi, 1964.

MAZUMDAR, KESHAB CHANDRA. *Imperial Agra of the Moguls.* 3rd rev. ed. Agra: Gaya Prasad & Sons, 1946.

MOINUL HAQ, S. *Prince Awrangzib: A Study.* Karachi: Pakistan Historical Society Publication no. 32, 1962.

MORELAND, W. H. *The Agrarian System in Moslem India.* Cambridge: W. Heffer & Sons Ltd., 1929.

MUKHERJEE, S. C. "The Architecture of the Taj and its Architect." *Indian Historical Quarterly* (1933), vol. 9, pp. 872–879.

NADVI, SAYYED SULAIMAN. "The Family of the Engineers who built the Taj Mahal and the Delhi Fort." *Bihar Research Society Journal,* Patna (1948), vol. 34, pt. 1–2, pp. 75–110.

NEHRU, JAWAHARLAL. *The Discovery of India.* New York: Anchor Books, 1960.

PANDEY, AWADH BIHARI. *Later Medieval India: A History of the Mughals.* Allahabad: Central Book Depot, 1963.

PENROSE, BOIES. *Travel and Discovery in the Renaissance 1420–1620.* New York: Atheneum, 1962.

PICKTHALL, MOHAMMED MARMADUKE. *The Meaning of the Glorious Koran: an Explanatory Translation.* New York: Mentor Books, 1953.

POSTANS, THOMAS. *Personal Observations on Sindh.* London: 1843, n.p.

PRASAD, BENI. "The Accession of Shah Jahan." *Journal of Indian History,* vol. 2 (November 1922), pp. 1–19.

QANUNGO, KALIKA-RANJAN. *Dara Shukoh.* Calcutta: S. C. Sarkar & Sons, 1935.

RICE, CYPRIAN, O. P. *The Persian Sufis.* London: Allen & Unwin, 1964.

SAKSENA, BANARSI PRASAD. *History of Shah Jahan of Dihli.* Allahabad: Central Book Depot, 1958.

SANGAR, S. P. "Religious Crimes during the Reigns of Shah Jahan and Aurangzeb." *Bharatiya, Vidya,* Bombay (November–December 1945), pp. 252–258.

[543]

Bibliography

SARKAR, JADUNATH. *Anecdotes of Aurangzib*. Calcutta: M. C. Sarkar & Sons, 1912.

―――. *History of Aurangzib*. 5 vols. Vols. 1–4, Calcutta: M. C. Sarkar & Sons, 1912–1919; Vol. 5, London: Longmans, Green, 1924.

―――. *Mughal Administration* (*First Series*). Patna University Readership Lectures, 1920. Calcutta: M. C. Sarkar & Sons, 1920.

―――. *Mughal Administration* (*Second Series*). Patna University Readership Lectures, 1921. Patna: Patna University Press, 1925.

―――. *Studies in Mughal India*. London: Longmans, Green, 1920.

SHAH, IDRIES. *The Sufis*. Introduction by Robert Graves. New York: Doubleday, 1964.

SITWELL, SACHEVERELL. *Great Temples of the East*. New York: Ivan Obolensky, Inc., 1963.

SLEEMAN, WILLIAM HENRY. *Rambles and Recollections of an Indian Official*. 2 vols. London: J. Hatchard & Son, 1844.

SMITH, VINCENT A. *Akbar the Great Mogul 1542–1605*. Oxford: Clarendon Press, 1917.

―――. Article. *Indian Antiquary* (1914), pp. 240–244.

SOLOMON, W. E. GLADSTONE. "Impressions of the Taj Mahal." *Islamic Culture*, vol. VI (April 1927), pp. 231–237.

―――. "In the Garden of the Taj Mahal." *Islamic Culture,* vol. VII (January 1923), pp. 147–159.

―――. "The Art and Colour of Gwalior." *Islamic Culture* (July 1933), pp. 380–394.

SPEAR, PERCIVAL. *A History of India*, vol. 2. Baltimore: Penguin Books, 1965.

―――. *Twilight of the Mughals: Studies in Late Mughal Delhi*. Cambridge: Cambridge University Press, 1951.

SRIVASTAVA, ASHIRBADI LAL. *The Mughal Empire*. 5th ed. Agra: Shiva Lal Agarwala & Co., 1966.

STACE, WALTER T. *The Teachings of the Mystics*. New York: Mentor Books, 1960.

THAPAR, ROMILA. *A History of India*, vol. 1. Baltimore: Penguin Books, 1966.

TRIPATHI, R. P. *Rise and Fall of the Mughal Empire*. 2nd ed. Allahabad: Central Book Depot, 1960.

VATS, M. S. "Repairs to the Taj Mahal." *Ancient India* (Bulletin of the Archaeological Survey of India), no. 1 (January 1946), pp. 4–7.

VILLIERS-STUART, CONSTANCE MARY. *Gardens of the Great Mughals.* London: A. & C. Black, 1913.

WALI, MAULAVI ABDUL, KHAN SAHIB. "A Sketch of the Life of Sarmad." *Journal and Proceedings of the Asiatic Society of Bengal,* N.S. vol. XX (1924), article no. 11, pp. 111–122.

WOODRUFF, PHILIP. *The Men Who Ruled India.* Vol. I: *The Founders of Modern India.* New York: St. Martin's Press, 1954.

ZIMMER, HEINRICH. *Philosophies of India.* Edited by Joseph Campbell. New York: Meridian Books, 1956.

Reference Works and Bibliography

BEALE, THOMAS WILLIAM. *An Oriental Biographical Dictionary.* New ed. rev. and enlarged by Henry George Keene. New York: Kraus Reprint Corporation (for the New York Public Library), 1965.

BHATTACHARYA, SACHCHIDANANDA. *A Dictionary of Indian History.* New York: George Braziller, 1967.

CROOKE, WILLIAM. *Herklots' Islam in India.* Text by Jafar Sharif, translated by G. A. Herklots; new rev. ed. rearranged, with additions, by William Crooke. London: Humphrey Milford and Oxford University Press, 1921.

PAMPHLETS OF THE PUBLICATIONS DIVISION. Ministry of Information and Broadcasting, Government of India.

SHARMA, SRI RAM. *A Bibliography of Mughal India (1526–1707 A.D.).* Bombay: Karnatak Publishing House, 1942.

THE TIMES ATLAS OF THE WORLD. Boston: Houghton Mifflin, 1967.

INDEX

[547]

Index

Index

Index

Index

Index

Miniature paintings
Mogul royalty, 96–99
See also illustrations for particular Moguls
Mir Jumla, 206, 208, 223, 224, 225, 226, 308
and Golconda politics, 169–177
death of, 326
pursuit of Shuja, 313, 314, 316–317, 319–320, 321, 322
Sarmad's prediction for, 402
viceroy of Bengal, 326
Mirza Ghiyas Beg. *See* Itimad-ud-Daulah
Mogul Empire, 19–20
court of, 22–24, 36–37, 56–58, 102–105
dissolution of, following Aurangzeb's death, 488
education, 24
Europe and, 49–51
first lady of the kingdom in, 436
Islamic justice, 24
Jahangir and, 15–28
lawlessness, 26–27
military personnel, 22–23
Mogul origins, 15
revenue of, 23–24, 25
Roe at Mogul court and trade writ with English, 51–66
seeds of destruction within, 197–198
Timur dynasty, end of, 491
Mohammed (Prophet), 9, 14, 150, 153
Sarmad on, 409, 410
Mohammed Akbar, marriage to Salima, 394
Mohammed Amin, 171, 172
joins Aurangzeb's forces, 260
Mohammed Azam, Prince, 439, 457, 471, 486
main events of life
Aurangzeb's final letter to, 485
Aurangzeb's heir apparent, 483–484
death of, 488

Mohammed Azam, main events of life (*continued*)
marriage to Jani Begum, 394, 449
Mohammed Beg, 401
Mohammed Kazim, 154
Mohammed Khan, Shaikh, 402
Mohammed Masum, 270n
Mohammed Said. *See* Sarmad
Mohammed Salih Kambu, 70
Mohammed Shah, reign of, 488
Mohammed Sultan, Prince, 172, 173, 247, 259, 265, 333, 415, 419, 439
main events of life
Battle of Khajuha, 304, 308
death of, 321, 470
defection to Shuja, 318, 463
engagement to Gulrukh Banu, 318
imprisonment of, 390
marriages, 394
pursuit of Shuja, 313
return to Aurangzeb's side, 320
Monserrate, *Commentary,* 399n
Muazzam, Prince, 431, 439, 446, 457, 467, 478, 481, 483, 484
characteristics, 463, 464
Golconda siege, 469–470
imprisonment of, 470
reign of, 488
Muhiuddin Mohammed Aurangzeb. *See* Aurangzeb, Muhiuddin Mohammed
Mukhlispur (Faizabad), 189–190
Mulla Shah, 150, 151–152, 185, 407
Mumtaz Mahal (Arjumand Banu Begum), 2, 55–56, 79, 86, 87, 436
death, funeral, and burial of, 106–115
family background, 36–38
first meeting with Shah Jahan, 38
marriage to Shah Jahan, 29–36

[555]

Index

Index